P9-DMV-778

THE QUEST

Also by Daniel Yergin

The Prize

Shattered Peace

Coauthored by Daniel Yergin

The Commanding Heights

Russia 2010

Global Insecurity

Energy Future

THE QUEST

. . .

ENERGY, SECURITY, AND THE REMAKING OF THE MODERN WORLD

DANIEL YERGIN

THE PENGUIN PRESS
NEW YORK
2011

THE PENGUIN PRESS
Published by the Penguin Group
Penguin Group (USA) Inc., 375 Hudson Street, New York, New York 10014, U.S.A. • Penguin Group (Canada), 90 Eglinton Avenue East, Suite 700, Toronto, Ontario, Canada M4P 2Y3 (a division of Pearson Penguin Canada Inc.) • Penguin Books Ltd, 80 Strand, London WC2R 0RL, England • Penguin Ireland, 25 St. Stephen's Green, Dublin 2, Ireland (a division of Penguin Books Ltd) • Penguin Books Australia Ltd, 250 Camberwell Road, Camberwell, Victoria 3124, Australia (a division of Pearson Australia Group Pty Ltd) • Penguin Books India Pvt Ltd, 11 Community Centre, Panchsheel Park, New Delhi – 110 017, India • Penguin Group (NZ), 67 Apollo Drive, Rosedale, Auckland 0632, New Zealand (a division of Pearson New Zealand Ltd) • Penguin Books (South Africa) (Pty) Ltd, 24 Sturdee Avenue, Rosebank, Johannesburg 2196, South Africa

Penguin Books Ltd, Registered Offices:
80 Strand, London WC2R 0RL, England

First published in 2011 by The Penguin Press,
a member of Penguin Group (USA) Inc.

Photograph credits appear on pages 722–23.

LIBRARY OF CONGRESS CATALOGING IN PUBLICATION DATA

Yergin, Daniel.
The quest :energy, security, and the remaking of the modern world / by Daniel Yergin.
p. cm.
Includes bibliographical references and index.
ISBN 978-1-59420-283-4
1. Power resources—Political aspects. 2. Money—Political aspects 3. Globalization. I. Title.
HD9502.A2Y47 2011
333.79—dc22
2011013100

MAPS BY VIRGINIA MASON
GRAPHICS BY SEAN MCNAUGHTON

Printed in the United States of America
1 3 5 7 9 10 8 6 4 2

DESIGNED BY AMANDA DEWEY

CONTENTS

PART ONE
The New World of Oil

PART TWO
Securing the Supply

PART THREE
The Electric Age

PART FOUR
Climate and Carbon

INTRODUCTION

They happened at the same time, halfway around the globe from each other. They both shook the world.

On March 11, 2011, at 2:46 in the afternoon Japan time, 17 miles below the seabed, the pressure between two vast tectonic plates created a massive violent upward force that set off one of the most powerful earthquakes ever recorded. In addition to widespread damage to buildings and infrastructure in the region north of Tokyo, the quake also knocked out the power supply, including that to the Fukushima Daiichi nuclear complex. Fifty-five minutes later, a huge tsunami unleashed by the quake swept over the coast, drowning thousands and thousands of people. At the Fukushima Daiichi complex, located at the very edge of the ocean, the massive tsunami surged above the seawall and flooded the power station, including its backup diesel generator, depriving the hot nuclear reactors of the cooling water required to keep them under control. In the days that followed, explosions damaged the plants, radiation was released, and severe meltdowns of nuclear rods occurred.

The result was the worst nuclear accident since the explosion at the Chernobyl nuclear plant in Soviet Ukraine a quarter century earlier. The Fukushima accident, compounded by damage to other electric generating plants in the area, led to power shortages, forcing rolling blackouts that demonstrated the vulnerability of modern society to a sudden shortage of energy supply. The effects were not limited to one country. The loss of industrial production in Japan disrupted global supply chains, halting automobile and electronics production in North America and Europe, and hitting the global economy. The accident at Fukushima threw a great question mark over the "global nuclear renaissance," which many had thought essential to help meet the power needs of a growing world economy.

On the other side of the world, a very different kind of crisis was unfolding. It had been triggered a few months earlier not by the clash of tectonic plates, but by a young fruit seller in the Tunisian town of Sidi Bouzid. Frustrated by constant harassment by the town's police and by the indifference of local officials, he doused himself with paint thinner and set himself aflame in protest in front of the city hall. His story and the ensuing demonstrations, transmitted by mobile phones, Internet, and satellite, whipped across Tunisia, the rest of North Africa, and the Middle East. In the face of swelling protests, the regime in Tunisia collapsed. And then, as protesters filled Tahrir Square in Cairo, so did the government in Egypt. Demonstrations against authoritarian governments spread across the entire region. In Libya, the protests turned into a civil war which drew in NATO.

The global oil price shot up in response not only to the loss of petroleum exports from Libya, but also to the disruption of the geostrategic balance that had underpinned the Middle East for decades. Anxiety mounted as to what the unrest might mean for the Persian Gulf, which supplies 40 percent of the oil sold into world markets, and for its customers around the globe.

These two very different but concurrent sets of events, oceans away from each other, delivered shocks to global markets. The renewed uncertainty and insecurity about energy, and the anticipation of deeper crisis, underscored a fundamental reality—how important energy is to the world.

This book tries to explain that importance. It is the story of the quest for the energy on which we so completely rely, for the position and rewards that accrue from energy, and for the security it affords. It is about how the modern energy world developed, about how concerns about climate and carbon are changing it, and about how different the energy world may be tomorrow.

Three fundamental questions shape this narrative: Will enough energy be available to meet the needs of a growing world and at what cost and with what technologies? How can the security of the energy system on which the world depends be protected? What will be the impact of environmental concerns, including climate change, on the future of energy—and how will energy development affect the environment?

As to the first, the fear of running out of energy has troubled people for a long time. One of the nineteenth century's greatest scientists, William Thomson—better known as Lord Kelvin—warned in 1881, in his presidential address to the British Association for the Advancement of Science in Edinburgh, that Britain's energy base was precarious and that disaster was impending. His fear was not about oil, but about coal, which had generated the "Age of Steam," fueled Britain's industrial preeminance, and made the words of "Rule, Britannia!" a reality in world power. Kelvin somberly warned that Britain's days of greatness might be numbered because "the subterranean coal-stores of the world" were "becoming exhausted surely, and not slowly" and the day was drawing close when "so little of it is left." The only hope he could offer was "that windmills or wind-motors in some form will again be in the ascendant."

But in the years after Kelvin's warning, the resource base of all hydrocarbons—coal, oil, and natural gas—continued to expand enormously.

Three quarters of a century after Kelvin's address, the end of the "Fossil Fuel Age" was predicted by another formidable figure, Admiral Hyman Rickover, the "father of the nuclear navy" and, as much as any single person, the father of the nuclear power industry, and described once as "the greatest engineer of all time" by President Jimmy Carter.

"Today, coal, oil and natural gas supply 93 percent of the world's energy," Rickover declared in 1957. That was, he said, a "startling reversal" from just a century earlier, in 1850, when "fossil fuels supplied 5 percent of the world's energy, and men and animals 94 percent." This harnessing of energy was what made possible a standard of living far higher than that of the mid-nineteenth century. But Rickover's central point was that fossil fuels would run out sometime after 2000—and most likely before 2050.

"Can we feel certain that when economically recoverable fossil fuels are gone science will have learned how to maintain a high standard of living on renewable energy sources?" the admiral asked. He was doubtful. He did not think that renewables—wind, sunlight, biomass—could ever get much above

15 percent of total energy. Nuclear power, though still experimental, might well replace coal in power plants. But, said Rickover, atomic-powered cars just were not in the cards. "It will be wise to face up to the possibility of the ultimate disappearance of automobiles," he said. He put all of this in a strategic context: "High-energy consumption has always been a prerequisite of political power," and he feared the perils that would come were that to change.

The resource endowment of the earth has turned out to be nowhere near as bleak as Rickover thought. Oil production today is five times greater than it was in 1957. Moreover, renewables have established a much more secure foundation than Rickover imagined. Yet we still live in what Rickover called the Fossil Fuel Age. Today, oil, coal, and natural gas provide over 80 percent of the world's energy. Supplies may be much more abundant today than was ever imagined, but the challenge of assuring energy's availability for the future is so much greater today than in Kelvin's time, or even Rickover's, owing to the simple arithmetic of scale. Will resources be adequate not only to fuel today's $65 trillion global economy but also to fuel what might be a $130 trillion economy in just two decades? To put it simply, will the oil resources be sufficient to go from a world of almost a billion automobiles to a world of more than two billion cars?

The very fact that this question is asked reflects something new—the "globalization of energy demand." Billions of people are becoming part of the global economy; and as they do so, their incomes and their use of energy go up. Currently, oil use in the developed world averages 14 barrels per person per year. In the developing world, it is only 3 barrels per person. How will the world cope when billions of people go from 3 barrels to 6 barrels per person?

The second theme of this book, security, arises from risk and vulnerability: the threat of interruption and crisis. Since World War II, many crises have disrupted energy supplies, usually unexpectedly.

Where will the next crisis come from? It could arise from what has been called the "bad new world" of cyber vulnerability. The complex systems that produce and deliver energy are among the most critical of all the "critical infrastructures," and that makes their digital controls tempting targets for cyberattacks. Shutting down the electric power system could do more than cause blackouts; it could immobilize society. When it comes to the security of energy supplies, the analysis always seems to return to the Persian Gulf region, which holds 60 percent of conventional oil reserves. Iran's nuclear program could upset the balance of power in that region. Terrorist networks have targeted its vast energy infrastructure to try to bring down existing governments and to drive up the price of oil and, in so doing, "bankrupt" the West. The region also confronts the turmoil arising from the dissatisfaction of a huge bulge of young people for whom education and employment opportunities are lacking and whose expectations are far from being met.

There are many other kinds of risks and dangers. It is an imperative to anticipate them, prepare for them, and ensure the resilience to respond—so as not to have to conclude after the fact, in the stark words of a Japanese government report on the Fukushima Daiichi disaster, that "consistent preparation" was "insufficient."

In terms of the environment, the third theme, the enormous strides have been made to address traditional pollution concerns. But when people in earlier decades focused on pollutants coming out of the tailpipe, they were thinking about smog, not about CO_2 and global warming. Environmental consciousness has expanded massively since the first Earth Day in 1970. In this century climate change has become a dominant political issue and central to the future of energy. This shift has turned greenhouse gases into a potent rationale for rolling back the supremacy of hydrocarbons and for expanding the role of renewables.

Yet most forecasts show that much of what will be the much larger energy needs two decades from now—75 to 80 percent—are currently on track to be met as they are today, from oil, gas, and coal, although used more efficiently. Or will the world shift toward what Lord Kelvin thought was needed and Admiral Rickover doubted was possible—a new age of energy, a radically different mix that relies much more heavily on renewables and alternatives—wind, solar, and biofuels, among others—perhaps even from sources that we cannot identify today? What kind of energy mix will meet the world's energy needs without crisis and confrontation?

Whatever the answers, innovation will be critical. Perhaps not surprisingly, the emphasis on innovation across the energy spectrum is greater than ever before. That increases the likelihood of seeing the benefits from what General Georges Doriot, the founder of modern venture-capital investing, called "applied science" being successfully applied to energy.

The lead times may be long owing to the scale and complexity of the vast system that supplies energy, but if this is to be an era of energy transition, then the $6 trillion global energy market is "contestable." That is, it is up for grabs among the incumbents—the oil, gas, and coal companies that supply the bulk of today's energy—and the new entrants—such as wind, solar, and biofuels—that want to capture a growing share of those dollars. A transition on this scale, if it does happen, has great significance for emissions, for the wider economy, for geopolitics, and for the position of nations.

The first section of this book describes the new, more complex world of oil that has emerged in the decades since the Gulf War. The essential drama of oil—the struggle for access, the battle for control, the geopolitics that shape it—will continue to be a decisive factor for our changing world. China, which two decades ago hardly figured in the global energy equation, is central to this new world. This is true not only because it is the manufacturing "workshop of the world," but also because of the "build-out of China"—the massive national construction project that is accommodating the 20 million people who are moving each year from rural areas into cities.

Part II centers on energy security and the future of supply. Will the world "run out" of oil? If not, where will it come from? The new supply will include natural gas, with its growing importance for the global economy. The rapid expansion of liquefied natural gas is creating another global energy market. Shale gas, the biggest energy innovation since the start of the new century, has turned what was an imminent shortage in the United States into what may be a hundred-year supply and may do the same elsewhere in the world. It is dramatically changing the competitive positions for everything from nuclear energy to wind power. It has also stoked, in a remarkably short time, a new environmental debate.

Part III is about the age of electricity. Ever since Thomas Edison fired up his power station in Lower Manhattan, the world has become progressively more electrified. In the developed world, electricity is taken for granted and yet the world cannot operate without it. For developing countries, shortages of electricity take their toll on people's lives and on economic growth.

Today, a host of new devices and gadgets that did not exist three decades ago—from personal computers and DVD players to smart phones and tablets—

all require increasing supplies of electricity—what might be called "gadgiwatts." Meeting future needs for electricity means facing challenging and sometimes wrenching decisions about the choice of fuel that will be required to keep the lights on and the power flowing.

Part IV tells the little-known story of how climate change, a subject of interest to a handful of scientists, became one of the dominating questions for the future. The study of climate began in the Alps in the 1770s out of sheer curiosity. In the nineteenth century, a few scientists began to think systematically about climate, but not because they were worried about global warming. Rather, they feared the return of an ice age. Only in the late 1950s and 1960s did a few researchers begin to calculate rising levels of carbon in the atmosphere and calibrate what that might mean for rising temperatures. The risk, they concluded, was not global cooling but global warming. But it was only in the twenty-first century that climate change as an issue started to have major effects on decisions by political leaders, CEOs, and investors—and even became a subject to be ruled upon by the U.S. Supreme Court.

Part V describes the new energies—the "rebirth of renewables"—and the evolution of technology. The history of the renewable industries is one of innovation, entrepreneurial daring, political battles, controversy, disappointment and despair, recovery and luck. They have become large global industries in themselves, but they are also reaching a testing point to demonstrate whether they can attain large-scale commerciality.

There is one key energy source that most people do not think of as an energy source. Sometimes it is called conservation; sometimes efficiency. It is hard to conceptualize and hard to mobilize and yet it can make the biggest contribution of all to the energy balance in the years immediately ahead.

The themes converge in Part VI on transportation and the automobile. It had seemed absolutely clear that the race for the mass-market automobile was decided almost exactly a century ago, with an overwhelming victory by the internal-combustion engine. But the return of the electric car—in this case fueled not only by its battery but also by government policies—is restarting the race. But will all-out electrification win this time? If the electric car proves itself competitive, or at least competitive in some circumstances, that outcome will reshape the energy world. That is not the only competitor. The race is also on to develop biofuels—to "grow" oil, rather than drill for it. All this sets a very big question: Can the electric car or biofuels depose petroleum from its position as king of the realm of transportation?

We can be sure that, in the years ahead, new "surprises" will upset whatever is the current consensus, change perspectives, redirect both policy and investment, and affect international relations. These surprises may be shocks of one kind or another—from political upheavals, wars or terrorism, or abrupt changes in the economy. Or they could be the result of accidents or of nature's fury. Or they could be the consequence of unanticipated technological breakthroughs that open up new opportunities.

But of one thing we can be pretty certain: The world's appetite for energy in the years ahead will grow enormously. The absolute numbers are staggering. Whatever the mix in the years ahead, energy and its challenges will be defining for our future.

PROLOGUE

Iraqi troops and tanks had been massing ominously for several days on the border with Kuwait. But Saddam Hussein, Iraq's dictator, assured various Middle Eastern leaders that they need not worry, that his intentions were peaceful, and that matters would get settled. "Nothing will happen," he said to Jordan's king. He told Egypt's president that he had no intention of invading Kuwait. To the U.S. ambassador, summoned on short notice, he raged that Kuwait, along with the United Arab Emirates, was waging "economic warfare" against Iraq. They were producing too much oil and, thus, driving down the price of oil, said Hussein—the results for Iraq, he added, were unbearable, and Iraq would have to "respond." The U.S. ambassador, citing Iraqi troop movements, asked "the simple question—what are your intentions?" Hussein said that he was pursuing a diplomatic resolution. The ambassador replied that the United States would "never excuse settlement of disputes by other than peaceful means." At the end of the meeting, Saddam told the ambassador that she should go on vacation and not to worry.[1]

However, a week later, in the early morning hours of August 2, 1990, Iraqi forces moved across the border and proceeded, with great brutality, to seize control of Kuwait. The result would be the first crisis of the post–Cold War world. It would also open a new era for world oil supplies.

Iraq proffered many rationales for the invasion. Whatever the justifications, the objective was clear: Saddam Hussein intended to annex Kuwait and remove it from the map. An Iraq that subsumed Kuwait would rival Saudi Arabia as an oil power, with far-reaching impact for the rest of the world.

"NOT SO FAST"

In the morning on August 2, Washington, D.C., time, President George H. W. Bush met with his National Security Council in the Cabinet Room at the White House. The mood was grim. The peace and stability so many around the world had hoped for was now suddenly and unexpectedly threatened. Just eight months earlier, the Berlin Wall had fallen, signaling the end of the Cold War. The key nations still had their hands full trying to peacefully wind down that four-and-a-half-decade confrontation.

With the annexation of Kuwait, Iraq would be in a position to assert its sway over the Persian Gulf, which at the time held two thirds of the world's reserves. Saddam already had the fourth-largest army, in number of soldiers, in the world. Now Iraq would also be an oil superpower. Saddam would use the combined oil reserves, and the revenues that would flow from them, to acquire formidable arsenals, including nuclear and chemical weapons; and, with this new strength, Iraq could project its influence and power far beyond the Persian Gulf. In short, with this invasion and annexation, Iraq could rewrite the calculations of world politics. Allowing that to happen would run counter to four decades of U.S. policy, going back to President Harry Truman, aimed at maintaining the security of the Persian Gulf.

The discussion in the Cabinet Room on August 2, perhaps reflecting the initial shock, was unformed and unfocused. Much of it seemed to turn toward various forms of economic sanctions, almost as though adjusting to a new reality. Or at least it seemed that way to some in the room, including President Bush himself, who was "appalled," as he put it, at the "huge gap between those who saw what was happening as the major crisis of our time and those who treated it as the crisis du jour."

"We will have to get used to a Kuwait-less world," said one adviser, acknowledging what seemed to be a fait accompli.

Bush raised up his hand.

"Not so fast," he said.[2]

DESERT STORM

Thereafter unfolded an extraordinary enterprise in coalition building—with some 36 nations signing on, in the form of either troops or money, under the auspices of the United Nations. The coalition included Saudi Arabia, whose largest oil field was only 250 miles from its border with Kuwait and whose ruler, King Fahd, told Bush that Saddam was "conceited and crazy" and that "he is following Hitler in creating world problems." It also included the Soviet Union, whose president, Mikhail Gorbachev, said something that would have been unthinkable only a couple of years earlier—that the Soviet Union would stand "shoulder to shoulder" with the United States in the crisis.[3]

Over the six months that followed, a coalition force steadily and methodically assembled in northern Saudi Arabia until it numbered almost a million strong. In the very early predawn hours of January 17, Operation Desert Storm commenced its first phase, with aerial bombardment of Iraqi military targets. On January 23, the Iraqis opened the valves on Kuwait's Sea Island Oil Terminal, releasing upwards of six million barrels of oil into the Persian Gulf, the largest oil spill in history, in an effort to foil what they expected to be an offensive from the sea by U.S. Marines. A month later, on February 23, coalition forces liberated Kuwait City. The next day, the coalition forces swept north from Saudi Arabia into Iraq, throwing back the Iraqi army. The invasion from the sea turned out to be a feint. The actual ground war took no more than a hundred hours, and it ended with Iraqi forces in full retreat.

But if Hussein could not have Kuwait, he would try to destroy it. Hussein's soldiers left Kuwait burning. Almost eight hundred oil wells were set aflame, with temperatures as high as three thousand degrees, creating a hellish mixture of fire and darkness and choking smoke and gross environmental damage. As much as six million barrels of oil a day were going up in flames—much more than Kuwait's normal daily production and considerably more than Japan's daily oil imports. The scale of this inferno was so much bigger than anything that even the most experienced oil-well fire-fighting firms had ever seen, and a host of new techniques had to be quickly developed. The last of the fires was put out in November 1991.

In the aftermath of the war, Saddam was boxed in; it seemed only a matter of time before the Iraqi dictator, weakened and humiliated, would be toppled by internal opponents.

A NEW AGE OF GLOBALIZATION

The outcome of the First Gulf War was a landmark for what was expected to be a more peaceful era—what, for a time, was called a new world order. The Soviet Union was no longer an adversary of the West. At the end of 1991, the Soviet Union disintegrated altogether. The talk was now of a new "unipolar world" in which the United States would be not only the "indispensable nation" but also the world's only superpower.

A new age of globalization followed: economies became more integrated and nations, more interconnected. "Privatization" and "deregulation," which had begun in the 1970s and gained momentum in the 1980s, became the watchwords around the world. Governments were progressively giving up the "commanding heights"—that is, control of the strategic sectors of their economies. Nations instead put increasing confidence in markets, private initiative, and global capital flows.

In 1991 India began the first phase of reforms that would unshackle its economy and eventually turn it into a high-growth nation and an increasingly important part of the global economy.

In the energy sectors of countries, as in so many other sectors, traditional government ministries were turned into state-owned companies, which in turn were partly or entirely privatized. Now many of these ministries-turned-companies worried as much about what pension funds and other shareholders thought as about the plans of government civil servants.

International barriers of all kinds came down. With the Iron Curtain gone, Europe was no longer divided between East and West. The European Community turned into a much more integrated European Union and established the principle of the euro as its currency. A series of major initiatives—notably, the

North American Free Trade Agreement—promoted freer trade. Overall, global trade grew faster than the global economy itself. Developing nations morphed into emerging markets and became the fastest-growing countries. Their rising incomes meant growing demand for oil.

Technology also drove globalization—in particular, the rapid development of information technology, the rise of the Internet, and the dramatic fall in the costs of international communications. This was changing the way firms operated, and it was connecting people in ways that had been inconceivable just a decade earlier. The "global village," a speculative concept in the 1960s, was now quickly becoming a reality. The oil and gas industry was caught up in these revolutions. Geopolitical change and greater confidence in markets opened new areas to investment and exploration. The industry expanded its capacity to find and produce resources in more challenging environments. It seemed now that an age of inexpensive oil and natural gas would extend much further into the future. That would be good news for energy supply but not such good news for higher-priced alternatives.

THE FADING OF RENEWABLES?

The energy crises of the 1970s had combined with rising environmental consciousness to give birth to a range of new energy options, known first as "alternative energy" and then, more lastingly, as "renewables." They covered a wide range—wind, solar, biomass, geothermal, etc. What gave them a common definition was that they were based neither on fossil fuels nor on nuclear power.

They had emerged out of the tumult of the 1970s with a great deal of enthusiasm—"rays of hope" in a famous formulation. But over the 1980s, the hopes had been dulled by the realities of falling costs of conventional energy, their own challenging economics, technological immaturity, and disappointment in deployment. With moderate prices and the apparent restoration of energy stability in the early 1990s, the prospects for renewable energy became even more challenging.

Yet environmental consciousness was becoming more pervasive. Most environmental issues were, traditionally, local or regional. But there was growing attention to a new kind of environmental issue, a global issue: climate change and global warming. Attention was initially confined to a relatively small segment of people. That would change in due course, with profound implications for the energy industry—conventional, renewable, and alternatives.

In other ways, the combination of energy policies launched in the 1970s and the dynamics of the marketplace had worked. In the face of much skepticism, energy efficiency—conservation—had turned out to be a much more vigorous contributor to the energy mix than most had anticipated.

A STABLE MIDDLE EAST

Mideast politics, which so often bedeviled security of supply, was no longer a threat. In the decade that followed the Gulf crisis, it seemed that the Middle East was more stable and that oil crises and disruptions were things of the past. No longer was there a Soviet Union to meddle in regional politics, and the outcome of the Gulf crisis and the weight of the United States in world affairs looked like an almost sure guarantee of stability.

The Palestinian Liberation Organization realized that it had driven itself into a dead end by supporting Saddam in the Gulf crisis, and, in the process, alienating many of the Arab countries that were its financial benefactors. It quickly reoriented itself, and swift progress thereupon followed in the Israeli-Palestinian peace process. In Washington, D.C., in September 1993, Yasser Arafat, chairman of the Palestinian National Authority, and Israel's prime minister, Yitzhak Rabin, signed the Oslo Accords, which laid out the route to a two-state solution to that long conflict. And then, standing in front of President Clinton with the White House as a backdrop, they did what would have seemed inconceivable three years earlier—shook hands. The following year, they shared the Nobel Peace Prize along with Israel's foreign minister, Shimon Peres. All this was a positive and powerful indicator of the world that seemed to be ahead. It might not have happened had Saddam not gone to war.

As for Saddam Hussein himself, he no longer seemed to be going anywhere.

CONTAINMENT

In 1991 the coalition's forces had stopped 90 miles short of Baghdad. The coalition had come together under the authority of the United Nations to eject Saddam from Kuwait; it had no mandate to remove Saddam and change the regime. Nor was there any desire to engage in the potentially bloody urban warfare that would be required for a final push. As it was, the television images of the destruction of the Iraqi army, and the backlash those images were engendering, were in themselves a further reason to call things to a halt—what has been dubbed the "CNN effect." Beyond all that, it was widely assumed that aggrieved elements of the Iraqi military would do what was expected—launch a coup—and that Saddam's days were numbered. But, such was his ruthlessness and iron control, that, contrary to expectations, he held tightly to power after the war.

Yet Saddam's position was much reduced. For Iraq was now hemmed in by a program of inspections, military force, and sanctions that amounted to what has been called "classic containment," evoking the policy that had checked Soviet expansion during the Cold War. In addition, some efforts were mounted over the next few years to support Saddam's opponents in toppling him, but that all ended in failure. Under the administration of Bill Clinton, the containment policy became more explicit. It also became conjoined with what now was described as "dual containment"—of Iran along with Iraq.

In principle, U.N. weapons inspectors could range freely around Iraq, looking for the elements that could go into weapons of mass destruction—colloquially known as WMD. In practice, obstructions were constantly put in the inspectors' way. There was only one moment of surprising cooperation: In 1995 the head of Iraq's unconventional weapons program, who happened to be Saddam's son-in-law, defected to Jordan. The regime panicked, fearing what he might tell. Trying to preempt any revelations, Baghdad suddenly released half a million documents (which had been hidden in a chicken coop) that detailed production of a variety of biological weapons. But after Saddam lured his son-in-law back to Iraq (in order to have him killed), obstruction once again returned as the norm.[4]

Still, the days of Saddam's capacity to try to control world oil had passed.

His continuing impact on oil came mainly in the form of his ability to manipulate prices at the margins. In the first few years after the Gulf War, with exports not permitted, petroleum output fell precipitously. In 1995 the United Nations established the Oil-for-Food Programme, which allowed Iraq to sell a defined amount of oil. Half of the revenues went for essentials, like medicine and food. Before Saddam seized power, Iraq had been an exporter of food to Europe and even shipped dates to the United States. But, under Saddam, agriculture had suffered, and oil exports provided the funding to import the food the country now required. The other half went to reparations and to fund the U.N. inspections. Thereafter Iraqi production recovered to something over two million barrels per day, with significant output smuggled into Jordan, Syria, and Iran. In addition, Saddam's regime benefitted from billions of dollars of secret kickbacks from those who had been granted contracts to sell Iraqi oil, ranging from mysterious Russian middlemen to a Texas oil tycoon to officials from countries seen as friendly to Iraq.[5]

But the program always seemed at risk. Would Saddam continue to cooperate with the U.N. program this time? Or would he break off cooperation, reducing or cutting off altogether Iraqi exports—thus abruptly sending the price up? The uncertainty created considerable price volatility.

By the end of the 1990s, the U.S. policy of containment was clearly fraying. Sentiment was growing in the Middle East and Europe that the sanctions were hurting not Saddam and his clique, and the Republican Guard that kept them in power, but the general Iraqi population. In 1998 Saddam permanently expelled the U.N. weapons inspectors. A 1998 U.S. National Intelligence Estimate concluded that Saddam's ambitions for weapons of mass destruction were unchecked.[6]

Yet Saddam had been contained, and it appeared that he would never again be able to renew his bid to control the Persian Gulf. Next door in Iran, in 1997, Mohammad Khatami, regarded as a reformer and a relative moderate, was elected president, and there seemed a possibility to reduce the mutual hostility that had so dominated relations between Washington and Tehran. With all these changes, Middle East petroleum now appeared much more secure—and that meant that the world's oil supply was more secure. Given this stability, it was thought that the price would circle around $20 or so a barrel. For American motorists, that meant relatively low gasoline prices, which they assumed were part of the natural order.

NEW HORIZONS AND THE "QUIET REVOLUTION"

At the same time, technology was increasing the security of oil supplies in a different way—by expanding the range of the drill bit and increasing recoverable reserves. The petroleum industry was going through a period of innovation, capitalizing on the advances in communications, computers, and information technology to find resources and develop them, whether on land or farther and farther out into the sea.

So often, over the history of the oil industry, it is said that technology has gone about as far as it can and that the "end of the road" for the oil industry is in sight. And then, new innovations dramatically expand capabilities. This pattern would be repeated again and again.

The rapid advances in microprocessing made possible the analysis of vastly more data, enabling geophysicists to greatly improve their interpretation of underground structures and thus improve exploration success. Enhanced computing power meant that the seismic mapping of the underground structures—the strata, the faults, the cap rocks, the traps—could now be done in three dimensions, rather than two. This 3-D seismic mapping, though far from infallible, enabled explorationists to much improve their understanding of the geology deep underground.

The second advance was the advent of horizontal drilling. Instead of the traditional vertical well that went straight down, wells could now be drilled vertically for the first few thousand feet and then driven at an angle or even sideways with drilling progress tightly controlled and measured every few feet with very sophisticated tools. This meant that much more of the reservoir could be accessed, thus increasing production.

The third breakthrough was the development of software and computer visualization that was becoming standard throughout the construction and engineering industries. Applied to the oil industry, this CAD/CAM (computer-aided design, computer-aided manufacturing) technology enabled a billion-dollar offshore production platform to be designed down to the tiniest detail on a computer screen, and its resilience and efficiency tested in multiple ways, even before welding began on the first piece of steel.

As the 1990s progressed, the spread of information and communications technology and the extraordinary fall in communication costs meant that geoscientists could work as virtual teams in different parts of the world. Experience and learning from a field in one part of the world could instantly be shared with those trying to solve similar problems in analogous fields in other parts of the world. As a result, the CEO of one company said at the time with only some exaggeration, scientists and engineers "would go up the learning curve only once."

These and other technological advances meant that companies could do things that had only recently been unattainable—whether in terms of identifying new prospects, tackling fields that could not be developed before, taking on much more complex projects, recovering more oil, or opening up entirely new production provinces.

Altogether, technology widened the horizons of world oil, bringing on large amounts of new supplies that supported economic growth and expanded mobility around the world. Billions of barrels of oil that could not have been accessed or produced a decade earlier were now within reach. All that proved to be "just in time" technological progress. For the world appeared to be on a fast track in terms of economic growth—and, thus, in its need for more oil.

The world was also changing fast in terms of geopolitics. Countries that had been closed or restrictive toward investment by international companies were now opening up, inviting the companies to bring their skills and technology along with their money. The seemingly immutable structure of global confrontation had suddenly buckled.

In particular, changes were unfolding in the successor states to the Soviet Union—Russia and the newly independent countries around the Caspian Sea—that would integrate the region with global markets. It was as if the twentieth century's end was being reconnected back to the century's beginning. The effect would be to broaden the foundations of the world petroleum supply. As an article in *Foreign Affairs* put it in 1993, "Oil is truly a global business for the first time since the barricades went up with the Bolshevik Revolution."[7]

This observation had particular significance for Russia, the country that had been home of the Bolshevik Revolution, and that now rivaled Saudi Arabia in its capacity to produce oil.

PART ONE

...

The New World of Oil

1

RUSSIA RETURNS

On the night of December 25, 1991, Soviet president Mikhail Gorbachev went on national television to make a startling announcement—one that would have been almost unimaginable even a year or two earlier: "I hereby discontinue my activities at the post of the President of the Union of Soviet Socialist Republics." And, he added, the Soviet Union would shortly cease to exist.

"We have a lot of everything—land, oil and gas and other natural resources—and there was talent and intellect in abundance," he continued. "However, we were living much worse than people in the industrialized countries were living and we were increasingly lagging behind them." He had tried to implement reforms but he had run out of time. A few months earlier, diehard communists had tried to stage a coup but failed. The coup had, however, set in motion the final disintegration. "The old system fell apart even before the new system began to work," he said.

"Of course," he added, "there were mistakes made that could have been avoided, and many of the things that we did could have been done better." But he would not give up hope. "Some day our common efforts will bear fruit and our nations will live in a prosperous, democratic society." He concluded simply, "I wish everyone all the best."[1]

With that, he faded out into the ether and uncertainty of the night.

His whole speech had taken just twelve minutes. That was it. After seven decades, communism was finished in the land in which it had been born.

Six days later, on December 31, the USSR, the Union of Soviet Socialist Republics, formally ceased to exist. Mikhail Gorbachev, the last president of the Soviet Union, handed over the "football"—the suitcase with the codes to activate the Soviet nuclear arsenal—to Boris Yeltsin, the first president of the Russian Federation. There were no ringing of bells, no honking of horns, to mark this great transition. Just a stunned and muted—and disbelieving—response. The Soviet Union, a global superpower, was gone. The successors would be fifteen states, ranging in size from the huge Russian Federation to tiny Estonia. Russia was, by far, the first among equals: it was the legatee of the old Soviet Union; it inherited not only the nuclear codes, but the ministries and the debts of the USSR. What had been the closed Soviet Union was now, to one degree or another, open to the world. That, among other things, would redraw the map of world oil.

Among the tens of millions who had watched Gorbachev's television farewell on December 25 was Valery Graifer. To Graifer, the collapse of the Soviet Union was nothing less than "a catastrophe, a real catastrophe." For half a decade, he had been at the very center of the Soviet oil and gas industry. He had led the giant West Siberia operation, the last great industrial achievement of the Soviet system. Graifer had been sent there in the mid-1980s, when production had begun faltering, to restore output and push it higher. Under him, West Siberia had reached 8 million barrels per day—almost rivaling Saudi Arabia's total output. The scale of the enterprise was enormous: some 450,000 people ultimately reported up to him. And yet West Siberia was part of an even bigger Soviet industry. "It was one big oil family throughout all the republics of the Soviet Union," he later said. "If anyone had told me that this family was about to collapse, I would have laughed." But the shock of the collapse wore off, and within a year he had launched a technology company to serve whatever would be the new oil industry of independent Russia. "We had a tough time," he said. "But I saw that life goes on."[2]

"THINGS ARE BAD WITH BREAD"

One of the lasting ironies of the Soviet Union was that while the communist system was almost synonymous with force-paced industrialization, its economy in its final decades was so heavily dependent on vast natural resources—oil and gas in particular.

The economic system that Joseph Stalin had imposed on the Soviet Union was grounded in central planning, five-year plans, and self-sufficiency—what Stalin called, "socialism in one country." The USSR was largely shut off from the world economy. It was only in the 1960s that the Soviet Union reemerged on the world market as a significant exporter of oil and then, in the 1970s, of natural gas. "Crude oil along with other natural resources were," as one Russian oil leader later said, "nearly the single existing link of the Soviet Union to the world" for "earning the hard currency so desperately needed by this largely isolated country."[3]

By the end of the 1960s, the Soviet economy was showing signs of decay and incapacity to maintain economic growth. But, as a significant oil exporter, it received a huge windfall from the 1973 October War and the Arab oil embargo: the quadrupling of oil prices. The economy further benefitted in the early 1980s when oil prices doubled in response to the Iranian Revolution. This surge in oil revenues helped keep the enfeebled Soviet economy going for another decade, enabling the country to finance its superpower military status and meet other urgent needs.

At the top of the list of these needs were the food imports required, because of its endemic agricultural crisis, in order to avert acute shortages, even famine, and social instability. Sometimes the threat of food shortages was so imminent that Soviet premier Alexei Kosygin would call the head of oil and gas production and tell him, "Things are bad with bread. Give me three million tons [of oil] over the plan."

Economist Yegor Gaidar, acting Russian prime minister in 1992, summed up the impact of these oil price increases: "The hard currency from oil exports stopped the growing food supply crisis, increased the import of equipment and consumer goods, ensured a financial basis for the arms race and the achievement of nuclear parity with the United States and permitted the realization of such risky foreign policy actions as the war in Afghanistan."[4]

The increase in prices also allowed the Soviet Union to go on without reforming its economy or altering its foreign policy. Trapped by its own inertia the Soviet leadership failed to give serious consideration to the thought that oil prices might fall someday, let alone prepare for such an eventuality.

"DEAR JOHN—HELP!"

Mikhail Gorbachev came to power in 1985 determined to modernize both the economy and the political system without overturning either. "We knew what kind of country we had," he would say. "It was the most militarized, the most centralized, the most rigidly disciplined; it was stuffed with nuclear weapons and other weapons."

An issue that infuriated him when he came into office—women's pantyhose—symbolized to him what was so wrong. "We were planning to create a commission headed by the secretary of the Central Committee . . . to solve the problem of women's pantyhose," he said. "Imagine a country that flies into space, launches Sputniks, creates such a defense system, and it can't resolve the problem of women's pantyhose. There's no toothpaste, no soap powder, not the basic necessities of life. It was incredible and humiliating to work in such a government."

But Gorbachev had very bad luck in timing. In 1986, one year after his ascension, oversupply and reduced demand on the world petroleum market triggered a huge collapse in the oil price. This drastically reduced the hard currency earnings that the country needed to pay for imports.

Even though the Soviet oil industry—which was now centered in West Siberia—continued to push up output, it was not enough to bail out the sinking economy. At the same time, Gorbachev was relaxing the grasp of communist repression on the society.[5]

While the collapse in oil prices was the "final blow," as Yegor Gaidar has written, the failure was of the system itself. "The collapse of the Soviet system," he said, "had been preordained by the fundamental characteristics of the Soviet economic and political system," which "did not permit the country to adapt to the challenges of world development in the late twentieth century. "High oil prices was not a dependable foundation for preserving the last empire."

By the end of the 1980s and the beginning of the 1990s, the word "crisis" in government and party documents was being replaced by "acute crisis," and then by "catastrophe." Food shortages were severe. At one point, the city of St. Petersburg nearly ran out of dairy products for children.

In November 1991, Gorbachev asked one of his aides to send British prime minister John Major, at that time head of the G7 group of industrial nations, a three-word message—"Dear John, Help!"[6]

It was just a month later that Gorbachev went on television to announce the dissolution of the Soviet Union.

A NEW RUSSIA: "NO ONE'S AT THE CONTROLS"

From January 1, 1992, Russia was an independent state, a huge one, traversing eleven time zones. The centrally planned socialist economy of the Soviet Union, where virtually every action in the entire economy was the result of bureaucratic decisions, had disintegrated, leaving economic chaos and uncertainty. There was no rule of commercial law, no basis for contracts, no established channels or rules for trade. Barter became the order of the day, not just for newly emerging traders and merchants out on the streets or working out of their apartments, but also factories, which traded goods and output back and forth as though it were all currency. It was also a free-for-all, a mad scramble, as most of the commercial assets of the state and of the *narod*—the Soviet people—were now up in play. It was a frightening time for the populace and a time of great hardship: their pensions and salaries, if paid at all, lost their value; and the low, but guaranteed, level of economic security on which they counted was disappearing before their eyes.

It was also frightening for the young reformers who came to power under Russian president Boris Yeltsin. "A nuclear superpower was in anarchy," said Gaidar, who was Yeltsin's first finance minister. "We had no money, no gold, and no grain to last through the next harvest, and there was no way to generate a solution. It was like travelling in a jet and you go into the cockpit and you discover that there's no one at the controls." The reformers couldn't even get into government computers because the passwords had been lost during the collapse.

There were two urgent needs in those days. One was to stabilize the economy, renew the flow of goods and services, keep people fed and warm, and establish foundations for trade and a market economy. The other was to figure out what to do with all the factories and enterprises and resources—the means of production that the government owned—and somehow move them into some other form of ownership—private ownership, which was more productive and appropriate to a market economy. Since the state owned most everything, it meant that all the assets of the Soviet Union were up for grabs.

And they were being grabbed. As President Yeltsin put it, the economic assets of the state were being privatized "wildly, spontaneously, and often on a criminal basis." He and his team of reformers were determined to regain control, to break up whatever remained from the command-and-control economy, and to replace it with a new economic system based upon private property. The objectives of privatization were not only economic; they also wanted to forestall any return to the communist past by removing assets from state control as quickly as possible. To make matters even more difficult, this economic upheaval took place against a backdrop of political turmoil: a standoff between the Yeltsin administration and the State Duma, or parliament, including a violent "siege" of the Duma; the first Chechnya war; and a 1996 presidential election that, until late in the campaign, seemed likely to end with a victory by resurgent communists.

The Soviet system had left many valuable legacies—a huge network of large industrial enterprises (though stranded in the 1960s in terms of technology); a vast military machine; and an extraordinary reservoir of scientific, mathematical, and technical talent, although disconnected from a commercial economy. The highly capable oil industry was burdened with an ageing infrastructure. Below ground lay all the enormous riches in the form of petroleum and other raw materials that Gorbachev had cited in his farewell address.[7]

RECONSTRUCTING THE OIL INDUSTRY

These natural resources—particularly oil and natural gas—were as critical to the new Russian state as they had been to the former Soviet Union. By the middle 1990s, oil export revenues accounted for as much as two thirds of the Russian government's hard currency earnings. What happened to these revenues "dominated Russian politics and economic policy throughout the 1990s and into the 2000s." Yet the oil sector was swept up in the same anarchy as the rest of the economy. Workers, who were not being paid, went on strike, shutting down the oil fields. Production and supply across the country were disrupted. Oil was being commandeered or stolen and sold for hard currency in the West. No one even knew who really owned the oil. Individual production organizations in various parts of West Siberia and elsewhere were busily declaring themselves independent and trying to go into business for themselves. The industry was suddenly being run by "nearly 2000 uncoordinated associations, enterprises and organizations belonging to the former Soviet industry ministry." Amid such disruption and starved for investment, Russian oil output started to slip, and then collapse. In little more than half a decade, Russian production plummeted by almost 50 percent—an astonishing loss of more than 5 million barrels a day.

Privatization here, too, would be the answer. But how to do it? The oil industry was structured to meet the needs of a centrally planned system. It was organized horizontally, with different ministries—oil, refining and petrochemicals, and foreign trade—each controlling its segments of the industry. The resources industry was as important to the new state as to the old and had to be handled differently from the other privatizations.

One person with clearly thought-through ideas about what to do was Vagit Alekperov. Born in Baku, he had worked in the offshore Azerbaijani oil industry until transferring at age twenty-nine to the new heartland of Soviet oil, West Siberia. There he came to the attention of Valery Graifer, then leading West Siberia to its maximum performance. Recognizing Alekperov's capabilities, Graifer promoted him to run one of the most important frontier regions in West Siberia. In 1990, Alekperov leapfrogged to Moscow, where he became deputy oil minister.

On trips to the West, Alekperov visited a number of petroleum companies. He saw a dramatically different way of operating an oil business. "It was a revelation," he said. "Here was a type of organization that was flexible and capable, a company that was tackling all the issues at the same time—exploration, production, and engineering—and everybody pursing the common goal, and not each branch operating separately." He came back to Moscow convinced that the typical organization found in the rest of the world—vertically integrated companies with exploration and production, refining and marketing all in one company—was the way to organize a modern oil industry. Prior to the collapse of the Soviet Union, his efforts to promote a vertically integrated state-owned oil company were rebuffed. Opponents accused him of "destroying the oil sector." He tried again after Russia became an independent state. For to stay with the existing setup, he said, would result in chaos.[8]

In November 1992, President Yeltsin adopted this approach in Decree 1403 on privatization in the oil industry. The new law provided for three vertically integrated oil companies—Lukoil, Yukos, and Surgut. Each would combine upstream oil production areas with refining and marketing systems. They would become some of the largest companies in the world. The state would retain substantial ownership during a three-year transition period, while the new companies tried to assert control over now semi-independent individual production groups and refineries; quell rebellious subsidiaries; and capture control over oil sales, oil exports, and the hard currency that came from these transactions. The controlling shares for other companies in the oil industry were also parked for three years in what was to be a temporary state company, Rosneft, buying time for decisions about their future.

This restructuring would have been hard to do under any circumstances. It was very hard to do in the early and mid-1990s, when the state was very weak and law and order was in short supply. There was violence at every level, as Russian *mafyias*—gangs, scarily tattooed veterans of prison camps, and petty criminals—ran protection rackets, stole crude oil and refined products, and sought to steal assets from local distribution terminals. As the gangs battled for control, a contract, all too often, referred not to a legal agreement but to a hired killing. In the oil towns, the competing gangs tried to take over whole swaths of the local economy—from the outdoor markets to the hotels and even the train stations. The incentives were clear: oil was wealth, and getting control of some part of the business was the way to quickly amass wealth on a scale that could not even have been dreamed about in Soviet days, just a few years earlier.[9]

But eventually the state reasserted its police powers, and the newly established oil companies built up their own security forces, often with experienced veterans of the KGB, and the bloody tide of violence and gang wars began to recede.

LUKOIL AND SURGUT

Meanwhile, following on Yeltsin's privatization decree, the Russian oil majors were beginning to take shape.

The most visible was Lukoil. Vagit Alekperov, equipped with a clear vision of an integrated oil company, set about building it as quickly as possible. The first thing was to pull together a host of disparate oil production organizations and refineries that had heretofore had no connection. He barnstormed around the country trying to persuade the managements of each organization to join this unfamiliar new entity called Lukoil. In order for Lukoil to come into existence, every single entity had to sign on. "The hardest thing was to convince the managers to unite their interests," said Alekperov. "There was chaos in the country, and we all had to survive, we had to pay wages, and keep the entities together. Without uniting, we would not be able to survive." They heard the message, all signed on, and Lukoil became a real company.

Alekperov recognized the heavy burdens that the new Russian companies carried—what he called their "Soviet legacy" of "aged equipment along with obsolete manpower and production management systems." Lukoil had to target "the best international practices." From the beginning, Alekperov put in place international standards and used international law firms, accountants, and bankers. In 1995 the chief financial officer of the American oil company ARCO came across an article about Lukoil in the *Economist* magazine. He found it intriguing enough that he followed up, and ARCO subsequently bought a share of Lukoil. From the early days, Lukoil also pursued an international strategy, first in the other new nations of the former Soviet Union and then in other parts of the world.

If Lukoil was the most international of the new Russian majors, Surgut was the most decidedly Russian. Its CEO, Vladimir Bogdanov, was called the "hermit oil man" by some. He had been born in a tiny Siberian village, made his name as a driller in Tyumen, and the enterprise he managed there became the basis of what emerged as Surgutneftegaz, better known by its short name, Surgut. He never moved to Moscow, instead keeping Surgut's headquarters in the city of Surgut. As he once explained, he liked to walk to work.[10]

Both Lukoil and Surgut were run by people who would have been qualified as "oil generals" under the Soviet system.

YUKOS: THE SALE OF THE CENTURY

Very different was a company called Yukos. It was one of the first oil companies to be run by one of the new oligarchs who had emerged not from the oil industry but out of the chaotic barter economy.

Mikhail Khodorkovsky had started off with orthodox Soviet ambitions: as a child, he announced that his objective was to rise to the highest levels of the Soviet industrial system and achieve the vaunted position of factory director. Later, while a student at the Mendeleev Institute for Chemistry, he jumped into business as a leader of the school's Komsomol, the communist youth organization, turning it into a commercial organization. He then moved into trading in imported computers and software and then, in the late 1980s, set up a bank called Menatep, which would soon be regarded as serious enough to be entrusted with government accounts. It also provided finance to one of the new oil companies, Yukos.

Khodorkovsky soon concluded that oil was an even better business than banking. The timing was right. By 1995 the Russian government was desperately short of funds, and some of the new businessmen and the Yeltsin government came up with a solution that went by the name of "loans-for-shares." Businessmen would loan the Russian government money, taking highly discounted shares in petroleum and other companies as collateral. When the government, as anticipated, defaulted on the loans, the shares would end up as the property of the lenders. They would thus control these new companies. The government meanwhile got the short-term funding it needed to keep afloat prior to the 1996 presidential election. It was certainly an unusual way to privatize assets, and loans-for-shares was immortalized as the "sale of the century." Khodorkovsky lent the Russian government $309 million and won control of Yukos's shares.[11]

Khodorkovsky set about task number one, which was to gain control of the flows of oil and money, which seemed to be going in all directions. Khodorkovsky had never attended the Gubkin Institute or any of the other Soviet oil academies, and he had no particular attachment to the Soviet approach to field development. And so he turned to Western oil field service companies to come in and apply Western development techniques, rather than Soviet techniques, to the oil fields. This would lead to dramatic improvements in output. (It would also, in later years, come back to haunt him, during his confrontation with the Russian government, with charges that he had violated recognized and sound "Russian" oil field production practices.) As his wealth and influence magnified, so did his ambitions.

These companies—Lukoil, Surgut, and Yukos—were the three majors. They were not alone by any means. There remained the state company, Rosneft; six "mini-majors"; and a number of other companies, including those owned or sponsored by oil-rich regional governments.

One of the mini-majors was TNK. A consortium of owners, the AAR group, came together to buy the company in 1997. They would become among the country's most prominent oligarchs. Three of them came from the Alfa Bank. Mikhail Fridman was a graduate of the Institute of Steel and Alloys. He had worked for a couple of years in a factory, but when it became possible to go into business in the late 1980s, he jumped in, starting a dizzying host of enterprises, ranging from a photo coop to window washing. Despite the chaos and being told that his businesses could not succeed, Fridman later said, "we did have an internal conviction." His partner German Khan, another graduate of the Institute of Steel and Alloys, ran what became the oil trading part of their new enterprise and would remain the most focused on the oil business itself. The money they made from trading commodities enabled them to set up the Alfa Bank. A third partner was Peter Aven, who had already established his reputation as an academic mathematician and had been minister of foreign trade in the early 1990s.

The other members of the consortium included Viktor Vekselberg, who trained in transportation engineering, and Len Blavatnik, who had emigrated to the United States at age 21 and worked his way through Harvard Business School after a stint as a computer programmer. Blavatnik made his first trip back to the Soviet Union in 1988. It was a different country. He returned again in 1991—now it was Russia—and became serious about investing in a newly independent Russia, which led him to join up with the others in TNK. For its part, TNK controlled half the Samotlor oil field in western Siberia. It was a most desirable jewel—among the half dozen largest oil fields in the world.

There was another prominent company—Sibneft, as in Siberian Oil.

This was the most classic of the loans-for-shares deals. Roman Abramovich, who had been trading everything from oil to children's toys, teamed up with Boris Berezovsky and lent $100 million to the impoverished Russian government for half the company. When, as anticipated, the government failed to repay the loans, these oligarchs had control. Berezovsky went into political exile after falling out with President Vladimir Putin. Abramovich followed a different path. He took on the additional duties of governor of an impoverished region in the Russian Far East. Abramovich eventually sold Sibneft to the Russian gas giant Gazprom and moved to England, where he was said to be the second-richest person in the country, exceeded only by the Queen herself.[12]

Overall, by 1998, within six years of the collapse of the Soviet Union, the Russian oil industry had gone from a system run by a series of ministries and subordinated to central planning to a system of large vertically integrated companies, organized, at least in rough outline, similarly to the traditional companies in the West. During these years, they all operated largely autonomously from the state. Eventually the Russian Federation would have five large energy companies, each of whose oil reserves were comparable to the size of the largest western majors.

The development of these companies was more than just a wholesale reconstruction of the Russian oil industry. It also brought visible changes in the larger cities. In Soviet times, those few lucky enough to own automobiles had to search out the rare and hard-to-find dingy service stations on the outskirts of the city. But now new, modern service stations were springing up at intersections and alongside the highways, bedecked with shiny corporate logos—Lukoil, Yukos, Surgut, TNK, and a number of others. The stations came equipped not only with high octane gasoline of dependable quality, but also in many cases things that people never expected to see, like convenience stores and, even more remarkable, automatic car washes. All of that would also have been unimaginable in Soviet times.

OPENING UP

How did this new Russian oil industry look to the rest of the world? In 1992 the head of one of the world's largest state-owned oil companies was asked what he thought about Russia and all the changes that were happening there. His answer was very simple. "When I think of Russia," he said without a pause, "I think of it as a competitor."

Others saw opportunity. For many decades after the 1917 Bolshevik Revolution, the Soviet Union had been closed off, an almost forbidden place, another world. The Soviet oil industry operated largely in isolation, with little of the flow of technology and equipment that was common in the rest of the world.

In the late Gorbachev years, at the end of the 1980s, the Soviet Union started to open the doors to joint ventures with Western companies. The objective was to bring in the technology it needed to improve the performance of the Soviet industry. Then came the collapse of the Soviet Union. This provided a vast new prospect to Western companies: the potential to participate in a region rich with hydrocarbons, perhaps comparable to the Middle East in the scale of resources, and world-class opportunities. They dispatched teams to research these opportunities.

Some concluded that, whatever the "Russian risk," they simply could not afford not to be in Russia. "When you looked at the opportunity, you became enthusiastic," recalled Archie Dunham, then CEO of the U.S. major Conoco. "It was just a huge opportunity." But, as time went on, the Western companies learned how difficult it was to work in the Russian Federation. As Dunham added, "You had a rule of law problem, you had a tax problem, and you had a logistical problem."

The uncertain political environment, the shifting cast of characters, the corruption, the security risks, the opaque and constantly changing rules, the uncertainty as to "who was who" and "who was behind who"—all of these made others more reluctant. "We had opportunities all over the world," said Lucio Noto, CEO of Mobil. "Once you sink a couple of billion dollars into the ground, you can't move it."[13]

When the Western companies looked across the panorama—at the operating conditions, the equipment, and the fields—they saw an industry that was suffering from decades of isolation and that lacked the most up-to-date equipment, advanced skills, and sufficient computing power. They recognized that Russian geoscientists were at the forefront of their disciplines, but that, in Russia, "theory" was quite separated from "practice." They also saw the dire situation in the Russian oil fields and the desperate need for investment. The Westerners were convinced that they would be welcome because they brought technology, capital, expertise, and management skills. That is not how Russian oil people looked at it, however. They took great pride in what the Soviet industry had accomplished, they were confident in their own skills, and they enormously resented the implication that they were not up to world standards. The Russian industry, in their view, did not need outsiders telling them what to do. Nor did it need substantial direct foreign participation in order to transfer technology. If the Russians needed technology, they could buy it on the world market from service companies.

Neither the government nor the emerging Russian business and political classes saw any reason to give up control over any substantial resources to Western companies. They may not have agreed among themselves as to who would ultimately own those resources and control the wealth so generated, but the one thing on which they could all agree was that it should not be the foreigners.

The major Western companies could not operate on any scale (with one major exception) in the core; that is, the traditional areas of current large production, the "brown fields" of West Siberia. Rather it was in those the areas where there was little development and major technical challenges to be overcome and where the Western companies thus had competitive advantage in terms of technology and execution of complex projects.

THE PERIPHERIES

In partnership with Lukoil, Conoco took on a project in the northern Arctic region. Conoco brought the know-how to Russia it had learned from Alaska, where new technologies had been developed in order to minimize the footprint in Arctic regions. Even so, the Polar Lights project was constantly bedeviled by an endless profusion of new tax charges and new regulations. The local regional boss, a former snowmobile mechanic, was known to demand a payment every time a new permit came up. Finally, Conoco had to tell Moscow that it was going to pull out altogether if the "extra-contractual" demands did not cease.[14]

Both Exxon and Shell went to Sakhalin, the six-hundred-mile-long island off the coast of Russia's far east, north of Japan, where there was some minor onshore production. While the technical challenges were immense there, so was the apparent potential, especially offshore. Though the region was almost totally devoid of the infrastructure that the planned megaprojects would need, it had other important advantages. Sakhalin was as far from Moscow as one could get and still be in Russia. It was also on the open sea, so that output could be exported directly to world markets.

Exxon became the operator for a project that also included the Russian state company Rosneft, Japanese companies, and India's national oil company. Within ExxonMobil, some considered this the most complex project that the company had ever undertaken up to that time—working in a remote, undeveloped subarctic area, where icebergs are a chronic problem, winds are hurricane strength for several months a year, and temperatures can drop to −40° or even lower. The conditions were so difficult, in fact, that work could only be done for five months a year. In the middle of development, as new complexities emerged, the engineers concluded that they needed to go back and redesign the whole project. The project, initially scoped out in the early 1990s, took a decade before it produced "first oil" and a decade and a half before it reached full production—all this at a cost approaching $7 billion.[15]

Shell's Sakhalin-2 also began in the early 1990s with the same environmental challenges. It would prove to be the largest combined oil and gas project in the world, not just a megaproject, but equivalent to five world-class megaprojects in scale and complexity. Shell faced the additional challenges of building two five-hundred-mile pipelines—one oil and one gas—that had to cross more than a thousand rivers and streams, through terrain frozen in the winter and soggy in the summer. To get the oil and gas to export facilities ended up costing more than $20 billion.

IN THE HEARTLAND

Only one Western company managed to gain a significant position in the heartland, West Siberia. Sidanco was a second-tier Russian major that had been bought by a group of oligarchs in one of the loans-for-shares deals in 1995. It had one jewel: partial ownership (along with TNK) of Samotlor, the largest oil field in West Siberia. BP bought ten percent of Sidanco for $571 million in 1997. Some members of BP's board thought it was a harebrained scheme; it was hard to make the case that Russia was a country with rule of law. But BP chief executive John Browne argued it was the only obvious way to get into West Siberia, and Russia was central to BP's overall global strategy. Nonetheless, he added, "we should consider it an outright gamble. We could lose it all."[16]

It soon appeared that Browne's caveat was even more warranted than he might have anticipated. For strange things began to happen. Under the guise of a newly approved Russian bankruptcy law, subsidiaries of Sidanco kept disappearing in a series of bankruptcy proceedings in various out-of-the-way Siberian courts. It became apparent that these were manufactured bankruptcies. The "creditors" were proving very adept at taking advantage of provisions in Russia's new bankruptcy law to take ownership of the subsidiaries. It looked as though Sidanco might end up a shell, and BP with little or nothing to show for its $571 million.

In due course it emerged that what was going on was a struggle between two groups of oligarchs who had jointly participated in the original loans-for-shares acquisition of Sidanco and then had a bitter falling-out. The AAR group believed that its partner, Interros, had tricked it into selling out at a greatly discounted price prior the BP deal. And now AAR wanted back in. BP was really a bystander, but its prospects for protecting its position in Russia did not look at all good. Outside Russia was a different matter. AAR also owned TNK. At this point, TNK had very few financial resources of its own but needed considerable investment to maintain and develop its share of Samotlor. So it was turning to Western credit markets to finance its activities. But then Western credit lines, on which TNK depended, were one after another shutting down. TNK could certainly prevail within Russia, but BP held high cards and influence outside Russia. That was sufficient to force the parties to the negotiating table: the dissident oligarchs and their company TNK gained a major share of Sidanco. Yet BP had preserved its role as the only Western company to have found a way into a significant position in the heartland of Russian oil—in West Siberia.

By this time, politics in Russia had changed, and so had the position of the Russian government.

"A GREAT ECONOMIC POWER"

With the end of the Cold War, Vladimir Putin, who had been a KGB officer stationed in Dresden in East Germany, returned to his home town of St. Petersburg and joined the city government. When the reformist mayor for whom he worked as a deputy mayor was defeated, Putin was without a job. Then his country house burned down. He enrolled to do a doctorate in the St. Petersburg Mining Institute. His studies there would help shape his view of Russia's future.

In 1999, Putin published an article in the institute's journal on "Mineral Natural Resources" that argued that Russia's oil and gas resources were key to economic recovery and to the "entry of Russia into the world economy" and for making Russia "a great economic power." Given their central strategic importance, these resources had to be, ultimately, under the aegis, if not direct control, of the state.

By the time the article was in print, Putin himself was already in Moscow, rapidly ascending in a series of jobs—including head of the FSB, successor to the KGB, and then prime minister. On the last day of December 1999 Boris Yeltsin abruptly resigned and Vladimir Putin, without a job just three years earlier, became Russia's acting president.

In July 2000, two months after his official election, Putin met in the Kremlin with some of the rich and powerful businessmen known by then as oligarchs. He very clearly laid down the new ground rules. They could retain their assets, but they were not to cross the line to try to become kingmakers or in other ways control political outcomes. Two of the oligarchs who did not listen closely were soon in exile.

TNK-BP "50/50"

Once its deal with TNK had been concluded, BP began looking at the possibility of a merger of interests. Given their recent struggle over Sidanco, there was wariness on both sides. After intense negotiations, the two groups agreed to combine their oil assets in Russia with 50/50 ownership of the new firm, TNK-BP. BP wanted 51 percent, but this was never going to be possible. As

John Browne later said, "We could not have it." On the other hand, it could not go ahead in a minority position of 49 percent. The result was equal ownership. President Putin gave his approval, though with a word of advice. "It's up to you," he said to Browne. But he added, "An equal split never works." The deal went forward. At a ceremony in Lancaster House in London in 2003, Browne and Fridman signed documents for the new company, with Vladimir Putin and British Prime Minister Tony Blair standing behind them, overseeing the signatures. The new TNK-BP represented the largest direct foreign investment in Russia. At the same time it was a Russian company. The new combination modernized the oil fields and increased production rapidly. It also increased BP's total reserves by a third, and it pushed BP ahead of Shell to be the second largest company, after ExxonMobil. But a few years later, bearing out Putin's adage, a fierce battle erupted over control and as to exactly what 50/50 meant. Eventually, after much tension, the two sides came to a new compromise that modified the governance, shifting the balance toward the Russian partners while preserving BP's position. Mikhail Fridman became the new CEO.[17]

YUKOS

By the time of Putin's election in 2000, Mikhail Khodorkovsky of Yukos was already on his way to becoming the richest man in Russia. He had the reputation as an aggressive and ruthless businessman; but with the beginning of the new century he seemed to be remaking himself. He would compress three generations—ruthless robber baron, modernizing businessman, and philanthropist—into one. He brought in Western technology to transform Yukos into a far more efficient company. By importing Western-style corporate governance and listing his company on Western exchanges, he could greatly increase the valuation of Yukos and thus multiply his wealth several times over. Through his Open Russia Foundation, he became the biggest philanthropist in Russia, supporting civic and human rights organizations.

His spending on politics was also well known, indeed almost legendary in its extent, most notably in the money spent to ensure that deputies in the Duma voted exactly the way he wanted on tax legislation in May 2003. He seemed to be pursuing his own foreign policy. He negotiated directly with China on building a pipeline, bypassing the Kremlin on something of great strategic importance, and on which Putin had very different views. He was moving fast to acquire Sibneft, one of the other new Russian oil majors, which would make Yukos possibly the largest oil company in the world. And he was in talks with both Chevron and ExxonMobil about selling controlling interest in Yukos. When Putin met with the CEO of one of the western companies, he had many, many questions about how a deal would work and what it would mean. For it would have moved control over a substantial part of the country's most important strategic asset, oil, out of Russia, which ran exactly counter to the principle that he had laid down in his 1999 article.

While moving on all these fronts at the same time, Khodorkovsky let it be widely known that he was prepared to spend money to move Russia toward being a parliamentary rather than a presidential democracy, with the implication that he intended to become prime minister. Selling part of Yukos would give him many billions of dollars that could go into that campaign.

And then there was what turned into a heated exchange with Putin at a meeting with the industrialists that was captured on video. "Corruption in the country is spreading," said Khodorkovsky. To which an angry Putin reminded him that he had won control over huge oil reserves for very little money. "And the question is, how did you obtain them?" said Putin. He then added, "I'm returning the hockey puck to you."[18]

Several months later, in July 2003, one of Khodorkovsky's business partners was arrested, and then others. Some of his advisers, fearing that he was becoming increasingly unrealistic, warned him to proceed with care, but he seemed to disregard them. On a visit to Washington in September 2003, he said that he thought there was a 40 percent chance he would be arrested. But he gave the impression that he did not believe that the real odds were anywhere near that high.

In the autumn of 2003, Khodorkovsky embarked on what looked like a campaign swing, with speeches and interviews and public meetings in cities across Siberia. In the early morning of October 23, his plane was on the ground in Novosibirsk, where it had stopped for refueling. At 5 a.m. FSB agents burst in and arrested him. In the spring of 2005, after a lengthy trial, Khodorkovsky was convicted of tax fraud and sent to a distant and isolated Siberian prison camp. In 2011, a second trial for embezzlement extended his sentence. By then, the case had become an international cause, exemplified when, after the trial, Amnesty International selected him as a "prisoner of conscience."

As for Yukos, it was no more. It was dismantled and became a noncompany and was absorbed into Rosneft, which is now Russia's largest oil company and, largely owned by the government, the national champion.

"STRATEGIC RESOURCES"

"Strategic resources" came to the fore in other ways as well. ExxonMobil's Sakhalin-1 project had a Russian company as partner, Rosneft. But Shell's Sakhalin-2 did not. Gazprom may have been the largest gas company in the world, but it had no representation in liquefied natural gas (LNG), and no capacity to market to Asia. Over several months in 2006, the Sakhalin-2 project was charged with a litany of various environmental violations that carried a variety of penalties, some of them severe. At the end of December 2006, Shell and its Japanese partners accepted Gazprom as majority shareholder. The project thereafter continued on course and in 2009 began exporting LNG to Asia and even as far away as Spain.

OIL AND RUSSIA'S FUTURE

By the second decade of the twenty-first century, Russia was back as an oil producer. Its output was as high as it had been in the twilight of the Soviet Union, two decades earlier, but on very different terms. The oil industry was integrated technologically with the rest of the world; and it was no longer the province of a single all-encompassing ministry, but rather was operated by a variety of companies with many differences in leadership, culture, and approaches. When it was all added up, Russia was once again the largest producer of oil and the second largest exporter in the world.

Once, as Russian production and oil revenues were ramping up, Vladimir Putin was asked if Russia was an energy superpower. He replied that he did not like the phrase. "Superpower," he said, was "the word we used during the Cold War," and the Cold War was over. "I have never referred to Russia as an energy superpower. But we do have greater possibilities than almost any other country in the world. If put together Russia's energy potential in all areas, oil, gas, and nuclear, our country is unquestionably the leader."

Certainly Russia's energy resources—and its markets—put it in a position of preeminence; and with a new uncertainty about the Middle East, it took on a renewed salience as an energy supplier and in terms of energy security.

Oil and gas were also what powered its own economy. As Putin had written in his 1999 article, they had indeed been the engine of Russia's recovery and growth—and the number one source of government revenues. High prices meant even more money flowing into the nation's treasury. The country's demographics made those revenues even more critical—in order to meet the pension needs of an aging population.

But the heavy reliance on oil and gas stirred a national debate about the country's heavy dependence on that one sector and about the need for "modernization," which meant, in part, diversification away from hydrocarbons. But modernization was hard to achieve without broad-ranging reforms of the economy and legal and governmental institutions, along with a nurturing of a culture of entrepreneurship. Some argued that high oil prices, by creating a cushion of wealth, made it easier to postpone reform. Whatever the progress on modernization, oil and gas would continue to be the country's greatest source of wealth for some years to come, as well as an arena in its own right for advanced technology.

But the very importance of oil and gas highlighted a different kind of risk: would Russia be able to maintain its level of output or was another great decline in the offing? The latter would threaten the economy. Some argued that Russia would not be able to sustain production without big changes—a step up in new investment, a tax regime that encouraged investment, augmentation of technology, and, of critical importance, the development of the "next generation" of oil and gas fields. One of the major targets for that next generation was the offshore, particularly in the Arctic regions, off the northern coast of Russia.

Developing those frontier regions would be challenging and costly and even more complex than the Sakhalin projects. Once again, here was the potential for a significant role for international companies. These would be the projects for which Western partners would be sought, especially the large majors with their capabilities to execute projects on that scale. Yet undertaking them would require considerable confidence on both sides. For these would be very long-term relationships; the development time would be measured not in years, but decades, and their full impact would likely be felt nearer the middle of the twenty-first century, rather than the beginning. But that was still prospect.

For the Western companies—save for those long-range projects in places like the Arctic—there was not much more in the way of large opportunities beyond what had already been launched in the 1990s. As things had turned out, the early expectations about Russia had proved to be much larger than the reality.

When it came to oil and gas, however, there had been more opportunity to be found in the former Soviet Union than just in the Russian Federation. Much more. And it was to the rest of the region that attention had also turned in the late 1980s and early 1990s as the Soviet system was disintegrating.

2

THE CASPIAN DERBY

In the late 1980s and the beginning of the 1990s, as the Soviet Union started to come unhinged, the first Western oil men had begun to drift down toward the south, to the Caspian and into Central Asia, into what would after 1991 become the newly independent countries of Azerbaijan, Kazakhstan, and Turkmenistan.

Historically, the most important city on the Caspian coastline was Baku. A century earlier, Baku had been a hub of great commercial and entrepreneurial activity, with grand palaces, built by nineteenth-century oil tycoons, and one of the world's great opera houses. But what these arriving oil men now found instead, amid the splintering of the Soviet Union, were the remnants of a once-vibrant industry and what seemed almost like a museum of the history of oil.

The interaction between these oil men and the newly emerging nations would help wrest these countries out of their isolated histories and connect them to the world economy. The results would redraw the map of world oil and bring into the global market an oil region that, by the second decade of the twenty-first century, would rival such established provinces as the North Sea, and would include the world's third-largest producing oil field.

The development of the Caspian oil and natural gas resources was inextricably entangled with geopolitics and the ambitions of nations. It would also help define what the new world—the world after the Cold War—would look like and how it would operate.

At the center is the Caspian Sea itself, the world's largest inland body of water, with 3,300 miles of coastline. Though not connected to any ocean, it is salty, and also subject to sudden, violent storms. Azerbaijan is on its western shore. To the west of Azerbaijan are Georgia and Armenia—the three together constituting the South Caucasus. On the northwest side of the Caspian, above Azerbaijan, are Russia and its turbulent North Caucasus region, including Chechnya. On the northeast side of the Caspian is Kazakhstan; and, on the southeast, Turkmenistan. On the southern shore is Iran, with ambitions to be a dominant regional power and with interests going back to the dynasties of the Persian shahs.

THE NEW GREAT GAME

The fierce vortex of competing interests in this region came to be known as the new "Great Game." The term had originally been attributed to Arthur Conolly, a cavalry officer in the British army in India turned explorer and spy, whose unfortunate end in 1842—he was executed by the local ruler in the ancient Central Asian town of Bukhara—captured both the seriousness and futility of the game. But it was Rudyard Kipling who took up the phrase and made it famous in *Kim,* his novel about a British spy and adventurer, at the front line in the late nineteenth century in the contest with the Russian Empire.[1]

But this purported new round in the Great Game, at the end of the twentieth century, included not just Russia and Britain, the two main contenders from the first round in the nineteenth century, but many more—the United States, Turkey, Iran, and, later, China. And of course the newly independent countries themselves were players, intent on balancing among these various contending forces to establish and then preserve their independence.

Then there were the oil and gas companies, eager to add major new reserves and determined not to be left out. And hardly to be overlooked was the jostling of the wheelers-dealers, the operators, the finders, and the facilitators, all of them out for their cut. This is a grand tradition established in the first decades

CASPIAN SEA AND THE CAUCASUS: THE "NEWLY INDEPENDENT STATES"

The breakup of the Soviet Union reconnected a resource-rich region to world energy markets.

of the twentieth century by the greatest oil wheeler-dealer of them all, Calouste Gulbenkian, later immortalized as "Mr. Five Percent."

Rather than the Great Game, others used the less dramatic shorthand of "pipeline politics" to convey the fact that the decisive clash was not that of weapons but of the routes by which oil and natural gas from the landlocked Caspian would get to the world's markets. But to some, watching the collisions and the confusion among the players, hearing the cacophony of charges and countercharges and the bluster and banging of deal making, it was better described as the Caspian Derby. Whatever the name, the prize was the oil and natural gas—who would produce it, and who could succeed in getting it to market.

THE PLAYERS

The Soviet Union was gone. But Russian interests were not. The economies of Russia and the newly independent nations were highly integrated in everything from infrastructure to the movements of people. Russian military bases, as legatees of the Soviet military, were scattered throughout the region. What would be the nature of Russia's relations with the newly independent states, many of which had been khanates in the centuries before their conquest by the Russian Empire but had never really existed as modern nation-states?

For the Russians, it was about power and position and restoring their country as a great power. They had hardly expected the Soviet Union to fall apart. Many Russians had come to regret this loss and regarded the dissolution of the Soviet Union as a nation (if not as a communist state) as a humiliation, as something that had been foisted upon them by malevolent forces from outside, specifically in the view of some, the United States. Immediately after the breakup, they began to describe these newly established countries as belonging to a newly conceived region, the "Near Abroad," over which they wanted to reassert control. That very name also conveyed a special status with special prerogatives for Russia—and all the more so because of the large numbers of ethnic Russians who lived in what were now independent countries. While there might now be formal boundaries, Russia and these new nations were bound together by history, education, economic and military links, the Russian language, and ideology and common culture—and a multitude of marriages. In Moscow's view, they belonged very much in Russia's sphere of influence and under its tutelage. Russians saw Western influence in the Near Abroad as an attempt to further undermine Russia and retard the restoration of its Great Power status.[2]

And there was the specific matter of oil. From the Bolshevik Revolution onward, the Caspian's petroleum resources had been developed by the Soviet oil industry with Soviet technology and Soviet investment. The Soviets had begun to bring on a very large, if also very difficult, new field in the Republic of Kazakhstan, and the Soviet oil generals had been talking, before the breakup, about renewed focus on the Caspian as a production area.

Some Russians also believed, or at least half believed, that the United States had deliberately orchestrated the collapse of the Soviet Union for the specific purpose of getting its hands on Caspian oil. Once, in the mid-1990s, the Russian energy minister was innocently asked what he thought of the development of Caspian oil. He pounded his fist down on his conference table.

"Eto nash neft," he replied. "It's our oil."

For the United States and Britain, the consolidation of the newly independent nations was part of the unfinished business of the post–Cold War and what was required for a new, more peaceful world order. This was these nations' opportunity to realize the Wilsonian dream of self-determination. An exclusive Russian sphere of influence would, in the American and British view, be dangerous and destabilizing. Moreover, there was the risk of Iran's filling a vacuum, which, though not often stated, was very much on their minds.

The energy dimension also loomed large for Washington in the early 1990s. Saddam's grab for Kuwait and the Gulf War, just concluded, had once again demonstrated the risks of the world's overdependence on the Persian Gulf. If the Caspian could be reintegrated into the world energy industry, as it had been prior to World War I, if major new petroleum resources from the region could be brought to the world market, that would be a very large step in diversification of petroleum supplies, making a most significant contribution to global energy security. To be prevented was the flip side—these resources slipping back under exclusive Russian sway or, even worse, under Iranian influence.

Yet at the same time, building a new relationship with Russia was at the very top of the priorities of the Clinton administration, and so there was little desire to have that relationship damaged by competition for Caspian oil and a modern Great Game. In a speech called "A Farewell to Flashman" (Flashman being a fictional swashbuckling British military man in the nineteenth-century Great Game), U.S. Deputy Secretary of State Strobe Talbott sketched out the goal of stable economic and political development in a critical crossroads of the world, and warned against the alternative—that "the region could become a breeding ground of terrorism, a hotbed of religious and political extremism, and a battleground for outright war." He added, "It has been fashionable to proclaim . . . a replay of the 'Great Game' in the Caucasus and Central Asia . . . fueled and lubricated by oil." But, he said, "Our goal is to actively discourage that atavistic outcome." The Great Game, he added firmly, belonged "on the shelves of historical fiction." Yet it would be very challenging to modulate the clash of interests and ambitions in this strategic terrain.[3]

For Turkey, locked out of the region for centuries, the breakup of the Soviet Union was a way to expand its influence and importance and commerce across the Black Sea into the Caucasus and onto the Caspian Sea and beyond—and also to connect with the Turkic peoples of Central Asia. And, for the Islamic Republic of Iran, here was the opportunity to expand its political and religious influence north into the other countries on the Caspian Sea and into Central Asia and to seek to proselytize among Islamic peoples whose access to Islamic religion had been tightly constrained during Soviet times.

Azerbaijan was of particular importance to Iran. Over 7.5 million ethnic Azeris lived there, now with the opportunity to interact with the outside world, while an estimated 16 million Iranians, a quarter of Iran's total population, were also ethnically Azeri. Though generally tightly policed by Iran's ruling theocracy, many Iranian Azeris had direct family relations in Azerbaijan. So for the regime in Tehran, an independent Azerbaijan, as an example of a more tolerant, secular and potentially prosperous society and one connected to the West, was something to be feared as a threat to its own internal control.

China's interests developed more slowly, but they became progressively more significant as the rapid growth of its economy made energy an increasingly important issue. The Central Asian states were "next door," and they could be connected by pipelines, providing critical diversification. China increasingly made its impact felt, but less through politics and more through investment.

The newly independent states were hardly mere pawns. Their leaders were determined to solidify their power. Although there were considerable differences among them, at home that meant what were essentially one-party states with power consolidated in the hands of the president. In foreign policy, the strategic objectives of these nations were very clear: maintain and consolidate their independence and establish themselves as nations. Whatever the differences in their views of the Kremlin, they did not want to find themselves reabsorbed one way or the other by the new Russian Federation. On the other hand, they were in no position to disengage from Russia or stoke its ire. They needed Russia. The connections were so many and so strong, and the geography so obvious. Moreover, they had to be concerned about their own ethnic populations in Moscow and the other Russian cities, whose remittances would become important components of their new national GNPs.

For many of the countries, oil and natural gas were potentially critical, an enormous source of revenues and the major driver of recovery and economic growth. The development of oil could bring in companies from many countries and generate not only cash but also political interest and support. As the Azeri national security adviser put it, "Oil is our strategy, it is our defense, it is our independence."[4]

If oil was the physical resource they needed for their survival as nation-states, they also required another kind of resource—wily diplomacy. For the game, always, required extraordinary skill in balancing in a difficult terrain. Azerbaijan, a secular Islamic state, was squeezed between Iran and Russia. Kazakhstan, with a huge territory but relatively small population, had to find its balance between Russia and an increasingly self-confident and rapidly growing China.

Yet in all the discussions about oil and geopolitics and great games, one could not lose sight of the more practical matters: that oil development took place not only on the stage of world politics but on the playing fields of the petroleum industry—on the computer screens of engineers and spreadsheets of financial analysts, in the fabrication yards where the rigs were built, and on the drilling sites and offshore platforms—where the key considerations were geology and geography, engineering, costs, investment, logistics, and the mastery of technological complexity. And the risk for the companies was large—not just political risk, but the inherent risk in trying to develop new resources that might be world class but also posed great enormous engineering challenges.

The companies had to operate against extremes of expectations. For at one point, the Caspian was celebrated as a new El Dorado, a magical solution, another Persian Gulf, a region of huge riches in oil and gas resources eagerly waiting for the drill bit. At another time, it was a huge disappointment, a giant bust, one great dry hole beneath the wet seabed. So in terms of expectations, too, one had to stay sober and keep one's balance.

"THE OIL KINGDOM"

In the late nineteenth century and early twentieth century, the Russian Empire, specifically the region around Baku on the Caspian Sea, had been one of the world's major sources of oil. Indeed, at the very beginning of the twentieth century, it had overtaken western Pennsylvania to be the world's number one source. Families with names like Nobel and Rothschild made fortunes there. Ludwig Nobel—brother of Alfred, the inventor of dynamite and endower of the Nobel Prizes—was known as the "Russian Rockefeller." It was Ludwig Nobel who conceived and built the world's first oil tanker, to transport petroleum on the stormy Caspian Sea. Shell Oil had been founded on the basis of oil from Baku, audaciously brought to world oil markets by an extraordinary entrepreneur and onetime shell merchant named Marcus Samuel. They shared the stage with prominent local oil tycoons of great influence.

The ascendancy of Baku would be undermined by political instability, beginning with the abortive revolution of 1905, what Vladimir Lenin dubbed the "great rehearsal." In the years immediately after, the region continued to be shaken by revolutionary activity. Among those most active was a onetime Orthodox seminarian from neighboring Georgia, Iosif Dzhugashvili, better known to the world as Joseph Stalin. As Stalin later said, he honed his skills as "a journeyman for the revolution" working as an agitator and organizer in the oil fields. What he did not add were his additional activities as a sometime bank robber and extortionist. It was thus with good reason that Stalin, recognizing the wealth that was to be extorted, anointed Baku as the "the Oil Kingdom."[5]

With the collapse of the Russian Empire at the outbreak of the Bolshevik Revolution during World War I, the region west of the Caspian Sea, including Baku, declared itself the independent Azerbaijan Democratic Republic. It established one of the first modern parliaments in the Islamic world. It was also the first Muslim country to grant women the right to vote (ahead of such countries as Britain and the United States). But Lenin declared that his new revolutionary state could not survive without Baku's oil, and in 1920 the Bolsheviks conquered the republic, incorporating it into the new Soviet Union and nationalizing the oil fields.

That same year, however, Sir Henri Deterding, the head of Royal Dutch Shell, confidently declared, "The Bolsheviks will be cleared, not only out of the Caucasus, but out of the whole of Russia in about six months." It soon became evident, however, that the Bolsheviks were not going anywhere soon, and that Western companies had no place in the new Soviet Union.

When, in June 1941, Hitler launched his invasion of the Soviet Union, Azerbaijan was one of his most important strategic objectives—he wanted to get his hands on an assured supply of oil to fuel his war machine. "Unless we get the Baku oil, the war is lost," he told one of his generals. His forces got very close to Baku, but not close enough, owing to fierce resistance by the Soviets and the natural barriers imposed by the high mountains of the Caucasus. The failure was costly for Nazi Germany, for its severe shortage of oil crippled its military machine and was one of the reasons for its ultimate defeat.[6]

By the 1970s and 1980s, the Caspian had become an oil backwater of the Soviet Union, thought to be depleted or technologically too difficult; its once prominent role had been assumed by other producing regions, most notably West Siberia. In the late 1980s and early 1990s, however, as Soviet power crumbled and Azerbaijan, Kazakhstan, and Turkmenistan were moving toward, and then into, independence, the region's potential—buttressed by advances in technology—once again loomed very large.

HISTORY ON DISPLAY

Baku and its environs stood at the historic center of what had been the Russian and then Soviet oil industry, and that entire history was on display for the wide-eyed Western oil men who were beginning to show up.

Some of it was at sea. A rickety network of wooden walkways and platforms, connected like a little city, extended out from the seafront in Baku. Farther offshore, 40 miles from the coastline, where the seabed became shallow again, was Oily Rocks, a great network of walkways and platforms, "a wooden and steel oil town on stilts, 15 miles long and a half mile wide," with 125 miles of road and a number of multistory apartment buildings built on artificial rock islands. Once it had been regarded as one of the great achievements of Soviet engineering, a "legend in the open sea." But now Oily Rocks was so dilapidated that parts of it were crumbling and falling into the sea, and some parts were considered so treacherous that they had been abandoned and closed off altogether.[7]

Onshore, in and around Baku, were innumerable antique "nodding donkeys," still bobbing up and down, helping to pump up oil from wells that had been drilled in the late nineteenth and early twentieth centuries. Hiking into the wide, dry Kirmaky Valley just north of Baku would take one back even earlier in time. There one would step over pipelines and clamber up barren hills that were pockmarked with hundreds of pits that been dug by hand in the eighteenth and nineteenth centuries. In those days, one or two men would be lowered into each of these narrow, dangerous pits, past walls reinforced with wood planks, 25 to 50 feet down to the claustrophobic bottom, where they would fill buckets with oil that would be hoisted out with primitive rope pulleys.

Down on the other side of the hill was the Balachanavaya Field, where a gusher had been drilled in 1871. That field was still crowded with old rigs, densely packed up against one another, some of them going back to the days of the Nobels and the Rothschilds. Altogether 5 billion barrels of oil had been extracted from the field, and it was still modestly producing away, while gas leaking from a nearby mountainside continued to burn in an "eternal flame."

Thus, awaiting the arriving oil men in Azerbaijan was an industry deep into decline and decay, starved of investment, modern technology, and sheer attention. Yet what the oil men also saw, if not altogether clearly, was the opportunity—though tempered by many risks and uncertainties.

"ALL ROADS ARE THERE"

Azerbaijan was ground zero for the Caspian Derby. As a Russian energy minister put it, it was the "key" to the Caspian, for "all roads are there." Every kind of issue was at play, and so many of them the result of geography. The most immediate problem was to the west, the newly independent state of Armenia, with which war had broken out over the disputed enclave Nagorno-Karabakh. Armenia, with some Russian support, was victorious; 800,000 ethnic Azeris, primarily from Nagorno-Karabakh, became refugees and "internally displaced peoples," living in tent cities and corrugated tin huts and whatever else Azerbaijan could find for them. This displacement—equivalent to 10 percent of the Azeri population—added to the woes of what was already an impoverished country, with a broken-down infrastructure and teetering on economic collapse.

In the first years of the 1990s, various consortia of international oil companies pursued what has been described as "disruptive and complex negotiations" with successive Azeri governments, which had largely come to naught. The country itself seemed to be entrapped in endemic instability and insurgencies, and, as various clans struggled for power, headed toward civil war.[8]

"THE NATIVE SON"

During Soviet times, Heydar Aliyev had risen to the pinnacle of power in Azerbaijan, initially as a KGB general and then head of the local KGB, and then as first secretary of the Azeri Communist Party. He had subsequently moved to Moscow and into the ruling Politburo, becoming for a time one of the most powerful men in the Soviet Union. But after a fiery falling-out with Mikhail Gorbachev and a spectacular fall from power, he was expelled not only from the Politburo but also from Moscow, and denied even an apartment back in Baku. He returned to his boyhood home, Nakhichevan, an isolated corner of Azerbaijan, which, after the collapse of the Soviet Union, was cut off from the rest of the country by Armenia and was reachable only by occasional air flights from Baku. While in this internal exile, he discovered his new vocation and identity—no longer as a "Soviet man," but, as he put it, as a "native son." He bided his time.

With the political battle in Baku getting even hotter and the country teetering on civil war, he returned to the capital city and, in 1993, amid an attempted insurrection, took over as president. At age seventy, Aliyev was back in power. He brought stability. He also brought great skill to the job. "I've been in politics a long time, and I've seen it all from inside out as part of the core leadership of a world superpower," he said not long after taking power. He was now an Azeri nationalist. He was also a proven master of tactics and a brilliant strategist. He would use Azerbaijan's oil potential to turn the country into a real nation, and to enlist key nations in support of its integrity, and, in the process of doing all of this, ensure his own primacy and control. But he also knew the Russians and the mentality of Moscow as well as anyone, and he understood clearly how to deal with the Russians and how far he could safely tread out on his own path.[9]

"THE DEAL OF THE CENTURY"

In September 1994, Aliyev assembled a host of diplomats and oil executives in the Gulistan Palace banquet hall in Baku for the signing of what he proclaimed the "deal of the century." The signatories included ten oil companies—representing six different nations—that belonged to what was now the Azerbaijan International Operating Company (AIOC) plus the State Oil Company of Azerbaijan Republic (SOCAR), the Azeri state company. BP and Amoco were the dominant Western companies, but also, and of great significance, in the deal was Lukoil, the Russian company. Later the Japanese trading company Itochu joined the AIOC, bringing the number of national flags to seven. Given the complexities and uncertainties, some mumbled that a better sobriquet than "deal of the century" would be "Mission Impossible." After all, how was this going to get done? And how was landlocked Azerbaijan ever going to get its oil to the world market? Yet as the CEO of one of the Western companies put it, "the oil had to go somewhere."[10]

Moreover, even with Aliyev in power, the political situation was far from stable. Baku was under nightly curfew, and, shortly after the signing of the "deal of the century," two of Aliyev's closest aides were assassinated, including his security chief, to be followed by a failed military coup.

The object of the "deal of the century" was the huge Azeri-Chirag-Gunashli field (ACG) in the Aspheron trend, seventy-five miles offshore. It had been discovered prior to the collapse of the Soviet Union, but it was a mostly undeveloped project, and a very challenging one. Much of it had proved well beyond the technological capabilities of the Soviet oil industry. However, during Soviet times, development had started in a more shallow corner of the field, and if the platform could be successfully refurbished and upgraded to international standards, some early production would be possible. This would become known as Early Oil. It was desirable, because it would create an early income stream and, perhaps even more important, build confidence among the AIOC shareholders.

WHAT ROUTE FOR EARLY OIL?

But Early Oil was also highly contentious, for it would create a big and immediate problem. How to get the oil out? Once ashore, some of it could be shipped in railway tank cars, just as in the nineteenth century, but that was a limited and hardly satisfactory alternative.

The only obvious answer was a pipeline. And, with that answer, the Caspian Derby turned clamorous. By reversing directions, the oil could go north through the existing Russian pipeline system, which is of course exactly what the Russians wanted. But that would also have given Russia very considerable leverage over Azerbaijan's economic and political fate, and the United States strenuously opposed it.

The other option for the Early Oil pipeline was to go west into Georgia and to the Black Sea, where tankers would pick up the oil and carry it through the Bosporus to the Mediterranean—a route that tracked what had been the main outlet for nineteenth-century Baku oil. But that would make Azerbaijan dependent on Georgia, which was wracked by separatist struggles and which had a very tense and uneasy relationship with Russia. This route would also be a great deal more expensive, entailing much more construction in difficult terrain. The AIOC was under great pressure to choose. The Azeris needed revenues; the companies needed clarity. But the United States and Russia were at loggerheads. Yet something needed to be done. One way or the other, Early Oil was coming.

THE TWO-TRACK STRATEGY: "OFFEND NO ONE"

In a nondescript conference room in central London, some senior AIOC staff and a small group of oil and regional experts debated the choices—"Early Oil

Goes North" and "Early Oil Goes West"—and the likely backlash to each. It was recognized that "an unequivocal choice in either direction would be perilous from the standpoint of political risk."

Finally, one of the participants who had sat quietly in the corner spoke up. Why choose? he asked. Why not do both? The more pipelines, the better. Even if the cost was higher, dual pipelines would provide more security. It would be a great insurance policy. That approach would also help assure speed and discourage foot dragging—since the AIOC could always threaten to go with the "other" option. So taken together, two routes made a lot of sense.[11]

Of course, one had to start somewhere. And that meant starting with the Russian route. After all, a pipeline was in place. The politics were right.

Heydar Aliyev saw it that way. On a dreary, cold February night in 1995, in his office in the hills above Baku, Aliyev gave his marching instructions both to Terence Adams, the head of the AIOC, and to the head of SOCAR. Nothing should be done that would "alienate" the Russians, said the president. It was too risky. A contract had to be signed with the Russians before anything else was done. "The geopolitical imperative could not have been made clearer for Baku oil diplomacy," Adams later said. The president made one other thing very clear. Failure in any form would be a major disaster for Azerbaijan, and thus would certainly also be a disaster for AIOC and personally for all those involved. He looked hard at both men. At the same time, Aliyev emphasized that the relationship with the United States was also essential to his strategy. His message to the oil companies was challenging but clear: "Offend no one."

Things were also changing with the United States. There had been a very sharp debate in Washington between those highly suspicious of Russia, who favored an "anything but Russia" pipeline policy, and those who believed that a collaborative approach with Moscow was required for the development of energy resources and transportation in the former Soviet Union. And, in the latter view, that development was necessary to meet the two objectives: helping to consolidate the nationhood of the newly independent states and enhancing energy security by bringing additional supplies to the world market. In due course, matters were generally—although never completely—resolved in favor of the more collaborative approach. In February 1996, the northern route won official approval.[12]

Agreement for the western Early Oil route soon followed. For its part, the

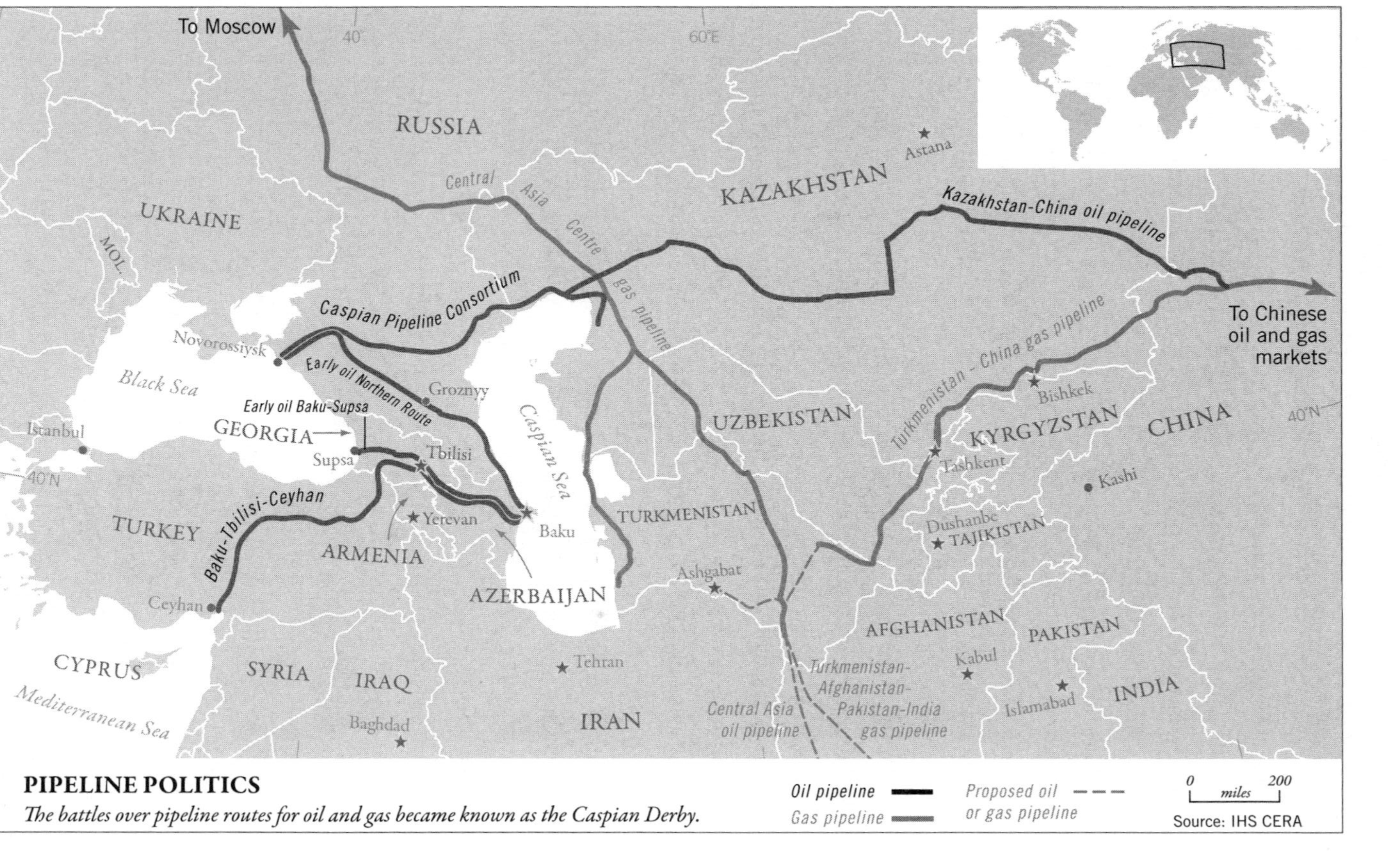

PIPELINE POLITICS

The battles over pipeline routes for oil and gas became known as the Caspian Derby.

Georgian route offered a counterbalance to the Russians. Getting this plan done drew upon the personal relationship between Aliyev and Georgian president Eduard Shevardnadze, whose career, like Aliyev's, had tracked from the local communist security service to leader of the Georgian communist party to the pinnacle of Soviet power in the Kremlin as Mikhail Gorbachev's foreign minister—and, thus, the opposite number of U.S. Secretary of State James Baker in negotiating the end of the Cold War. Now Shevardnadze, who had returned as president to Georgia after the breakup of the Soviet Union, was negotiating a pipeline whose transit fees would be important to keeping impoverished, independent Georgia afloat. Even more important was the geopolitical capital that Georgia gained from U.S., British, and Turkish engagement with which to balance against the Russian giant to the north.

By 1999 both Early Oil export lines were operating. The western route tracked the old wooden pipeline built by the Nobels in the nineteenth century. The Russian northern line passed through Chechnya, where in that same year the second Chechen War would erupt between Russian forces and Islamic rebels. That conflict forced the shutdown of the Russian pipeline. This proved the insurance value of a second, western Early Oil line through Georgia.

That took care of Early Oil. Meanwhile, as the decade progressed, the technical challenges were being surmounted offshore of Azerbaijan, and it was clear that very substantial additional production would begin in the new century. The resources had been "proved up": oil could actually be economically extracted in large volumes from beneath the Caspian Waters.

WHAT ROUTE FOR THE MAIN PIPELINE?

Now that the resources were bankable, a main export pipeline capable of transporting much greater volumes had to be built. It was back to the same battles as over Early Oil. This time, however, there could be only one pipeline. Given the costs and scale, the difference could not be split between two lines. The Russians, of course, wanted the pipeline to go north and flow into their national pipeline system, which would give them some degree of control and leverage over the Caspian resources. Another option was to go through Georgia. But in both cases, the oil would have to be picked up by tankers that would carry it across the Black Sea and then sail through the Bosporus, the narrow strait that runs through the middle of Istanbul. And that was a big problem.

The Bosporus, which connects the Black Sea and the Mediterranean and is the demarcation between Europe and Asia, has loomed large throughout history. It was on its banks that, in the fourth century A.D., the Roman emperor Constantine established his new eastern capital—Constantinople—in order to better manage the far-flung Roman Empire. In more recent centuries, it was of great strategic importance for both the Russian and Soviet empires, as the only warm-water ports for their fleets were on the Black Sea, and their warships had to pass through the Bosporus to reach the world's oceans.

But the Bosporus was becoming increasingly crowded with the growing fleet of oil tankers that would carry Russian and Caspian oil to the world's markets. And the Bosporus was no isolated waterway; it ran right through the middle of Istanbul (as Constantinople had been officially renamed in 1930), a city of 11 million people. Turkey was apprehensive of a major tanker accident in what in effect was Istanbul's living room. And with good reason. The 19-mile waterway has 12 turns. Its narrowest point is 739 yards, which requires a 45-degree turn. Another turn is 80 degrees, almost a right angle.[13]

There was still another option for the main outlet, and in dollars and cents, the cheapest of all. Go south and deliver oil to refineries in northern Iran, which would supply Tehran. And then swap an equivalent amount of oil from fields in the south of Iran for export via the Persian Gulf. Hence, it would not be necessary to build a pipeline through Iran. Such a swap was the least cost option in economic terms. But it was wholly unacceptable to the United States and other Western countries, and thus a complete nonstarter. It would not only have bolstered Iran, but would have given the nation the trigger finger over Azerbaijan's future, which was hardly something that Heydar Aliyev wanted. Moreover, it would have completely undercut the whole quest for diversification and energy security by putting more oil into the Persian Gulf and increasing dependence on the Strait of Hormuz, when the whole point was to diversify away from it.

There was one more option—go west, skirting around Armenia into Georgia, and then turn left near the Georgian capital of Tbilisi and head south down through Turkey to its port of Ceyhan on the Mediterranean. This was the most logical route. The problems with the proposed BTC pipeline—Baku to Tbilisi to Ceyhan—were two: First, it would be one of the longest oil export pipelines in the world, and the engineering challenges over the tall peaks of the Caucasus were enormous. And, second, it was by far the most expensive route. It was very difficult to make the economics work.

As decision time approached, the arguments over the main pipeline became increasingly fierce. The Russians were out to scuttle the project. The Azeris clearly wanted it, as did the Turks. Both pressed BP to push it forward. For a time, it seemed that the United States was most vociferous proponent of all for Baku-Tbilisi-Ceyhan. Its representatives took every opportunity to argue the case, sometimes with a force that surprised and even shocked other participants in the debate. For Washington, the thought that the main export pipeline could possibly go through Russia was unacceptable. The risk was too great.

Madeleine Albright, Bill Clinton's secretary of state, privately summed up the matter at the time. One afternoon, sitting in a little room on the seventh floor of the State Department, she said, "We don't want to wake up ten years from now and have all of us ask ourselves why in the world we made a mistake and didn't build that pipeline."

"NOW IS THE MOMENT"

For half a decade, an annual conference, the "Tale of Three Seas" (Caspian, Black, and Mediterranean), had been convening in Istanbul each June. It would start in the evening, as the sun went down, in a hillside garden overlooking the Bosporus, with a soothing outdoor concert by what was called the "Orchestra of the Three Seas." Its music was meant to symbolize the healing of all the historic breaches that needed to be healed, for its members were drawn from the Caucasus and Central Asia and from a number of Arab countries, as well as Israel.

And then, the next day, all the harmonies would disappear as the raucous Caspian Derby began in earnest. Year after year, the conference sessions and the corridors were the scene of agitated arguments and increasingly vocal debate over pipeline routes—and, at least once, a shoving match among very senior people.

The conference dinner, on a warm summer night in June 2001, was held in the Esma Sultan Palace, with a sweeping view over the Bosporus. The speaker was John Browne, the chief executive of BP, now the dominant company among the shareholders of the AIOC. He stressed that the Bosporus simply could not take any more tanker traffic. "The risks of relying solely on this route would become too high. Another solution is necessary," he said. And that solution was "a new export pipeline"—the Baku-Tbilisi-Ceyhan line.

The oil companies, he announced, were ready to begin the engineering, with the objective of beginning construction as soon as possible. As he made this declaration, almost as if on cue, on the dark historic waters behind him the shadowy silhouette of a large tanker glided by, illuminated only by its own lights. Its silent message seemed to be, How many more of these tankers could the Bosporus take? The pipeline had to be built.

Many obstacles had to be overcome. The first was to convince a sufficient number of the AIOC partners that the pipeline was commercial and get them to sign up for it. Another was the sheer enormity of negotiating so many incredibly complex multiparty agreements that were required to build and operate and finance the pipeline, involving countries, companies, localities, engineering firms, banks, and financing agencies, among other parties. Here the United States played a key role by facilitating an intergovernmental agreement, and myriad other agreements, which otherwise, in the words of one of the company negotiators, would have taken "years to arrange and negotiate."[14]

Another continuing obstacle was the opposition of nongovernmental organizations (NGOs) on various environmental and political grounds. Would the pipeline be buried three feet underground, where it was accessible to repairs, or fifteen feet, where it would not be? (Three feet won out.) Much intense debate ensued as to whether the proposed route was a threat to the Borzhomi springs, the source of Georgia's most famous mineral water. One tense negotiating session with the president of Georgia went on until 3:00 a.m., and then had to be extended another hour when a functioning photocopier could not be found in the presidential palace. The route, in the end, was not changed, but the consortium ending up paying the Borjomi brand water company about $20 million to cover the potential "negative reputational impact" of the pipeline. As it turned out, the reputational impact was surprisingly positive; the head of the Borjomi water company is said to have later described the episode as the best global advertising the mineral water could have ever gotten, and, better yet, it was free advertising.[15]

"OUR MAJOR GOAL": PETROLEUM AND THE NATION-STATE

The BTC pipeline has been described as "the first great engineering project of the twenty-first century." The 1,099-mile-long pipeline had to cross some 1,500 rivers and water courses, high mountains, and several major earthquake fault zones, while meeting stringent environmental and social impact standards. Four years and $4 billion later, the pipeline was finished. The first barrels arrived at the Turkish oil port Ceyhan, on the Mediterranean coast, in the summer of 2006, where they were welcomed in a grand ceremony. It had been twelve years since the "deal of the century" had been signed.

As would be expected, an Aliyev was there at the very forefront among the dignitaries who proclaimed the importance of the day for the countries involved, the region, and the world's energy markets. But it was not Heydar Aliyev; it was his son Ilham, the new president of Azerbaijan. Heydar Aliyev had not lived to see that day. For Aliyev, the KGB general and Soviet Politburo member who had gone on to become Azerbaijan's premier "native son," had passed away three years earlier at the Cleveland Clinic in the United States. But this day was the demonstration that his strategy had worked, that oil—and how he had played it—had given Azerbaijan a future that in 1994 had seemed almost unattainable. Petroleum had consolidated Azerbaijan as a nation and established its importance on the world stage. Or, as Ilham Aliyev had put it before taking over as president, "We need oil for our major goal." Which was, he said, "to become a real country."[16]

Azerbaijan is also strategically important because it is a secular, Muslim-majority state situated between Russia and Iran. Today Azerbaijan's offshore ACG field—a $22 billion project—ranks as the third-largest producing oil field in the world. Petroleum flows ashore at the new $2.2 billion Sangachal Terminal, just south of Baku, then moves into a forest of pipes and a series of tanks where it is cleaned and prepared for transit. Then the oil, now fit for export, all converges into a single forty-two-inch, crisp white pipeline. That is it—the much-debated Baku-Tbilisi-Ceyhan pipeline. The pipeline extends flat out on the ground for fifty feet and then curves down into the earth and disappears from sight. It bends and twists its way, mostly underground, until it surfaces again, 1,768 kilometers—1,099 miles—later at Ceyhan, where more than a million barrels a day flow into the storage tanks that fleck the Mediterranean shore, waiting for the tankers that will pick up their cargoes and take them to world markets. After all the battles of the great game, all the clash and clamor of the Caspian Derby, all the maneuvering and diplomacy, all the negotiating and trading and deal making, it all comes down to science and engineering and construction—the platforms and oil complexes in the Caspian Sea, and the $4 billion underground steel tubular highway that has reconnected Baku to the global market. As it carries oil, that pipeline also seems to be carrying the cargo of history, connecting not only Baku and Ceyhan but also the beginning of the twenty-first century back to the beginning of the twentieth.

Subsequently, a second pipeline was built parallel to the BTC to carry gas from the offshore Caspian Shah Deniz field, one of the largest gas discoveries of recent decades, to Turkey. The pipeline, known as the South Caucasus Pipeline, was no less challenging technically, but politically a good deal easier. The hard work had been done by the oil line. The South Caucasus Pipeline further consolidated the Caspian with the global energy market.

But Azerbaijan was only part of the Caspian Derby. Another round was being played out across the Caspian Sea.

3

ACROSS THE CASPIAN

In the summer of 1985, spy satellites spinning high above the earth picked up something startling—a huge column of flames on the northeastern corner of the Caspian Sea, with plumes that stretched a hundred miles. It was an oil field disaster on a scale visible from space. A well being drilled—Well 37—in the newly opened oil field of Tengiz, in the Soviet Republic of Kazakhstan, had blown out, sending up a powerful gusher of oil, mixed with natural gas. It had caught fire, creating a flaming column that reached 700 feet or more into the air. The gas was laden with deadly hydrogen sulfide, which inhibited recovery efforts. The USSR Ministry of Oil had neither the capability nor the equipment to bring it under control. At one point the Ministry, desperate and at wit's end, considered an "atomic explosion" to get the well under control.

That option was never implemented. "We managed to intercede in time," said Nursultan Nazarbayev, then the republic's premier.

Eventually American and Canadian experts were recruited to help. It took two months to put out the fire and four hundred days to get the well fully under control. This disastrous and costly blowout underlined the technical challenges facing the Soviet oil industry. But the burning "oil fountain" also illuminated something else: Kazakhstan might have world-scale petroleum potential.[1]

KAZAKHSTAN AND THE "FOURTH GENERATION" OF OIL

Kazakhstan today, one of the newly independent countries of the former Soviet Union, is a large nation in terms of territory, physically almost the size of India, but with a population of 15.5 million. A little over half is ethnically Kazakh, 30 percent ethnically Russian, and the rest other ethnic groups. With the exception of the new capital Astana, most of the population lives on the periphery of the country; a good part of the country is grassy steppe. During Soviet times, "each of the Union republics occupied a particular place in the division of labor," as Nazarbayev put it, and Kazakhstan's role was as "a supplier of raw materials, foodstuffs, and military production." A quarter of its population had died during Stalin's famine in the early 1930s. It was where Stalin exiled ethnic groups he did not like, where Nikita Khrushchev unleashed his disastrous "virgin lands" program to try to rescue Soviet agriculture, and where the Soviet Union tested its nuclear weapons. It was the place from whence the Soviet Union launched its spy satellites and where Russia today shoots tourists into space, at $20 million a shot.

Kazakhstan had had a small local oil industry going back to the nineteenth century, an eastern extension of the great Azeri boom that had made the Nobels and the Rothschilds into oil tycoons. If West Siberia had been the giant "third generation" of Soviet oil, then it was expected that Kazakhstan, centered in Tengiz, would be a key part of the "fourth generation."

But Kazakhstan's development was held back in the 1980s by lack of investment and technology in the face of difficult and unusual challenges, as evidenced at Tengiz. As former Soviet oil minister Lev Churilov wrote: "Exploration and production equipment stood frozen in time, with few technological advances after the 1960s." In the effort to bolster the faltering economy and facilitate technology transfer, in the final years of the Soviet Union, Mikhail Gorbachev had tried to lure in foreign investors. Under that umbrella, a controversial American promoter named James Giffen brought together a group of U.S. companies that would serve as an investment consortium.[2]

TENGIZ: "A PERFECT OIL FIELD"

One of the companies in the consortium was Chevron, which after looking around the Soviet Union came to focus on Tengiz. The company was deeply impressed by the huge potential. A "perfect oil field" is the way one Chevron engineer described it. With what was finally estimated as at least 10 billion barrels of potential recoverable reserves, Tengiz would rank among the ten largest oil fields in the world.[3]

There were, unfortunately, a few ways in which it was not quite perfect. One was the problem of the "sour gas," so-called because of the heavy concentrations of poisonous hydrogen sulfide. Sickeningly noxious with its rotten-egg-like smell, hydrogen sulfide is so toxic in large concentrations that it deadens the sense of smell, potentially dulling the ability of people to respond to inhaling it before it is too late. It would take considerable engineering ingenuity and a good deal of money to solve that problem. Other problems included the generally poor condition of the field and the enormous investment that would be required. There was an additional problem that would come to loom quite large—location. Tengiz was a far-off field with no real transportation system.

In June 1990, the Soviets signed a pact with Chevron that gave the company exclusive rights to negotiate for Tengiz. It was a very high-priority deal. For in the words of Yegor Gaidar, Moscow regarded Tengiz as "the Soviet Union's trump card in the game for the future."

But the Soviet Union was experiencing what Nazarbayev called "the distinctive symptoms of clinical death throes. The state organism sank into a coma." When it collapsed altogether, Nursultan Nazarbayev became president of the independent nation of Kazakhstan. His communist days were over. He was now a nationalist, who would now look not to Marx or Lenin for his role model, but to Lee Kuan Yew and the emergence of modern Singapore. And never again, he said, would Kazakhstan be "an appendage."

The Tengiz field loomed as absolutely crucial to the new nation's future; it was what Nazarbayev called the "fundamental principle" underpinning the country's economic transformation. But it was in very poor shape. In many parts of the oil field, electric power was available only two hours a day. Tens of billions of dollars of investment would be required to bring the field up to its potential.[4]

THE PIPELINE BATTLE

After arduous negotiations, Kazakhstan and Chevron came to agreement on how the immense and immensely expensive field would be developed. It would be a 50-50 deal in terms of ownership but not in terms of the economics. Eventually, after various costs were recovered, the government take would be about 80 percent of the revenues. Chevron would fund much of the estimated $20 billion investment until Kazakhstan started receiving cash flow, which would fund its share. Nazarbayev hailed this as "truly . . . the contract of the century." It was certainly a very big deal, with the objective of increasing output tenfold. Extraordinarily complex engineering was necessary to produce from very deep, very high-pressure structures, and then to treat the sour gas and separate the toxic hydrogen sulfide from petroleum.

Geography presented an additional challenge—getting the oil out of the country to world markets. The route was obvious—a 935-mile putative pipeline that would go north out of Kazakhstan, curve west over the top of the Caspian Sea, and then straight west for 450 miles to the Russian port of Novorossiysk on the northern coast of the Black Sea. From there oil would be transshipped by tanker across the Black Sea through the Bosporus Strait and into the Mediterranean. In other words, the pipeline would have to traverse Russian territory.

What was not obvious was how to get it done—not physically, but commercially, and even more so, politically. The battle would be no less contentious than the struggle over the pipelines out of Azerbaijan, no less complicated in the clash of ambitions and politics. It would also be caught up in the complex post–Cold War geopolitical struggle to redefine the former "Soviet space" and the relationships among Moscow, the Near Abroad, and the rest of the world. The players here would include Kazakhstan, Russia, the United States, and, later, China; Chevron and other oil companies; as well as the Persian Gulf oil-producing nation of Oman. Improbably, at the center of it all, at least for a time, was a flamboyant Dutch oil trader, John Deuss, whose penchant for high living included stables with champion jumping horses, two Gulfstream jets, yachts, ski resorts, and a variety of homes. His involvement in Kazakhstan was bankrolled by Oman, with which he had developed a very close relationship.

Chevron, so focused on the Tengiz field itself and also the risks that went with it, had left it to Kazakhstan to finance and organize the pipeline. "We hadn't planned on building a pipeline," said Richard Matzke, the head of Chevron Overseas Petroleum. "We felt that the pipeline would be a national asset, and there would be objections to foreign ownership across Russian territory."

Kazakhstan, still building its institutional capability as an independent nation-state, had turned to Deuss, who, with Oman, would be the "principal sponsor" of the pipeline. What, one might ask, was a Dutch oil trader with Omani money doing trying to build a pipeline across Russia? Deuss had been functioning as a senior oil adviser to the newly independent nation of Kazakhstan and had helped arrange an Omani line of credit for Kazakhstan in its first months of independence. Deuss had won the Kazakhs' trust. His Omani backer put up the money to initiate what would be called the CPC—the Caspian Pipeline Consortium.

Deuss and Chevron were soon at loggerheads. Chevron now realized that Deuss would be able to extract high tariffs and make a huge profit on the pipeline and also get what he was really after—control of the pipeline. "That wasn't going forward," said Matzke.

What followed has been called "one of the most prolonged and bitter confrontations of the era."

Kazakhstan loomed large to Russia. The two countries shared a 4,250-mile border, and the large ethnic Russian population testified to Kazakhstan's close links. The Russians resented the growth of U.S. influence in the newly independent states, including in Kazakhstan, and what they saw as an American initiative to cut them out of the action in their natural sphere, the Near Abroad.

More specifically, the Russians regarded Tengiz as "their oil." They had found it, they had drilled for it, they had begun to develop it, they had put money and infrastructure into it—and it would have been the great new field. But it had been snatched from their hands by the collapse of the Soviet Union. They were determined to extract maximum recompense and ensure that they participated in Tengiz. The two sides were constantly at odds. "It took six years to talk the Russian side round to building the oil pipeline," recalled Nazarbayev. "The oil lobby in Russia put tremendous pressure on Boris Yelstin to get him to convey the ownership of the Tengiz oil field to Russia. I had many disagreeable conversations . . . about this."

Once, at a meeting in Moscow, Yeltsin said to Nazarbayev, "Give Tengiz to me."

Nazarbayev looked at the Russian president and realized that he was not joking. "Well," Nazarbayev replied, "if Russia gives us Orenburg Province. After all, Orenburg was once the capital of Kazakhstan."

"Do you have territorial claims on Russia?" Yeltsin shot back.

"Of course not," Nazarbayev replied.

With that, the presidents of independent countries, both of whom had risen up together in the Soviet hierarchy, burst out laughing. But Nazarbayev had no intention of giving way. For, if he did, Kazakhstan would have become Russia's "economic hostage"—and, once again, "an appendage."[5]

"THE MAIN THING IS THAT THE OIL COMES OUT"

But with no progress on resolving the ownership and economics of the pipeline, Kazakhstan's frustration was growing. It needed a go-ahead on oil; its economic situation was desperate. GDP had shrunk almost 40 percent since 1990, and its nascent enterprises could not get international credit. Nazarbayev's anger over the impasse between Deuss and Chevron mounted. "The problem is that the money has to be invested," the irate Nazarbayev declared. "What difference is it to me if it is Americans, Omanis, Russians? The main thing is that oil comes out."[6]

As it was, the oil was coming out, but only with great difficulty and improvisation. As production rose, Chevron started shipping 100,000 barrels a day by tanker across the Caspian to Baku. Then, what seemed to be the entire Azerbaijani and Georgian rail systems were mustered to move the oil on to the Black Sea. Chevron was also leasing six thousand Russian rail tank cars to move additional oil to the Black Sea port of Odessa, which, to make things more complicated, was now part of Ukraine. Once again, it seemed back to the nineteenth century in terms of logistics. And that just would not do.

John Deuss had a particular patron in Oman, the deputy prime minister. But then this minister was mysteriously killed in an auto collision in the middle of the desert. Thereafter Oman's support for Deuss dwindled away at remarkable speed. At the same time, Kazakhstan canceled Deuss's exclusive rights to negotiate for financing for the pipeline. The United States was becoming alarmed at the delay in getting the transportation issue settled and the resulting risks to the financial stability and thus the nationhood of Kazakhstan, which had been very cooperative on a number of issues—most notably in disposing of the nuclear weapons left behind in its territory after the collapse of the Soviet Union. Without the oil pipeline, this particular "newly independent" state was certainly going to be less independent. Having a freebooter—oil trader John Deuss—ending up with control of something so strategic and significant for global energy security as the major export route for Kazakh's future oil was definitely seen as a problem. Finance would be key to whether Deuss's plan would go ahead. It became clear that Western loans were never going to be available to finance John Deuss to become the pipeline arbiter of Kazakh oil. With that, Deuss faded out of the picture.

But Moscow still needed to agree to a pipeline running through Russian territory. United States Vice President Al Gore used his co-chairmanship of a joint U.S.-Russian commission to successfully convince Premier Viktor Chernomyrdin that this was in Russia's interests. It also became very apparent that Russian participation in the project itself would be an asset. Russia's Lukoil, in partnership with the American company ARCO, came in and purchased a share of Tengiz.

Meanwhile, Kazakhstan had asked Mobil to help put up money for the pipeline. "I finally said we were not going to help on the pipeline in order to help Chevron crude to get out of Tengiz," said Mobil's CEO, Lucio Noto. "Tengiz was an absolutely world-class opportunity." Mobil paid a billion dollars, part of it up front, and bought a quarter of the oil field itself.[7]

In 1996 a new agreement dramatically restructured the original consortium. The oil companies were now members in a 50-50 partnership with the Russians, the Kazakhs, and Oman. The companies paid for the construction of the new pipeline—$2.6 billion—while Russia and Kazakhstan contributed the right-of-way and such pipeline capacity as was already in place. There was still much that was difficult to get done, including securing the actual route.

Matzke and Vagit Alekperov, the CEO of Lukoil, barnstormed by plane, visiting the interested parties all along the proposed pipeline route. Each stop required a banquet or a heavy reception, which sometimes meant as many as eleven meals a day for the traveling oil men, leaving them stuffed and groggy by nighttime. With the door thus opened, the Caspian Pipeline Consortium had to follow up and go into every locality and to negotiate right-of-way agreements for the new pipeline.[8]

Nonetheless, in 2001 the first oil from Tengiz passed into the pipeline. This was a landmark. Kazakhstan now, too, was integrated into the global oil industry. In the years that followed, there were many points of contention about Tengiz, which continue to the present day, but they were about the traditional issues—about how much the government's "take," or share of revenues and profits, would increase. By 2011 production was up to about 630,000 barrels of liquids per day—ten times what it had been when Chevron had begun to work in the field a decade and a half earlier—and planning was well advanced for the next stage of increase. The difficulties of dealing with the sour gas, laden with hydrogen sulfide, had, however, driven the price tag for Tengiz up from the anticipated $20 billion to more like $30 billion.

Tengiz is not the only supplier into the Caspian Pipeline. Another significant field, Karachaganak, feeds into it, as do other smaller fields.

KASHAGAN

The largest single oil field discovered in the world since 1968 is also in Kazakhstan. This is the immense Kashagan field, fifty miles offshore in the waters in the northeast of the Caspian. The Soviet oil industry had done seismic testing there but did not have the technology to explore the offshore region. In 1997 a consortium of Western companies had inked a deal with the Kazakh government to explore and develop the northern Caspian. In July 2000 they struck oil. Subsequently, Kashagan's recoverable reserves have been estimated at 13 billion barrels, as big as the North Slope of Alaska.

Kashagan's potential may be great, but it has also been the subject of continuing contention and discord among the international partners—ENI, Shell, ExxonMobil, Total, ConocoPhillips, and Japan's Inpex—and between all of them and the Kazakh government. For while Kashagan may be immense, so are its challenges. They dwarf by far those of Tengiz. A whole new production technology has had to be designed for the complex, fragmented field in what has been described as "the world's largest oil development." The petroleum resources are buried two and a half miles beneath the seabed, under enormous pressure and suffused with the same dangerous hydrogen sulfide found onshore at Tengiz. After many difficulties and setbacks, and in the face of ballooning costs and much acrimony and debate, the companies had to start over and reallocate roles. The project has taken almost a decade longer than anticipated to complete; first oil is not expected before 2012; and anticipated costs have increased to more than $40 billion for the first phase. All of this has infuriated the Kazakh government, which is having to wait years longer than it had anticipated for Kashagan revenues to start flowing into its treasury. But when Kashagan does start up production, it could add 1.5 million barrels of oil a day to world supplies.[9]

ONE MORE DEAL

There was one other notable Kazakh deal, though not understood as such at the time. In 1997 China National Petroleum Corporation, a state-owned oil company little known to the outside world at the time, bought most of a Kazakh oil company called Aktobe Munaigas, and committed to build a pipeline to China. Production in 1997 was only about 60,000 barrels a day, but the Chinese have since doubled it. Little attention was paid to that first entry of China into Kazakhstan, and even that attention was mixed with much skepticism about the pipeline and the overall prospects. As one keen observer of Caspian oil was to note almost a decade and a half later, "How wrong we were."

But, then, centuries earlier a Russian geographer had caught a glimpse of the future. He had written that the people of the steppes would also need to look to the East for the markets for their natural resources.[10]

TURKMENISTAN AND THE PIPELINE THAT NEVER WAS

One other major source of hydrocarbons was, at least potentially, unleashed by the breakup of the Soviet Union—Turkmenistan. There, too, a plan emerged for major pipelines. It would connect the world in new ways. But that project, too, was complicated and even more contingent, and ever since wrapped in many legends, including that it was part of a grand strategy. In fact, it was much more of a great flyer—a Hail Mary pass of transcontinental proportions.

Turkmenistan sits on the southeast corner of the Caspian, immediately north of Afghanistan. It was highly isolated in Soviet times. Endowed with significant oil resources, it is truly rich in natural gas. This was recognized even in the early 1990s—and even more so today, as Turkmenistan now ranks as the fourth-largest holder of conventional natural gas resources in the world. Immediately after the breakup of the Soviet Union, Turkmenistan managed to earn some money and barter for goods by delivering gas into the Russian pipeline system, just as it had supplied gas to the Soviet system. This was the new country's major revenue source. But then, in 1993, the Russians abruptly shut down such imports. With their economy in freefall, the Russians did not need the Turkmen gas. Turkmenistan managed to stay afloat economically—just barely—by selling cotton and its limited output of oil.

TAP AND CAOP

Turkmenistan's entire existing pipeline system, built for the integrated Soviet economy, flowed north into Russia. An alternative export route looked like a very good idea. But given the geography and the neighbors, it was just very hard to see what the alternative route might be. As one Western oil man put it at the time, "Certainly there is no easy way out of Central Asia." The U.S. government lent support to a project to ship gas from Turkmenistan across the Caspian Sea to Azerbaijan and on to Europe, but that never eventuated.

There was one possibility that recommended itself, but, along with all the other normal inputs of money and engineering capabilities and diplomatic skills, this particular transit route would require something else—very substantial amounts of political imagination. For the envisioned track would take the gas south through Afghanistan and into Pakistan, where some of it would be used domestically and some exported as liquefied natural gas (LNG). The rest would be exported farther south by pipeline into India. Moreover, the proposed 1,040-mile oil pipeline could help move the landlocked petroleum resources of Central Asia south to global markets, closer to Asia, but without having to go through Iran and the Persian Gulf. "Only about 440 miles of the pipeline would be in Afghanistan," one oil man optimistically said in congressional testimony. And the route had one more decided advantage: it looked to be "the cheapest in terms of transporting oil."

It was a very big idea that appealed to a company called Unocal, one of the smaller of the U.S. majors. Started as a California company, it had already developed a significant position as a natural gas producer in Southeast Asia, and had also been one of the pioneers of the AIOC, of which it owned about 10 percent. Once the Baku-Tbilisi-Ceyhan Pipeline project got going, recalled John Imle, Unocal's president, "We asked ourselves, What's the next project? Turkmenistan had a lot of gas, but all the pipelines were going north, and the Russians were not taking the gas. Our premise was that Central Asia needed an outlet to the Indian Ocean." So convinced was Unocal of the potential of additional transport routes that it embraced what became a famous slogan, "Happiness Is Multiple Pipelines."

For Unocal, a project with Turkmenistan could be the game changer, an enormous opportunity that could leapfrog Unocal into the front ranks of international companies. Marty Miller, the Unocal executive with the responsibility for the project, described it as the "moon shot" in the company's portfolio of possible future projects. It was an $8 billion idea, for it would also be a "twofer"—twin natural gas and oil pipelines. The natural gas line was dubbed the Trans-Afghan Pipeline; and the oil, the Central Asian Oil Pipeline.

Together TAP and CAOP (the latter pronounced as "cap") would open global markets to Turkmen resources; they would provide significant transit revenues to Afghanistan, an alternative to the revenues that the nation derived from opium cultivation. TAP would deliver natural gas to the growing economies of Pakistan and India, where, the economics indicated, it would be cheaper than imported LNG. CAOP would move a million barrels per day of oil south from Turkmenistan and elsewhere in Central Asia, perhaps even Russia.[11]

Unocal could already clearly see that the great growth markets of the twenty-first century would be in that region. Yet reflecting the perspectives of the times, the main markets for Turkmen oil were thought to be Japan and Korea. China, as a market at that point, was still little more than a footnote. After all, it was only two years earlier that China had stopped exporting oil and become an importer. The gas project was particularly compelling to some policymakers in India, who hoped that a natural gas link would tie India and Pakistan together with common interests that would help to offset decades of conflict and rivalry. They called it a "peace pipeline."

To say the project was "challenging" was an understatement.

TURMOIL EN ROUTE

The main transit country for TAP and CAOP was Afghanistan, but Afghanistan in the mid-1990s was hardly a functioning country. For ten years the country had been torn apart by a war between Soviet troops, which had invaded in 1979, and Afghan mujahedeen, supported by Pakistan, the United States, and Saudi Arabia, among others. "The greatest mistake [of the Soviet intervention] was failing to understand Afghanistan's complexity—its patchwork of ethnic groups, clans and tribes, its unique traditions and minimal governance," Soviet president Mikhail Gorbachev later said. "The result was the opposite of what we had intended—even greater instability, a war with thousands of victims and dangerous consequences for our own country." Gorbachev knew of what he spoke. The retreat of the last Soviet troops over the Termez Bridge back into the Soviet Union in February 1989 was the final act in the projection of Soviet military power beyond its borders, and it had failed—that retreat would be a grim landmark on the way toward the collapse of the Soviet Union.[12]

But, then, with the war over, and the world caught up in both the collapse of communism and the Gulf War, Afghanistan slipped off the international agenda and was forgotten—an omission that would have enormous global consequences a decade later. The country degenerated into civil war and lawlessness as warlords struggled for primacy. In 1994 a group of Islamists—the "students" or "Taliban"—came together as vigilantes to take matters into their own hands and restore order, but also, as it turned out, to establish a very strict Islamic order. They rallied supporters in a campaign against corruption and crime and hated warlords. Very quickly, operating with a cavalry of Toyota pickup trucks equipped with machine guns, they turned themselves into a zealous militia, already battle-hardened by the war against the Soviets. They gained control over much of the southern part of the country, largely dominated by the Pashtuns, which they renamed the Islamic Emirate of Afghanistan.[13]

There was yet another obstacle to TAP and CAOP—the historic enmity, sometimes punctuated by war, between India and Pakistan, the two countries that were intended to be the main outlet for the gas and oil flowing from Turkmenistan. Their militaries were designed mainly to fight each other, and conflict too often seemed imminent.

Pakistan itself, with its very contentious politics, was in a state of continuous political turmoil. The ISI, the Pakistani security services, was sponsoring the Taliban to pursue what it saw as Pakistan's own strategic interests—in particular, as a Pashtun buffer against what they feared would be an India-dominated government in Kabul. Events would later demonstrate that this was a mistake of historic proportions. For Al Qaeda and a combined Afghan and Pakistan Taliban would, a decade and half later, challenge the very legitimacy of Pakistan as a nation and seek to destabilize and overturn it and replace it with an Islamic caliphate.

THE "TURKMENBASHI"

In Turkmenistan itself, there was one additional issue: the resources had to be secured. And that meant dealing with one of the most unusual figures to emerge from the collapse of the Soviet Union—Saparmurat Niyazov, the former first secretary of the Turkmenistan Communist Party, who had, after the Soviet breakup, taken over as president and absolute ruler. He had also anointed himself "Turkmenbashi"—"the Leader of All the Turkmen." His cult of personality rivaled any in the twentieth century. (He once privately explained that it was part of his drive to create identity and legitimacy for the new Turkmen nation.) His picture was everywhere; his statues, plentiful. He renamed the days of the month after his mother and other members of his family, all of whom had been killed in a 1948 earthquake. Niyazov himself had been raised in an orphanage. He had been selected as head of the Community Party in Soviet times after his predecessor was removed because of a nepotism scandal involving many relatives; it was said that Niyazov's accession was helped because he had no relatives. Once Turkmenistan became independent, Niyazov emptied school libraries, refilling them with his *Ruhnama,* a rambling combination of autobiography and philosophical rumination on Turkmen nationality. Medical doctors had to renounce the Hippocratic oath and instead swear allegiance to him. He also ordered a reduction in the number of school years for children, banned opera and ballet as "alien," and prohibited female television news anchors from wearing cosmetics on air.

While highly authoritarian in most ways, Niyazov was rather liberal in one way—and that was with the country's physical resources. For Turkmenistan was thought to sell the same natural gas to more than one buyer. In this particular case, Unocal thought it had obtained rights to export key gas resources. But so did Bridas, an Argentine company, which had additional support from Pakistan. Unocal worried that Niyazov did not understand, as one Unocal negotiator put it, what was required to "implement a project of such magnitude."[14]

HOPE AND EXPERIENCE

Nevertheless, by the autumn of 1995, Unocal had a preliminary agreement with Turkmenistan. Niyazov was in New York City for the fiftieth anniversary of the United Nations, and Unocal organized a signing ceremony at the Americas Society on Park Avenue. The ceremony was immediately followed by a lunch in the grand Salon Símon Bolivar. Dominating the room was a large map of the region, set up on easels, that showed the proposed routes for TAP and CAOP. The lunch was presided over by John Imle, Unocal's president, a man of some enthusiasm. Struggling to find common ground with the Turkmenbashi, which was not at all an easy thing to do, Imle came up with at least one thing they absolutely and indubitably shared in common—both were fifty-five years old, he declared with a big smile.

The guest of honor was former Secretary of State Henry Kissinger, who was escorted to the map, which he spent some time examining, including the route by which TAP and CAOP would snake down from Turkmenistan through Afghanistan, over the mountains into Pakistan, and then branch to the sea and down farther into India. After the meal, Kissinger delivered the luncheon address. He offered best wishes on the project. He then added his own assessment of its prospects. "I am reminded," he said, "of Dr. Samuel Johnson's famous comment on second marriages—that they are 'the triumph of hope over experience.'"

Imle turned a little white. He wasn't sure if it was a joke or a prophecy.

"NO POLICY"

There was little interest in the project on the part of the U.S. government, which was much more preoccupied with the breakup of the Soviet Union and the other energy initiatives involving Azerbaijan and Kazakhstan and that possible gas pipeline across the Caspian. This mirrored the larger disinterest toward Afghanistan, so different from just a few years earlier, when it had been the last battleground of the Cold War. Once that struggle was over in 1989, the United States just packed up and seemed to forget about Afghanistan and its postwar reconstruction. Much of Afghanistan's educated middle class was long gone, and the country fell back into battle among the warlords who had led the mujahedeen. As the U.S. ambassador to Pakistan later said, "There basically was no policy" toward Afghanistan in the 1990s.

Unocal recognized that it could not operate in a vacuum. It needed someone to negotiate with—that a condition for the implementation of the pipeline project is "the establishment of a single, internationally recognized entity" running the country that is "authorized to act on behalf of all Afghan parties." Who would it be? Trying to implement this transformative project both for the region and itself, Unocal was struggling to understand the competing factions, especially the Taliban. Were the Taliban "pious people" who would bring some order and stability to the chaotic, violence-wracked country? Or were they militants and fanatical zealots with an altogether incompatible agenda?

It often happens that when a U.S. oil company is entering a new country, the company will invite representatives from that country to the United States to tour its facilities and learn more about how the company and the industry operates—and to begin to establish the kind of working dialogue that is required when hundreds of millions and then billions of dollars start getting invested. But in Afghanistan, this was much more challenging than is typically the case. In an effort to build some bonds—"these guys had never seen the ocean," said Imle—Unocal brought a delegation of Taliban to the United States. Included was a trip to Houston to show them the modern oil and gas industry, and to Washington for a visit to the State Department. But Unocal recognized at the time, "no high level US involvement [had] materialized." Unocal similarly helped sponsor a visit by the Taliban's hated rival, the Northern Alliance, that followed the same route. Imle gave a similar message to both groups. "We can only deal with you when you stop fighting, form a government that is representative of all factions, and recognized by the United Nations." Unocal also gave both sides the same present, a piece of communication technology that was a very practical symbol of the advancing technology of the 1990s—a fax machine. The message to both groups was the same: Stay in touch.[15]

WHICH SCENARIO?

In the spring of 1996, Unocal examined a report outlining several scenarios, with a range of probabilities, for the future of Afghanistan. None of them were promising. The highest probability was "a continuation of the warlordism scenario." In another the non-Pashtuns would break off and form their own state, Khorastan, which would orient itself toward Central Asia. There was also a scenario in which Iran and Pakistan would become much more directly involved on the ground in Afghanistan.

The least likely scenario in the report was a "triumphant Taliban." Under that unlikely scenario, it was thought, the Taliban would need economic development to consolidate its hold and "gain popular support"—which, rationally, would lead it to "seek foreign aid and investment." But that effort would be hampered by the Taliban's "major human rights violations in their dealings with women, Shiites, and Tajiks." Yet a Taliban victory seemed dubious, impeded among other things by factionalism and infighting among the Taliban. But the Taliban's odds might improve for a variety of reasons, including if it were to "receive a substantial increase in outside assistance without similar increase in support" for the government in Kabul.

One source of support was the ISI, Pakistan' intellegence agency, which stepped up to offer the Taliban "unlimited covert aid." But in the spring of 1996, another source materialized. Unbeknownst to most of the world, the virtually unknown Osama bin Laden, avoiding extradition by Saudi Arabia, had moved his retinue from Sudan to Afghanistan and set up shop. He began to substantially bankroll the Taliban. There he also built his own organization, Al Qaeda. It was from his new redoubt in Afghanistan that, in the summer of 1996, he issued his then-obscure fatwah—his "declaration of Jihad against Americans Occupying the Two Sacred Places" and an attack on the Saudi royal family as "the agent" of an alliance of imperialistic Jews and Christians—a document that was faxed to newspapers in London, though with little notice.

Months later, in the largest mosque in Kandahar, Mullah Omar, the one-eyed leader of the Taliban, would, during his sermon, embrace Bin Laden as one of "Islam's most important spiritual leaders."[16]

THE END OF THE ROAD

By the early autumn, the formerly least likely of the scenarios examined by Unocal now seemed the most likely. On September 27, 1996, the Taliban captured Kabul. They wasted no time imposing their strict version of Islamic law. No cigarettes, no toothpaste, no television, no kite flying. Eight thousand women were summarily expelled from Kabul University, and religious police would beat women pedestrians who were unaccompanied by men.

But the battle for Afghanistan was not over. The Taliban was still at war with the Northern Alliance; the country was not consolidated; and perhaps there was still the opportunity to engage with some factions within the Taliban. At the same time, Turkmenistan president Niyazov was stoking Washington's alarm by threatening to turn to Iran as a major export market and transport route for Turkmen gas. Toward the end of 1996, Unocal mustered its confidence and, in an effort to build momentum and diplomatic support, announced that, with partners from Saudi Arabia, South Korea, Japan, and Pakistan, it hoped to start building a pipeline by the end of 1998.

But this plan was becoming increasingly problematic. In the United States, the entire project was becoming a target of criticism, including from a movement, which was led by the wife of talk-show host Jay Leno, that attacked Unocal for associating with a regime so repressive of women. Unocal sponsored skill training for Afghan women as well as men. It retained an Islamic scholar to try to communicate with the Taliban what the Koran really said about women, but the Taliban wasn't interested. "Once we understood who the Taliban were, and how radical, this project didn't look so good," said Marty Miller.

Many years earlier, in 1931, a British scholar of Central Asia had observed: "In Afghanistan, both European clothing and unveiling are anathema, and there has been a strong reaction in favor of Islam, the old customs and the old abuses." That still seemed true 65 years later. The Westerners could not fully grasp how deep-seated were the cultural antagonisms into which they were treading—and how much these antagonisms resonated across history—and what was ahead. Nor did they know how much money Osama bin Laden was already spending on the Taliban—nor what he was brewing in the Afghan city of Kandahar.

On August 7, 1998, two teams of suicide bombers hit U.S. embassies in Kenya and Tanzania. The attacks were highly coordinated, just nine minutes apart. Kenya was worst hit, with 211 dead and 4,000 wounded. The attack had been masterminded from Afghanistan by Al Qaeda. A few days later, the United States retaliated with cruise missiles aimed at a suspected chemical weapons facility in Sudan and at an Al Qaeda training camp in Afghanistan.

"It didn't take us five minutes to know that it was all over," said Unocal's John Imle. "We were in regular contact with the U.S. embassy in Pakistan, and no one had ever said anything about terrorism. But now we understood what Bin Laden was doing in Kandahar." Imle called Unocal's chief representative, who happened to be on vacation in the United States, and told him to forget about going back to Islamabad, Pakistan, let alone to Kandahar. It was too dangerous for any U.S. businessman promoting a project that so clearly was anathema to the Taliban. A few months later, instead of starting construction, Unocal declared that it was withdrawing altogether from the project.

Thus, TAP and CAOP were finished before they started. A project that would have opened a wholly new route for Central Asian resources to the great growth market of Asia was never to be. The moon shot never got off the ground. It was aborted before launch by the Taliban and its ally, Al Qaeda, both armed with a militant ideology and a version of religion that was determined to return to the middle ages.[17]

What happened in the 1990s—with the offshore field in Azerbaijan and the Baku-Tbilisi-Ceyhan Pipeline, and Tengiz and the Caspian pipeline—was very significant for the supplies they brought to the markets. Today the total output of Azerbaijan and Kazakhstan is 2.8 million barrels of oil—equivalent to more than 80 percent of North Sea production, and four times what they were producing a little more than a decade earlier. But these deals were significant as turning points—for the way in which they redrew the map of world oil, for their geopolitical impact, for the consolidation they provided to the newly independent states, and for the way in which they reconnected the hydrocarbons of the Caspian to the world economy—on a scale that could never have been imagined during the first great boom a century earlier.

More than a decade later, Turkmenistan is still negotiating with Western companies over the development of its natural gas resources. Pakistan is struggling with a domestic Taliban insurgency. And NATO forces, primarily American, are fighting in Afghanistan.

4

"SUPERMAJORS"

Asia had been the target market for TAP and CAOP—the "pipelines that never were." For Asia was booming. But in July of 1997, one of the most buoyant of the economies, that of Thailand, was slammed by a financial crisis that threatened to destroy much of the country's recent economic progress. Soon the crisis spread, threatening the whole region and the entire Asian Economic Miracle, with far-reaching impact on global finance and the world economy. It would also detonate a transformation in the oil industry.

THE "ASIAN ECONOMIC MIRACLE"

The title of a popular business book, *The Borderless World,* captured the abounding optimism about the process of globalization in the 1990s that was knitting together the different parts of the world economy. World trade was growing faster than the world economy itself.[1] Asia was at the forefront. The "Asian tigers"—South Korea, Taiwan, Hong Kong, and Singapore, and behind them the "new tigers" of Malaysia, Indonesia, Thailand, and the Philippines, plus China's Guangdong Province—were emulating Japan's great economic success.

The Asian Economic Miracle was providing a new playbook for third world economic development. Instead of the inward-looking self-sufficiency and the high trade barriers that had been the canon of development in the 1950s and 1960s, the "tigers" embraced trade and the global economy. In turn, they were rewarded with rapidly rising incomes and remarkably fast growth. Singapore was a beleaguered city-state when it gained independence in 1965. By 1989 its per capita GDP, on a purchasing power parity basis, was higher than that of Britain, which, as the birthplace of the Industrial Revolution, had a two-hundred-year head start. Asia also became the foundation for "supply chains," extending from raw materials to components to final goods. The world was truly being knit together in ways not imagined even a decade earlier.

The high growth rates in Asia meant rising demand for energy, and, specifically, for oil. These countries became the growth market for petroleum, and there was every reason to think that this Asian economic growth would continue at its fevered pace.

JAKARTA: "OPEC'S ECONOMIC STARS"

OPEC petroleum ministers convened for one of their regular sessions in Jakarta, Indonesia, in November 1997. Asia's buoyant prospects were much on the minds of the delegates. Many of them were considering how to reorient their trade more to the East. Here, after all, it seemed, was their future. But, as if to symbolize how bumpy the road to fast growth could be, they found themselves booked into a not-quite-finished luxury hotel in which the water supply was quite unpredictable.

After four days of discussion in Jakarta, they agreed to raise their production quota by two million barrels per day. This decision was intended to end the wrangling over quotas and overproduction among members. It was read by some as a bet on Asia's future, but it also had another, much more specific purpose. Some of the countries, notably Saudi Arabia, were quite aggravated that other countries, particularly Venezuela, were producing at their maximum capacity, not at their quotas, and thus taking market share at Saudi Arabia's expense. Raising the quota at Jakarta would level the playing field. Now all the exporters could officially essentially produce at their maximum. Market conditions seemed to necessitate the increase. World consumption had risen more than two million barrels per day between 1996 and 1997, and the International

Energy Agency was predicting that the world's consumption would rise by another two million barrels per day in 1998. "Price will hold up," the oil minister from Kuwait said confidently after the decision was announced. "The rise is a very reasonable one."

That judgment was widely shared. An observer described market conditions as nothing less than "the alignment of OPEC's economic stars." But, in the heavens above, the stars were silently moving.[2]

"ESSENTIALLY ALL GONE": THE ASIAN FINANCIAL CRISIS

During the course of the Jakarta conference, two of the delegates to the meeting were taken to dinner by the head of the local International Monetary Fund office. He told them in no uncertain terms that the currency crisis that had begun a few months earlier was only the beginning of a far more devastating crisis—and that the Asian economic miracle was about to crash on the rocks. The two delegates were shaken by what they heard. But the decision to raise production, based upon an optimistic economic scenario, had already been taken. It was too late.

"Asia was the darling of foreign capital during the mid-1990s," and it became the beneficiary of a "capital inflow bonanza," a great flood of lending by international banks. As a result, Asian companies and property developers had taken on much too much debt—and much of it dangerously short-term and denominated in foreign currency.

It was overleverage in the overheated and overbuilt condo and office building sectors in Bangkok that caused the collapse in July 1997 of Thailand's currency, which in turn triggered the fall of currency and stock markets in other Asian countries. By the end of 1997, a vast panic was raging over large parts of Asia. Companies tumbled into bankruptcy, businesses closed, governments teetered, people were thrown out of work, and the high economic growth rates gave way to a virtual economic depression in many countries.

At the end of 1997, Stanley Fischer, the deputy director of the International Monetary Fund, hurriedly flew to Seoul. He was taken into the vault of the South Korean central bank so he could see with his own eyes the state of the country's financial reserves—that is, how much money was left. He was stunned by what he discovered. "It was essentially all gone," he said.

By then the panic and contagion was spreading beyond Asia. In August 1998, after teetering on the edge of crisis, the Russian government defaulted on its sovereign debt, sending that country into a sudden downward spiral. The ruble plummeted in value, and the Russian stock market fell by an astounding 93 percent. The new Russian oil majors could not pay their workers and suppliers. Salaries were slashed; some of the most senior managers were down to $100 a month.

Wall Street teetered on the edge when the highly levered hedge fund Long-Term Capital Management collapsed. Panic in the United States was averted by fast action by the New York Federal Reserve. In early 1999 the contagion seemed about to sweep over Brazil, threatening what U.S. Treasury Secretary Robert Rubin called an "engulfing world crisis." An immense rescue effort, mobilizing very large financial resources, was mounted to prevent Brazil from going down. It worked. Brazil was spared. By the spring of 1999, the panic and contagion were over.[3]

THE JAKARTA SYNDROME

The Asian financial crisis had generated enormous economic ruin. As a result, the assumptions at the end of 1997, embodied in the Jakarta agreement, were all wrong. By implementing the Jakarta agreement, OPEC had been increasing its output—just as demand was falling.

Now there was way too much oil in the world. When there was no more room in storage tanks, seagoing tankers that normally transported oil were turned instead into floating storage. And still there was too much oil. And not enough demand. The price collapsed to $10 a barrel and, for some grades of oil, to as low as $6. These were the kinds of prices that had been seen during the 1986 collapse and had been thought would never be seen again.

The 1997 meeting in Jakarta would be remembered thereafter by the exporters as a cautionary tale—the "Jakarta Syndrome"—the danger of increasing production when demand was weakening or even just uncertain. It was a mistake they intended never to repeat.

THE SHOCK

The price collapse did something else as well. It set off the most far-reaching reshaping of the structure of the petroleum industry since the breakup of the Standard Oil Trust by the U.S. Supreme Court in 1911. The result was something that would have been unimaginable without the circumstances created by the price crash.

As oil prices plummeted, the finances of the oil industry collapsed. " 'Bloodbath' may be an understatement," said one Wall Street analyst. Companies slashed budgets and laid off employees. One of the major companies shrank its annual Christmas party down to some snacks in the cafeteria. DROWNING in OIL was the load lines a the cover of *The Economist*. With some exaggeration, that captured what had become the widespread conviction that prices were going to be low for the foreseeable future and that the future of the industry was bleak.[4]

To some, though, it was an opportunity, not an easy one by any means, but a window through which to get things done. After all, people would still need petroleum, and, indeed, they would need more petroleum when economic growth resumed, which would mean higher prices. But the industry would need to be more efficient, managing its costs better, and leveraging skills and technology across a larger span. That pointed in one direction—toward greater scale. And the way to get there was through mergers.

"WERE HE ALIVE TODAY . . ."

Sanderstolen is a rustic mountain resort in central Norway, reached only by a twisting two-lane highway that has to be laboriously plowed during the winter. In the years after discovery of North Sea oil in Norway's offshore, it became the venue for the Norwegian government and the oil companies operating in the Norwegian sector to get together and thrash out industry issues—talk in the morning, cross-country skiing in the afternoon.

One morning in February 1998, two investment bankers, Joseph Perella and Robert Maguire, offered a view of the industry that caught the attention of the executives gathered there that year. "The roster of the top publicly traded firms in the oil industry is largely the same as it has been since the breakup of the Standard Oil Trust," they said in their presentation. "Were he alive today, John D. Rockefeller would recognize most of the list. Carnegie, Vanderbilt, and Morgan, on the other hand, would have difficulty with similar lists for their industries."

The bankers and their colleagues had been talking about something more than "mergers"—about the imminent emergence of what they had started to call the "supermajors." For a year, Doug Terreson, an analyst at Morgan Stanley, had been laboring over a paper that declared the "Era of the Super-Major" was at hand. "Unparalleled globalization and scale"resulting from mergers—combined with greater efficiency and a much wider book of opportunities—would lead to "superior returns and premier valuations." In short, larger companies would be more highly valued by shareholders. And, by implication, those companies that were smaller and less highly valued would be at risk.[5]

Someone would need to go first. But how could mergers be done? Hostile takeovers looked very difficult to do, so companies would have to agree on a price. There was also a formidable obstacle—what is variously called antitrust in the United States and competition policy in Europe. After all, the most famous antitrust case in history was that involving John D. Rockefeller's Standard Oil Trust that the Supreme Court had decided in 1911.

Beginning in the mid-1860s, Rockefeller had marched out of Cleveland with "our plan," a concept for transforming the volatile, chaotic, and individualistic new American oil industry into one highly ordered company, operating under his leadership. "Methodical to an extreme," in the testy words of a former partner, Rockefeller had proceeded with cold-eyed and single-minded determination, a mastery of strategy and organization, and a bookkeeper's love of numbers. The result was a massive company, the Standard Oil Trust, that controlled up to 90 percent of the U.S. oil industry and dominated the global market. In doing all this, Rockefeller really created the modern oil industry. He also invented the "integrated" oil company in which the oil flowed within the corporate boundaries from the moment it came out of the ground until finally it reached the consumer.

Rockefeller became not only the richest man in America but also one of the most hated, and, indeed, the very embodiment of monopoly in the robber baron age. In 1906 the administration of the trust-buster, President Theodore Roosevelt, launched the momentous case charging the Standard Oil Trust with restraint of trade under the Sherman Antitrust Act. In May 1911, the

U.S. Supreme Court upheld lower court decisions and ordered the Standard Oil Trust broken up into thirty-four separate companies.[6]

Ever since the dissolution of the Standard Oil Trust, virtually every American law student interested in antitrust has studied that case. And, again and again, in the decades since 1911, the industry had been investigated for allegations and suspicions of colluding and restraining trade. Wouldn't combinations, creating larger companies, only fan the flames of suspicion? But times had changed. The global playing field was much larger. Altogether, the large international oil companies now controlled less than 15 percent of world production; most of it was in the hands of the national oil companies, which had taken control in the 1970s. Some of these government-owned companies, such as Saudi Aramco, were becoming effective and capable competitors in their own rights, backed up by those immense reserves that dwarfed anything held by the traditional international oil companies.

In order to gain efficiency and bring down costs—and with the approval of antitrust authorities—some of the companies had combined, in key markets, their refineries and networks of gasoline stations. But none of these had sought to overturn the established lay of the land, the demarcations of corporate boundaries so clearly set in place by the 1911 Supreme Court decision.

THE MERGER THAT WASN'T

The chief executive of BP, John Browne, was among those who were convinced that something radical needed to be done. Trained first as a physicist at Cambridge University and then subsequently as a petroleum engineer, Browne had considered a career in academic research. But, instead, he had gone to work in BP, where his father had been a middle-level BP executive, for some time based in Iran. His mother was a survivor of the Auschwitz concentration camp, although this was known only to a very few until after her death in 2000.

Browne had entered BP on what was called an "apprentice program." He quickly proved himself what the British called a high-flier, moving rapidly up in the organization. In 1995 he became chief executive. He was convinced, he said, that "we had to change the game. BP was stuck as a 'middleweight insular British company.' It was either up or out."

During a BP board meeting, Browne laid out the rationale for a merger: BP was not big enough. It if did not take over another company, it was in danger of being taken over. BP needed to become bigger to achieve economies of scale, bring down costs, and take on larger projects and risks. And it needed the clout that came from scale to be taken "seriously" by the national companies. Browne was apprehensive that the board members would conclude that just one year after choosing him as CEO, he had taken leave of his senses. But, somewhat to his surprise, the board gave a contingent go-ahead.

The best fit for BP seemed to be Mobil, the second-largest of the successor companies to the Standard Oil Trust. In the many decades since the breakup, it had turned itself into one of the largest international integrated oil companies in its own right. It was also one of the most visible. Its flying horse insignia was known around the world; it had invented the "advertorial" in the right-hand bottom corner of the *New York Times;* and it was one of the biggest supporters of PBS, public broadcasting in the United States, most notably, of *Masterpiece Theater*. Moreover, BP had already established a joint venture with Mobil in European refining and marketing operations that had saved $600 million and had proved that the two companies could work together.

Mobil's CEO was Lucio Noto. Known throughout the industry as "Lou," he had wide international experience and his avocations were notably broad, extending from the opera to rebuilding the engines of old sports cars.

Mobil faced big strategic problems. A significant part of its income came from one source—the Arun LNG project on the island of Sumatra, in Indonesia. But, as Noto put it, "Arun was going downhill." It was in decline and would require new investment, and that meant that there would be a large gap in profitability until new projects came on stream. This threatened Mobil with its shareholders and would make it vulnerable to a hostile takeover.

The company needed time. "To have one really good upstream asset," Noto said, "you have to have six projects in the frying pan to bring experience, money, and talent to bear." Moreover, Mobil's new growth projects were in Nigeria, Kazakhstan, and Qatar, as well as Indonesia, meaning that the company's future prospects would be susceptible to geopolitical risks of one kind or another.

Qatar's vast offshore natural gas field, at the northern end of the Persian Gulf, would be a particular challenge. Because of the field's immense size, the investment bill would be enormous. "The more we learned about Qatar," said

Noto, "the more we realized that it would be beyond the capacity of a single company."

"We had to do something," recalled Noto. "We could survive. But we couldn't really thrive."

Mobil was ready to talk to BP. Secrecy was essential. If any news leaked, it would be damaging to the companies involved and could wreak havoc with the stock price. Browne and Noto sketched plans for a two-headed company, with listings on both the New York and London stock exchanges. Finally, after lengthy negotiations and much consideration, Mobil concluded that while BP would be taking over Mobil, there would be no premium to shareholders.

Noto met Browne at the Carlyle Hotel in New York City. His message was very simple: Without a premium, there could be no deal.

"I can't do it," Noto said. Browne was stunned. Just to be sure that there was no misunderstanding, Noto handed him a short, carefully drafted "Dear John" letter, which expressed great appreciation for the discussions but made clear, absolutely clear, that they were over.

There was not much else to say as they stood there. But Noto had one other thought. "I don't know what will happen," he said.

Browne flew home in silence. What would his own board, which he had worked so hard to convince, think when he broke the news? Maybe they would conclude that he really had taken leave of his senses.[7]

THE BREAKOUT: BP AND AMOCO

As soon as he was back in London, Browne called Laurance Fuller, the CEO of Amoco, which was headquartered in Chicago. The former Standard Oil of Indiana, Amoco was one of the largest American-based oil companies. Although its assets were heavily weighted to the United States, it had been one of the pioneering oil companies to go into the Caspian after the collapse of the Soviet Union, and it was now one of the major partners, along with BP, in Azerbaijan.

Fuller and Browne chatted first about the state of their project in Azerbaijan. That was the warm-up. Then Browne popped the question.

"What are your thoughts about the future of Amoco?" Browne asked. "Because it seems to me it's a good time for a few oil companies to get together."

Fuller showed no surprise over the phone. Fuller reminded Browne that in the early 1990s, Amoco and BP had discussed combining their petrochemical operations, but BP had broken off the talks.

"What's new?" Fuller asked.

"Strategically," Browne replied, a merger is "something we ought to do."

"Well, it's not on my agenda," Fuller said. "But why don't we talk?"

"When would be convenient?"

"How about the day after tomorrow?"

Two days later they met in British Airways' Concorde lounge at JFK Airport in New York. Amoco had gone through a series of restructurings and major strategy projects to try to find a way forward but without clear success; Fuller, a lawyer who had been CEO for almost a decade, was personally pessimistic about the future of the industry. BP was bigger than Amoco, so it was going to be a 60-40 deal. But the negotiations foundered on structure—whether it would be a two-headed company, with headquarters in both Chicago and London, and whether Fuller would share power with Browne.

In early August 1998, Browne, surrounded by his team, called Fuller from his home on South Eaton Place in London. "This only works if it's a British company, based in London, and we get one more director on the board," said Browne. "That's it." He asked Fuller to let him know within the next twenty-four hours. Several hours later, Fuller called back. It was a go, he said. He was getting on his plane.

A few days later, August 11, 1998, BP convened a press conference in the largest venue it could find, on short notice, in London—the Honourable Artillery Company, in the city of London—in order to accommodate a huge press corps. It was clear that something very big was about to be announced. London was in the midst of a heat wave, and it was another hot day, blazing hot, and the circuits in the building were overloaded by the temperature and all the television cameras. As Browne stood up to announce the deal, a fuse blew. The whole room went dark. Not an auspicious start for what was, up to that point, the largest industrial merger in history. But the sensational news got out far and wide—a $48 billion merger, a potentially transformative step for the world oil industry. And, although not said publicly, it was what BP needed if it was to become a heavyweight.

The implementation proceeded quickly. The Federal Trade Commission found no major antitrust issues. The businesses of the two companies "rarely overlap," said the chairman of the FTC, and consumers will continue to "enjoy the benefits of competition." The BP-Amoco deal closed on the last day of December 1998.[8]

TOO GOOD TO BE TRUE

John Browne was scheduled to speak in February 1999 at a major industry conference in Houston. Two days before the conference, he called the organizers. He was very apologetic. Something urgent had come up in London and unfortunately he wouldn't be able to make it. He would send one of his senior colleagues to read his speech in his place.

It was an excuse. The real reason was that Browne was scheduled to be the keynoter on Tuesday, and the keynoter on Wednesday was Michael Bowlin, the president of one of the major U.S. oil companies, ARCO. And Browne could not take the risk of being on the same program with Bowlin, not given what both were then engaged in.

A month earlier, in January 1999, Bowlin had called Browne from Los Angeles, which was ARCO's hometown. Bowlin had a simple message: "We would like BP to buy ARCO," he said.

Unlike Browne, Bowlin did appear at the Houston conference. His speech was on the future of natural gas, which was a little ironic: for Bowlin, it seemed, had concluded that oil did not have much future. Bowlin and the ARCO board had lost confidence in the company's prospects. ARCO's major asset was its share of the North Slope oil in Alaska, and with oil around $10 a barrel amid the price collapse, management worried that it would not be able to survive.

"It seemed too good to be true," Browne later observed. ARCO "simply wanted to drop into the lap of BP." This was a superb opportunity for BP, especially because of the efficiencies that would come through combining ownership and operatorship of their large North Slope oil resources. The North Slope was the largest oil field ever discovered in North America, but its production had fallen from a peak of 2 million barrels per day to a million, and a combined operatorship would save several hundred million dollars a year.[9]

If ARCO had hung on for another six weeks, it would have seen the beginning of a recovery in its fortune. For, in March 1999, OPEC started to cut back production, which in turn would begin to lift the oil price off the floor. But by then the deal was just about done. The purchase of ARCO for $26.8 billion by BP Amoco (as it was then) was officially announced on April 1, 1999.

"EASY GLUM, EASY GLOW": EXXON AND MOBIL

The announcement of the BP-Amoco deal the previous August proved to be a historic juncture. The taboo against large-scale mergers had been broken, or so it appeared. Perhaps the greater risk, really, was to *not* merge.

Lee Raymond, the CEO of Exxon, was at a conference at the Gleneagles golf course in Scotland when the BP-Amoco announcement broke in August 1998. He knew exactly what he should do: get in touch with Lou Noto.

Raised in South Dakota, Raymond had joined Exxon after earning a Ph.D. in chemical engineering in three years from the University of Minnesota. His first jobs were in research. In the mid-1970s, he was drafted to work on a project for the CEO. The oil-exporting countries were nationalizing Exxon's reserves, and the company needed a strategic direction going forward. Thereafter, Raymond began to play an increasingly key role in reshaping the company. From the mid-1970s onward, the dominant issue for the company had become not only how many barrels of reserves did it have, although that was still critically important, but how financially efficient it was. And how much more financially efficient could it be, compared with its competitors? Success on those criteria would enable it to deliver steadily growing returns to pension funds and all the other shareholders. "The industry had to exist," Raymond later explained. "If you were the best of the lot, you'll always be there."

Raymond became president of Exxon in 1987 and its chairman and CEO in 1993. During the years that Raymond led the company, Exxon's investment process became known for its highly disciplined and long-term focus. Indeed, Exxon's "discipline" became a benchmark against which the rest of the industry was measured. The long-term focus meant that it kept its investment very steady, whether the price was high or low. It did not suddenly increase its spending when prices went up or abruptly cut it when prices fell. This reflected Raymond's own steadiness. One of his favorite maxims, whether in boom times or a price collapse, was "Easy glum, easy glow." Don't get overexcited and hyperactive when prices are shooting up, or overly depressed and catatonic when they're headed down.

But by the mid-1990s, Raymond was coming to the conclusion that financial efficiency in itself had limits. Something more was needed, and that something was a merger. Mobil was a candidate. And as Lou Noto liked to say, "Business is about making something happen."

A couple of months after the breakdown of negotiations with BP, Noto had run into Lee Raymond at a conference. After chatting about various challenges facing the industry, Raymond had said, in his own steady, measured way of speaking, "Something will happen." Not long after, Raymond phoned Noto and said he was coming to Washington and hoped they could have lunch. Sure, Noto replied. Afterward, Noto happened to ask what would be bringing Raymond to Washington.

"To have lunch with you," he was told.

On June 16, 1998, over the meal at Mobil's headquarters in Fairfax, Virginia, Raymond turned to the immeadiate subject of the joint venture they shared with a Japanese company. Eventually they got to the subject of combining their own companies. They concluded that three questions would have to be answered in the affirmative: First, could they work out a satisfactory deal? Second, would such a deal win the approval of the Federal Trade Commission in the United States and the competition directorate at the European Union in Brussels? The third was the most daunting: "Were we wise enough to mold one organization out of two businesses?" A number of closely held conversations followed. But it became apparent that the two companies were far apart on the all-important question of valuation; that is, on what premium would be paid to Mobil shareholders. The discussions petered out. On August 6, Noto told the Mobil board the he and Raymond "had mutually agreed to discontinue discussions."

Five days later, BP and Amoco announced their merger.

As soon as Raymond heard the news, he placed that call to Noto from Gleneagles. The valuations in the BP-Amoco deal provided an external yardstick for resolving their differences on the relative prices of Exxon and Mobil shares.

"Your neighbor just sold his house," is the way Raymond put it. "And now we have another benchmark for what houses are selling for."

The two companies quickly moved into overdrive on negotiating what was code-named "Project Highway." A key decision was to create a wholly new structure so that it would be a new company for everybody.

Antitrust was a major concern. BP's combining with Amoco was one thing. Exxon and Mobil was quite another: it would be a much bigger company, and it would bring together the two largest companies to have emerged from the 1911 breakup of the Standard Oil Trust, which meant it would be a very big news story—and a much bigger subject for regulators.

Noto was deeply worried about the impact on Mobil if they tried to do a merger and it failed because of rejection by the Federal Trade Commission. "Exxon would be okay," said Noto, "but we would be dead meat."

But Raymond reassured him. "This merger is going to happen," said Raymond. "Come hell or high water."

There was an unwritten understanding within the fraternity of antitrust lawyers that 15 percent of the total U.S. gasoline market was the limit that the FTC would allow for any combination, and this deal would fall below that line.

But what immediately preoccupied the two sides was the third question—getting to a valuation and then figuring out who would own what share. Months of hard negotiation followed, often conducted by Raymond and Noto with just a couple of aides. Finally, on the evening of November 30, the two CEOs came to agreement: Exxon would account for 80 percent of the new company, and Mobil, 20 percent. (This proportion was remarkably similar to their relative proportions in the original breakup of the Standard Oil Trust in 1911.) Mobil's shareholders would get about a 20 percent premium on their stock. The negotiations were very intense; indeed, so intense that the final valuation on a share of stock went out to six decimal places.

On December 1, 1998, even before the FTC had ruled on the BP-Amoco deal, Exxon and Mobil announced their intention to merge. It was a very big deal. "The New Oil Behemoth," headlined the *New York Times*.

At the huge press conference presenting the deal, Noto was asked if it was true that, prior to this deal, there had been discussions with BP and other companies. Noto looked out on the audience with what seemed a very long pause.

"I'll tell you what my mother told me," he said. "That you never talk about your old flames on the day you announce your engagement."

The room erupted in laughter. In general, the managements of the two companies were prepared for just about every question during the press conference—except for one. What would happen, Raymond was asked, to Mobil's longtime support of *Masterpiece Theater* on Friday nights on PBS? He uncharacteristically fumbled for an answer.

At another press conference a few hours later, he was asked the same question. This time he answered with a strong affirmation about continuing the commitment. As a follow-up, he was asked what had changed since the previous press conference.

"I talked to my wife," Raymond said.[10]

THE GHOST OF JOHN D. ROCKEFELLER

But there remained a huge potential barrier to these deals, and that was the U.S. government—specifically the Federal Trade Commission, which would rule whether they violated antitrust laws. The spirits of John D. Rockefeller and the 1911 U.S. Supreme Court hovered over the consolidations that were transforming the industry, but the world had changed enormously in the years since.

The FTC's focus was predominantly on refining and the networks of gasoline stations and whether any of the companies would have undue market power, which meant the ability to control the price, in the words of the FTC, "even a small amount." What was of "intense interest" to the regulators was pricing in the downstream—that is, the cost of fuel coming out of the refineries and gasoline at the pump.[11]

But the central rationale of these deals was not about refining and marketing—the downstream—in the United States. It was about the global upstream—exploration and production of oil and gas around the world. The companies were seeking efficiency and cost reduction—the ability to spread costs over a larger number of barrels. No less important was the quest for scale—the ability to take on larger and more complex projects (Lou Noto's "six projects in the frying pan")—and the ability to mobilize the money, people, and technology to execute those projects. Also, the bigger and more diversified the company, the less vulnerable it was to political upheavals in any country. Such a company could take on more and bigger projects. It was already clear that projects themselves were getting larger. A megaproject in the 1990s might cost $500 million. In the decade that was coming, they would be $5 billion or $10 billion or even more. The BP-Amoco deal sailed through the FTC in a matter of months with only minor requirements for divestiture. But Exxon-Mobil was of entirely different scale—much larger. And just to mention together the names of the two largest legatees of the original Standard Oil Trust seemed enough to evoke the ghost of John D. Rockefeller.

The FTC launched an enormous probe into the proposed merger, in cooperation with twenty-one state attorneys general and the European Union's competition directorate. As part of its investigation, the FTC mandated the largest disclosure project in history, which altogether required millions of pages of documents from the two companies from operations all over the world, ranging from refinery operations in the United States to a decade's worth of documents on all lubricant sales in Indonesia. It took almost a year, but finally the FTC came to its decision. In order for Exxon and Mobil to merge, they had to divest 2,431 gasoline stations, out of a total of about 16,000, and one oil refinery in California, plus a few other things. But to those who feared the reincarnation of John D. Rockefeller, the FTC replied that this was not 1911 but rather a very different world. The Standard Oil Trust, explained FTC chairman Robert Pitofsky, "had 90 percent of the U.S. market, while this company after the merger will have about 12 or 13 percent"—below that unstated 15 percent limit. On November 30, 1999, ExxonMobil came into existence as one company.

But at the same time, Pitofsky sent out a warning: a high degree of market concentration would "set off antitrust alarms."[12]

THE ALARMS

Those "antitrust alarms" had already been set off by BP's bid for ARCO. BP-Amoco had moved very fast with its ARCO deal—too fast for the FTC, as it turned out. After a heated internal debate, the commission, by a 3-to-2 vote, decided that the absorption of ARCO would enable BP to manipulate the price of Alaskan oil sold into the West Coast and keep "prices high." What did "high" mean? According to the mathematics of the FTC's witness, a combined company would have been able to increase the price of gasoline by about half a cent a gallon for a few years.

In the view of the majority at the FTC, BP had overreached, and before it could close the deal, it would be required to divest the premier asset, the crown jewel, the whole reason that it had wanted ARCO in the first place—the North Slope oil. A chastened BP realized that it had no choice. It proceeded to close the deal in April 2000, but without the North Slope.

The director of the FTC's Bureau of Economics, writing afterward about the deal, offered a considered judgment that extended to the other mergers of the era: "It is fair to say that in each of these cases, the companies agreed to divestitures that went well beyond what many believed were necessary to protect competition." But politics, the inherent suspicion of the oil industry, and the sense that the mergers were coming too fast—all these were decisive factors.[13]

THE FRENCH RECONNECTION: TOTAL AND ELF

Not everyone depended upon the approval of the Federal Trade Commission. In France, what counted was the assent of the prime minister.

France had two major oil companies, Total and Elf, both of which had been state controlled but were now fully privatized. The reason for the two companies was, as Thierry Desmarest, then Total's CEO, put it, a "historical accident." After World War II, France's president, General Charles de Gaulle, was intent on restoring French "grandeur." He decided that Total, or CFP, as it was known at the time, was "too close to the American and British companies," and he orchestrated the creation of a second French company, a new national champion, which eventually became Elf.

"We were already convinced at the time of the BP-Amoco deal of the need to grow through consolidation," recalled Total's Desmarest. When we heard about the BP-Amoco deal, it confirmed for us intellectually that we had to consolidate, that we had to grow."

The first step, at the end of 1998, was to acquire the Belgian oil company Petrofina, which was primarily a European downstream company. By June 1999, Total had worked out a takeover plan for its main target, Elf. By Friday lunchtime, on July 2, a few senior Elf executives were hearing worrying rumors that Total was about to move.

But nothing could happen without the advance approval of the government. Although Elf had been privatized in 1986, the government still held what was called a "golden share," which gave it a veto over any change of control. Even if there had been no golden share, for a French company to proceed without a green light from the French government would have been career destroying for the managements involved.

The first person who needed to be convinced was Dominique Strauss-Kahn, the finance minister. An economist by profession, Strauss-Kahn quickly understood the competitive economic imperatives of consolidation. Worse, if the French companies did not merge, one of them might well be absorbed by a non-French company, which would be *"un suicide politique"* for any government that allowed it to happen.

The French prime minister, Lionel Jospin, was another matter. A onetime Trotskyite and one of the founders of the modern French Socialist Party, he was not at all familiar with the oil business and its circumstances. It was made clear to Desmarest that he would personally have to make the case to the prime minister about "the importance to France" of a merger.

Time was very short, as Total was on the very eve of launching its takeover bid. But the prime minister was in Moscow.

On Friday evening, Desmarest flew to Moscow and went directly to the National Hotel, opposite the Kremlin, for a middle-of-the-night meeting with the prime minister and Finance Minister Strauss-Kahn. Desmarest set about explaining the urgency, given what was happening with BP and Amoco, and Exxon and Mobil, and with the national oil companies. "Isn't this just a matter of the egos of the CEOs?" asked the prime minister. Desmarest was prepared to answer the question. But under the circumstances, he judged it wiser to leave that particular answer to Strauss-Kahn. The finance minister, a former economics professor, gave the prime minister a short and persuasive lecture on the economic reality and global competitive dynamics that made a deal essential for French national interest. The French prime minister absorbed the lesson. He gave the requisite green light.

By Saturday morning, Desmarest was back in Paris, where the team was putting the last touches on the offer. On Monday, Total launched its takeover bid for Elf. The Elf CEO, Philippe Jaffré, was shocked. Elf mounted a counteroffer; it would take over Total.

In the war for shareholder support, the battle was on. Despite the bitter accusations back and forth, the two sides were privately exchanging plans, since it was foreordained that there would be a merger, and a single French company would emerge out of the struggle. With that in mind, Desmarest and Jaffré worked out a private understanding: neither would personally attack the other publicly, since one of them would actually have to run the combined company.

In September 1999 the deal was done. TotalFina took over Elf, and Desmarest became CEO of the combined company. After a short while, TotalFinaElf would come to be known simply as Total, one of the world's supermajors.[14]

"WE HAD TO CONSOLIDATE": CHEVRON AND TEXACO

For Chevron, the former Standard of California and the nation's third-largest oil company, it was the Exxon-Mobil merger that had really galvanized action. "What surprised me of all of the deals was Mobil's selling themselves to Exxon," said David O'Reilly, who would later become CEO of Chevron. "I thought of Mobil as a sizable company, with a good portfolio, and good growth prospects."

For Chevron, the obvious partner was Texaco, with which it shared the Caltex joint ventures—oil production in Indonesia, refining and marketing throughout Asia, now the fastest-growing market in the world. These joint ventures were five decades old and considered among the most successful such operations involving any kind of companies in the world.

A merger made the same sense to Texaco. The larger companies, the supermajors, would indeed have a higher stock market valuation than the traditional majors. In the spring of 1999, Texaco reached out to Chevron.

The companies secretly dispatched teams to rendezvous in Scottsdale, Arizona. After several days, they concluded that the fit would be excellent. But this would be no merger of equals. Texaco had gone through difficult times. It had lost a $3 billion lawsuit to an independent oil company, Pennzoil, and then, to fend off a hostile takeover from the financier Carl Icahn, it had taken on billions more in debt. As a result, it had to sell its Canadian subsidiary and slash its exploration budget, which would have painful consequences. "It's a pretty simple rule," said William Wicker, then CFO of Texaco. "If you cut your exploration budget in Year Zero, you're not growing in Year Seven and Eight." Texaco had just started to invest again, but the impact would be years away. Texaco was still a very big company, but Chevron was nearly twice as large and would be the acquirer.

While there was a good fit between the companies, the same could hardly be said of the two CEOs, Chevron's Kenneth Derr and Texaco's Peter Bijur. At best, the relationship between them was frosty. Moreover, the two sides could not agree on price, and the discussions broke down. Texaco, Bijur said, was developing a strategy that would get back on a solid growth course.

In the autumn of 1999, Derr retired. The new CEO, David O'Reilly, had been hired by Chevron many years earlier directly out of University College, Dublin, and was immediately dispatched to its Richmond, California, refinery. Now, as CEO, he devoted his first strategy meeting to relaunching a merger plan. "I had already known," recalled O'Reilly, "that we had to consolidate because otherwise we'd become less relevant and marginalized compared with the competition. You have to be committed and have the stomach to go after assets even in lean times."

O'Reilly asked for his board's authorization to pursue a merger. The board's reply was pretty clear: Yes. And the sooner the better.

Over the years, O'Reilly had become known for his unusual ability to connect with all sorts of people. Now his immediate job was to reconnect with Peter Bijur, the Texaco CEO. The senior managements of the two companies met in San Francisco in May 2000 to review their two Caltex joint ventures in Asia. It was clear that the joint venture structure was a very inefficient way to run such an important—and growing—business in the most dynamic growth region in the world. They needed to change it. At the end of the meeting, O'Reilly suggested to Bijur that they talk privately and then brought up the subject of a merger. Bijur allowed that Texaco's go-it-alone strategy was going to be hard going in the new business environment. Negotiations were reopened. The Chevron-Texaco merger was finally signed in October 2000. As Bijur somewhat ruefully summed it up, "It's apparent that scale and size are important as the supermajor oil companies have come on the scene."[15]

THE LAST ONES STANDING: CONOCO AND PHILLIPS

The FTC decision in the spring of 2000, forcing BP to divest ARCO's North Slope assets, inadvertently helped foster the last major merger in the United States. On one side was Phillips Petroleum. Headquartered in Bartlesville, Oklahoma, Phillips was regarded as a mini-major. On the other side was Conoco, which had been owned by the DuPont chemical company since 1981. DuPont had constrained Conoco's spending and growth, using the profits from oil and gas to build up its life-sciences business. When Archie Dunham became CEO in 1996, he later said, "My number one objective was to free the company from DuPont." He convinced DuPont that liberating Conoco would be a very good deal for DuPont's shareholders. On Mother's Day, May 11, 1998, DuPont announced that it would begin selling off the company.

When the first 20 percent was sold, it constituted the largest IPO in U.S. history until that point. The company took as its mantra "Think big and move fast." It celebrated the efficiencies that came from being nimble and keeping a direct "line of sight" from top management down into the front line of operations—not possible in a company with the scale of a supermajor. Its television commercials featured agile, nimble cats, which was said to be irritating to the much bigger Exxon, whose own emblem was a tiger.

But there were two obvious risks. One came from being in the position of being able to bet only on three or four big projects, instead of ten or fifteen. The second was the danger of being absorbed in a hostile takeover. Phillips faced the same risks. And these were not theoretical risks. After all, the reason Conoco had fallen into DuPont's arms in 1981 was to ward off hostile bids. And later in the 1980s, Phillips had been the target of hostile tenders by both T. Boone Pickens and Carl Icahn. And, thus, Dunham and Phillips's CEO, James Mulva, had begun discussing a possible combination in 2000. But the talks had foundered in October 2000.

Instead, the two companies went head to head as finalists in bidding for the Alaskan assets that BP and ARCO had to shed in order to consummate their merger. Phillips was the winner. That meant a strategic transformation. For the acquisition doubled its reserves and gave it a bulk that made it commensurate with Conoco in size. But how were talks to get going again?

During World War I, the state of Oklahoma had run short of money and, as a result, had left its capital's building in an embarrassingly unfinished condition—that is, without a dome. Eighty-five years later, in June 2001, a celebration was being held in Oklahoma City for a newly built dome that was to be hoisted atop the capitol. Both Phillips and Conoco were financial contributors to this historic rectification, and the two CEOs, Dunham and Mulva, both in town for the event, ran into each other in the lobby of the Waterford Hotel.

"We need to talk again," said Mulva.

Months of negotiations followed. In November 2001, the two companies announced their merger, creating ConocoPhillips, the third-largest oil company in the United States with, in fact, the largest downstream system in the nation. Dunham become chairman. Mulva, who was now the CEO of the combined company, was very clear as to the purpose of this merger: "We're going to do this so we can compete against the biggest oil companies."[16]

STANDING ASIDE: SHELL

One company was notably absent from the fray, Royal Dutch Shell, which had been, prior to the mergers, the largest oil company of all. There were several reasons. An internal analysis had concluded that the long-term oil price would be determined by the cost of new non-OPEC oil, which it pegged at $14 a barrel; and so it used a $14 oil price to screen investments. It had also concluded that size mattered, but only up to a certain threshold. But there was a still more important reason—the structure of the company itself.

When Mark Moody-Stuart would introduce himself at conferences, he would say, "I'm the chairman of Shell. I'm also the closest thing you'll ever see to a CEO of Shell." That was the problem. Shell had a unique structure. Although it operated as one company, it was actually owned by two separate companies with two separate boards—Royal Dutch and Shell Transport and Trading. It had no CEO; it was run by committee. This was the compromise reached to carry out a much earlier merger, in 1907, and then modified in the late 1950s. This "dual structure" had worked well for many decades, but had become increasingly inefficient. The dual ownership also made it "very difficult," as Moody-Stuart put it, to do a stock-based merger with another large company. In fact, it had made such a merger virtually impossible. During the merger years, Moody-Stuart had tried to push through an internal restructuring, but the reaction from many of the directors was, as he said, "quite stormy."[17] Nothing happened. After all the mergers were done, Shell was no longer the largest oil company.

What had unfolded between 1998 and 2002 was the largest and most significant remaking of the structure of the international oil industry since 1911. All the merged companies still had to go through the tumult and stress of integration, which could take years. They all came out not only bigger but also with greater efficiencies, more thoroughly globalized, and with the capacity to take on more projects—projects that were larger and more complex.

Looking back a decade later on the consolidation, on this earthquake in the industry structure, Chevron CEO David O'Reilly observed, "A lot of it has played out as was expected. The part that hasn't quite played out relates to the national oil companies. Are these larger companies competitive with the national oil companies?"[18]

When a minor corner of the world economy—the overleveraged Bangkok commercial real estate market—began to convulse, and the overvalued Thai baht began to plummet from speculative attacks, no one expected that the consequences would lead to an Asian, and then a wider global, financial crisis. Certainly none of the managements of the world's major oil companies would ever have expected that the distress of this rather obscure Southeast Asian currency would trigger a collapse in the price of oil and the massive restructuring of their own industry. Yet more was to come. For the consequences would also transform national economies and countries, including one of the world's most important oil producers.

5

THE PETRO-STATE

For oil-importing countries, the price collapse was a boon to consumers. Low prices were like tax cuts. Paying less for gasoline and home-heating oil meant that consumers had extra money in their pockets, which was a stimulus to economic growth. Moreover, low oil prices were an antidote to inflation, allowing these countries to grow faster, with lower interest rates and less risk of inflation.

CRISIS FOR THE EXPORTERS

What was a boon for the consumers was a disaster for the oil producers. For most of them, oil and gas exports were the major source of government revenues, and the petroleum sector was responsible for 50 or 70 or 90 percent of their economies. Thus, they experienced sudden large drops in GDP. With that came deficits, budget cuts, considerable social turmoil, and, in some cases, dramatic political change.

The most dramatic change of all would be in Venezuela. Because of the scale of its resources, Venezuela could be described as the only OPEC "Persian Gulf country" not actually in the Persian Gulf. In 1997 it was actually producing more petroleum than either Kuwait or the United Arab Emirates, and almost as much as Iran. Its position in the Gulf of Mexico and its role as a Western Hemisphere producer made it a bulwark of U.S. energy security, as it had been going back to World War II. But Venezuela had also become the very embodiment of what is called a petro-state.

The term "petro-state" is often used in an abstract way, applying to nations that differ widely in everything—political systems, social organization, economy, culture, religion, population—except for one thing: they all export oil and natural gas. Yet certain common features do make the petro-state a useful lens. The common challenge for these exporters is to ensure that the opportunities for longer-term economic development are not lost to economic distortion and the ensuing political and social pathologies. That means having the right institutions in place. It is very challenging.

Venezuela's national saga illuminates the difficulties.

"The Venezuelan economy since 1920 can be summed up in a word: oil," the economist Moises Naim has written. Prior to that, it had been an impoverished, underpopulated, agricultural nation—a "cocoa-state" and then a "coffee-state" and "sugar state"—highly dependent on those commodities for its national income, such as it was. Local *caudillos* ran their little fiefdoms as if they were their own countries. Of the 184 members of the legislature in the mid-1890s, at least 112 claimed the rank of general. Afflicted by innumerable military coups, Venezuela was ruled by a series of dictators, such as General Cipriano Castro, who after taking power in 1900, proclaimed that he was "the man raised by God to fulfill the dreams of Bolivar" and reunite Venezuela, Colombia, and Ecuador as a single country. He was soon pushed aside by another general, Vicente Gómez, who ruled the country as his "personal hacienda" from 1908 until his death in 1935.[1]

The decisive event for Venezuela's fortunes came in 1922. The giant Barroso well in the Maracaibo basin blew out with an uncontrolled flow of 100,000 barrels a day. (It was discovered by the same engineer, George Reynolds, who in 1908 brought in the first oil well in Iran.) With the Barroso gusher, Venezuela's oil age had begun. Thereafter, increasing wealth poured into the country as more and more oil flowed out of the ground.

Yet why did Juan Pablo Pérez Alfonso, the influential energy minister after the restoration of democracy in 1958, and one of the founders of OPEC, decry petroleum in his retirement years as "the excrement of the devil"? It was because he saw the impact of the influx of revenues on the state, the economy, and society, and the psychology and motivations of the people. The oil wealth could be wasted; it could distort the nation's life. In his view, Venezuela was already becoming a petro-state, a victim of the alluring and malevolent "resource curse."[2]

THE "REVERSED MIDAS TOUCH"

In the 1980s and 1990s, oil could generate more than 70 percent of Venezuela's central government's revenues. In a petro-state, the competition for these revenues and the struggle over their distribution becomes the central drama of the nation's economy, engendering patronage and clientelism and what is called "rent-seeking behavior." That means that the most important "business" in the country (aside from oil production itself) is focused on getting some of the "rents" from oil—that is, some share of the government's revenues. Entrepreneurship, innovation, hard work, and the development of a competitively oriented growth economy—all these are casualties of the system. The economy becomes inflexible, losing its ability to adapt and change. Instead, as the edifice of the state-controlled economy grows, so do subsidies, controls, regulations, bureaucracy, grand projects, micromanagement—and corruption. Indeed, the vast amounts of revenues connected with oil and gas create a very rich brew for corruption and rent seeking.

A group of Venezuelan academics summed up the problem this way: "By the middle of the twentieth century, there was already a deeply rooted conviction that Venezuela was rich because of oil, because of that natural gift that does not depend on productivity or the enterprising spirit of the Venezuelan people." They added: "Political activity revolved around the struggle to distribute the wealth, rather than the creation of a sustainable source of wealth that would depend upon the commercial initiatives and the productivity of the majority of the Venezuelan people."[3]

The petro-state and its attendant resource curse have two further characteristics. One is called the Dutch disease. The term describes an ailment that the Netherlands contracted in the 1960s. Around that time, the Netherlands was becoming a major natural gas exporter. As the new gas wealth flowed into the country, the rest of the Dutch economy suffered. The national currency became overvalued and exports became relatively more expensive—and, thus, declined.

Domestic businesses became less competitive in the face of the rising tide of cheaper imports and increasingly embedded inflation. Jobs were lost and businesses couldn't survive. All of this came to be known as Dutch disease.

A partial cure for the disease is to segregate some of these earnings. The sovereign wealth funds that are now such important features of the global economy were invented, in part, as preventative medicine—to absorb this sudden and/or large flow of revenues and prevent it from flooding into the economy and thus, by so doing, insulate the country from the Dutch disease.

The second, even more debilitating ailment of the petro-state is a seemingly incurable fiscal rigidity, which leads to more and more government spending—what has been called "the reversed Midas touch." This is the result of the variability of government revenues, owing to the volatility of oil prices. When prices soar, governments are forced by society's rapidly–rising expectations to increase their spending as fast as they can—more subsidies to hand out, more programs to launch, more big new projects to promote. While the oil can generate a great deal of revenues, it is a capital-intensive industry. This means it creates relatively few jobs, adding further to the pressure on governments to spend on projects and welfare and entitlements.

But when world oil prices go down and the nations' revenues fall, governments dare not cut back on spending. Budgets have been funded, programs have been launched, contracts have been let, institutions are in place, jobs have been created, people have been hired. Governments are locked into ever-increasing spending. Otherwise they face political backlash and social explosions. The governments are also locked in to providing very cheap oil and natural gas to their citizens as an entitlement for living in an energy-exporting country. (In 2008 gasoline in Venezuela went for about eight cents a gallon.) This leads to wasteful and inefficient use of energy, as well as reducing supplies for export. A government that resists the pressures to spend—and increase spending—puts its very survival at risk.

There are easier ways than cutting spending to alleviate the "reversed Midas touch." But they work well only in the short term. One way is by printing money, which leads to high inflation. Another is by international borrowing, which keeps the money flowing. But that debt needs to be serviced and repaid, and as the debt balloons, so do the interest payments, leading of potential debt crises.

In the petro-state, no constituency is in favor of adjusting spending downward to the lower levels of income—except for a few economists who understandably become very unpopular. On the contrary, across society most hold the conviction that oil can solve all problems, that the tide of oil money will rise forever, that the spigot from the finance ministry should be kept wide open, and that the government's job is to spend the oil revenues as fast as possible even when more and more of those revenues have become a mirage.

As Ngozi Okonjo-Iweala, former finance minister and foreign minister of Nigeria, summed it up: "If you depend on oil and gas for 80 percent of government revenues, over 90 percent of exports are one commodity, oil, if that is what drives the growth of your economy, if your economy moves up and down with the price of oil, if you have volatility of expenditures and of GDP, then you're a petro- state. You get corruption, inflation, Dutch disease, you name it."[4]

While these are the general characteristics that define a petro-state, there are wide variations. The dependence on oil and gas of a small Persian Gulf country is obvious, but its population is also small, which reduces pressures. And it can insulate itself from volatile oil prices through the diversified portfolio of its sovereign wealth fund. A large country like Nigeria that depends heavily on oil and natural gas for government revenues and for its GDP has much less flexibility. Spending is very difficult to rein in.

There is also a matter of degree. With 139 million people and a highly developed educational system, Russia possesses a large, diversified industrial economy. Yet it does depend upon oil and natural gas for 70 percent of its export revenues, almost 50 percent of government revenues, and 25 percent of GDP—all of which means that the overall performance of its economy is inordinately tied to what happens with the price of oil and gas. And while Russia is much more than a petro-state, it has some of the characteristics of a petro-state—from which it can benefit and with which it must contend—and which generates a constant debate about how to diversify the economy away from oil and gas.

"WE COULDN'T LOSE TIME"

But it is Venezuela that is as identified as any nation with the very idea of the petro-state. And it was Carlos Andrés Pérez who embodied the petro-state—at least the first time around. His first term as president of Venezuela was during the height of the oil boom in the 1970s, when revenue far greater than anyone had ever contemplated was flowing into the national treasury. As a result of the quadrupling of the oil price in 1973–74, he had gained, on an annualized basis, four times as much money to spend as his immediate predecessor. And he was determined to spend it. "We are going to change the world!" he would say to his cabinet. Venezuela's human capital made the ambitions more credible. Even before the price increases, the government was taxing the oil companies as much as 90 percent, and as part of the policy of "sowing the oil," a good deal of money had been spent on education, and as a result, Venezuela had an educated and growing middle class.

As much as anyone, Pérez was the architect of what became the modern Venezuelan petro-state, "the kingdom of magical liquid wealth." Some called it "Saudi Venezuela." Pérez proclaimed his vision of *Le Gran Venezuela,* an increasingly industrialized, self-sufficient nation that would march double-time, fueled by oil, to catch up with the developed countries. Oil had "given us," he said, the opportunity to "pull Venezuela out of her underdevelopment... We couldn't lose time."

In 1976 Pérez engineered the government takeover of the oil industry, in accord with the great wave of resource nationalism that was sweeping the developing world in that decade. But Venezuela carried out its nationalization in a careful and pragmatic way. Considerable talent had been built up throughout the industry during the years that the international majors ran the sector. Prior to nationalization, 95 percent of the jobs in the industry, right up to the top management, were held by Venezuelans. So nationalization would be a change of ownership but not of personnel. The new state-owned company, Petróleos de Venezuela, S.A. (PDVSA), was generally run on professional grounds. It was the holding company, overseeing a series of cohesive, operating subsidiaries.[5]

"IT IS A TRAP"

When Pérez left the presidency in 1979, the money was still flowing. But in the 1980s, the oil price plummeted and so did the nation's revenues. Yet the edifice of the new petro-state was locked in place and indeed had expanded. Pérez was out of office during the 1980s, and the ills of the petro-state now became all too evident to him. As he traveled the world, he looked at different models for economic development and the struggle for reforms, and reflected on the costs and inefficiencies and defects of the overweening, oil-fed state. "An [oil] price spike is bad for everyone but worst for developing countries that have oil," he had concluded. "It is a trap."

By the end of the 1980s, Venezuela was the very paradigm for the petro-state. It was in deep crisis. Inflation and unemployment were rising rapidly, as was the share of the population below the poverty line. The widening income gap was evident in the massive emigration from the countryside to the cities and in the ever-expanding slums and shanty towns that climbed up on the hills surrounding the capital city of Caracas. Meanwhile, a substantial part of Venezuela's current revenues was being diverted to meet interest payments due to international lenders.

All these pressures were made worse by one other factor—Venezuela's rapid rise in population, which had, over two decades, almost doubled. Such an increase would have required heroic economic growth under any circumstances to keep per capita incomes constant. (Although sometimes overlooked, the growth in population was an indicator of social improvement—of better health and lower infant mortality.) To prevent explosive social protest, the government ran an ever more complex system of price controls that made the economy even more rigid. The price of almost everything was set by the government, right down to ice, funerals, and the price of a cup of coffee in a coffee shop.[6]

At the end of the 1980s, Pérez won a return term as president. By the time he moved back into the Miraflores, the presidential palace, in 1989, it was evident how severe the slippery "trap" of oil had become. Despite all the oil money, the economy was in terrible shape and getting worse. Per capita incomes were back to where they had been in 1973. In his inaugural address, Pérez had declared that he would administrate the nation's wealth as though he were "administrating scarcity." Determined to reverse course, Pérez immediately launched a program of reform, which included reducing controls on the economy, cutting back on spending, and strengthening the social safety net for the poor. After a very turbulent first year, marked by major riots in Caracas that left hundreds dead, the economy started to respond to the reforms and began to grow at high rates.

But undoing the petro-state was very difficult. The traditional political parties, interest groups, and those who benefited from the special distribution of rents united to oppose him and obstruct his program at every turn. Even his own party turned on him. The party activists were outraged that he had appointed technocrats to economic ministries, denying them access to the favors and rents to which they had become accustomed.

But those were not Pérez's only opponents.

THE COUP

On the night of February 4, 1992, Pérez, just returned from a speech in Switzerland, was falling asleep in the presidential residence when he was awakened straight up by a phone call. A coup was in process. He raced to the Miraflores, the presidential palace, only to find it under attack. A group of ambitious young military officers had brought a long-planned conspiracy to a head and launched a coup against the state. The assault on the palace was coordinated with attacks elsewhere in Caracas and in other major cities.

A number of soldiers were killed in the bloody assault on the presidential palace. Pérez would have likely been killed too—he was certainly the prime target—save that he was spirited out of the building through a back door and hidden under a coat in the backseat of an unmarked car.

While the conspirators elsewhere in the nation achieved their objectives, those in Caracas were not able to capture the presidential palace. And they failed in one of their other most decisive objectives: to seize the broadcasting companies in order to announce their "victory". But when a group of the rebels arrived at what they thought was one of the television stations, they discovered they had the wrong address; the station had moved three years earlier. Another group went to the right address of another station. But the station manager succeeded in persuading them that their videotape was the wrong format and that it would take some time to convert the tape to broadcast format—long enough, as it turned out, for the station to be recaptured by loyal forces. Before the night was out, it was evident that the coup had failed, at least in Caracas.

The next day, the leader of the Caracas part of the coup, the thirty-eight-year-old Lieutenant Colonel Hugo Chávez, now in custody, was put on national television, "impeccably dressed in uniform," in order to deliver a two-minute statement urging the rebels in other cities, who were still holding their targets, to surrender. The message was heeded. But Chávez's two minutes on the airwaves did something more: they transformed him from a failed conspirator into an instant celebrity, a charismatic *caudillo,* very different from the maneuvering politicians of the traditional parties that the cynical public was accustomed to seeing. "Unfortunately, *for now,* the objectives we sought were not achieved in the capital city," Chávez calmly told the other rebels—and the nation. "We will have new situations. The country definitely has to embark on the road to a better destiny." The for now reverberated around the country.

At that particular moment, however, Chávez's own road was leading to a prison cell.[7]

HUGO CHÁVEZ

Son of schoolteachers, Hugo Chávez Frías had grown up in the sparsely populated savannah region of Venezuela. As a youth, he had proved himself a formidable baseball player, with dreams of signing in the American major leagues. He was also a budding artist and caricaturist. But those were not his only interests. Two of his best friends in the city of Barinas were named Vladimir, in honor of Lenin, and Federico, in honor of Friedrich Engels, Karl Marx's coauthor. During his teenage years, Chávez spent hours in the library of their father, a local communist, discussing Karl Marx and South America's "Liberator" Simón Bolívar, and revolution and socialism. All this had a lasting impact, as evidenced by the book he carried with him on the day he entered the military academy as a cadet, *The Diary of Che Guevara.* And, already, as a new cadet, he was writing in his diary of his ambition that "one day I will be the one to bear responsibility of an entire Nation, the nation of the great Bolivar." At the academy, he imbibed the careers of other ambitious young officers from modest circumstances—Ghaddaffi in Libya, Juan Velasco Alvarado in Peru—who had gone on to seize power.

It did not take Chávez long after graduating from the military academy to connect with other like-minded conspirators. "As far as anyone knows," his biographers have written, "Hugo Chávez began to lead a double life when he was around twenty-three." By day, he was a hardworking, dutiful, and obedient officer. At night, he was meeting secretly with other young officers, as well as extreme left-wing activists, plotting his way to power. One day, in the early 1980s, Chávez was out jogging with a group of other junior officers when they broached the idea that some of them, including Chávez, had been harboring for some time—that they secretly launch a revolutionary movement. And right there, in front of a tree much favored for its shade by Simón Bolívar, they took an oath to that effect. From that moment onward, Chávez saw himself as the future leader of Venezuela. He formed a clandestine officers' group, the Bolivarian Revolutionary Army, that built its network in the army.[8]

It was in 1992, a decade or so after that jog, that Chávez and his co-conspirators launched their failed coup. In the subsequent two years that followed his arrest, Chávez spent his time in prison reading, writing, debating, imagining his victory, receiving a continuing stream of visitors who would be important to his cause—and basking in his new glory as a national celebrity.

Later in 1992, a second coup attempt, this by more senior officers, also failed. But its very fact demonstrated how unpopular Carlos Andrés Pérez had become. Perez had alienated the public with his policies, especially the cutbacks in the spending that was the hallmark of the petro-state. He also continued to infuriate his opponents with his economic reforms and decentralization of political power. They got their revenge: they impeached him for corruption. The specific charge: he had provided $17 million to the new president of Nicaragua, Violeta Chamorro, who had taken over from the Marxist Sandinistas, and, fearing for her life, had asked for help in setting up a presidential security service to prevent her assassination. Here, with Pérez's removal from office, was proof anew of the old maxim that no good deed goes unpunished.

Pérez's opponents celebrated their victory in deposing him. But it would eventually prove a costly victory for these defenders of the old order of the petro-state. For the impeachment would further discredit the political system, ultimately leading to their own ruin.

On Palm Sunday, 1994, Rafael Caldera, Pérez's successor and longtime rival, freed Chávez and the other plotters and provided an amnesty. It is possible that Caldera simply thought that these were young military officers led astray. There is also the possibility that Caldera acted out of a degree of personal sentiment. Hugo Chávez's father had been a leader of Caldera's old party in the state of Barinas and was the person who would have received him when he campaigned there. Curiously, Caldera did not add to the amnesty what might have been the normal restriction—permanently banning Chávez and the others from political life. It was a significant omission. But Caldera certainly never imagined that any of the plotters could ever navigate their way through Venezuelan electoral politics.

Now out of prison, the former conspirator, guided two seasoned politicians of the left, was determined to win political power not with bullets but at the ballot box. This time, instead of guns and conspiracy, Chávez's weapons would be his new popularity, organization, unstoppable personal drive, and sheer charisma. He put himself at the head of what he called the Bolivarian political movement, and with endless energy, crisscrossed the country denouncing corruption, inequality, and social exclusion. He also traveled abroad. In Argentina, he spent time with a sociologist who propounded a theory of the mystical union of the "masses and the charismatic leader"—and also denied the Holocaust.[9]

But his most important trip was to Cuba, where he forged a deep bond with one of his heroes and another baseball fanatic, Fidel Castro. Castro would be his mentor, and indeed embrace him as his political son. For his part, Chávez would come to see himself as Castro's legatee in the Hemisphere, but different in one crucial aspect—a Castro who would be bolstered with tens of billions of dollars of oil revenues.

LA APERTURA

Meanwhile, things had gotten worse for Venezuela's economy, leading to a severe banking crisis. By the middle 1990s, it was clear that Venezuela urgently needed to increase its oil revenues to cope with the country's problems. Since world petroleum prices were not going up, the only way to raise additional revenues was to increase the number of barrels that Venezuela produced. The new president of PDVSA, a petroleum engineer named Luis Giusti, embarked on a campaign to rapidly step up investment and output.

The most significant initiative, and one with global impact, was *la apertura*—"the opening" (really, a reopening)—inviting international oil companies to return to Venezuela to invest in partnership with PDVSA, to produce the more expensive and technologically challenging reserves. This was not a winding back of nationalization, but rather reflected the trend toward greater openness in the new era of globalization. It was also a pragmatic effort to mobilize very large-scale investment that the state could not shoulder by itself.

La apertura was highly controversial. To some it was anathema, heresy. After all, the traditional route that had been followed—nationalization, state control, expulsion of the "foreigner"—was enormously popular. But to Giusti, this was all ideology. What mattered was not appearances and symbolism, but revenues and results. The state did not have the resources to fund the full range of required investment, and social programs were a huge competing call on the government's money. Moreover, despite its competence, PDVSA did not have the advanced technology that was needed. *La apertura* would bring in international capital and technology. Output would increase from older fields. And, at last, Venezuela would be able to use technology and large-scale investment to liberate the huge reserves of very heavy oil in what is called the Faja, the Orinoco region, that up to then could not be economically produced. "The Orinoco was dormant," said Giusti. "We had known for one hundred years that the oil was there, but nothing had been done."

With *la apertura,* Venezuela might be able to double its production capacity by five million barrels over six or seven years, and the state would capture the lion's share of the additional revenues through taxation and partnership. But none of this could be accomplished without foreign investment. As Giusti summed it up, "There was only so much money, and we had so much to do."[10]

PAINTING THE PICTURE

The hardest part was the politics, starting with President Rafael Caldera. Giusti had to convince the president, who knew the nationalistic politics all too well. Giusti had the detailed plan for *la apertura* printed in two handsomely bound volumes, with blue covers and gold letters. At a meeting with the president, he saw that Caldera had put paper clips on many, many pages. This sent Giusti into something of a panic. He knew that Caldera was a very skilled lawyer and that he would lose if he got into a detailed legal discussion with the president.

How was he going to persuade the president to reverse what was one of the most fundamental and popular principles of national politics and public opinion? Somehow he had to get to the essence; he had to paint the whole picture for Caldera. Then he had an idea. Why not actually paint a picture? He knew a brilliant geologist who was also a talented landscape painter, Tito Boesi. On a Thursday, Giusti called Boesi and said that he wanted the geologist to paint a large canvas mural that would depict every stage of the country's oil technology development, from the seepages that had enticed the original explorers to the application of the various generations of technologies, up to what might be imagined for the future of the Orinoco. The purpose would be to vividly demonstrate how increasingly complicated and expensive would be the further development of Venezuela's petroleum patrimony.

Giusti told Boesi that he needed the painting right away.

"Are you crazy?" said Boesi.

"I need it," insisted Giusti. "I know you're a very good artist, Tito. But it doesn't have to be a masterpiece."

Summoned to the president's house the following Saturday, Giusti appeared with Boesi's canvas painting rolled up under his arm. When called upon, he asked the president if he could show him something. To the perplexed look of many in the room, including the president, he rolled out the canvas on the long conference table and explained its story.

When Giusti finished, he could see that President Caldera was angry. At first he thought it was directed at him, but then realized that Caldera was angry with his own entourage, which, the president had concluded, had not properly briefed him on the scale of the challenge facing the industry on which Venezuela depended.

Several days later, the president approved *la apertura.* Over the next few years, as the contracts were negotiated and implemented, *la apertura* would bring tens of billions of dollars of international investment into the country, jump-starting the development of the vast oil sands, the Faja, and "reactivating" older oil fields, which needed injection of new technologies to reverse their decline.[11]

THE OIL WAR

There was a second very important aspect to oil policy as well. Venezuela would produce at its maximum rate, irrespective of OPEC output quotas, indeed disregarding the country's quota. Venezuela argued that its quota had been set a decade earlier and did not reflect changes in its population and social needs. Of course, other OPEC countries, wanting to maximize their own output, vehemently disagreed. Between 1992 and 1998, Venezuela increased its oil production by an astonishing 40 percent. That engendered an acrimonious battle within OPEC. Observers began to write about an "oil war" for market share between the two countries that had taken the lead in founding OPEC—Venezuela, now ignoring quotas; and Saudi Arabia, insisting that they be observed. That was the battle that culminated in the November 1997 Jakarta meeting and was resolved with the agreement that all exporters could produce flat out, which by now they were all more or less already doing.[12]

But by then the Asian financial crisis had already begun to trigger an oil price collapse, ravaging the budgets of the oil-exporting countries. At this point, Venezuela recognized that it could no longer afford its market share strategy. In March 1998 Venezuela, Saudi Arabia, and non-OPEC Mexico met in Riyadh and worked out a set of production cutbacks for exporters, OPEC and non-OPEC alike. Most of the other exporters went along, out of self-interest and sheer panic. But it was not enough to deal with the drop in demond from the Asian crises. Then the oil prices, after a brief recovery, fell to $10 and then further to something that, for the exporters, was intolerable—single digits.

THE ELECTION: NOT EVEN "THE REMOTEST CHANCE"

By late 1998 Venezuela was deep into an economic crisis, poverty was rising rapidly, and social tensions were high—and mounting. "Economically, Venezuela is reeling, with oil prices under $10 a barrel," reported the *New York Times* in December 1998. It was just at this moment that Venezuela was going to the polls to elect a new president. The two dominant parties, Acción Democrática and Copei, were thoroughly discredited. They were also depleted; they seemed to have run out of ideas, energy, and conviction. For a time, the presidential frontrunner was a mayor best known for having once been Miss Universe, but she faded as the campaign progressed.[13]

Chávez, unrelenting in his attacks on the political system, had risen from a few percentage points to the top of the polls. As was customary during a presidential election campaign, PDVSA provided briefings to the candidates. By this point, Giusti himself had become a controversial figure because of his championing of *la apertura* and wide-open production, and because he was seen by some as pursuing his own political agenda. When Chávez arrived at PDVSA's headquarters, he told Luis Giusti he wanted his briefing to be one-on-one, with each just having one aide there. For ninety minutes, Giusti took him through the industry's situation. At the end, Chávez thanked him for an excellent presentation and then, just before they went through the door, grabbed him by the arm and warmly added that he wanted to express his appreciation and personal affection. Chávez then went downstairs to the waiting press; he announced that as soon as he was elected president, he was going to fire Giusti.

In the December 1998 presidential election, with just a 35 percent turnout, the deep economic and social distress that came with the oil price collapse gave Hugo Chávez, who had been released from prison only four years earlier, a 56 percent victory. In his victory speech that night, Chávez denounced Luis Giusti as the devil who had sold the soul of Venezuela to the imperialists.

The next month, standing next to Chávez at the inauguration, was the outgoing president, Rafael Caldera, who had amnestied the lieutenant colonel in 1994. Caldera looked nothing so much as stunned. "Nobody thought that Mr. Chávez had even the remotest chance of becoming president of the republic," he later said. As for Luis Giusti, he made a point to resign as president of PDVSA before Chávez could fire him.[14]

CHÁVEZ IN POWER

But how would the forty-two-year-old lieutenant colonel govern? Was he a democrat or an authoritarian? His initial comments were not clear: "If you try to assess me by traditional canons of analysis, you'll never emerge from the confusion," he said. "If you are attempting to determine whether Chávez is of the left, right or center, if he's a socialist, Communist or capitalist, well, I am none of those, but I have a bit of all of those." At another time he added, "I absolutely refuse, and will refuse to my grave, to let myself be labeled or boxed in. I cannot accept the notion that politics or ideology are geometric. To me, right and left are relative terms. I am inclusive, and my thinking has a little bit of everything."

Whatever the ideology, Chávez moved swiftly to consolidate all power in his hands, keeping the formal institutions of the state—"worm-eaten" though he called them—but depriving them of any independent role. He quickly pushed through a new constitution, which eliminated the upper house of the congress. He turned the remaining chamber into a rubber stamp. He increased the number of Supreme Court judges from twenty to thirty-two, packing it with *revolucionistas.* He took direct control of the National Electoral Council, ensuring that his personal political machine would count the ballots in future elections. He removed any congressional oversight of the army and then proceeded to set up a second parallel military force of urban reservists. And he rechristened Venezuela as the Bolivarian Republic.

He made a triumphant visit to Cuba, where he declared, "Venezuela is traveling toward the same sea as the Cuban people, a sea of happiness and real social justice and peace." He also played ball with Fidel Castro—in this case, baseball. Although Chávez did the pitching for the Venezuelan team, the Cubans won, 5-4. The Cubans won something else as well—a Venezuelan subsidy. With the end of Soviet communism, Russia no longer had any ideological bonds with Cuba and had stopped providing cheap oil. Chávez stepped in to become Castro's oil banker, delivering petroleum at a steep discount.[15]

In turn, Cuba provided advisers of many different kinds—health workers, teachers, gymnastic instructors, and a wide variety of security personnel operating under various guises. For Cuba, this was a return to Venezuela, for it had provided aid to guerrillas during the "violent years" of the 1960s. Castro had relished Venezuela's oil wealth, and he had repeatedly tried to open a beachhead. Indeed, one attempt to insert Cuban military into Venezuela in 1967 had led to the death of Castro's personal chief of security. This time, however, Cuba was there to bolster the government—Chávez's government. Chávez also adopted the Cuban system of local neighborhood control. And in case it was still not clear where he stood, Chávez clarified matters. "There is only revolution and counterrevolution," he declared, "and we are going to annihilate the counterrevolution." When Roman Catholic bishops urged him to be less confrontational, he dismissed them as "devils in vestments."[16]

Castro was a role model in many ways. As the Cuban president specialized in speeches that went five or six hours, Chávez adopted a variant with his Sunday-afternoon television broadcast, *Alo Presidente*. Over the course of four hours or more, in a weekly demonstration of his manic energy, he would joke, sing revolutionary songs, tell anecdotes from his boyhood, and talk about baseball. He would also denounce his opponents as the *corruptos* and position himself as the leader of the revolutionary vanguard opposing the United States or what he calls the "North American empire . . . the biggest menace on our planet." At one and the same time, he wrapped himself in the cloak of the nineteenth-century liberator Simón Bolívar and propounded his new theory of "socialism for the twenty-first century."

And then there was oil, the soul of the Venezuelan state. The economic engine was PDVSA and Chávez quickly asserted his control. He was much influenced by a German-born energy economist, Bernard Mommer, who made the case for a highly nationalistic oil policy and argued that Venezuela had fallen prey to "liberal policies" that urgently needed to be reversed. Chavez attacked PDVSA as "a state within a state" and then proceeded to subordinate it to his state, politicizing what had been the professionally run company. PDVSA's treasury became the cash box of the state, and Chávez moved financial control of the company into the central government, giving him direct control over its vast revenues. There was no accountability or transparency. He could use the money as he wanted, shifting investment from the oil industry to whatever purposes he thought best, whether social spending and subsidies for favored groups at home or pursuit of his political objectives within the country and abroad. More than ever before, Venezuela was truly a petro-state.[17]

THE RECOVERY OF OIL

Chávez made a decisive policy change that would reverberate throughout the world. Venezuela would no longer pursue a strategy of increasing revenues by increasing outputs. Indeed, it now became the strongest advocate in OPEC for cutting back on production and observing quotas.

As prices started to recover, Chávez left no doubt of his explanation: "The increase in the oil price has not been the result of a war or the full moon," he said. "No. It is the result of an agreed strategy, a change of 180 degrees in the policy of previous governments and of Petróleos de Venezuela . . . Now the world knows that there is a serious government in Venezuela."[18]

Chávez had moved OPEC to the center of Venezuelan oil policy, but in fact, Venezuela had already started to cut back on production before Chávez was elected, beginning in Riyadh in March 1998. Also, Venezuela was one element in a larger tableau. For faced with plummeting revenues, all the OPEC countries—and some non-OPEC countries—had gotten religion about quotas and restraint.

Moreover, the overall picture was certainly changing. While OPEC was reining in production, Asia started to recover. Demand started to snap back. And so did prices. This particular oil crisis—the crisis of the producers—was ending.

The exporters, who before had been dismally staring at $10 a barrel or less, were now talking more confidently about a $22-to-$28 "price band" as their target. But by the autumn of 2000, spurred by economic recovery in Asia and OPEC's new policy, the price of oil had surged over the band, above $30 a barrel, a threefold-plus increase from where it had been just two years previously. The big increase in demand—a surge of 2.5 million barrels per day between 1998 and 2000—was having a decided impact on the oil market.

The "soaring oil prices," as they were described in the press, were setting off alarms in consuming countries, which had rather quickly become accustomed to lower prices. Now they feared a "brewing energy crisis." Such was the alarm that the rising prices—and the gasoline and home-heating oil prices they drove—were becoming a contentious issue in the hotly contested 2000 U.S. presidential battle between George W. Bush and Al Gore. On September 22, 2000, two days after prices spiked to what seemed a shocking $37 a barrel and in the midst if the campaign, the Clinton administration released some oil from the Strategic Petroleum Reserve, aimed at blunting price increases in the weeks before the arrival of winter.[19]

By that point Hugo Chávez had already established himself as a force in world oil and in the Western Hemisphere. Yet without the oil price collapse of 1997–98, it is not at all clear that he would have had the chance, just seven years after his coup attempt had landed him in jail, to act on what he had written in his diary decades before, while a cadet in the military academy, and take "responsibility" for Venezuela. Now, like the dictator General Cipriano Castro a century earlier, he aimed for his Bolivarian project to extend beyond Venezuela's borders, to the rest of Latin America. But unlike that general, he was seeking global reach as well. And the rising price of oil would give him the wherewithal to try.

6

AGGREGATE DISRUPTION

As the twenty-first century opened, except for the brief price spike, oil had faded away as a policy issue. Moreover, the resolution of the 1990–91 Gulf crisis appeared to have taken energy security off the table.

Instead attention was riveted on new things and in particular on "new new things." That meant the revolution in information technology and in how people communicated with one another in a world that was now continually interconnected twenty-four hours a day. And it meant, more than anything else, the Internet. Silicon Valley and cyberspace—those were the places to be. All this, along with the end of the Cold War and rapidly growing world trade, inaugurated a new self-confident era of globalization. "Distance" was disappearing, along with borders, as both finance and supply chains tied production and commerce together around the planet. It was an increasingly open world, freely communicating, freely trading, freely traveling—and, as it turned out very definitely, "visa-lite." It was a world of rising living standards and ever-wider possibilities. It was an optimistic time.

THE DAY THAT CHANGED EVERYTHING

On September 11, 2001, two jets hijacked by Al Qaeda operatives slammed into the twin towers of the World Trade Center, and a third into the Pentagon.

The fourth, aimed at the Capitol, was brought down by passengers in a cornfield in Pennsylvania. For the first time since the Japanese air raid on Pearl Harbor, December 7, 1941, which had taken the United States into World War II, America had been directly attacked, and with a greater loss than on that unsuspecting Sunday morning in Hawaii.

In retrospect, the warnings had been there with a series of attacks—initially on the World Trade Center in 1993; then on the embassies in Kenya and Tanzania in 1998, where hundreds perished; and on the U.S. destroyer *Cole* in a port in Yemen in 2000—along with an attempt to blow up Los Angeles International Airport on New Year's Eve 2000 that had been aborted by an alert guard at the Canadian border. And there were also all the pieces of intelligence that were not connected—ranging from the CIA and FBI databases that did not talk to each other, to the Arab students at flying schools in the United States who were interested in learning only how to take off but not how to land.

That morning transformed international relations. Security now became the central preoccupation. Borders and barriers went up. The world was no longer so open a place. In the autumn of 2001, in what became known as the "war on terror," the United States and its allies counterattacked in Afghanistan, the base from which Al Qaeda operated. They pushed the Taliban, Al Qaeda's ally, from power, and in just a matter of weeks achieved a decisive victory. Or so it seemed at the time.

Globalization suddenly looked different. The world might be much more interconnected, but new vulnerabilities arose out of the much-denser network of trade and communication lines on which this interconnected world relied. "Homeland security" went from being a title for think-tank reports to the name of a massive new U.S. cabinet agency. September 11 revealed a dark underside to globalization. Empowered with the tools of globalization, shadowy groups with militant ideologies could take advantage of the openness—easy travel, easy movement, cheap cellular communication, and easy Internet access—to disrupt globalization and seek to undermine the more open world.

Petroleum had, since the beginning of the twentieth century, been entwined with security and the power and position of nations. But 9/11 led to a new emphasis on oil's risks, including the fact that the world's biggest oil region, the Middle East, was also the region from which Al Qaeda had emerged. One of Al Qaeda's original grievances, in addition to the impact of modernity on the region, was the presence in Saudi Arabia of U.S. troops, which had remained after the 1991 Gulf War to help contain Saddam Hussein. The militant messages and sermons in some of the Mideast mosques were very similar to those of Al Qaeda, and recruits and money came from that region. Some fifteen of the nineteen suicide hijackers on 9/11 had been Saudi Arabian nationals.

The "special relationship" between the United States and Saudi Arabia went back to the meeting between President Franklin Roosevelt and King Ibn Saud on the Great Bitter Lake, in the Suez Canal, in February 1945. From Harry Truman onward, U.S. presidents had made the security of Middle East, and in particular Saudi Arabia and its oil, a fundamental national interest. Jimmy Carter made the commitment much more explicit in response to the Christmas Eve 1979 Soviet invasion of Afghanistan, which was seen as a possible "stepping stone" for the Soviet Union to try to gain control over the Persian Gulf and "much of the world's oil supplies."

"An attempt by any outside force to gain control of the Persian Gulf region," said the Carter Doctrine, "will be regarded as an assault on the vital interests of the United States, and such an assault will be repelled by any means necessary, including military force." Saudi Arabia, in turn, had tied its long-term security to the United States. There were many other ties as well. During the late 1970s, the Saudi cabinet was said to have more members with American Ph.D.s. than the U.S. cabinet.[1]

The Carter Doctrine was pointedly directed at an "outside force," the Soviet Union. But what about "inside forces" within the Gulf region? Here, with the attack of September 11, was evidence that some part of the population in Arab countries was outrightly, indeed violently, hostile to the United States and the rest of the industrial world. No one knew the actual proportions. Yet in the aftermath of 9/11, some in Saudi Arabia initially denied that fifteen of the hijackers were even Saudi. This added to the tension between the United States and Saudi Arabia that strained the energy and security relationship. The rift did not fully end until May 2003, when Al Qaeda–linked operatives launched terrorist attacks in the Saudi capital of Riyadh, followed within a year by other attacks, including one on a police headquarters in the capital city. Saudi Arabia recognized that it was a prime target and that Al Qaeda was its dangerous enemy.

From an energy perspective, the lasting impact of 9/11 in the United States was a renewed conviction that oil consumption and oil imports in particular were a security risk. At the time, Mideast oil represented about 23 percent of imports and 14 percent of total U.S. oil consumption. But it had become symbolic of "dependence" and the dangers thereof. Many Americans thought that *all* U.S. imports came from the Mideast. And thus the mantra of "energy independence," which had been a fixture of American politics since the 1973 oil embargo, took on new urgency.

September 11 itself did not have much impact on oil price. (In the months that immediately followed, oil prices actually fell below $20 a barrel and did not get back over $20 until March 2002.) Even into 2004, the widespread expectation was that market conditions would ensure that prices remain in that "moderate" range. Yet over four years, between 2004 and 2008, prices would shoot up, reaching a historic high of $147.27, with far-reaching impact on the world economy. They would redistribute global economic and political power, and shake people's confidence and raise anxiety about the future. The extraordinary increase both reemphasized the centrality of oil and at the same time gave new impetus to move beyond oil.

As with most great developments in human affairs, there is not a single explanation for the massive leap in prices. It was driven first by supply and demand, and huge but largely unanticipated change in the world economy. Disruptions and a return to resource nationalism were critical elements. But then more and more momentum was provided by forces and innovations coming out of the financial market. The story of what happened to price is also a narrative about profound changes both in the oil industry and in the wider world.

September 11 disrupted security and international affairs and altered thinking about oil and dependence and the uses that could be made with oil revenues. But 9/11 did not interrupt supply. In the autumn of 2002, more than a year after 9/11, there was little hint that supply problems would begin to take a toll on the flow of oil. Indeed, anything but. "Oil Prices Fall as Global Supplies Soar" headlined an industry trade publication. But that would very shortly change.[2]

A series of crises in three major exporting countries would spur supply losses, compounded by the the forces of Mother Nature. None was large enough on its own to upset the balance in the oil market. Yet when tallied together, they would constitute a significant loss of supply, what added up to an "aggregate disruption" that would have notable impacts over the next half decade, reducing supplies that would have otherwise been available to a growing world economy.

"ALO PRESIDENTE"—VENEZUELA

Reelected president of Venezuela in 2000, Hugo Chávez moved to further consolidate power in his hands. As he did so, opposition became more vocal. Parents protested the Ministry of Education's plans to revise history textbooks in a way that would demonize Venezuela's first forty years of democracy—"Cubanizing" the textbooks, it was said. In the face of parental opposition, the government retreated, temporarily. The government also established local militias called Bolivarian circles, modeled on Cuba's Committees for the Defense of the Revolution, in order, as Chávez announced, to create "a great human network" to defend the revolution. New controls on the media included a ruling that the press could be punished for spreading "false news" or "half truths." But particularly alarming was a package of 49 laws that greatly extended state power and that was put into effect without approval by the National Assembly. At the same time, Chávez extended his control over Petróleos de Venezuela—PDVSA—the state oil company. The continuing politicization of PDVSA was eroding the effectiveness and professionalism for which the company had developed a worldwide reputation.

By this time, a broad coalition of opposition had emerged, encompassing both trade unions and business groups, as well as the Catholic Church. Segments of the senior military leadership were becoming wary of the way in which Chávez was taking power into his own hands and the way he was wielding it. On April 7, 2002, Chávez used his Sunday television talk show, *Alo Presidente,* to fire seven members of the board of PSVSA. He ridiculed each by name and then dismissed them one by one to the cheers of the studio audience.[3]

Four days later, on April 11, 2002, opposition to Chávez and popular discontent exploded into a mass march of upwards of a million people in Caracas. As the march approached Miraflores, the presidential palace, guards loyal to Chávez started shooting, killing, and wounding some of those at the forefront of the crowd. Chávez went on television to denounce the marchers. But a split scene on the screen simultaneously showed the carnage in front of the presidential palace while Chávez orated, further inflaming the outrage.

"CALL FIDEL!"

As tension mounted, Chávez ordered the implementation of Plan Ávila, what has been described as "a highly repressive security operation." Military units began to rebel against both the plan and the idea that soldiers would turn their guns on civilians. At 3:25 a.m., on April 12, 2002, the nation's top military officer went on television. In light of the "appalling incidents that occurred yesterday in the nation's capital," he said, "the president of the republic has been asked to resign, and he has agreed to do so." By this time Chávez had been taken into custody and was being hustled from one military base and then to another. At one point he managed to borrow a cell phone from a soldier, and reaching one of his daughters, asked her to "call Fidel . . . Tell him I haven't resigned." Over the next several hours, various resignation letters were presented to Chávez and negotiated over, but he never quite signed any of them.[4]

Although described as a coup, what had ensued was not expected or planned, and the opposition scrambled to fill the sudden power vacuum. A prominent business figure emerged as head of a provisional civilian-military government. He proceeded to make what proved to be a fundamental mistake by dissolving the government but failing to announce that elections would be held soon, thus losing the mantle of constitutionalism—alienating the military, in particular. And there was still no resignation letter signed by Chávez.

Chávez had been moved to the military island of La Orchila, from whence it was thought he was going to be flown out of the country, probably to exile in Cuba. But, on the mainland, confusion and fissure started to appear among the opposition, suddenly thrust into power. The military began to waver and split. Finally, in the very early morning hours of April 14, Chávez had apparently agreed to a final document that embodied his resignation. However, a couple of hours earlier, a general, one of the original members of Chávez's group of conspirators, had already dispatched helicopters carrying commandos to La Orchila. While the letter was going through retyping, the helicopters touched down on the island, where they picked up Chávez. He was not going to Cuba after all. Instead, he headed back to the presidential palace in Caracas.[5]

Less than three days after his arrest, Hugo Chávez was once again in control of the country, and he set out to quickly tighten his grip. That included further extending his direct control over the management of PDVSA, the engine of the economy and by far the largest source of government revenues. The months that followed were turbulent, for Chávez showed no interest in reconciliation. The country was deeply divided, and the opposition was very restive.

THE GENERAL STRIKE

Later in 2002, with the normal channels of political opposition closed in what was increasingly becoming a one-party governmental system, the unions and business community joined together to call a general strike in order to try to force Chávez into a referendum on his governance.

Much of the country shut down. PDVSA just stopped working. Over the next few weeks, the country's oil output plummeted from 3.1 million barrels a day to around 200,000 barrels a day—perhaps even less. Venezuela was forced to import gasoline on an emergency basis. The loss of almost three million barrels a day shifted the world market from surplus to shortage. Oil prices, which had been declining, started to rise sharply again and soon were higher than any prices seen since the Gulf crisis in 1990.

In Washington, the disruption ignited a sharp debate within the U.S. government as to whether to release oil stored in the U.S. Strategic Petroleum Reserve to compensate for the oil lost from one of America's biggest suppliers. The Department of Energy recommended use of the SPR. But the final decision was not to do so. The oil in the strategic reserve needed to be retained, it was said, for the possibility of a much greater disruption that could occur somewhere else—in the Middle East.

Meanwhile in Caracas, Chávez would not budge: as the weeks went on, the general strike eroded; people drifted back to work and after sixty-three days, the strike ended altogether. By mid-February 2003, PDVSA was back up to about half its prestrike level. In the aftermath of the shutdown, Chávez was now even more intent on eliminating any political opposition to his march toward his "socialism for the twenty-first century." He was determined to end whatever independence PDVSA still had left. About twenty thousand workers—almost half the workforce—were summarily fired and replaced with less-experienced workers; from then on, the company would be operated not as a state-owned company, but as an arm of the state. The vast amounts of money that the company generated would become inseparable from the state.

The crisis of production was over. But due to the haphazard way in which production was shut down, and the inexperience of many new managers brought on after Chávez's purge, Venezuela would not regain its prestrike levels of output, let alone approach what had been its ambitious expansion goals. Still by mid-April 2003, enough oil was being produced and refined that Venezuela could once again start exporting petroleum to its customers. But by then supply was being disrupted elsewhere on the world market.

NIGERIA: "YOU'RE A PETRO-STATE"

Nigeria, the eighth-largest exporter in OPEC and one of the major sources of U.S. petroleum imports, certainly has the attributes of a petro-state. Oil and natural gas account for 40 percent of GDP.

As finance minister from 2003 to 2006, Ngozi Okonjo-Iweala sought to set the budget based on a lower oil price assumption, impose fiscal discipline, and build up the government's financial reserves. All that made her highly unpopular—and a political liability. "The pressures were enormous, which is part of the reason I'm not there today," she later recalled. "Politicians were not happy with me. I was quite controversial for maintaining discipline. I'm sure that on the day I resigned there were more than a few high-fives."[6]

ETHNIC CONFLICT

But oil is only part of the picture. Nigeria is a dominant force in Africa. With 155 million people, it is the most populous country on the continent; one out of every seven Africans is Nigerian. But many of them do not think of themselves as Nigerian but rather define themselves by language, religion, and tribal group.

Nigeria is a country of 250 ethnic groups, split among an Islamic north and a Christian south, with further divisions between east and west in the southern part. It was defined as a unit by the British colonial administration, but is a nation tied together with weak institutions and a weak sense of national unity, and divided by strong religious and ethnic identities. Nigeria became independent in 1960, four years after the discovery of oil there. Its history has thereafter been defined by violent conflict over the distribution of power and resources and over the state itself. In 1967 the southeastern part tried to secede and become a separate nation of Biafra. After three years of civil war, and the loss of more than three million lives, the north won, and the country stayed whole.

Nigeria has gone through five constitutions and seven military coups. The country's experience demonstrates the Dutch disease in many ways. The once-vibrant agricultural-export sector has collapsed, and the country is a net importer of food. An effective and dedicated civil service, one of the legacies of colonial rule, was weakened, contributing to the poor governance. Oil revenues were stolen and squandered on a massive scale. The huge Ajaokouta steel complex is the poster child for revenues wasted. Built in the 1970s, it has yet to produce commercial steel. Between 1970 and 2000, Nigeria's population more than doubled; over the same period, on a per capita basis, income actually declined.[7]

Through all this, the country's oil industry has been caught up in the struggle among regions, ethnic groups, national and local politicians, and violent groups—militias, gangs, and cults—for power and primacy, for identity—and for the money. The Nigerian government takes over 80 percent of the sale price of a barrel, but there is a constant battle over how those earnings should be split between the federal government, the states, and local communities.

But that is only part of the battle. Violent clashes between Christians and Muslims, including massacres in which hundreds are slain, are a recurrent feature. So is the struggle over the application of Islamic sharia law in the north. Corruption is deeply embedded throughout the fabric of national life.

The epitome of state failure was the brutal dictatorship of General Sani Abacha, who seized power in 1993. In the five years prior to his sudden death, he proved himself a champion at corruption; it is thought that he amassed as much as $5 billion. Most notoriously, in 1995 he oversaw the brutal execution of Ken Saro-Wiwa, author and environmental campaigner for the Ogoni people, and eight other Ogoni activists. His death resounded for years ofter. Abacha himself died three years later. Over the next several years, Nigeria struggled to recover some of the stolen money. Abacha's family stubbornly maintained that the money had been honestly gained, insisting that Abacha, in addition to being Nigeria's full-time dictator, had also been a very astute investor.[8]

In 1999, in the first election in sixteen years, Olusegun Obasanjo, a former general, was elected president. Obasanjo had earned a unique position in Nigerian annals, for during a previous spell in power, he proved to be the only military ruler in Nigeria's history to hand over power to a constitutionally elected civilian government. Prior to his return as an elected president, he served as chairman of the advisory board of Transparency International, a prominent NGO that focuses on combating corruption in developing countries. It was not an inappropriate preparation: when he returned to power as a civilian and as an elected president in 1999, corruption was one of the most intractable problems.

VIOLENCE IN THE DELTA

And nowhere was it more intractable than in the Niger Delta. The Delta is a vast, swampy region formed by the Niger River, Africa's largest, as it flows into the Gulf of Guinea. The Delta is where most of Nigeria's oil is produced, and where regional and local politicians have habitually siphoned off a great deal of wealth for their own bank accounts, and which is why a governorship of one of the Delta states is a much-sought-after position: it is a ticket to wealth.

Officially, however, only 13 percent of total oil revenues accrue to the local states. The Delta's decrepit infrastructure and endemic poverty, combined with the high population density, fueled hostility both toward the oil industry, which had no say over how the oil money was allocated between the federal and state governments, and the regional and national governments. There was also a legacy of environmental degradation from oil production of the 1960s and 1970s.

The Delta had been subject to recurrent outbreaks of violence. With an estimated forty ethnic groups in the area, there was plenty of tinder for conflict. But the violence became more organized and more lethal in the first decade of this century. "Bunkering"—stealing oil from the maze of pipelines and flow stations that carry the oil to barges and on to the world market—turned into a very profitable business, and an increasingly violent one. Bands of young men began to attack the flow stations, drilling sites, and oil camps to extract money and pressure companies and local governments. They formed gangs under names like the Bakassi Boys, the Icelanders, the Greenlanders, and the Niger Delta's People's Volunteer forces; and they waged war with rival gangs, fueled by drugs, alcohol, demonic initiations, and occult superstitions.

In the run-up to elections in 2003, as had become the custom, local politicians patronized various armed groups to violently promote their victories and steal oil as a way to raise campaign funds. In March 2003, gangs attacked a series of production sites in the Delta. The oil companies evacuated their personnel, and more than a third of Nigeria's production—over 800,000 barrels a day—was shut down.

After the 2003 elections, the militias, operating independently, began to acquire more weapons and build themselves into more formidable forces. They stole increasing amounts of oil—sometimes estimated at over 10 percent of Nigeria's total production (which in 2010 would amount to over $5 billion stolen oil)—in collaboration with former oil workers, corrupt government officials, an international network of oil smugglers, and pirates operating widely in the Gulf of Guinea. Stealing and sabotage were largely responsible for the oil spills that despoiled the Delta. Violence was already so endemic and at such a level that by the end of 2003, an internal report for one of the major oil companies said that "a lucrative political economy of war in the region is worsening" and warned of "increasing criminalization of the Niger Delta conflict."

The funds from the bunkering, in turn, enabled the militia leaders to further increase their arsenals and acquire much more lethal weapons and, in the words of one observer, "take militia activity to a new dimension of criminality." As the head of one of the most notorious militias put it, "We are very close to the international waters and it's very easy to get weapons."

The wells and gathering systems are strung out through the swampland, mangrove forests, and shallow waters of the Delta, crisscrossed by creeks and streams—all of which provides for good cover and quick getaways on speedboats mounted with machine guns. The region is very densely populated, the birth rate is very high, and poverty is widespread. The inequities breed anger and resentment, on which the militias feed.

In September 2004 a leader of one of the gangs, a self-described admirer of Osama bin Laden and an advocate that the Ijaw ethnic group should secede and form its own country, threatened "all-out war" against the Nigerian state. That threat "pushed oil over $50 per barrel for the first time."[9]

That was it for President Obasanjo. He summoned the leaders of two of the most violent groups to the federal capital of Abuja, where he met with them in the cabinet room and hammered out a peace accord. It lasted through part of 2005. But then the Delta began to descend back into violence and gang warfare.

"THE BOYS"

In January 2006, four foreign oil workers were kidnapped from a platform in the shallow waters of the Niger Delta, and then gunmen aboard speedboats attacked another oil facility in the Delta, killing 22 people, setting buildings afire, and severely damaging the equipment for managing the flow of oil.

A heretofore unknown group took credit—the Movement for the Emancipation of the Niger Delta. MEND, as it became known, declared that it sought "control of resources to improve the lives of our people." Claiming several thousand men under arms, MEND warned that it would unleash further attacks that would "set Nigeria back 15 years and cause incalculable losses," and said it aimed "to totally destroy the capacity of the Nigerian government to export oil."[10]

A few days after the January 2006 attacks, in the snow-covered Swiss Alpine village of Davos, at the World Economic Forum, Olusegun Obasanjo, Nigeria's president, was meeting in a seminar room to discuss his country's economic prospects. Two of the participants, a venture capitalist from Silicon Valley and a world-famous entrepreneur from Britain, urged Obasanjo to get off oil and emulate Brazil and launch large-scale cultivation of sugarcane to make ethanol. A bemused Obasanjo, president of one of the world's major oil producers, nodded with feigned enthusiasm and promised to give the idea serious consideration.

Toward the end of the meeting, as Obasanjo was about to leave, he was asked about the those recent attacks a few days earlier in Nigeria and whether they presaged a new wave of violence.

It was nothing to get too concerned about, he said with confidence. "The Boys," as he called them, would be brought under control.

That was not an unreasonable expectation. After all, some of the militia and vigilante groups, including the Bakassi Boys, had been subdued over the previous few years. Moreover, it was difficult to distinguish among all those who attacked the oil industry infrastructure. They all operated with the same kind of tools—those fast speedboats, sometimes with machine guns mounted on them, AK-47s, and stolen dynamite. The picture was further complicated by the shadowy connections between those in speedboats and those in power.

But this time, "the Boys" did not cooperate. The January 2006 attacks were the beginning of a wave of bloody intimidation, kidnappings, and murder. Violence in Nigeria became a key factor in the world oil market. "The balance of world oil supply and demand has become so precarious," U.S. Federal Reserve chairman Alan Greenspan warned in June 2006, "that even small acts of sabotage or local insurrections have a significant impact on prices." The dense swamps and intricate network of creeks and waterways made it easy for MEND and such similar organizations as the Martyrs Brigade to attack and then fade back into the jungle—and they did so with impunity. One night shortly after the presidential election in 2007 of Nigeria, the family home in the Delta of Goodluck Jonathan, the new vice president (and now Nigeria's president), was burned to the ground by one of the gangs. It was meant as a demonstration of power—and as a warning.[11]

In the face of constant violence in the Delta and the killing and kidnapping of their workers, the international oil companies repeatedly evacuated their employees, closed down facilities, and declared force majeure on shipments. Plans for substantial expansion of capacity were shelved. As it was, without physical security, the oil could not flow. At some points, upward of one million barrels per day—40 percent of Nigeria's total output—was shut in and lost to the world market. That deficit was one of the key factors in the rise of prices. And it was certainly a loss for the United States, for which Nigeria had just moved up in the rankings to become its third-largest source of imported oil.

NATURAL DISASTER

Somewhere above the west coast of Africa, unseen and unnoticed on a cloudless day, solar radiation penetrated the earth's atmosphere and struck an expanse of surface of the southern Atlantic. The sun's rays transferred their energy to an enormous number of water molecules, transforming liquid into gas and sending these molecules back into the sky as a gaseous vapor. Winds off the dry Sahara and the power of the earth's rotation pushed these clouds of water, now coalescing into large bands of tropical moisture, westward, toward the American continent.

No one took notice until August 13, 2005, when a forecaster at the National Hurricane Center in Miami identified a mass of clouds over the tropical Atlantic, 1,800 miles east of Barbados. Ten days later, those same clouds once again caught the attention of the National Hurricane Center as they merged with another tropical storm and began to slowly churn. On Thursday morning, August 25, what had now been christened Hurricane Katrina made landfall near Miami Beach but without heavy devastation. The storm gained scope as it passed into the Gulf of Mexico.

By August 28, it had been transformed into a huge storm, a frighteningly ominous black mass, sprawling across the map—from the Yucatán Peninsula in Mexico to the southern United States. With winds as powerful as an EF4 tornado, Katrina was already one of the most powerful storms ever recorded by the National Oceanic and Aeronautics Administration.

America's largest energy complex is in and around the Gulf of Mexico, and it was right in the bull's-eye. Over more than six decades, thousands of oil and gas production platforms had been built offshore, in both shallow waters, within sight of shore, and deepwater far out at sea. At the time, almost 30 percent of U.S. domestic oil production and 20 percent of natural gas production came from the Outer Continental Shelf in the Gulf of Mexico. Almost a third of the country's entire refining capacity—which turns the crude into gasoline, jet fuel, diesel, and other products—stretches along the shores of the Gulf.

Now, with Katrina approaching, the entire offshore industry went into emergency mode. Workers rushed to shut in the wells, secure the platforms, and activate automatic systems; they then hurriedly climbed into helicopters and raced the increasingly powerful winds back to shore.

As winds reached a peak strength near 175 miles per hour, Katrina hit the offshore energy complex and then slammed with devastating force and surging seas along the Louisiana, Mississippi, and Alabama coasts, blowing down buildings, washing away homes, overturning cars, ripping out power lines, flooding the entire region, and forcing 1.3 million to flee as temporary refugees.[12]

What ensued was a human tragedy of far-reaching proportions. The worst violence was reserved for New Orleans, where the levies were breached, opening the way for the waters to flood into streets and homes built below sea level, submerging large parts of the city under water, forcing up to 20,000 people to seek refuge in the Superdome and leaving more than 1,800 dead.

Rita, a new storm, also one of the most violent hurricanes ever recorded, similarly spawned in the South Atlantic, headed straight down the center of the Gulf. Once again, the industry sprang into emergency mode. Rita hit the platforms that had been spared on Katrina's course and then tore through onshore oil refining centers, leaving some of them severely damaged and flooded.

Altogether, more than 3,000 platforms and 22,000 miles of undersea pipeline were in the direct path of the two storms. A total of 115 platforms were completely destroyed (most of them older ones, not built to 1988 standards); 52 were damaged, as were 535 pipeline segments of pipeline. Yet so effective were the environmental containment measures that the offshore production facilities did not leak. At the peak, the hurricanes knocked out 29 percent of total U.S. oil production and almost 30 percent of U.S. refining capacity. Months later, a significant part of the production and refining operations was still not back on line.[13]

Onshore, some 2.7 million people were left without electricity. With electric power down, the long-distance pipelines that carry gasoline and other refined products to the East Coast could not operate, and supplies became very tight in the Southeast and the Mid-Atlantic states. The gasoline may have been sitting there in the underground tanks at the stations. But without electric power there was no way to pump it out and into the tanks of the ambulances and police cars and fire engines and repair trucks so that they could carry out their rescue and repair missions amid the chaos and devastation.

Oil prices surged upward, both because of the disruption itself and as word of shortages sent tremors of panic and fears of gas lines through the public. The two storms sparked the largest disruption of oil supply in the history of the

United States—a loss, at its peak, of 1.5 million barrels per day. Other countries took the unprecedented step of shipping emergency stocks of oil to the United States to help make up for the shortfall.

By 2006 production was recovering in the Gulf of Mexico, and supplies from offshore were once again making their way to consumers. But the market continued to feel the impact of the various losses of supply from the aggregate disruption. Moreover—in addition to Venezuela, Nigeria, and Katrina and Rita—another disruption was having a big impact on the world market. This one was in the very heart of the Middle East.

7

WAR IN IRAQ

In late 2002, Philip Carroll received a phone call from an official in the Pentagon. The Department of Defense was putting together an advisory group on oil, and Carroll was a sensible stop. Twice retired—first as CEO of Shell Oil USA and then the engineering company Fluor—Carroll came equipped with considerable international experience in the logistics and infrastructure of energy supply, as well as a reputation for diplomatic skill.

The questions were about how and what to plan for, in terms of oil, in the event of war. Two things were known: Iraq was highly prospective but had not really been explored since the 1970s and indeed was one of the least explored of all the major oil-exporting countries. And its industry was in poor condition, although no one really knew how poor. Carroll recommended that the DOD do an in-depth study and think through how the industry could be managed during postwar transition. A few months later, in early 2003, Carroll was formally asked if he would go out to Iraq as oil adviser following U.S. military action. He would become one of about twenty other senior advisers, each to advise and help direct an Iraqi ministry. By that time it was more than clear that the United States, along with Britain, Australia, Japan, and a score of other nations, in what was called "the coalition of the willing," would shortly be going to war.

WHY THE WAR?

Iraq was an oil country. Its only export was oil. It was a nation defined by oil, and as such was a country of great significance to the global energy markets. But the ensuing war was not about oil. It resulted from a convergence of factors: the primary ones were the September 11, 2001, attack and its consequences, the threat of weapons of mass destruction, the way the 1991 war ended, the persistence of Saddam's intransigent and ruthless rule, and the way in which analysis was, and was not, carried out.

Saddam had an "addiction to weapons of mass destruction," as the head of the U.N. weapons inspection program put it on the eve of the war. For decades the Iraqi dictator had devoted a significant part of the country's resources to the development of chemical, biological, and nuclear weapons. Despite his agreements with the United Nations after the Gulf War, both Western and neighboring countries believed that Saddam was continuing to develop WMD and that, if not restrained, would indeed acquire them. For instance, a 1998 National Intelligence Estimate reported that while Iraq's WMD capability had been damaged by the Gulf War, "enough production components and data remain hidden and enough expertise has been retained or developed to enable Iraq to resume development and production of WMD . . . Evidence strongly suggests that Baghdad has hidden remnants of its WMD programs and is making every effort to preserve them."

For the war planners, the likely use of such weapons by the Iraqi regime was a central factor in military planning, right up to and into the war itself, when, as a result of intercepted signals, some units carried bulky, cumbersome masks, impermeable gowns, and individual antidotes for chem-bio attacks. The postwar failure to find WMD capabilities, despite much effort, undermined the credibility of the decision making in the eyes of many. Some parts of the U.S. intelligence community—notably the State Department's Bureau of Intelligence and Research and some in the CIA—had dissented, arguing the view that Saddam was probably still not pursuing the weapons but their arguments were discounted. The general view was that Saddam certainly was acting on his addiction. And there was within the U.S. intelligence community, the Middle

East National Intelligence Officer Paul Pillar wrote, "a broad consensus that such programs existed." There was, however, no agreement on their scale, timing, effectiveness, and utility.[1]

France and Germany—along with Russia—opposed the decision to go to war at every step. French president Jacques Chirac emerged as a particular foe to supporters of war, stating that "nothing today justified a war," and that there was, in his view, "no indisputable proof" of weapons of mass destruction. But Chirac was reflecting the view of the French intelligence service. "We had no evidence that Iraq had weapons of mass destruction," recalled a senior French policymaker. "And we had no evidence that it did not. It may be that sanctions had worked much better than we had thought."[2]

But Saddam made several miscalculations. He thought that the scale of the antiwar demonstrations in Europe would somehow ensure that the coalition would not actually invade. In what proved to be a massive miscalculation, he chose to convey ambiguity as to what he was doing about such weapons—and what he was covering up. To do otherwise, he apparently thought, would have weakened his regime vis-à-vis both Iran and domestic opponents. As he told his inner circle, "The better part of war was deceiving." To an interrogator after the war, who asked him why the illusion, he had a one-word reply: Iran.

There was also the matter of assuming that others saw the world the way he did. It has been suggested that Saddam could never have believed that the 1991 coalition would have stopped short of Baghdad for something so mushy as the "CNN effect" on television viewers around the world and because of the fear of splintering the coalition. He would not believe it because he would not have acted on such reasons. It had to be because they feared that he had equipped his forces with chemical and biological weapons for the final defense of Baghdad. This was a very compelling reason to maintain the illusion.[3]

From the coalition side, there was good cause to proceed on a worst-case assumption: in the aftermath of the First Gulf War, it was discovered, with some shock, that the Iraqi regime was six to eighteen months away from a crude nuclear weapon. In retrospect, had Saddam not been so hasty but instead waited to invade Kuwait until 1993 or 1994 rather than 1990, he would have been in a much stronger position—equipped with some kind of nuclear weapon capability, and operating in a much tighter world oil market. All this would have reduced the flexibility of his opponents.

With the United States' having underestimated Saddam's capabilities once, the Bush administration was not going to repeat that mistake. There was all the more reason for such a response given 9/11 and in light of Saddam's evident appetite for WMD and his hunger for revenge after 1991. Laura Bush later wrote of her husband, "What if he gambled on containing Saddam and was wrong?" Bush himself said, "That was not a chance I was willing to take." This gamble seemed all the more risky in the state of permanent anxiety and tension that followed 9/11: after the attacks, a daily litany of reports flowed into the U.S. government about plots and attacks prevented, which only added to the constant apprehension about those plots that might not be nipped in time. "We lived with threat assessments more disturbing than any ever spoken on the air," said Laura Bush.

As a senior State Department official wrote to Secretary of State Colin Powell prior to the war, "September 11 changed the debate on Iraq. It highlighted the possibility of an Iraqi version of September 11, and underscored concerns that containment and deterrence will be unable to prevent such an attack." Some argued that Iraqi intelligence had direct links to, and had perhaps even coached, Al Qaeda. Others said that such a link was highly dubious, indeed unlikely, and certainly unsubstantiated. "The intelligence community never offered any analysis that supported the notion of an alliance between Saddam and al Qaeda," said Paul Pillar, the national intelligence officer. But that did not mean that, under the premise of "the enemy of my enemy is my friend," there could not be cooperation in the future given their common enmity toward the West.[4]

Iraq was already at the top of the agenda of some of the senior policymakers prior to their taking office in the administration of George W. Bush. A policy review of options related to Iraqi sanctions had been launched in the summer of 2001. A few days after 9/11, at a meeting of President Bush with his senior advisers at Camp David, some sought to add Iraq as a target for counterattack, alongside Al Qaeda and Afghanistan. At that point Bush was firm in his rejection. In early October 2001, the U.S. ambassador to the United Nations was instructed to read "the toughest message I'd ever been asked to deliver" to Iraq's ambassador, warning of the dire consequences for Iraq if it tried to take advantage of the 9/11 attacks. But it was not until 2002, fueled with the confidence from what seemed to be the very successful and very short campaign to evict the Taliban from Afghanistan that plans really began to congeal around a war with Iraq. And, in the aftermath of 9/11, it was going to be a preventative war—launched under what became known as the policy of preemption.[5]

To the inner circle of decision makers, 9/11 demonstrated the risks of not acting in advance to prevent Saddam's acquisition of such weapons. Vice President Dick Cheney, who had been secretary of defense during the Gulf crisis, was central to the Iraq decisions. "As one of those who worked to assemble the Gulf War coalition," he said in 2002, "I can tell you that our job then would have been infinitely more difficult in the face of a nuclear-armed Saddam Hussein."

President Bush laid out the fundamentals of the new policy in a speech at West Point in June 2002. Traditional "deterrence" did not work against "shadowy terrorist networks." And "containment" did not work "when unbalanced dictators with weapons of mass destruction can deliver these weapons on missiles or secretly provide them to terrorist allies." The only answer was "preemptive action," Bush added, "if we wait for threats to fully materialize, we will have waited too long."

There was also a conviction among some that the existing political systems and stagnation in the Middle East were the breeding grounds for the likes of Al Qaeda and terrorism. A "new" Iraq could be the beginning of the answer. The skillful and clever Iraqi émigré Ahmed Chalabi, claiming to speak both for the exile community and those within the country, convinced some policymakers that an Iraq without Saddam would welcome the coalition as liberators and would quickly embrace representative democracy. These decision makers were convinced that "a pluralistic and democratic Iraq" would have a transformative effect in the Middle East, and in something akin to the fall of communism, set off a process of "reform" and "moderation" throughout the region.[6]

Contrary intelligence and analyses that did not fit this vision were pushed aside. Moreover, after thirty-five years of Baathist dictatorship, some could argue that, in any event, not much was really known about such "facts on the ground" as religious cleavages, sectarian rivalries, the importance of tribal loyalties, and the role of Iran. Those who did know something about these details, or who questioned the basic policy convictions, or who warned that these assumptions were too optimistic, were progressively squeezed out of the decision-making process.

The shock of 9/11 created a determination to demonstrate the strength of the United States, reassert a balance of power, and seize the initiative. There was also the desire to finish the "unfinished business" of 1991. After the 1991 Gulf War, Saddam conducted a brutal war against the disenfranchised Shia, which might have been prevented had the armistice not permitted Saddam's forces to use helicopters in the south.

Some critics said that the war was conducted for the benefit of Israel. The elimination of Saddam's military power would certainly be a boon for Israel, on which Iraqi Scud rockets had rained during the 1991 Gulf War. But Saddam was already contained and his military much weakened. Israel was much more worried about the Iranian nuclear program. As Richard Haass, the head of policy planning in the State Department, wrote, "The Israelis did not share the administration's preoccupation with Iraq. Actually, it was just the opposite. The Israelis . . . feared that Iraq would distract the United States from what they viewed as the true threat, which was Iran." Both Israeli officials, including the minister of defense, who happened to be Iraqi-born, and Israeli experts warned that the administration was greatly underestimating the postwar troubles that would await them in Iraq. As one of Israel's leading specialists put it at a prewar conference in Washington, D.C., someone needed to tell the U.S. president that American forces would have to be in Iraq for up to five years and "they will not have an easy time there."[7]

"OIL"

Oil did not play the same role as these other factors in defining policy. The significance of oil was because of the nature of the region—the centrality of the Persian Gulf in world oil and thus the critical importance of the balance of power in that region. It had been determined U.S. policy since Harry Truman to prevent the Persian Gulf and its oil from falling under the sway of a hostile power. But the possibility of a hostile power—Iraq—achieving dominance in the region, and thus over the region's oil, loomed much larger during the Gulf crisis of 1990–91, when Iraq had conquered Kuwait and was threatening the Saudi oil fields, than in the run-up to the subsequent Iraq War. At the same time, in 2003, neither the Americans nor the British were pursuing a mercantilist 1920s-style ambition to control Iraqi oil. The issue was not who owned the oil at the wellhead, but whether it was available on the world market. Iraqi oil could be purchased on the world market, albeit managed under the U.N. sanctions program. Indeed, in 2001 the United States imported 800,000 barrels per day from Iraq. A democratic Iraq, it was certainly thought, would be a more reliable provider and, not being under sanctions, could expand its capacity. In the minds of some policymakers, noting the number of Saudi nationals involved in 9/11, the prospect of Iraq's becoming a much larger exporter that would counterbalance Saudi Arabia was attractive, but this was far from a well-shaped—or well-informed—strategic objective.[8]

While a variety of ideas were being tossed around for the postwar organization of the industry, the clear policy determination was that the decisions about the future of Iraq's oil would be made by a future Iraqi government. Nothing should be done to prejudice the prerogatives of the eventual government—even including the subject of OPEC membership—although a nongovernmental oil industry was seen as highly preferable in order to facilitate the introduction of the technology and the tens of billions of dollars of investment that the industry would need. Even in that case, however, a liberated Iraq, with its strong nationalist tradition, was likely to offer terms to investors that were as tough as those of any other petroleum-exporting countries, or tougher.

As war approached in 2002–3, the dominant attitude among the major international oil companies was one of skepticism and caution, and some alarm over the entire idea of war. Many of them were familiar with the region and feared a backlash. They were very doubtful that a stable, peaceful, new-style democracy could be quickly created from the wreckage of the Baathist state.

"You know what I'll say to the first person in our company who comes to us with a proposal to invest a billion dollars in Iraq?" asked the CEO of one of the supermajors a month before the war. "I'll say, 'Tell us about the legal system, tell us about the political system. Tell us about the economic system and about the contractual and fiscal systems, and tell us about arbitration. And tell us about security, and tell us about the evolution of the political system. Tell us all those things, and then we'll talk about whether we're going to invest or not.' "[9]

"BEYOND NATION BUILDING"

The immediate issue in 2003 was the state of the Iraqi oil industry and the need to ensure that it operated to provide the revenues that the country required. That, however, would depend upon overall conditions in Iraq.

In overseeing the planning for the war, Defense Secretary Donald Rumsfeld was driven by an imperative—to prove that his design for the light and lethal "new model army" (to borrow a term from Oliver Cromwell) was the model for the army of the future. Rumsfeld was intent on prevailing over the uniformed leadership in the Pentagon, which he considered too cautious, too risk averse, and much too conservative. He was determined to overturn the "overwhelming force" doctrine championed by the then-chairman of the Joint Chiefs of Staff Colin Powell during the 1990–91 Gulf crisis (and now Secretary of State). Instead he wanted to demonstrate on the battlefield that smaller but highly skilled and disciplined, technologically advanced forces—with "speed and agility and precision," in his words, were more than sufficient to win a swift victory. And, indeed, a very effective fighting force successfully demonstrated that capability on the battlefield in Iraq in 2003.

But war and postwar—defeating an army on the field and occupying a country—were two very different propositions. In cultural, logistics, training, and regional political terms, little had been done to prepare the military or the civilian arms of the U.S. government for an occupation of open duration. As it turned out, the troop levels required for a swift victory were much less, perhaps only a third, of what was needed after the war to occupy and stabilize the country. Shortly before the war, Army Chief of Staff Eric Shinseki had told a Senate committee that, based on U.S. experience ranging from post–World War II Germany to Bosnia in the 1990s, "several hundred thousand" troops—on the order of 260,000—was the right size. To say his comments were unwelcome would be an understatement. He was immediately disavowed and summarily retired. For good measure, the secretary of the army, who had supported his view, was also fired.

Rumsfeld was also determined to denigrate and banish the kind of "nation building" that had engaged U.S. forces in the Balkans during the Clinton administration in the 1990s. A month before the Iraq War, Rumsfeld delivered a speech titled "Beyond Nation Building," in which he proclaimed Afghanistan a complete victory and contrasted that to what he said was the "culture of dependence" in the Balkans in the 1990s. The prime example that he cited to prove what was wrong with nation building was that of a driver who, while shuttling aid workers around Kosovo, earned more than a university professor. "The objective is not to engage in what some call nation building," he declared. "If the United States were to lead an international coalition in Iraq," he added, the objective would be "to leave as soon as possible."

Afghanistan, he said, was the proof of the right way to do things. For what seemed to be the remarkably swift victory in Afghanistan in the autumn of 2001 had reinforced Rumsfeld's assumptions—and the self-confidence that underlay them. As Rumsfeld put it, the Soviets had hundreds of thousands of troops in Afghanistan "for year after year after year," while the United States, with "tens of thousands" did in "eight, nine, ten, twelve weeks what [the Soviets] weren't able to do in years." (Some pointed out that the USSR had also made short work of its invasion; it was in the long occupation that it failed.)

But the intervention in the Balkans in southeast Europe, as difficult as it was, was a much simpler situation than invading Iraq, a major Arab country in the Middle East that had been under tight dictatorial control for thirty-five years, and then proceeding to demolish all of its institutions, creating a giant vacuum, all under the premise that, as one U.S. official in Iraq put it, a "Jeffersonian democracy" would sprout almost overnight.

Rumsfeld's position was reinforced by the U.S. commander Tommy Franks, who made clear that his intention was to pull U.S. troop levels down as fast as possible after the initial victory. Some advocates within the Bush administration were further propelled by the belief that the war would not be difficult—that a "lightning victory" would be followed by a quick withdrawal and the emergence of that new Iraqi democracy. With such a mind-set, not much thought needed to be given to the planning for what would happen after the war.[10]

Nor was much thought given to the budgetary implications, for a quick war would surely also be cheap. As it turned out, the war was not quick and the subsequent occupation cost more than a trillion dollars in direct outlays.

NOT A CAKEWALK

Some voices in and around the U.S. government urged caution. The intelligence community on its own initiative developed an analysis of "the principal challenges that any postwar authority in Iraq" would likely face. Among the principal conclusions: Iraq was not a "fertile ground for democracy" and any transition would be "long, difficult, and turbulent." The intelligence analysts could feel "a strong wind consistently blowing," but it was not in their direction.

One of the most widely respected senior statesmen in Washington was Brent Scowcroft. He had been national security adviser to two former presidents—Gerald Ford and George H. W. Bush. He had worked closely with Dick Cheney when Cheney was secretary of defense during Desert Storm, and the current national security adviser Condoleezza Rice had been one of his deputies during the George H. W. Bush administration. Moreover, he spoke with considerable current authority. He was, after all, chairman of the President's Foreign Intelligence Advisory Board. "An attack on Iraq at this time would seriously jeopardize, if not destroy, the global counterterrorist campaign we have undertaken," he wrote in a *Wall Street Journal* article in August 2002. "If we are to achieve our strategic objectives in Iraq, a military campaign in Iraq would likely have to be followed by a large-scale, long-term military occupation." He added, "It will not be a cakewalk."

Scowcroft had been among the key policymakers in the decision not to go to Baghdad and depose Saddam during the Gulf War in 1991. In Scowcroft's mind, it was not only because of the "CNN factor" and the likely splintering of the coalition. It was exactly because of the risks of a long occupation. During the 1991 war, the first President Bush had ordered up a study on the lessons from previous conflicts. "Don't change objectives in the middle of a war just because things are going well," was one of the prime lessons that Scowcroft had taken away from that study. "We learned that from Korea." In 1991 Scowcroft had been convinced that capturing Baghdad would "change the character of what we were doing. We would become the occupiers of a large country. We don't have a plan. What do we do? How do we get out?" Those were the same questions that troubled Scowcroft in 2002.

The month following Scowcroft's article, Richard Haass, head of policy planning in the State Department, wrote to Secretary of State Colin Powell.

"Once we cross the Rubicon by entering Iraq and ousting Saddam ourselves, we will have much greater responsibility for Iraq's future. . . . Without order and security, all else is jeopardized."

The inadequacy of forces would have far-reaching impact on what would transpire over the next several years in Iraq, including the fate of its oil industry and the direction of the global oil market. And, in turn, what would happen to the oil industry would be central to Iraq's future.

Iraq was a petro-state—about three quarters of its GDP was derived from oil around the time of the war, and 95 percent of government revenues would come from oil after the war. There were extremely optimistic expectations about how quickly production and exports could be restored and put on a growth track. Just prior to the war, Deputy Defense Secretary Paul Wolfowitz had declared that, with restored oil exports, Iraq "can really finance its own reconstruction." He suggested that Iraq could soon be at 6 million barrels per day, double its current capacity.[11]

The war began on March 20, 2003, Baghdad time, some twelve years after the end of the first Gulf war. By April 9, U.S. forces had captured Baghdad. That same day, American soldiers helped Iraqis pull down the giant statue of Saddam Hussein in a downtown square, a scene reminiscent of the end of communism in Eastern Europe and one that seemed to promise that a "pluralistic and democratic Iraq" was at hand. Up to this point, things had gone according to plan.

But what would happen thereafter? General Franks, the U.S. commander, thought he had the answer. Not long after that initial victory, he posited U.S. forces would be drawn down to 30,000 by September 2003—a little more than a tenth of what, others argued, historical experience suggested was the prudent number.[12]

THE OIL INDUSTRY: "DILAPIDATED AND DEPLORABLE"

The actual conditions of the oil industry ensured that it was in no condition to meet the heady prewar expectations. The industry was suffering from years of neglect and lack of investment. With the collapse of Saddam's regime, communication had broken down, the country was in chaos, and no one was in charge. Most of the government buildings in Baghdad were looted and burned. A notable exception was the oil ministry, which was secured by units of the U.S. Army's 3rd Infantry.

A few days after the fall of Baghdad, an experienced Iraqi technocrat showed up at the gate of the ministry and asked to speak to someone about getting the industry restarted. This was Thamir Ghadhban, who had been chief geologist and then head of planning for the Iraq National Oil Company. He eventually connected over a satellite phone with Phil Carroll, who at this point had not yet arrived in Iraq. After several conversations, Carroll finally asked Ghadhban if he would like to be "chief executive" of the Iraqi oil industry, with Carroll as chairman. They became the core of the team charged with getting the oil sector up again. It was hard going.

Although Iraq's potential was considerable, it had not been seriously explored since the 1970s. Out of eighty discovered oil fields, only twenty-three were put into production. In 1979–80 the Iraqi oil industry had worked out a plan to raise output to six million barrels per day, but it had never been put into effect because of the Iran-Iraq War in the 1980s and then the 1990–91 Gulf crisis. Instead the industry went into a long decline. Now, after the invasion, workers were frightened to go to work because of the lack of security. Carroll and Ghadhban concluded that the physical capacity of the Iraqi industry was just under 3 million barrels a day, less than half of the 6 million barrels per day that had been cited as a "reasonable" target. They set a series of more-reasonable targets aimed at reaching that 3 mbd level by the end of 2004.[13]

But the obstacles were formidable. Despite fears prior to the war that Saddam's forces might blow up the wells and then set oil fields on fire, as they had done in departing Kuwait in 1991, the oil infrastructure, in fact, went through the war largely unscathed. Yet the overall conditions of the industry were, in Carroll's words, "dilapidated and deplorable." The underground reservoirs had been damaged by years of mismanagement. The sanctions had also had their impact. Equipment was rusting and malfunctioning. The machinery and systems were obsolete. The control room in the key Daura Refinery, near Baghdad, said Carroll, "was a time warp, right out of the 1950s." Indeed, it had been installed by an American company in the mid-1950s, when Iraq was still ruled by a king. Environmental pollution was also widespread. From a practical standpoint, what kept the industry going was the skill of Iraqi engineers; they were geniuses at improvisation. But now, with the looting and the breakdown in the infrastructure of the country in the aftermath of the war, conditions were even worse. There were no phone links to the refineries or the oil fields. Even the normal tools for measuring the flow of oil were absent.

As Carroll saw it from his vantage point, there were three priorities for the restoration of the Iraqi oil industry—and the rest of the economy—"security, security, and security." But none of the three was being met. The collapse of the organized state and the inadequacy of the allied forces left large parts of the country very lightly guarded, and the forces that were there were overstretched.[14] And what crippled everything else was the disorder that was the consequence of two decisions haphazardly made by the Coalition Provisional Authority, the entity set up to run the American-led occupation.

"DE-BAATHIFICATION" AND THE ARMY'S DISSOLUTION

The first was "Order #1—De-Baathification of Iraqi Society." Some two million people had belonged to Saddam's Baath Party. Some were slavish and brutal followers of Saddam; some were true believers. Many others were compelled to join the Baath Party to get along in their jobs and rise up in the omnipresent bureaucracies and other government institutions that dominated the economy, and to ensure that their children had educational opportunities in a country that had been ruled by the Baathists for decades. The very choice of the name of the edict showed its model—the denazification program in Germany after World War II. But that program had actually been applied quite differently in very different circumstances. Postwar Iraq was not postwar Germany, nor for that matter postwar Japan; and the Coalition Provisional Authority under L. Paul Bremer III was not the military administration of General Lucius Clay, America's proconsul in postwar Germany, or the occupation in Japan under General Douglas MacArthur.

Initially, de-Baathification was meant only to lop off the top of the hierarchy, which needed to be done immediately. But as rewritten and imposed, it reached far down into the country's institutions and economy, where support for the regime was less ideological and more pragmatic. The country was, as one Iraqi general put it, "a nation of civil servants." Many schoolteachers were turned out of their jobs and left with no income. The way the purge was applied removed much of the operational capability from government ministries, dismantled the central government, and promoted disorganization. It also eliminated a wide swath of expertise from the oil industry. Broadly, it set the stage for a radicalization of Iraqis—especially Sunnis, stripped of their livelihood, pensions, access to medical care, and so forth—and helped to create conditions for the emergence of Al Qaeda in Iraq. In the oil industry, the result of its almost blanket imposition was to further undermine operations.

Aleksander Kwaśniewski, president of Poland, one of the countries in the "coalition of the willing," argued with Defense Secretary Rumsfeld that the post–World War II German model was misunderstood and was being misapplied. Rather, said Kwaśniewski, the United States should pay attention to the more recent model from Eastern Europe, where reformist wings of the former communist parties had been successfully integrated into the new political systems—an approach that had brought both cohesion and stability. Kwaśniewski's Polish troops were welcomed into the coalition, but not his argument.[15]

The U.S. occupation arrived with a mélange of many ideas and analogies and lessons—ranging from a vision of a "New Middle East" to remembered film images of the joyous French tossing flowers at the U.S. soldiers liberating them from Nazi rule. Whatever their actual relevance to conditions in Iraq in 2003, these ideas nevertheless shaped the approach on the ground after the hostilities. Important realities of culture, history, and religion featured less.

The problem of inadequate troop levels was compounded by Order #2 by the Coalition Provisional Authority—"Dissolution of Entities"—which dismissed the Iraqi Army. Sending or allowing more than 400,000 soldiers, including the largely Sunni officer corps, to go home, with no jobs, no paychecks, no income to support their families, no dignity—but with weapons and growing animus to the American and British forces—was an invitation to disaster. The decision seems to have been made almost off-hand, somewhere between Washington and Baghdad, with little consideration or review. It reversed a decision made ten weeks earlier to use the Iraqi Army to help maintain order. In bluntly criticizing the policy to Bremer, one of the senior U.S. officers used an expletive. Rather than responding to the substance of the objection, Bremer said that he would not tolerate such language in his office and ordered the officer to leave the room.

The immediate effect of the army's dissolution was "incendiary," and the consequences would prove enormous. A plan was formulated to create a new military, but the ambition was pathetically small—initially just 7,000 troops, later lifted to 40,000. A separate oil police had guarded the entire petroleum sector. That too was dissolved, adding to the risks for the workers in the oil industry and leaving the oil system even more vulnerable to pillage and sabotage.[16]

RAMPANT LOOTING

Looting seemed to have been endemic in Iraq whenever authority broke down, going back to the 1958 revolution. Widespread looting had broken out in the aftermath of the 1991 Gulf War. Yet that risk too seems to have gone largely unnoted in the planning for the postwar situation. In 2003 looting and vandalism started immediately, and on a massive scale. There was no Iraqi Army to help prevent the looting, but now a large number of disgruntled and unemployed former soldiers. When it first began, Defense Secretary Rumsfeld dismissed it with the famous phrase "Stuff happens." But it undermined the entire economy and highlighted the immediate lack of security. Two of the three sewage plants in Baghdad were so thoroughly looted that they had to be rebuilt. Even police stations were stripped of their electric wires, phones, light fixtures, and doorknobs. The oil industry was a prime target for this stripping. For instance, all the water pumps, critical to its operation, were stolen from the giant Rumaila oil field. Only by mustering his workers with their private arms did the head of the Daura Refinery succeed in standing off an army of looters at the refinery gate.

One of the most devastating impacts resulted from the wholesale looting of the electric system, on which the whole economy depended. Vandals took down the electric wires and pulled down the transmission towers and carted their booty off to Iran or Kuwait to sell as scrap. Even the computerized control room of the power station that controlled Baghdad's electric grid was looted. This continuing disruption hit the oil industry hard. Without electricity, many of the oil fields and the three surviving refineries simply could not operate. It also crippled the irrigation on which agriculture depended.[17]

Despite the looting, in the first several months or so, the occupation seemed to be making some progress. And, such was the ingenuity of the Iraqi oil people that, even in the face of deprivation, petroleum production was being restored and was actually ahead of target. By late summer, one could detect a certain note of triumphalism in some commentaries along with a growing confidence that Iraq really did presage a "new" Middle East.

INSURGENCY AND CIVIL WAR

But the occupation was not going according to plan. Rumsfeld had called the emerging insurgents "dead-enders." But soon the U.S. commander in Iraq was talking about "a classical guerilla-type campaign," and one of the senior British representatives was warning that "the new threat" was "well-targeted sabotage of the infrastructure." Unemployment was running at 60 percent. Yet this unemployment, even with all its obvious risks, was not the top economic priority. Instead U.S. officials were focused on transforming Iraq, which had a totally state-dominated economy, into a free-market state, and doing so as rapidly as possible. Meanwhile, as one American general warned, "the liberators" were coming to be seen as something else—"occupiers."

By the autumn of 2003, a new, more difficult phase was beginning. In due course, some would call it a civil war; others, an insurgency. As events played out, it would be both—a civil war between Shia and Sunnis, and an insurgency manned by Baathists and other Sunni activists, increasingly conjoined with foreign jihadists, abetted by unemployed young men (who, for a hundred dollars or even fifty dollars, could be hired to open fire on the Americans).[18]

By the spring of 2004 it would become a war against the occupation. Private militias were battling each other. Foreign jihadists were infiltrating into the country. Killings and revenge killings became a daily occurrence. Roadside bombs were becoming increasingly lethal. Car bombs were going off outside restaurants and offices. The leadership of the occupation withdrew into the safety of the heavily secured Green Zone. In May 2004, Jeremy Greenstock, who had been the senior British representative in Baghdad, lamented that Bremer, as the U.S. head of the occupation, did not have a plaque on his desk that said "Security and jobs, stupid."[19]

THE INDUSTRY UNDER ATTACK

The oil industry was by then under attack. The former Baath Party put high priority on sabotaging the industry in a plan it called its Political and Strategic Program for the Armed Iraqi Resistance. Pipelines were being blown up; the export line, from Iraq into Turkey and to the Mediterranean, was shut by repeated bombings. The great expectations for the rapid expansion of Iraqi output were being punctured. Increasingly, the struggle was to maintain exports, especially in the north.

With his term as oil adviser over, Phil Carroll returned to the United States in the autumn of 2003. He was succeeded by Rob McKee, who had headed exploration and production for ConocoPhillips around the world.

"From the moment I got there, I saw that we didn't have enough people on the ground to do what needed to be done," said McKee. "Everything was broken. There was no police, no order, no courts, no infrastructure, and lack of electricity and water. Every day was a firefight, literally and figuratively. You'd come in the morning and get word that something had been blown up or looted. And then you'd figure out how to get that fixed before you could turn back to the longer-term, bigger issues."

On top of that were the procedures of the U.S. government. "All the bureaucracy over bidding and contracting, all that slowed things down to a crawl," said McKee. "That was the most frustrating thing I had to deal with."[20]

THE IRAQI DISRUPTION

But such was the effort that output in 2004 did come close to the prewar levels in several months but, for the year—as a result of the violence and of the economic disarray and electricity shortages—was more than 20 percent lower. Exports were often disrupted. In what could have been a disaster, two suicide bombers in a motorized dinghy came close to blowing up part of the critically important offshore oil export terminal, but the craft exploded short of its target. Naval patrols, thereafter, were much tighter.

As the insurgency stepped up its attacks, the effect was being felt in the world oil market. "Last week's attacks on key pipelines," reported *Petroleum Intelligence Weekly* in June 2004, "have reduced exports of around 1.6 million barrels per day to zero with no immediate prospect that they will resume. While bad enough for Iraq, the export outage has left world oil markets with a tiny sliver of spare capacity concentrated in Saudi Arabia. . . . Global oil supplies have relatively little slack."[21]

Again and again, exports were reduced or temporarily halted. In the years following the invasion, Iraqi production remained, at best, at only two thirds of capacity. It was not until 2009 that it was able, on an annual basis, to reach the prewar level of 2001, itself still considerably below the kind of potential that the country could achieve with investment. Before the war there had been high expectations about how Iraq's growing output would contribute to stability in the world oil market. Instead Iraq's beleaguered oil industry, producing well below its capacity, ended up contributing, on a sustained basis, to the toll of the aggregate disruption.

WHAT DID YOU LEARN?

In the autumn of 2003, when Phil Carroll, the first oil adviser, finished his tour, he stopped in Washington on his way back to Houston to visit the Pentagon. He was taken in to see Defense Secretary Rumsfeld. The secretary mainly had two questions for Carroll: "Did you enjoy it?" And, "What did you learn?"

There was not much more to the discussion than that. Carroll headed on home.

8

THE DEMAND SHOCK

On one still afternoon under an Oklahoma sun, neither a cloud nor an ounce of "volatility" was in sight. All one saw were the somnolent tanks filled with oil, hundreds of these tanks, spread over the rolling hills, some brand-new, some more than seventy years old, and some holding, inside their silver or rust-orange skins, more than half a million barrels of oil each.

Here, in a physical sense, was ground zero for the world oil price. For this was Cushing, Oklahoma, the gathering point for the light, sweet crude oil known as West Texas Intermediate—or just WTI. This was the price that one heard announced every day, as in "WTI closed today at . . ."

Cushing proclaims itself, as the sign on the main road into town says, the "Pipeline Crossroads of the World." Through this quiet town passes the network of pipes that carry oil at the stately speed of four miles per hour from Texas and Oklahoma and New Mexico, from Louisiana and the Gulf Coast, and from Canada, too, into Cushing's tanks. From there the oil flows onward to refineries where the crude is turned into gasoline, jet fuel, diesel, home heating oil—all the products that people actually use. But that is not what makes Cushing so significant. After all, there are other places where still more oil flows. Cushing plays a unique role in the new global oil industry because WTI is a preeminent benchmark against which other barrels are priced.

Soon after its discovery in 1912, the Cushing oil field achieved star status as

"The Queen of the Oil Fields." For a time, it produced almost 20 percent of all U.S. oil. The town of Cushing became one of the classic wild oil boomtowns of the early twentieth century, a place where, as one journalist wrote at the time, "any man with red blood gets oil fever."[1]

After Cushing's production declined, the town turned into a key petroleum pipeline junction. When the futures market started to trade oil futures in 1983, it needed a physical delivery point. Cushing, its boom days long gone, but with its network of pipelines and tank farms and blessed by its central location, was the obvious answer. As much as 1.1 million barrels per day passes in and out of Cushing—a great deal of oil in absolute terms, but equivalent to only about 6 percent of total U.S. oil consumption. That oil is the physical commodity that provides the "objective correlative" to the "paper" barrels and "electronic" barrels traded around the world.

A couple of other types of crudes are also used as markers, most notably Brent based on North Sea oil. Notwithstanding, prices for a good deal of the world's crude oil are set against the benchmark of the WTI oil—also known as domestic sweet—sitting in those tanks in Cushing, making what is today a quiet little Oklahoma town, its fever long gone, one of the hubs for the world economy. But Cushing's sedateness would stand in increasing contrast to the growing clamor and controversy that would be set off by the ascending price of oil in the global market. And what a clamor and controversy it was.

THE SURGE

The remarkable ascent of oil prices that began in 2004 ignited a furious argument as to whether the great surge was the result of supply and demand or of expectations and financial markets. The right answer is all of the above. The forces of supply and demand were very powerful. But over time they were amplified by the financial markets, embodying the new dynamics of oil.

The twenty-first century brought a profound reshaping of the oil industry—the "globalization of demand"—that reflected the reordering of the world economy. For decades, world consumption had been centered in the industrial countries of what was called the developed world—primarily North America, Western Europe, and Japan. These were the countries with most of the cars, most of the paved roads, and most of the world's GDP. But, inexorably, that predominance was ebbing away with the rise of the emerging economies of the developing world and the growing impact of globalization.

Even though total world petroleum consumption grew by 25 percent between 1980 and 2000, the industrial countries were still using two thirds of total oil as the new century began. But then came the shock—the demand shock—that hit the world oil market in 2004. It propelled consumption upward, with—when combined with the aggregate disruption—a startling impact on price. It was also a shock of recognition for a new global reality. Between 2000 and 2010, world oil demand grew by 12 percent. But by now, the split between the developed and the developing world was 50–50.

As far back as 1973, it seemed that whenever an upheaval shook the world oil market, sending prices flying up, it was always some kind of "supply shock"—in other words, a disruption of the supply lines. This was true whether it was the oil embargo at the time of the 1973 October War, or the turmoil that came with the Iranian Revolution in 1978–79, or the Gulf crisis of 1990–91. The last significant demand shock had been the swiftly rising consumption in Europe and Japan at the end of the 1960s and early 1970s that had tightened the global supply-demand balance, setting the stage for the 1973 oil embargo. But that was a long time ago.

The new demand shock was powered by what was the best global economic performance in a generation and the shift toward the emerging market nations as the engines of global economic growth. Yet this had taken the world by surprise.

As 2004 began, the consensus expectation was still centered on what OPEC had taken as its $22-to-$28 price band. Market projections were for standard growth in consumption. In February 2004, OPEC ministers met in Algiers. "Every piece of paper we had," said one minister, "indicated we are going into a glut." Fearing a price "rout," OPEC announced plans for a substantial production cut.

"The price can fall, and there is no bottom to it," warned Saudi petroleum minister Ali Al-Naimi after the meeting. "You have to be careful." He added, alluding to the Jakarta meeting and the Asian financial crisis, "We can't forget 1998."

Prices rose after the announcement of the production cut, as would have been anticipated. But then, unexpectedly, they continued to rise. The reason was not immediately obvious. Shortly after Algiers, Naimi went to China.

What he encountered there convinced him that what was needed was not a cutback in world production but additional output. "We had seen the trend in China since the early 1990s," said one Saudi. "But the cumulative effect was greater than any of us had realized. China was facing a shortage at the time. It was a structural change in the oil market."[2] China was on a red-hot growth streak. Economic growth in 2003 was 10 percent; in 2004, another 10 percent. Coal, the country's main source of energy, simply could not keep up with the demands of China's export machine. Compounding shortages, the railway system that carried the coal was overloaded and gridlocked, and long trains of coal cars were sidetracked on tracks across the country. Oil was the only readily available alternative for electricity generation, whether in power plants or diesel generators at factories. As an insurance policy, enterprises were also stockpiling extra petroleum supplies. Oil demand normally grew at 5 or 6 percent a year in China. In 2004 it was growing at an awesome 16 percent—a rate even more rapid than the overall economy. The world market was not prepared. By August headlines were reporting soaring prices in "the incredibly strong crude market."

The world economy was moving into a new era of high growth. Between 2004 and 2008, Chinese economic growth averaged 11.6 percent. India, entering on the "growth turnpike," would average over 8 percent during those same years. Strong global growth translated into higher oil demand. Between 1999 and 2002, world oil demand increased 1.4 million barrels per day. Between 2003 and 2006, it grew by almost four times as much—4.9 million barrels.

That was the demand shock.

THE TIGHTEST MARKET

All the elements were there for an oil boom: Spending to develop new supplies had been held in check by the trauma of the 1998 price collapse. But demand was now surging, and the disruptions—in Venezuela, Nigeria, and Iraq—were taking supplies off the market. The result would be a historically tight market.

Usually the global oil industry operates with a few million barrels of shut-in capacity—that is, production capability that is not used. Between 1996 and 2003, for instance, spare capacity had averaged about 4 million barrels per day. That shut-in capacity is a security cushion, a shock absorber to manage sudden surges in demand or some kind of interruption. One supplier country has made an explicit commitment to hold significant spare capacity. Saudi Arabia's policy is to build and maintain spare capacity of between 1.5 and 2 million barrels per day in order to promote market stability. But for other countries, spare capacity is somewhat inadvertent. In 2005, however, the surge in demand and disruptions of supply shrank spare capacity to no more than a million barrels a day. In other words, the cushion was virtually gone. In terms of absolute spare capacity, the oil market was considerably tighter than it had been on the eve of the 1973 oil crisis. In relative terms it was even tighter, as the world oil market was 50 percent bigger in 2005 than in 1973.

In such circumstances the inevitable happens. Price has to rise to balance supply and demand by calling forth more production and investment on one side of the ledger, and on the other, by signaling the need for moderation in demand growth. By the spring of 2005, OPEC's $22-to-$28 price band was an artifact of history. Many now may have thought that $40 to $50 was the "fair price" for oil. But that was only the beginning.

Other factors reinforced the rising price trend. In the aftermath of the 1998 price collapse, the industry had contracted, and then had continued to do so, on the basis of expectations for low prices. It was focused on keeping spending under tight control. As late as August 2004, the message from one of the supermajors was that "our long-term price guidelines are around the low $20s." Or, as the chief financial officer of another of the supermajors put it, "We remain cautious." The industry continued to fear another price collapse that would undermine the economics of new projects. Investors exerted tremendous pressure on managements to demonstrate "capital discipline" and hold back spending. The reward was a higher stock price. And if companies did not heed the admonition, they would be punished with a lower stock price. As one such investor warned in mid-2004, if companies started increasing investment because of higher oil prices, "I'd look at that skeptically."[3]

WHERE ARE THE PETROLEUM ENGINEERS?

"Capital discipline" translated into caution. The mantras were "take out costs" and "reduce capacity." That meant reductions in people, drilling rigs, and everything else. In the late 1990s and early years of the 2000s, not only did many skilled people leave the industry, but university enrollments in petroleum engineering and other oil-related disciplines plummeted. If there were no jobs, what was the point?

But the sharp increase in demand in 2004 and 2005 delivered an abrupt jolt. No longer was the fear about going back to 1998 and a giant surplus that would tank prices. Now it was just the opposite—not having enough oil. Hurriedly switching gears, the industry went into overdrive to develop new supplies as fast as possible. Companies started competing much more actively for acreage and access to resources. As would be expected, the price of entry for new production opportunities went up. Nations were making more money than they had anticipated and thus were tougher in their financial demands on companies, and in this more competitive environment, they could get the terms they wanted. Competition for exploration and production opportunities was made even more intense by the arrival of new entrants in the international business—national oil companies based in emerging-market countries—which were willing to spend to gain access.

The industry was hamstrung in its ability to respond. Contraction had taken its toll. There were not enough petroleum engineers, not enough geologists, not enough drilling rigs, not enough pipe, not enough supply ships, not enough of everything. And so the cost of everything was bid up. Shortages of people and delays in the delivery of equipment meant that new projects took longer than planned, adding to the budget overruns.

On top of that, the cost of the inputs—such as the steel that went into platforms, and nickel and copper—was also rising dramatically as China's appetite for commodities continued to draw in supplies from all over the world. This was the era of the great bull market for commodities.

The economic impact of all these shortages was stunning. Total costs for doing business ended up more than doubling in less than half a decade. In other words, the budget for developing an oil field in 2008 would have been twice what the budget for the same field would have been in 2004. These rising costs also, inevitably, contributed to the rising price of oil.[4]

"FINANCIALIZATION"

Then there was the matter of currencies; in particular, the dance between oil and the dollar. In this period, commodity prices would, in the jargon of economists, "co-move negatively with the U.S. dollar exchange rate." Put more plainly, it meant that when the dollar moved down, oil prices moved up. Petroleum is priced in dollars. For part of this period the dollar was weak, losing value against other currencies. Traditionally during times of political turmoil and uncertainty, there is a "flight to the dollar" in the search for safety. But during this period of dollar turmoil, the flight was to commodities, most of all to petroleum, along with gold. Oil was a hedge against a weaker dollar and the risks of inflation. So as the "price" of the dollar went down against other currencies, particularly the euro, the price of oil went up.[5]

More generally the financial markets and the rising tide of investor money were having increasing impact on the oil price. This is often described as speculation. But speculation is only part of the picture, for oil was no longer only a physical commodity; it was also becoming a financial instrument, a financial asset. Some called this process the "financialization" of oil. Whatever the name, it was a process that had been building up over time.[6]

THE RISE OF OIL TRADING

Into the 1970s, there really was no world oil market in which barrels were traded back and forth. Most of the global oil trade took place inside each of the integrated oil companies, among their various operating units, as oil moved from the well into tankers, and then into refineries and into gasoline stations. Throughout this long journey, the oil remained largely within the borders of the company. This was what was meant by "integration." It was considered the natural order of the business, the way the oil industry was to be managed.

But politics and nationalism changed all that. In the 1970s the oil-exporting countries nationalized the concessions held by the companies, which they regarded as holdovers from a more colonial era. After nationalization, the companies no longer owned the oil in the ground. The integrated links were severed. Significant amounts of oil were sold under long-term contracts. But oil also became an increasingly traded commodity, sold into a growing and variegated world oil market. Those transactions, in turn, were handled both by newly established trading divisions within the traditional companies, and by a host of new, independent commodity traders.

A change in the United States gave a further boost to this new business of oil trading. From the early 1970s onward, the federal government controlled and set the price of oil. These price controls were originally imposed during the Nixon administration as an anti-inflation initiative. They did succeed in creating a whole new federal bureaucracy, an explosion in regulatory and litigation work for lawyers, and much political contention. But the controls did little for their stated goals of limiting inflation—and did nothing for energy security. In 1979, after a bruising political battle, President Jimmy Carter implemented a two-year phase-out of price controls. When Ronald Reagan took over as president in January 1981, he speeded things up and ended price controls immediately. It was his very first executive order.

This shift from price controls to markets was not just a U.S. phenomenon. In Britain, the government shifted from a fixed price for setting petroleum tax rates to using spot price. As its benchmark, it used a North Sea stream called Brent.[7]

FROM EGGS TO OIL: THE PAPER BARREL

Now oil was becoming "just another commodity." Although OPEC was still trying to manage prices, it had a new competitor—the global market. And, specifically, a new marketplace emerged to help buyers and sellers manage the risk of fluctuating prices. This was the New York Mercantile Exchange—the NYMEX. The exchange itself wasn't exactly new. It had actually begun its life as the Butter and Cheese Exchange, founded in 1872 by several dozen merchants who needed a place to trade their dairy products. It soon expanded its offerings and became the Butter, Cheese, and Egg Exchange. By the 1920s, in a little-noticed innovation, egg futures were added to the trading menu, at what was now the more grandly renamed New York Mercantile Exchange.

By the 1940s the NYMEX was also the trading place for a motley group of other commodities, ranging from yellow globe onions to apples and plywood. But the exchange's mainstay was the Maine potato. Yet potatoes had progressively less skin in the game: for in the late 1970s, scandals hit the Maine potato contract, including the mortifying failure of the potatoes to pass the basic New York City health inspection. It looked like the exchange was going to go under. Just in time, the NYMEX started trading futures contracts in home heating oil and gasoline. This, however, was only the beginning.

March 30, 1983, was the historic day when the exchange began trading a futures contract for light, sweet crude, tied to a stream called West Texas Intermediate—WTI—and linked back to those tanks in Cushing, Oklahoma. Now the price of oil was being set by the interaction of the floor traders at the NYMEX with other traders and hedgers and speculators all over the world. Thus was the beginning of the "paper barrel." As technology advanced over the years, the price would be set not only daily and hourly, but eventually on a second-by-second basis.

HEDGERS VERSUS SPECULATORS

Today's futures markets go back to the futures markets for agricultural products established in the nineteenth century in Midwestern cities of the United States. By availing himself of the futures market, a farmer planting his spring wheat could assure himself of his sales price for the following fall. He might lose the upside if the price of wheat shot up. But by using futures, he avoided financial ruin in case a bumper crop tanked the price.

The petroleum futures market on the NYMEX now provided what is called a "risk-management tool" for people who produced oil or who used it. An airline would buy contracts for oil futures to protect itself against the possibility of rising prices of the physical commodity. It would put down the fraction of a cost of a barrel for the right to buy a hundred contracts—equivalent to 100,000 barrels—a year or two years from now at the current price. The price of oil—and jet fuel—might go up 50 percent a year from now. But the futures contracts would have gone up by about the same value, and the airline could close out its position, accruing the same amount as the price increase—minus the cost of buying the futures. Thus the airline would have protected itself by buying the futures, although putting the hedge in place did cost money. But that cost was, in effect, what the airline was willing to pay to insure itself against a price increase.

For an airline, or an independent oil producer protecting itself against a fall in the price, or a home-heating oil distributor worrying about what would happen in the winter, someone needed to be on the other side of the trade. And who might that person be? That someone was the speculator, who had no interest in taking delivery of the physical commodity but is only interested in making a profit on the trade by, as the NYMEX puts it, "successfully anticipating price movements." If you wanted to buy a futures contract to protect against a rising price, the speculator would in effect sell it. If you wanted to sell to protect yourself against a falling price, the speculator would buy. The speculator moved in and out of trades in search of profits, offsetting one position against another. Without the speculator, the would-be hedger cannot hedge.[8]

Often, it seems, the word "speculator" is confused with "manipulator." But "speculation" is, in its use here, a technical term with rather precise meaning. The "speculator" is a "non-commercial player"—a market maker, a serious investor, or a trader acting on technical analysis. The speculator plays a crucial role. If there is no speculator, there is no liquidity, no futures market, no one on the other side of the trade, no way for a hedger—the aforementioned airline or oil producer or the farmer planting his spring wheat or the multinational company worried about currency volatility—to buy some insurance in the form of futures against the vagaries of price and fortune.

Futures and options trading in oil rose from small amounts in the mid-1980s to very large volumes. By 2004 trading in oil futures on the NYMEX was 30 times what it had been in 1984. Similar growth was registered on the other major oil futures market. This was the ICE exchange in London, originally called the International Petroleum Exchange, where Brent, the North Sea oil stream, is traded. The Brent contract in London and the "sweet crude" contract in New York became the global standards for oil against which other crudes were benchmarked. WTI was oriented toward North America; Brent, toward the Eastern Hemisphere. Later a Dubai contract was introduced in the Middle East.

After the stock market bust of 2000, investors wanted to find alternative investments. It was observed at the time that the prices of commodities did not move in coordination with other investment choices; that is, they were not correlated with stocks and bonds. So according to theory, if the value of a pension fund's equity holdings declined, the value of the commodities would not. They might even go up. Thus commodities would protect portfolios against declines in stock markets and help pension funds to assure the returns on which their retirees depended. In the years that followed, diversification into commodities became a major new investment strategy among many pension funds.

Investors were trying to purchase other forms of "insurance" as well. A large European state pension fund, for instance, was buying futures contracts to protect its portfolio against, as its chief investor officer put it, "a conflict in the Middle East"—which really meant a war involving Iran. Were such an event to occur, the value of the fund's equity holdings would likely drop dramatically, while oil prices would likely soar. This pension fund thought it was acting as a prudent investor, hedging its portfolio against disruption and allocating among assets to protect its retirees. But, by the definition of the futures market, it was a speculator.[9]

THE "BRICs": THE INVESTMENT OPPORTUNITY OF A GENERATION

Putting money to work in oil-based financial instruments was also seen as a way to participate on the greatest economic trend of a generation: globalization and economic growth in China, India, and other emerging markets.

In November 2001 an economist at Goldman Sachs, Jim O'Neill, put out a research paper hatching a new concept: "the BRICs"—Brazil, Russia, India, and China. These four large-population economies, he said, were destined to grow faster than the main industrial economies. He made the startling prediction that within a few decades they would, as a group, overtake the combined GDP of the United States and the world's five other largest economies.

O'Neill came to the BRICs idea in the aftermath of 9/11. "I felt that if globalization were to thrive, it would no longer be American-led," he said. "It had to be" based on the reality that "international trade lifts all." There was also what he called the "odd insight" that provided a lightbulb moment: on flights to China, he had noticed continuing improvements in the standards and quality of service, rising toward world levels. "Rightly or wrong, I associated that with China's involvement." Something new was happening in the world economy.

Initially, many people found the whole concept of BRICs wacky. They shook their heads and asked what these diverse countries could possibly have in common. "They thought it was just some kind of marketing gimmick," said O'Neill. But by 2004 the concept of BRICs was providing a different—and powerful and compelling—framework for looking at the world economy and international growth. Competing banks, which had previously made fun of the idea, were now launching their own BRIC funds. And in the ultimate stamp of approval, leaders of the four BRIC-anointed countries eventually started to meet for their own exclusive BRICs-only summits.

"BRICS," said the *Financial Times,* became "a near ubiquitous term, shaping how a generation of investors, financiers and policymakers view the emerging markets." Investors started to buy equities linked to the BRICs. They also bought financial instruments linked to oil. For the growth of these countries—especially the "C," China—was driving the demand for commodities and thus prices. Thus for investors—whether running hedge funds or pension funds, or retail investors—the commodity play was not just about oil itself, but about the booming economies that were using more and more oil.[10]

TRADING PLACES

And now there were a lot more people in the oil market—the paper barrel part of the market—investing with no intention nor any need of ever taking delivery of the physical commodity. There were pension funds and hedge funds and sovereign wealth funds. There were the "massive passives"—the commodity index funds, heavily weighted to oil and with all the derivative trading around them.

There were also exchange-traded funds; there were high net-worth individuals; and there were all sorts of other investors and traders, some of them in for the long term, and some of them very short term.

Oil was no longer just a physical commodity, required to fuel cars and airplanes. It really had become something new—and much more abstract. Now these paper barrels were also, in the form of futures and derivatives, a financial instrument, a financial asset. As such, prudent investors could diversify beyond stocks, bonds, and real estate, by shifting money into this new asset class.

Economic growth and financialization soon came together to start lifting the oil price higher. With that came more volatility, more fluctuations in the price, which was drawing in the traders. These were the nimble players who would, with hair-trigger timing, dart in and out to take advantage of the smallest anomalies and mispricings within these markets.

This financialization was reinforced by a technological push. Traditionally, oil had been traded in the pit at the NYMEX by floor traders, wearing variously colored jackets, yelling themselves hoarse, wildly waving their arms and making strange hand gestures, all of which was aimed at registering their buys and sells. This system was called "open outcry," and it was enormously clamorous.

But around 2005 the importance of the floor traders began to decline rapidly with the introduction of the electronic trading platforms, which directly connected buyers and sellers through their computers. Now it was just push a button and the trade was done, instantaneously. Even the "button" was a metaphor, for frequently the trade was executed by a commodity fund's algorithmic black box, operating in microseconds and never needing any sleep, let alone any human intervention once it had been programmed. The paper barrel had become the electronic barrel.[11]

OVER THE COUNTER

Futures contracts on commodity exchanges were only part of the new trading world. There were also over-the-counter markets, which did not have the regulatory and disclosure requirements of the futures market. Those who were critical of them dubbed them the "dark markets" because of this lack of regulatory oversight and transparency, and because they were suspicious of how they worked and of their impact. These were, after all, a form of financial derivative—a financial asset whose price is *derived* from one or more underlying asset. The cumulative risk and systemic impact of such derivatives could be very large because of their leverage, complexity, and lack of transparency.

The over-the-counter off-exchange markets were the place for tailored, bespoke transactions where participants could buy oil derivatives of one kind or another, specifically designed to meet a particular market need or investment strategy. Banks became the "swap dealers," facilitating the *swapping* of one security, currency, or type of interest rate for another between investors. They would then turn around and hedge their risks in swap deals on the futures markets. The over-the-counter market began to grow very substantially around 2003 and 2004. These markets had several attractive traits. It could be less expensive for hedgers to go to the over-the-counter market, as the costs might be lower and more predictable. They could make deals that were tailored to their particular needs and specifications and timing. For instance, someone might want to hedge jet fuel in New York Harbor, and WTI at Cushing was not a clear enough approximation in its pricing. It was also possible to do much larger deals without calling attention to oneself and thus prematurely forcing the price up or down, depending on the nature of the hedge.

Overall, more and more money was coming into the oil market, through all the different kinds of funds and financial instruments. All this engendered increased activity, and more and more "investor excitement," to borrow a phrase from Professor Robert Shiller, the student of financial bubbles and the explicator of the term "irrational exuberance." Traders saw momentum in the market, which meant rising prices, and as they put money to work and prices went up, it added to the momentum, providing yet more reason to put more money to work, further fueling the momentum. And so prices kept going up.

THE BELIEF SYSTEM

There was method in all this momentum, a well-articulated belief system that explained rising prices. Or rationalized them. In his studies of bubbles and market behavior, Shiller refers to the common characteristic of what he calls "new era thinking"—the conviction that something new and different has arrived that justifies a rapid rise in asset prices in a particular market. New era thinking has been a consistent feature of bubbles—in stock markets and real estate and many other markets—going back to tulips in Holland in the early 1600s and the South Sea land bubble in the early 1700s. "A set of views and stories are generated that justify continuation of the bubble," says Shiller. "But it's not perceived as a bubble."[12]

In the case of the oil market, an explanatory model, a set of new-era beliefs, took particular hold on the financial community with an almost mesmerizing effect. The beliefs came in the form of catechisms:

> *That oil was going to be in permanently short supply* (just the opposite of a decade earlier).
>
> *That the world was running out of oil.*
>
> *That China was going to consume every barrel of oil that it could get its hands on—and then some.*
>
> *That Saudi Arabia was misleading the world about its oil reserves, and that Saudi production, the great balancer of world markets, would soon begin to decline.*
>
> *That the world had reached, or would soon reach, "peak oil"—maximum output—and the inevitable decline in output would begin even as the world wanted more and more oil.*

The last—"peak oil"—was the great unifying theme that tied all the rest together. As prices climbed, this view became more and more pervasive, especially in financial markets, and in a great feedback loop, reinforced bullish investor sentiment and helped to push prices up further.

For all the above reasons together, it made sense, powerful sense, for prices to keep going up. That, after all, is what the most publicized predictions said would happen. Data that did not fit the model—for instance, an analysis of eleven hundred oil fields that failed to find a "peak" on a global basis—were disregarded and dismissed.[13]

DOES PRICE ACTUALLY MATTER?

At this point the oil world split in two. Some thought that prices did not matter, and some thought they did. Those who thought "not" worked on the assumption that prices would continue to go up, for all the reasons noted above, with little impact on consumers and on producers—and on the global economy.

Those who believed that prices still mattered were pretty sure that the impact would be felt, though perhaps not immediately. But rising prices would eventually do what they always did—encourage more supply, more investment, stimulate alternatives, while damping down demand. They also feared that rising prices would have a wider cost in terms of reduced economic growth or even recession, which in turn would also bring down demand.

Yet that latter position seemed to be losing the argument. On the first trading day of 2007, WTI had closed at $61.05. A year later, on the first day of trading, January 2, 2008, oil briefly hit $100 and then slid back. A month later it really broke through $100. And kept going. The oil fever that had struck Cushing, Oklahoma, after 1912 was coming back in 2008 in the form of a global epidemic that was sweeping the planet.[14]

It was in the last part of 2007 and around the beginning of 2008 that the forces driving the oil price up shifted decisively from the fundamentals into something else—"hyperappreciation in asset prices." Or what is more colloquially known as a bubble.

"GOING TO EXPLODE"

Even the biggest, most sophisticated institutional investors were embracing commodities. In February 2008, CalPERS, the California State retirement fund, the largest pension fund in the United States, announced that it now deemed commodities part of a distinct asset class. As a result it was going to increase its commitment to "commodities" as much as sixteenfold. "The actual importance of the energy and materials sector we believe is going to explode," CalPERS's chief investment officer had previously explained.

Gasoline prices in the United States finally broke through the $3 a gallon barrier in February 2008 and headed higher. By April 2008, 70 percent of Americans described higher gasoline prices as a financial hardship and blamed "greedy oil companies for" "gouging the public." A month later gasoline breached $4 a gallon. The public was agitated and enraged; gasoline prices dominated the news; they looked to become an issue in the presidential campaign. They had already become a subject of a host of congressional hearings. In a deliberate replay of the political theater that had followed the 1973 oil crisis, oil company executives were summoned to congressional hearings, made to raise their right hands and put under oath, and then interrogated for hours. But now the executives were no longer alone. Fund managers and executives from the financial industry were also called to testify. The Commodity Futures Trading Commission, which regulates futures, was charged with assessing whether new controls on speculators were required.

Still the drumbeat of predictions continued, as though casting and recasting a spell. A Wall Street analyst predicted that the coming superspike made $200 oil "increasingly likely" within the next two years.

That forecast struck terror into the heart of the airline industry, which was reeling from the effects of the surge in jet fuel, made even worse by constraints in the refining system. "Scary" was the one-word reaction of David Davis, Northwest Airlines' chief financial officer at the time. "We kept saying to ourselves that the price had to fall back, but it kept going up. The market was looking for any opportunity to take the price up."[15]

"YOU NEED BUYERS"

In the middle of May—with oil prices now the top domestic political issue in the United States—President George W. Bush went to Saudi Arabia. There at a meeting at the ranch of Saudi King Abdullah, Bush talked about the risks to the world economy of rising prices. He urged the Saudis to lift output to help cool the fever. He did not get the answer he wanted. The Saudis had already upped production by 300,000 barrels per day but were having trouble finding customers. "If you want to move more oil, you need a buyer," said Saudi petroleum minister Ali Al-Naimi. After the meeting, the president's national security assistant Steven Hadley ruefully commented, "There is something going on in the oil market that is much more complicated than just turning on the spigot." There was no relief after Riyadh. The price of oil kept going up. "One concern that has prompted traders to bid up oil prices," reported the *Wall Street Journal* from Jeddah, "is Saudi Arabia's long-term production capacity. Some analysts believe the kingdom's best fields could hit a production peak in the years ahead."

At almost exactly the same time, one of the most prominent Wall Street oil analysts added to the fever with a report declaring that a "structural re-pricing" of oil—reflecting long-term expectations for shortage of oil and "continued robust demand from the BRICS"—meant a "structural bull market" on top of the "super cycle" that would take prices "to ever-higher levels." The surge continued. By the end of May, oil prices had hit $130. New cars sales in the United States were plummeting.[16]

"OIL DOT-COM"

A few contrarian voices on Wall Street warned that these prices had become seriously divorced from reality. Edward Morse, a veteran analyst, in a paper titled "Oil Dot-com," wrote: "As during the dotcom period, when 'new economy' stocks became popular, a growing band of Wall Street analysts who are significantly raising" their forecasts were "partially responsible for new investor flows, driving . . . prices to perhaps unsustainable levels." He continued: "We are seeing the classic ingredients of an asset bubble. Financial investors tend to 'herd' and chase past performance. . . . But when peak prices hit, they are also likely to fall precipitously. That's the way cyclical turning points always occur." But the analysis could only go so far. "Getting that timing right is the difficult part," he added.

Morse did not sway many people. Some of his clients did not merely disagree; they literally shouted at him that he was wrong. The price continued its sharp ascent. Ever more money flooded into the market on the premise that prices would climb still higher. "Perhaps the biggest ramification of current oil prices is the stoking of fears over 'peak oil,' " said one petroleum industry publication. "This mindset has spurred investors to buy."[17]

"IT NEEDS TO STOP"

There seemed no respite. High gasoline prices—combined with the imminence of Memorial Day and the opening of driving season—infected the entire nation with a virulent case of road rage. That made it an "ideal time," said the *New York Times,* "for Congress to show its solidarity with angry American motorists." At one hearing, a congressman bluntly told oil company executives, "You are gouging the American public and it needs to stop." Another announced that the industry should be nationalized outright.

At a hearing on the other side of Capitol Hill, a senator asked the empanelled oil company executives, "Does it trouble any of you when you see what you are doing to us?" One executive tried to frame a reply: "I feel very proud of the fact that we are investing all of our earnings. We invest in future supplies for the world, so I am proud of that."

"You," snapped another senator, "have no ethical compass about the price of gasoline."[18]

CHINA IN 2014

In other parts of the world, high prices were seen as a boon. Every year in June in St. Petersburg, during the white nights, when it is light even at midnight, the Russian government hosts its own version of Davos—the St. Petersburg Economic Forum. The setting is the sprawling modernistic Lenexpro congress center that juts out into the Gulf of Finland and looks toward the Baltic Sea. In June 2008 Russia was booming from the high oil and natural gas prices, which was reflected in the buoyant atmosphere of the forum. Wall Street may have been showing signs of growing distress. But, seen from St. Petersburg, that was only further reason for the global financial markets to become more anchored in Russia and the other BRICs.

Over coffee between one of the sessions, the head of a very large commodities-trading firm was asked why he thought prices were still going up. He had a very clear explanation: As markets generally do, he replied, the oil market was anticipating what would happen in the future. In this case, it had pulled forward into

2008 the prices that would be associated with China's huge oil demand in the year 2014. It just seemed so obvious.

A few days later, the head of one of the world's largest state-owned energy companies declared that oil would hit $250 a barrel in the "foreseeable future." Were that to happen, a leader of the travel industry said in reply, the airline industry would collapse and would have to be nationalized. Otherwise there would be no planes in the air.

On June 15, oil prices reached $139.89. The airline industry certainly had its back against the wall. In earlier years, fuel prices had been about 20 percent of operating costs; now they were up around 45 percent, bigger even than labor costs. Bankruptcies seemed inevitable—the only way out.[19]

JEDDAH VERSUS BONGA

On Sunday, June 22, a hastily organized conference involving 36 countries convened in Jeddah, Saudi Arabia, at the invitation of King Abdullah. The Saudis, among others, were acutely concerned with what oil prices would do to the demand for oil and to the world economy, in which they had a very significant stake.

To open the conference, King Abdullah and British Prime Minister Gordon Brown entered, side by side, to the music of a military band. But there was little harmony. The producers blamed the prices on "speculators" and said that there was no shortage of crude oil. The consuming countries blamed the prices on a shortage of crude oil. The Saudis announced that they would put another 200,000 barrels a day into the market if they could find buyers. But that would take time. The next morning the price in Singapore opened higher than it had closed in New York the previous Friday.

Within hours of the Jeddah meeting, a dramatic reminder of the physical risks to supply shook the market and added to the widespread anxiety. One third of Nigeria's production was already shut in by violence and criminal attacks. But surely it was thought, the new multibillion-dollar offshore projects were secure from assault, insulated from violence by their distance from land. That sense of security was misplaced.

Members of MEND, the Movement for the Emancipation of the Niger Delta, moving fast in heavily armed speed boats, evaded such security as there was and launched an attack on Bonga, the most prominent of all the platforms, 70 miles from the shore. They managed to climb onto the platform, but they were repelled before they could blow up the computerized control room. It was a close call, and a very scary one. The Bonga attack sent new shockwaves through the market. In an e-mail to journalists, a spokesman for MEND warned, "The location for today's attack was deliberately chosen to remove any notion that offshore oil production is far from our reach." Bonga trumped Jeddah and prices continued to go up.[20]

The physical market had turned. Although hardly recognized, the demand shock was over. World oil demand was going down and supply was increasing. Spare capacity—the gap between world capacity and world demand—was beginning to widen. But none of that seemed to matter. Prices continued to rise. "I kept staring at my Bloomberg, looking at the prices all the time," recalled the CFO of Northwest Airlines. "It was unbelievable."

And it was all happening very fast. "This is like a highway with no cops and no speed limits, and everybody is going 120 miles per hour," lamented one senator, citing a Wall Street analyst, at a hearing on June 25. By the beginning of July, prices exceeded $140. Prediction after prediction reinforced that conviction, as the crescendo of incantations about higher prices reverberated around the world.[21]

BREAK POINT

In truth, the gears had already started to grind in the other direction. The break point was at hand. Prices did matter after all. They mattered economically—and, as the public's ire and fear rose, they mattered politically.

The most immediate evidence of the break point would be in the decisions by energy users—whether large industrial firms, which found new ways to reduce energy use; or airlines, which cut back on the number of planes in the air; or individual consumers, who could change their behavior.

And that consumers were doing. They were driving less. In June 2008

California motorists used 7.5 percent less gasoline than in June 2007. Consumers were also voting with their feet. They were no longer walking into auto showrooms, and when they were, they were steering clear of SUVs. They wanted fuel-efficient vehicles, if they wanted anything at all. That left Detroit, which had focused on the popular SUVs, scrambling to try to gear up to produce the cars that consumers now desired and that would meet the new fuel-efficiency targets—something that would take billions of dollars and several years to implement. The torrid romance with the SUV had suddenly gone cold. The oversize Hummers were becoming targets of vandalism.[22]

Meanwhile, oil companies were dramatically increasing their spending to develop new supplies, although they had to contend with the big increase in costs. The market was no longer tight. World oil supply in the first quarter of 2008 was more than a million barrels higher than it had been in the first quarter of 2007. In June 2008 U.S. oil demand was a million barrels less than it had been in June 2007. These prices were providing both a political and commercial stimulus to the longer-term development of renewables and alternatives.

CHANGING THE CAR FLEET

The turmoil in the market had a major impact on public policy and on the politics of energy, and nowhere more significantly than in regard to the American automobile.

The United States has the world's largest auto fleet—about 250 million out of a global total of 1 billion. Despite growth in emerging markets, one out of every nine barrels of oil used in the world every day is burned as motor fuel on American roads. In 1975, during the first oil crisis, fuel-efficiency standards were introduced, requiring a doubling from the then-average of 13.5 miles per gallon to 27.5 miles per gallon over ten years. And there the standards sat for more than three decades, with some minor tinkering around the edges.[23]

But circumstances were changing. In his 2006 State of the Union Address, President George W. Bush denounced what he called the nation's "addiction to oil." And new players became engaged. The most notable group was the Energy Security Leadership Council, an affiliate of another group, SAFE—Securing

America's Future Energy. The council was chaired by P. X. Kelley, a former commandant of the Marine Corps, and Frederick Smith, the founder and CEO of FedEx. The members were retired military officers and corporate leaders, not exactly fitting the traditional mode of environmentalists and liberals who had traditionally campaigned for higher fuel-efficiency standards.

In December 2006 the council issued a report advocating a balanced energy policy. Raising auto-fuel standards was the first chapter. Five weeks later, to Detroit's shock and notwithstanding opposition from within his own administration, Bush used his 2007 State of the Union to endorse a fuel-efficiency increase. A week later, Bush met with some of the council's members. The president made clear the geopolitical thinking behind his energy policies. He wanted, he said, to get Iranian president Mahmoud Ahmadinejad and Venezuelan president Hugo Chávez "out of the Oval Office."

The Council took its campaign to the Senate. At one hearing, council member Retired Admiral Dennis Blair, former commander of the Pacific Fleet (and later director of National Intelligence in the Obama administration), argued that excessive dependence on oil for transportation was "inconsistent with national security" and that nothing would do more than "strengthen fuel economy standards" to reduce that dependence.[24]

Fuel-efficiency standards were no longer a left-right issue. Now they were a national security and a broad economic issue. New standards flew though both houses of Congress. In December 2007, almost exactly one year to the day after the Energy Security Leadership Council's report, Bush signed legislation raising fuel-efficiency standards—the first such increase in 32 years.

Of course, the new fuel-efficiency standards would take years to make a sizable impact. Automakers would have to retool, and then, in normal years, only about 8 percent of the vehicle fleet turns over annually. But when their impact was felt, it would be very large.

THE GREAT RECESSION

What was happening in the economy would also lower the demand for oil. The Great Recession, at least in the United States, is now reckoned to have begun in December 2007, well before most anybody had recognized it. It was primarily a credit recession, the result of too much debt, too much leverage, too many derivatives, too much cheap money, too much overconfidence—all of which engendered real estate and other asset bubbles in the United States and other parts of the world.

But the surge in oil prices was an important contributing factor to the downturn. Between June 2007 and June 2008, oil prices doubled—an increase of $66—in absolute terms, a far bigger increase in oil prices than had ever been seen in any of the previous oil shocks, going back to the 1970s. "The surge in oil prices was an important factor that contributed to the economic recession," observed Professor James Hamilton, one of the leading students of the relation between energy and the economy. The oil price shock interacted with the housing slowdown to tip the economy into a recession. The sudden increase of prices at the pump took purchasing power away from lower-income groups, making it more difficult for many of them to make payments on their subprime mortgages and their other debts. The higher cost of the gasoline they needed to get to work meant trade-offs in terms of what else they could spend elsewhere. The effects also showed up, as Hamilton has noted, in "a deterioration in consumer sentiment and an overall slowdown in consumer spending."

As gasoline prices rose, car sales nosedived. Discounting and rebates by auto dealers did little good. June 2008 was the worst month for sales for the auto industry in seventeen years.

"The auto industry was under siege," said Rick Wagoner, the former CEO of General Motors. "While we had a comprehensive scenario planning process at GM, we had no scenarios in which oil prices went up so much, so fast. People weren't coming into showrooms as oil prices skyrocketed in part because their disposable incomes were going down. The rate and size of the decline in auto sales was unprecedented. Demand was collapsing." Wagoner continued, "The only question was how high oil prices would go and when they came down, to what level. Our view of the future was that it was either going to be difficult or very, very difficult."[25]

The effects of the downturn in the automobile industry reverberated throughout the supply chains of companies that supplied it and at dealers across America. Many hundreds of thousands of jobs were abruptly lost across the economy.

The direct impact was felt less in other developed countries because so much of the price at the pump is actually tax. Many European governments use gasoline stations as subbranches of their treasuries. Thus while government tax on gasoline averages 40 cents in the United States, it is more like $4.60 a gallon in Germany. Thus a doubling in the price of crude oil would only raise the retail price in Germany by a fraction of what it would in the United States.

Many developing countries subsidize retail fuel prices; oil-exporting countries, generously so. To allow prices to rise would mean social turmoil and perhaps strikes and riots. Thus these governments had to absorb the growing gap between the world price for oil and the prices that their citizens paid. Subsidies cost India's government about $21 billion in 2009.[26]

SOVEREIGN WEALTH

When it was all added up, these high prices transferred a great deal of income from consuming countries to producing countries. The total oil revenues of the OPEC countries rose from $243 billion in 2004 to $693 billion in 2007. Halfway through 2008, it looked as though it could reach $1.3 trillion.

What were they going to do with all this money? Part of the answer was embodied in the initials SWF, shorthand for "sovereign wealth funds." These were essentially government bank accounts and investment accounts set up to receive oil and gas revenues that would be kept separate from the national budget. For some countries, they were cast as stabilization funds to be held for "rainy days." Some funds were explicitly created to prevent inflation and the Dutch disease that can result from a resource boom. These funds transformed oil and gas earnings into diversified portfolios of stocks, bonds, real estate, and direct investment.

But with oil prices rising to such heights, they had become truly giant pools of capital, swollen with tens of billions of dollars of unanticipated inflows, and now with tremendous financial capacity that would have far-reaching impact on the global economy. They faced their own particular quandary—how to invest all these additional revenues in a timely and prudent fashion. But the flip side was that their expansion meant a very large reduction of spending power in the oil-importing countries, which contributed to the downturn.

THE PEAK

Still the spell held. On July 11, 2008, oil reached its historic peak of $147.27—many times higher than the $22-to-$28 band that had been assumed to be the "natural price" for oil only four years earlier. The headlines told of more economic troubles ahead: Then something did happen. "Shortly after 10 a.m., as Mr. Bernanke was speaking to Congress," the *New York Times* reported on July 16, "investors did a double-take as oil prices, previously trading at record highs, suddenly plunged." But, said the oil bulls, it was "only a minor meltdown."[27]

And then the fever broke. Demand for oil was going down in response to the higher prices. And now it was going down for another reason too. The world economy was clearly beginning to slow. The United States was already in a recession. In China's Guandong Province, the new workshop of the world, orders were drying up, exports were declining, and workers were being laid off. Even electricity demand in that formerly booming province was declining. That was a message with global implications, for it meant that world trade was contracting. And the world's financial system was beginning to shudder and shake, the spasms of a coming cataclysm. Financial investors began ditching "risky" assets such as equities and oil and other commodities.

In September 2008 came the decisive event. The venerable Lehman Brothers, the fourth-largest U.S. investment bank, 158 years old, failed. No one came riding to its rescue. The insurance behemoth AIG looked as though it might go down the very next day; the Federal Reserve stepped in to save it at the last moment.

"A COLD WIND FROM NOWHERE"

In the aftermath of the Lehman collapse, the world's financial system simply froze up. Finance stopped flowing, whether to fund the daily operations of major companies or to provide the lubricant for trade. The Great Depression of the early 1930s, which had seemed to belong distantly in history, something that happened a very long time ago, now seemed to have happened only yesterday.

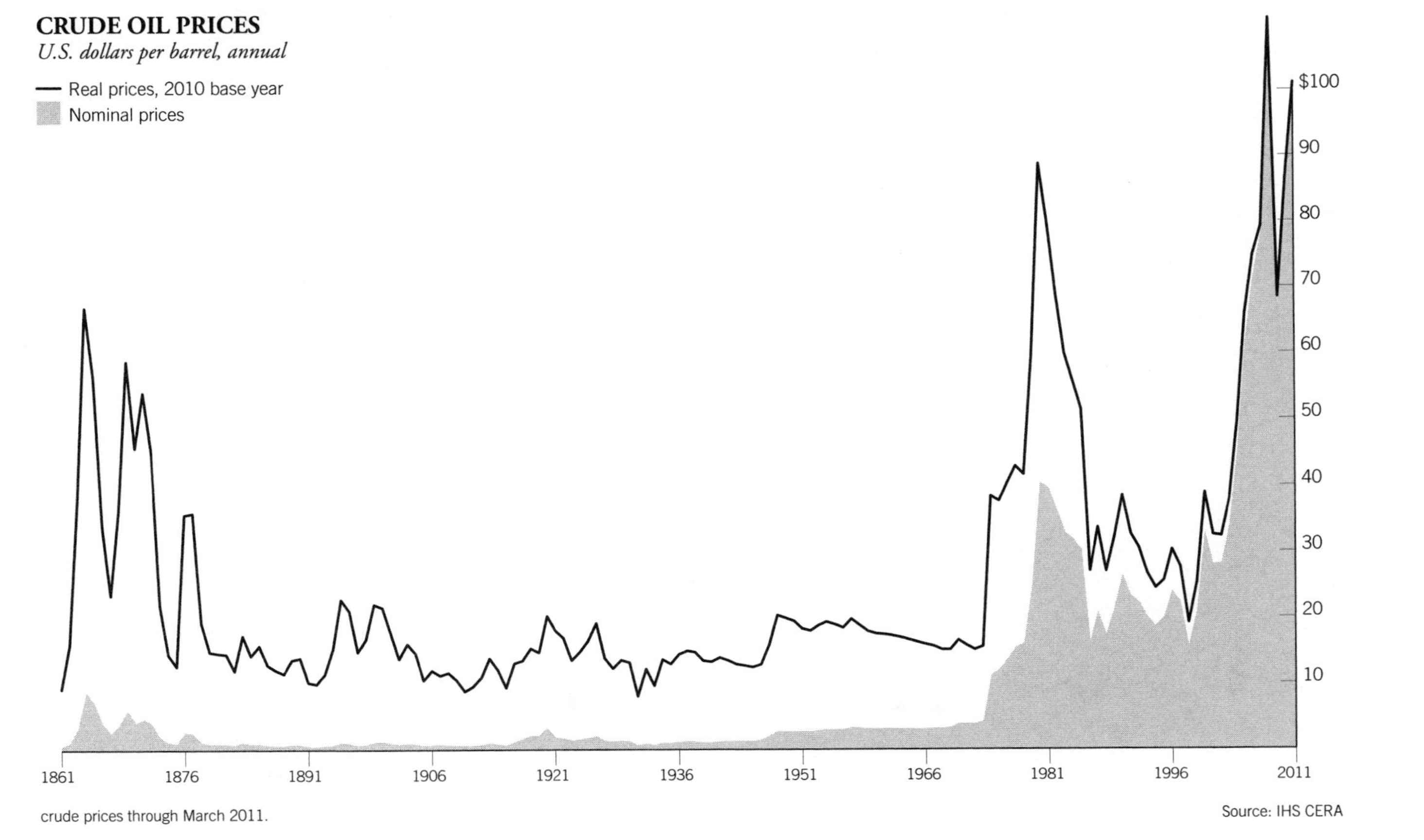
CRUDE OIL PRICES
U.S. dollars per barrel, annual
Real prices, 2010 base year
Nominal prices
$100
90
80
70
60
50
40
30
20
10
1861
1876
1891
1906
1921
1936
1951
1966
1981
1996
2011
crude prices through March 2011.
Source: IHS CERA

U.S. GASOLINE PRICES

U.S. dollars per gallon, annual

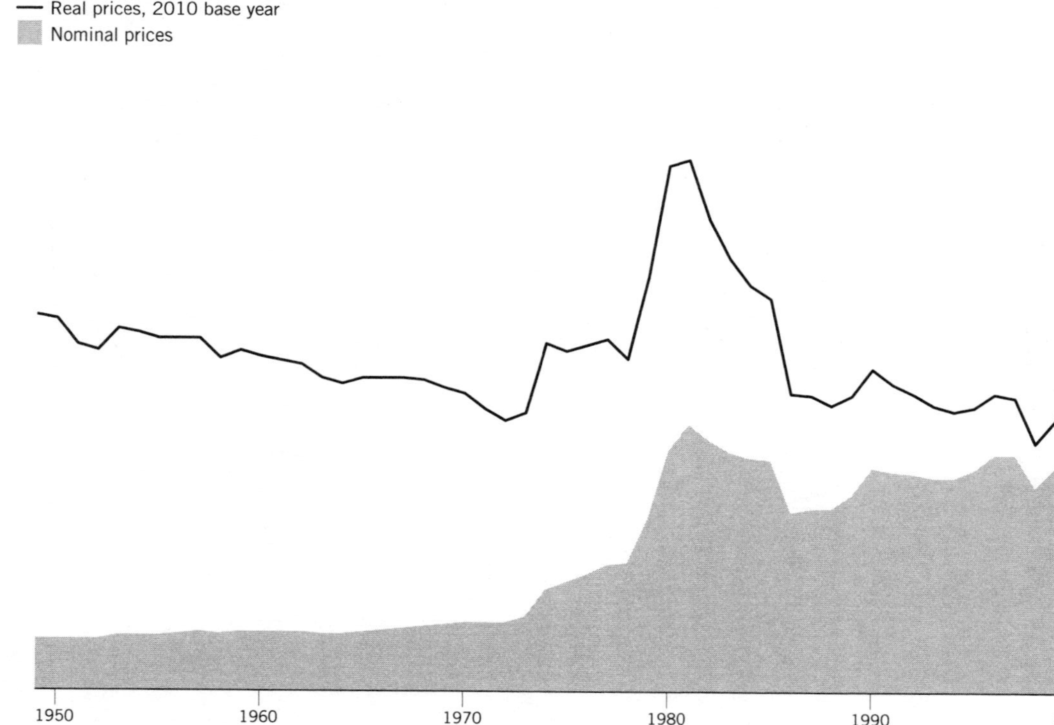

*Leaded Regular Prices used through 1975. Unleaded Regular prices used from 1976–March 2011.

Source: IHS CERA

History books and economic texts were hurriedly scoured for immediate and urgent lessons on how to rescue a failing banking system. The crisis was turning into a global panic of the sort that had not been seen for many decades. The impact on what had been healthy economies, including the BRICs, was, as Federal Reserve Chairman Ben Bernanke said, like "a cold wind from nowhere."

In the midst of what would become known as the Great Recession, demand for oil continued to decline while supplies continued to build up. Yet even in the week that Lehman collapsed, a prediction of "$500 per barrel oil" managed to make its way prominently onto the cover of a leading business magazine. At that moment, however, oil was heading down, and precipitously so. Before the year was out, as the tanks at Cushing, Oklahoma, ran out of storage space and crude backed up in the system, the price of WTI fell to as low as $32 a barrel.

Even though prices subsequently recovered, the spell had been shattered.

For some, prudence paid off, when prices came tumbling down. Indeed, there is no better example of the value to an oil producer of hedging its production forward than the sovereign nation of Mexico. Its government is very vulnerable to the price of oil, as about 35 percent of its total revenues are generated by Pemex, the state company. A sudden fall in the price of oil can create budgetary and social turmoil. For years, Mexico had been hedging part of its oil output. In 2008 Mexico went all out and hedged its entire oil exports and locked in a price. It was not cheap; the cost of this insurance was $1. 5 billion. But when the price plummeted, Mexico made an $8 billion profit on its hedge, thus preserving $8 billion for its budget that, without the hedge, would have otherwise disappeared. It could only have done that huge trade over the counter. If it had tried to do it on the futures market itself, the scale would have set off a scramble by other market participants before Mexico could even begin to get all of its hedges in place.

That transaction was, on Mexico's part, an act of prudence but also audacity. On the basis of the transaction's success, Mexico's finance minister received a unique honor—he was dubbed the "world's most successful, but worst paid, oil manager."[28]

How much of what happened in the oil market can be ascribed to the fundamentals, to what was happening in the physical market, and how much to financialization and what was happening in the financial markets? In truth, there is no sharp dividing line. Price is shaped by what happens both in the physical and financial markets.[29]

A couple of years later, Robert Shiller, who had become prominent for calling the Internet stock bubble and then the real estate bubble, was having breakfast in the restaurant of the Study, a new hotel on Chapel Street in New Haven, before walking over to lecture in his famous Yale class on financial markets. By then, with recovery well along in the global economy, the price of oil had more than doubled from its lows back to a range of $70 to $80 a barrel. Handed a piece of paper, Shiller looked carefully at what it showed—a plot depicting the movement of oil prices since 2000 culminating in the sharp ascent to its peak in mid-2008, and then its precipitous fall. It was superimposed on a plot of stock prices that culminated in the market boom that went bust in 2000. The fit was very tight. The two curves looked very similar. But the steep, bell shape of the curve instantaneously reminded Shiller of something else as well.

"That looks very much like what happened with real estate prices," he said. A bubble.[30]

The rise in oil prices had not begun as a bubble. For the price had been driven by powerful fundamentals of supply and demand; by the demand shock arising from unexpectedly strong global growth and major changes in the world economy, led by China and India; and by geopolitics and the aggregate disruption. But it was a bubble before it was over.

9

CHINA'S RISE

It was one of those sharp, cold nights in Beijing when the smell of burning, crisp and a little sweet, wafted through the dark. This was the very end of the 1990s when the swelling hordes of cars were beginning to fill the new eight-lane highways and push the bicycles to the side. The burning still mainly came not from the cars but rather from the many hundreds of thousands of old-fashioned coal ovens throughout the city that people were still using to cook and heat their homes.

The dinner had gone on for a long time in the China Club, once the home of a merchant, and then a favorite restaurant of Deng Xiaoping, who had launched China's great reforms at the end of the 1970s. Coal may have been in the air that night, but oil was on the agenda. With the dinner over, the CEO of one of China's state-owned oil companies had stepped out into the enclosed courtyard with the other guests. Everybody's overcoats were buttoned to the top against the cold. He and his management team were facing something he would never have anticipated when he started as a geologist in western China, more than three decades ago. For now they were charged with taking a significant part of China's oil and gas industry—built to serve the command-and-control centrally planned economy of Mao Tse-tung—and turning it into a competitive company that would meet the listing requirements for an IPO on the New York Stock Exchange.

The reasons for this sharp break with the past were clear—the specter of China's future oil requirement and the challenge of how to meet it—although that evening they could not visualize how rapidly consumption would grow. As the group paused in the courtyard outside the restaurant, the CEO was asked a pertinent question: Why go to all the trouble of becoming a public company? For then the management would be responsible not only to the senior authorities in Beijing but also to young analysts and money managers in New York City and London, and in Singapore and Hong Kong, all of whom would scrutinize and pass judgment on strategies, expenses, and profitability—and on the job they all were doing.

It wasn't at all obvious that the CEO relished such an "opportunity." But he replied, "We have no choice. If we are going to reform, we have to benchmark ourselves against the world economy."

That was still the time when China was moving from being a minor player in the world oil market to something more, although how much more was not at all clear. What was clear, however, was that China was fast integrating with the world economy and beginning to transition to a new and far larger role in it.

Over the years that followed, these changes would transform calculations about the world economy and the global balance of power. Would all of this mean a more interdependent world? Or, people would ask in the years to come, would it lead to intensified commercial competition, petro-rivalry, and a growing risk of a clash of nations over access to resources and over the sea-lanes through which those resources are borne?

"CHINA RISK"

None of these questions were much in the air that night, on the very eve of the new century, at least in terms of energy. Indeed, at that moment, the prospects for the IPOs of the three state-owned companies looked, at best, quite problematic, and even somewhat dubious.

The IPO for PetroChina, the new subsidiary of China National Petroleum Corporation (CNPC), the largest of the companies, would be the first one successfully out of the gate. But getting ready for the IPO was proving harder than might have been imagined. Financial accounts that could satisfy the requirements of the U.S. Securities and Exchange Commission had to be carved out and formulated from the undigested, confusing, and poorly organized data of a vast Chinese state organization that had never had to pay attention to any such metrics—and certainly never had any reason to heed to the U.S. agency that regulated the New York Stock Exchange. Management knew that a whole new set of values and norms had to be inculcated into the organization. Add to this the fact that some of the company's overseas investments were generating protests, and the picture became exceedingly unclear. It took a long prospectus—384 pages—to spell out all the risks.[1]

For their part, the international investors in the United States and Britain, and even those closer to China, in Singapore and Hong Kong, were skeptical. They worried about the China risk—uncertainty about the political stability and economic growth of the country. Also, this was an oil company at a time when the new economy—the Internet and Internet stocks—was booming. By contrast, the oil business was seen as quintessential old economy—stagnant, uninteresting, and stuck in what was thought to be the doldrums of permanent overcapacity and low prices.

As 2000 began, the appetite of global investors appeared tepid. The IPO was scaled back, substantially. But, finally, in April 2000 it went forward, though just barely, and PetroChina was launched as a public entity, partly owned by international investors but still majority owned by CNPC.

Over the next year, it was followed by the IPOs of the other two companies also cut from the once-monolithic ministries—Sinopec (the China Petroleum and Chemical Company) and CNOOC (China National Offshore Oil Corporation). They received the same tepid welcome. But as the years went on, the skepticism among investors disappeared, and with good reason. A decade after its IPO, PetroChina's market capitalization had increased almost seventy times over. Its market value by that point was greater than that of Royal Dutch Shell, which is a century older, greater than Walmart's, and was second only to ExxonMobil.

That increase in value calibrates the growing importance of the People's Republic of China (PRC) in the balances of world energy and the rise of China itself. Since reforms began in 1979, more than 600 million Chinese people have been lifted out of gripping poverty, with as many as 300 million people in the middle-income level. Over that same time, China's economy has grown more than fifteenfold. By 2010 it had overtaken Japan's to become the second-largest economy in the world.[2]

"THE BUILD-OUT OF CHINA"

This great economic expansion has changed China's oil position. Two decades ago China was not only self-sufficient in oil but an actual exporter of petroleum. Today it imports about half of its oil, and that share will go up as demand increases. The People's Republic of China is now the second-largest oil consumer in the world, behind only the United States. Between 2000 and 2010, its petroleum consumption more than doubled. All this reflects what happens when the economy of a nation of 1.3 billion expands at 9 or 10 or 11 percent a year—year after year after year.

As China continues to grow, so will its oil demand. Sometime around 2020 it could pull ahead of the United States as the world's largest oil consumer. It is an almost inevitable result of what can be described as the "great build-out of China"—urbanization at a speed and scale the world has never seen, massive investment in new infrastructure, and mass construction of buildings, power plants, roads, and high-speed rail lines—all of it reshaping China's economy and society.

This build-out of China over the next two or three decades will be one of the defining forces not just for China but for the world economy. It is certainly one of the main explanations for a long-lasting boom in commodities. China's urban population is growing very fast. In 1978 the country was only 18 percent urbanized. Today it is almost 50 percent urbanized, with more than 170 cities over a million people, and a number of megacities with populations exceeding 10 million. Every year another 20 million or so Chinese move from the countryside looking for work and housing and a higher standard of living. Asked by George W. Bush what worry kept him up at night, President Hu Jintao said that his biggest concern was "creating 25 million new jobs a year." That was the basic requirement for both development and social stability.[3]

As a result of this build-out, the country has become a vast construction site for homes and factories and offices and public services, requiring not only more energy but also more commodities of all kinds—a seemingly endless demand for concrete, steel, and copper wiring. An expansion on this scale will likely mean real estate booms and bubbles and busts. It is only when it is largely finished and China, mainly urbanized, sometime in the 2030s and 2040s, that the tempo of demand will slow.

All this growth, all this new construction, all these new factories, all these new apartments and their new appliances, and all the transportation that comes with this—all of it depends upon energy. This is on top of the huge energy requirements of all the factories that make China the world's leading manufacturing country and supplier of goods to the global economy. It all adds up—more coal, more oil, more natural gas, more nuclear power, more renewables. Today coal remains the backbone of China's energy. But in terms of the relationship with international markets and the world economy, the dominating factor is oil.

GROWTH AND ANXIETY

China's rapid growth in oil demand generates great anxiety, both for China and for the rest of the world. For Chinese oil companies, and the government, assuring sufficient oil supplies is a national imperative. It is crucial to Beijing's vision of energy security—guaranteeing that shortages of energy do not constrain the economic growth that is required to reduce poverty and tamp down the social and political turbulence that could otherwise ensue in such a fast-changing society. At the same time, a sharp awareness has developed that rising energy demand must be balanced with greater environmental protections.

In other countries, some fear that the Chinese companies, in their quest for oil, could preempt future supplies around the world—and deny access to other countries. Some also worry that the inevitable growth in Chinese demand, along with that of other fast-growing emerging markets, will put unbearable and unsustainable pressure on world oil supplies—leading to global shortage.

These anxieties suddenly burst into view in 2004—the year of the global demand shock, when world oil consumption grew in a single year by what normally would have been the growth over two and a half years. The surge in Chinese consumption was one of the central elements in the jump in demand.

The demand shock forced perceptions to catch up with a fundamental reality. Until then, many had seen China mainly as a low-cost competitor, a manufacturer of cheap goods, a challenge to wages in industrial countries, and the supplier for the shelves in Walmart and Target and other discount stores around the world. China, with its low costs, had become the Great Inflation Lid, giving central bankers the comfort to allow faster economic growth than they otherwise would feel safe doing.

But now one also had to look at China as a market of decisive importance, with the heft to significantly affect the supply and demand—and, therefore, the price—of oil, along with other commodities and all sorts of other goods. Until 2004 it would never have occurred to motorists in the United States or Europe that the prices they paid at the pump could be so strongly influenced by bottlenecks in coal supplies and shortages of electricity in China that would force a sudden switch to oil. And it certainly would never have occurred to the management of General Motors, the prototypical American car company, that within just a few years it would be selling more new cars in China than the United States. But such is the new reality of today's global economy. This is also true for trade in general. China is the biggest export market for countries like Brazil and Chile—not necessarily surprising for countries that export commodities. For countries like Germany, China is now also a key export market.

For the oil market, there is only one meaningful analogy for China's rapidly growing importance. It was the massive growth in petroleum demand—and imports—in Europe and Japan in the 1950s and 1960s that resulted from the rapid economic growth during the years of their economic miracles. That growth in demand certainly had a transformative impact on the world energy scene and on global politics.

But there is a risk around this change in the balance in the world oil market: that commercial competition could turn into a national rivalry that gets cast in terms of "threats" and "security," disrupting the working relationships that the world economy requires. As always in international relations, the danger is that miscalculation and miscommunication can in turn escalate security "risks" into something more serious—confrontation and conflict.

This emphasizes the importance of not recasting commercial competition into petro-rivalry and a contest of nation-states. After all, change is inevitable as a result of China's rapidly growing economy and from the new balance that will inevitably result. Moreover, the global oil and gas markets do not exist in a vacuum. They are part of a much larger and ever more dense network of economic linkages and connections, including huge trade and financial and investment flows—and, indeed, flows of people. These connections, of course, generate their own tensions, particularly around trade and currencies. Yet overall, the mutual benefits and common interests much outweigh the points of conflict.

Whatever the tensions today, this degree of integration and collaboration would have been inconceivable in the earlier era of confrontation, when Mao proclaimed that "the east is red" and the Bamboo Curtain closed off China from the rest of the world.

"POOR IN OIL"

On a Sunday night, from the top floor of the China World Hotel, one looks down at an endless stream of headlights, gliding in multiple streams, from the four lanes in each direction of Chang'an Avenue, Beijing's most important road, onto the elevated Third Ring Road expressway, which is constantly at capacity. This is the new China. Satisfying these streams of demand is part of China's preoccupation when it comes to oil.

There was no way that Zhou Qingzu, the venerable chief economist of China National Petroleum Company, could have imagined the panorama he was watching, twenty floors down, when he joined the oil industry as a geologist in 1952. At that time, China's entire production was less than 3,500 barrels a day. As his first assignment, he was sent to China's far west to join an early exploration effort. He was one of just a small handful of geologists going into an industry whose prospects were hardly promising. Decades earlier, after World War I, a Stanford University professor had delivered what had been taken as the definitive verdict: "China will never produce large quantities of oil." The meager experience of the succeeding decades seemed to bear out that conclusion.

Yet after the Second World War, no one could doubt that oil was essential for a modern economy—and for military might and political power. But China had virtually no oil of its own and had to depend on imports to meet its needs. Following the victory of Mao Tse-tung's communist revolution in 1949, the United States sought to limit Western oil exports to China and then, after the outbreak of the Korean War, to cut them off altogether, which constrained Chinese military operations during the war. "Self-reliance" became an urgent imperative, and Mao's five-year plans made the development of the oil industry a very high priority. Despite disappointing results from exploration, the Chinese leadership simply refused to accept that China was "poor in oil."

The Chinese Revolution did have one asset on which to draw in the search for oil—its fraternal relations with its communist brethren, the Soviet Union, which was a large oil producer. "We were just getting started," recalled Zhou. "Our major teachers were the Russians. We called the Russians 'our big brothers.'" The Soviets sent experts, equipment, technology, and financial aid to China, and a whole generation of young Chinese went off in the other direction, to Moscow, to be trained in petroleum.[4]

Some new fields were developed in the remote west, with Soviet help, but the overall results, as Zhou found from personal experience, were almost negligible. Pessimism was so rife that some Chinese experts thought the country should turn to synthetic oil, making petroleum from its abundant coal resources, as the Germans had done during the Second World War.

DAQING: THE "GREAT CELEBRATION"

But then, unexpectedly, in the grasslands of the northeast, in Manchuria, a vast new oil field was found. It was called Daqing—which means "Great Celebration."

The development of the field, arduous as it was, became even more difficult when the "brotherhood" with the Soviet Union splintered and the two countries became bitter rivals for leadership of the communist world. Moscow abruptly pulled out its people and equipment, and demanded repayment of debts. Mao repaid the Soviets in vituperation, denouncing them as "renegades and scabs . . . slaves and accomplices of imperialism, false friends and double-dealers."

The Chinese were now on their own for Daqing. No modern technology. No nearby urban areas. No housing. Thousands and thousands of oil field workers were hastily dispatched like troops in a military campaign. Despite the harsh cold, they slept in tents or huts or holes in the ground or just out in the open; they used candles and bonfires for light and heat; they scrounged the countryside for wild vegetables. Operations were headquartered in cattle sheds. And they worked terribly hard. To make matters worse, the Soviets reduced their oil exports to China. "Once imports are cut off, airplanes could be forced to stop flying," warned one senior official, "certain combat vehicles could be forced to stop operating." He added, "We should not rely on imports again." From then on, self-sufficiency and the determination represented by the "Spirit of Daqing" became the guiding principles of China's oil development.[5]

"IRON MAN" WANG

The embodiment of the Spirit of Daqing became a driller named Wang Jinxi. He achieved fame across China as the "Iron Man of Daqing oilfield" and was celebrated as the "national model worker." According to legend, when Wang had once visited Beijing, he had seen buses with large units on top that burned coal to make gas to power the vehicles. To Wang, this clear evidence of China's shortage of oil was an outrage. "I simply want to now open the earth with my fist," he declared, "to let the black oil gush out and dump our backwardness in petroleum into the Pacific."

Wang's team drilled at a furious rate. Wang himself would not be stayed. After one injury, it is said, he crept out of the hospital and went back to the drilling site, where he directed operations from his crutches. In his most famous exploit, in order to prevent a blowout that would have destroyed the drilling rig, he ordered bags of cement to be poured into a pit. Since there was no mixer, Wang jumped in and mixed the cement with his legs, forestalling the blowout and further injuring himself. Following the success of Daqing, Premier Zhou En Lai welcomed Iron Man Wang and his fellow Daqing workers to Beijing as national heroes. Mao himself declared that Chinese industry should "learn from the Daqing oil field."

Many other fields followed, the pace pushed by a famous oil minister and later vice premier, Kang Shien. China succeeded in becoming self-sufficient in petroleum, which, the *People's Daily* announced, had "blown the theory of oil scarcity in China sky high." Another publication declared that, "The so-called theory that China is poor in oil only serves the U.S. imperialist policy of aggression and plunder." The United States was not the only antagonist. The victory in the oil campaign was also hailed as a fusillade against "the Soviet revisionist renegade clique."[6]

RED GUARDS

In the mid-1960s, Mao recognized that he was being pushed aside because of the dismal failure of his disastrous economic policy, the Great Leap Forward, which had caused an estimated 30 million people to die from starvation. In 1966 he counterattacked and declared war on the Communist Party itself, charging that it had been captured by renegades with "bourgeois mentality." To carry out his "Cultural Revolution," Mao mobilized youthful zealots, the Red Guards, who waged a vicious battle against all the institutions of society, whether enterprises, government bureaus, universities, or the party itself. Prominent figures were humiliated, paraded around with donkey heads, beaten up, sent to do manual labor, or killed. Universities closed, and young people were dispatched to factories or the countryside to toil with the masses. The nation was in turmoil.[7]

But because of the oil industry's importance to national security, Premier Zhou En Lai took it under his personal protection, using the army to insulate the industry and ensure that it kept working. This led to notable incongruities. "During the day, I organized production as usual," recalled Zhou Qingzu, the chief economist at CNPC. "At night, I would sit in front of the students and workers and say I was wrong and apologize and write out my errors and apologies. I would listen very attentively to their criticism and write notes. During the day, I was a boss. At night, I was a nobody."[8]

Eventually the Cultural Revolution went too far even for Mao, in terms of the chaos it had created, and he used the army to throttle back the Red Guards.

"EXPORT AS MUCH OIL AS WE CAN"

Henry Kissinger, President Nixon's special assistant for national security, fell ill during a dinner in his honor in Pakistan in July 1971. Pakistan's president, the dinner's host, strenuously suggested that Kissinger, in order to escape the heat and thus speed his recovery, should recuperate in an estate up in the much cooler hills. This was very definitely a diplomatic illness. The supposed trip to the hills was a ruse, to provide cover for Kissinger's real purpose. Meanwhile, Kissinger himself—now code-named "Principal Traveller"—was given a hat and sunglasses to disguise himself at the airport prior to taking off for his actual destination, although the disguise might have seemed a little excessive since it was 4 a.m. in the morning.[9]

Only a week later did the sensational news break. From Pakistan, Kissinger had flown secretly over the Himalayas to Beijing, creating an opening in the Bamboo Curtain that had surrounded China since the communist victory in 1949. Half a year later, President Richard Nixon went through that opening. In the course of his historic visit to Beijing, Nixon supped with Mao, clinked glasses with Zhou En Lai, and dramatically reset the table of international relations.

For both sides it was a matter of realpolitik. The United States, looking for a way out of the stalemated Vietnam War, wanted to create a balance against the Soviet Union. For China, this was a means to strengthen its strategic position against the Soviet Union and reduce the risk of a "two-front war" with the Soviet Union and the United States. This was no mere theoretical matter, for Russian and Chinese military forces had already clashed on the border along the Amur and Ussuri rivers.

The Chinese had a second set of reasons as well. The most virulent phase of the Cultural Revolution was over. Vice Premier Deng Xiaoping and others were trying to get the country working again. They knew that self-reliance could not work. China needed access to international technology and equipment to modernize the economy and restore economic growth. But a very big obstacle stood in the way: How to pay for such imports?

"Petroleum export–led growth"—that was Deng's answer. "To import, we must export," he said in 1975. "The first to my mind is oil." The country must "export as much oil as we can. We may obtain in return many good things."

By this time, Deng was already becoming the manager-in-chief of the new strategy of opening toward the world. A stalwart communist since his student and worker days in France after World War I, he had emerged as one of the top leaders after the communists came to power. He then became one of the foremost targets of the Cultural Revolution and of his leftist rivals. His family had suffered much; his son had been pushed out of an upper-floor window and left paralyzed. Deng himself had spent those years variously working in a tractor repair shop and by himself, in solitary confinement. He had spent many hours pacing his courtyard, asking himself what had gone so wrong under Mao and how China's economy could be restored. In some ways, he had always been a pragmatist. (Even while organizing underground communist activities in France after World War I, he had also started and run a successful Chinese restaurant.) The traumas of the Cultural Revolution—national and personal—only reinforced his pragmatism and realism. His fundamental mottos were about being practical—"crossing the river by touching the stones"—and the most famous maxim of all: that he didn't care whether a cat was black or white so long as it caught mice.[10]

Following Mao's death and after a brief struggle with the radical "Gang of Four," Deng secured his position as paramount leader. He could now initiate the great transformation that would lead to China's integration with the global economy—which the 11th Congress of the Communist Party, in 1978, would proclaim as the historic policy of "reform and opening."

The oil industry was central to the opening. By that time, China—no longer "poor in oil"—was producing petroleum in excess of its own needs and could start exporting it. There was a waiting market nearby—Japan—which wanted to reduce its reliance on the Middle East and, at the same time, develop export markets in China for its own manufactures. Buying Chinese oil would help on both counts.

As the door began to open to the outside world, the Chinese oil industry discovered, to its shock, how wide was the technology gap that separated it from the international industry. But now, bolstered by its oil-export earnings, it could buy from abroad the drilling rigs, seismic capabilities, and other equipment that would lift its technical abilities.

While Mao's death and Deng's ascension were critical to the opening of China, those events did not put an end to the turmoil. Inflation, corruption, and inequality emboldened opponents of reform. So did the bloody 1989 confrontation with students in Tiananmen Square. In the aftermath, amid the indecision of the leadership, the efforts to continue market reform stagnated. Seeking to jump-start the faltering reforms, Deng, in January 1992, launched his last great campaign—the *nanxun,* or "southern journey." This trip showcased the booming Special Economic Zone of Shenzhen, which was becoming a manufacturing center for exports, and sought, fundamentally, to erase the stigma from making money. His message was that "the only thing that mattered is developing the economy." It was during this tour that Deng also made a stunning revelation—he had never actually read the bible of communism, Karl Marx's *Das Kapital.* He never had the time, he said. He had been too busy.[11]

WORKSHOP OF THE WORLD

In the years after Deng's "southern journey," China consolidated its course of reform and moved toward integration with the global economy. The 1990s was a decade of a new, much more interconnected economy. On January 1, 1995, the World Trade Organization was established to bring down barriers and facilitate global trade and investment. World trade was growing much faster than the global economy itself. American and European companies were setting up supply chains that gathered components from different parts of the world, assembled them in still other parts, and then packed the finished goods into containers and shipped them across oceans to customers anywhere in the world. Although China did not formally join the WTO until 2001, it had by then already become the linchpin in this new system of global supply chains.

As factories went up all along the coastal region, the inscription "Made in China" became ubiquitous on all sorts of products shipped all over the world. China had now become what was said of Britain two centuries earlier—"the workshop of the world." In due course, these new trade and investment linkages would have much greater impact on world energy than anyone might have imagined. For any workshop needs energy on which to run, and this new workshop of the world would run on fossil fuels.

THE END OF SELF-SUFFICIENCY

Already, however, a few years earlier, China had crossed a great divide in terms of energy. By 1993 petroleum production could no longer keep up with the rising domestic demand of the rapidly growing economy. As a result, China went from being an oil exporter to an oil importer. Though not at first noticed by the rest of the world, it was for China an immediate shock. "The government thought it was a disaster," remembered one Chinese oil expert. "It was very negatively received. From an industry point of view, we felt very shamed. It was a loss of face. We couldn't supply our own economy. But some scholars and experts told us, 'You can't be self-sufficient in everything. You import some things, and export others.' "[12]

This added greatly to the urgency to further modernize the structure of the oil industry—to move from the all-encompassing ministries of the petroleum and chemical industries, based on rigid central planning, to a system based on companies and rooted in the marketplace. The foundation for this shift had already been laid in the 1980s. The three state-owned companies had emerged from the ministries: the China National Petroleum Company, CNPC; Sinopec, the China Petrochemical Corporation; and CNOOC, the China National Offshore Oil Company. The next move, beginning in the late 1990s, was to dramatically restructure the three companies into more modern, technologically advanced companies—and more independent enterprises. "They would need to earn a living," said Zhou Qingzu. It was at this point that they would go through IPOs, opening partial ownership to shareholders around the world. CNPC's subsidiary was given a new name—PetroChina—while Sinopec and CNOOC used their existing names for their listed subsidiaries. There was also an enormous cultural change. "Now you'd have to be competitive," said Zhou. "You never had to be competitive before."[13]

THE "GO OUT" STRATEGY: USING TWO LEGS TO WALK

China has become a growing presence in the global oil and natural gas industry. This new role goes by the name of the "go out" strategy. It was enunciated as policy around 2000, though the policy's roots extend back to the original reforms of Deng Xiaoping.

The first steps abroad were very small ones, beginning in Canada, then

Thailand, Papua–New Guinea, and Indonesia. In the mid-1990s, CNPC acquired a virtually abandoned oil field in Peru. By applying the kind of intense recovery techniques it had honed to coax more oil out of complex older oil fields in China, it took the field from 600 barrels a day to 7,000. But these projects were small and did not get much attention. It took time and experience for the confidence to build for significant international activities. "We knew that, from its beginning in the mid-nineteenth century, the oil industry was always an international industry," said Zhou Jiping, the president of PetroChina. "If you wanted to become an international oil company in the real sense, you had to go out." By the beginning of the new century, a policy consensus had formed around the idea of international expansion, along with confidence in the capabilities of the Chinese companies to implement it.[14]

In general, the "go out" phase meant the internationalization of Chinese firms—that they should become competitive international companies with access both to the raw materials required by the rapidly growing economy and to the markets into which to sell their manufactures. For energy companies more specifically, it meant that the partly state-owned, partly privatized oil companies should own, develop, control, or invest in foreign sources of oil and natural gas. For the oil industry, this was complemented by another slogan—"using two legs to walk"—one, to further development of the domestic industry; the other, for international expansion.

Today the impact of the "go out" strategy is evident worldwide. Chinese oil companies are active throughout Africa and Latin America (as are Chinese companies from other sectors). Closer to home they have acquired significant petroleum assets in neighboring Kazakhstan and have achieved some positions in Russia after repeated tries. They are developing natural gas in Turkmenistan. As latecomers into the international industry, the Chinese come equipped not only with oil field skills but a willingness and the financial resources to pay a premium to get into the game. Also, particularly in Africa, they make themselves partners of choice with very significant "value added." That is, they bring government-funded development packages—helping to build railroads, harbors, and roads—something that is not in the tool kit of traditional Western companies. This has engendered controversy. Critics charge that China is colonizing Africa and using Chinese rather than local labor. Chinese reply that they are doing much to create markets for African commodity exports, and that export earnings are better than foreign aid and do more to stimulate lasting economic growth. (Some of these packages have fallen apart.) Chinese banks, in coordination with the Chinese oil companies, have also made multibillion-dollar loans to a number of countries that will be paid back in the form of oil or gas over a number of years. (One such deal took fifteen years to work out.)[15]

The energy security strategy is also taking an obvious route—building pipelines to diversify, reduce dependence on sea-lanes, and strengthen connections with supplier countries. A new set of pipelines, built in record time, brings oil and gas from Turkmenistan and Kazakhstan to China. Russia's $22 billion East Siberia–Pacific Ocean Pipeline will, in addition to supplying oil to the Pacific (Japan and Korea primarily), also deliver Russian oil to China—guaranteed by a $25 billion loan that China advanced to Russia. In September 2010 Chinese president Hu Jintao and Russian president Dmitry Medvedev jointly pushed the button to start the flow of oil over the Russian-Chinese border. The potential for a large trade in natural gas was also hailed. At the ceremony, Hu proclaimed a "new start" in Chinese-Russian relations. A relationship that was once based upon Marx and Lenin was now rooted in oil and possibly gas.[16]

"LIKE THROWING A MATCH"

But the greatest controversy over the "go out" strategy came not in Africa but in the United States. In 2005 Chevron and CNOOC—Chinese National Offshore Oil Corporation—were locked in a battle royal to acquire the large U.S. independent company Unocal, which had significant oil and gas production in Thailand and Indonesia but also had some in the Gulf of Mexico. The competition between the two companies was very tough, with sharp arguments about the financial terms and the role of Chinese financial institutions, as well as the timing of the respective offers. For some in Beijing, a global takeover battle was not only unfamiliar but disconcerting. The price that CNOOC put on the table was greater than the entire cost of the huge Three Gorges Dam project, which had taken decades to build. After months of battle, Chevron emerged victorious with a $17.3 billion bid.

But in the course of takeover battle, a fiery political controversy erupted in Washington that was out of scale compared with the issues. After all, Unocal's entire production in the United States amounted to just 1 percent of the total U.S. output. Much of it was in the Gulf of Mexico, in joint ventures with other companies, and the only market for that output was the United States. Yet when the contest got to Washington, as one of the American participants said, it was "like throwing a match into a room filled with gasoline." For it became the focus of a firestorm of anti-Chinese sentiment on Capitol Hill that was already supercharged by the contentious hot-button issues of trade, currencies, and jobs. The heated rhetoric showed the intensity, at least in some quarters, of suspicions of China's motives and methods. One critic told a congressional committee that CNOOC's bid fit "into a pattern" of "activity around the globe" that is "ominous in its implication." Another charged that CNOOC's bid was part of China's strategy for "domination of energy markets and of the Western Pacific." Whatever the specifics of the takeover battle, the takeaway for the Chinese at the end of the political battle was that the United States itself was less hospitable to the openness toward foreign investment that it preached to others and that the Chinese companies should redouble their investment effort—but elsewhere. "The world was shocked that a Chinese company could make this kind of bid," said Fu Chengyu, at the time the CEO of CNOOC. "The West was saying that China is changing in terms of such things as building highways. But it was not paying attention to China itself and how China had changed."

In the years that followed, the changes became much more evident. China's president made highly visible state visits to a number of oil and commodity-exporting countries in the Middle East and Africa, beginning with Saudi Arabia. And when China convened a summit of African presidents to discuss economic cooperation, 48 of the presidents made the trip. "China should buy from Africa and Africa should buy from China," said Ghana's president. "I'm talking about the win-win."

The world moves on. In 2010, five years after the fiery battle over Unocal, Chevron and CNOOC announced that they were teaming up to explore for oil not in the Gulf of Mexico but in the waters off China. "We welcome the opportunity to partner with CNOOC," said a senior Chevron executive.[17]

"INOCs"

In the decade-plus since the shaky days of the original IPOs, the Chinese companies have become highly visible players in the world oil market.

Their international roles have instigated a vigorous debate outside China as to what drives them. One agenda is established by the government (which remains the majority shareholder) and the party, both of which maintain oversight. They are to meet national objectives in terms of energy, economic development, and foreign policy. The CEOs of the major companies also hold vice ministerial government rank—and many also hold senior party rank.

At the same time, the companies are driven by strong commercial, competitive objectives that are similar to those of other international oil companies, and, increasingly, their commercial identities define them. They are indeed benchmarked against the world economy and other international oil companies by the investors in their listed subsidiaries, and they have to be responsive to their investors' interests. In addition, they are subject to international regulation and international governance standards. And they manage large and complex businesses that, increasingly, are operating on a global scale.

As Zhou Jiping put it, "As a national oil company, we have to meet the responsibilities of guaranteeing oil and gas supply to the domestic market. As a public company listed in New York, Hong Kong, and Shanghai, we must be responsible to our shareholders and strive to maximize shareholder value. And, of course, we have a responsibility to the 1.6 million employees of our company."

In short, Chinese oil companies are hybrids, somewhere between the familiar "international oil companies," IOCs, and the state-owned national oil companies, NOCs. They have become a prime example of a new category called INOCs—the international national oil companies. "There has been a great change in people's overall psychology and philosophy since the IPO," said the CEO of one of the companies. "We used to focus on how much we produced. Now it's the value of what we do."

Today walk into the headquarters of some of the companies in Beijing and what one sees are not exhorting slogans but the epitome of the international benchmarking—flashing displays of the stock price in New York, Hong Kong, and Shanghai. Yet in the lobby of CNPC, one is also greeted by a very strong reminder of how the industry was built—a massive statue of Iron Man Wang.

What is the balance in these INOCs? The Chinese companies are sometimes portrayed mainly as "instruments" of the state. A new study from the International Energy Agency concludes otherwise—that "commercial incentive is the main driver" and that they operate with "a high degree of independence" from the government. As the IEA puts it, they are "majority-owned by the government" but "they are not government-run." As they become increasingly internationalized, they operate more like other international companies.

For all concerned, the development of the Chinese companies has been an evolution. Fu Chengyu, now the chairman of Sinopec, summed up the changes this way: "Evolving so completely from full state-ownership to join the ranks of major international corporations is a huge transformation—one that, back when I started in the oil business in the oil fields of Daqing, we never thought could be possible. Back in those days, China's largest source of foreign exchange was not manufacturing, but in fact sales of oil to Japan! Today everything around us has changed. But so have we."[18]

PROPORTION

Chinese companies will likely become bigger, more prominent players; they will certainly compete; but they will also be sharing the stage with established American, European, Middle Eastern, Russian, Asian, and Latin American companies—and often in partnerships.

For all the talk about China "preempting" world supplies, its entire overseas production is less than that of just one of the supermajor companies. It's very hard to conceive of China ever being in a position to preempt world supplies. Moreover, while some of Chinese overseas production is shipped to China, most of it is sold into world markets at the same prices as similar grades of petroleum. Destination is determined by the best price, local and international, taking into account transportation costs. And that is all the more true of oil from joint ventures, in which much of China's international oil is produced.

There is a further critical consideration. Chinese investment and effort in bringing more barrels to the markets contribute to stability in the global market. For were those barrels not forthcoming, the growing demand from China (and elsewhere) would add more pressure and lead to higher prices. Additional investment means more supply and adds to energy security. The Chinese oil companies are committing more capital and resources to expanding Iraq's oil output, and taking more risk, than the companies of any other nation.

Indeed, it would be quite surprising if a country in China's position—rapidly rising demand, rapidly growing imports, a well-established domestic industry, huge holdings of dollars—did not venture out into the rest of the world to develop new resources. Indeed, were they not doing so, they would likely be roundly criticized around the world for not investing.

Moreover, "go out" is not the sole strategy of the Chinese companies. About 75 percent of the companies' output is within China. Altogether, China's domestic oil production makes it the fifth-largest in the world—ahead of such large producers as Canada, Mexico, Venezuela, Kuwait, and Nigeria. Within the Chinese industry itself there is talk about the "second age of Chinese oil." This means the application of new technologies and new approaches to the discovery and development of domestic petroleum resources, as well as a much greater focus on what are increasingly seen as abundant but undeveloped domestic resources of natural gas, including shale gas.

These are the new commercial realities—China as a growing consumer of oil, China as an increasingly important participant in the world oil industry. But there is also a security dimension, which arises from growing dependence for a country for which "self-reliance" had been such a strong imperative for so many years.

10

CHINA IN THE FAST LANE

In the late 1990s, when energy security proposals were presented to the Chinese government, they were tabled. "They said there was no energy security issue," said a senior adviser, "and that was partly right. It was a benign market."

But that changed as oil consumption surged, increasing the reliance on imports, and prices started their upward trek. A country that had been self-sufficient in oil as a matter of policy found itself increasingly dependent upon the global market—something that was anathema in its earlier and very different stage of development. This dependence made energy security a central concern in Beijing. As one of the country's top officials put it, "China's energy security issue is oil supply security."

By 2003 a new factor had further increased the anxiety about energy security—the war in Iraq. For Beijing, it was hard to believe that the promotion of democracy in the Middle East was what propelled the United States into Iraq in March 2003. If not that, it had to be something more concrete, more urgent, more critical, more threatening. In short, it had to be oil. And if the United States was worried enough about oil to launch a full-scale invasion, then, in the view of many Chinese, energy security was clearly much more important—and urgent.[1]

Part of the new insecurity arose from apprehension about the sea-lanes, the economic highways for the world commerce that were increasingly important as the lifelines for Chinese oil imports—and indeed for Chinese trade in general. Half of the country's GDP depends on sea-lanes. In November 2003, seven months after the invasion of Iraq, President Hu Jintao reportedly told a Communist Party conference that the country had to solve what became known as the Malacca Dilemma. This referred to China's reliance on the Malacca Strait, the narrow waterway connecting the Indian Ocean and the South China Sea and through which passes more than 75 percent of China's oil imports. "Certain powers have all along encroached on and tried to control navigation through the strait," Hu is said to have declared. "Certain powers" was an obvious euphemism for the United States.[2]

The growing attention to risk was reinforced by what happened in 2004: the unanticipated jump in both Chinese and global demand for oil and the consequent rapidly rising prices. An energy problem had already become evident in China from late 2002. But initially it was a coal and electricity problem, not an oil problem. China depends on coal for 70 percent of its total energy and about 80 percent of its electricity. The economy was growing so fast that tight supplies of coal turned into outright shortages. At the same time, electric power plants and the transmission network could not keep up with the demand for power. The country simply ran out of electricity. As brownouts and blackouts hit most of the provinces, a sense of crisis gripped the country. Factories were working half days or even shutting down because of shortages of energy, while sales of diesel generators soared as desperate industrial enterprises resorted to making their own electricity. Power was so short in some parts of the country that traffic lights weren't working, and children were back to doing their homework by candlelight. Hotels in Beijing were requested to keep room thermostats above 79 degrees Fahrenheit, and their staffs ordered to use the stairs rather than the elevators.[3]

Only one short-term alternative to coal was available for satisfying the accelerating energy demand—oil. That is why China's oil demand in 2004 grew not by the anticipated 7 or 8 percent but that much higher 16 percent, requiring a rapid rise in petroleum imports. The Chinese oil companies hurriedly stepped up their efforts both to increase domestic production and to access additional supplies internationally.

Around this time, the theses about peak oil and limitations on future supply were permeating discussions in Beijing, as elsewhere in the world. The overlay of a fear of imminent and permanent shortage, which was so common in this period, added to a pervasive sense of crisis about the adequacy and availability of future supplies and whether a new rivalry would emerge.

PETRO-RIVALRY?

But what would a "new-energy-security strategy" look like? This became part of what has become a continuing debate about the possibility of a petro-rivalry between the United States and China. Some strategists in Beijing worry about China's depending on a world oil market that they assert is unreliable, rigged against them, and in which the United States has, in their view, excessive influence. Some of them even argue that the United States has a strategy to interdict sea-borne Chinese oil imports—cut off China's overseas "oil lifeline"—in the event of a confrontation over what has been for decades the most critical issue between the two nations, the self-governing island of Taiwan and its relationship to mainland China. They criticize the presence of the U.S. Navy in the regional seas and U.S. support for Taiwan—even as economic links between Taiwan and the People's Republic continue to grow. Some of the military leaders denounce the United States, in the words of one admiral, as a "hegemon."

The reverse of such fears can be found among some strategists in the United States. There are those who argue that China, driven by a voracious appetite for resources and control, has a grand strategy to project its dominance over Asia while also seeking to preempt substantial world oil supplies. China is said to be pursuing this strategy with a single-minded mercantilism, backed up by growing military power. They point, for evidence, to double-digit increases in Chinese defense spending, a rapid naval buildup, China's pursuit of naval and aviation technology, and its potential for developing a "blue water navy" that would project naval power far beyond China's neighborhood. Moreover, China has established a network of strategic ports, bases, and listening posts along the Indian Ocean. These critics specifically cite the development of new missiles that seem aimed directly at U.S. sea power—specifically aircraft carriers—and at upsetting the security of sea-lanes that U.S. sea power protects—security from which China, as much as any nation, directly benefits.

All this could stir up the specter of a naval arms race reminiscent of the Anglo-German naval race that did so much to inflame the tensions that ignited the First World War. Despite an extensive and growing economic relationship in the years that led up to August 1914, Britain and Germany were driven apart by rivalry and the suspicions aroused by their naval race, by anxiety over control of sea-lanes and access to resources, by competition over who would have what place in the sun—and by growing nationalistic fervor. Echoes of the Anglo-German naval race can be heard in today's arguments.

Controversy over the South China Sea has already created some tension between the United States and China. That sea's 1.3 million square miles are bounded on the west by China, Vietnam (which calls the region the East Sea), and Malaysia, down to Singapore and the Strait of Malacca; and then, coming up on the east, by Indonesia, Brunei, the Philippines, and at the top, by Taiwan. Through its waters pass most of the trade between East Asia and the Middle East, Africa, and Europe—including most of the energy resources shipped to China, Japan, and South Korea. "It's really a lifeline of our commerce, of our transport, for all of us, China, Japan, Korea, and Southeast Asia, and the countries beyond to the west," said the secretary general of ASEAN, the association of ten Southeast Asian countries.[4]

In 2002 China and the ASEAN countries signed an agreement that seemed to settle rival claims. But later some Chinese military officials began to speak of China's "undisputed sovereignty" over the South China Sea, control of which they elevated to what they called *hexin liyi,* a "core interest." Others in the China foreign policy community have subsequently described the assertion of "core interest" as "reckless" and "made with no official authorization." If China were to successfully assert such an interest, it would control the critically important merchant shipping lanes as well as be in a position to deny freedom of passage to the U.S. Navy. Not surprisingly, the ASEAN countries, as well as the United States, have rejected China's claims. Still, to underline those claims, a Chinese submarine went down to the deepest part of the sea, where its crew planted a Chinese flag.[5]

Energy resources are an increasingly important part of the argument. Substantial oil and gas resources are produced around the South China Sea, notably in Indonesia, Brunei, and Malaysia. Estimates of the undiscovered oil in the South China Sea range between 150 billion and 200 billion barrels, which is more than enough to stir competition, although far from proven. Although China and Vietnam have worked out some joint-production agreements, they are at odds over ownership of other exploration areas. Particularly contentious are the Spratly Islands, whose waters are thought to be rich in resources and are claimed in whole or in part by several countries. Meanwhile, in the East China Sea, Japan and China have had a long dispute, which recurrently flares up, over sovereignty and drilling rights.

It is exactly these kinds of tensions that can fester, blow up into incidents, and lead to much more serious and disruptive consequences. That explains the urgency for finding frameworks that can meet the interests of the various nations involved.

"RESPONSIBLE STAKEHOLDERS"

While these tensions persist, China's direct anxiety over energy security appears to have eased. Hu Jintao offered his own answer to the Malacca Dilemma when he presented, at a G8 meeting in 2006, a definition of what he called global energy security in which importing countries like the United States and China are interdependent. Energy insecurity for China, he has said, also means energy insecurity for the United States—and vice versa. Thus collaboration is one of the main answers to the dilemmas of energy security.

Part of this shift is based on China's growing realization that it can obtain the additional energy it needs by participating in the same global economy from which it has benefited so considerably. In simple words, China can buy the energy it needs. That was not so obvious a few years ago, but experience since has shown that it is eminently feasible. This applies not only to oil but also to natural gas, the imports of which are growing. "There's no other solution but to rely on the marketplace," said an energy strategist in Beijing. "What's different about exporting to America and importing energy from elsewhere? China is part of world markets."

Moreover, China has very large coal reserves. Adding in domestically produced oil and hydropower, China is more than 80 percent self-sufficient in terms of overall energy. A sign of greater confidence is the change in the discussion about making synthetic oil from coal. This was a very high priority when oil prices were spiking and some people were predicting permanent shortage, but now the Chinese talk about its development more as an insurance policy against disruption rather than a large-scale substitution.[6]

An effort to reduce the tensions is evident within the larger framework of relations. It is built on the recognition of the new reality—China's prominent place in the global economy and the world community. The administration of George W. Bush initially described China as a "strategic competitor" with all the implications that went with that. But as the years passed, a more cooperative approach emerged, based upon a mutual understanding of the interdependence. "Rising power" and "peaceful rise" were the way that senior Chinese had come to describe their country's new role and position. Some Chinese strategists have emphasized the need to manage and ameliorate the inevitable tensions that would arise between a latecomer and an established power. For its part, the United States proffered the concept of "responsible stakeholder," an idea first proposed by Robert Zoellick, at the time deputy secretary of state and subsequently president of the World Bank. The argument was that China could play a larger constructive role in diverse international arenas that was commensurate with its new stature. The Chinese came to interpret "responsible stakeholder" as meaning shared "international responsibilities" for the international system from which they are benefiting—and which they are helping to shape.

This new orientation has become embodied in a set of arrangements for addressing issues, defusing tensions, and fundamentally providing strategic reassurance. These include a "strategic and economic dialogue" between the two countries and an "energy and environment cooperation framework," which was launched at the end of the Bush administration and continued by the Obama administration. China's collaboration with the International Energy Agency and its participation in the International Energy Forum enable greater alignment and less tension on energy-security issues. On a global basis, the G7 and the G8 club of the major industrial countries now shares the stage with the G20, which expands the table to include the major developing countries, with China obviously in a very prominent position. The relevance of the G20 was made clear when it became an essential forum for coordination during the financial crisis of 2008–9.

All of this does not guarantee that competition over energy, and tensions about access and security, will not flare up and become more threatening. But it does mean that an established framework exists to handle such issues and to help prevent their escalation into something more serious. One Chinese decision maker summed up the evolution of thinking this way: "The government considers energy security very important, a first priority. But there is a change of understanding. Now we recognize that we have lots of options and choices to solve energy security issues."[7]

This is all the more important as China's oil consumption is destined to rise as it moves at record speed into the auto age.

THE FAST LANE

China is making the transition to a mass automobile culture as other countries have already done, but it is doing so at an extraordinary rate and on a scale never seen before. In the United States, oil accounts for about 40 percent of total energy consumption. In China, despite rapid demand growth, oil is only 20 percent of total energy use, and the largest part of that oil is used as fuel in industry or as diesel in trucks and farm equipment. But that is changing swiftly. As the Chinese automobile industry moves into the fast lane, the impact will be felt not only across the nation but globally.

In 1924 Henry Ford, already known worldwide for his Model T, received an unexpected letter. "I have . . . read of your remarkable work in America," wrote China's president Sun Yat-sen. "And I think you can do similar work in China on a much vaster and more significant scale." He continued: "In China you have an opportunity to express your mind and ideals in the enduring form of a new industrial system." The invitation was all the more gracious as Sun himself was highly partial to Buick, made by Ford's great rival, General Motors. By the late 1920s, Ford Motor was already shipping cars to China and had opened a sales and service branch in that country. But Sun Yat-sen's dream was not to be realized.

In the "new industrial system" that the triumphant Mao imposed after 1949, the automobile had virtually no place. Even as late as 1983, China produced fewer than 10,000 cars. By then, however, Mao was gone, and the creation of an automobile industry had been identified as necessary to the reforms that Deng Xiaoping was introducing. It was part of a modern society, one of the "pillars" of economic development, critical to technical advance and to creating jobs for those moving from farms into cities.

But how to do it? China was so far behind the United States and Japan in terms of technology and industrial capability, and had been so isolated, that there was no point in trying to start from scratch.

And so the answer turned out to be joint ventures. The first one, however, Beijing Jeep, never fulfilled the original hopes. Volkswagen scored the first successful joint ventures when it teamed up, beginning in the mid-1980s, with Shanghai Automotive Industry Corporation and China's First Auto Works. Yet by 1990 China was still producing only 42,000 cars a year, and the roads still belonged to the great swarms of bicyclists. But General Motors, Toyota, and Hyundai were also establishing joint ventures, to be joined by Nissan and Honda, among others.

China's accession to the WTO in 2001 really ignited the growth of the auto industry—fueled by the emergence of distinctly local companies with such names as Chery, Geely, Great Wall, Lifan, Chang'an, and Brilliance. As the Chinese sales grew, the other international automakers realized that they could not afford to be left out of the most dynamic automobile market in the world, and they too signed up for joint ventures.

Indeed, auto executives could now see a point on the horizon when China might actually overtake the United States as the world's largest automobile market. It was inevitable, they said. It was just a matter of time. In 2004 General Motors predicted that it could happen as early as 2025. Some went further and said it could happen as early as 2020. Maybe even 2018. But, they would add, that would be a real stretch.

As things turned out, it happened much sooner—in 2009, amid the Great Recession. That year China, accelerating in the fast lane, not only overtook the United States but pulled into a clear lead. The massive and swift Chinese economic stimulus program targeted the automobile industry as one of the "core pillars of growth" with tax cuts on new vehicles, cash subsidies, and price reductions on some vehicles. Car sales increased 46 percent over the previous year,

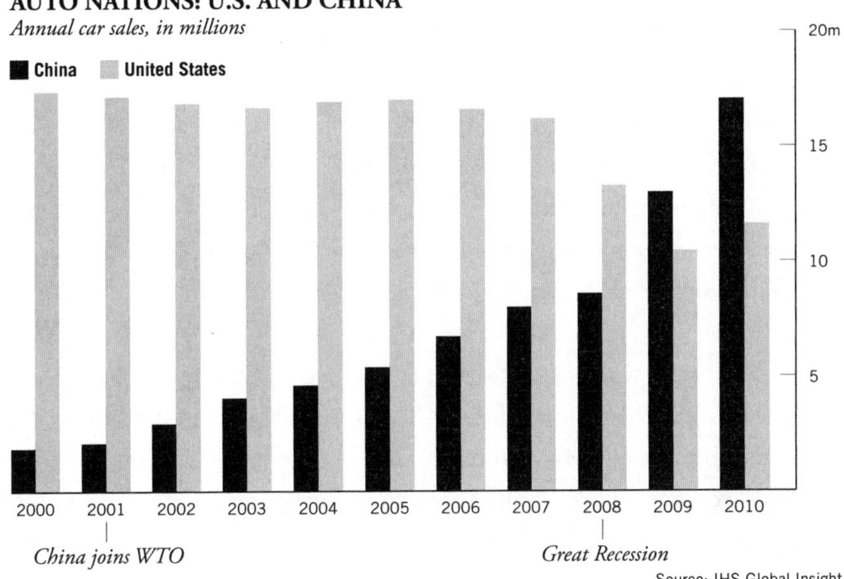

while in that same year U.S. sales plummeted to the lowest level since 1982. Seen in perspective, the shift in relative positions was staggering. In 2000, 17.3 million new cars were sold in the United States, compared with 1.9 in China. By 2010 only 11.5 million were sold in the United States, while China had reached 17 million. By 2020 sales in China could reach 30 million—and keep going.

American automakers may be struggling at home but not in the booming Chinese market. General Motors now does sell more automobiles in China than in the United States. The name Buick may not anymore exude class to American or European ears, but the black Buick Xin Shi Ji ("New Century") luxury sedan had a powerful allure for Chinese. Buick was so dominant a brand that by the early 1930s, one out of every six cars on China's streets was an imported Buick. Not only had Buick been Sun Yat-sen's favorite car, but also much favored by Zhou En Lai. Indeed, when GM first started manufacturing cars in the country, the Chinese insisted that Buick be the brand name, and for several years Buick led as a luxury car. Audi, Mercedes, and BMW might have overtaken the luxury segment, but Buick still remains a stalwart in the market.[8]

GOING OUT—ON WHEELS

Some of the Chinese companies are already producing inexpensive automobiles that are being sold in increasing numbers into developing countries. Chinese companies, like Indian manufacturers, also have their eye on a new, potentially very big market—cars priced from $2,500 to $7,500 and aimed at the hundreds of millions of people climbing up the rungs of the income ladder.

But the specter that haunts Detroit and Tokyo and Stuttgart and the other auto cities is whether—and when—China's auto companies (supported by local components suppliers) will reach a level of sophistication at which they can directly compete in the United States and Europe against the likes of GM, Ford, Toyota, and Daimler. Price will likely not be enough. Assuring quality and safety will also be essential. Fuel efficiency will be a criteria. They will also have to build dealer networks.

One Chinese company that has partly solved that problem is Geely, which got started in 1986 making components for refrigerators and only produced its first car in 1998. Within a decade it was one of the top domestic Chinese manufacturers. In 2010 Geely purchased Volvo from cash-strapped Ford, giving it an instant global sales and dealer network. It is not clear whether that means Geelys will eventually go into American and European showrooms. But by producing Volvos in China, Geely would have a potentially upmarket brand with which to challenge BMW and Mercedes at home.

The rapid expansion in China's auto industry is adding many jobs and stimulating domestic consumption—two steps that China's trading partners have, for years, been calling for. At the same time, this is causing worry among China's leadership about adding to future oil imports as well as about the quality of life. China's major cities are already clogged with traffic for which they were not built, and the delays and congestion—and growing pollution—embody the costs of such success. Some predict that if Beijing continues to add cars at its current rate of 2,000 vehicles a day, average speeds in the city could drop to nine miles an hour.[9]

THE PRICE OF SUCCESS

The abstract GDP and energy consumption numbers tell an extraordinary story. Never has the world seen so many people moving so quickly out of poverty into a world of economic growth and expanding opportunities. The scourges of hunger and malnourishment are receding rapidly. But there is an environmental price. Water is a great problem, both because of potential shortages and because of pollution from untreated waste. But it is the air that carries the burden of the rapidly growing energy consumption. Individual Chinese feel the pollution in their lungs and in their health.

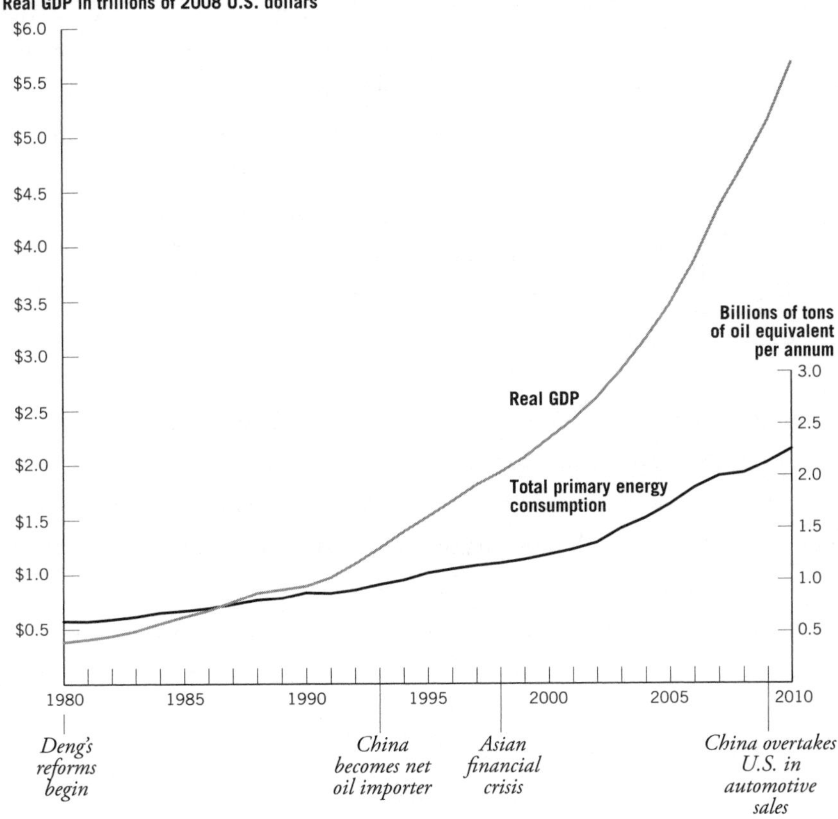

Source: IHS CERA, IHS Global Insight, International Energy Agency, China National Bureau of Statistics

The major source of air pollution is coal, whether burned in individual homes for cooking and heating or used to generate electricity or burned in factories. Electricity demand is growing at about 10 percent. The rapidly growing automobile fleet is adding to the pollution in major cities. Regulations are seeking to push new cars to European levels of pollution control, but with mixed results.

Meanwhile, in recent years China has become less energy efficient, reversing a long trend. Between 1980 and 2000, China's economy quadrupled, and its energy use only doubled. Such a record in energy efficiency was a considerable achievement. With the new century, however, the relationship suddenly reversed. Energy consumption started growing much more rapidly than the economy. From 2001 onward, a huge wave of investment stimulated enormous expansion in industry, particularly heavy industry. Many of the factories—old and new—were quite inefficient in how they used energy. As China became the workshop of the world, its energy-intensive heavy industries were operating at double-time supplying the world's market. China, for instance, became the largest producer of steel—almost half of the world's entire output—and the biggest exporter of steel in the world. Thus it would be correct, at least in part, to say that as Chinese production has supplanted energy-intensive output in the United States and Europe, some share of energy consumption that used to take place in the United States and Europe has in effect migrated to China. Or to put it more sharply, the United States and Europe have outsourced part of their energy consumption to China. As a result of the rapid rise in energy use, Beijing has put conservation—energy efficiency—at the very top of its priorities.[10]

As in other countries, climate change and emissions are becoming an increasingly important factor in reshaping China's energy policies. But climate change is also a mechanism to tackle other more immediate and, from the Chinese point of view, much more urgent problems—environmental degradation, rising energy demand, and energy security. To reduce carbon is also to reduce air pollution and contain energy use, and thus modulate imports of energy.

POWER SURGE

In the second decade of the twenty-first century, one of China's great challenges is to ensure that it has the electricity its rapidly growing economy needs and at the same time protect the economy against the environmental consequences of fast economic growth. For a number of years, China was adding on an annual basis the equivalent of the entire installed capacity of a France or a Britain. This averaged out to another new, full-sized coal-fired plant going into service every week or two. The tempo has slowed down somewhat, but enormous capacity is still being added on an annual basis.

It is hard to comprehend the scale and pace of growth. A dozen years ago, China's generating capacity was not much more than a third that of the United States. Today it exceeds the United States. Between 2005 and 2010, China's total electricity capacity doubled. It is as though the country built in just half a decade a new electrical system of identical size to the system in place in 2005! About 22 percent of new capacity added in 2009 was hydropower, and about 11 percent wind. Natural gas has just 2 percent. Still, the bulk of the new capacity—65 percent—is coal (lower than the 77 percent in 2005). But this also means that new, highly efficient, supercritical and ultra-supercritical coal plants, with more pollution controls, are being brought on line, while older, more-polluting and less-efficient coal plants are being retired early.

Coal will continue to be the mainstay of the electric power industry. As a result of growing demand for coal, China is no longer self-sufficient in that resource either. Once a significant coal exporter, China is the world's second largest importer of coal.

But greater diversification among fuel sources will still be sought. A substantial part of the country's target for non-fossil-fuel energy will be met by large hydropower plants. The Three Gorges Dam, which began producing electricity in 2003, has an installed power-generation capacity equivalent to about twenty nuclear plants. About 80 nuclear power plants are either under construction or in planning.

State Grid, the largest utility in the world, is spending about $50 billion a year to build what some consider the most technologically advanced grid system in the world. This is another way to promote efficiency. China needs what State Grid chairman Liu Zhenya calls a "strong *and* smart grid" to transport power thousands of miles from the west and the north across the country to the load centers on the east coast and in the center of the country. This would also reduce the heavy burden of coal transport by truck or rail. The huge wind potential of the sparsely populated Northwest is seen as particularly desirable.

It is not only clean energy, but is also an accessible domestic source that can be harnessed to meet China's future need. But it is only accessible with a vast expansion of long-distance transmission.[11]

In its 12th Five Year Plan, adopted in 2011, China put further emphasis on what it called its emerging-energy policy—to disproportionally push for alternatives to coal and oil, which means renewables (including hydropower), nuclear, natural gas, electric vehicles—and efficiency.

ENERGY AND FOREIGN POLICY

When it comes to oil, there are risks of a clash of interests between China and other countries, notably with the countries of Southeast Asia and Japan. How real these risks become will depend upon how the nations involved define and adjust their maritime positions.

In terms of relations with the United States, the real risks would come not from competition in the marketplace but would more likely arise when oil and gas development becomes embroiled in geopolitical concerns, foreign policy, and human rights issues. One of those issues was Sudan, where a Chinese-led consortium produces substantial amounts of oil. Venezuela could become an issue, as Hugo Chávez is deliberately trying to play a "China card"—bringing in Chinese investment and promoting China as an alternative market in his campaign against the United States. But that does not seem all that strong a hand.

But currently there is only one country where the risk of energy and foreign policy interests colliding is high. That country is Iran, in light of its nuclear program and pursuit of nuclear weapons. As a result, Iran presents the most complex, contentious, and potentially most difficult issue. Western and Japanese oil and natural gas companies have withdrawn or are in the process of withdrawing from Iran owing to its standoff with the United Nations over nuclear weapons and the growing body of sanctions. This creates a vacuum, and thus an opportunity for China to secure a significant position for its "go out" strategy in one of the major Middle East oil and gas producers. Chinese companies have negotiated, at least on paper, tens of billions of dollars of contracts for investment in the Iranian oil and gas industry that would provide access to substantial oil and gas resources, but they are not moving fast. At the same time, China has a larger interest in the stability of the entire Gulf region, on which it depends for a significant amount of its imports. Chinese companies have prominent roles in Iraq.

China has generally gone along with U.N. sanctions but has opposed them on the energy sector. As tensions mount, and votes come up in the U.N. Security Council, China's economic links with Iran, and its willingness or unwillingness to restrict its own dealings with Iran, could become a critical focal point in its relations with the United States and Europe. That could engender, if not managed carefully, much wider tensions, affecting the structure of overall collaboration in the world community. In the words of the International Energy Agency, "what will happen to the largest investment" to which the Chinese companies "have committed remains unclear."[12]

THE OVERLAP OF INTERESTS

So much has happened since the discussion that night at the end of the 1990s, in the chilly courtyard of the China Club restaurant in Beijing, about China's need to benchmark itself against the global oil industry. Then China was only a minor part of a global industry. Today it is the single most dynamic, rapidly changing element in the global oil market. Yet the fast growth of Chinese energy consumption and surging oil imports brings uncertainty, both for China and for the other major importers. The potential for conflict gets most of the attention.

Yet there are also the common interests between China and other oil consumers, particularly the United States. These two countries are bound together—much more connected perhaps than many recognize—in the global networks of trade and finance that fuel economic growth. More specifically, they have shared interests as the world's two largest petroleum consumers. The United States and China each import about half of their oil requirements. In the case of China, that share is likely to increase. Altogether, between them, they account for 35 percent of world petroleum consumption. Both benefit from stable markets, open to trade and investment, and improved energy security. But Chinese confidence needs to be enhanced in the reliability of the global market and the institutions maintaining its security. In turn, greater transparency about energy use and inventories in China would build confidence and create greater clarity for other importers. Both countries share common interests in encouraging greater energy efficiency, promoting innovation in renewables and alternative energy as well as conventional energy, and in managing carbon to reduce the threat of climate change. They have defined a common clean-energy agenda. Moreover, as holders of the world's largest and second-largest coal reserves, they depend upon coal for substantial parts of their electricity generation, and thus share interests in finding a pathway to commercial clean coal.

When all this is added up, there is much room for cooperation. Such collaboration would improve the energy and economic positions of both countries. And that, in turn, would contribute to the security and well-being of both countries as well as that of the global community.

PART TWO

...

Securing the Supply

11

IS THE WORLD RUNNING OUT OF OIL?

Since the beginning of the twenty-first century, a fear has come to pervade the prospects for oil and also feeds anxieties about overall global stability. This fear, that the world is running out of oil, comes with a name: peak oil. It argues that the world is near or at the point of maximum output, and that an inexorable decline has already begun, or is soon to set in. The consequences, it is said, will be grim: "An unprecedented crisis is just over the horizon," writes one advocate of the peak oil theory. "There will be chaos in the oil industry, in governments and in national economies." Another warns of consequences including "war, starvation, economic recession, possibly even the extinction of homo sapiens." The date of the peak has tended to move forward. It was supposed to arrive by Thanksgiving 2005. Then the "unbridgeable supply demand gap" was expected to open up "after 2007." Then it would arrive in 2011. Now some say "there is a significant risk of a peak before 2020."[1]

The peak oil theory embodies an "end of technology/end of opportunity" perspective, that there will be no more significant innovation in oil production, nor significant new resources that can be developed.

The peak may be the best-known image of future supply. But there is another, more appropriate, way to visualize the course of supply: as a plateau. The world has decades of further production growth before flattening out into a plateau—perhaps sometime around midcentury—at which time a more gradual decline will begin.

ABOVEGROUND RISKS

To be sure, there's hardly a shortfall of risks in the years ahead. Developing the resources to meet the requirements of a growing world is a very big and expensive challenge. The International Energy Agency estimates that new development will require as much as $8 trillion over the next quarter century. Projects will grow larger and more complex and there is no shortage of geological challenges.[2]

But many of the most decisive risks will be what are called "above ground." The list is long, and they are economic, political, and military: What policies do governments make, what terms do they require, how do they implement their choices, and what is the quality and timeliness of decision making? Do countries provide companies with access to develop resources and do companies gain a license to operate? What is happening to costs in the oil field? What is the relationship between state-owned national oil companies and the traditional international oil companies, and between importing and exporting countries? How stable is a country, and how big are threats from civil war, corruption, and crime? What are the relations between central governments and regions and provinces? What are the threats of war and turmoil in different parts of the world? How vulnerable is the supply system to terrorism?

All of these are significant and sober questions. How they play out—and interact—will do much to determine future levels of production. But these are not issues of physical resources, but of what happens above ground.

Moreover, decision making on the basis of a peak oil view can create risks of its own. Ali Larijani, the speaker of Iran's parliament, declared that Iran needs its nuclear program because "fossil fuels are coming to an end. We know the expiration date of our reserves." Such an expectation is surprising coming from a country with the world's second-largest conventional natural gas reserves and among the world's largest oil reserves.[3]

This peak oil theory may seem new. In fact, it has been around for a long time. This is not the first time that the world has run out of oil. It is the fifth.

And this time too, as with the previous episode, the peak presumes limited technological innovation and that economics does not really matter.

RUNNING OUT AGAIN—AND AGAIN

The modern oil industry was born in 1859 when "Colonel" Edwin Drake hit oil near the small timber town of Titusville in northwest Pennsylvania. It grew up in the hills and ravines surrounding Titusville in what has become known as the Oil Region. Other production centers also emerged in the late nineteenth century—in the Russian Empire, around Baku, on the Caspian Sea and in the Caucasus; in the Dutch East Indies; and in Galicia, in the Austro-Hungarian Empire. But Pennsylvania was the Saudi Arabia of the day—and then some—supplying Europe and Asia, as well as North America. The primary market for oil its first 40 years was illumination, to provide lighting, replacing whale oil and other fluids used in oil lamps. Petroleum quickly became a global business. John D. Rockefeller became the richest man in the world not because of transportation but because of illumination.

Yet oil flowing up from the earth's interior was mysterious. Wells might send oil shooting up into the sky and then run dry for reasons no one knew. People began to fear that the oil would run out. The State Geologist of Pennsylvania warned in 1885 that "the amazing exhibition of oil" was only a "temporary and vanishing phenomenon—one which young men will live to see come to its natural end." That same year, John Archbold, Rockefeller's partner in Standard Oil, was told that the decline in American production was almost inevitable. Alarmed, he sold some of his Standard Oil shares at a discount. Later, hearing that there might be oil in Oklahoma, he replied, "Why, I'll drink every gallon produced west of the Mississippi." Yet not long after, new fields were discovered—in Ohio, Kansas, and then the huge fields of Oklahoma and Texas.[4]

Those new supplies appeared just in time, for an entirely new source of demand—the automobile—was rapidly replacing the traditional illumination market, which in any event was being crushed by electricity. The arrival of the motor car turned oil from an illuminant into the fuel of mobility.

In 1914 the European nations went to war thinking it would be a short conflict. But World War I turned into the long, arduous, and bloody battle of trench warfare. It also became a mechanized war. The new innovations from the late nineteenth and early twentieth centuries—cars, trucks, and planes—were, more rapidly than anyone had anticipated, pressed into large-scale military service. One of the most important innovations first appeared on the battlefield in 1916. It was initially code-named the "cistern" but was soon better known as the "tank." As oil went to Europe to support the mobility of Allied forces, a gasoline famine gripped the United States. In fact, 1918 saw the highest gasoline prices, in inflation-adjusted terms, ever recorded in the United States. In order to help relieve the shortage, a national appeal went out for "Gasolineless Sundays," on which people would abstain from driving. In response, President Wilson ruefully announced, "I suppose I must walk to church."

By the time the war ended, no one could doubt oil's strategic importance. Lord Curzon, soon to become Britain's foreign secretary, summed it up: "The Allied cause had floated to victory upon a wave of oil." But for the second time, the fear took hold that the world was running out of oil—partly driven by the surging demand growth from the internal combustion engine. Between 1914 and 1920, the number of registered motor vehicles in the United States grew fivefold. "Within the next two to five years," declared the director of the United States Bureau of Mines, "the oil fields of this country will reach their maximum production, and from that time on we will face an ever-increasing decline." President Wilson lamented, "There seemed to be no method by which we could assure ourselves of the necessary supply at home and abroad."[5]

Securing new supplies became a strategic objective. That is one of the major reasons that, after World War I, the three easternmost oil-prospective provinces of the now-defunct Ottoman Turkish Empire—one Kurdish, one Sunni Arab, and one Shia Arab—were cobbled together to create the new state of Iraq.

The permanent shortage did not last very long. New areas opened up and new technologies emerged, the most noteworthy being seismic technology. Dynamite explosions set off sonic waves, enabling explorers to identify prospective underground formations and map geological features that might have trapped oil and gas. Major new discoveries were made in the United States and other countries. By the end of the 1920s, instead of permanent shortage, the market was beginning to swim in oil. The discovery of the East Texas oil field in 1931 turned the surplus into an enormous glut: oil plunged temporarily to as little as ten cents a barrel; during the Great Depression some gasoline stations gave away whole chickens as premiums to lure in customers.

The outbreak of World War II turned that glut into an enormous and immensely valuable strategic reserve. Out of seven billion barrels used by the Allies, six billion came from the United States. Oil proved to be of key importance in so many different aspects of the struggle. Japan's fear of lack of access to oil—which, in the words of the chief of its Naval General Staff, would turn its battleships into "nothing more than scarecrows"—was one of the critical factors in Japan's decision to go to war. Hitler made his fateful decision to invade the Soviet Union not only because he hated the Slavs and the communists, but also so that he could get his hands on the oil resources of the Caucasus. The German U-boat campaign twice came close to cutting the oil line from North America to Europe. The Allies, in turn, were determined to disrupt the oil supplies of both Germany and Japan. Inadequate supplies of fuel put the brakes on both General Erwin Rommel's campaign in North Africa ("Shortage of petrol," he wrote his wife; "It's enough to make one weep") and General George Patton's sweep across France after the D Day landing.[6]

World War II ended, like World War I, with a profound recognition of the strategic significance of oil—and, for the third time, widespread fear about running out of oil. Those fears were heightened by the fact that, immediately after the war, the United States crossed a great strategic divide. No longer self-sufficient in petroleum, it became a net importer. But for a number of years, quotas limited imports to about 10 percent of total consumption.

Once again, the specter of global shortage receded, as the opening up of the vast fields of the Middle East and the development of new technologies led to oversupply and falling prices. This downward trend culminated in cuts in the world oil price in 1959 and 1960 by the major oil companies that brought five oil-exporting countries together in Baghdad in 1960 to found the Organization of Petroleum Exporting Countries—OPEC—in order to defend their revenues. Oil remained cheap, convenient, and abundant, and it became the fuel for the postwar economic miracles in France, Germany, Italy, and Japan.

But by the beginning of the 1970s, surging in petroleum consumption, driven by a booming world economy, was running up against the limits of available production capacity. At the same time, nationalism was rising among exporting countries, and tensions were mounting in the Middle East. The specter of resource shortage was in the air, prominently promoted by the Club of Rome study *The Limits of Growth* on "the predicament of mankind." To wide acclaim, it warned that current trends would mean not only rapid resource depletion but also portended the unsustainability of industrial civilization.[7]

In October 1973 Arab countries launched their surprise attack on Israel, initiating the October War. In response to U.S. resupply of armaments to a beleaguered Israel, Arab exporters embargoed oil shipments. The oil market went into a hyperpanic, and within months petroleum prices quadrupled. They doubled again between 1978 and 1981 when the Iranian Revolution toppled the pro-Western shah and disrupted oil flows. All this seemed to be proof of the Club of Rome thesis of looming shortages. One most prominent scientist, a former chairman of the Atomic Energy Commission, warned: "We are living in the twilight of the petroleum age." The CEO of a major oil company put it differently. The world, he said, had reached the tip of "the oil mountain," the high point of supply, and was about to fall down the other side. This was the fourth time the world was said to be running out of oil.[8]

The fear of permanent shortage ignited a frantic search for new supplies and the double-time development of new resources. Major new provinces were discovered and brought on stream from Alaska's North Slope and from the North Sea. At the same time, government policies in the industrial countries promoted greater fuel efficiency in automobiles and encouraged electric utilities to switch away from oil to increased use of coal and nuclear power.

The impact was enormous—and surprisingly swift. Within half a decade, what was supposed to be the permanent shortage turned into a huge glut. In 1986 the price of oil collapsed. Instead of the predicted $100 a barrel, it fell as low as $10 a barrel. Prices recovered in the late 1980s, spiked with the Gulf crisis in 1990, and then seemed to stabilize again. But, in the late 1990s, the Asian financial crisis precipitated yet another price collapse.

THE FIFTH TIME

By the beginning of the twenty-first century, oil prices were once again rebounding. It was around that time that fear about running out of oil began to gain prominence again, for the fifth time. But it was no longer "the oil mountain."

It was now something loftier—"the peak." Accelerated growth of oil consumption in China and other emerging economies—and the sheer scale of prospective demand—understandably reinforced the anxiety about the adequacy of future supplies. Peak oil also became entwined with the rising concerns about climate change, and the specter of impending shortage provided further impetus to move away from carbon-based fuels.

The peak theory, in its present formulation, is pretty straightforward. It argues that world oil output is currently at or near the highest level it will ever reach, that about half the world's resources have been produced, and that the point of imminent decline is nearing. "It's quite a simple theory and one that any beer drinker understands," one of the leaders of the current movement put it. "The glass starts full and ends empty and the faster you drink it the quicker it's gone." (Of course, that assumes one knows how big the glass is.) The theory owes its inspiration and structure, and indeed its articulation, to a geologist who, though long since passed from the scene, continues to shape the debate, M. King Hubbert. Indeed, his name is inextricably linked to that perspective—immortalized in "Hubbert's Peak."[9]

M. KING HUBBERT

Marion King Hubbert was one of the eminent earth scientists of his time and one of the most controversial. Born in Texas, he did all his university education, including his Ph.D., at the University of Chicago, where he folded physics and mathematics into geology. In the 1930s, while teaching at Columbia University in New York City, he became active in a movement called Technocracy. Holding politicians and economists responsible for the debacle of the Great Depression, Technocracy promoted the idea that democracy was a sham and that scientists and engineers should take over the reins of government and impose rationality on the economy. The head of Technocracy was called the Great Engineer. Members wore uniforms and saluted when the Great Engineer walked into the room. Hubbert served as its educational director for 15 years and wrote the manual by which it operated. "I had a box seat at the Depression," he later said. "We had manpower and raw materials. Yet we shut the country down." Technocracy envisioned a no-growth society and the elimination of the price system, to be replaced by the wise administration of the Technocrats. Hubbert wanted to promote a social structure that was based on "physical relations, thermodynamics" rather than a monetary system. He believed that a "pecuniary" system, misinformed by the "hieroglyphics" of economists, was the road to ruin.

Although cantankerous and combative, Hubbert was, as a teacher, demanding and compelling. "I found him to be arrogant, egotistical, dogmatic, and intolerant of work he perceived to be incorrect," recalled one admiring former student. "But above all, I judged him to be a great scientist dedicated to solving problems based on simple physical and mathematical principles. He told me that he had a limited lifetime in which to train and pass on what he knew, and that he couldn't waste his time with people that couldn't comprehend."

Hubbert did not have an easy relationship with his Columbia colleagues. When Columbia failed to give him tenure, he packed up and went to work as a geologist for Shell Oil.[10]

Collegiality was not one of his virtues. Coworkers found him abrasive, overly confident in his own opinions, dismissive of those who disagreed with him, and ill disguised in his contempt of those with different points of view.

"A gifted scientist, but with deep-seated insecurities," in the words of one scholar, Hubbert was so overbearing that it was almost painful for others to work with him. At Shell, the young geologists assigned to him never managed to last more than a year. Finally, the first female geologist to graduate from Rice University, Martha Lou Broussard, was sent to him. "Overpopulation" was one of Hubbert's favorite themes. During her job interview, he asked Broussard if she intended to have children. Then, in order to convince her not to, he told her to go to the blackboard to calculate at exactly what point the world would reach one person per square meter.

From Shell he moved to the U.S. Geological Survey, where he was in a permanent battle with some of his colleagues. "He was the most difficult person I ever worked with," said Peter Rose, his boss at the USGS.

Yet Hubbert also became recognized as one of the leading figures in the field and made a variety of major contributions, including a seminal paper in 1957, "The Mechanics of Hydraulic Fracturing." One of his fundamental objectives was to move geology from what he called its "natural-history phase" to "physical science phase," firmly based in physics, chemistry, and in particular, in rigorous mathematics. "King Hubbert, mathematician that he is," said the chief geophysicist of one of the oil companies, "based his look ahead on facts, logically and analytically analyzed." Four decades after turning him down for tenure, Columbia implicitly apologized by awarding him the Vetlesen Prize, one of the highest honors in American geology.[11]

AT THE PEAK

In the late 1940s, Hubbert's interest was piqued when he heard another geologist say that 500 years of oil supply remained in the ground. This couldn't possibly be true, he thought. He started doing his own analysis. In 1956 at a meeting in San Antonio, he unveiled the theory that would forever be linked to his name. He declared that U.S. oil production was likely to hit its peak somewhere between 1965 and 1970. This was what became Hubbert's Peak.

His prediction was greeted with much controversy. "I wasn't sure they weren't going to hang me from the nearest light post," he said years later. But when U.S. production did hit its peak in 1970, followed by the shock of the 1973 embargo, Hubbert appeared more than vindicated. He was a prophet. He became famous.[12]

The peaking of U.S. output pointed to a major geopolitical rearrangement. The United States could no longer largely go it alone. All through the 1960s, even with imports, domestic production had supplied 90 percent of demand. No longer. To meet its own growing needs, the United States went from being a minor importer to a major importer, deeply enmeshed in the world oil market. The rapid growth of U.S. oil imports, in turn, was one of the key factors that led to the very tight oil market that set the stage for the 1973 crisis.

Hubbert was very pessimistic on the prospects for future supply. In tones reminiscent of the State Geologist of Pennsylvania in 1885, he warned that the era of oil would be only a brief blip in mankind's history. In 1978 he predicted that children born in 1965 would see all the world's oil used up in their lifetimes. Humanity, he said, was about to embark upon "a period of non-growth."[13]

WHY SUPPLIES CONTINUE TO GROW

Hubbert used a statistical approach to project the kind of decline curve that one might encounter in some—but not all—oil fields, and then assume that the United States was one giant oil field. Hubbert's followers have adopted that approach to global supplies. Hubbert's original projection for U.S. production was bold and, at least superficially, accurate. His modern-day adherents insist that U.S. output has "continued to follow Hubbert curves with only minor deviations." But it all comes down to how one defines "minor." Hubbert got the date right, but his projection on supply was far off. Hubbert greatly underestimated the amount of oil that would be found—and produced—in the United States.

By 2010, U.S. production was four times higher than Hubbert had estimated—5.9 million barrels per day versus Hubbert's 1971 estimate of no more than 1.5 million barrels per day—a quarter of the actual number.[14]

Critics point out that Hubbert left two key elements out of his analysis—technological progress and price. "Hubbert was imaginative and innovative in his use of mathematics in his projection," recalled Peter Rose. "But there was no concept of technological change, economics, or how new resource plays evolve. It was a very static view of the world." Hubbert also assumed that there was an accurate estimate of ultimately recoverable resources, when in fact it is a constantly moving target.

Although he seemed a stubborn iconoclast, even a contrarian, Hubbert was actually a man of his times. He made his key projections during the 1950s, an era of relatively low, and flat, prices and a period of technological stagnation. He claimed that he had fully assumed innovation, including innovation that had not yet occurred. Yet the impact of technological change was missing from his projections. The mid-1960s marked the beginning of a new era in technological advance and capabilities.[15]

Hubbert also insisted that price did not matter. Economics—the forces of supply and demand—were, Hubbert maintained, irrelevant to the finite physical cache of oil that can be extracted from the earth. Indeed, in the same spirit, those today who question the imminence of decline are often dismissed by peak adherents as "economists"—even if they are in fact geologists. Yet it is not clear why price—with all the messages it sends to people about allocating resources and making choices and developing new technologies—would apply in so many other realms but not in terms of oil. Activity goes up when prices go up; activity goes down when prices go down. Higher prices stimulate innovation and encourage people to figure out ingenious new ways to increase supply. The often-cited "proved reserves" are not just a physical concept, accounting for a fixed amount in the "storehouse." They are also an economic concept—how much can be recovered at prevailing prices—and they are booked only when investment is made. And they are a technological concept, for advances in technology will take resources that were not physically accessible or economically viable and turn them into recoverable reserves.

The general history of the oil and gas industry, as with virtually all industries, is one of technological advance. New technologies are developed to identify new resources and to produce more from existing fields. For instance, in a typical oil field, only about 35 to 40 percent of the oil in place is produced using traditional methods. Much technology is being developed and applied to raising that recovery rate. That includes the introduction of the digital oil field of the future. Sensors are deployed in all parts of the field, including in the wells. This dramatically improves the clarity and comprehensiveness of data and the communication between the field and a company's technology centers, and allows operators to utilize more powerful computing resources to process incoming data. If widely adopted, the "digital oil field" could also make it possible to recover, worldwide, an enormous amount of additional oil—by one estimate, an extra 125 billion barrels of oil—almost equivalent to Iraq's reserves.[16]

THE SUPERGIANT

In the 2000s, the imminent decline of output from Saudi Arabia became a central tenet of peak oil theory. The argument focused on the supergiant Ghawar field, the largest oil field in the world. The first well was drilled in Ghawar in 1948, ten years after the original discovery of oil in Saudi Arabia. It took decades to really understand the extent of this extraordinary field, made more complicated by the fact that it is really a network of five fields, which have been developed over decades owing to Ghawar's colossal size. The latest segment went into development only in 2006.[17]

The contention that Saudi Arabia's overall production is in decline is somewhat odd, for Saudi capacity has increased in recent years. After more than sixty years, Ghawar is still, in the words of Saudi Aramco President Khalid Al-Falih, "robust in middle age." Investment requirements are going up. But at a production rate of over 5 million barrels per day, Ghawar continues to be highly productive. The application of new technologies continues to unlock resources and open up new horizons.[18]

DISCOVERIES VERSUS ADDITIONS

As proof for peak oil, its advocates argue that the discovery rate for new oil fields is declining. But this obscures a crucial point. Most of the world's supply is not the result of discoveries, but of reserves and additions. When a field is first discovered, very little is known about it, and initial estimates are limited and generally conservative. As the field is developed, better knowledge emerges about its reserves and production. More wells are drilled, and with better knowledge, proven reserves are very often increased.

The difference in the balance between discoveries and revisions and additions is dramatic. According to one study by the United States Geological Survey, 86 percent of oil reserves in the United States are the result not of what is estimated at time of discovery but of the revisions and additions that come with further development. The difference was summed up by Mark Moody-Stuart, the former chairman of Royal Dutch Shell, recalling his own days as an exploration geologist out in the field: "We used to joke all the time that much more oil was discovered by the petroleum engineers, developing and expanding the fields, than by us explorers, who actually found the fields."

The examples provided by many fields and basins point to another fundamental weakness of Hubbert's argument and its application to the entire world. In 1956 Hubbert drew a bell-shaped curve; the decline side would be the mirror image of the ascending side. Indeed, he made it so sharp on both sides that for some years it was called "Hubbert's Pimple." Some oil fields do decline in this symmetrical fashion. Most do not. They eventually do reach a physical peak of production and then often plateau and more gradually decline, rather than falling sharply in output. As one student of resource endowments has observed,

"There is no inherent reason why a curve that plots the history of production of a type of fossil energy should have a symmetrical bell-shaped curve."[19]

The plateau is less dramatic. But, based on current knowledge, it is a more appropriate image for what is ahead than the peak. And the world is still, it would seem, many years away from ascending to that plateau.

HOW MUCH OIL?

At the end of 2009, after a year's worth of production, the world's proved oil reserves were 1.5 trillion barrels, slightly more than were at the beginning of that year. That means that the discoveries and revisions and additions were sufficient to replace all the oil that was produced in 2009—a pattern common to many years. Replacing that production is one of the fundamental jobs of the worldwide oil industry. It is challenging and requires enormous investment—and a long time horizon. Work on a field whose reserves were judged proved in 2009 might have begun more than a decade earlier. Replacing reserves is even more challenging because of a natural decline rate in oil fields—on a worldwide basis, about 3 percent.

What are the prospects for the future? One answer is drawn from an analysis using a database that includes 70,000 oil fields and 4.7 million individual wells, combined with existing production and 350 new projects. The conclusion is that the world is clearly not running out of oil. Far from it. The estimates for the world's total stock of oil keep growing.

The world has produced about 1 trillion barrels of oil since the start of the industry in the nineteenth century. Currently, it is thought that there are at least 5 trillion barrels of petroleum resources, of which 1.4 trillion is sufficiently developed and technically and economically accessible to count as proved plus probable reserves. Based upon current and prospective plans, it appears the world liquid production capacity should grow from about 93 million barrels per day in 2010 to about 110 mbd by 2030. This is about a 20 percent increase.[20]

But—and there are many *buts*—beginning with all the political and other aboveground risks that have been enumerated earlier. Moreover, attaining such a level in 2030 will require further development of current and new projects,

WORLD LIQUIDS PRODUCTION* 1946–2011

Millions of barrels per day

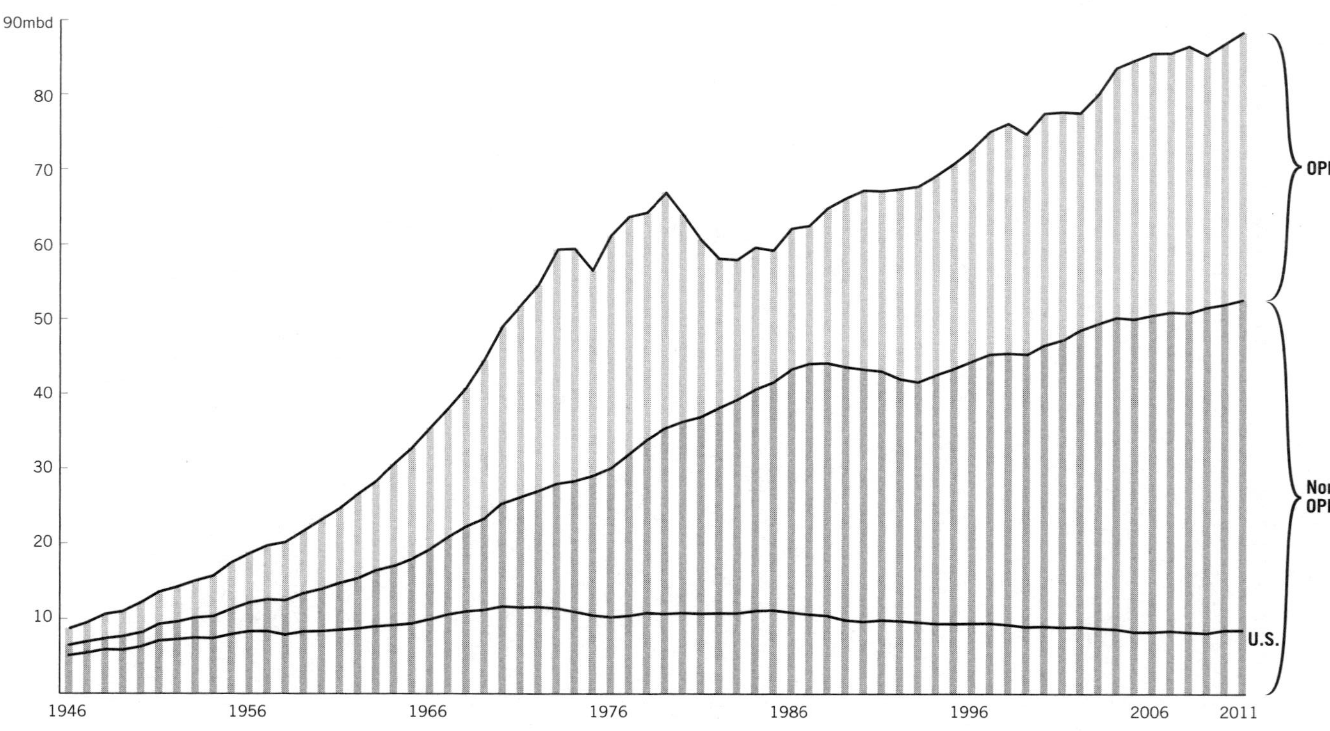

*Total liquids production includes crude oil, natural gas liquids, condensates, and other liquids.

Source: IHS CERA, EIA

which in turn requires access to the resources. Without access, the future supply picture becomes more problematic.

Achieving that level also requires the development of more challenging resources and a widening of the definition of oil to include what are called non-traditional or unconventional oils. But things do not stand still. With the passage of time, the unconventionals become, in all of their variety, one of the pillars of the world's future petroleum supply. And they help explain why the plateau continues to recede into the horizon.

12

UNCONVENTIONAL

H. L. Williams was both a spiritualist and a shrewd businessman. In the 1880s he began to organize séances on a ranch he had bought south of Santa Barbara, California, which he had named Summerland. He also went into real estate. He wrote other spiritualists, promising that Summerland could be "a beacon light to the world" and that there they could "better both the spiritual and material condition of mankind." To make it easy for prospective members to gather for séances and summer camps, he sold them lots to build their own cottages for $25 each. But soon the lots were being feverishly resold for up to $7,500 each. Oil had been discovered beneath the lots.

Williams jumped into the oil business. The most productive wells were the ones closest to the beach. Why not go right out into the ocean? Williams built a series of piers and began drilling into the seabed.

Unfortunately, the offshore drilling did not work out that well, and production petered out within a decade or so. The piers were left derelict for many decades until they were finally washed away in a fierce storm. Yet while Summerland never fulfilled Williams's great vision, he had achieved something else. He had pioneered offshore drilling.[1]

Today about 30 percent of total world oil production—26 million barrels per day—is produced offshore, in both shallow and deep waters. The total global deepwater output in 2010 was almost six million barrels per day—

larger than any country except for Saudi Arabia, Russia, and the United States. Altogether, deepwater production could reach 10 million barrels by 2020.

Deepwater production is one of the building blocks of what is known as unconventional supply. These unconventionals are a varied lot. What joins them is that their development depends on the advance of technology. The unconventionals are an important part of today's petroleum supply and will become even more important in the future.

LIQUIDS WITH GAS

The biggest source of nonconventional oil is something that has been part of the energy business for a long time, though not very well known. These are the liquids that accompany the production of natural gas. Condensates are captured from gas when it comes out of the well. Natural gas liquids are separated out when the gas is processed for injection into a pipeline. Both are similar to high-quality light oils.

Their output is increasing very fast, owing to the growth of natural-gas production worldwide and the building of new facilities in the Middle East. In 2010 these gas-related liquids added up to almost 10 million barrels per day. By 2030 they could be over 18 million barrels per day, roughly 15 percent of total world oil—or liquids—production.[2]

OUT OF SIGHT OF LAND

In the first decades of the twentieth century, following the early efforts of H. L. Williams and other pioneers, oil had continued to move offshore, but offshore had been limited to platforms in lakes in Texas and Louisiana and in Venezuela's oil-rich Lake Maracaibo.

Drilling out in the ocean on freestanding platforms, subject to wave pressures and the tides, was an altogether different matter. After World War II, an independent company named Kerr-McGee decided to go out to sea because it figured that its best shot at "real class-one" acreage was offshore—mainly because the larger companies thought drilling offshore, out of sight of land, was probably impossible.

On a bright Sunday morning in October 1947, working ten and a half miles offshore with a cobbled-together little flotilla of surplus World War II ships and barges, Kerr-McGee struck oil. "Spectacular Gulf of Mexico Discovery," headlined *Oil and Gas Journal.* "Revolutionary" was its judgment.[3]

An extended legal battle between the federal government and the coastal states, which went all the way up to the Supreme Court, slowed the development of the offshore industry in the United States. The fight was over turf—that is, as to whom the waters "belonged" and thus to whom would go the royalties and tax revenues. One result was the invention of the concept of the outer-continental shelf—the OCS—which was deemed the exclusive province of the federal government. The coastal waters of the states extended out just three miles—except in the cases of Florida and Texas, both of which had the heft to wrest nine miles from their struggle with Washington. By the end of the 1960s, the shallow waters of the offshore were starting to become a significant source of oil.

In January 1969 drillers at work on a well off the coast of Santa Barbara, not far from the original Summerland play, lost control. The well suffered a blowout, an uncontrolled release of oil. The well itself was capped. But then oil started to leak through a nearby fissure, creating an oil spill that blackened local beaches, put a halt to new drilling off the coast of California, and increased offshore regulation. The ooze on the beaches—and on oil-soaked birds—became one of the emblematic images in the nation's new environmental consciousness. Santa Barbara also marked the beginning of a never-ending battle over offshore drilling that pitted environmental activists against oil and gas companies.

THE NORTH SEA AND THE BIRTH OF NON-OPEC

Yet nine months after Santa Barbara, toward the end of 1969, a new era opened in waters much harsher and challenging than those found off Santa Barbara—the stormy North Sea, between Norway and Britain. By then, oil companies had drilled 32 expensive wells in the Norwegian sector of the North Sea. All had come up dry. One of the companies, Phillips Petroleum, after drilling yet another dry hole, was about to give up and go back home to Bartlesville, Oklahoma. But then it decided to drill one more well—since it had already prepaid for the drilling rig. At the end of October 1969, it struck the Ekofisk oil field. It turned out to be a giant.

The offshore industry developed with remarkable speed—spurred by the 1973 oil embargo and the quadrupling of price, and by the push by Western governments for the development of secure, new sources of oil. Giant platforms, really mini-industrial cities, were built, some of them hundreds of miles out at sea. These structures, and the infrastructure that supported them, had to be designed to withstand winds up to 130 miles per hour and the terrifyingly destructive "100 Year Wave." The North Sea came on line extraordinarily fast. By 1985 the North Sea—British and Norwegian sectors combined—was producing 3.5 million barrels per day, and it had become one of the pillars of what had already become known as "non-OPEC."

TO THE FRONTIER

The North Sea was still in relatively shallow waters. In the United States, it seemed as though the "offshore" had gone about as far as it could—into depths of 600 feet of water, at the edge of the continental shelf. Beyond that the seabed falls away sharply, to depths of thousands of feet, which seemed well beyond the reach of any technology. Despondent about what seemed bleak future prospects, oilmen began to refer to the Gulf of Mexico as the "dead sea."

But a few companies were trying to find a way to push beyond the shallow waters—both in the Gulf of Mexico and elsewhere, most notably the Campos Basin off the northeast coast of Brazil. Petrobras, Brazil's state-owned oil company, was charged with reducing the nation's heavy dependence on petroleum imports. In 1992, after years of work, Petrobras broke the deepwater barrier by successfully placing the Marlim platform in 2,562 feet of water.

Meanwhile, Shell Oil was using new seismic technologies to identify promising prospects in the deeper waters of the Gulf of Mexico. In 1994 its Auger platform—which towered twenty-six stories above the sea—went into production in 2,864 feet of water. It had taken nine years from the acquisition of the leases and an expenditure of $1.2 billion, and even within Shell it had been regarded as a huge gamble. Yet the resource proved much richer than anticipated, and eventually the complex was producing over 100,000 barrels a day. Augur opened up the deepwater frontier in the Gulf of Mexico and turned it into a global hot spot of activity and technological advance. The federal government's lease sales for the deep waters of the Gulf of Mexico led to intense competitions for prospects among companies. The bonus payments and royalties made it a major revenue source for the government.[4]

The growth of the deepwater sector worldwide was extraordinary—from 1.5 million barrels a day in 2000 to 5 million by 2009. By that point, some 14,000 exploratory and production wells had been drilled in the deep waters around the world. It became customary to describe deepwater production as the great new frontier for the world oil industry. Among the most prospective areas were at the corners of what was called the Golden Triangle—the waters off Brazil and West Africa and the Gulf of Mexico. By 2009 the shallow and deep waters of the Gulf of Mexico together were supplying 30 percent of U.S. domestic oil production. That year, for the first time since 1991, U.S. oil production increased, instead of declining, and the deepwater was the largest single source of growth. In fact, in 2009 the Gulf of Mexico was the fastest-growing oil province in the world.[5]

DEEPWATER HORIZON

On the morning of April 20, 2010, a helicopter took off from the Louisiana coast and headed out over waters so smooth as to be almost glassy. Its destination was the Deepwater Horizon, a drilling platform operating 48 miles off the Louisiana coast. A fifth-generation semisubmersible drilling rig, the Deepwater Horizon was a marvel of scale and sophisticated engineering. The passengers that morning included executives from Transocean, which owned the drilling rig, and BP, which had been the contractor of the rig since it had been launched nine years earlier. They were flying out to honor the Deepwater Horizon and its team for its outstanding safety record.

The location was Mississippi Canyon Block 252, on a prospect known as

Kuwaiti oil fields were set afire by retreating Iraqi troops at the end of the Gulf War in 1991. Nine months later, the flames were extinguished, seeming to point to a new era of peace and stability in the Middle East.

"Mistakes were made that could have been avoided," said President Mikhail Gorbachev on Soviet television in December 1991. He announced his resignation and the end of the Soviet Union.

Heydar Aliyev went from being a high-level Soviet official to the president and "native son" of Azerbaijan. He sought to use its oil to turn Azerbaijan into a "real country"—recalling when the region, a century earlier, was the world's leading oil producer.

Nursultan Nazarbayev (right), president of the newly independent Kazakhstan, signed in 1993 with Chevron what he called "the contract of the century" for the huge Tengiz oil field. He said that it was the "fundamental principle" for his country's future.

Before he became Russia's president, Vladimir Putin declared that natural resources would be the basis to "make Russia a great economic power."

Two huge projects on Sakhalin island, off Russia's east coast, required Western technology to overcome harsh subarctic conditions and complex technical challenges. The projects marked the return of Western energy companies to Russia.

In a "moon shot," the American company Unocal tried to lay oil and gas pipelines from Turkmenistan across Afghanistan to Pakistan and India. In 1996, Unocal vice president Marty Miller (left) signed an agreement in Afghanistan with the Northern Alliance. The company also negotiated with their archenemy, the Taliban, giving both sides a fax machine.

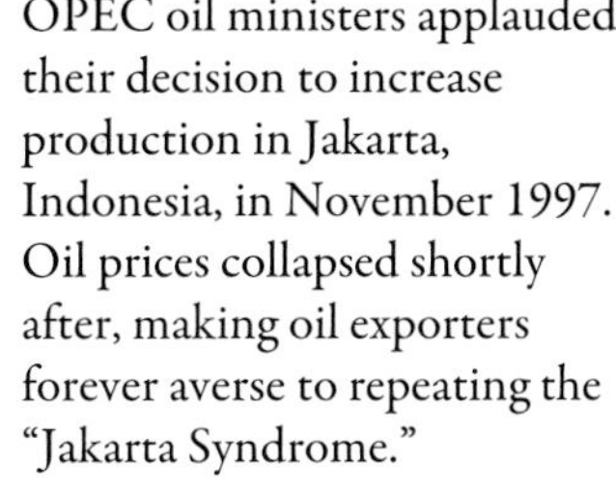

OPEC oil ministers applauded their decision to increase production in Jakarta, Indonesia, in November 1997. Oil prices collapsed shortly after, making oil exporters forever averse to repeating the "Jakarta Syndrome."

BP's John Browne (left) and Amoco's Laurance Fuller merged their companies in August 1998, setting off the biggest reshaping of the oil industry since the breakup of Standard Oil in 1911.

In December 1998, Exxon's Lee Raymond (left) and Mobil's Lucio Noto announced the largest industrial merger in history, confirming the era of the oil supermajor.

On the creeks in the swampy Delta region of Nigeria, heavily armed MEND rebels sought to "totally destroy the capacity of the Nigerian government to export oil."

In 2005, Hurricane Katrina (pictured here), followed by Hurricane Rita, knocked out virtually all oil production in the Gulf of Mexico, the biggest oil disruption in U.S. history.

Venezuelan President Hugo Chávez promotes his Bolivarian Revolution, accompanied by a parrot wearing a matching red beret.

After the U.S.-led invasion of Iraq in 2003, looting and and sabotage targeted the country's oil infrastructure, setting back reconstruction.

President George W. Bush decried the nation's "addiction to foreign oil" in his 2006 State of the Union address. One of his solutions was ethanol, made not only from corn but also from switchgrass.

Mexican Finance Minister Agustín Carstens (later head of the country's central bank) hedged Mexico's entire oil output in 2008, saving the country $8 billion. It earned him a unique honor: "world's most successful, but worst paid, oil manager."

THE BUTTER AND CHEESE EXCHANGE IN NEW YORK—A HEAVY OPERATION.

In 1872, merchants set up the Butter and Cheese Exchange in New York City. In 1882, it became the New York Mercantile Exchange—later the NYMEX.

In 1960, eggs underwent inspection as the exchange expanded its menu to include egg futures.

The NYMEX (below) began trading oil futures—"paper barrels"—in 1983. The raucous action in the trading pit, bolsterered by electronic trading around the world, is linked to the oil stored in Cushing, Oklahoma (above). In July 2008, the price of a barrel of West Texas Intermediate hit $147.27.

Sun Yat-sen, the father of modern China (far right), invited Henry Ford to repeat his success on "a vaster and more significant scale" in China. Sun himself rode in General Motors' Buick, to which he was highly partial.

"Iron Man" Wang Jingxi, "national model worker," leaped into a pit of liquid cement to forestall a blowout by turning himself into a human mixer. The 1959 discovery of the giant Daqing oil field launched China's modern oil industry. China is now the fourth largest oil producer in the world.

Deng Xiaoping, here meeting with U.S. President Gerald Ford, led the revolution that made China an economic superpower. He used oil exports to jump-start growth, saying, "We may obtain in return many good things."

China still depends primarily on coal, which provides 70 percent of its energy.

In 2009, China overtook the United States as the world's largest automobile market. Where bicycles once swarmed, automobiles now crowd the streets of China's megacities.

"Attach Great Importance, Pay Close Attention to Implementation, and Further Strengthen Energy Conservation and Emission Reduction" was the title of Chinese Premier Wen Jiabao's speech to the nation on energy. Conservation has become a national priority for China's leadership.

Russia's President Dmitry Medvedev and China's President Hu Jintao in September 2010 start the new pipeline carrying oil from East Siberia to China, now the world's second largest oil importer.

When a seemingly permanent oil shortage gripped the United States during World War I, "gasolineless Sundays" were introduced. President Woodrow Wilson ruefully announced, "I suppose I must walk to church."

PETROLEUM WEEK

March 16, 1956

Is Oil Nearing a Production Crisis?

Ultimate U.S. Crude Oil Production

(Assumed total: 150-billion bbl.)

Billions of bbl. per year

3
2
1
0

1850
1900
1950
2000
2050

PROVEN RESERVES 30-billion bbl.

CUMULATIVE PRODUCTION 52½-billion bbl.

AT-A-GLANCE © PETROLEUM WEEK

U. S. CRUDE PRODUCTION is continuing to rise steadily, but the rise is slowing, and some experts fear the peak may be only a decade or so away.

In 1956, geologist M. King Hubbert, the father of peak oil, first proposed his theory of a decline in U.S. oil output. His forecast that the United States would peak around 1970 proved correct. But his longer-term predictions of U.S. and global production have proved far too pessimistic.

In November 1973, in the face of rising oil prices, President Richard Nixon called for the United States to become "energy independent"—as have all presidents since.

Wells drilled from piers near Santa Barbara, California, in the 1890s pioneered the offshore oil industry.

The first well out of sight of land was successfully drilled in 1947, 11 miles offshore from Louisiana.

The Petrobras platform, atop 2,562 feet of water in the Marlim field off the coast of Brazil, opened the deepwater frontier in 1992. Today offshore oil accounts for 30 percent of global oil supply.

The explosion aboard the Deepwater Horizon drilling rig in April 2010 unleashed the largest oil spill in U.S. history. The Macondo well gushed millions of barrels of oil into the Gulf of Mexico before it was capped in July 2010.

The oil sands in Canada's Alberta province use the largest trucks in the world to "mine" oil. The oil sands, also produced with heat underground, have become the United States' largest source of oil imports.

The Bosporus, the waterway that runs through the middle of Istanbul and divides Europe from Asia, is a critical choke point. It is the gateway for Russian and Central Asian oil headed to world markets.

The control room in Dhahran in Saudi Arabia (above) manages oil production for Saudi Aramco, the world's largest oil company, including the new giant Shaybah oil field (right) in the desert known as the Empty Quarter. Saudi Arabia is the world's biggest oil exporter.

Hundreds of thousands of protesters gathered in Tahrir Square in Cairo in February 2011 to watch a televised speech by Egyptian President Hosni Mubarak. Eleven days later, he resigned after 30 years in power—a great victory for the "Arab Spring" but portending new uncertainty for the region.

Supertankers pass through the Strait of Hormuz, the most important choke point in the global oil market. Forty percent of world oil exports move from the Persian Gulf through this narrow waterway between Iran and Oman.

Iran's President Mahmoud Ahmadinejad tours centrifuge facilities, which can enrich uranium for use in a nuclear bomb. Such a weapon would help Iran realize its ambition to be the dominant power in the Persian Gulf.

Emir Hamad bin Khalifa al-Thani (right) and Minister Abdullah bin Hamad al-Attiyah turned the small desert sheikdom of Qatar into a powerhouse of natural gas. From the huge Ras Laffan complex, liquefied natural gas is shipped in special LNG tankers to world markets.

George P. Mitchell, celebrating his 3,000th well in North Texas, drove the shale gas revolution. Shale gas wells like this one in Pennsylvania (below) now provide a quarter of the U.S. natural gas supply.

In 1882, the "Jumbos" in Thomas Edison's Pearl Street station, the world's first generating plant, began delivering electricity to Lower Manhattan, providing light "graceful to the eye" and "without a particle of a flicker."

Samuel Insull, who started as office boy to Thomas Edison, created the modern electric power business. When his debt-laden empire collapsed in the 1930s, he fled the country, but was brought back and put on trial.

LIVE BETTER ELECTRICALLY

In a 1957 television commercial for General Electric, Ronald Reagan and his wife Nancy demonstrate a portable radio. Before becoming the champion of freedom, Reagan was the advocate of the "all-electric home," marking electricity's transformation of American life.

Admiral Hyman Rickover, the "greatest engineer of all time," explained a nuclear reactor aboard the U.S.S. *Nautilus,* the first nuclear submarine. He was the father of the nuclear navy and civilian nuclear power.

A nuclear plant at Belleville-sur-Loire in central France. After the 1973 oil crisis France made nuclear power a priority. Today nuclear power provides almost 80 percent of French electricity.

In March 2011, one of the most powerful earthquakes ever recorded generated a massive tsunami in Japan, triggering a major nuclear accident at the Fukushima Daiichi nuclear complex.

Macondo. The Deepwater Horizon had been on site for eighty days. The well had descended through almost five thousand feet of water and then had pushed on through more than another 13,000 feet of dense rock under the seabed, where it had made another major Gulf of Mexico discovery and it was now almost at the end of the job. All that was left to do was plug the well with cement, and then the rig would move on to another site. At some later date, when a permanent production platform was in place, the Macondo well would be unplugged and would begin producing. The crew had encountered some frustrating problems along the way, notably what were called gas kicks from pockets of natural gas. At times Macondo had been called the "well from hell." But now that all seemed behind them.

A decade earlier, Macondo would have been at the very edge of the frontier, but by 2010 the frontier in the Gulf of Mexico had moved beyond Macondo to discoveries as deep as 35,000 feet—twice that of Macondo.

Now, on board the Deepwater Horizon, it was a matter of wrapping up over the next few days—highly exacting and technically complex work, but also familiar in terms of what needed to be done. The night before, April 19, it was decided to dispense with a cement bond log, which would have provided critical data to determine if the well was sealed is a secure way. It was deemed unnecessary. Overall, things seemed to be proceeding normally.

At 7:55 p.m. the evening of April 20, final tests were concluded on the pressure in the well. After some discussion, the results were judged satisfactory. That was a misinterpretation. For deep down in the earth, many thousands of feet below the seabed, something insidious, undetected, was beginning to happen. Oil and, even more dangerous, gas were seeping through the cement that was meant to keep the well sealed.

At 9:41 p.m., the captain of a neighboring ship, the Damon Bankston, saw mud shooting up above the drilling rig with extraordinary force. He hurriedly called the Deepwater Horizon. The officer on the brig told him there was "trouble" with the well and to pull away as fast as possible. Then the line went dead.

"WE HAVE A SITUATION"

On the rig itself, one of the drillers called a superior in a panic. "We have a situation. The well has blown out." People began to scramble, but the response in those critical minutes was hampered by confusion, poor communication, unclear information, and lack of training for that kind of extreme situation.

Yet there was still one last wall of defense—the 450-ton, 5-story-tall blowout preventer, sitting on the bottom of the ocean floor. Equipped with powerful pincerlike devices called shear rams, it was meant to slice into the pipe and seal the well, containing any potential blowout of surging oil and gas. It was the fail-safe device if all else failed, the final impregnable line of protection. The blowout preventer was activated. The unimaginable happened. The pincers failed to fully cut into the pipe—by 1.4 inches.

At about 9:47 p.m. there was a terrifying hissing sound. It was the worst sound that the crew could possibly hear. It meant that gas was escaping up from the well. The gas encountered a spark. At 9:49 a thundering explosion rocked the rig, and then a second blast, and a series more. The rig lost all its power. It heaved and shook violently. Whole parts of the structure were blown to pieces; stairways crumbled and disappeared altogether. Workers were tossed this way and that. The entire rig was engulfed in fierce flames.

Some crew members dove directly into the sea. Many piled into the two lifeboats, some dreadfully injured and in awful pain, and eventually made it to the Damon Bankston. Others were pulled from the sea. The Coast Guard arrived just before midnight and began a search-and-rescue mission. On April 22, two days after the accident, the Deepwater Horizon, gutted and deformed, sank. The next day the search for additional survivors was called off. Eleven of the 126 crew members had perished.[6]

THE RACE TO CONTAIN

At the time of the accident, no established methods existed for staunching the flow of a deepwater accident, other than the proper operation of the blowout preventer. If it failed, the only option was to drill a relief well that would intercept the damaged well so that it could be sealed. But that would take three months or more. Both industry and government seem, in retrospect, to have assumed that a catastrophe of such dimensions was impossible. It was an accident, said BP's then chief executive Tony Hayward, that "all our corporate deliberations told us simply could not happen."[7]

Over recent decades, a handful of serious accidents and major blowouts had occurred. The worst in terms of loss of life was a fire on the Piper Alpha platform in 1988, off the coast of Scotland, that took 167 lives. That disaster had led to major reforms in North Sea regulation and safety practices. The last big blowout in the Gulf of Mexico was a Mexican well in the Gulf of Campeche, off the Yucatán, in 1979. In August 2009, a well in the Timor Sea between Australia and Indonesia spilled up to 2,000 barrels a day for ten weeks. But no noteworthy blowouts had occurred in U.S. waters since Santa Barbara in 1969. Between 1971 and 2009, according to the U.S. Department of the Interior, the total number of barrels of oil that had spilled in federal waters as the result of blowouts was a miniscule 1,800 barrels—an average of 45 barrels a year.[8]

But now the unthinkable had happened, and the flow had to be stopped. The result was an overdrive process of high-tech engineering improvisation by BP, its contractors, other companies, outside specialists, government experts, and government scientists who knew little about oil to begin with but quickly became experts.

A whole host of approaches for stemming the flow were tried. They all failed. Finally, in mid-July, eighty-eight days after the accident, a newly designed capping stack was put in place. That ended the spill. No more oil was leaking out of the Macondo well. Two months later, on September 19, after the relief well connected with the original well, the government pronounced Macondo "effectively dead."[9]

"FIGHTING THE SPILL"

In the Gulf itself, the fishing industry, whose boats could not go out, was hardest hit economically, along with tourism at beach resorts. The marshy coastal waters of Louisiana were among the areas worst affected.

As with the blowout itself, both government and industry were unprepared to deal with the environmental consequences. The Oil Pollution Act and the Oil Spill Liability Trust Fund had been established two decades earlier, in the aftermath of the Exxon Valdez accident in Alaska, to respond to an accident involving a tanker. But the loss of oil from a tanker, however serious, was a finite affair. A tanker only held so much oil.

The response to a blowout on this scale had to be invented. A vast navy of ships of all sorts, 6,700 in all, were deployed to intercept and capture the oil;

onshore, a small army was similarly raised to clean up the beaches. Altogether, the clean-up campaign enlisted 45,000 people.

Some said that it would take decades for the Gulf to recover and that some parts of it might never recover. But in August 2010, the National Academies of Sciences estimated that three quarters of the spilled oil had already evaporated, been captured, or had dissolved. It was becoming clear that the consequences of Macondo would not be as severe as had first been feared.[10]

The sea itself provided a major solution. The natural seepage of oil from fissures in the bottom of the Gulf—estimated to be as much as a million barrels of oil a year—combined with the warm waters, had nurtured microbes known as hydrocarbonolostic, whose specialty is feasting on oil. For them, Macondo oil was an unexpected bonanza, and they went to work on it. As a result, the oil biodegraded and disappeared much faster than had been expected. On September 20, 2010, the day after the official announcement that the well had been killed, the *New York Times* reported that the environmental consequences were proving far less long lasting than feared. "As the weeks pass, evidence is increasing," said the *Times,* that "the gulf region appears to have escaped the direst predictions of the spring."[11] Over the next several months, further research confirmed that the microbes had eliminated much of the oil and gas that had leaked from the well. As one scientist put it, "The bacteria kicked on more effectively than we expected."[12]

Many uncertainties about the longer-term consequences remain—as to whether a damaging carpet of Macondo oil has settled over the Gulf's floor around the well, the impact on the delicate marshes and wetlands along the coast, and the long-term effect on aquatic life and wildlife. Only time will tell.

THE GOVERNMENT AND THE COMPANY

For many years, 85 percent of the U.S. outer-continental shelf had been closed to drilling. On March 31, 2010, three weeks prior to the accident, President Barack Obama had begun the process of opening areas off the coast of Virginia and in the eastern Gulf for future exploration. The opposition from his own political base was intense. After the accident, these areas were quickly withdrawn and once again put off-limits.[13]

The Obama administration placed a moratorium on all drilling in the Gulf of Mexico. In due course, the moratorium was officially lifted. But it seemed clear that a de facto slow pace was going to prevail for some time, as a result of more thorough reviews and re-reviews, more complex and time-consuming regulation, a slowing-down of decision making, and a possible immobilization of decision making altogether. The Obama administration reorganized the regulatory apparatus for the offshore to avoid any hint of "coziness" between regulators and industry. Safety officials now had to carry their own lunches when they flew a couple of hundred miles out to inspect platforms, and they were prohibited from accepting anything once there, even a bottle of cold water on a hot day.

The accident and its consequences demonstrated that the abilities to explore and produce in the deep water had run ahead of the capacity to deal with a failure of all the safety systems. Under extreme duress, the learning about what to do had been compressed from years into months. Several companies came together in the aftermath to establish, with an initial billion dollars, a nonprofit Marine Well Containment Corporation that would have the skills and tools, in the event of a major accident, to close a well quickly and clean up the spill. Two dozen other companies formed the Helix Well Containment Group, a deepwater containment consortium that can rapidly provide expertise and equipment in the event of an accident. Helix is the company whose equipment was used to actually shut the Macando well.

As to the cause of the accident, the conclusion (as is so often the case in a postmortem on a major accident) is that the cause was not one thing but rather a series of errors, omissions, and coincidences—human judgment, engineering design, mechanical, and operational—all interacting to build to a crescendo of disaster. Were one single incident not to have occurred, there might not have been a disaster.[14]

That was certainly the conclusion of the national commission appointed by President Obama. "The well blew out because a number of separate risk factors, oversights, and outright mistakes combined to overwhelm the safeguards meant to prevent just such an event from happening," it said. The commission continued, "But most of the mistakes and oversights at Macondo can be traced back to a single overarching failure—a failure of management." It added, "A blowout in deep water was not a statistical inevitability." The diagnoses and debate about what had gone wrong—and what could be learned from the experience—will go on for years.[15]

The resource-rich deep waters of the Gulf of Mexico will likely remain one of the main pillars of domestic U.S. energy supply. The offshore oil industry has considerable economic as well as energy significance. In 2010 about 400,000 jobs depended upon the offshore industry just in the four Gulf states of Texas, Louisiana, Mississippi, and Alabama. Moreover, the offshore oil and gas industry could generate as much as a third of a trillion dollars of government revenues in taxes and royalties over a ten-year period.[16]

But the Gulf of Mexico was clearly going to be more quiet and less active, at least for a few years ahead. In response, some of the drilling rigs, the workhorses of exploration, began to leave the Gulf and migrate to other parts of the world that still saw the deep water as one of the great frontiers of world energy.

THE PRESALT: THE NEXT FRONTIER

The most obvious destinations were the other points in the Golden Triangle—West Africa and, more than anything else, Brazil. By this time, Brazil had already leapfrogged ahead of the United States to become the world's largest deepwater producer. "We had to find oil," said José Sergio Gabrielli, the president of Petrobras. "We didn't find any onshore and so we had to go offshore." Today Brazil is on track to become one of the world's major oil producers, exceeding Venezuela, which for almost a century has been the dominant producer in Latin America. The reason is a major advance in capabilities that has opened up a massive new horizon.

The offshore Santos Basin stretches 500 miles, paralleling the southern coast of Brazil. Beneath the seabed is a layer of salt, averaging more than a mile thick. Oil had been produced beneath salt in other areas, including the Gulf of Mexico, but never through so large a section. It was thought that there might be oil below the salt layer in the Santos Basin, but it seemed impossible to do the seismic work—mapping the underground structures—because the salt dispersed the seismic signals so much that they could not be interpreted. "The breakthrough was pure mathematics," said Gabrielli. "We developed the algorithms that enabled us to take out the disturbances and look right through the salt layer."

The first discovery was the Parati field. Petrobras was also drilling with its partners BG and Galp in the Tupi field, the most difficult well the company had ever undertaken. It cost $250 million and went through 6,000 feet of water and then another 15,000 feet under the seabed. It required significant new technologies to cope with the peculiarities of the salt layer, which, like sludge, keeps shifting.

When Guilherme Estrella, Petrobras's head of exploration, reported to the board on the outcome of the well, he began with a long discussion about what had happened 160 million years ago when the continents of Africa and Latin America had pulled apart, depositing the salt above the oil reservoirs, which were already in place and thus became known as the presalt.

"As we listened to him," said Gabrielli, "we thought that Estrella is a great geologist, but that he was dreaming. But then he told us the numbers, and we were thrilled."

That well had discovered a supergiant field—at least 5 billion to 8 billion barrels of recoverable reserves—the biggest discovery since Kashagan in Kazakhstan in 2000. As other wells have been drilled, it has become clear that the presalt in the Santos Basin could be a huge new source of oil. Brazil's then president, Luiz Inácio Lula da Silva, described it as "a second independence for Brazil."[17]

If development proceeds more or less as planned and there are no major disappointments, Brazil could, within a decade and a half, be producing close to six million barrels per day, which would be twice the current output of Venezuela. The investment would be huge—half a trillion dollars or more—but it would catapult Brazil to the top rank among the world's oil producers, making it one of the foundations of world supply in the decades ahead.

FROM FRINGE TO MAINSTREAM: CANADIAN OIL SANDS

In April 2003, a few weeks after the start of the Iraq War, a U.S. Senate hearing convened to examine international energy security issues. The chairman of the foreign relations subcommittee was startled by what he heard. "Something very dramatic has happened that people have not much focused on," said one witness. It was "the first major increase in world oil reserves since the mid-1980s." But it was not in the Middle East. It was often said that Iraq had the second-largest oil reserves in the world. But that was no longer true. Canada had just made an extraordinary upward adjustment in its proven oil reserves—from 5 billion barrels to 180 billion, putting it in the number two position, right after Saudi Arabia.[18]

At first, surprise, even skepticism, greeted the Canadian announcement. But it has come to be generally accepted in the years since. This particular unconventional petroleum resource—Canadian oil sands—also happens to be strategically placed on the doorsteps of the United States.

For many years, oil sands—sometimes called tar sands—had seemed, at best, almost beyond the fringe of practicality and were generally dismissed as of little significance. Yet over the last few years, the oil sands have proved to be the fastest-growing source of new supplies in North America. Their expanding output will push Canada up in the rankings to be the fifth-largest oil-producing country in the world. The significance for the United States is great. If the "oil sands" were an independent country, they would be the largest single source of U.S. crude oil imports.[19]

The oil sands are found primarily in the northern part of the Canadian province of Alberta, including an area known as the Athabasca region. These sands are composed of viscous bitumen embedded in sand and clay. This asphaltlike bitumen, a form of very heavy oil, is a solid that for the most part does not flow like conventional oil. That is what makes its commercial extraction so challenging. But when the weather is warm, a little bit of the bitumen does ooze out of the ground as thick, tarlike liquid. In earlier centuries local Indians would use that seep to caulk their canoes.

In the first decades of the twentieth century, a few scientists intrigued by these seeps, along with promoters lured by the visions of riches, began to make the trek to the Athabasca River in northern Alberta and the isolated outpost of Fort McMurray—a cluster of a dozen log buildings connected to the outside world by mail delivery four times a year, weather permitting. The expeditions found indications that the sprawling swampy lowlands around Fort McMurray were rich in oil sand deposits, but there was no obvious way to extract the resource. In 1925 a chemist at the University of Alberta finally found a solution for separating the bitumen from the sand and clay and getting it to flow—but only in his laboratory. Decades of research failed to overcome the baffling challenge of extracting a liquid oil out of the sands in any commercial way.

But a few refused to give up on the oil sands. One of them was J. Howard Pew, the chairman of Sun Oil, who, as one of his colleagues said, was "enamored of the resource up there." In 1967 Sun launched the first at-scale oil sands project. "No nation can be long secure in this atomic age unless it is amply supplied with petroleum," said Pew. "Oil from the Athabasca area must of necessity play an important role." The sands at what was called the Great Canadian Oil Sands Project were mined, and then treated above ground so as to turn the bitumen into a liquid. But for many years the results from the Great Canadian Oil Sands were anything but great. The venture encountered one engineering problem after another.[20]

In addition to the great technical challenges, the operating conditions were daunting. In the winter, the temperature dropped to –40°F. The swampy terrain, known as muskeg, freezes so hard that a truck can be driven on it. In the spring, it turns into such a swampy bog that a truck can sink so far into it that you lose it.

The business environment was also tough. In the 1970s Canada adopted a highly nationalistic, high-tax national energy policy. It may have reflected the temper of the time, but it was ill suited for a high-risk, multiyear, multibillion-dollar enterprise. Development stalled as companies packed up and went elsewhere to invest.

MEGA-RESOURCE

It was not until the late-1990s that the oil sands finally began to prove themselves as a large-scale commercial resource, facilitated by a crucial tax reform and less-rigid government intervention, and by major advances in technology. The mining process was modernized, expanded in scale, and made more flexible. Fixed conveyer belts were replaced with huge trucks with the biggest tires in the world, and with giant shovels that gather up oil sands and carry them to upgraders that separate out the bitumen. Refining processes then upgrade the bitumen into higher-quality synthetic crude oil, akin to light, sweet crude oil, which can be processed in a conventional refinery into gasoline, diesel, jet fuel, and all the other normal products.

At the same time, a breakthrough introduced an alternative way of producing oil sands—not with mining but rather in situ (Latin for "in place"); that is, with the crucial link in the production chain done in place—underground. This was very significant for many reasons, including the fact that 80 percent of the oil sands resource is too deep for surface mining.

The in situ process uses natural gas to create superhot steam that is injected to heat the bitumen underground. The resulting liquid—a combination of bitumen and hot water—is fluid enough to flow into a well and to the surface. The best-known process is SAGD—for steam-assisted gravity drainage, and pronounced as *"sag-dee."* It has been described as "the single most important development in oil sands technology" in a half century.[21]

Altogether, since 1997, over $120 billion of investment has flowed into Alberta's oil sands, now defined as a "mega-resource." Oil sands production more than doubled from 600,000 barrels per day in 2000 to almost 1.5 million barrels per day in 2010. By 2020 it could double again to 3 mbd—an output that would be higher than the current oil production of either Venezuela or Kuwait. Adding in its conventional output, Canada could reach almost 4 mbd by 2020.

Yet the development of oil sands brings its own challenges. The projects are large industrial developments in relatively remote areas. In terms of new oil development, they are among the highest in cost, especially when competition heats up for both labor and equipment. The offsetting factor is that there is no exploration risk, the resource does not deplete in the way that a conventional oil well does, and the projects will have a very long life.

One environmental challenge arises from the local impacts of mining development, which are visually dramatic. But they are also limited. To date, the entire footprint from mining oil sands is an area that adds up to about 230 square miles of land in a province of Alberta that is about the size of Texas. When part of a surface mine is exhausted, the operators are required to restore the land to its original condition. Mining wastes, a sort of yogurtlike sludge, are deposited in tailing ponds. These toxic ponds, like the rest of the industry, are regulated by the province. Recently the regulatory authorities have required new processes to further reduce the impact of these pools. Altogether the tailing ponds cover an area equivalent to about 66 square miles.[22]

The other significant environmental issue is definitely not local and is also the most controversial. This is greenhouse gas emissions, in particular carbon dioxide (CO_2), associated with the in situ production process. These emissions are higher than the emissions released from the production of the average barrel of oil because of the heat that must be generated underground to get the bitumen to flow.

How much greater is the impact compared with conventional oil? The best way to assess the impact is from a "well to wheels" analysis. That measures the total CO_2 emitted along the entire chain, from the initial production to what is burned in the auto engine and comes out the tailpipe. A range of studies finds that a barrel of oil sands adds about 5 to 15 percent more CO_2 to the atmosphere than an average barrel of oil used in the United States. The reason the difference is so small is that, by far, most of the CO_2 is produced by the combustion in an auto engine and comes out of the tailpipe.[23]

The technologies for producing oil sands continue to evolve, and increasing ingenuity is being applied to shrinking the environmental footprint and reducing the CO_2 emissions in the production process. As the industry grows in scale, it will require wider collaboration on the R&D challenges not only among companies and the province of Alberta but also with Canada's federal government.

Yet the very scale of the resource, and its reliability, puts a premium on its continued evolution of this particular industry. Oil sands are, after all, an enormous resource. For the 175 billion barrels of recoverable oil sands is only 10 percent of the estimated 1.8 trillion barrels of oil sands "in place." The development of the other 90 percent requires further technological progress.

ABOVEGROUND RISKS

The only other concentration of unconventional oil resources in the entire world that rivals Canada's oil sands is the Orinoco belt in the interior of Venezuela.

There, too, the oil is in the form of bitumen embedded in clays and sands. With new technologies and a good deal of investment, the potential output of the Orinoco is huge. Yet what might have been anticipated in terms of supplies from the Orinoco has been much reduced in recent years—not because of limits of the resource itself but because of what has happened aboveground.

May Day, 2007, began in Venezuela with a show of strength. The army swept in to seize oil facilities in the Faja, the Orinoco Oil Belt. This was a prelude to the moment when President Hugo Chávez, dressed in red fatigues, took to the platform in the industrial complex of José to announce to assembled oil workers what was already obvious—he was taking over this vast industrial enterprise. "This is the true nationalization of our natural resources," he proclaimed as jets streaked overhead. To underline the point, behind him hung a giant banner that read, "Full Oil Sovereignty. Road to Socialism." His audience was oil workers who had traded their normal blue helmets for revolutionary-red helmets and had donned red T-shirts celebrating nationalization.

This was one of a long series of steps by Chávez to subordinate the country's political institutions and economy to his Bolivarian Revolution. But the Orinoco was a unique prize. Covering 54,000 square miles and stretching 370 miles, it contains an estimated 513 billion barrels of technically recoverable reserves. But that is far larger than what currently is economically recoverable. And, as in Canada, the overall potential is still that much greater—as much as 1.3 trillion barrels.

The Orinoco's bitumen is very difficult to produce. Like the oil sands in Canada, the extra heavy oil (EHO) of the Orinoco Belt is so heavy and gunky that it cannot easily flow. Limited production began in the 1970s, but was greatly constrained by costs and technology.

To extract significant amounts of resource and then refine it into flowing oil would require a great deal of investment and advanced technology. In the 1990s Venezuela had neither. The Orinoco was too big and complex for the state oil company, PDVSA, to go it alone. The Orinoco became the most high-profile part of the petroleum opening, or *la apertura,* under which in the 1990s Venezuela invited international companies back as partners or service providers.

A half dozen international companies partnered there with PDVSA, investing upwards of $20 billion. They also pushed the technology. Within a decade, the joint ventures had gone from nothing to more than 600,000 barrels a day, with the promise of much more to come.

But with Chávez's Bolivarian Revolution, it was clearly only a matter of time before the Orinoco was taken over. And what better day than May Day to announce, as Chávez did, that the Orinoco had to be nationalized "so we can build Venezuelan socialism." He declared, "We have buried the 'petroleum opening.'" And for good measure, he thundered, "Down with the U.S. empire."

Some of the Western companies remained, but in more subordinate roles. New operators—Vietnamese and Russians, among others—came in. The Venezuelan government held out the objective of tripling the Orinoco's output to 2 million barrels per day by 2013. Others questioned if even current production levels could be maintained, given the financial and technical challenges. After all, oil output elsewhere in Venezuela was already in decline because of lack of investment and loss of managerial talent.

Still, May 1, 2007, was a day of triumph for Chávez. It was a little more uncertain for the workers, who had to listen to his speech for an hour and a half under the hot sun and were unsure about their new owner. "Our bosses made us come," said one worker. "We didn't want to get fired." And, to make sure that everyone showed up, attendance was taken on the buses that ferried them to the speech.

And so there, under that hot sun at the Jose Industrial Complex, was both the spectacle of another victory for the Bolivarian Revolution and its leader, and at the same time, a very visible demonstration, amid one of the world's richest concentrations of resources, of the meaning of aboveground risk—in this case clad in revolutionary red.[24]

MOTHER NATURE'S PRESSURE COOKER

Despite the diversity of the range of unconventional oils, a common theme ties them together. It is all about finding a way to unlock resources whose existence may have long been recognized but for which recovery on a commercial scale had seemed impossible.

Those breakthroughs are yet to happen with what is called oil shale. Oil shale contains high concentrations of the immature precursor to petroleum, kerogen. The kerogen has not yet gone through all the millions of years in Mother Nature's pressure cooker that would turn it into what would be regarded as oil. The estimates for the oil shale resource are enormous: 8 trillion barrels, of which 6 trillion are in the United States, much of it concentrated in the Rocky Mountains. During the gasoline famine of World War I, *National Geographic* predicted that "no man who owns a motor-car will fail to rejoice" because this oil would provide the "supplies of gasoline which can meet any demand that even his children's children for generations to come may make of them. The horseless vehicle's threatened dethronement has been definitely averted." But then early hopes for oil shale were completely buried by its high costs, lack of appropriate technology, and an abundance of conventional oil.

At the end of the oil crisis decade of the 1970s, amid the panic and shock of the Iranian Revolution, a vigorous campaign was launched in Washington, D.C., to create a new industry that would provide 5 million barrels per day of synthetic fuels and, in addition, give the nation "a psychological lift of 'doing something' instead of just doing without." The Carter administration instituted an $88 billion program that would cost many tens of billions of dollars to develop those "synfuels" as the way to ensure energy independence. Oil shale was at the top of the list. Petroleum companies announced major projects. But within a couple of years, the projects were abruptly terminated. The oil shale campaign was done in by the rising surplus of petroleum in the world market, the falling price, and the way in which the costs for developing oil shale were skyrocketing—even without any commercial production having begun.[25]

Yet today a few hardy companies, large and small, are at work on oil shale again. They are still trying to find new and more economic approaches for speeding up nature's time machine and turning kerogen into a commercial fuel without having that several-million-year wait. One line of research parallels the in situ process for oil sands and seeks to heat the kerogen underground.

There are still other types of unconventional oils that may grow in scale and importance over the next few years, notably oil made by processing coal or natural gas. The former is done, notably, in South Africa; and the latter, in Qatar. Both require heavy engineering. But high costs hold back both processes from further significant expansion, at least so far.

TIGHT OIL

The newest breakthrough is opening the prospect of a big new source of oil, something that was not even expected a few years ago. This new resource is often confusingly called "shale oil," which can be totally mixed up with "oil shale," which it is not. Thus, both for clarity's sake and because it is found in other kinds of rocks as well, it is becoming better known as tight oil. People have recognized for a long time that additional oil was locked inside shale and other types of rock. But there was no way to get this oil out—at least not in commercial volumes.

The key was found on the fringes of the industry, in a huge oil formation called the Bakken, which sprawls beneath the Williston Basin across North and South Dakota and Montana and into Saskatchewan and Manitoba in Canada. The Bakken was one of those places where smaller operators drilled wells that delivered just a few barrels a day. By the late 1990s, most people had given up on the Bakken, writing it off as "an economically unattractive resource."[26]

But then the impact of the technology for liberating shale gas—horizontal drilling and hydraulic fracturing—became evident. "As shale gas began to grow, we asked ourselves 'Why not apply it to oil?' " said John Hess, CEO of Hess, one of the leading players in the Bakken. The new technologies worked. Companies rushed to stake out acreage, and a boom in tight oil began to sweep across the Bakken. Production in the Bakken increased dramatically, from less than 10,000 barrels per day in 2005 to more than 400,000 in 2010. In another several years it could be 800,000 barrels per day or even more.[27]

The technique is spreading. Formations similar to the Bakken, with such names as the Eagle Ford in Texas, and Bone Springs in New Mexico, and Three Forks in North Dakota, are becoming hot spots for exploration.

Although still in the early days of tight oil, initial estimates suggest that there might be as much as 20 billion barrels of recoverable tight oil just in the United States. That is like adding one and a half brand-new Alaska North Slopes, without having to go to work in the Arctic north and without having to build a huge new pipeline. Such reserves could potentially be reaching two million barrels per day of additional production in the United States by 2020 that was not even anticipated even half a decade ago. Although there is hardly any calculation of the tight oil resources in the rest of the world, the numbers are likely to be substantial.

What all the unconventional resources have in common is that they are not the traditionally produced onshore flowing oil that has been the industry staple since Colonel Drake drilled his well in Titusville in1859. And they are all expanding the definition of oil to help meet growing global demand. By 2030 these nontraditional liquids could add up to a third of total liquids capacity. By then, however, most of these unconventional oils will have a new name. They will all be called conventional.[28]

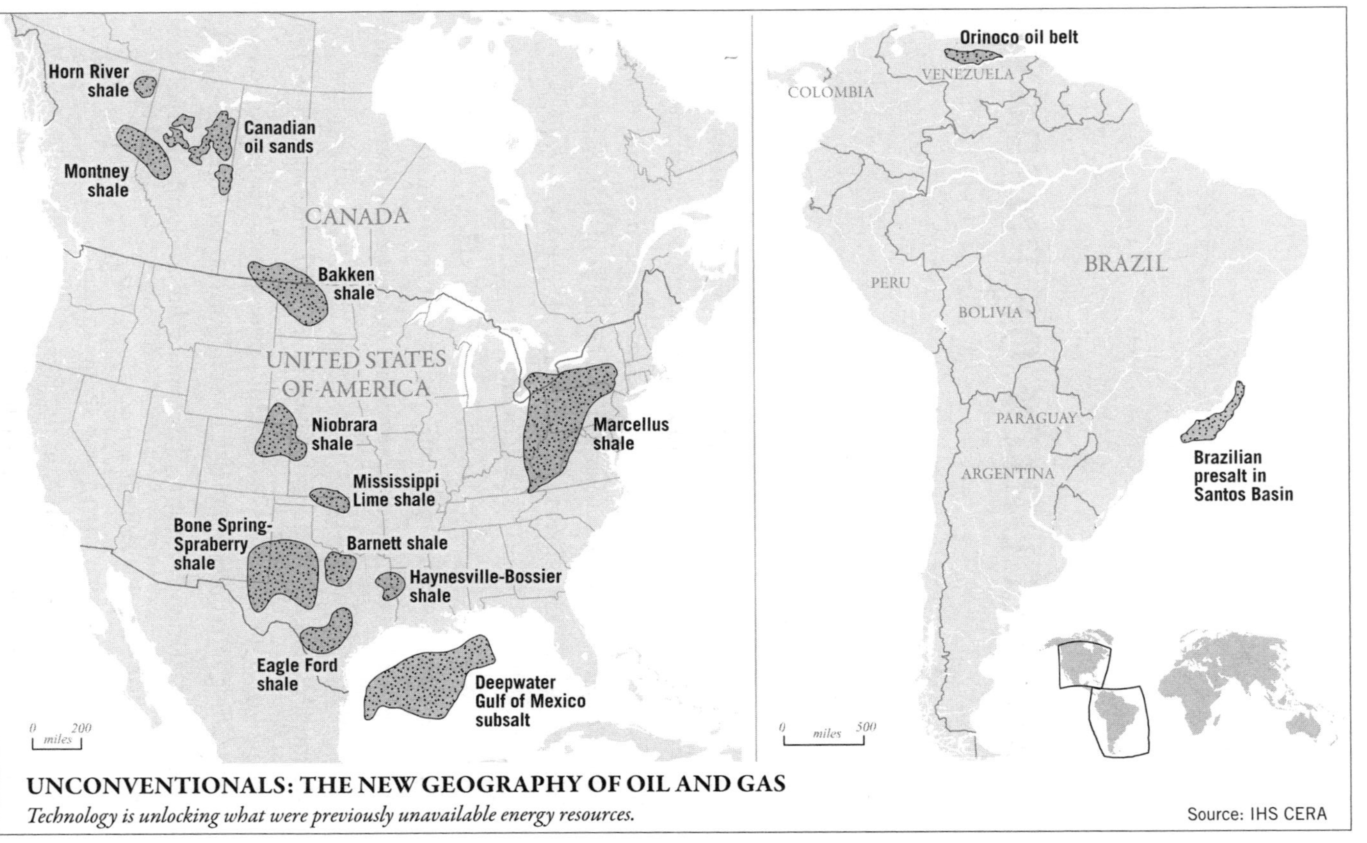

UNCONVENTIONALS: THE NEW GEOGRAPHY OF OIL AND GAS

Technology is unlocking what were previously unavailable energy resources.

Source: IHS CERA

13

THE SECURITY OF ENERGY

Energy security may seem like an abstract concern—certainly important, yet vague, a little hard to pin down. But disruption and turmoil—and the evident risks—demonstrate both its tangibility and how fundamental it is to modern life. Without oil there is virtually no mobility, and without electricity—and energy to generate that electricity—there would be no Internet age.

But the dependence on energy systems, and their growing complexity and reach, all underline the need to understand the risks and requirements of energy security in the twenty-first century. Increasingly, energy trade traverses national borders. Moreover, energy security is not just about countering the wide variety of threats; it is also about the relations among nations, how they interact with each other, and how energy impacts their overall national security.

The interdependence of energy has been a fact of international life for centuries. Beginning in the sixteenth century, the boom in the need for wood—used for shipbuilding and construction but, most important, for domestic heating—led to the integration of Norway and Sweden, and then North America to some degree, into the European economy.[1]

But the point at which energy security became a decisive factor in international relations was a century ago, in the years just preceding the First World War. In 1911 Winston Churchill, then First Lord of the Admiralty, made the historic decision, in his words, to base Britain's "naval supremacy upon oil—that is, to convert the battleships of the Royal Navy from coal to oil." Oil would make the ships of the Royal Navy faster and more flexible than those of Germany's growing navy, giving Britain a critical advantage in the Anglo-German naval race. As Churchill summed it up, switching to oil meant "more gun-power and more speed for less size or cost."[2]

But the move to oil created a new challenge: a daunting problem of supply. While the U.S. Navy was behind the Royal Navy in considering the move from coal to oil for its battleships, it at least could call on large domestic supplies. Britain had no such resources. Conversion meant that the Royal Navy would rely not on coal from Wales, safely within Britain's own borders, but rather on insecure oil supplies that were six thousand miles away by sea—in Persia, now Iran.

Critics argued at the time that it would be dangerous and foolhardy for the Royal Navy to be dependent upon the risky and insecure nation of Persia—what one official called "an old, long-mismanaged estate, ready to be knocked down." That was hardly a country on which to rely for a nation's most vital strategic resource.

Churchill responded with what would become a fundamental touchstone of energy security: diversification of supply. "On no one quality, on no one process, on no one country, on no one route, and on no one field must we be dependent," he told Parliament in July 1913. "Safety and certainty in oil lie in variety and variety alone." That precept has proved itself again and again.[3]

THE RETURN OF ENERGY SECURITY

Since the start of the twenty-first century, a periodically tight oil market and volatile prices have fueled new concern about energy security. Other factors also add to the concern: the instability in some oil-exporting nations, jihadist terrorism, the rebirth of resource nationalism, fears of a scramble for supplies, the costs of imported energy, and geopolitical rivalries. The turmoil that swept over much of North Africa and the Middle East in 2011 disrupted supplies and added a fear premium to the oil price. Underlying everything else is the fundamental need of countries—and the world—for reliable energy with which to power economic growth.

Energy security concerns are not limited to oil. Natural gas was formerly a national or regional fuel. But the development of long-distance pipelines and the growth of liquefied natural gas (LNG) have turned natural gas into much more of a global business. Electric power blackouts in North America—such as the one that shut down the northeast of the United States in 2003—and in Europe and Russia, generate worries about the reliability of electricity supply systems.

Hurricanes Katrina and Rita, which struck the Gulf of Mexico's energy complex in a one-two punch in 2005, created something that the world had not seen, at least in modern times: an integrated energy shock. Everything seemed connected, and everything was down at the same time: oil and natural gas production and undersea pipelines in the Gulf of Mexico, and—onshore—receiving terminals, refineries, natural gas processing plants, long-distance pipelines, and electricity. The storms showed how fundamental was the integrity of the electricity system on which the operation of everything else depended, be it the refineries and communications systems, or the pipelines that take supplies to the rest of the country—or the gas stations, which lacked the electric power to operate their pumps. The huge earthquake and tsunami that struck Japan in 2011 killed more than 15,000 people, devastated a major part of the country, and set off a nuclear accident. It also took down the region's power system, knocking out services, immobilizing communication and transportation, disrupting the economy and global supply chains, and paralyzing efforts to respond to the tragedy.

In China, India, and other developing countries, chronic shortages of electric power demonstrate the costs of unreliability. The Internet and reliance on complex information-technology systems have created a whole new set of vulnerabilities for energy and electric power infrastructure around the world by creating entry paths for those who wish to disrupt those systems.

THE DIMENSIONS

The usual definition of energy security is pretty straightforward: the availability of sufficient supplies at affordable prices. Yet there are several dimensions. First is physical security—protecting the assets, infrastructure, supply chains, and trade routes, and making provision for quick replacements and substitution, when need be. Second, access to energy is critical. This means the ability to develop and acquire energy supplies—physically, contractually, and commercially. Third, energy security is also a system—composed of the national policies and international institutions that are designed to respond in a coordinated way to disruptions, dislocations, and emergencies, as well as helping to maintain the steady flow of supplies. And, finally and crucially, if longer-term in nature, is investment. Energy security requires policies and a business climate that promote investment and development to ensure that adequate supplies and infrastructure will be available, in a timely way, in the future.

Oil-importing countries think in terms of security of supply. Energy-exporting countries turn the question around. They talk of "security of demand" for their oil and gas exports, on which they depend to generate economic growth and a very large share of government revenues—and to maintain social stability. They want to know that the markets will be there, so that they can plan their budgets and justify future levels of investment.

THE LIMITS OF "ENERGY INDEPENDENCE"

In the United States, the issue of energy security often gets framed in terms of energy independence. That phrase has been a political mantra since first articulated by President Richard Nixon in his November 1973 "Project Independence" energy policy speech. Just three weeks earlier, an unthinkable—and yet also foreseeable—event had occurred. The Arab oil exporters, wielding the "oil weapon," had embargoed oil supplies to Western countries in response to the United States' hurried resupply of weapons to a beleaguered Israel, reeling from a surprise attack on Yom Kippur in October 1973. Oil prices were on a trajectory to quadruple. In his speech, Nixon deliberately modeled his Project Independence plan on the goal that his old rival John F. Kennedy had set for the Apollo project in 1961, of "landing a man on the moon and returning him safely to the earth" within ten years. But Nixon sought to outdo Kennedy, pledging in his own speech that the United States would "meet our own energy needs without depending on any foreign energy source"—and do it not in ten years, but in seven.

This bold promise startled his own advisers, for they did not see how it could be achieved. "I cut the reference to 'independence' three times from the drafts," recalled one of his speechwriters, "but it kept being put back in. Finally, I called over, and was told that it came from the Old Man himself."

The phrase not only stayed in the speech but has remained part of the political vocabulary ever since. Every president after Nixon has evoked energy independence as a prime objective. It resonates powerfully with the American public and comes imbued with a nostalgia for a more manageable time when prices were low and the United States really could go it alone. After all, the United States had once been the world's number one oil exporter.[4]

As events have turned out, getting a man on the moon proved easier than making a nation energy independent—or at least oil independent. (In terms of overall energy—including natural gas, coal, nuclear, and renewables—the United States was 78 percent self-sufficient in 2011.) In the almost four decades since Nixon's speech, the United States has gone from importing a third of its oil to importing, on a net basis, to about 60 percent at the peak. In 2011 imports had declined to about 50 percent.

Is energy independence a realistic goal for a country with a $15 trillion economy that is deeply enmeshed in the global economy? Some argue that the term "energy independence" is misconstrued, that it should not be taken as meaning virtually import-free, but rather as connoting "not vulnerable." Generally, however, it is understood to mean self-sufficiency. Yet its promotion, no matter how compelling, can lead to expectations about quick fixes and easy adjustments that are at odds with the realities of the U.S. energy position and the complexity and scale of its energy system. The result can be disappointment and cynicism that, together, drive cycles of inconsistency in energy policy and leave the United States no less vulnerable. Overemphasizing something that is an aspiration, rather than a goal that can be realized in a reasonable time frame, can corrode the international relations that are critical to energy security in an interdependent world. And it runs the risk of diverting attention from the more complex agenda of energy security. But perhaps the imperatives of political communication require the mantra of energy independence. As one senator put it, "Energy independence really means energy security."[5]

STRATEGIC SIGNIFICANCE

The 1973 oil crisis may have provided the proof that the era of energy self-sufficiency for the United States was already over. Yet it seemed that most Americans did not know, at least until the crisis, that the United States imported oil—or they simply did not believe it. Thus, they concluded, the price surge had to be the result of price manipulation by oil companies. Nor did they know that the gas lines in which they waited (and in which they were to wait again in 1979, after the Iranian Revolution) were mainly the result of government price setting and allocations that prevented supplies from getting to the cities where they were needed, and instead sent them to the country-side, where they were not needed. Those gas lines set off a chain reaction of anger, accusations, and rumors of all kinds ("tankers brimming with oil were circling offshore, just beyond the horizon"), multiple congressional hearings, many investigations, acrimonious battles over price controls, and a tumultuous ocean of litigation.

The shock was hardly limited to the United States. The embargo—and the massive disruption that it engendered—created surprise, panic, chaos, shortages, and economic disarray around the world. It generated a mad scramble for oil among companies, traders, and countries. Government ministers climbed on planes and personally scoured the world for petroleum supplies. The shock was further aggravated by what it seemed to portend—a massive shift in the global political and economic balance of power away from the importing countries and the "North" scorned to the exporters and the "South," to what was then known as the Third World.

Among the Western governments themselves, the embargo created enormous strain and antagonism as they struggled to respond, blamed one another, and sought to outmaneuver each other in securing supplies. Some sought special relationships with the exporting countries that would give them what they thought would be privileged access to supplies. Indeed, this was widely regarded as the worst crisis, and the most fractious, to afflict the Western alliance since its foundation after World War II.

The acid spirit of the times was captured during the hurriedly convened

Washington Energy Conference of 1974 when the French foreign minister, angry that the other European countries were cooperating with the United States, greeted his fellow European ministers with *"Bonjour, les traîtres"*—"Hello, traitors."[6]

TOWARD AN INTERNATIONAL REGIME

Yet out of the rancorous Washington energy conference emerged the International Energy Treaty of 1974. It outlined a new energy security system that was meant to deal with disruptions, cope with crises, and avert future bruising competitions that could destroy an alliance. It provided for coordination among industrialized countries in the event of supply interruptions, and encouraged parallelism and collaboration among their energy policies. At the same time, it was meant to serve as a deterrent against any future use of an "oil weapon" by exporters. That system—refined, updated, and broadened in the years since—remains the foundation for energy security today and provides the ballast of confidence during times of uncertainty and danger. At its most basic, this system is meant to keep member nations supplied with energy and the global economy functioning, and thus prevent deep recessions—or worse.

The treaty established the International Energy Agency (IEA) as the main mechanism for meeting these objectives. The IEA was also meant to provide a common front for the industrial countries and thus counterbalance OPEC, the Organization of Petroleum Exporting Countries. OPEC had been founded in 1960 after the major oil companies cut the price of oil, the major source of income for the countries. In the first decade after its founding, OPEC had labored in obscurity. Indeed, it even failed to gain diplomatic recognition from the Swiss and ended up having to move its headquarters from Geneva to Vienna. But at the beginning of the 1970s, with the tightening oil market and rising nationalism, the major oil-exporting countries took control of the world market, and OPEC was their mechanism to do so. So dominant did OPEC appear to be in the mid-1970s that some spoke about an "OPEC Imperium." The IEA was intended to provide a means for the consuming countries to counteract that new imperium.

Now headquartered on the Left Bank in Paris and looking up from its windows toward the Eiffel Tower, the IEA currently numbers 28 industrial countries as members. It provides continued monitoring and analysis of energy markets, policies, technologies, and research. As such it operates as a kind of "energy conscience" for national governments.

EMERGENCY STOCKS

One of the IEA's core responsibilities is to coordinate the emergency sharing of supplies in the event of a loss of supplies. Under the International Energy Treaty, each member is meant to hold strategic oil stockpiles, either government-owned public stocks, such as the Strategic Petroleum Reserve in the United States, or in government-controlled stocks that private companies are required to hold. These stocks can be released on a coordinated basis in the event of a disruption and can be complemented, in a severe disruption, with measures to help temporarily bring down demand. Of course, it is up to national governments to decide whether to implement any of the measures.

Currently, IEA nations have about 1.5 billion barrels of public stocks, of which about 700 million barrels are in the U.S. Strategic Petroleum Reserve. Were Iranian exports to disappear from the market, the 1.5 billion could compensate for the shortfall for more than two years.

The U.S. Strategic Petroleum Reserve (SPR), along with the other IEA stocks, can be thought of as a giant insurance policy. Yet, often enough, when prices rise at the gasoline pumps, so do temptations and calls to "do something"—which means release oil from the SPR in order to bring prices down. That would have the effect of turning the reserve into a de facto tool for price controls. Tempting, for sure, but not the wisest policy.

Releasing oil under those circumstances would prevent price signals from reaching consumers with the message that there is a problem in the marketplace so that they can modulate their consumption. That could make a bad situation get worse. It would also drain oil from the reserves that might be needed in a more serious situation in the future. Hasty use of the SPR could well dissuade friendly producing countries from stepping up their own output because petroleum from the SPR is going to flow into the market. Putting SPR oil into the market might

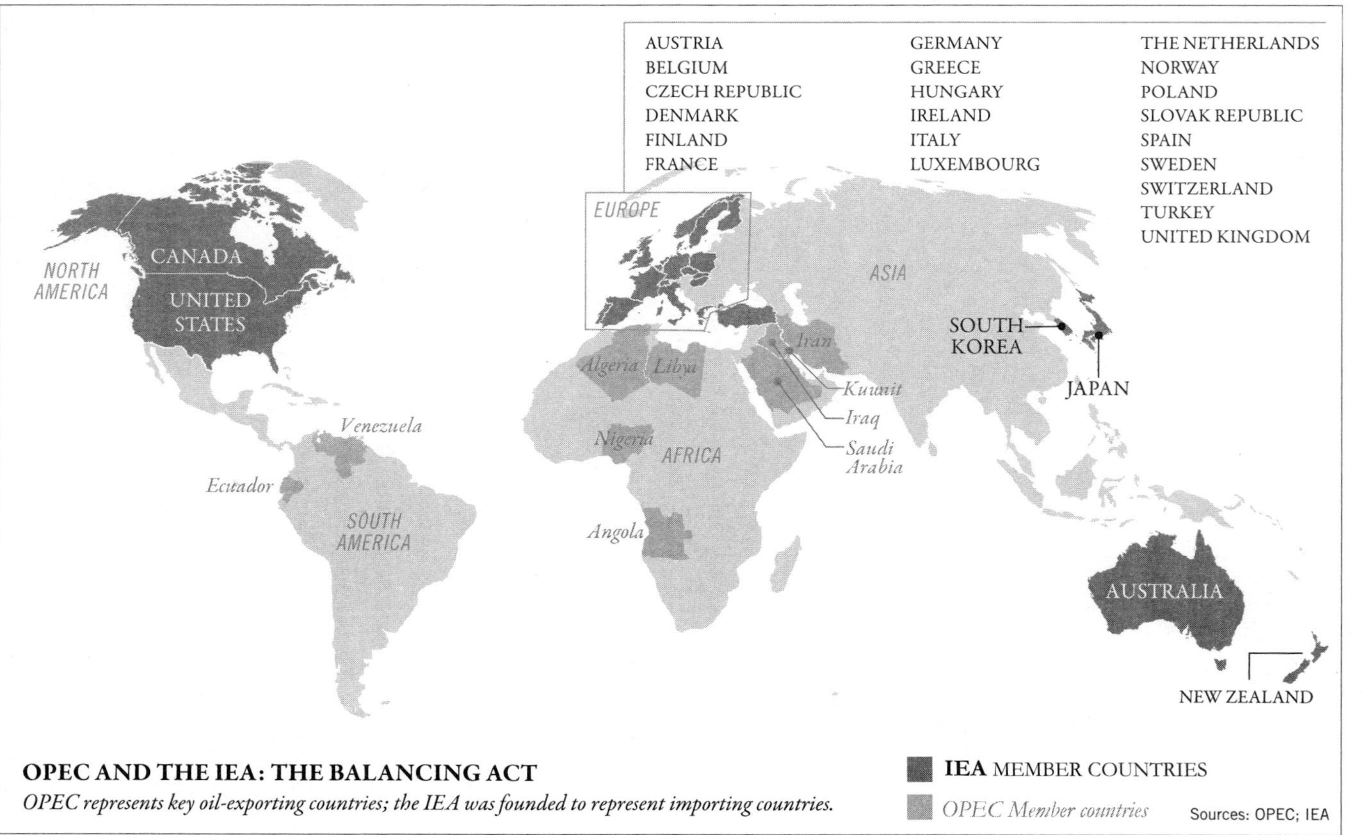

OPEC AND THE IEA: THE BALANCING ACT

OPEC represents key oil-exporting countries; the IEA was founded to represent importing countries.

temporarily send prices down, but then they might bounce right back, raising the question of whether to drain yet more oil from the reserves. Finally, the whole history of price controls does not provide much confidence about how deft government can be at using strategic stocks as a tool of market management.

Decisions about the use of strategic reserves will always require judgment, an evaluation of a wide variety of factors, including the level of commercial inventories, and consultation among consumers and with key producing nations. Ambiguity about its use can help to temper a "sky's the limit" psychology. But the essential point was made by Lawrence Summers, when he was treasury secretary in the Clinton administration, during a White House debate about using the reserves: "The SPR was created to respond to supply disruptions," and not as a means "simply to respond to high prices or a tight market." These stockpiles are an antidote to panic, a source of confidence, and a deterrent to actions that might otherwise interrupt supplies.[7]

Since the system's inception 30 years ago, IEA members have only three times triggered an actual emergency drawdown of strategic stockpiles. The first time was during the Gulf crisis of 1990–91. In January 1991, just before hostilities commenced, the IEA coordinated a release from strategic stockpiles around the world. The other coordinated release occurred in the summer of 2005, to deal with a different kind of disruption—that of Hurricanes Katrina and Rita. One can be sure that the founders of the IEA never contemplated that the emergency sharing system would be used for a disruption in the United States. The third time it was used was 2011, in response to the persisting loss of supply from the Libyan civil war and concern about the impact of high prices on economic recovery.

Over time, the IEA has evolved, and today one of its missions is to help promote dialogues with non-IEA consuming countries and with energy-exporting countries, OPEC and non-OPEC alike. This reflects a larger shift in relations among oil-importing and oil-exporting countries, away from the confrontation of the 1970s to what has become known as consumer-producer dialogue.[8] If the International Energy Treaty was the foundation for the development of a global energy security system, then the development of the producer-consumer dialogue represented the next stage in its development.

The first public step toward a producer-consumer dialogue was a seminar at the Hotel Kleber in Paris in the first two days of July 1991. The Gulf War had ended just a few months earlier. As the October War had set the framework for confrontation, so now the Gulf War had reset the framework and opened the door to dialogue. For in coordination with consumers, OPEC countries had ratcheted up production to compensate for the loss of output from Iraq and Kuwait. (Of course, several of them, led by Saudi Arabia, were also members of the coalition, and protecting Saudi Arabia's oil fields against Iraq was one of the major objectives of the coalition.) This demonstrated what was now perceived as shared interests in energy security and stability in oil markets. After the meeting the French minister of industry reported that the seminar had allowed the delegates to "break certain taboos and even to propose joint projects. The era of confrontation, we hope, is over; dialogue and communication must take its place." Not everyone was ready to break all the taboos. To maintain a certain distance, the U.S. delegation insisted on not sitting at the main table but rather at a sort of little "children's table" off to the side.

Efforts at a dialogue gained momentum, although, initially, somewhat furtively. It took a year to arrange, but in 1994 the head of the IEA went to Vienna to meet with the head of OPEC. Still, it was a secret get-together and it was conducted out of the office, over a private out-of-sight lunch at a Viennese restaurant. That was the beginning of a continuing exchange, in a variety of forums, on everything from energy security, investment regimes, and volatility in oil prices, to the aging of the workforce, carbon capture and storage, and—of some importance—improving the transparency and quality of energy data. The exporting countries had come to hold significant stakes in the growth and health of the global economy, which, after all, is the market for their oil and where much of their sovereign wealth funds are invested. For the consuming countries, lingering taboos dissipated with time. By 2009 the G8 industrial countries were calling upon "both producers and consumers to enhance transparency and strengthen their dialogue" and move "toward a more structured dialogue" among "producing, transit and consuming countries."[9]

The mechanism for this dialogue became the International Energy Forum. One of its missions is to spearhead JODI—the Joint Oil Data Initiative. The objective is to provide a more complete and transparent view of supply and demand and inventories so that world markets can operate on the basis of better information. The countries participating in the forum represent 90 percent of global oil and natural gas production and demand. Both the IEA and OPEC are members.

The producer-consumer dialogue provides a framework for communication; it responds to the interests that both sides have owing to their interdependence in terms of a vital commodity. But it certainly has its limits. The real test is not how it works during a time of stability but during a time of stress. During the price spike of 2008, it provided a mechanism for trying to restore stability to the market. Without it, the spike might have gone even higher, with greater damage to the global economy. The renewed oil market turmoil of 2011 and the sharp division among OPEC exporters—particularly Saudi Arabia versus Iran and Venezuela—showed those limits. Saudi minister Ali Naimi captured that when he described the June 2011 OPEC meeting as "one of the worst meetings we ever had." This was a demonstration that any dialogue really depends on the relationships not among blocs but among specific nations and how they see their interests and the degree to which they can act upon those interests.

OPERATING SYSTEMS

Experience in the decades since the creation of the IEA has highlighted broad principles that underpin the emergency system and inform all of the dimensions of energy security.

The starting point is what Winston Churchill urged a century ago—diversification of supply. Multiplying one's sources of oil, and one's sources of energy, reduces the impact of a disruption by providing alternatives. This should serve the interests not only of consumers but also of those producers for whom stable markets are a long-term concern.

Resilience should be ingrained in the energy system, ensuring a security margin that provides a buffer against shocks and facilitates flexibility and recovery after disruptions. Resilience can include sufficient spare production capacity in oil-exporting countries and, of course, strategic reserves like the SPR. It extends to adequate storage capacity along the supply chain and backup stockpiling of equipment and critical parts for electric power production and distribution, such as transformers for substations. Hurricanes Katrina and Rita and the 2011 Japanese earthquake and tsunami highlight the need to develop plans for recovery from disruptions that devastate large regions.

Overall, the reality of integration needs to be recognized. Only one oil market exists. This market is a complex, worldwide system that moves and consumes almost 90 million barrels of oil every day. Let there be a disruption in one part of the world, and the effects will reverberate throughout the market. Security resides in the stability of this market. Secession from the global market is not an option, except at very great cost.

Experience has consistently demonstrated the importance of high-quality information and data for well-functioning markets and future investment. The Energy Information Administration, an independent arm of the U.S. Department of Energy, and the International Energy Agency, along with the new International Energy Forum, contribute to meeting that need. Access to reliable and timely information becomes particularly urgent in a crisis, when a mixture of actual disruptions, rumors, media imagery, and outright fear stokes panic among consumers. Accusations, acrimony, outrage, the pressures of the news cycle, the dusting off of familiar scripts, and a fevered hunt for conspiracies—all these can obscure the realities of supply and demand, transforming a difficult situation into something much worse. Particularly at such times, governments and the private sector need to collaborate to counter the tendency toward panic and guesswork with the antidote of high-quality, highly timely information.

Markets—large, flexible, and well-functioning energy markets—contribute to security by absorbing shocks and allowing supply and demand to respond more quickly and with much greater ingenuity than is possible within a controlled system. Markets can often more efficiently and effectively—and more quickly—resolve shortfalls and disruptions than more centralized direction.

When troubles do arise and the calls "to do something" grow loud, governments do well to be cautious, to the degree they can, in responding to the short-term political pressures and the temptation to micromanage markets. However well meaning, intervention and controls can backfire, slowing and even preventing the moving around of supplies to mitigate disruptions and speed adjustment.

The gas lines in the 1970s were, as already noted, self-inflicted by rigid government policies—price controls and a heavy-handed federal allocation system that seriously misallocated gasoline. In other words, policy prevented markets from working.

In 2005 the huge disruption to supply resulting from Hurricanes Katrina and Rita seemed destined to create shortages, which—compounded by rumors of price gouging and stations' running out of supplies—could have swiftly generated gas lines. But that is not what happened. In contrast to the 1970s, steps were taken to help markets shift supplies around more quickly and reduce the impact of the crisis.

Instead of adding new regulatory restrictions—two critical ones were eased. Non-U.S.-flagged tankers were permitted to pick up supplies trapped on the Gulf Coast by the nonoperation of pipelines and carry them around Florida to the East Coast. The "boutique gasoline" regulation, requiring different blends of gasolines for different cities, was temporarily lifted to allow the shifting of supplies from cities that were relatively well supplied to cities where there were potential shortages. Overall, the calls for controls were resisted. The markets moved back into balance much sooner, and prices came down much faster, than had been generally expected.

Energy security still needs to be expanded in response to changes in the infrastructure of information technology, the transformation of the world economy itself, and the need to protect the entire supply chain.

CYBERATTACK: "A BAD NEW WORLD"

The sea-lanes are not the only kind of routes that are vulnerable. The threats to energy security loom large in a different kind of geography—cyberspace. In 2010 the U.S. director of national intelligence identified cybersecurity as one of the top threats to the United States. The "information infrastructure," warned his Annual Threat Assessment, is "severely threatened." The assessment added: "We cannot be certain that our cyberspace infrastructure will remain available and reliable during a time of crisis." Since then, one of the authors of the report has said "the situation has become worse." Even those entities that are considered to be the most highly protected, such as financial institutions and sophisticated IT companies, have been subject to successful attacks. After Sony suffered a major cyberattack, its CEO summarized the situation this way: "It's not a brave new world; it's a bad new world."

For obvious reasons, the electric power system is ranked among the most critical of all infrastructures. One report described the vastness of the North American power infrastructure this way: "Distributed across thousands of square miles, three countries, and over complex terrain (from the remote plains and Rocky Mountains to major urban areas), the bulk power system is comprised of over 200,000 miles of high-voltage transmission lines, thousands of generation plants, and millions of digital controls." It is also one of the most complicated to secure. After all, it has been built up over decades. In the 1960s and 1970s, computers were deployed to manage the generation and distribution of electricity and to integrate the grid. In the years since, the system has become more sophisticated and integrated. This makes the system far more efficient, but it also makes it more vulnerable.[10]

The potential marauders may be recreational hackers, who, despite their benign appellation, can do great damage, as can a disaffected employee. They can be cybercriminals, seeking to steal money or intellectual property, or gain commercial advantage, or create situations from which they can profit. They can be governments engaged in espionage or positioning for, or actually conducting, cyberwarfare. Or they can be terrorists or other non-state actors using digital tools to wreak havoc and disrupt their avowed enemies. For all of these, the electric grid is a very obvious target, for its disruption can immobilize a large segment of a country and do great harm.

The tools available to the cyberattacker are extensive. They can mobilize networks of computers to mount a "bot attack" aimed at denial of service, shutting down systems. They can introduce malware—malicious software—that will cause systems to malfunction. Or they can seek, from remote locations, to take control of and disrupt systems.

One point of entry is through the ubiquitous SCADA systems, the supervisory control and data acquisition computer systems that monitor and control every kind of industrial process. Originally, they were site specific, but now they are connected into larger information networks. Malicious intruders may gain access through a thumb drive and a desktop computer. A multitude of new entry points are provided by the proliferation of wireless devices and possibly by the smart meters that are part of the smart grid and that provide two-way communications between homes and the electrical distribution system.[11]

A test at a national laboratory in 2007 showed what happened when a hacker infiltrated an electric system. A SCADA system was used to take control of a diesel generator and cause it to malfunction; it shook and shuddered and banged until it eventually blew itself up in a cloud of smoke. The Stuxnet virus that slipped into the Iranian centrifuges in 2010 caused them to spin out of control until they self-destructed.

It is not just the power system that is at risk. Obviously, other systems—involving energy production, pipelines, and water—share similar vulnerabilities, as do all the major systems across an economy.

In response to this threat, nations are struggling to design the policies to meet this threat. The U.S. Department of Defense has created a Cyber Command. It is also developing a new doctrine in which a major attack on critical infrastructure, including energy, could constitute an "act of war" that would justify military retaliation. The Council of Europe has established a convention on cybersecurity to guide national policies. But these need to be matched by efforts by companies and bolstered with considerable investment and focus. New security architectures have to be introduced into systems that were designed without such security in mind. And they need to be coordinated with other countries. After all, it takes only 135th of a millisecond for an attack to hit a server from anywhere in the world.

Can active defense prevent a cyberattack that seriously damages electricity or some other major energy system, with all the dangerous consequences that can flow from it? Will the risks be properly anticipated and acted upon? Or will the analysis have to wait until a national commission goes back after a "cyber Pearl Harbor" and assesses what went wrong and what was missed—and what could have been done. "In the nineteenth century, steamboats regularly blew up," one study noted, "but Congress waited 40 years until a long series of horrific accidents led to safety regulations." At a recent meeting of 120 experts on cybersecurity, the question was asked: How long before a destructive cyberattack on the country? The consensus answer was bracing: within three years.[12]

BRINGING CHINA AND INDIA "INSIDE"

One of the fundamental reasons for establishing the IEA in the 1970s was to prevent that mad scramble for barrels that had sent prices spiraling upward and threatened to rip apart the Western alliance. It worked, establishing a system for more durable and constructive cooperation. That same kind of approach is needed now with China and India to help ensure that commercial competition does not turn into national rivalries, thus preventing future scrambles that inflame or even rupture relations among nations in times of stress or outright danger. Both China and India have moved from the self-sufficiency and isolation of a few decades ago to integration into the global economy. The energy consumption of both is rising rapidly; in 2009 China became the world's largest energy consumer. Neither China nor India is a member of the IEA, and neither looks likely to become one anytime soon, both because of membership rules and their own interests.

Yet even if they do not join, they can collaborate closely. If they are to engage on energy security, they have to come to the conclusion that their interests can be served and protected in global markets—that the system is not rigged against them and that they will not be disadvantaged compared with other countries in times of stress. And they would have to decide that participation, either formally or informally, with the international energy security system will assure that their interests will be better served in the event of turbulence than going it alone. China, India, and Russia all now have memorandums of understanding with the IEA. Given their growing scale and their importance, their participation is essential for the system to work more effectively.

SECURING THE SUPPLY CHAIN

Energy security needs to be thought of not just in terms of energy supply itself but also in terms of the protection of the entire chain through which supplies move from initial production down to the final consumer. It is an awesome task. For the infrastructure and supply chains were built over many decades without the same emphasis on security as would be the case today. The system

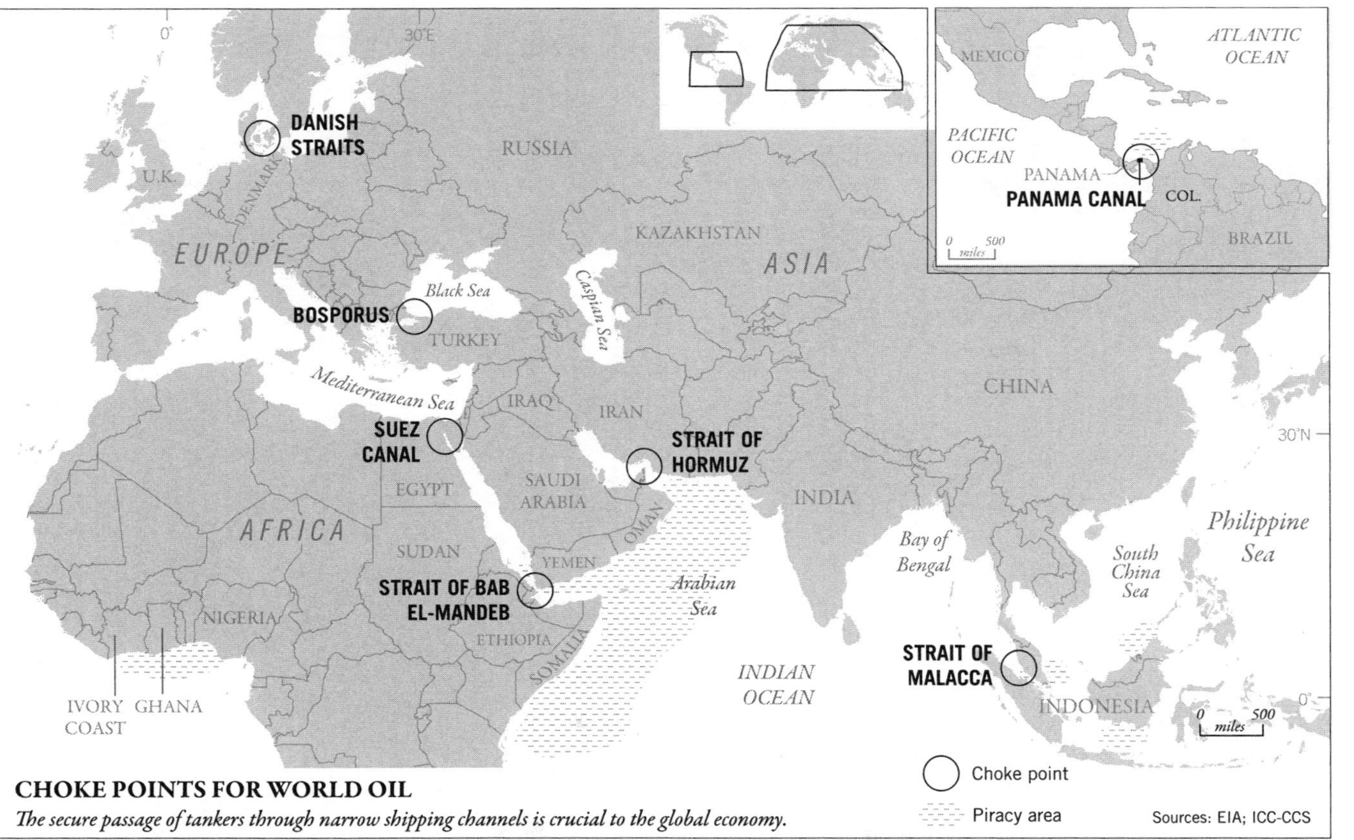

CHOKE POINTS FOR WORLD OIL

The secure passage of tankers through narrow shipping channels is crucial to the global economy.

is vast—electric power plants, refineries, offshore platforms, terminals, ports, pipelines, high-voltage transmission lines, distribution wires, gas storage fields, storage tanks, substations, etc. The vulnerabilities of such extensive infrastructure take many forms, from outright hostile assaults to the kind of small events that can trigger a massive blackout.

As the energy trade becomes more global and crosses more borders and grows in scale on both land and water, the security of the supply chains is more urgent. Ensuring their safety requires increased collaboration among both producers and consumers. Critical choke points along the sea routes create particular vulnerabilities for the transport of oil and LNG, whether from accidents, terrorist attacks, or military conflict.

The best known of these choke points is the Strait of Hormuz, which separates the Persian Gulf (with more than a quarter of world oil production) from the Indian Ocean. Another key point is the Malacca Strait—the five-hundred-mile-long, narrow, and constricted passage between Malaysia and the Indonesian island of Sumatra that funnels in from the Indian Ocean, curves up around Singapore, and then widens out again into the open waters of the South China Sea. At its most narrow, it is only 40 miles in width. About 14 million barrels per day pass through this waterway, as does two thirds of internationally traded LNG—and half of all of world trade. Some 80 percent of Japan's and South Korea's oil and about 40 percent of China's total supply traverse the strait. Pirates prey upon these waters, and there have been reports of terrorist plans to seize an oil tanker and wreak havoc with it.

Another key choke point is the Bosporus Strait—just 19 miles long, a little over two miles at its widest, and a half mile at its most narrow, connecting the Black Sea to the Sea of Marmara and on into the Mediterranean. Every day more than three million barrels per day of Russian and Central Asian oil pass through it, right down through the middle of Istanbul. Two other critical choke points are both in the Middle East: the Bab el-Mandeb Strait, which provides entrance at the bottom of the Red Sea between Yemen and Somalia for up to three million barrels per day, and the hundred-mile-long Suez Canal and Sumed Pipeline, which together connect the top of the Red Sea to the Mediterranean and through which pass about two million barrels per day of oil plus major shipments of LNG. There is also the Panama Canal, with 0.6 million barrels per day.[13]

Recent years have revealed a new risk—or really the return of an old one.

More open ocean waters—the world's ungoverned geographical spaces—have become noticeably more dangerous. The area around the Horn of Africa—the Gulf of Aden, which leads to the Bab el-Mandeb Strait, and the western waters of the Indian Ocean, south of the Arabian Peninsula—has become the arena for pirates operating out of Somalia and neighboring countries. With that has come what has been described as a "radicalization of maritime piracy," as cooperation increases between pirates and terrorist groups. Pirate attacks on shipping, including oil and LNG tankers, seem almost a daily occurrence. Using larger mother ships, the pirates operate as far as a thousand nautical miles from their bases on shore. European, U.S., Russian, Chinese, and Indian naval forces are all now active in those waters seeking to repel and deter pirate attacks.[14]

Because these waters are the main route for the tankers carrying oil and LNG from the Persian Gulf to Europe and North America, and because of the proximity to the Gulf itself, this surge in piracy adds a further dimension to the security concerns for the region that holds well over half of the world's proved oil reserves. The energy security of the region known as the Gulf is truly a global question.

14

SHIFTING SANDS IN THE PERSIAN GULF

Even as the dimensions of energy security have become wider, the world's concerns always seem to circle back to oil, and that means, as it has for so many years, back to the Middle East and the Persian Gulf. The risks today center on terrorism, the stability of societies, and Iran's nuclear program and its drive to dominate the Gulf.

The Gulf countries produce more than a quarter of total world oil output and hold almost 60 percent of proved reserves, making the region of central importance to the world oil market and the global economy. North Africa produces another 5 percent. But over the decades, out of the Gulf and the larger Middle East have come a series of crises that disrupted global oil supply.

The first was the 1956 Suez crisis. Egypt's expropriation of the Suez Canal triggered an invasion by Britain and France—along with Israel, which was threatened by Egyptian military pressure. The closure of the Suez Canal created an oil shortage in Europe. It was relieved by a surge in output from the United States, which at that point had surplus capacity. One consequence of the Suez crisis was to spur a technological advance in the development of larger tankers that could sail around Africa instead of using the canal.

In 1967 Arab oil exporters reacted to Israel's victory in the Six Day War with an oil embargo against the United States, Britain, and West Germany.

However, this embargo failed, owing to what was at the time a large surplus in the world petroleum market. Seven years later, the 1973 embargo responded to the U.S. resupply of Israel following the Yom Kippur surprise attack. In contrast to 1967, the embargo was highly successful, owing to the tight market. It triggered a fourfold increase in the price of oil. The embargo, combined with the price increases, shook the structure of international relations and sent shock waves through the global economy, followed by several years of poor economic performance. The 1978–79 Iranian Revolution, which toppled the shah and ushered in the theocratic Islamic Republic, also ignited a worldwide panic in the petroleum market and another oil shock that contributed mightily to the difficult economic years of the early 1980s.

Saddam Hussein's 1990 invasion of Kuwait set off the Gulf crisis, leading to the loss of five million barrels a day of supply from Iraq and Kuwait. Other producers, notably Saudi Arabia, cranked up output and largely replaced the missing barrels over the next several months, even before Operation Desert Storm evicted Saddam's forces from Kuwait. It was in anticipation of that military operation that the International Energy Agency organized the first-ever coordinated release of strategic stocks.

For more than a decade thereafter, there were no petroleum disruptions in the region. Then the 2003 invasion of Iraq shut down its oil industry. Production resumed, though erratically. The reduced output from Iraq was part of the aggregate disruption that contributed to the price spike of 2008.

All this transpired over the course of a half century in the region that is the breadbasket of world oil production.

The unique energy position of the Gulf is the product of a peculiar geologic history that has made it the most prolific hydrocarbon basin on the planet. Over hundreds of millions of years ago, what is now much of the Arabian Peninsula and the Persian Gulf basin was submerged beneath a vast, shallow sea. The recurrent expansion and shrinking of this sea created excellent conditions for the deposit of organic material in successive layers of sediment. During the times when the sea receded, the land was not a desert but a warm and humid jungle. Temperatures much hotter than they are today encouraged lush growth, which added to the organic sediments. Pressure and heat turned this organic material into hydrocarbons—oil and gas. The shifts in the earth's crust and the clash of tectonic plates, on a geological time scale, created huge structures for trapping these hydrocarbon deposits. And it was in those structures that in the twentieth century the drill bit found the extraordinary accumulations of oil and gas that define the modern Persian Gulf.

"THE CENTER OF GRAVITY OF WORLD OIL"

In 1943, in the middle of World War II, the Roosevelt administration dispatched Everette Lee DeGolyer to the Persian Gulf to assess the petroleum potential of the region. DeGolyer was America's preeminent geologist; he had made the discovery in 1910 that opened up Mexico as a great oil producer, and in the 1920s he did more than anyone else to promote the introduction of seismic technology.

Oil had originally been discovered in Iran in 1908; then in Iraq, in 1927; then in Bahrain, in 1932. Still, some were skeptical of what might be found in Saudi Arabia. In 1926 the senior management of one petroleum company decided that Saudi Arabia was "devoid of all prospects" of oil and that big reserves would most likely be found in Albania. In the 1930s, after several years of disappointment and dry holes, even the companies exploring in Saudi Arabia debated "whether the venture should be abandoned" and "written off as a total loss." But then came the transformative discoveries—Anglo-Persian (later BP) and Gulf Oil hit petroleum in Kuwait, at a well called Burgan Number One, in February 1938. The next month, Chevron and Texaco did the same in Saudi Arabia, with Dammam Number Seven. Although many of the wells were capped and operations suspended during World War II, some people, including DeGolyer, suspected that these discoveries might rewrite the geopolitics of world oil. "It is uncertain," he wrote his wife as he embarked on the trip, "and a little bit hazardous." Yet "it seemed pretty important," he added, "for some American to make this trip and size up the situation."

The survey confirmed DeGolyer's conviction about the scale of the resource. "The center of gravity of world oil production," he reported at the end of his mission, "is shifting from the Gulf-Carribean area to the Middle East—to the Persian Gulf area." Another member of DeGolyer's team summed it up more simply: "The oil in this region is the greatest single prize in all history."[1]

ONE QUARTER OF WORLD RESERVES

The decades that followed proved these predictions on a massive scale. On the western side of the Gulf, towering over all the other exporters, is Saudi Arabia, with about a fifth of the world's proven oil reserves. Its output averaged 8.2 million barrels per day in 2010—almost 10 percent of total world production. It has the capacity to produce to 12.5 million barrels per day. It also has the great advantage of having the lowest production costs in the world. Although in recent years, Saudi Arabia's costs for exploration and production have risen, they are still well below those of most other regions in the world.

As a matter of ongoing policy, Saudi Arabia maintains a cushion of 1.5 to 2 mbd of spare capacity that can be brought quickly into production. That extra capacity is meant to be a stabilizer—or what Saudi petroleum minister Ali Al-Naimi calls an "insurance policy"—to counteract "unforeseen supply disruptions" in the global oil market, such as "wars, strikes, and natural disasters." It is the producer's analogy to a Strategic Petroleum Reserve.[2]

Almost the country's entire industry is operated by the state-owned Saudi Aramco, by far the world's largest oil company. Saudi Aramco, which took over operations from the consortium of U.S. companies that had developed the oil industry prior to nationalization, has established itself at the forefront in terms of its technical capability and in its capacity to execute large-scale, complex projects.

Saudi Aramco still has a substantial portfolio of untapped fields and reservoirs, with over 100 fields that contain nearly 370 reservoirs. It produces from only 19 of the fields, albeit the largest and most productive among the discovered fields, the largest of which is Ghawar. The development of three new mega-projects—Shaybah, Khurais, and Manifa—is adding over 2.5 million barrels a day of capacity, which just by itself would rank as a major OPEC exporter. The application of new technologies continues to unlock resources and open up new horizons. The part of Saudi Arabia that is heavily explored is relatively small. The company has committed close to $100 billion for investment in the oil sector for the five-year period, 2011–15, including new exploration in the northeast of the country and the Red Sea, aimed at increasing its oil and gas reserves.

THE GULF

Sixty percent of conventional oil reserves are located in the Gulf.

The other major Arab producers are strung out along the western shore of the Persian Gulf. But Kuwait and Abu Dhabi, which is the largest member of the United Arab Emirates, each produce about 2.3 million barrels per day; Qatar pumps 0.8 mbd. Oil and gas have given these countries the wherewithal to play a major role in the world economy well beyond hydrocarbons. Significant amounts of their export earnings go into their sovereign wealth funds, which have become among the largest pools of capital in the world. Lesser amounts of oil are produced by Dubai and Bahrain and, on the southern end of the Arabian Peninsula, Oman and Yemen. Algeria and Libya are the main producers in North Africa.

THE "HINGES" OF THE WORLD ECONOMY

Al Qaeda has targeted what it has called the "hinges" of the world's economy—its critical infrastructure. However, when Al Qaeda first emerged in the 1990s, energy systems, specifically, were not targets. In his 1996 statement, "Declaration of War Against the Americans Occupying the Land of the Two Holy Places," Osama bin Laden argued against attacking oil infrastructure in the Middle East, which, he said, embodied "great Islamic wealth" that would be needed "for the soon-to-be-established Islamic state." The attacks that did take place were aimed at foreign interests.

Then a new jihadist work appeared in 2004 that called for a change in strategy. Titled "The Laws of Targeting Petroleum-Related Interests and a Review of the Laws Pertaining to the Economic Jihad," it proclaimed the oil industry a legitimate target so long as certain "rules" were followed. Long-term oil production capability should not be damaged. That needed to be preserved for the Islamic caliphate. But it advocated conducting operations that would drive up the price of oil, thus hurting Western countries.

Several months later Bin Laden, embracing this new doctrine, urged attacks on oil targets as part of an economic jihad against the United States. He cited the war in Afghanistan, which had "bled Russia for 10 years until it went bankrupt and was forced to withdraw from Afghanistan in defeat" and called for the same kind of policy "to make the US bleed profusely to the point of bankruptcy." He later declared that the West sought to dominate the Middle East in order to steal oil and urged his adherents "to give everything you can to stop the greatest theft of oil in history." He called for terror attacks that would drive oil to $100 a barrel with the aim of bankrupting the United States. In 2005 Ayman al-Zawahiri, Bin Laden's deputy, declared that the mujahedeen should "focus their attacks on the stolen oil of the Muslims," in order to "save this resource" for the time when an Al Qaeda caliphate would rule the Arabian Peninsula.

A raid in September 2005 on a safe house near the largest Saudi oil field discovered the practical tools for this new doctrine: charts and maps for the oil infrastructure not only of Saudi Arabia but of the other Gulf Arab oil producers as well. The Saudis were taken aback by how detailed the information was.[3]

A CRITICAL NODE

On a Friday in February 2006, shortly after afternoon prayers, three vehicles—a Toyota Land Cruiser SUV and two pickup trucks—made their way toward a little-used service gate at the vast Abqaiq processing plant, 60 miles from Saudi Arabia's largest oil field. Abqaiq is one of the most critical nodes in the global supply system. Up to 7 million barrels of oil—8 percent of total world supply—pass through this sprawling industrial facility every day.

Once at the gate, the gunmen jumped from the Land Cruiser and started shooting, killing the guards, while the two pickups rammed through the fence and into the Abqaiq facility. One of the pickup drivers apparently took a wrong turn and ended up in the dead end of a parking lot. His engine, leaking oil, stalled. At that point, with nowhere to go, the driver detonated his bomb, committing suicide and destroying his vehicle. Meanwhile, the second pickup driver, trying to outrun pursuing security guards, was barreling down the road so fast that, by the time he detonated his bomb, killing himself, he had already driven past his target, and the resulting explosion did no damage to the facilities.

But the shooters escaped in the Land Cruiser and raced back to Riyadh, where they holed up in a small compound in the eastern part of the city. Police kept them under surveillance for a few days and then moved in. In the ensuing shoot-out, the jihadists were killed. One of them, it was discovered, was among the most wanted terrorists in Saudi Arabia. Inside the compound, the authorities found a trove of terrorist tools.

The Abqaiq facility is so big and spread out that even if the suicide drivers had been more adept, the damage would have been localized. Moreover, the Saudis maintain several levels of security at Abqaiq and other sensitive installations. Nevertheless, the attempt demonstrated the intent of the jihadists. In the aftermath of the Abqaiq attack, the Saudi government moved to further enhance security, including the creation of a new 35,000-man force specifically charged with protecting the kingdom's oil infrastructure. In the years since, the jihadists further codified their doctrine of economic warfare. This was most obvious in the constant attacks on the oil infrastructure in Iraq. In 2008 an Arabian affiliate of Al Qaeda reiterated the call for attacks on the oil infrastructure. In July 2010 a suicide bomber in a small skiff, apparently taking off from an isolated part of Oman's coast, rammed into a large Japanese oil tanker. Though little damage was done, it was the first such attack inside the strait itself.

For their part, the Arab oil-exporting countries along the Gulf have, in general, substantially deepened security, hardened targets, and much honed their intelligence operations. "The terrorists have begun to focus on disrupting our energy infrastructure," Petroleum Minister Ali Al-Naimi said after the attempt at Abqaiq. "The threat from terrorists to the world's energy infrastructure is not limited to any one country or region. We must all be vigilant."[4]

In May 2011, Osama bin Laden was killed by U.S. Navy Seals in a villa in Pakistan. He had lived there, hidden with no Internet connection, for several years, just 35 miles from Islamabad, Pakistan's capital. His communications with Al Qaeda were by couriers. Among the materials seized in the raid were plans for attacking oil tankers.

THE SOCIAL FOUNDATIONS

In December of 2010, Mohammed Bouazizi, a young fruit vendor in the Tunisian town of Sidi Bouzid, reached the breaking point. For years, the police had been harassing him and stealing his fruit, along with that of the other vendors in the fruit market on the main street. When he tried to stop a policewoman from stealing two baskets of apples, two other policemen held him down while the policewoman slapped him. He went to the city hall to complain but was told to go away. He did leave but returned shortly after and, standing in front of the municipal building, set himself ablaze. He died a few weeks later in the local hospital.[5]

But footage of protests over his fate and the way he had been treated was quickly posted on Facebook. The government did not know how to block the footage. Bouazizi's self-immolation set off a blaze that burned across the Middle East, shaking the political order and bringing down part of the geostrategic structure of the region.

Bouazizi's plight was the match that ignited the kindling whose accumulation had been building up for years: A huge bulge in the number of young people for whom educational options were limited and for whom there were no jobs, no prospects, no economic opportunity; pervasive corruption, lack of political participation, overwhelming and inefficient bureaucracies, and low quality of government services; a "freedom deficit" and a "women's empowerment deficit"; arbitrary political power, secret police, and permanent "states of emergencies"; economic stagnation and enormous obstacles to entrepreneurship and initiative.[6]

All these were the factors that set in motion what has been called the "Arab Spring" among young people who had also reached the breaking point. It quickly gained momentum. Massive street demonstrations toppled the long-ruling government in Tunisia.

The protest movement spread to Egypt, where, day after day, hundreds of thousands of people packed into Tahrir Square in Cairo to demand the resignation of President Hosni Mubarak, who had ruled Egypt for 30 years. All of this played out on television and the Internet. The Arab world was transfixed, for Egypt plays a unique role in the region. It is a quarter of the total Arab population, and its influence reaches throughout the area. As one Saudi said, "We were all taught by Egyptians." It had also signed a treaty with Israel, and a kind of cold peace existed between those two former belligerents. Egypt's size—and the scale of its armed forces—make it the foundation of the geostrategic balance of the region. Finally, on February 11, 2011, Mubarak gave up power. The nature of Egypt's future government would have great significance for the entire Middle East.

The events in North Africa triggered protests and demonstrations across much of the Middle East. Syria was racked by constant protests against the Assad government, which were met with bullets. Three countries of particular significance to the Gulf were Iran, Bahrain, and Yemen. Iran used whatever force was necessary to put down demonstrations. In Bahrain, the longtime tense relationship between the Sunni elite and the majority Shiite population make it a proxy for contention between Saudi Arabia and Iran. It is a very small country in terms of population but it is only a couple of dozen miles by causeway from Saudi Arabia and the world's largest oil field. It is also the home of the U.S. Fifth Fleet, the mission of which is to maintain freedom of the seas in the Gulf. When protests turned into protracted violence, the Gulf Cooperation Council, led by Saudi Arabia, sent troops into Bahrain to help restore order.

Yemen was particularly vulnerable because of its strong tribal tensions and regional splits, the 33-year rule of the autocratic Ali Abdullah Saleh, its low per capita incomes, and what is thought to be the strongest Al Qaeda affiliate. Adding to the significance of what happens to Yemen is its position on the narrow Bab el-Mandab choke point, the entrance into the Red Sea, and its rugged 1,100-mile border with Saudi Arabia. The specter of chaos and violence in Yemen leads some Saudis to talk about the threat of having "our Afghanistan" on its frontier.

Altogether, unfolding events throughout the region had demonstrated that social instability had become a critical factor for energy security. In Libya protests turned quickly into a civil war that divided the country between rebels in the east and Ghaddaffi forces in the west. As Ghaddaffi's forces advanced on Benghazi and what seemed likely to be a bloodbath, the Arab League called for a no-fly zone, and U.S. and European forces, operating under U.N. and NATO authorization, intervened on the side of the rebels.

By March of 2011, virtually all of Libya's oil production was disrupted, removing about 1.5 percent of supplies from the market. But that, combined with rising demand, started to narrow once again spare capacity. As unrest and turmoil continued in the Middle East, anxiety rose about the potential for further disruptions to supply. Oil prices surged once again both on the actual disruption and on fear of "what would happen next," taking the Brent price at least for a time, toward $130 a barrel. The rising oil prices were now seen as the biggest risk to global economic recovery. And, as long as there was uncertainty about the Middle East, oil prices would reflect the risk premium. Thus, the social foundations and the now uncertain geostrategic balance of the region would prove to be crucial in the formation of world oil prices, which in turn would have much wider impact.

Yet there is no single answer to how the uncertainty will be resolved. The differences among the countries in the region are very great. Egypt, like Iran, has about 80 million people, and per capita income in Egypt is about $5,800 a year. By contrast, many of the key oil producers have small populations; depend on a large number of expatriates to make their economies work; and are, in effect, cradle-to-grave welfare states with high per capita incomes.

What all the countries share, whatever their differences, is an enormous youth bulge. About a third of the population in the region is between the ages of ten and twenty-four. Historians have observed, going back to the European revolutions of 1848, the link between such bulges and turmoil and upheaval. In addition, what these countries lack is jobs, especially for frustrated and educated young people. Unemployment may range as high as 30 percent, and many of those who are not unemployed are underemployed. In addition to disappointed expectations and economic difficulties, the mass lack of employment feeds smoldering resentment against the governing system for all the reasons already noted.[7]

What made the critical difference was the galvanizing power of new communications technologies, which eroded the control of information that is so essential to authoritarian regimes. The development of Arab satellite networks, beginning in the 1990s, was already bringing both views of the outside world and domestic news that was not censored by the ministries of information. For many, these networks became the most important source for news. But then cell phones and the Internet—in particular e-mail, Facebook, and Twitter—provided a way to share information, mobilize for action, and outwit the traditional instruments of control. Lack of political participation was offset by participation through these new channels, as social networks came to challenge the traditional prerogatives of national sovereignty.[8]

It has been recognized for years that creating opportunity and jobs is a challenge in much of the Middle East, owing both to rapid population growth and the nature of the economies. This need has now gone from chronic to acute. But industries like oil and gas and petrochemicals are capital intensive; that is, they create good jobs but not a lot of jobs. This is where countries face the

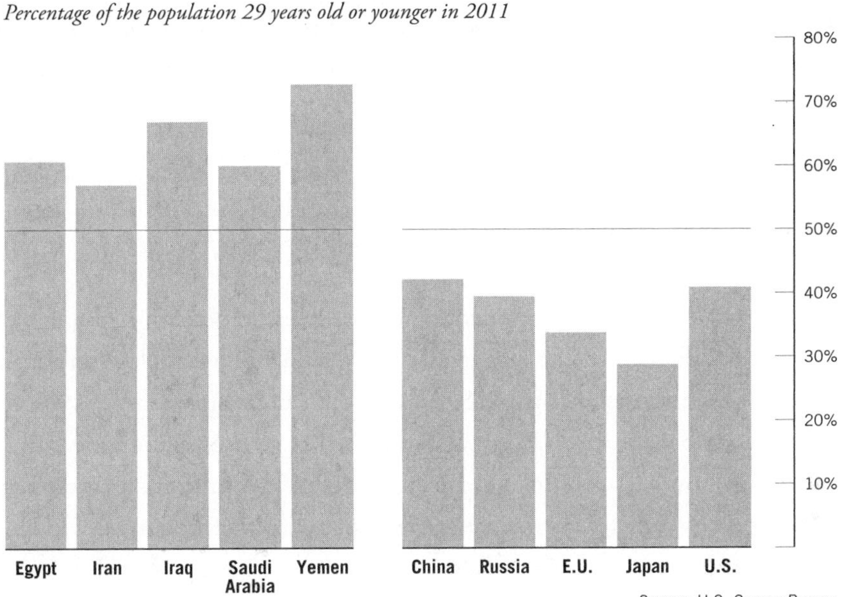

risk of the resource curse and the structural problems of the petro-state. That applies even to the wealthy petro-state that can provide cradle-to-grave welfare. These industries are so big and so dominant that an entrepreneurial economy gets squeezed out. Subsidies can ease the tensions, but they are not a substitute for job creation.

But jobs, on a large scale, cannot be created overnight. That takes both higher economic growth rates and time, along with openness, stimulation of entrepreneurship, reduced regulation and control, and dampening down of corruption. China and the other countries of East Asia have created jobs by intensively integrating with the global economy. Taiwan and South Korea were at the same stage of development as Egypt in the 1960s. Now Taiwan and South Korea export more to the world economy in two days than Egypt does in a year. But opening to the world economy brings with it the forces and values of globalization, which in the Middle East are seen as threatening and are resisted, sometimes fiercely, and often with religious exclusions. This stagnation leaves the young—especially young men—with no jobs and often no spouses, no homes of their own, alienated, and nowhere to go.[9] The potential of political participation brings the possibility of moving beyond stagnation. But the expectations for economic improvement are way ahead of how fast economies can actually change and generate opportunity. So the hopes and optimism of the Arab Awakening will have to contend with the disillusionment that comes with the uncertain pace of economic improvement.

IRAQ'S POTENTIAL

For decades, Iraq's potential to rank among the very top producers has been recognized—along with the fact that it was producing well below its potential. By 2009, six years after the U.S.-led invasion, and a after years of violence and sabotage, output was almost back to the 2001 level of 2.5 million barrels per day. The postwar government realized that it needed enormous investment and technology transfer from outside the country, and starting in 2009 it held bidding rounds for a number of fields. As would have been expected, the winners included oil companies from all over the world. Surprisingly, however, U.S. companies were notably underrepresented. Iraq was asking among the stiffest terms of any oil-exporting country, and a number of the U.S. companies could not make the economics work.[10]

Some of the projections bruited about for Iraqi output are exceedingly optimistic. To make the leap from 2.5 million or 3 million barrels per day to 12 million barrels a day, as one Iraqi minister had suggested, seems almost impossible. Much more reasonable is that by 2020 Iraq could be around 6.5 million barrels per day.

Yet even that lower target faces considerable obstacles and uncertainties: Development on such a scale requires political stability and physical security for the oil fields and pipelines and loading terminals. There needs to be a political consensus about the need for international investment and the fiscal terms so that the whole effort is not undone by subsequent changes in the rules of the game. These risks are further compounded by the sheer logistical complexity of delivering people, services, skills, and equipment—and the building of pipelines and export facilities—in a country that was technologically shut off from the global industry for decades. The companies that are investing recognize these risks. But they also see the potential and have concluded that it would be too risky to find themselves sidetracked from what may be one of the biggest oil opportunities of the twenty-first century.[11]

One further obstacle could well stand in the way of the steady development of Iraq's resources: Iran. And that may be the most important of all. Iran regards any substantial expansion in Iraqi output as a threat because that could lead to lower oil prices. From a geopolitical point of view, Iran does not want Iraq to supplant it as the second-largest producer in the Gulf and in OPEC. Tehran made this clear in 2010 when Iraq decided, based upon the bids and new exploration, to raise its estimated oil reserves from 115 billion barrels to 143 billion. Iran waited hardly a week to leapfrog back over Iraq, lifting its own reserve estimates from 138 billion to 150 billion barrels.[12]

The longer-run question is to what extent Baghdad will come under the lasting sway of Tehran. Although Iraq is at least 75 percent Arab, and Iran is primarily Persian and Azeri, religion and religious authority tie Shia Iran together with the majority Shia population of Iraq. Since 2003 Iran's deep involvement in Iraq, and its support of various groups, has not been a secret. Moreover, geography is inescapable. As one Iranian official told a U.S. diplomat, "Eventually, you will have to leave Iraq. But we're not going away."

SEEKING HEGEMONY

For decades, under the rule of the shah, Iran had competed with Saudi Arabia to be the dominant oil producer in the Gulf. In the 1970s Iran tried to do more—to take on the role of "regional policeman" of the Gulf and fill the security vacuum created by the withdrawal of the British military umbrella from the region in 1971. The ambitions were suspended by the Iranian Revolution of 1978–79 and then by the eight-year Iran-Iraq War.

Iran's oil production had peaked under the shah at six million barrels per day; it plummeted to as low as 1.3 million barrels per day during the Iran-Iraq War, and in recent years it has fluctuated around four million barrels per day. But given the country's petroleum reserves, the Iranian industry also produces well below its potential. It has been hamstrung by a host of factors: political battles among the factions ruling the country; lack of investment; the tough and painful way in which Iran negotiates with international companies; and, in more recent years, international sanctions that have sharply reduced its access to technology and finance. All this has hampered the development of the industry. Moreover, it has to import about 25 percent of its gasoline to make up for a shortage of refining capacity at home.

While Iran has the second largest conventional natural gas reserves in the world and is a founding member of the newly formed Organization of Gas Exporting Countries, it exports negligible quantities of gas, and only to immediate neighbors. In fact, it actually has to import some gas to make up for its domestic shortfall.

"THE GREAT SATAN"

In the first months of the Iranian Revolution in 1979, it was not clear whether the new regime would be reformist or fundamentalist. But the path was clearly set when militants stormed the U.S. Embassy in November 1979 and took 66 U.S. diplomats hostage, holding them until January 1981. The country's new leader was the stern cleric Ayotollah Ruhollah Khomeini, who had returned to Iran after 15 years of exile. Khomeini and his followers used the seizure of the hostages—and the immediate cleavage it created with the United States—to consolidate power and eliminate effective opposition to the new theocratic fundamentalist regime. At one point, in a "letter to clergy," Khomeini wrote, "When theology meant no interference in politics, stupidity became a virtue." In the new Iran, ultimate political power lay in the hands of mullahs and, specifically, the Supreme Leader, Ayatollah Khomeini.[13]

Khomeini's hatred for the shah, who had exiled him in 1963, was matched by his hatred for Israel, and for the United States. America as the implacable enemy—the "Great Satan"—became one of the organizing principles of the Islamic Republic and indeed a backbone of its legitimacy, critical to holding together the apparatus of control. The U.S. support for the 1953 coup that toppled the nationalist prime minister Mohammad Mossadegh and brought back the shah was a powerful historical memory that the fundamentalists could manipulate, and that story became part of the catechism of Iranian politics.

In the early 1990s, with the war with Iraq over, Iran resumed its revolutionary campaign. It stepped up its efforts to subvert other regimes along the Persian Gulf, fostered terrorism, targeted U.S. interests, and embarked on a military buildup. The hand of its clandestine Qods forces, the international arm of the Revolutionary Guards, could be seen in terrorism around the world. By 1993 Iran had earned the sobriquet of "the most dangerous sponsor of state terrorism."[14]

NORMALIZATION?

Khomeini died in 1989. He was succeeded as Supreme Leader by one of his acolytes, Ali Khamenei, who had been president for eight years and who embraced the hard line of his predecessor.

Yet at various moments, glimmers of normalization appeared. The market-oriented president Hashemi Rafsanjani thought that a reduction in tensions with the United States was in Iranian interests and that commercial relations was the way to begin. That seemed to accord with the Clinton administration's new policy of using economic engagement to improve relations with adversaries. Tehran sought to communicate its signal through oil. Iran deliberately awarded the first contract to a foreign company since the revolution not to a French oil company, but to an American one—Conoco.

Under U.S. sanctions policy, no Iranian oil could be imported into the United States, but it was legal for an American oil company to do business in Iran. For three years Conoco had been negotiating with Iran for rights to develop two offshore oil and gas fields. The two sides finally signed the deal on March 5, 1995, in the dining room of a government guesthouse that had formerly belonged to a Japanese auto company. In factionalized Iranian politics, a deal with an American company was a considerable victory for Rafsanjani. The contract could not have been signed without the approval of the Supreme Leader, Ayatollah Ali Khamenei. But that approval must have been very reluctantly given. For Khamenei deeply hated what he called the "Great Arrogance"—the United States—which he declared wanted to impose its "global dictatorship" on Iran. In his worldview, as he once said, that "enmity with the United States" was essential to the survival of the regime.[15]

The internal struggle within the Iranian leadership may well be why Conoco did not know, almost to the last moment, whether it would win the contract.

The competitor, the French company Total, was told that Iran had chosen an American company to send a "big message."[16]

Conoco executives had briefed State Department officials a couple of dozen times over the course of its negotiations with Iran, but those briefings turned out to be insufficient. Members of Congress attacked the deal with fury. Secretary of State Warren Christopher, who years earlier had led the arduous negotiations for the release of the American hostages, now denounced the oil deal as "inconsistent with the containment policy." He added that in the Mideast, "Wherever you look you find the evil hand of Iran." The deal did not even survive two weeks. On March 15, 1995, President Clinton signed an executive order forbidding any oil projects with Iran. The deal was seen in Washington not as an opening, an opportunity for economic engagement, but rather in the context of Iran's support for terrorism, exemplified vividly in the attack on a Jewish center in Buenos Aires several months earlier that had killed 85 and wounded hundreds of others. Moreover, at that time, the United States was trying to persuade other countries to restrict trade with Iran.[17]

With Conoco abruptly forced to withdraw, the deal went instead to Total. Subsequently, at an OPEC meeting in Vienna, Gholam Reza Aghazadeh, Iran's then oil minister and a Rafsanjani man, summoned two American journalists to his suite in the middle of the night. Speaking in a slow, gravelly tone amid the shadowy light, he talked about the now failed deal and asked, "What is it that I don't understand about America? Tell me what I don't understand about America." Why had the United States rejected the opportunity to open a door? The answer was that, whatever the signal, the door could not be opened; terrorism made economic engagement impossible. Soon after, a 1996 terrorist assault in eastern Saudi Arabia, which was apparently engineered by Iran's own Hezbollah, killed 19 U.S. servicemen and injured another 372. That seemed to seal the door even more tightly shut.[18]

But then in 1997, unexpectedly, some possibility of normalization emerged with the overwhelming—and totally unanticipated—electoral victory of Mohammad Khatami as president. A cleric, Khatami was a reformist who wanted to move toward what has been called a "proper constitutional government." He was also an accidental president, having previously been dismissed as minister of culture for being too lenient toward the arts and the film industry, and then relegated to an insignificant position as head of the national library.

His presidential victory seemed to represent a rejection of the harsh theocracy by a large majority of the public. After his election, he reached out to the United States with words about a "Dialogue of Civilizations." After some delay, Washington positively reciprocated with encouraging words of its own, including a call by President Clinton for an end to "the estrangement of our two nations."[19]

It was difficult, however, to assess how to deal with a Tehran in which power was divided between the president and the Supreme Leader. A coalition of hardline clergy, Revolutionary Guards, security services, and judiciary—all under the control of the Supreme Leader—mounted a determined campaign of violence and intimidation to block Khatami's reforms, neutralize his presidency, limit his flexibility on foreign policy, and undercut his chances for achieving some degree of normalization.[20]

Thus it was all the more surprising when, in the immediate aftermath of 9/11, Tehran stepped forward to provide limited support for the U.S. campaign in Afghanistan. The Iranians saw the Taliban as an immediate and dangerous enemy that mobilized Sunni religious fervor against Iran's own Shia religious zeal, and it was an enemy that the United States was prepared to eliminate. Iran provided intelligence about the Taliban, urged the U.S. to move faster to attack the Taliban, cooperated militarily in some ways, and collaborated in establishing a provisional post-Taliban government. For the first time since the revolution, Iranian and American officials met regularly face-to-face. In the third week of January 2002, at a conference in Tokyo on Afghan economic reconstruction, Iranians approached the U.S. Treasury Secretary Paul O'Neill and James Dobbins, the most senior U.S. diplomat at the meeting, and suggested wider negotiation over "other issues."

But several days earlier, the *Karine A,* a freighter carrying fifty tons of Iranian arms to Gaza, had been intercepted in the Mediterranean. The message was conveyed that Khatami and his circle did not know about the shipment. But for Washington, the *Karine A* had a much bigger impact than Tehran's diplomatic probes. The ship and its cargo further confirmed Iran's commitment to terrorism. It also came at a critical moment in the definition of policy.

A week after that exchange in Tokyo, President George Bush delivered his State of the Union Address. It was the first since 9/11, and it was a call to mobilization in a new struggle, the war on terror. Bush's defining phrase was the "axis of evil," which was deliberately meant to echo the 1930s' axis of Nazi Germany, fascist Italy, and Japan. This new axis included Iraq and North Korea. Iran, the archenemy of Iraq, was the third. The phrase "axis of evil," with its clear implication of "regime change," undercut those in Tehran who wanted some détente with the United States and largely squelched the unusual U.S.-Iranian collaboration on Afghanistan—but not quite. In Geneva, at another Afghan donors' meeting, a senior Iranian general from the Revolutionary Guards suggested to the Americans that Iran could still work with the United States, including training 20,000 Afghan troops under U.S. leadership. He added that Iran was "still paying the Afghan troops your military is now using to hunt down the Taliban."[21]

Moreover, some dialogue was resumed during the early phase of the Iraq War, when the United States removed Saddam Hussein, Iran's main regional enemy and the biggest obstacle to the expansion of its influence.

RENEWED MILITANCY

Whatever door to dialogue that might have existed was firmly closed with the 2005 election of Mahmoud Ahmadinejad as president. The former mayor of Tehran and a civil engineer by training, with a doctorate in traffic management, he had been a Revolutionary Guard and remained closely aligned with the guards. That he was determined to return to an aggressive and militant path was made clear by his continuing fusillade of rhetoric. The 9/11 attacks, he told the United Nations, were probably "orchestrated" by elements in the U.S. government "to reverse the declining American economy and its grip on the Middle East." The mission of Iran was "to replace unworthy rulers" and ensure that the whole world embraces Shia Islam. He threatened that Iran would "wipe Israel off the map"—or in another translation, be "erased from the page of time"—a slogan that also adorned missiles during military parades.[22]

With Iraq demolished as its regional rival, Iran communicated its ambition to dominate the Gulf. In December 2006, at a meeting in Dubai of a regional group, the Arab Strategy Forum, Ali Larijani, the sometime Iranian nuclear negotiator and later speaker of the Parliament, told his Arab audience that America's time in the Middle East was finished, it would be leaving, and that Iran would assume the leadership of the region. But, he pledged, Iran would be guided by the principle of "good neighborliness." The stony-faced Arab audience was clearly not thrilled by the prospect of being under the stewardship of their Iranian neighbor.[23]

THE STRAIT OF HORMUZ

For many years, both oil-consuming and -exporting countries have been concerned about the security of the Strait of Hormuz, through which ships pass on their way from the Persian Gulf on to the high seas and on to world markets. Twenty-one miles across at its most narrow, the Strait is the number one choke point for global oil supplies. About 20 tankers pass through it daily, carrying upward of 17.5 million barrels of oil. This is equivalent to 20 percent of world oil demand—and 40 percent of all the oil traded in world commerce. On the northern shore of the strait is Iran. The southern shore belongs to Oman and the United Arab Emirates.[24]

The strait is also a target for Iranian threats. "Enemies know that we are easily able to block the Strait of Hormuz for an unlimited period," one Revolutionary Guard general has warned. Strategists argue, however, that Iran's ability to disrupt the strait is more limited than its rhetoric. The physical characteristics and geography of the strait and its environs would limit the effectiveness of Iran's arsenal of cruise missiles; mines; submarines; and small, high-speed, explosive-packed boats. Any attacks would be met with overwhelming military force, including from the U.S. Fifth Fleet, which is headquartered in Bahrain and whose primary mission is to maintain freedom of the seas in the region. Moreover, an assault on the flow of oil today would be an attack not just on the West, as might have been the case two decades earlier, but also on the East, including China, which gets about one quarter of its oil from the Gulf. Here is one strategic point where U.S. and Chinese interests as consumers coincide. An effort to disrupt or close the strait would be seen as an assault on the world economy and would likely stimulate a global coalition, as happened in response to Iraq's invasion of Kuwait in 1990.[25]

In addition to all this, any effort to stem the flow of oil would be very costly for Iran itself. Iran depends on the strait to export its own oil, which generates about $80 billion in earnings and about 60 percent of its budget. Unlike other

Gulf countries, Iran does not have the financial reserves that would enable it to easily withstand any cessation of export earnings.

To be sure, attacks on shipping and efforts to disrupt the flow through the strait would very likely panic markets and cause prices to spike, at least initially. And there are many oil assets that could be targeted within the Gulf. But any effort to block the Strait of Hormuz would probably fall well short of the kind of catastrophe sometimes feared.

THE GAME CHANGER

But what really threatens to upset the balance of power in the Gulf—and thus the security of world oil—is Iran's pursuit of nuclear weapons. Iran's initial nuclear program, launched in the 1950s on a minor scale by the shah under America's Atoms for Peace, was aimed primarily at developing atomic power. It was driven more intensively in the 1970s by the shah's conviction that Iran's oil and gas resources would be exhausted within three decades.[26]

In the mid-1980s, amid the Iran-Iraq War, the Khomeini regime made the decision to seek nuclear weapons capability. It obtained know-how and technology from the Pakistani A. Q. Khan network. In 2002 a dissident Iranian group revealed that Iran was secretly developing the capability to produce enriched uranium. Under pressure from the Europeans, Iran temporarily halted its enrichment program in 2003.

After his election, Ahmadinejad restarted enrichment. Iran's repeated assertion that its nuclear program is for peaceful purposes is met with total disbelief by its Arab neighbors. Ahmadinejad has also accelerated the development of missiles, some of which could carry nuclear payloads. The nuclear program entered a new phase in 2006 with the activation of a large number of centrifuges to enrich uranium. Enrichment is the process by which the ratio of the U-235 isotope to the far more common U-238 is increased. A 3 percent to 5 percent U-235 concentration is required to provide the fuel for a civilian nuclear reactor. A 20 percent level is needed for medical purposes. An atomic bomb needs 90 percent. It is much easier, once having reached the 20 percent level, to go from 20 percent to 90 percent than it is to go the initial distance from 3 percent to 20. In 2010 Iran announced that it had reached the 20 percent level.

This was not long after the discovery by Western intelligence of a secret enrichment facility near the holy city of Qom.

Iran claims that the enriched uranium is exclusively for its civilian nuclear program. Its first large nuclear reactor at Bushehr went online in 2010, with more plants supposed to follow. Iran's nuclear power program will take many years to develop and will be very costly. Yet Iran is rich in natural gas, and it is to gas that many other countries are turning as one of the most desirable and low-cost fuels for electric power. This mismatch between Iran's rich hydrocarbon resources and its plans for atomic energy—and the haste to enrich uranium—reinforces the Arab and Western conviction that it is pursuing nuclear weapons.

THE BALANCE OF POWER

An Iran with nuclear weapons would change the balance of power in the Gulf. It would be in a position, to borrow a phrase that Franklin Roosevelt had used prior to World War II, to "overawe" its neighbors. It could assert itself as the dominant regional power. Iran could directly threaten to use the weapons in the region—or actually use them—although the latter would likely trigger a massive and devastating response. But such weapons would also provide it with a license to project its power and influence with what it might regard as impunity throughout the region—both directly and through its proxies. On top of all of that, Iran, as a hegemonic nuclear power, would likely try to more directly assert dominance over the flow and price of oil, displacing the Saudis. In short, Iranian possession of such weapons would, at the very least, create insecurity for the region and for world oil supplies.

Many governments fear that elements in the Iranian government would, if they have not already done so, go into the proliferation business and provide fissile material to other governments, to its proxies like Hezbollah in Lebanon, or to terrorist groups.

When all is added up, the assessment of the impact of a nation's acquiring nuclear weapons depends not only on the possession of the weapons themselves but also on the intentions of those who hold them. And that is why the rhetoric from Tehran would take on new significance were Iran to have those weapons. Ahmadinejad has said that the ultimate mission of the Islamic Republic is to prepare the way for the return of the Hidden Imam, who disappeared in the ninth century but whose reappearance will be necessarily preceded by a period of violent chaos and fiery war that will culminate in "the end of times"—and that this moment is imminent. When the Mahdi returns, Ahmadinejad has added, he will destroy the unjust "who are not connected to the heavens"—which means the United States, the rest of the West, and Israel—and lead survivors to "the most perfect world." All this can only increase the deep anxiety about his finger being anywhere close to the nuclear button.

Adding to the danger is the lack of communication with Tehran, which could increase the likelihood of an "accidental" nuclear confrontation. Even during the tensest moments of the Cold War, the United States and the Soviet Union had communication channels, including, after the Cuban Missile Crisis in 1962, the "hotline" between the White House and the Kremlin to assure immediate contact during a crisis. No such channels exist with Iran. Indeed, there is very little understanding of how the regime functions, who makes decisions, and how the factions compete for power. All this adds to the risk. The lack of understanding also extends to the Gulf Arab states. The great worry, observed a leader of one of the Gulf nations, "is not how much we know about Iran, but how much we don't."[27]

The alarm among the other Gulf countries, as well as in Israel, about Iran's objectives has been rising in direct proportion to Iran's progress toward nuclear weapons capability. They fear that Iran will become more and more aggressive in seeking to assert its dominion over the region and in trying to destabilize other regimes. As one Saudi put it, "They want to dominate the region, and they express it strongly and clearly." Many of the Arabs believe that intermittent "negotiations" is a standard Iranian tactic to create a cover while it proceeds with its nuclear program—what one official described as "their usual strategy" of "leading you on with false promises, designed to buy more time."

Some Gulf Arabs are convinced that Iran is pursuing a strategy of encirclement, from its presence in Iraq and subversion among the Shia populations in Bahrain and eastern Saudi Arabia and in Yemen to promoting insurgency on Saudi Arabia's southern border to financing and supplying weapons to Hezbollah in Lebanon and Hamas in Gaza. This encirclement would pressure the Arab Gulf states and, at the same time, put assets in position that Iran could activate during some future time of tension or crisis.

For years, the Israelis have spoken of a nuclear Iran as an "existential threat" to the very survival of their nation and its people. Now some Arabs also describe Iran as an "existential threat." As a leader of one of the emirates put it, his country is only "46 seconds from Iran as measured by the flight time of a ballistic missile."[28]

INCENTIVES AND SANCTIONS

The United States and Europe have been trying for several years to find a mix of policies sufficient to persuade Iran to stop short of the red line—nuclear weapons capability—and thus avoid a situation where another country concludes that it has no choice but preemptive military action. The offers include expanded trade, membership in the World Trade Organization, and—recognizing the broad public embrace in Iran of a nuclear program—support for the development of peaceful atomic energy in Iran under an acceptable international regime. At the same time, they have mounted an increasing array of sanctions, both under the United Nations and unilaterally, that restrict investment, trade, and the flow of finance. In addition to their general impact on the economy, these sanctions have put pressure on Iran by retarding the modernization of Iran's conventional military forces and by greatly constraining international investment in Iran's oil and gas industry and Iran's access to international finance and capital markets.

Sabotage is another way, short of military action, of slowing Iran's progress toward the red line. In 2010 a sophisticated Stuxnet computer virus was introduced into the software programs running the centrifuges, causing them to speed up, perform erratically, and self-destruck. Israel, the United States, or possibly a European country is considered the most likely author.

After intense negotiation, Russia and China have supported the United Nations sanctions but not the unilateral sanctions. As Western oil companies wound down and backed out of Iran in the face of the unilateral sanctions, Chinese companies—not governed by those sanctions—have signed a variety of large oil and gas deals with Iran that would, if implemented, bring much of the technology and investment that the Iranian industry needs. Yet at the same time, China does have many other interests, including avoidance of a conflict in the Gulf that would disrupt oil and gas supplies coming out of the region. While a number of major contracts have been signed, the Chinese companies have been moving slowly to act on them.

An alternative to conflict is a policy of containment, which would use sanctions and other restrictions to hold Iran in check until such time as Iran concludes that the advantages of real negotiations outweigh the purported benefit of nuclear weapons—or until the political situation in the country changes. That, after all, is what containment meant when George Kennan propounded it in 1947, at the beginning of the Cold War, when he outlined "a policy of firm containment" designed to confront "the Soviet Union with inalterable counterforce at every point" and increasing "the strains under which Soviet policy must operate"—until a settlement was possible or until the "seeds of its own decay" brought down the Soviet Union.[29]

This kind of containment would also involve the extension of guarantees, nuclear shields, and extended deterrence to other nations in the region. The prospect of a nuclear Iran has already ignited a conventional arms buildup in the region. The reality of a nuclear Iran could well provoke a nuclear arms race, which, by the very numbers of countries involved, would increase the chances of such weapons actually being used. The nuclear standoff in the Cold War, despite the grave risks, had a certain stability. It was essentially between two parties, each of whom understood the meaning of deterrence and the second-strike capability of the other side. And neither wanted to risk suicide. The deterrence of the Cold War is not necessarily a good analogy at all for the highly unstable—and not very predictable—situation that a nuclear Iran would create.[30]

What then might reduce the risk and encourage Iran to stop somewhere short of the red line? It could be a combination of containment and external pressure, economic difficulties within Iran, and widespread domestic discontent that foments a political change. The potential for change was vividly demonstrated by the overwhelming victories of the reformist Khatami in 1997 and 2001, and then the mass "Green" protests after the bitterly contested and much-disputed reelection of Ahmadinejad in 2009. But in all those instances, the tools of violence and repression, wielded by the religious establishment and the powerful Revolutionary Guards and their allies, demonstrate how strong is the resistance and the determination to defend the system now in place. This leaves the unnerving risk that nuclear weapons would be in the hands of those who are bent on overturning the regional and international order and who believe in the necessity of an apocalypse to usher in a "perfect world."

The whirring of the centrifuges may also be the ticking of a clock. The timing as to when Iran would cross a red line in its nuclear program is uncertain, as is the response of those who feel most threatened by it. Sometimes it is said to be two years away. But containment and other measures may stretch out the time by a few more years. Still, as one senior official from the region put it, "Whatever the time frame, time is running out."

Here is one of the preeminent risks for regional security and the world's energy security, and one that inescapably becomes part of the calculations for the energy future.

15

GAS ON WATER

From the moment they left Doha, the capital of Qatar, the cars took just a little over an hour speeding on a new four-lane highway that crossed the desert with tight curves. This desert motorcade carried members of the Qatari royal family; senior officials from the government and from RasGas and Qatargas, the country's two gas-exporting companies; along with a range of other dignitaries, including bankers and executives from the international companies that are Qatar's partners in the greatest concentrated natural gas development the world has ever seen.

The cars slowed as they passed through several gates where identifications were checked again and again. A little distance off, rising, as though a mirage in the desert, was a huge assortment of pipes and machinery, the nearest part half assembled with tall cranes, and the rest arranged in neat lines, stretching down across the sand. Beyond all this, on the other side of the road, was the sea.

Out there, below those waters of the Persian Gulf, was the North Field, one of the world's major energy assets. But it ends abruptly. For some forty miles off this placid coast is an imaginary demarcation line, invisible except on maps, on the other side of which is Iran and, specifically, its offshore South Pars Field. In political terms they are two separate fields. In geological terms, they are one and the same. But still, North Dome by itself constitutes the largest conventional natural gas field in the world. The median line between the two countries was negotiated before the gas field was discovered, and Iran has never been happy that it does not have a larger share.

Once out of their cars, the group was ushered into a huge tent, filled with chairs. After everyone was seated, there was a stir. The emir, Sheikh Hamad bin Khalifa al-Thani, swept in, a big, husky man in a dishdasha. He paused to shake hands and kiss people. Next to him was Abdullah bin Hamad al-Attiyah, deputy prime minister and at the time minister of petroleum. For many years, al-Attiyah's true vocation had been natural gas, and he had driven this development. Everyone was there to celebrate an industrial feat: the building of a massive new LNG train—as the facilities for transforming natural gas into a liquid at very cold temperatures are called—ahead of schedule and on budget. Another notch for one of the largest production facilities of any kind anywhere in the world.

Qatar is a mostly flat, sandy, stony peninsula that juts out from Saudi Arabia a hundred miles into the Persian Gulf. Through the nineteenth century, Qatar had been under the overlapping rules of the Ottoman Empire, the neighboring island of Bahrain, and Great Britain, which sought to maintain its influence in the Persian Gulf in order to protect the routes to India. Qatar itself managed to eke out a livelihood from fishing and pearl diving. After a military clash between Bahrain and Qatar tribesmen, a merchant family from Doha, the al-Thanis, emerged as the ruling clan. With the collapse of the Ottoman Empire at the end of the First World War, Qatar became a British protectorate; it did not gain full independence until 1971, when the British withdrew their military presence from east of Suez.

At that time, Qatar was still a poor country. No longer. In recent years, its economy has been growing at a furious pace—some years reaching double digits. Today Qatar has the highest per capita gross domestic product in the world and has become one of the main commercial hubs of the Persian Gulf. At the same time, this small principality of about 1.5 million people (of which at least three quarters is composed of foreigners with temporary residence status) also rivals Russia to be the Saudi Arabia of world natural gas. For Qatar has emerged as the central player in what is becoming, after oil, the world's second global energy business—natural gas, specifically liquefied natural gas, or LNG.

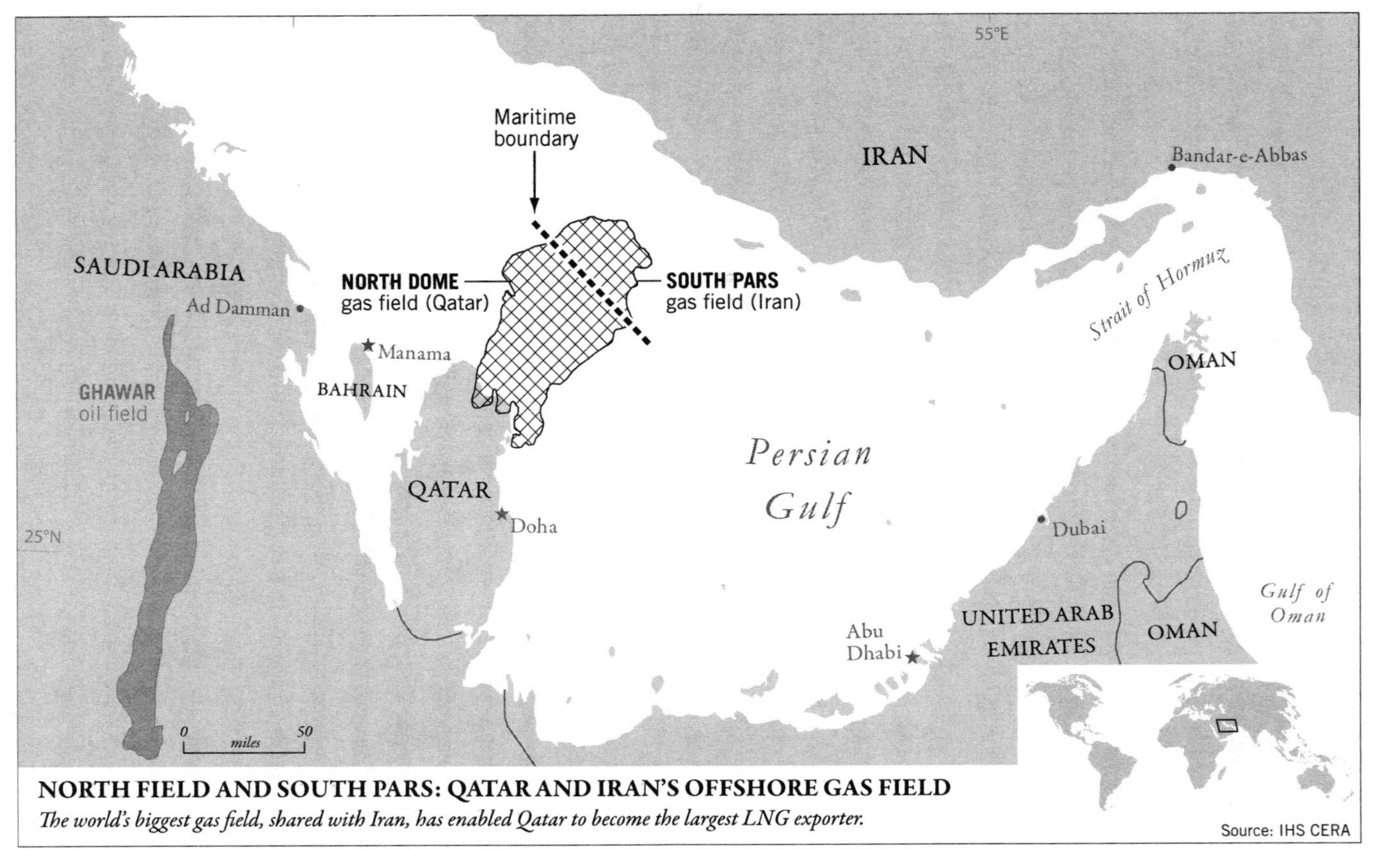

NORTH FIELD AND SOUTH PARS: QATAR AND IRAN'S OFFSHORE GAS FIELD

The world's biggest gas field, shared with Iran, has enabled Qatar to become the largest LNG exporter.

Source: IHS CERA

This corner of desert at the very edge of the Arabian Peninsula, just two decades ago mostly dunes, was now well on its way to being one of the strategic junctures in the world economy.

Qatar is also a key element in the larger mosaic of the world natural gas market. Not so many years ago, there were three distinct gas markets. One was Asia, mainly fed by LNG. The second was Europe, with a mix of domestic gas, long-distance pipeline gas, notably from Russia, plus some LNG. And North America, with virtually all gas delivered by pipeline. Each had its own distinctive pricing system. But then the development of LNG, represented most notably by Qatar, appeared to be tearing down the walls. The markets looked like they were coming together and would eventually be integrated into a single global natural gas market in which prices were converging. That seemed irreversible—until a major innovation in the United States made it reversible.

After the inaugural ceremonies, the emir boarded a minibus to tour the new facility. The bus crossed the sand and then turned into the site. It was like driving into a dense forest, but one that was not damp and whose colors were not varieties of green but rather silver and steel glinting under the dry desert sun. For this forest had none of the vagaries of nature but rather was an intricately planned maze of interconnected pipes and towers and turbines and, occasionally, what looked like huge white Thermos bottles. That image was appropriate enough since the liquefaction train was in effect a giant-sized refrigerator, into which was pumped the natural gas from the North Field, after it had been scrubbed and cleaned of impurities. There, through a facility that stretched more than a half mile, the gas would step by step be compressed and refrigerated. It would come out the other end as a liquid that could be pumped into ships and transported around the world. And it was a very expensive forest. Adding up all the trains together, some $60 billion of engineering and hardware has been compressed into this small area in a remarkably short number of years.

This train—70,000 tons of concrete, 440 kilometers of electric cable, 13,000 metric tons of piping—was one stage in the great complex at Ras Lafan, which in its entirety is the single largest node in the expanding global LNG business that involves more and more countries. The growing list of LNG suppliers ranges from Malaysia, Indonesia, and Brunei in Asia; to Australia; to Russia (from the island of Sakhalin); to Qatar, Oman, Abu Dhabi, and Yemen in the Middle East; to Algeria, Libya, and Egypt in North Africa, and Nigeria and Equatorial Guinea in West Africa; to Alaska; to Trinidad and Peru in the Western Hemisphere. Other countries may join in the queue, including Israel, after a major new gas discovery offshore that could turn the Eastern Mediterranean into a new frontier for gas development.

This global expansion of LNG is a very big business. Projects today can easily run $5 billion or $10 billion—or even more—and take five to ten years to complete. The Gorgon prospect in Australia is budgeted at $45 billion. Altogether, the price tag for LNG development worldwide could add up to as much as half a trillion dollars over the next fifteen years.

Yet the very possibility of this huge global LNG business derives from a single physical phenomenon—that when natural gas is compressed and brought down to that temperature of −260°F, it turns into a liquid, and, as such, takes up only 1/600th of the space it occupies in its gaseous state. That means it can be pumped into a specifically designed tanker, shipped long distances over water, and then stored or re-gasified and fed into pipelines and sent to consumers.

But very few of the participants in this business today would know that the industry owes its existence to someone whose fascination with LNG long predated theirs.

CABOT's CRYOGENICS

Just after World War I, Thomas Cabot, a graduate of both Harvard and the Massachusetts Institute of Technology, had headed down to West Virginia to sort out a natural gas pipeline business owned by his father, Godfrey, who, to Thomas's distress, had lost all interest in it. Returning to Boston, Thomas found that he had other pressing family business to attend to—keeping his father from going to jail. It turned out that Godfrey had had no use for the federal income tax, which Woodrow Wilson had signed into law in 1913, and for the next several years Godfrey had simply not bothered to pay it. "Income is only a matter of opinion," he would say to government agents. In return, the Internal Revenue Service had expropriated Godfrey's bank accounts.

While wrestling with this problem, Thomas had some time on his hands, and he started writing a scientific paper that related to one of his father's other failed ventures. This concerned cryogenics—the study of very low temperatures, at which various gases turn into liquids. During the First World War, Godfrey Cabot had built a plant in West Virginia to liquefy natural gas and patented a design. "My father had dreamt of liquefying components of natural gas," Thomas Cabot later said. As a business, however, it had proved to be a total bust.[1]

Cryogenics was based on the work of Michael Faraday, who in the 1820s had used cold temperatures to turn gases into liquids. In the 1870s the German scientist Carl von Linde had done further work on refrigeration. His research attracted interest from brewing companies, which, along with their customers, decidedly liked the idea of cold beer. Linde was soon supplying the brewers with refrigerators. He later patented processes for liquefying oxygen, nitrogen, and other gases at very low temperatures and making them available on a commercial scale. His work provided the basis for practical applications of cryogenics.

It was back to his father's dream of liquefying natural gas that Cabot turned, while also fending off the IRS. Cabot specifically wanted to explore how extreme refrigeration could be used during the summer season, when demand was low, to compress natural gas into a liquid, enabling it to be held in storage and then returned to its gaseous state in winter, when demand was high.

Cabot's father, who rarely demonstrated positive responses to anything his son did, showed his characteristic lack of interest in his son's paper. Seeking to interest someone, Cabot passed it to the chief engineer of a natural gas pipeline company who was "intrigued to the greatest possible extent" by the idea of compressing natural gas in order to store it. But it was not until 1939 that the first pilot plant was built.

During World War II, in order to meet the energy needs of factories working two or three shifts a day to supply the war effort, the East Ohio Gas Company built an LNG storage facility in Cleveland. In October 1944 one of the tanks failed. Stored LNG seeped into the sewer system and ignited, killing 129 people and creating a mile-long fireball. Subsequently, the causes of the accident were identified: poor ventilation, insufficient containment measures, and the improper use of a particular steel alloy that turned brittle at very low temperatures. The design and safety lessons would be seared into the minds of future developers.[2]

After World War II, such interest as remained in LNG shifted from using refrigeration to store gas for consumers to quite a different purpose; instead, using it as a way to transport gas over water over long distances.

KILLER FOG

In December 1952 a killer fog gripped London, making it difficult for people even to find their homes, let alone breathe, killing thousands and making many more ill. The fog resulted from the interaction of weather conditions and coal smoke. Rapidly reducing the burning of coal and replacing it with cleaner fuels became a critical priority. The government-owned British Gas Council teamed up with an American company to import natural gas from Louisiana into Britain in the form of LNG. The first shipment to Britain, aboard the *Methane Pioneer,* arrived in 1957. This may have proved the concept, but importing LNG was a very small business. Yet demand, stimulated by a promotional campaign for "High Speed Gas," was exceeding all expectations. If this new LNG business in the UK was going to get anywhere, it needed a much larger source of gas.

Royal Dutch Shell bought controlling interest in the nascent LNG company and started developing a large natural gas deposit in Algeria far out in the Sahara Desert. In 1964, two years after Algeria gained its independence from France, its first shipment of liquefied natural gas was loaded on a tanker in Arzew for a month-long, 1,600-mile trip to Canvey Island in the lower Thames. A few months later, another shipment left for La Havre in France.[3]

This was the real beginning of the international LNG trade. It demonstrated what would become the characteristic practice in the business. It is expensive to turn gas into liquid, transport the liquid, and then turn the liquid back into gas. These large costs require predictability about prices and markets. Thus the business model for LNG projects has traditionally involved long-term (often twenty-year) contracts among all the interested parties—countries, international oil companies, utility customers, and sometimes trading houses. They share overlapping ownership of tankers and liquefaction and regasification facilities. This model, quite distinct from the international oil business, would last a half century.

In the mid-1960s, Europe certainly looked poised to become a growing LNG consumer. But what might have been an LNG boom was abruptly stymied—by competitive gas that was cheaper and more accessible. In 1959 a huge gas field—at the time the largest in the world—had been discovered under the flat farmlands in Groningen in the northern part of the Netherlands. Then in 1965 natural gas deposits were also found in the British sector of the North Sea. With that, Britain made a wholesale shift to natural gas for appliances and heating. Subsequently, the Soviet Union and then Norway began to deliver growing volumes of natural gas, via pipeline, to Western Europe. LNG now had to compete in Europe.

Asia was a different story. Japan, in the midst of its amazing postwar economic boom, saw natural gas as a way to reduce the stifling air pollution produced by its coal-fired electric-generation plants. Lacking any significant gas or oil resources of its own, Japan turned to LNG. The first LNG arrived in Japan in 1969. The source was the United States—the Cook Inlet in southern Alaska, in a project developed by Phillips Petroleum. After the 1973 oil crisis, Japan was determined to reduce its dependence on Middle East oil and diversify its energy supplies. LNG, along with nuclear power, was a key part of the prescription. By the end of the 1970s, Japan was importing large volumes of LNG.[4]

As they entered their economic miracle phases, both South Korea and Taiwan—two other hydrocarbon-poor countries—also became major LNG importers. All the projects followed the original model, based on overlapping long-term contracts. Because the imported gas was replacing not only coal but also oil in electric generation, the LNG price was indexed to oil prices, meaning that the price of LNG followed oil's.

THE "FUEL NON-USE ACT"

The natural gas industry in the United States was very different. Natural gas, produced like oil, had become an important energy resource but a largely local one. During World War II, when gasoline was rationed and fuel shortages in the fighting theaters were a constant threat for the Allies, President Franklin Roosevelt urgently wrote to his secretary of the interior: "I wish you could get some of your people to look into the possibility of using natural gas. I am told that there are a number of fields in the West and Southwest where practically no oil has been discovered but where an enormous amount of natural gas is lying idle in the ground because it is too far to pipe to large communities."[5]

But this had to wait until after World War II. It required the development of long-distance pipelines, stretching halfway across the country, in an industry for which "long distance" had heretofore meant 150 miles. Pipelines connected the Southwest to the Northeast, and New Mexico and West Texas to Southern California. Thus natural gas became a truly continental business, in which the main population and industrial centers were connected to gas fields that were far across the country. As the nation's economy grew and suburbs rolled out around major cities, natural gas consumption increased at a rapid pace.

By the beginning of the 1970s, natural gas provided fully 25 percent of America's total energy. It was produced either jointly with oil or from pure gas wells. But then a natural gas shortage gripped the country. In the cold winter of 1976–77, parts of the Midwest ran so short that schools and factories had to shut down. Companies were already scrambling to find new supplies. LNG looked to be a very good—and timely—answer. Several utilities, including the Cabot Corporation (the company Thomas Cabot had created in sorting out his father's taxes) contracted with Algeria for supplies. The Texas-based pipeline company El Paso ordered enough LNG tankers to constitute a virtual floating pipeline. Receiving terminals for re-gasifying the liquid gas were built on the Gulf Coast and the East Coast. The most visible, designed to help meet New England's gas deficit, was Cabot's in Everett, Massachusetts, right across Boston Harbor from the USS *Constitution* ("Old Ironsides"), the famed frigate launched in 1797. Another big project was planned for the West Coast, at Point Conception, California's elbow into the Pacific, north of Santa Barbara.

But it turned out the natural gas shortage was not an act of nature but manmade, the consequences of inflexible regulation. The federal government, which regulated natural gas prices, had set them at such an arbitrarily low level as to stifle supply. The obvious solution was to let the market determine prices. But what was straightforward economics was hardly the same when it came to politics. The single biggest domestic political battle during the presidency of Jimmy Carter was over natural gas price deregulation. "I understand now what Hell is," Energy Secretary James Schlesinger said in 1978 amid the battle over natural gas pricing between House and Senate negotiators. "Hell is endless and eternal sessions of the natural gas conference."[6]

Finally, the Natural Gas Policy Act of 1978 started to decontrol prices. The act was a wonderful example of what happens when economics and politics interact in the same test tube. It provided distinct pricing schedules for some 22 different categories of a commodity that, in molecular terms, was more or less all the same—one carbon atom and four hydrogen atoms. Still, the end point was pretty clear: deregulation.

As part of the compromise, Congress enacted the Fuel Use Act. But the law might as well have been called the "Fuel Non-Use Act" as it banned the burning of natural gas in power plants to generate electricity. Natural gas was deemed the "prince of hydrocarbons" and was to be kept for higher uses—heating and cooling, cooking, and industrial processes. It was too "valuable" to be used to make electricity.

To the surprise of some, markets actually worked. Deregulation of prices led to a surge in supplies. Moreover, as supplies increased, prices did not shoot through the roof but settled at lower levels. Indeed, so much additional natural gas came onto the market that it created an extended oversupply that was known as the gas bubble. After a time, it seemed that this was one bubble that would never burst.

The oversupply of low-cost domestic gas did in the prospects for LNG, for LNG was simply too expensive to compete. The expected boom in the U.S. LNG business turned into a bust. Projects were canceled; companies defaulted on contracts for LNG tankers. Companies that had committed to LNG teetered on bankruptcy. Cabot Corporation was losing $5 million on every cargo of LNG.[7]

Yet by the 1990s, the market was changing again. The fears of shortage had long since faded away, and the prohibition on using natural gas in electric generation was lifted. Instead of being banned, natural gas became the fuel of choice for electric power. New technologies made natural gas turbines much more efficient and thus lowered costs. Gas was seen as a cleaner, more environmentally attractive fuel than coal, and the development of new nuclear power in the United States had already come to a stop. In contrast, power plants fired by gas could be built more quickly and at a much lower cost than the competitors'.

By the mid-1990s the U.S. economy was booming, and, as a result, electricity demand was growing. To meet this demand, power generators were frenetically building natural gas-fired power plants. But where was the gas supply to come from? In response to rising prices, drilling did increase, but in contrast to the traditional pattern, new drilling brought forth only a paltry increase. It was proving harder to step up gas output from existing basins, which were said to be mature. Access to new areas was difficult, owing to increasing regulatory delays. Moreover, many prospective areas, both onshore and offshore, were closed off to drilling altogether for environmental reasons.

In the face of rising demand and flat supply, the market tightened. Consumers saw their bills increase dramatically. Even harder hit were energy-intensive industries, like petrochemicals. They could no longer compete against products from the Middle East that were made from far less expensive gas. Chemical plants were shut down in the United States. If supplies did not increase, and costs did not come down, companies would have to close even more of their U.S. plants and lay off still more workers.

The answer once again seemed to be LNG. Innovation had made it available by attacking costs at dramatically increasing scale. Cabot, which only a few years earlier had been desperately trying to extricate itself from unviable LNG contracts, now started to look for new LNG supplies.

One possible source was Trinidad, where significant natural gas reserves had been discovered offshore. But could gas from Trinidad be competitively landed in the United States? "The conventional wisdom was that the cost of LNG was going to continue to rise," recalled Gordon Shearer, who worked for Cabot at the time. "But then we realized that the cost structure of LNG didn't make sense." Cabot succeeded in bringing down these costs substantially by simplifying designs and promoting much more competitive bidding.[8]

Trinidad demonstrated that LNG need not be the high-priced alternative but rather could compete with conventional pipeline gas. By 1999 this cheaper LNG was starting to flow in growing volumes into the terminal at Everett, near Old Ironsides, across the bay from Boston.

"THE CROWN JEWELS"

But then there was Qatar.

The North Field was discovered by Shell in 1971 in the waters off Qatar. At first no one knew how vast it was; indeed, it took decades for the full dimensions to be recognized. Today its reserves are estimated at 900 trillion cubic feet.

This makes the State of Qatar the third-largest resource owner of conventional natural gas in the world. Ahead of it are only Russia and Iran, whose South Pars Field is really the same structure as the North Field.

In the 1970s and 1980s, there was no obvious market for the North Field gas, no demand for it, and no way to get it to market. Eventually, Shell relinquished the North Field and moved on to the more immediately attractive Northwest Shelf project in Australia.

In 1971, the same year that Shell discovered Qatar's North Field, Mobil Oil discovered Arun, a huge offshore natural gas field in the northern part of Sumatra, the largest of the 17,000 islands that comprise the nation of Indonesia. As billions of dollars flowed into the project, Arun turned into the largest LNG development of the 1970s and 1980s. The onshore liquefaction plants were in the province of Aceh, and the supplies went to Japan. The project was absolutely crucial to the fortunes of Mobil and its profitability. "It was the crown jewels, no question," recalled one Mobil executive.[9]

But a problem emerged—Arun's output appeared set to decline. Thus, with increasing urgency, Mobil searched for another supply of natural gas, unreachable by pipeline and thus stranded from markets, where its LNG skills could be applied. North Field stood out; Shell was now gone, and a discouraged BP had just pulled out of an LNG project there that existed only on paper. Mobil proposed a structure that would allow it to take a share in two Qatari companies, Qatargas and RasGas. This kind of structure made sense to the Qataris, especially as RasGas did not yet exist as a company. They did their deal.

The new partnership needed to find customers, but it was very hard going. "We weren't able to do much," recalled one of the Qatari marketers.

Every decade or so, however, Japan sought to add another major source of LNG not only to meet demand but also as part of its diversification strategy. Chubu Electric, which serves the territory next to Tokyo and whose biggest customer is Toyota, contracted for the first gas from the North Field. A Korean utility, Kogas, signed on next.

With these deals, Qatar had gotten in the door in Asia, the biggest LNG market in the world. But Qatar was a latecomer, and it ran a real risk that it would be relegated to a secondary position as a supplemental supplier. And Qatar had too much gas for that. But where else could they go? Finally, after a couple of years of study and debate, a senior Qatari settled the matter: "We should be heading west," he said. That meant to Europe—and beyond.[10]

During this same period, Qatar was going through political change that would reinforce its commercial drive. In 1995 Crown Prince Hamad bin Khalifa al-Thani sent a message to his father, the emir, Sheikh Khalifa bin Hamad, then vacationing in Switzerland. It was actually a pretty simple message: Don't bother coming back. The crown prince had just deposed his father, who had been in power since overthrowing his cousin in 1972 and was not seen as a very competent ruler. Nevertheless, Sheikh Khalifa had insisted on being in charge of everything. Indeed, it was said that he personally signed all checks over $50,000. He was also thought to have been bleeding the country of revenues, and indeed, after the bloodless coup in 1995, the new emir, Sheikh Hamad, sued his father for return of the state's money. That case was settled out of court, and the aged father found a new life for himself based in London.[11]

Now in power, Sheikh Hamad initiated a far-reaching program of modernization and reform, ranging from permitting women candidates in municipal elections to the opening in Qatar of the Mideast branches of New York's Weill Cornell Medical School, Georgetown University's School of Foreign Service, and Texas A&M University. Qatar became home to the forward headquarters for the U.S. Central Command, which has responsibility for the Middle East. It also became home to, and indeed financed, the Al Jazeera satellite news network.

The emir was determined to turn his small Persian Gulf principality into a global energy giant, based on LNG, with the revenue stream that would go with it. Accelerating LNG was the way to do that. But a huge amount of money would have to be invested. That meant that LNG costs—considered absolutely irreducible—had to be reduced. Even so, the capital costs would be enormous. "The more I learned about Qatar," recalled Lucio Noto, former CEO of Mobil, "the more I realized the scale was beyond the capacity of an individual company."[12]

The merger of Mobil with Exxon in 1999 made the great expansion much more doable. The combination brought critical Mobil assets—the gas resource, LNG expertise, and relationships—together with Exxon's financial strength and its skill in project execution. The combined company now had the size and wherewithal to think big in terms of scale and risks. Actually, very big. And scale was the way to bring costs down—much bigger ships, much bigger liquefaction trains, and much bigger turbines. Projects were managed with great discipline, capturing the learning and bringing down the costs of subsequent projects. One way to do that was by making facilities as standard as possible, doing the design very carefully, and then sticking to it. As one of the senior managers put it, "The rule was no change orders."

Hungry at the time for work, Korean shipyards tendered for much bigger LNG carriers—two times the size of those then afloat—at a very attractive price. RasGas accepted the bids. Higher volumes meant lower costs. Now, as they put it, Europe was "reachable." The joint venture knew that it could compete against pipeline gas in Europe, and even beyond Europe. For with sufficient scale (and bolstered by the liquids with the gas) Qatar could deliver competitively priced gas anywhere in the world.

By 2002 Qatar had emerged as a potent new competitor in the global gas market. It could dispatch large amounts of LNG into any major market—Asia, Europe, and the United States. Breaking with the traditional business, it could also do so without necessarily being tied to a long-term contract. It built its own receiving terminal, in Europe. Qatar was at the forefront in creating a new business model in which both buyers and sellers were willing to buy or sell LNG without complete reliance on long-term contracts. And the numbers are huge: By 2007 Qatar had leapfrogged over Indonesia and Malaysia to become the world's number one supplier of LNG, and this small emirate of 1.5 million people was on its way to being able to provide almost a third of the world's LNG supply.

It was not just the physical resources and technical capabilities that projected Qatar into this premier position. It was also the result of what those on the other side of the negotiating table recognized to be efficient and determined decision making. Qatar could be very tough, but it was also intent on closing deals and getting things decided quickly, not in multiple years. As Minister Al-Attiyah put it, "If we do a deal one day, we don't wait, we sign it the next day." Reliability was one of the critical pillars on which the Qatari industry was built. Once a deal was done, stability of contracts underpinned confidence and facilitated investment. The importance of this approach was made clear by comparison to the other side of the median line, off the coast of Qatar, where Iran after forty years has yet to be able to turn South Pars gas into exports.[13]

By the 2000s, it seemed that natural gas, carried around the world on tankers, was on its way to becoming a truly global industry. Historically, due to the high cost of transporting gas over long distances, natural gas has been traded regionally. By bringing down costs so significantly, this no longer applied.

What this meant was vividly demonstrated in July 2007. On July 16, 2007, a large earthquake hit central Japan, damaging the Kashiwazaki-Kariwa Nuclear Power Station—the world's largest, home to seven reactors. The entire facility was shut down, creating an immediate shortage of electric generation. The owner of the power station, Tokyo Electric Power Company (TEPCO), began buying heavily from the short-term LNG market to fuel stand-by natural gas–fired power plants that could make up for the nuclear power shortfall. LNG tankers intended for elsewhere immediately changed course on the high seas and headed for Japan. Also in that same month, July 2007, half a world away, outages of natural gas pipelines flowing from the natural gas fields in the North Sea interrupted supplies to Europe. This too triggered a quick diversion of LNG supplies from their intended routes.

Almost four years later in March 2011, a giant earthquake and tsunami shook Japan, knocking out power and setting off a major nuclear accident at the Fukushima Daiichi plant. Natural gas supplies were redirected to Japan on an even more massive scale.

What had been an inflexible regionally based LNG industry had turned into a flexible international business. Natural gas had become a global commodity.[14]

16

THE NATURAL GAS REVOLUTION

George P. Mitchell, a Houston-based oil and gas producer, could see the problem coming. His company was going to run short of natural gas, which would put it in a very difficult position. For it was contracted to deliver a substantial amount of natural gas from Texas to feed a pipeline serving Chicago. The reserves on which the contract depended were going down, and it was not at all clear where he could find more gas to replace those depleting reserves. But he did have a strong hunch, piqued by a geology report that he had read.

That was in the early 1980s. Three decades later, Mitchell's relentless commitment to do something about the problem would transform the North American natural gas market and shake expectations for the global gas market. Indeed, the stubborn conviction of this one man would change America's energy prospects and force recalculations around the world.

The son of a Greek goat herder who had somehow ended up in Galveston, Texas, Mitchell had grown up dirt-poor. He had worked his way through Texas A&M University waiting tables, selling candy and stationery, and doing tailoring for his fellow students. After World War II, Mitchell had started in the oil-and-gas business in Houston, working out of a one-room office atop a drugstore. Over the years he had built it into a very substantial company, Mitchell Energy and Development, that focused much more on natural gas than oil.

For Mitchell, natural gas was virtually a cause. He was such a believer that when he suspected someone of speaking too kindly of coal, he would reach for the phone and set him straight in a few short sentences. What he wanted to see was more natural gas use. And he simply would not accept the notion that supplies were constrained by scarcity.

But where was he going to get more gas? The geological report that he had read in 1982 pointed to a possible solution. For a very long time it had been recognized that natural gas was to be found not only in productive reservoirs but also trapped in hard, concretelike shale rock. This shale rock served as the source rock, the "kitchen," where the gas was created, and also as the cap that sat on top of reservoirs that prevented the gas (and oil) from leaking away.[1]

Gas could certainly be extracted from shale rock. In fact, it is thought that the very first natural gas well in the United States, in Fredonia, New York, in 1821, drew from a shale formation. The problem was the economics. It was inordinately difficult and thus very expensive to extract gas from shale. It just was not anywhere near commercially viable. Yet maybe it was possible with the right mixture of technological innovation and persistence.

Mitchell's "laboratory" was a large region called the Barnett Shale, around Dallas and Fort Worth, Texas, which sprawled under ranches, suburbs, and even Dallas–Fort Worth International Airport. Despite Mitchell's efforts, the Barnett Shale proved continuously unforgiving. Mitchell insisted that his engineers and geologists keep plugging away in the face of ongoing disappointment and their own skepticism. "George, you're wasting your money," they would say to him over the years. But when they raised objections, he would reply, "This is what we're going to do."[2]

Fortunately, something of a carrot was available, what was called Section 29. This was a provision in the 1980 windfall profits tax bill that provided a federal tax credit for drilling for so-called unconventional natural gas. Over the years, that incentive did what it was supposed to do—it stimulated activity that would otherwise not have taken place. In the 1990s, the tax credit mainly supported the development of two other forms of unconventional natural gas, and gas from tight sands, the very name of which conveys the challenge.

"FIGURE A WAY"

But even with the incentive of the Section 29 tax credit, producing commercial-scale shale gas—another form of unconventional gas—was proving so much more difficult. In addition to Mitchell, a few other companies were also tackling the problem, but they became discouraged and dropped out. In 1997 the only one of the major companies working on shale gas development efforts in the Barnett region shut down its office. Only Mitchell Energy and a few other smaller independents were left. George Mitchell would just not give up. "It was clear to him that Barnett held a lot of gas, and he wanted us to figure a way to get it out," recalled Dan Steward, who led the development team. "If we couldn't, then he would hire other people who could. He had a way of getting things out of people they might not know they could deliver on."

The introduction of 3-D seismic much improved the understanding of the subsurface. Still, Mitchell Energy had not yet cracked the Barnett's code. "All sorts of experienced, educated folks," said Steward, "wanted to bail out of the Barnett."

Indeed, by the late 1990s the area was so much off the radar screen that when people did forecasts of future natural gas supplies, the Barnett did not even show up. Mitchell Energy's board of directors was becoming increasingly skeptical. After all, when almost two decades of effort were added up, it was clear that the company had lost a good deal of money on the Barnett play. But George Mitchell would not give up; he insisted that they were getting closer to cracking the Barnett's code.[3]

BREAKTHROUGH

Fraccing—otherwise known as hydraulic fracturing—is a technique that was first used at the end of the 1940s. It injects large amounts of water, under high pressure, combined with sand and small amounts of chemicals, into the shale formation. This fragments underground rock, creating pathways for otherwise trapped natural gas (and oil) to find a route and flow through to the well.

Mitchell Energy had been experimenting with different methodologies for fraccing. By the end of 1998, the company finally achieved its breakthrough: it successfully adapted a fraccing technique—what is known as LSF, or light sand fraccing—to break up the shale rock. "It was the trial-and-error approach that Mitchell Energy used that ultimately made the difference," said Dan Steward.

George Mitchell recognized that developing the Barnett was going to take a lot of capital. He had also been at it as an independent for sixty years and that was a long time. He had other interests; he had developed the Woodlands, the twenty-five-thousand-acre new community north of Houston. He put Mitchell Energy up for sale. Three other companies looked at the company but they all decided, after due diligence, to pass. It appeared to all of them that while Mitchell's pursuit of shale gas, fraccing included, may have been an interesting idea, it was a commercial flop.

The team at Mitchell went back to work on the shale, further developing its capabilities, deepening its understanding—and producing a lot more natural gas.

One of the companies that had passed was another independent, Devon Energy, from Oklahoma City. But in 2001, its CEO, Larry Nichols, noticed a sudden surge in gas supply from the Barnett Shale area. "I challenged our engineers as to why this was happening," said Nichols. "If fraccing was not working, why was Mitchell's output going up?" The answer was clear: Mitchell Energy had indeed cracked the code. Nichols did not waste any more time. In 2002 Devon acquired Mitchell Energy for $3.5 billion. "At that time," added Nichols, "absolutely no one believed that shale drilling worked, other than Mitchell and us."

Devon, for its part, had its own strong capabilities in another technology, horizontal drilling, which had begun to emerge in the 1980s. Advances in controls and measurement allowed operators to drill down to a certain depth, and then drill on at an angle or even sideways. This would expose much more of the reservoir, permitting much greater recovery of gas (or oil) from a reservoir.

Devon combined the fraccing know-how (and the team) it had acquired from Mitchell with its own skills in horizontal drilling. All that required a good deal of experimentation. Devon drilled seven such wells in 2002. "By 2003," said Nichols, "we were becoming very confident that this drilling truly worked." Devon drilled another fifty-five horizontal wells in the Barnett that year. It did work.[4]

Shale gas, heretofore commercially inaccessible, began to flow in significant volumes. Combining the advances in fraccing and horizontal drilling is what would unleash what became known as the unconventional gas revolution.

Entrepreneurial independent oil and gas companies jumped on the technology and quickly carried it to other regions—in Louisiana and in Arkansas, and Oklahoma, and then to the "mighty Marcellus" shale that sprawls beneath western New York and Pennsylvania down into West Virginia.

THE "SHALE GALE"

Something was very strange about the numbers. As they rolled in for 2007 and then 2008, they showed something unexpected that did not make sense—a sudden surge in domestic production of U.S. natural gas. How was that possible? Where was that coming from? The United States was supposed to be facing a sharp decline in domestic production—for which LNG was the only sure answer. Then it started to become clear: a technological breakthrough was beginning to make its impact felt. The rest of the industry now realized that something new was happening. And that included both major oil and gas companies, which had heretofore been more focused on big international LNG projects, and which was thought to be required to offset the apparent shortfall in North American natural gas.

Over the next few years, the output of shale gas continued to increase. Some now started to call it the "shale gale." As the supply increased and skills were further developed, costs came down. Shale gas was proving to be cheaper than conventional natural gas. In 2000 shale was just 1 percent of natural gas supply. By 2011 it was 25 percent, and within two decades it could reach 50 percent.

The shale gas transformed the U.S. natural gas market. Perennial shortage gave way to substantial surplus, which turned the prospects for LNG in North America upside down. Just a few years earlier, LNG had seemed destined to fill an increasing share of the U.S. market. Instead it became a marginal supply rather than a necessity. Electric utilities, remembering gas shortages and price spikes, had been reluctant to use more natural gas. But now, with the new abundance and lower prices, lower-carbon gas seemed likely to play a much larger role in the generation of electric power, challenging the economics of nuclear power and displacing higher-carbon coal, the mainstay of electric generation. As a source of relatively low-priced electric power, it created a more difficult competitive environment for new wind projects. Shale gas also began to have an impact on the debate on both climate change and energy security policy. By the beginning of this decade, the rapidity and sheer scale of the shale breakthrough—and its effect on markets—qualified it as the most significant innovation in energy so far since the start of the twenty-first century. As a result of the shale revolution, North America's natural gas base, now estimated at 3,000 trillion cubic feet, could provide for current levels of consumption for over a hundred years—plus. "Recent innovations have given us the opportunity to tap larger reserves—perhaps a century's worth—in the shale under our feet," President Obama said in 2011.[5] The potential here is enormous.[6]

At the same time, the rapid growth in shale gas has stoked environmental controversy and policy debate. In part, demographic differences have brought the controversy to the fore. Lower-density states like Texas are accustomed to energy development, and encourage it as a major source of income for the population and revenues for the state government. Residents in more populated eastern states, like New York and Pennsylvania, are not accustomed to drilling in their region (although Pennsylvania is certainly long experienced with coal mining and was the birthplace of the oil industry. While some welcome the jobs, royalties, and tax revenues, others are taken aback by the surface disruption and the sudden increase in large truck traffic on what had been quiet country roads.

But, more than traffic, the environmental debate is centered on water. Critics warn that fraccing may damage drinking water aquifers. The industry argues that this is highly unlikely, as the fraccing takes place a mile or more below drinking water aquifers and is separated from them by thick layers of impermeable rock. Moreover, the industry has a great deal of experience with fraccing: more than a million wells have been fracced in the United States since the first frac job six decades ago. Fraccing uses small amounts of chemicals; the general trend now is to disclose those chemicals.

Although most of the discussion is about fraccing, the biggest issue has become not what goes down, but what comes back—the water that flows back to the surface. This is the "flow back" from the fraccing job, and then the "produced water" that comes out of the well over time. This water needs to be handled properly, managed, and safely disposed.

Three things can be done with the flow back and produced water. It can be injected into deep disposal wells; it can be put through treatment facilities; or it can be recycled back into operations. In traditional oil and gas states, the wastewater has often been reinjected. But the geology of Pennsylvania does not, for the most part, lend itself to reinjection. And so water that cannot be recycled has had either to be put through local treatment facilities or trucked out of state.

Aboveground management of waste has to keep pace with the rapid development of the shale industry. New large-scale water treatment facilities are being developed. The industry is now recycling 70 to 80 percent of the flow back. There is also intensive focus on innovation. These include developing new methods to reduce the amount of water going in and to treat the water coming out, and the drilling of more wells from a single "pad" to reduce the footprint.

A more recent concern is "migration"—whether methane leaks toward the surface and into some water wells as a result of fraccing. This is a controversial subject. Methane has been found in water wells in gas-producing regions but there is no agreement on how this can happen. Some cases of methane contamination in water wells have been tied to shallow layers of methane, not the mile-deep deposits of shale gas where fraccing takes place. In other cases, water wells may have been dug through layers of naturally occurring methane without being adequately sealed. It is difficult to know for certain because of a lack of "baseline" data—that is, measurements of a water well's methane content before a shale gas well is drilled in the neighborhood. Gas developers are now routinely taking such measurements before drilling begins in order to establish whether methane is preexisting in water aquifers. A new question concerns whether there are significant "fugitive emissions" or whether those emissions are captured.

One other subject of controversy is regulation itself. Some argue that drilling is an unregulated activity. In fact, the entire drilling process—including the water aspects—is heavily regulated by a mixture of state and federal agencies. The states are the primary regulators of drilling, including hydraulic fracturing as well as all other activities inherent in the production of oil and gas.

While the federal government has ultimate authority over water treatment and disposal, it has delegated its authority to many states whose own regulations meet or exceed federal standards. The next few years will see much argument about whether the federal government should have more responsibility. There will also be much more research on the water issues, and continuing focus on advancing the technology, both for drilling and for environmental protection in areas where shale gas is produced.[7]

The shale gale had not only taken almost the entire natural industry by surprise; it also sent people back to the geological maps. Very large potential supplies of shale gas have been identified in the traditional energy areas of Canada, in Alberta and British Columbia, as well as in eastern Canada, in Quebec. Chinese oil companies, recognizing significant potential for shale gas as well as coal-bed methane, have signed agreements with Western companies to develop both. Altogether the base of recoverable shale gas outside North America could be larger than all global conventional natural gas discovered to date. But only a portion is likely to be developed. Even so, the next several years are surely to see a substantial addition to the world's supply of natural gas.[8]

GLOBAL GAS

While shale gas is, thus far, a North American phenomenon in terms of large-scale production, it is already changing the dynamics of the global gas business. For its emergence as a new supply source coincided with a rapid buildup of LNG. In 2010 Qatar celebrated reaching 77 million tons of LNG capacity—28 percent of the world total. Australia is emerging as a new LNG powerhouse, number two only to Qatar and well positioned to supply Asia—and to continue to expand. Altogether, between 2004 and 2012, the world's LNG capacity will double. That means that what was accomplished in the first forty years of LNG development is being replicated in just eight years. But assumptions that helped underpin and drive this rapid buildup are now somewhat unhinged. The United States was supposed to be a major guaranteed market because of a projected domestic shortfall. But instead it is a marginal market.[9]

This puts much more LNG at sea, literally, in search of markets. Growing

Asia will absorb a significant amount, more than most had anticipated a few years ago. But far from all. Thus, the immediate impact is on Europe, which is now the world's number one contestable market. Freely available LNG, sold on a spot basis, can take some market share away from pipeline gas, whose price is, according to twenty-year contracts, indexed to more-expensive oil.

This not only creates greater competition among gas suppliers, pushing down price. It also has wide geopolitical impact, for it upsets a four-decade-old economic and political balance that has proved so durable that it even survived the upheaval that was set in motion by the collapse of the Soviet Union and the fall of communism. The new gas competition is central to the complex and evolving relationship among a much-expanded European Union, the Russian Federation, and the other newly independent states of the former Soviet Union, some of whom are now members of the European Union.

The development of the gas market in Europe is embodied in the web of pipelines that crisscross the European Continent. Look at the pipeline map from the 1960s, and all one sees are a few strands of string. Today such a map looks like a big bowl of spaghetti. Local gas markets had earlier developed in different parts of Europe. But the real European gas market only began with the development of the Groningen field in Holland in the 1960s, followed by the offshore oil and gas fields in the British sector of the North Sea.

In the 1970s, a new pipeline brought the first Soviet gas into Europe in the 1970s. It came with a strong geopolitical tone. West German Chancellor Willy Brandt signed the first Soviet gas deal in 1970 as a key element in his Ostpolitik, aimed at reducing Cold War tensions, normalizing relations with the Soviet Union and Eastern Europe, and creating some common interest between East and West. "Economics," as Brandt put it, was "an especially important part of our policy." He specifically, if indirectly, wanted to reestablish contact with communist East Germany, which had been cut off completely by the construction of the Berlin Wall in 1961. The dependence flowed in both directions; this gas trade, for the Soviets, became a major—and crucial—source of hard currency earnings.[10]

Over the years that followed, the gas business would be built up and managed by a handful of Western European transport and distribution companies joined together by 25-year contracts with the gas export arm of the Soviet Ministry of Gas Industry.

"WOUNDED BY A FRIEND"

By the early 1980s, major discoveries in West Siberia had propelled the Soviet Union ahead of the United States as the world's largest gas producer. Inevitably, those big new supplies provided further impetus to sell more gas into Western Europe.

The Soviets and the Europeans began to plan for a large, new, 3,700-mile pipeline from the great Urengoy field in West Siberia. But before it was ever built, the proposed pipeline created a bitter rupture in the Western alliance, prefiguring the controversies over the geopolitics of European natural gas that continue to the present.

The Reagan administration became alarmed at the prospect of a much larger East-West gas trade. It had launched a major arms buildup to counter Soviet military expansion; the last thing the administration wanted was additional hard currency earnings from natural gas financing the Soviet military-industrial complex. It also feared that greater reliance on Soviet gas would create vulnerable dependence that the Soviets could exploit to pry apart the Western alliance and that—in a time of crisis—would give the Soviets crucial leverage. The American administration warned that the Soviet Union could use dependence on its natural gas to "blackmail" the Europeans by threatening to turn off the heat and stoves in Munich.[11]

The Reagan administration struck back at the proposed new pipeline. It imposed a unilateral embargo that prohibited companies from exporting the billions of dollars of equipment that was essential to the construction and the operations of the pipeline. It applied not only to U.S. companies, but to European companies whose equipment was based on U.S. technology.

The Europeans, however, were as determined as the Soviets to go ahead. They wanted both the diversification away from the Middle East and the environmental benefits from reduced coal use. They also wanted the revenues and the jobs, as well as the opportunity to expand their export markets in the Soviet bloc. Even Reagan's closest ally, British Prime Minister Margaret Thatcher, looking at the loss of jobs in an area of Scotland with 20 percent unemployment, pushed back. Given her relationship with Reagan, she took the embargo very personally. "We feel particularly wounded by a friend," she said. The British government ordered the British companies that had contracts with the Soviets to ignore the embargo and to go ahead and ship their goods. Moreover, it became apparent that the Soviets could replicate some of the supposedly proprietary technology, albeit at higher cost. Thus the embargo would only delay, not prevent, the new pipeline from going ahead.[12]

By the end of 1982, a solution would be found. The Western allies would very seriously "study" the problem in order to determine what would be a "prudent" level of dependence on the Soviet Union. After much discussion, the study eventually established a dependence ratio of 25 percent, which just happened to be higher than the share of Soviet gas even with the new pipeline. It was also understood that natural gas from a major new source, Norway's Troll field, would begin to flow into European markets.

The Urengoy pipeline was indeed built, and the flow of Soviet gas into Europe more than doubled over a decade. Even when the Soviet Union collapsed, the gas continued to flow. In the 1990s the earnings from gas exports would prove a critical source of revenues for Russia as the government of Boris Yeltsin struggled to stay afloat in those difficult years.

THE EMERGENCE OF GAZPROM

Out of the Soviet collapse, and specifically out of the Ministry of Gas Industry, a new Russian gas company emerged: Gazprom. Eventually it would have private shareholders not only in Russia but around the world, and would become, for investors and fund managers, a proxy stock for the overall performance of the Russian stock market and economy. At one point, in mid-2008, Gazprom's stock market capitalization catapulted to more than $300 billion, and it ranked as the third-largest company in the world by that measure, behind ExxonMobil and PetroChina.[13]

Gazprom remains just over 80 percent owned by the Russian state with which it is closely aligned and to which it pays taxes of one kind or another equivalent to about 15 percent of the total government budget. In many meetings with Western businessmen, Prime Minister Vladimir Putin has demonstrated a deep interest and an extraordinarily detailed knowledge about the gas business. For his part, Dmitry Medvedev, before becoming Russia's president, was chairman of Gazprom. The company produces over 80 percent of Russia's total natural gas output. It also has a monopoly over gas transportation within Russia and over all gas exports. It is, thus, Russia's interlocutor with the global gas market. Gazprom, while retaining its primacy at home, has also been moving to become a global diversified energy company. That began with the establishment of a joint marketing company in Germany in 1993 with Wintershall, a German energy company.

By 2005 European gas supply appeared to be in political balance. Domestic European production was 39 percent; Russia supplied 26 percent; Norway, 16 percent; Algeria, 10 percent; and about almost another 10 percent from other sources, largely LNG. But by then the system that had created the European gas market was disintegrating, and many of the premises on which it had been built were progressively dissipating, creating new tensions and conflicts.

For one thing, Europe was going through great change. The European Union had grown to 27 members; the new additions being either former Soviet satellites or, in the case of the Baltic nations, former constituents of the Soviet Union. These new members have a high degree of dependence on Russian gas, but their energy relations are wrapped up in overall unsettled and sometimes tense relations with Russia.

The gas market was also changing in somewhat unpredictable ways. In order to promote "competition," the European Union was seeking to break up the integrated companies that had helped build the market and move away from the stability of 25-year contracts that the companies had used as the building blocks. Instead the EU wanted to promote trading, hubs, and spot markets. But it was not clear how the next generation of expensive new gas fields in Russia (or elsewhere) could be developed without the guarantee of such long-term contracts. At the same time, gas supplies from the North Sea were declining. In addition, the dominance of pipeline gas could erode as increasingly large volumes of LNG sought entry into Europe.

And the Soviet Union was gone. The region through which the critical pipelines transited was no longer either part of the Soviet Union or its satellites, but rather independent countries. They were dependent on Russia for their gas, but history of Soviet domination weighed heavily on their relations.[14] And Russia was dependent on them for access to the European market.

UKRAINE VERSUS RUSSIA

No relationship was more complex than that with Ukraine. Russia and Ukraine were bound together by history. The Russian state had actually been founded in Kiev, now the capital of Ukraine, and Ukraine had been part of the Russian Empire from 1648. Russian, and not Ukrainian, was the daily language of life in Soviet Ukraine. After independence in 1991, the country seemed to have a natural split: eastern Ukraine still looked to Russia; western Ukraine gravitated increasingly toward Europe.

Gas much complicated the new relationship between the two countries. Since the breakup of the Soviet Union in 1991, Russia and Ukraine had often been at odds, and sometimes rancorously so, over gas pricing and supply, and over the tariffs and indeed control of the crucial pipeline to Europe.

The victory by the Western-oriented Orange Revolution in the December 2005 Ukraine presidential election put the two countries on a path to confrontation. The Orange Revolution aimed at reducing Russian influence and reorienting toward Europe. The new president, Viktor Yuschenko, had, prior to the election, barely survived a mysterious poisoning with deadly dioxin, and he built much of his campaign on turning away from Russia.

Natural gas became the inevitable focus for rising tensions. Ukraine was heavily dependent on gas from Russia. It has the most energy-intensive economy in the world, three times more energy intensive than that of neighboring Poland. The previous government had negotiated a deal with Moscow that gave Ukraine the gas at a steep discount from the price charged to Western Europe. This was really a subsidy to the aged Soviet-era industrial infrastructure and one that was essential to keeping it competitive in world markets. For years, international institutions like the World Bank had been urging Ukraine to raise domestic gas prices to improve energy efficiency, but Ukraine had resisted from fear of the impact on its industries and on jobs.

In its relations with Russia, Ukraine had one trump—the pipeline network, which carried over 80 percent of Russia's gas exports to Europe. Yuschenko had described this system as Ukraine's "crown jewels," and he had no intention of letting Russia gain control.[15]

But for Russia, greater control over those pipelines was a decisive objective, exactly because it was so central to its export position. Ukraine owed Russia billions of dollars in unpaid bills for gas. Moreover, it was buying gas at much lower prices than the Europeans. That might have been acceptable were Ukraine still aligned with Russia. But it was not. Therefore, Moscow asked why it should provide what was, in effect, a $3 billion–plus annual subsidy to a hostile Orange Revolution, thus depriving Gazprom and the Russian government of revenues that they would otherwise have. For months after Yuschenko became president, increasingly angry negotiations on gas prices dragged on between Gazprom and Ukraine, with no resolution. Complicating things further was the existence of a strange and nontransparent company called RosUkrEnergo, which appeared to control the flow of gas in and out of Ukraine.

At 10:00 a.m. on the cold winter Sunday of New Year's Day, January 1, 2006, pipeline pressure suddenly began to go down at the border into Ukraine. Gazprom had begun to cut gas deliveries directed to Ukraine itself. Moscow immediately warned Ukraine not to siphon off any of the gas that was meant to flow on to Europe. Notwithstanding, Ukraine proceeded to do exactly that, and some shortfalls of gas became evident not only in Ukraine but also in Central Europe.

The showdown was resolved within a few days and the gas shipments resumed. But the shock waves reverberated across the entire Continent. Russian delivery of gas to some former constituents of the former Soviet Union had been disrupted at times of tension. But never in four decades had there been a decision that would disrupt supplies to Europe. Such disruptions as had occurred were the result of weather or technical malfunctions. Here now, it seemed to some, was concrete proof of the dangers of dependence that had animated the pipeline battle of the 1980s. "Europe needs a clear and more collective policy on the security of our energy supply," said Andris Piebalgs, the EU energy commissioner. Austria's economic minister was blunter: "Dependence on Russia should be reduced," he declared. Over the next couple of years, natural gas became a heated subject of contention and suspicion between East and West. At one point, Alexei Miller, the CEO of Gazprom, told the Europeans, "Get over your fear of Russia, or run out of gas."[16]

For their part, Russia and Ukraine had had further standoffs over natural gas pricing. Even the subsequent government of President Viktor Yanukovych, which had better relations with Moscow, still continued to describe its pipeline network as "our national treasure."

DIVERSIFICATION

The lasting impact of the gas controversies was to fuel a new campaign of diversification on both sides of the argument. That meant a new round of pipeline politics that was elevated to the geopolitical level. The Russians were determined to get around Ukraine and Poland with a series of new pipelines. Gazprom and ENI had already built Blue Stream, which crosses the Black Sea from Russia to Turkey and is the deepest underwater pipeline in the world. They now bruited the idea of South Stream, which would cross the Black Sea from Russia to Bulgaria and deliver gas to Italy. Russia also launched a large new pipeline project, Nord Stream, in partnership with major Western European gas companies and chaired by former German Chancellor Gerhard Schröeder. Nord Stream travels under the Baltic Sea from near St. Petersburg to northern Germany.

But most contentious of all are the EU and European proposals aimed at bringing non-Russian gas to Europe by skirting Russia's southern border and involving countries that were formerly part of the Soviet Union, countries that Russia continues to see as part of its sphere of influence. The European Union calls this the Fourth Corridor and emphasizes that it is not a challenge to Russia but just an appropriate diversification. Some European companies have combined to promote the Nabucco project. This odd name was borrowed from a Verdi opera that some of the original planners had seen one night while meeting in Vienna. Nabucco would pick up gas in Turkey and carry it all the way to Germany.

But where would the gas come from to fill the Fourth Corridor pipeline system? That is the central question and a source of great uncertainty—in terms of price, availability, and reliability—and politics. It could be from Turkmenistan, which has immense resources but has made exporting east to China its number one priority. It could be Azerbaijan, but it has its own plans. The gas resources in Kurdistan, in northern Iraq, could potentially be very large, but both the politics and security situation are very unsettled. The transit fees across Turkey need to be reasonable, both for shippers and buyers. The European market has to be large enough to absorb the gas and thus justify the billions of dollars in investment. In the meantime, Russia's interest is to discourage the Fourth Corridor, which would somewhat erode its own market position in Europe, and move quickly to preempt with its own new pipelines.[17]

This clash of pipeline politics is further unsettled by the potential for alternative new supplies—from the global LNG market. These supplies could greatly increase, both because of the growing LNG capacity around the world and the disappearance of the U.S. market owing to shale gas. These additional volumes of LNG would compete with present and future pipeline gas, putting downward pressure on all gas prices and thus making the economics of new pipeline projects more problematic. In addition, a major new source of gas might be opening up on Europe's doorstep in the eastern Mediterranean. The deepwater Leviathan field offshore Israel is one of the largest discoveries so far this century.

And then there is the potential for shale gas. There is no geologic law that restricts shale gas to North America. Only around 2009 did serious work on shale gas begin to determine how abundant shale gas is in Europe, and how difficult to extract. A new study suggests that Europe's endowment of unconventional gas—shale gas and coal-bed methane—may be as large as that of North America. Development of these resources could provide an alternative to gas imports, whether they come by pipeline from the east or by ship in the form of LNG.[18]

But it is still early days, and a great deal of effort will be required to develop such resources. Obstacles will range from local opposition and national policy to lack of infrastructure and sheer density of population. Still the imperatives of diversification will likely fuel the development of unconventional gas resources in some parts of Europe, as elsewhere—most notably in Poland and Ukraine. The new supplies will compensate for declining conventional domestic supplies. Moreover, by enhancing the sense of security and diversification around gas supplies, the development of unconventional gas could end up bolstering confidence in relying on expanded gas imports.

A FUEL FOR THE FUTURE

Natural gas is a fuel of the future. World consumption has tripled over the last thirty years, and demand could grow another 50 percent over the next two decades. Its share of the total energy market is also growing. World consumption on an energy-equivalent basis was only 45 percent that of oil; today it is about 70 percent. The reasons are clear: It is a relatively low-carbon resource. It is also a flexible fuel that could play a larger role in electric power, both for its own features and as an effective—and indeed necessary—complement to greater reliance on renewable generation. And technology is making it more and more available, whether in terms of advances in conventional drilling, the ability to move it over long-distance pipelines, the expansion of LNG onto much larger scale, or, most recently, the revolution in unconventional natural gas.

A few years ago the focus was mainly on rapid growth in LNG. With that went a widespread belief that a true world gas market was in the making, one in which supplies would easily move to one market or another, and one in which prices would converge. The arrival of shale gas has, for the time being, disproved that assumption. Yet the emergence of this new resource in North America is certainly having a worldwide impact—demonstrating that the gas market is global after all—just not quite in the way that would have been expected.

PART THREE

...

The Electric Age

17

ALTERNATING CURRENTS

Electricity underpins modern civilization. This fundamental truth is often expressed in terms of "keeping the lights on," which is appropriate, as lighting was electricity's first major market and remains a necessity. But today that phrase is also a metaphor for its pervasiveness and essentiality. Electricity delivers a precision unmatched by any other form of energy; it is also almost infinitely versatile in how it can be used.

Consider what would not work and would not happen without electric power. Obviously, no refrigerators, no air-conditioning, no television, no elevators. It is essential for every kind of industrial processing. The new digital world relies on electricity's precision to drive everything that runs on microprocessors—computers, telephones, smart phones, medical equipment, espresso machines. Electricity makes possible and integrates the real-time networks of communications, finance, and trade that shape the world economy. And its importance only grows, as most new energy-consuming devices require electricity.[1]

Electricity may be all-pervasive. But it is also mostly taken for granted, much more so than oil. After all, gasoline usage requires the conscious activity once or twice a week of pulling into the filling station and filling up. To tap into electricity, all one needs to do is flip a switch. When people think about power, it's usually only when the monthly bill arrives or on those infrequent times when the lights are suddenly extinguished either by a storm or some breakdown in the delivery system.

All this electrification did indeed begin with a flip of a switch.

THE WIZARD OF MENLO PARK

On the afternoon of September 4, 1882, the polymathic inventor Thomas Edison was in the Wall Street offices of the nation's most powerful banker, J. P. Morgan. At 3:00 p.m., Edison threw the switch. "They're on!" a Morgan director exclaimed, as a hundred lightbulbs lit up, filling the room with their light.[2]

Nearby, at the same moment, 52 bulbs went on in the offices of the *New York Times,* which proclaimed the new electric light "soft," and "graceful to the eye . . . without a particle of flicker to make the head ache." The current for these bulbs flowed underground, through wires and tubes, from a coal-fired electric generating plant that Edison had built a few blocks away, on Pearl Street, partly financed by J. P. Morgan, to serve one square mile of lower Manhattan. With that, the age of electricity had begun.

The Pearl Street station was the first central generating plant in the United States. It was also a major engineering challenge for Edison and his organization; it required the building of six huge "dynamos," or generators, which, at 27 tons each, were nicknamed "Jumbos" after the huge elephant from Africa with which the circus showman P. T. Barnum was then touring America.

Another landmark event in electric power occurred a few months later, on January 18, 1883. That was the first electricity bill ever—dispatched to the Ansonia Brass and Copper Company, for the historic sum of $50.44.[3]

It had required a decade of intense, almost round-the-clock work by Thomas Edison and his team to get to that electric moment on Pearl Street. Still only in his midthirties at the time, Edison had already made himself America's most celebrated inventor with his breakthroughs on the telegraph and the phonograph. He was also said to be the most famous American in the rest of the world. Edison was to establish the record for the greatest number of American patents ever issued to one person—a total of 1,093. Much later, well into the twentieth century, newspaper and magazine polls continued to select him as America's "greatest" and "most useful citizen."

Edison was largely self-taught; he had only a couple of years of formal schooling, plus six years as an itinerant telegrapher, making such achievements even more remarkable. His partial deafness made him somewhat isolated and self-centered, but also gave him an unusual capacity for concentration and creativity. He proceeded by experiment, reasoning, and sheer determination, and, as he once said, "by methods which I could not explain." He had set up a research laboratory in Menlo Park, New Jersey, with the ambitious aim, as he put it, of making an invention factory that would deliver "a minor invention every ten days and a big thing every six months or so."[4]

"THE SUBDIVISION OF LIGHT"

That was not so easy, as he found when he homed in on electricity. He wanted to replace the then-prevalent gas-fired lamp. What he also wanted to do, in his own words, was to "subdivide" light; that is, deliver electric light not just over a few large streetlights as was then possible, but make it "subdivided so that it could be brought into private homes."

Many scoffed at Edison's grand ambition. Experts appointed by the British Parliament dismissed Edison's research as "good enough for our transatlantic friends" but "unworthy of the attention of practical or scientific men."

To prove them wrong and successfully subdivide light, Edison would have to create an entire system—not just the lightbulb but also the means to generate electricity and distribute it across a city. "Edison's genius," one scholar has written, "lay in his ability to direct a process involving problem identification, solution as idea, research and development, and introduction into use." His aim was not just to invent a better lightbulb (there had already been 20 or so of one kind or another) but to introduce an entire system of lighting—and to do so on a commercial basis, and as quickly as possible.[5]

The inventor had to start somewhere, which did mean with the lightbulb. The challenge, for a practical bulb, was to find a filament that, when electricity flowed through it, would give off a pleasing light but that also could last not just one hour but for many hours. After experimenting with a wide variety of possible sources—including hairs from the beards of two of his employees—he came up with a series of carbon filament, first made from cotton thread and then from cardboard and then bamboo, that passed the test.

Years of acrimonious and expensive litigation followed among Edison and other competing lightbulb inventors over who had infringed whose patents. The U.S. Court of Appeals finally resolved the legal fight in the United States in 1892. In Britain, however, the court upheld competing patents by the English scientist Joseph Wilson Swan. Rather than fight Swan, Edison established a joint venture with him to manufacture lightbulbs in Britain.

To create an entire system required considerable funding. Although not called such at the time, one of the other inventions that could be credited to Edison and his investors was venture capital. For what he developed in Menlo Park, New Jersey, was a forerunner of the venture capital industry that would grow, coincidentally, around another Menlo Park—this one in Silicon Valley in California. As an Edison biographer has observed, it was his melding of the "laboratory and business enterprise that enabled him to succeed."[6]

Costs were a constant problem, and as they increased, so did the pressures. The price of copper, needed for the wires, kept going up. "It is very expensive experimenting," Edison moaned at one point. The rising costs strained his relations with his investors, leading him to complain, "Capital is timid."

But he did keep happy his lead investor—J. P. Morgan—by wiring up Morgan's Italianate mansion on Madison Avenue in the East 30s in New York City with 385 bulbs. That required the installation of a steam engine and electric generators in a specially dug cellar under the mansion. The clanging noise irritated not only the neighbors but also Mrs. Morgan. Moreover, the system required a technician to be on duty from 3:00 p.m. to 11:00 p.m. every day, which was not exactly efficient. Making matters worse, one night Edison's wiring set J. P. Morgan's library on fire. But, through it all, Morgan remained phlegmatic, with his eye on the objective. "I hope the Edison Company appreciates the value of my house as an experimental station," the banker dryly remarked.[7]

"BATTLE OF THE CURRENTS"

Except for Morgan's mansion, Edison concentrated on developing central generating stations that would supply part of the city. But Edison's system had a major limiting flaw. Because of its low voltage, Edison's direct current electricity could not travel very far. If Edison had had his way, every square mile of a city would have needed its own generating plant, which would have certainly minimized the economies of scale and much slowed the spread of electric power.

Alternating current—otherwise known as AC—provided an alternative. The Pittsburgh industrialist George Westinghouse had acquired the patent of a brilliant but eccentric Serbian inventor, Nikola Tesla, that made alternating current practical. A transformer would step up electricity to much higher voltage, which meant it could be economically transported long distances over transmission lines, and then stepped down at the other end for subdivision into individual homes. That made possible larger generating plants, serving a much greater area. With that came true economies of scale and much lower costs.

What followed was a titanic struggle between Edison and Westinghouse. Because electricity was a networks system, there could be only one winner, and the outcome would be winner takes all.

Edison threw all his formidable prestige into his furious battle against alternating current, denouncing it as unsafe and warning that it would lead to people's accidental electrocution. At that time, electrocution happened to be much in the news, as the state of New York was considering the electric chair as the preferred method for executions. The state's electrocution expert, also secretly working for Edison, sought to inextricably link alternating current with electrocution and death by the electric chair. As part of the campaign, Edison himself electrocuted animals to demonstrate the dangers of alternating current. Edison's group went further and tried to dub the electric chair "the Westinghouse" and to describe execution by electrocution as being "Westinghoused."[8]

Yet the superiority of alternating current was so clear that Westinghouse's alternating current system prevailed. Westinghouse grabbed market share from Edison and established the foundations for large-scale generation. Edison's technological stubbornness weakened his company financially during a time of business difficulties. His company, Edison General Electric—against his own fervent protestations—was forced into a merger with a competitor. To add to the ignominy and Edison's pain, the merger stripped his name from the merged company. Thereafter, it would be known simply as General Electric.

Electricity's ascendancy was on display at the Chicago World's Fair of 1893, which was so popular that the number of people attending it over six months was equivalent to more than a third of the entire population of the United States. The throngs were amazed by the demonstrations of all the versatile things electricity could do. One of them was something remarkable that most had never seen before: the world's fair emblazoned the night, earning Chicago the nickname "the white city." At the fair's center the General Electric Company erected the "Tower of Light" as a tribute to Edison. But the exposition also demonstrated Westinghouse's victory over Edison, for it was Westinghouse and Tesla's alternating current that powered most of the lighting and the exhibits.[9]

The technical pieces were now in place for the growth of electric power. But what would be the business model?

THE METER MAN

Samuel Insull first went to work in London at the age of fourteen as an office boy at the British magazine *Vanity Fair*. Then, answering a classified advertisement, he was hired as a secretary in the office of the European representative of Thomas Edison. There he made such a good impression that the chief engineer recommended him to the inventor, and in 1881 Insull emigrated to America to work as Edison's secretary. The first day Insull arrived in Menlo Park, Edison kept him up to midnight, dictating to him, and then told him to get some rest, as they would start again at six in the morning. The 117-pound Insull quickly established himself as the dynamo in Edison's organization. After Edison lost control of the company in 1892, Insull moved to Chicago to take over one of the 20 or so competing generating companies in the city.[10]

In the early 1890s, electricity was still a luxury product. Customers were charged by the number of bulbs installed in their homes or offices. Insull had much grander ambitions. He wanted scale: he wanted to lower prices and sell to as many people as he could and by so doing democratize electricity. He couldn't get there by having people pay by the bulb. But how to do it? As often happens in innovation, Insull stumbled upon the answer by accident.

On a trip to England in 1894, Insull, worn out by his frenetic pace, decided to go down to the seaside resort of Brighton for a little rest. As evening rolled in, he was stunned to see the town light up. All the shops, no matter what their size, were bright with electric lights. How could this be? The manager of the local power plant, it turned out, had invented a meter that could measure how much electricity each store or home used. This made possible a new business model: instead of paying by the bulb, people could pay by their usage, along with an additional charge covering the capital invested in the project. "We had to go to Europe," Insull explained afterward, "to learn something about the principles underlying the sale of the product."[11]

The meter, imported by Insull to Chicago, would become the interface, the middleman so to speak, between the generating company and the customer. Electricity could be priced by consumption, not by the number of bulbs. This facilitated the scale that Insull wanted and helped propel the vast growth in his business. Insull did everything else he could to get scale, from aggressive marketing to installing the world's largest generators to gaining new customers like the rapidly expanding trolley lines, which he could electrify—all in order to sell to the most people he could, at the lowest prices possible. Insull assured other utility executives in 1910 that if they priced their product cheaply enough, they would greatly increase their sales and "you will begin to realize the possibilities of this business, and these possibilities may exceed your wildest dreams."[12]

"NATURAL MONOPOLY": THE REGULATORY BARGAIN

To build his empire, Insull used the great financial innovation of the day—the holding company—a company that controls part of or all the interest in another company or companies. Insull constructed a pyramid of these holding companies, with each tier holding a controlling interest in the one below, on down to the base—the power plants themselves. In such a way, Insull, through his holding companies, could control a huge amount of assets with a relatively small outlay of capital, and thus reap outsize returns.

To build out the pyramid base, Insull would acquire local electric utilities and close their small, inefficient power plants, and build much larger central stations plus the transmission lines to serve groups of localities. Access to electricity would be much expanded, and prices would come down. In this way his companies became the provider of electricity to millions of Americans.

But chaotic competition threatened this new model. An electric generating company typically had to obtain a franchise from the municipality, and the municipality might grant franchises to a number of competing companies. Moreover, in many cases, the whole business of franchising could become quite corrupt—a franchise granted could also be a franchise withdrawn.

Altogether, between 1882 and 1905, the city of Chicago granted 29 power franchises, plus another 18 from towns that it had absorbed. Some of the franchises were as small as "a few blocks on the northwest side" or "the old twelfth ward." Three of them covered the entire city. At one point, members of the Chicago City Council and their friends set up a competitive power company with the obvious purpose of forcing Insull to purchase it at vastly inflated prices. Such was Insull's muscle, however, that he was able to knock down the price. The political instability surrounding a franchise made capital raising difficult; yet this industry had an enormous appetite for investment capital in order to expand and achieve the greater efficiencies and lower costs that came from larger scale.[13]

Faced with such a treacherous business environment, Insull promoted yet another innovation—this, not technical, but political: it was the regulatory bargain. Because of the large investment required by the business, the economics of this industry dictated, in his view, that it be a monopoly. But he argued it was a particular kind of monopoly—a "natural monopoly." It was very wasteful to have two companies laying wires down the same alley and building capacity and competing head to head to supply the same customer. Costs to the customer would end up higher, not lower. By contrast, because of the efficiency of its investment, a natural monopoly would deliver lower prices to the consumer.

This was where the bargain came in. Insull recognized the political reality: If "the business was a natural monopoly," he said, "it must of necessity be regulated by some form of governmental authority"—specifically a state public utility commission, which would determine the "fairness" of its rates. For, he said, "competition is an unsound economic regulator" in the electricity business.

This call for government regulation hardly endeared him to many of his fellow electricity entrepreneurs, but it became the way the business worked. In due course, this regulatory bargain was ingrained into public policy: as a natural monopoly, the electric power business had to be treated as a regulated industry with its rates and its profits determined by a public utility commission. What was required of the regulators in turn was, as Supreme Court Justice Oliver Wendell Holmes Jr. wrote in 1912, "fair interpretation of a bargain."[14]

Wisconsin and New York established the first such commissions in 1907. By the 1920s, about half the states had done so, and eventually all of them did. This new regulatory bargain imposed a fundamental responsibility on the natural monopolist—the utility had the obligation to "serve"—to deliver electricity to virtually everyone in its territory and provide acceptable, reliable service at reasonable cost. Otherwise, it would lose its license to operate.

ELEKTROPOLIS: TECHNOLOGY TRANSFER ACROSS THE SEAS

Chicago, lit up by Insull, became the world's showcase for electricity. It had only one rival: Berlin, which became known around the world as Elektropolis.

The inventor Werner von Siemens and an engineer named Emil Rathenau would be decisive figures in Berlin's—and Germany's—electrical preeminence. Rathenau acquired the German rights to Edison's electrical inventions. His company achieved recognition in 1884 when it succeeded in lighting up the popular Café Bauer, on the Unter den Linden, the most prominent boulevard in Berlin. Rathenau built up what eventually became AEG—Allgemeine Elektrizitäts Gesellschaft—German for the "General Electric Company."

By 1912 Berlin would be described as "electrically, the most important city" in Europe. Siemens and AEG became formidable companies, competing head-on for contracts to electrify cities and towns throughout Germany.

Electricity was the hallmark of progress in the late nineteenth and early twentieth centuries. Illuminating that progress, Berlin, with three million people, and Chicago, with two million, easily outshone London, which, with seven million people, was the largest—and most important—city in the Western world.

Whereas Chicago and Berlin both had centralized systems, London was highly fragmented, with 70 generating stations, about 70 different methods of charging and pricing, and 65 separate utilities, including such variegated firms as the Westminster Electric Supply Corporation, the Charing Cross Electric Supply Company, and the St James and Pall Mall Company, and many more. "Londoners who could afford electricity toasted bread in the morning with one kind, lit their offices with another, visited associates in a nearby office building using still another, and walked home along streets that were illuminated by yet another kind."

London lagged because of the lack of a regulatory framework that would have promoted a more rational unified system. A prominent engineer complained in 1913 that London used "an absurdly small amount of electricity" for a city its size. "There is a very great danger of our not only being last, but of our remaining last." London continued to lag for years after.[15]

"AIM FOR THE TOP"

In the United States by the 1920s, Samuel Insull had implemented his formidable business model—taking advantage of the economies of scale derived from centralized, mass production to provide an inexpensive product to a diverse customer base—on a grand scale. His great electric power empire stretched across the Middle West and into the East. Chicago itself showed the scale of what had been achieved. When Insull took over Chicago Edison in 1882, there were just 5,000 customers in the entire city, and they paid by the number of electric bulbs. The optimistic view at that time was "as many as 25,000 Chicagoans might ultimately use electricity."

But by the 1920s, 95 percent of the homes in Chicago were wired for electricity. And they paid by usage. This was the prototype of Insull's vision for the world: "Every home, every factory and every transportation line will obtain its energy from one common source, for the simple reason that that will be the cheapest way to produce and distribute it." By the boom years of the 1920s, Insull himself had become not only one of the most famous businessmen in the world but also an icon of capitalism. Many saw him as the greatest business statesman of the age, his words were venerated like those of a sage, and "Insullism" was applauded as the future of capitalism.[16]

At the peak, in 1929, Insull's empire of holding and operating companies, valued in the billions, controlled power companies in 32 states; and he held 65 chairmanships, 85 directorships, and 11 presidencies. He was a man of wide renown and a great benefactor. He was the "presiding angel" of the Civic Opera House in Chicago and was responsible for its building.

Reporters constantly sought out his wisdom. Asked by one reporter for his advice to young men starting out, he said, "Aim for the top." And what was his "greatest ambition in life"?

"To hand down my name as clean as I received it," he replied.

That was not quite to be.[17]

"I HAVE ERRED": TOO MUCH DEBT

In the booming late 1920s, Insull's empire went on a buying spree, acquiring new companies and consolidating control of its holdings—all of this at higher and higher prices. In December 1928 he created a new company, Insull Utilities Investments, and to assure his control over his empire, he issued shares to the public at $12. Before the summer of 1929 was out, the stock had hit $150.[18]

The business required continually greater scale to bring down costs, deliver cheaper power, expand the customer base—and to assure profits. But such expansion created enormous capital needs, which Insull met by taking on more debt and by selling common stock to customers and the public. Insull relentlessly pursued growth. Even after the 1929 stock crash, his companies were still making investments, and taking on still more debt with some abandon. The enterprise became leveraged to an extraordinary degree. Moreover, Insull's accounting practices were suspect. His companies, it was said, would overcharge each other for services. They would also sell assets among themselves, marking up the book values after the sales; they virtually ignored accounting for the depreciation of assets. The whole business was predicated on Insull's ability to continue raising massive sums, even as investors had little understanding of the actual finances of the companies. But time was running out.

As the Great Depression deepened and the stock market continued to decline, banks began to call in their loans from Insull. The ugly reality became clear: the debt he had taken on for acquisitions far exceeded the value of the stock that had been pledged as collateral, for the value of this stock had been plummeting. "I have erred," Insull said. "My greatest error was in underestimating the effect of the financial panic."[19]

In 1932 Insull's whole empire collapsed, done in by its debt and intricately complex corporate structure. When the bankers, at a meeting in New York, told Insull that they would give him no more respite and were pulling his loans, he is reported to have said, "I wish my time on earth had already come."

The *New York Times* had described Insull as a man of "foresight and vision . . . one of the foremost and greatest builders of American industrial empires." But now Insull was disgraced; "too broke to be bankrupt," said one banker. Insull's fall from the pinnacle was as precipitous and calamitous as any in American history.[20]

Thousands of small investors were left holding securities worth only pennies on the dollar. The federal government launched criminal charges against him for fraud and embezzlement. Not only was he now poor, he had also become, according to both prosecutors and much of the public, a scoundrel, an embezzler, and a crook. Everything else was forgotten.

But Insull was more than the scapegoat for the Great Depression. He had very quickly become the very embodiment of the evils of capitalism in an economically prostrate country that was close to losing faith in the system. Franklin Roosevelt, campaigning for president in 1932, pledged "to get" the Insulls.

Insull fled the country. He chartered a Greek freighter to cruise the Mediterranean while considering taking up an offer to become minister of power of Rumania or seeking political asylum elsewhere. When he docked in Istanbul, the Turkish authorities arrested him and packed him back to the United States, where the small, white-haired 74-year-old was transited, under armed guard, to a Chicago courthouse. Formidable prosecutorial talent was arrayed against Insull.

The jury took just five minutes to come to its decision. But the jurors, in order to avoid any suspicion, used various ruses to stall, including ordering in a cake and coffee and holding a birthday party for one of them. Finally, the jurors walked back into the courtroom with their decision. Insull was not guilty.

Despite his acquittal, Insull decided it would be better to live out his life in Paris. He had lost virtually all his money; even the ownership of his shirt studs became the subject of a lawsuit. In order to save money, Insull made his way around the city on the Paris Metro. In 1938 he collapsed from a heart attack at the Place de la Concorde station. There he died clutching a subway ticket in his right hand. The press pounced on the fact that the great capitalist, the architect of the modern electric power industry, had died so poor that he was found virtually penniless, with just a few centimes in his pocket. He had little in personal effects to leave behind. His legacy was the business model for electric power.[21]

THE NEW DEAL: COMPLETING THE ELECTRIFICATION OF AMERICA

The hostility toward Insull and the holding-company structure was enormous. It was widely believed that speculators and bankers had used the holding-company system to gouge customers, loot the utilities, and make inordinate and unconscionable profits. The Federal Trade Commission left no doubt of its view of the system epitomized by Insull with the following words—"fraud, deceit, misrepresentation, dishonesty, breach of trust and oppression."[22]

But Insull's vision had also made electricity available to millions of Americans. "The decades of complex system-building were easier to ignore or forget," wrote one scholar of the electric power industry. "They involved difficult concepts, esoteric technology, uncommon economics, and sophisticated management." Insull's empire, and the business model he developed, brought the U.S. public affordable reliable electric power in a remarkably short period of time.

A top New Deal priority was to eliminate the holding-company system pioneered by Insull and by which most of the U.S. power industry operated. The utilities and their supporters fought back in the most contentious and bitter domestic political battle of the entire New Deal. "I am against private socialism of concentrated power as thoroughly as I am against governmental socialism," Roosevelt declared. And in the end the New Deal did prevail with the historic Public Utility Holding Act of 1935, which defined the new legal structure of the electric power industry. Designed to get the Insulls out of electric power, it dealt what was triumphantly called "the death sentence" to the kind of complex holding-company network that Insull had masterminded. Holding companies were effectively permitted only for utilities that were geographically adjacent and in some way physically integrated.[23]

But when it came to electricity, the nation was divided in two. City dwellers had easy access to power, provided either by investor-owned utilities or municipality owned. But rural dwellers had almost no access. Investor-owned utilities were not stringing lines out into the countryside because, they said, the costs were too high and the load density too low.

This left farmers stuck in the nineteenth century with endless hours of back-breaking labor. Cows had to be milked by hand. There were no refrigerators to keep food fresh long enough to get it to market. It was even worse for the farmer's wife. Hours had to be spent tending the hot stove; more hours beating the laundry clean outside. By one estimate, it took 63 eight-hour days a year per farm to pump and haul water back to the house. Half of all farm families did their laundry and bathed their children outside. All because there was no electricity.[24]

This changed with the New Deal, beginning with a federally owned dam at Muscle Shoals, in Alabama, which had been built to provide power for manufacturing explosives during the First World War. After a bruising political battle, it became the starting point for the government-owned Tennessee Valley Authority, with another 20 or so dams to be built as part of the system.

In 1936 Roosevelt signed legislation creating the Rural Electrification Administration. It provided loans to rural cooperatives, which built transmission and distribution lines to isolated farms across America that, until then, had had to depend upon kerosene lamps for their light and exhausting labor for their power. Some of the co-ops also went into electricity generation.

Other legislation established marketing authorities that gave preference to rural cooperatives and municipals for the power generated by the big new federal dams, like Bonneville and Grand Coulee in the northwest, and the Hoover Dam on the Colorado. The REA and the cooperatives that worked with it transformed the life of rural America.

"LIVE BETTER ELECTRICALLY"

The 1950s and 1960s were the years in which America really became an electrified society. With the end of World War II, millions of U.S. soldiers returned home. Rising marriage and birth rates, combined with the G.I. Bill that made it easier for veterans to purchase homes, led to a surge in demand for new houses. A great suburban house-building movement rolled out from the cities, with more than 13 million new homes built in the United States between 1945 and 1954—and with electricity playing an increasingly important role in the American home and American life. During the postwar years of the 1950s, U.S. electricity demand grew at an astounding annual rate of 10 percent (compared with about 1 percent in recent years) as more and more uses were found for electricity in homes, offices, and factories.[25]

Nothing so much captured the build-out of electricity in the postwar era as General Electric's "Live Better Electrically" campaign, launched in the mid-1950s and supported by 300 utilities. But such a campaign needed a spokesman, indeed a national champion. It turned toward Hollywood.

In the early 1950s, Ronald Reagan's movie career was not going all that well. Yes, he was a well-known screen actor, but not quite a top leading man. As president of the Screen Actors Guild, the actors union, he had certainly honed his political skills behind the scenes, but that had done nothing to advance his presence on the silver screen. He and his wife Nancy had a baby at home, but no scripts or paychecks were coming into the house. Finally, his agent landed him a job at the Last Frontier Hotel in Las Vegas, doing stand-up comedy and opening for a singing group called the Continentals. Though Reagan protested that he neither sang nor danced, the money was good, and the two-week show was sold out, but he found the work boring, and he and Nancy had no interest in the gaming tables. This was not why he had become an actor.

Then his agent called with a more interesting offer: to host a proposed television series called *GE Theater* and become the roving ambassador for General Electric. The pay was very good—$125,000 a year ($1 million in today's money). He took it. Over the next eight years he spent a great deal of time on the road—the equivalent of two years—visiting 135 GE plants around the country, giving speeches, and meeting 250,000 GE workers. The time away from home was lengthened by his contract, which permitted him to avoid airplanes and crisscross the country only by train and car because of his fear of flying. (As he wrote to a friend in 1955, "I am one of those prehistoric people who won't fly.") In the course of those years on the road for GE, he developed "the speech"—the thematic amalgam of patriotism, American values, criticism of big government and regulation, and anecdotes and affable good humor—that would launch him into the governorship of California and then onto the presidency. But that was all in the future. In the meantime, *GE Theater,* with Ronald Reagan at the helm, became one of the top-rated shows on Sunday night.[26]

General Electric also turned the Reagan home in the Pacific Palisades section of Los Angeles into a stunning showcase for the all-electric home—"the most electric house in the country," Reagan called it. "We found ourselves with more refrigerators, ovens and fancy lights than we could use," Nancy Reagan said. GE kept finding new appliances to deliver—a color television, a refrigerated wine cellar, and an amazing new innovation, an electric garbage disposal. So great was the extra electric load that it had to be accommodated with additional wiring and a three-thousand-pound steel cabinet on the side of the house. Reagan would joke that they had a direct electric line to Hoover Dam.[27]

And so, long before Ronald Reagan became the fortieth president of the United States and the global proponent for freedom and free markets, he already became the fervent advocate for the "all-electric home." In a series of television commercials, he and Nancy invited viewers into their all-electric home, where they extolled many of their GE appliances, ranging from a toaster oven to a vacuum cleaner to a waffle iron to a portable television that they proudly carried onto their patio and out by the pool.

"My electric servants do everything," said Nancy Reagan, as her husband savored the coffee from an electric coffee maker.

"That's the point of living better electrically," replied a beaming Reagan.

After giving their young daughter, Patti, a tour around the house, and letting her identify all their household appliances, Nancy Reagan said, "It makes quite a difference in how we live."

To those who had lived through the deprivation of the Depression in America's cities and on its farms, the electric home and those "electric servants" truly did mean a veritable revolution in the quality and ease of domestic life. With what was already that characteristically affable shake of his head, Reagan summed it up, "You really begin to live when you live better . . ." And then his daughter jumped in to enthusiastically add, "Electrically!"[28]

Here it was—the American Dream and what would become a dream around the world—all electric. Or, at least, increasingly electric. Living better electrically was reflected in the rapid growth in the nation's consumption of electricity. But how to generate the electricity to meet the nation's growing demands for power?

18

THE NUCLEAR CYCLE

It was an odd location for a president-elect to be briefed on the most dire threat facing the world. But the small office belonging to the club manager was the only place readily available at the Augusta National Golf Club in Georgia, where Dwight Eisenhower was on a golfing vacation after his electoral victory in 1952.

What Eisenhower learned that morning was very sobering. The subject was the growing risk of nuclear war.

Seven years earlier, two atomic bombs detonated over the Japanese cities of Hiroshima and Nagasaki had brought the Second World War to a sudden conclusion. In the immediate postwar years, the United States, with its ally Britain, held what seemed to be an atomic monopoly. But then in 1949, in what was a stunning shock, the Soviet Union, abetted by a network of spy rings, tested its first atomic bomb well ahead of what was anticipated.[1]

That November morning in 1952, Eisenhower began by asking the briefer, a senior official from the Atomic Energy Commission, about the pluses and minuses of combining in a single facility the generation of civilian nuclear electricity with the production of weapons-grade fuel. Then, getting down to the immediate business at hand, the briefer pulled the top-secret documents from an oversize envelope. The topic, on which the new president needed to be urgently informed, was the state of the nuclear arsenal and the fearsome rate at which destructive power was growing.

. . .

A little more than a week earlier, the United States had tested "Mike"—"the first full-scale thermonuclear device," said one of the documents—the prototype of a far more powerful hydrogen bomb, 150 times more powerful than the atomic bomb. The Pacific island on which "Mike" had been tested was now, in the stark words of the document, "missing," replaced by an underwater crater almost a mile in diameter. Eisenhower instantly absorbed the significance. There was now, he said, "enough destructive power to destroy everything." He worried about the dangerous temptation to think that such weapons "could be used like other weapons."

After the meeting, the first thing that the briefer did, even before getting back on the plane, was to burn the secret documents.[2]

The dangers of nuclear conflict would deeply preoccupy Eisenhower throughout his presidency. He had been Supreme Commander in Europe during World War II, and he knew that the U.S. nuclear arsenal was already several times more destructive than all the munitions exploded during the war. The Russians were headed down the same path.

Was there not some way to temper the arms race and move the "atom" onto a more peaceful path? The death of Joseph Stalin in March 1953 held out that prospect, possibly. But then in August 1953, a Soviet weapon test—nicknamed "Joe 4"—set off new alarms, since it seemed to indicate that the Soviet Union was also far along in developing a hydrogen bomb. There was much discussion in the U.S. government about how to slow down the arms race, including a set of proposals code-named "Project Wheaties" and the seemingly endless redrafting of a major presidential address for the United Nations on the nuclear danger. "We don't want to scare the country to death," Eisenhower instructed his speechwriter. But he was determined to take the initiative. "The world is racing towards catastrophe," he wrote in his diary. "Something must be done to put a brake on this movement." At the same time, as the Atomic Energy Commission put it in a memo to the president, achieving "economically competitive nuclear power" was "a goal of national importance."

In his address at the United Nations, delivered in December 1953, Eisenhower tried to sketch out that different path. It might or might not work, but it had to be tried. "Atoms for Peace" is what Eisenhower called it. He summarized the buildup of the nuclear arsenals. But he also called for U.S.-Soviet cooperation to modulate the nuclear arms race and to commit to the development of the peaceful atom for people around the world. That meant, primarily, the generation of electricity with nuclear power. "Peaceful power from atomic energy is no dream of the future," he promised.[3]

The way nuclear energy was developed after World War II still shapes its role—present and potential—in the twenty-first century. That begins with designs themselves. At the heart of all of the reactor designs is a core where radioactive material generates a controlled chain reaction, releasing a great amount of energy and heat. Where the designs differ is in the coolant that flows around the core, keeping it from getting too hot while at the same time becoming hot enough itself to produce steam, which in turn drives a turbine and produces electricity. For its coolant, Canada's CANDU reactor used heavy water, a variant of natural water that occurs rarely in nature. A British design used gas rather than water as the coolant.

But the most common type of reactor, developed in the United States, uses light water—which is another term for normal water—for the coolant. As the water circles the core, it is heated to such a level as to produce, either directly or indirectly, the steam to drive a turbine. The light-water reactor is the basis for about 90 percent of the 440 or so nuclear reactors currently operational in the world, and virtually all those presently planned.

Whatever the coolant, it is typical to speak of the nuclear-fuel cycle. For the light-water reactor, the cycle begins with the mining of uranium and then moves to enrichment to increase the concentration of the isotope U-235 to a level that will be able to sustain a controlled chain reaction. This more-concentrated fuel is then fabricated into fuel rods that will be inserted into the reactor. The cycle continues through the use of the fuel in the reactor all the way through to the deposition of the spent fuel in some form of storage or possible reuse.

The origins of the light-water reactor go back to the way in which the U.S. Navy, after World War II, set out to harness the atom to power its submarine fleet. It owes its predominance to the single-minded drive of one person, an intensely focused engineer, Admiral Hyman Rickover. "Widely considered to be the greatest engineer of all time" is how President Jimmy Carter described him. Rickover, who achieved the virtually unheard-of feat of spending 63 years on active duty, was not only, as he is remembered today, the father of the nuclear navy; he is also, to a very considerable degree, the father of today's nuclear power industry.[4]

THE ADMIRAL

"Everything in my life has been sort of a coincidence," Rickover once said. Hyman Rickover was born Chaim Rickover in a small village in a Jewish shtetl of czarist-ruled Poland, most of whose inhabitants would eventually perish in the Holocaust. At age six Rickover immigrated to the United States with his mother and sister. His father, a tailor, who had gone ahead to New York, did not know they had arrived. His mother, tricked out of her money on the ship over and now penniless, was being held in detention with her children. Just before they were to be deported back to Poland, his father learned by chance that they were stuck in immigration and eventually stumbled on them on Ellis Island. The Rickovers settled in Chicago. The family was so poor that the boy had to take his first job, age nine, holding a lantern in a machine shop. While in high school, Rickover worked the night shift, from 3:00 to 11:00, at the Western Union telegraph agency. A picture from the 1916 Republican convention in Chicago shows him standing stiffly at attention in his Western Union uniform as he would later stand in his naval uniform. Through a lucky fluke, he won a nomination to the Naval Academy at Annapolis.[5]

Anxious, fearful of failure, and certainly no athlete—and subject to extra hazing because he was Jewish—Rickover spent every moment he could at the academy studying. He was, as he later put it, "trying to get by, stay alive." At night when the library closed, he even crammed himself into an unused shower stall to get in extra time with his books. Rickover may not have been the most popular midshipman in his class, but he graduated with distinction. However, as a result of a naval disarmament treaty, it looked as though there would be few career berths in the navy for the Annapolis graduates, including Rickover. Deeply disappointed, he secured an entry-level engineering job at Chicago's Commonwealth Edison, the linchpin of Samuel Insull's empire. But then, a naval posting became available. Rickover subsequently served on two submarines—one, the

S-48, of such faulty, sooty, dangerous and repellent engineering as to sear into Rickover's soul a fanaticism about the absolute importance of high engineering standards. This conviction would infuse everything he did thereafter.[6]

During World War II, Rickover headed the Electrical Section in the Bureau of Ships. There he honed his zealotry for excellence and an obsession with precision. "An organizer & leader of outstanding ability," said his final fitness report, and "one of the country's foremost engineers." What this report did not include was his driving, domineering, irascible, abrasive, sometimes hypersensitive, extremely confident personality. This was the flip side of his single-minded focus on mission and extraordinarily demanding nature. This combination of qualities would make some forever loyal to him and others, bitter enemies—later including much of the senior Navy brass. But, he would say, "my job was not to work within the system. My job was to get things done and make this country strong."

"I have the charisma of a chipmunk," Rickover, late in life, told newscaster Diane Sawyer. He added, "I never have thought I was smart. I thought the people I dealt with . . . were dumb, including you." Sawyer quickly replied, "To be called dumb by you is to be in very good company."[7]

Rickover had a distinctive gift that made him, in the eyes of many, the best engineer in the Navy. "I believe I have a unique characteristic—I can visualize machines operating right in my mind," he once explained. "I do not think there has been anyone in the U.S. Navy who has had as much engineering experience as I have had."[8]

THE NUCLEAR NAVY

After World War II, despite the dislike that many had for him, Rickover's name was added at the last minute to the roster of naval officers dispatched to the secret atomic research city at Oak Ridge, Tennessee. Their mission was to learn about the mysteries of nuclear energy and what role it might have if harnessed in peaceful power generation.

Rickover quickly recognized the strategic potential of a nuclear navy and thereafter committed himself to realizing it. In particular, he understood that nuclear submarines could offer a range and capability that far exceeded that of the diesel-fueled submarines of World War II. By so doing, nuclear power offered an extraordinary solution to an intractable problem that bedeviled contemporary submarines—the constraints of conventional batteries, which limited the amount of time that submarines could spend at full speed underwater. By contrast, it was thought, nuclear subs should be able to cruise underwater at full speed for hours, days, or even months.

Rickover was given double duty; he was put in charge of the nuclear propulsion programs for both the navy and for the new Atomic Energy Commission. This double posting helped him to overcome the formidable engineering and bureaucratic obstacles to realizing the nuclear submarine. It was said that he would write letters to himself and then answer them, ensuring instant sign-off from both the navy and the AEC. The urgency of the program increased in 1949 with the first Soviet atomic bomb test.

It was one thing to build an atomic bomb. It was quite another to harness a controlled chain reaction of fission to generate power. So much had to be invented and developed from scratch—the technology, the engineering, the know-how. It was Rickover who chose the pressurized light-water reactor as the propulsion system. He also imposed "an engineering and technical discipline unknown to industry or, except for his own organization, to government."[9]

To accomplish his goals, Rickover built a cadre of highly skilled and highly trained officers for the nuclear navy, who were constantly pushed to operate at peak standards of performance. If that meant being a taskmaster and a martinet, Rickover would be a taskmaster and a martinet. Even a minor oversight or deviation from Rickover's very high standards would likely mean that an officer would be "denuked"—ejected from the nuclear service.

When interviewing candidates for the nuclear navy, Rickover would, in order to throw them off and test them, seat them in chairs with shortened front legs and at the same time position them so that the sunlight streamed through specially adjusted venetian blinds straight into their eyes. That way "they had to maintain their wits," he explained, "while they were sliding off the chair."[10]

Once, when a young submarine officer was applying to the nuclear navy, he proudly told Rickover that he had come in 59th in his class of 820 at the Naval Academy. Rickover acidly asked him if he had done his best. After a moment's hesitation, the taken-aback officer, named James Earl Carter, admitted that he had not.

"Why not?" Rickover asked.

That question—Why Not the Best?—became the title of his campaign autobiography when, as Jimmy Carter, he ran for the presidency decades later.[11]

In Rickover's tireless campaign to build a nuclear submarine and bulldoze through bureaucracy, he so alienated his superiors that he was twice passed over for promotion to admiral. It took congressional intervention to finally secure him the title.

Rickover's methods worked. The development of the technology, the engineering, and construction for a nuclear submarine—all these were achieved in record time. The first nuclear submarine, the USS *Nautilus,* was commissioned in 1954. The whole enterprise had been achieved in seven years—compared with the quarter century that others had predicted. In 1958, to great acclaim, the *Nautilus* accomplished a formidable, indeed unthinkable, feat—it sailed 1,400 miles under the North Pole and the polar ice cap. The journey was nonstop except for those times when the ship got temporarily stuck between the massive ice cap and the shallow sea bottom. When, on the ship's return, the *Nautilus*'s captain was received at the White House, the abrasive Rickover, who was ultimately responsible for the very existence of the *Nautilus,* was pointedly excluded from the ceremony.

At a separate meeting, the ship's captain presented Admiral Rickover with a piece of polar ice, carefully preserved in the ship's freezer. It was one of the rare times that those who reported to him ever saw the frosty admiral smile. By the time Rickover finally retired in 1986, 40 percent of the navy's major combatant ships would be nuclear propelled.[12]

THE REACTOR AT OBNINSK

The *Nautilus* was the first controlled application of nuclear power for vehicle propulsion. However, in the summer of 1954, Soviet radio announced another "first" for "Soviet science": the first civilian reaction anywhere in the world had gone into operation in the science city of Obninsk, south of Moscow. The Soviet Union, declared the Soviet news agency TASS, had "leaped ahead of Britain and the United States in the development of atomic energy."

But the actual reactor at Obninsk was tiny, capable of supplying power only to some local collective farms and factories and a few thousand residents. It was also a forerunner of a particular type of Soviet reactor called the RBMK, which would achieve unfortunate notoriety some decades later.[13]

"TOO CHEAP TO METER"

Even before the launch of the *Nautilus,* the development of a civilian nuclear reactor was beginning. It too was under the firm control of Admiral Rickover. The civilian reactors were based upon the navy's designs. The design is often attributed to the submarine reactors, but there was an intermediate step. After work had already begun on developing a reactor for aircraft carriers, the Eisenhower administration decided that the program would be too expensive and instead concluded that the quickest way to get to nuclear power would be by stripping the carrier propulsion project of its distinctive naval features and making it the basis for a civilian reactor.

The reaction to the Atomic Energy Commission's announcement of the civilian program was enthusiastic. *Time* magazine called it a "new phase" of the atomic age; the *New York Times* went even further, announcing the coming age of atomic power. The optimism of the times was captured in 1954 when the head of the Atomic Energy Commission, Lewis Strauss, made what would turn into the famous prophecy that nuclear power would, within 15 years, deliver "electrical energy too cheap to meter."[14]

The first U.S. nuclear plant was built at Shippingport, Pennsylvania. It went into operation in 1957, just three years after the launch of the *Nautilus.* The British actually beat it by a year, with the first commercial production of nuclear power in the world at Calder Hall in Britain, which Queen Elizabeth dedicated in 1956. But Calder Hall was a small power plant (built with a design now considered obsolete).

Shippingport, by contrast, ranks as "the world's first full-scale atomic power station." The design and construction of the power plant was directed by none other than Admiral Hyman Rickover, who retained operational oversight for the next twenty-five years. Though the reactor had been scaled up from the one designated for an atomic-powered aircraft carrier, it had also been fundamentally rethought and redesigned to produce electric power. It performed far above its rated design and operated virtually fault free. This was credit to Rickover, with his determined exactitude, and to the team he assembled.[15]

The real commercial turning point for nuclear power came in 1963, when a New Jersey utility ordered a commercial plant to be built at Oyster Creek. That reactor was also based upon the design developed under Rickover.

THE GREAT NUCLEAR BANDWAGON

Over the next few years, about 50 nuclear power plants were ordered, as utilities clambered all over each other to jump onto what was becoming known as the "great bandwagon market." It was Thomas Edison versus George Westinghouse all over again, with General Electric and Westinghouse battling for market share with their respective versions of light-water reactors. Westinghouse championed the PWR, the pressurized-water reactor; and GE, the BWR, the boiling water reactor. Atomic energy, some projected, could provide almost half of total U.S. electricity by the first decade of the twenty-first century. One leading scientist declared, "Nuclear reactors now appear to be the cheapest of all sources of energy" with the promise of "the permanent and ubiquitous availability of cheap power."[16]

But nuclear power, it turned out, was not cheap at all. Costs went up—way up. The reasons were many and interconnected. There was not enough standardization in plants and designs. Many utilities did not have the heft and experience to take on projects that were much bigger than they had anticipated and more complex and difficult to manage. The vendors were promising more than they could deliver in a time frame that they could not meet. And there was insufficient operating experience.

At the same time, the question of "how safe is safe enough?" emerged as a burning issue. What were the risks of an accident and radiation exposure? At both the federal and state levels, licensing and permitting took much longer than expected. Growing environmental and specifically antinuclear movements prompted constant regulatory delays, reviews, and changes. Concrete walls that had already been laid in had to be rebuilt and thickened; piping had to be taken out and reworked. Plants had to be redesigned and then redesigned again and again during construction, meaning that costs went up and then went up again, far exceeding the original budgets.

The plants also became more expensive because of the general inflationary pressures of the era, and then high interest rates. Instead of six years, plants were taking ten years to build, further driving up financing costs. Plants that were supposed to cost $200 million ended up costing $2 billion. Some cost much more. "The evolution in the costs," said an economist from the Atomic Energy Commission, with some understatement, could be "classified as a traumatic, rather than a successful, experience."[17]

"THE BUDDHA IS SMILING": PROLIFERATION

Another concern was emerging as well—about the risks of nuclear proliferation and the diversion of nuclear materials and know-how. Members of what was becoming known as the arms-control community, focusing on proliferation, added their voices to those of the antinuclear activists.

For a number of years, there was confidence that the nuclear weapons "club" was stable and highly exclusive, limited to just five members—the United States, the Soviet Union, Britain, France, and China. The doctrine of mutually assured destruction—known as MAD—offered the stability of deterrence between the United States and the Soviet Union. But then, in May of 1974, the Indian foreign minister received a cryptic phone message: "The Buddha is smiling." He knew what that code meant; India had just exploded a "peaceful nuclear device" in the Rajasthan Desert, 100 miles from the border with Pakistan. The nuclear monopoly of the five powers had been broken, and the prospect for further proliferation was now very real.[18]

It was now eminently clear that a strong link—if that link was sought—existed between "peaceful nuclear power" and a nuclear weapon. There was only one atom; and the same nuclear plant that produced electricity could also produce plutonium in its spent fuel, which could be used as a weapons fuel. That was the way the Indians had done it. Moreover, an enrichment facility that turned out nuclear fuel with the 3 percent to 5 percent concentration required for a reactor could keep enriching the uranium over and over until it reached an 80 percent or 90 percent concentration of U-235. That was weapons-grade uranium, and out of that could be made an atomic bomb.

Influential scientists and members of the foreign-policy community in the United States and other countries began to question the promotion of nuclear power—not on grounds of safety, but because of the risks of proliferation. During World War II, Harvard chemistry professor George Kistiakowsky, known as "Kisty," had been one of the chief designers of the atomic bomb at the secret Los Alamos laboratory. Later he was the White House science adviser to President Eisenhower. But now, in 1977, troubled by second thoughts, he said, "We must hold back on great expansion of nuclear power until the world gets better. It's just too damn risky right now."[19]

THREE MILE ISLAND

Whatever their bitter differences, on one thing proponents and opponents of nuclear power could absolutely agree: The core of an operating reactor had to be kept "constantly supplied with copious amounts of coolant to dissipate the heat produced by fission." Otherwise, something terrible could happen.

And that nightmare scenario suddenly seemed about to become a reality—in the predawn hours of March 28, 1979, in Unit 2 at the Three Mile Island nuclear power plant, on the Susquehanna River, near Harrisburg, Pennsylvania. The chain reaction of events started at 4:00 a.m. with a shutdown in the feedwater pumps that were meant to keep the reactor core cool. Initially the problems were dismissed as a "normal aberration." Then a whole series of further malfunctions and operator errors ensued, one piling on top of the next. At one point, the instrumentation misled the operators into thinking that there was too much water in the cooling system, instead of too little. They turned off the emergency cooling system and shut down the pumps that were circulating water, which eliminated their ability to remove heat from the reactor core. All this generated a sequence of events that melted part of the reactor's core, forced a complete shutdown of the plant, and led to a minor release of radioactive steam. It also ignited fears of a major radioactive leak and a total meltdown.[20]

The result was immediate panic. "Nuclear Nightmare" was the cover of

Time magazine. The *New York Post* headlined "Nuclear Leak Goes Out of Control." Thousands of people fled their homes; residents over a wide area were instructed to keep their windows tightly shut and turn off air conditioners to prevent intake of contaminated air. Almost a million people were told to prepare for immediate evacuation.

A few days after the accident, Jimmy Carter, the nuclear engineer–turned–president, arrived by helicopter at Three Mile Island. He viewed the crippled reactor from a school bus and then, along with his wife, Roslynn, toured the plant's control room with his shoes garbed in yellow plastic booties. The president promised to "be personally responsible for informing the American people" about the accident. Fears were further stoked by the coincidental release of a motion picture, *The China Syndrome,* about a nuclear meltdown. The film and its message became a national sensation, helping to feed the panic.[21]

THE AFTERMATH

The accident at Three Mile Island riveted the world. It also led to an overhaul of safety management, including much greater focus on human factors and preventing operator errors. Who better to provide understanding of what had gone wrong and what needed to be done than Admiral Hyman Rickover? Jimmy Carter asked his old boss to help him with the investigation.

Rickover wrote a lengthy private letter to the president "to put the issue in perspective as I see it based on my own experience." In a letter of lasting value for its insight into disasters, Rickover wrote:

> Investigations of catastrophic accidents involving man-made devices often show that:
>
> 1. The accident resulted from a series of relatively minor equipment malfunctions followed by operator errors.
> 2. Timely recognition and prompt corrections . . . could have prevented the accident from becoming significant.
> 3. Similar equipment malfunctions and operator errors had occurred on prior occasions, but did not lead to accidents because the

starting conditions, or sequence of events, were slightly different. If the earlier incidents had been heeded, and prompt corrective actions taken, the subsequent catastrophic accident would have been avoided.

4. To reduce the probability of a repetition of similar or worse catastrophic accidents, adequate technical standards must be established and enforced, and increased training of operators must be provided.

This pattern has been characteristic of broken dams, aircraft crashes, ship sinkings, explosions, industrial fires etc.

"As was predictable," the admiral said, the investigation into Three Mile Island "revealed the same pattern." Rickover went on to identify many problems, from lack of training and discipline in operations to lack of standardization. "For example, it makes no sense that the control room for Unit 1 at Three Mile Island is designed much differently than the control room for Unit 2, even though both reactor plants were designed by the same manufacturer."

Rickover did warn the president against relying upon a " 'cops and robbers' syndrome" between government regulators and the nuclear power industry. Government regulators would never be sufficient and could not adequately do the job. Instead the admiral advocated that the utilities come together to create a central organization that could provide "a more coordinated and expert technical input and control for the commercial nuclear power program than is presently possible for each utility with its limited staff"—a position that he had advocated for years.[22]

Shortly after, the nuclear power industry founded the Institute of Nuclear Power Operations to serve exactly that purpose. The institute became the industry's own watchdog, and a very tough one, with the utilities stringently evaluating one another. The companies all understood that the viability of nuclear power in the United States was at stake and that they were all in it together. The industry could not withstand another accident. It would operate at Rickover standards.

The accident at Three Mile Island brought the great nuclear bandwagon to a screeching halt. Orders for more than 100 new reactors in the United States were eventually canceled. The last nuclear power reactor to go into operation in the United States was one that had been ordered in 1976.

The next several years proved to be a time of agony for the U.S. power industry. A few utilities went bankrupt. Others came very close. Construction was halted on plants that were as much as 90 percent completed. The Shoreham plant on Long Island was actually fully completed and underwent low-level testing. But in the face of local opposition, after producing only a small amount of power, it was shut down forever. Eventually the $6 billion plant was sold off for a grand total of one dollar to the Long Island Power Authority.

Still, over 100 nuclear power reactors did end up operating in the United States, although often at far higher cost than originally expected and with construction extended over much longer time spans than planned. They became part of the base load of the nation's power supply. But they were not operating anywhere near their full capacities. Improving operations became the top priority for the industry. To do so it drew on the most obvious pool of talent—the alumni from Admiral Rickover's nuclear navy. The mission of the retired naval officers was to make the fleet of existing nuclear power plants work better, at Rickover standards.

Still what was remarkable was how fast the nuclear power industry had developed and how large it had grown. The design and building program had commenced only in the early 1960s. Yet within little more than two decades, nuclear power was supplying about 20 percent of U.S. electricity, and that remained the case even after the brakes were slammed on.

FRANCE'S TRANSFORMATION

Nuclear development was also stymied in other countries. Popular opposition to nuclear power had emerged in Europe prior to Three Mile Island. Austria completed a nuclear power plant at Zwentendorf, 20 miles from Vienna. But it was never turned on and it has sat idle ever since. In many other countries, political stalemate and indecision were also slowing ambitious programs.

One country that went resolutely ahead was France. In the immediate aftermath of the 1973 embargo, Jean Blancard, the senior energy official in the government, made the case to President Georges Pompidou that France had to decisively move away from oil—especially oil in electrical generation. The nation's electricity supply could not depend on oil, which could be cut off. "The period from here on will be quite different—a transformation, not a crisis," Blancard said to the president. "It is not reasonable," he continued, for France to be "dependent" on decisions from the Middle East. "We must pursue a policy of diversification." Pompidou was more than receptive to Blancard's argument. Though seriously ill with cancer and swollen from the effects of treatment, he convened his senior advisers and confirmed nuclear power as the way to eliminate oil from French electricity and restore autonomy to the nation's energy position. Nuclear power, rather than oil, would increasingly be the basis of France's energy supply, complemented by a return to coal and a new emphasis on energy efficiency.

Yet, to the government's consternation, the nuclear program immediately ignited determined opposition across the country. Four hundred scientists signed a proclamation demanding that the government postpone the installation of new plants until all safety questions could be answered.[23]

Despite the protests, and large demonstrations around the country, France's centralized political system, bolstered by the prestigious engineering culture in the upper reaches of French government, locked in the commitment. Even the election in 1981 of the Socialist François Mitterrand as president did not alter the commitment to nuclear power. Labor unions and the communists, who were part of his coalition, were already onboard, as they saw nuclear as a promoter of jobs and energy security. The fact that the state company, Électricité de France, operated the entire power industry also greatly helped. "People trusted EDF," said Philippe de Ladoucette, chairman of France's Commission for the Regulation of Energy. "It was seen as the ultimate French champion." France continued to build dozens of reactors over the decades. One striking result of this continuing commitment was to propel France into the vanguard of the global nuclear supply industry.[24]

"BLACK STALKS"

The other European country that continued to move ahead on nuclear power was the Soviet Union. In 1963–64 the first standard-size civilian reactors in the

Soviet Union were commissioned. By the middle of the 1980s, 25 reactors were operating in the Soviet Union.

One type of Soviet civilian reactor was so similar to Westinghouse's pressurized light-water reactor that it was dubbed the "Eastinghouse." Another design was the RBMK, a prototype of which was that first tiny reactor in the scientific city of Obninsk. The RBMK was based on a reactor developed for manufacturing weapon-grade nuclear fuel. As it was being adapted for civilian nuclear power, some Soviet scientists had warned that it was not safe and argued strongly against using it for civilian nuclear power. But the political authorities overruled the scientists. It was much cheaper to build, and it became a mainstay of Soviet nuclear power.

Four such RBMK reactors were built at the little village of Pripyat, about 65 miles north of Kiev, then the capital of the Soviet republic of Ukraine. But the plant became better known by the name of the nearby town, Chernobyl, which in Ukrainian means "black stalks," for a long grass that was common to the region.

In the early morning hours of April 26, 1986, operators were carrying out a poorly designed experiment aimed, ironically, at enhancing the safety of the plant. Through a series of mistakes, they lost control. The first of two explosions blew the top off the reactor, followed by a fire. These reactors did not have the kind of containment vessels that were standard in the West to prevent a catastrophe. Radioactive clouds were released and carried by the winds across vast stretches of the European Continent. The first indications that something had gone seriously wrong were heightened radioactivity readings on sensors in Sweden. The word spread quickly, including back into the Soviet Union. Terrified crowds packed the railway station in Kiev, trying to squeeze onto overcrowded trains and flee the region. Fear and panic spread throughout the Soviet Union. Without any news or information, the rumors became more and more sensational.

But for more than two weeks the Soviet leadership and media denied that anything serious had happened—it was all the creation of the Western press. One senior Soviet energy official, meeting Westerners in Moscow, pounded his fist down on the table and insisted that any notion of a nuclear accident action was a total fabrication by the Western newspapers.

Then, on May 14, 1986, Soviet leader Mikhail Gorbachev went on television and in sober, somber tones did something that Soviet leaders never did: gravely reported what had actually happened. While attempting to dispel some of the sensationalism surrounding the event in the Western media, Gorbachev talked about the now-evident perils of what he called "the sinister power of uncontrolled nuclear energy."[25]

This was a historic turning point. Within the Soviet Union, this accident—which according to dogma could never happen—was a major political and social shock that contributed to shattering confidence in the communist system and the myths that helped to hold it together.

THE EXCEPTIONS

Across Western Europe, Chernobyl's impact on the energy sector was immense; it fueled and solidified the opposition to nuclear power. Italy pledged no new nuclear power plants and eventually shut down its capacity. Sweden and Germany introduced moratoria on nuclear power and aimed at a phaseout. Britain's Atomic Energy Commission prepared to devote the rest of its days to the decommissioning of plants. Chernobyl had done in Europe what Three Mile Island had done in the United States: brought the development of new nuclear power to a stop.

In Europe, only France plowed on with its program. "France's commitment to nuclear energy was never reconsidered, in spite of major accidents," said Philippe de Ladoucette. "Ever since the end of World War I, energy independence had become a motto." Bolstering all of this was the fact that so many policymakers came from a technocratic engineering background.[26]

With its political foundation secured, nuclear would become the indispensable baseload of French power supply. Its 58 reactors supply almost 80 percent of France's electric power. France is also the largest exporter of electricity in the world: those sales to neighboring countries constitute France's fourth-largest export.

In Japan, too, nuclear power plants continued to come online—with more than a dozen in the decade following Chernobyl's meltdown. But Japan's cultural legacy regarding nuclear power was more complicated. It was the only country to have ever suffered a nuclear attack, and the politics of nuclear power could engender a powerful emotional response from voters and politicians alike. But the oil shocks of the 1970s, which threatened to undermine Japan's postwar economic miracle, were deeply traumatic. Indeed, so much so that the political will to support the nuclear program remained strong.

"Unlike the United States or the United Kingdom, Japan had no choice but to depend on imports for virtually all of its fossil-fuel supply," said Masahisa Naitoh, a formerly senior energy official in Japan. Accordingly, Japan has viewed nuclear energy as "an affordable, stable electricity source and as essential for Japan's energy security." Rather than abandon the nuclear plan, Japan strengthened safety regulations and moved ahead. To a large extent opposition was "neutralized." By the beginning of 2011 Japan's 54 operating nuclear reactors were delivering 30 percent of Japan's total power, and the official target was for nuclear power to provide 50 percent of Japan's electricity by 2030.[27] Japan's commitment seemed immutable and unshakeable.

But Japan, along with France, was the big exception.

WHAT FUEL FOR THE FUTURE?

In the United States, the shuttering of nuclear development left a big question: If not uranium, what would be the fuel of the future in electric power? Oil was already being driven out of the electric power sector in response to the oil crises of the 1970s. Natural gas was an obvious answer. Except that in 1978, Congress had banned its use in new power plants due to the sharp increase in natural gas prices in the 1970s and the conviction that there was a shortage. Natural gas, it was said, was too valuable to be burned in power plants, but rather should be saved for higher purposes—heating homes. Nuclear power was far from being "too cheap to meter" and was now subject to a de facto moratorium.

That left only one resource: coal, which once again became the mainstay for much of the new capacity. It was domestic, it was abundant, and it provided security and dependability. But for how long? The costs of new capacity would trigger changes in the regulatory bargain that underlay the power industry in the United States—and, once again, in the decisions about fuels. The most dramatic impact would be in California.

19

BREAKING THE BARGAIN

Almost 1.5 million voters—it was the biggest win ever recorded in a California gubernatorial election: that was the overwhelming margin by which Democrat Gray Davis defeated his Republican opponent in 1998. Because of California's importance, that triumph automatically started talk of him as a potential future president. Davis was a career Sacramento politician. He had been chief of staff to Governor Jerry Brown in the 1970s and painstakingly climbed his way up the political ladder thereafter. Indeed, so entrenched was Davis in California politics that on his election as governor, an aide joked that in the days since Davis had been chief of staff, it had taken the new governor "23 years to walk 15 feet."[1]

After his first 100 days in office, Davis was more popular than his boss, Jerry Brown, had been in the same time frame and even more popular than California's best-known former governor, Ronald Reagan. As for being governor, Davis had a plan: do nothing radical. It certainly made sense. After a deep recession, the state's economy was surging.

But so, by the way, was its electricity demand. Although the implications were little understood, the impact would soon not only shake California but would be felt throughout the United States and in the rest of the world. It would also starkly dramatize fundamental realities of electric power.

. . .

By the 1990s the regulatory bargain that had long been the foundation of the electrical power business in the United States was more than half a century old. Electric power prices were established not in the marketplace but rather by a state's public utility commission (PUC), in accord with the model originally promoted by Samuel Insull. They did so by allowing utilities to pass on, in their rates to consumers, the cost of service—that is, the cost of everything, including plants, fuel, and operations, plus an additional sum that was the permitted profit. The PUC would then decide how those costs were to be allocated in terms of the prices paid by the different classes of customers—residential, commercial, and industrial.

On their side of the bargain, the utilities were required to provide reliable service, universally available, at reasonable cost. They would ensure that the lights stayed on. If the power went off because a storm had knocked down the power lines or a blizzard had disrupted the system, the linemen would be out as fast as their trucks could roll, and the utility would scramble to get the power back on. This was all based on the concept of natural monopoly. Competition was definitely not part of the bargain.

RATE SHOCK

But change was coming. For many years electricity prices in the United States had been declining dramatically—between 1934 and 1970, by an astonishing 86 percent. That was testament to the impact of scale, technology, and lower costs that came with higher volumes. But in the 1970s and 1980s, prices abruptly turned up: New power plants—whether nuclear or coal—were proving to be expensive, sometimes very expensive. Costs were also driven by the 1978 Public Utility Regulatory Policies Act (PURPA). That law had forced utilities to buy power at high "avoided" costs from small-size generators of renewable power—largely wind and small hydro plants.

Avoided costs were a very interesting concept: It was an estimate of how much the same amount of power would cost were it generated from an oil- or gas-fired facility. It was not an actual price, but an expected price sometime in the future. These avoided costs were often pegged at stratospherically high anticipated oil prices. But in the 1980s, oil and gas prices had declined, meaning that PURPA avoided-cost power prices were far above actual market costs. All this meant that consumers, in many parts of the country, were hit by "rate shock"—steep rises in electricity rates, as the costs from new nuclear and coal plants, and from the PURPA machines, were passed on to them in their monthly bills.

Residential consumers may have complained about their bills, but there was little they could really do, aside from being more careful in their use of electricity. For industries that used a good deal of electricity, rate shock hit their bottom line and made them less competitive against companies in lower-cost states. They needed to do something to bring down their power prices. Their answer was to promote what was variously called "deregulation" or "restructuring," which would allow them to find a way to buy cheaper power from someone else rather than more expensive power from their local utility. In a historic shift, that would lead toward electric rates being determined in a marketplace, not by the PUC—that is, toward competition in what had heretofore been assumed to be a natural monopoly. Getting deregulation right, however, would not prove so easy for electric power. Even competitive markets are, after all, not exactly free. They depend, crucially, on the rules by which they operate.

Deregulation was made even more compelling by the appearance of a shift in the fuel mix for electric power. As new nuclear plants came online they contributed a growing share of power generation—leveling out at 20 percent of supply nationally. But the big growth was in coal. In the fifteen years following the natural gas shortages of the mid-1970s, coal consumption in electric generation literally doubled and was responsible for about 55 percent of all electricity produced in the United States. Coal's great advantage was that it was abundant and it was a domestic fuel.

But natural gas too was now abundant, and it too was also domestic. It was a fuel well suited for the deregulated power business. The gas bubble, the long-lasting surplus of natural gas following its deregulation, made gas cheap. In the face of the changing economics, the prohibition on the use of natural gas in power generation was clearly irrational, and the ban was lifted. At the same time, a new generation of highly efficient combined-cycle gas turbines—based on engines designed for jets, combined with steam turbines that run on "rejected heat"—started to enter the market. Gas plants were much less costly to build than coal and nuclear power plants, they could be constructed more quickly, and natural gas was a cleaner fuel than coal.

Thus electricity from a new gas-fired power plant was cheaper than that from a nuclear power plant that had been constructed in the 1970s—or, for that matter, a coal plant that was built in the 1980s. But the existing regulatory system did not easily allow buyers to get access to the lower-cost power. At least not yet.

TOWARD MARKET

Thinking about the role of governments and markets was, at that time, undergoing a decisive change around the world. Increased confidence in markets stimulated a movement toward deregulation and privatization. In the United States, financial services were deregulated in the 1970s, after which stockbrokers could offer lower rates to customers if they wanted to. The airline industry was also deregulated, a transformation championed by Senator Edward Kennedy, Senate staffer (and later Supreme Court justice) Stephen Breyer, and the regulatory economist Alfred Kahn. As a result, the federal government stopped regulating everything from the cost of airline tickets to the size of sandwiches that could be served on planes. And, as already observed, price controls on oil as well as natural gas were abandoned in the 1980s. This same shift was even more evident in other countries. State-owned companies in Western Europe were privatized; communism collapsed in the Soviet Union and Eastern Europe; and both China and India opened up to the world economy.[2]

But what laid out the path for the United States was what happened in the United Kingdom. Of all the privatizations set in motion in Britain by Prime Minister Margaret Thatcher's market revolution, the biggest was that of the Central Electricity Generating Board (CEGB). The British power industry had been nationalized after World War II to end wasteful fragmentation, modernize the industry, and give virtually everyone access to the benefits of electric power. All of this it had done. It was an engineering-driven organization whose mandate was "to keep the lights on no matter what the cost." The downside was that, in the process, it was racking up big losses and was in constant turmoil with trade unions.

Beginning in 1990, the British industry was privatized. "Again and again I insisted that whatever structure we created must provide genuine competition," said Prime Minister Thatcher. The government broke the generating part of the CEGB into three private companies. These generation companies competed both among themselves and against new independent generating companies to sell electricity into the wholesale market. As for the retail side of the market, the government converted "area boards," which distributed electricity to the customers in a particular part of the country, into independent companies. It then gradually introduced competition among these companies.[3]

The UK's approach became the global model of how to bring market competition into electric power. It was a forceful and compelling model—including for the United States. Members of the Federal Energy Regulatory Commission, visiting Britain on a study trip, were much impressed by how the once-monolithic state-owned monopoly had been turned into a competitive business, with prices constantly changing in response to supply and demand. The FERC decided to open up the U.S. industry to competition as fast as possible. "The Brits' enthusiasm about the early successes of their restructuring definitely emboldened us to embark upon restructuring," said Elizabeth Moler, the FERC chair at the time. "We learned from both the successes and failures of the U.S. natural gas restructuring and from what the British did." Other visitors from the U.S. power industry made the same trek to Britain and came back with similar conclusions. This seemed to be the new future for electric power.[4]

ENTER THE MERCHANT GENERATORS

In the United States, policy at both the federal and state level now began to move toward deregulation. The biggest change was to allow new competitors to get into the generation business and sell their power either to utilities or to end users. And since electricity is an undifferentiated commodity, then new entrants would compete on price. The big idea here was to drive down costs through competition. And in the process, these new entrants were determined to disprove Insull's dictum that competition was an "unsound economic regulator."

The Federal Energy Policy Act of 1992 specifically allowed these newcomers to sell electricity into interstate transmission lines regulated under federal laws. These were given the name "merchant generators" because they did not own the wires and distribution system but rather would sell to those who did. The merchants might be either independent companies or subsidiaries of utilities in some other part of the country. Whichever, they either built new power plants or bought existing ones from utilities. These merchants were selling into second-by-second electronic markets. To implement the competitive intent of the 1992 Energy Policy Act, the Federal Energy Regulatory Commission promoted "wheeling." That allowed local utilities in one part of the country to contract with a cheaper generator in another part and wheel—that is, transport—the less expensive power over wires across the United States.

Both merchant generators and traditional utilities realized that they could become more competitive by fueling the new power plants with cheap natural gas. That set off a mad "dash to gas" across the country. In just six years, between 1998 and 2004, the United States added an enormous amount of new generating capacity—equivalent to a quarter of all the capacity that had been built since Edison's Prince Street station in 1882! Over 90 percent of that capacity burned natural gas. Although not recognized at the time, the dash to gas was also a very big bet on cheap natural gas prices. It led to the overbuild—which produced much more generating capacity than was necessary.

Yet by the end of the 1990s, cheap gas was disappearing. Prices started to rise sharply once again. The wager on cheap natural gas prices proved costly. Many of the independent merchant generators that had made that bet were caught out. Some went bankrupt. Nowhere did the bet on gas go so badly, or more disastrously, than in California.

CALIFORNIA'S STRANGE RESTRUCTURING

A power crisis that erupted in California in 2000 threw the state into disarray, created a vast economic and political firestorm, and shook the entire nation's electric power system. The brownouts and economic mayhem that rolled over the Golden State would have been expected in a struggling developing nation, but not in the state that was home to Disneyland, and that had given birth to Silicon Valley, the very embodiment of technology and innovation. After all,

California was, if an independent country, the seventh-largest economy in the world.

What unfolded in California graphically exposed the dangers of misdesigning a regulatory system. It was also a case study of how short-term politics can overwhelm the needs of sound policy.

According to popular lore, the crisis was manufactured and manipulated by cynical and wily out-of-state power traders, the worst being Enron, the Houston-based natural gas and energy company. Its traders and those of other companies were accused of creating and then exploiting the crisis with a host of complex strategies. Some traders certainly did blatantly, and even illegally, exploit the system and thus accentuated its flaws. Yet that skims over the fundamental cause of the crisis. For, by then, the system was already broken.

The California crisis resulted from three fundamental factors: The first was an unworkable form of partial deregulation that explicitly rejected the normal power-market stabilizers that could have helped avoid or at least blunt the crisis but instead built instability into the new system. The second was a sharp, adverse turn in supply and demand. The third was a political culture that wanted the benefits of increased electric power but without the costs.

This was not the way it was supposed to be. California enacted deregulation, or restructuring, as it was more commonly called, in 1994. At the time, the state was in a bad way economically. Unemployment hit 10 percent, real estate was a bust, and more people were moving out of the state than were moving in. Spending for defense, one of the state's main industries, had been cut back sharply with the end of the Cold War, and Sacramento was running big deficits. High electricity prices were partly blamed for the state's economic slump. Manufacturing companies were fleeing California, in part because of high energy costs, taking jobs with them. Meanwhile people did not worry much about increases in electricity demand. After all, in 1993 demand hadn't grown at all.

Competition, it was thought, would bring down the price of power, helping to revive the state's fortunes. California's brand of deregulation was fashioned out of a complex negotiation and a great compromise, involving stakeholder democracy, although the stakeholders varied much in terms of their understanding of how power markets worked. Politically, the great compromise worked brilliantly; the deregulation bill sailed through the state legislature in

1996 with not a single dissenting vote and was signed into law by Republican Governor Pete Wilson.[5]

Under California's restructuring, consumer advocates got lower prices; big industrial customers would get access to cheaper power. But in a deregulated market traditional utilities would be stuck with legacy costs of their contracts for PURPA power and the cost overruns on building other new plants—such as the Diablo Canyon nuclear facility on the central California coast that was caught in a regulatory morass and had ended up costing about $11.5 billion. These costs would prevent them from being competitive. The legislation gave the investor-owned utilities the relief they needed—various ways to extricate themselves from the burden of what was called "stranded costs." They too embraced restructuring. As for the new entrants, the merchant generators, there were two great prizes. One was the ability to sell power into the large California market; and the other, the opportunity to buy the power plants that the state was strongly "encouraging" the utilities to sell. "Every major group got what they wanted most," said Mason Willrich, who later became chairman of the California grid operator. "But no one connected the dots."

This restructuring was an extraordinary edifice in terms of political support. The entire California congressional delegation signed a letter urging the Federal Energy Regulatory Commission not to use federal authority to interfere with the plan. The political forces were so finely balanced that any alteration could cause the whole edifice to come tumbling down.

The objective was to dismantle the traditional natural monopoly in electric power. The new system, in the words of economist Paul Joskow, was "the most complicated set of wholesale market institutions ever created on earth and with which there was no real world experience." It yoked together a deregulated market with a regulated market. Some compared it to having a bridge designed by consensus. The subsequent collapse of this particular bridge would demonstrate the hard-earned lessons of power markets.[6]

THE IRON CURTAIN

Wholesale markets were deregulated—along with the markets in which the generators that operate the power plants that sold power to utilities that distributed it to customers. Prices in those markets would be free to fluctuate, in response to supply and demand. But the traditional retail markets—those between the utilities and their customers (home owners, factories, offices, and others)—were not deregulated. This meant that these consumers were to be protected—insulated—from rising prices. They, after all, were the ones who cast votes for governors and state legislators.

The result was to build an economic iron curtain between the wholesale and retail markets. The ultimate consequences would be devastating. Changes in wholesale markets, which would reflect those changes in supply and demand, would not flow as price signals into the retail markets—that is, to consumers. Thus consumers would have no incentive, no wake-up call, to make adjustments that would normally happen in response to rising prices (buying a more efficient air conditioner, putting a little more insulation in their walls). They would not get the message because it would not be transmitted to them.

In order to make the wholesale system function like a competitive market, the state's utilities were ordered to shear themselves of a substantial number of their in-state power plants and sell them to other companies, which would operate them and in turn sell electricity into the open market. Here was the dissolution of the formerly vertically integrated utility—the kind of utility invented by Samuel Insull, which traditionally combined generation, transmission, and distribution within the borders of a single company. Many of these new merchant generators were out-of-state companies, a number of which had arisen during the era of deregulation.

Other key elements in the deregulation would make matters still worse. The first is that the scheme did not worry about capacity. Electricity is different from other commodities. Oil can be stored in tanks; grain, in silos; natural gas, in underground caverns. But electricity is the instantaneous commodity; here one second, gone the next. It is a business that operates with virtually no inventory.

Therefore, a "reserve margin" is needed. Reserves are the stabilizers, the extra production capacity—above projected peak demand—that can be called into operation in order to avoid a shortage. Maintaining such a margin is a basic rule of operations—the power system in its entirety needs to be large enough not just to cover average demand but the extremes of demand, with an additional reserve to allow for accidents or malfunctioning equipment. A state like California, which depends upon hydropower for part of its electricity, needs about a 20 percent reserve margin—20 percent extra capacity—in order to be ready for a spike in demand brought about by a heat wave or a drop in hydropower production because of drought. California's new system, however, included no incentive or encouragement to ensure sufficient extra capacity to help deregulation work. At some points during the crisis, the reserve margin got as low as 1 percent—which was frighteningly low—essentially no reserve margin at all.

As part of the deregulation compromise, California also forbade utilities from signing with generating companies any long-term contracts for electricity supply. This was a truly fundamental flaw. It is standard practice—and, indeed, good practice—to hold a portfolio of contracts, some that go out just a few months, others that go out for a couple of years. This kind of portfolio helps to provide a buffer against major surges in market prices that would result if capacity became tight. But since the California model assumed that prices would remain low forever, the state would not permit long-term contracts, which, while more expensive than the spot prices at the time, would have provided an insurance policy for consumers if spot prices shot up.[7]

"We had to sell our power plants, which was the heart of a reliable power system, but we were forbidden from doing long-term contracts," said John Bryson, who was CEO of the parent of Southern California Edison, one of the state's three major utilities. "Utilities have an obligation to serve their clients, but now there was no way for us to source power except from a spot market."

California's restructuring, with its disconnect between wholesale and retail markets, and its prohibition of the buffers against rising prices, meant that an enormous amount of risk was unintentionally being built into the new system for supplying electricity to the most populous state in the nation. One report did warn in 1997 that this system was "likely to lead to extended periods of low prices followed by periods of very high prices, as supply shortages and surpluses develop. Price volatility will not be conducive to a smooth transition to competition." But few were listening.

The system would work well so long as no major changes in the supply-demand balance occurred and prices stayed down, which would have occurred if California had remained mired in an economic downturn. But how quickly markets can change.

"Deregulation, California-style" officially went into effect in 1998. By then, California's economy was already starting to recover, real estate was sizzling again, and the Internet was beginning to take off, giving a big boost to the Bay Area. All this was reflected in electricity consumption and a radical shift in the balance of supply and demand. Over a six-year period, California's economy grew by 29 percent; its electricity use by 24 percent. But no significant new electricity generation was added. Indeed, after 1997 the state's capacity actually went down as some older, inefficient plants were retired.[8]

California was arguably the most difficult state in the Union to site a new project; the process was time consuming and costly, the environmental review process was open-ended, and local community opposition could usually prevail. So for the additional supplies it needed, California drew on other western states and British Columbia—turning them into a sort of vast energy farm to feed its growing economy. That was fine as long as the out-of-state power was abundant and cheap. But states like Arizona were growing fast, and thus they were consuming more and more of their own power production. The year 1999 had been great for hydropower in the Northwest and British Columbia: mild winter, cool summer, and a lot of rain—which meant a lot of cheap hydropower.

"IT WAS MADNESS"

But 2000 was something else. A drought in the Northwest and Canada curbed the availability of hydropower. Meanwhile, power demand was surging in California, partly because of a hot summer, partly because of economic growth. More natural gas had to be pulled into power production. But natural gas supplies were tightening, and the price started to go up, which meant that the price of additional electricity—made from natural gas—also started to rise sharply.[9]

During the hot summer of 2000, the staff at the agency that managed the state's power grid frantically shopped for additional power supplies. "We simply couldn't make enough phone calls," said one of its managers. "It was a Turkish bazaar. It was madness." It was at this point that the state began to experience the first convulsions from the physical shortages of electricity. Utilities had to source power "on an hour-to-hour basis," said John Bryson. And "no one knew what price would be bid in the next hour." Moreover, the new market had been structured so that utilities had no visibility beyond an hour on the availability of power.

Many businesses had "interruptible" contracts, which meant that in exchange for lower rates they could be cut off if electricity went short. A steel company east of Los Angeles, which had had its electricity interrupted only once over fifteen years, now found its electricity cut off eighteen times in 2000—with only fifteen-minutes' notice to shut down all its operations. "We cannot run a business like this," the president of the company declared. Infrastructure constraints in transmission, particularly between Northern and Southern California, added to the woes. The system was clearly breaking down. Yet still the state government did not react.

The crisis worsened as the year progressed. Utilities were spending five times as much to buy electricity in the wholesale market as they could sell it to retail customers for—an obviously untenable situation. But they could not do much about it. They were certainly not allowed to raise rates. Seven times Southern California Edison requested permission from the state's public utility commission to gain protection by signing long-term power-supply contracts, and seven times the commission said no.[10]

"PIRATES" AND "PLUNDER": CALIFORNIA AT SEA

By the beginning of 2001, the state was in the grip of a full-blown electricity crisis. It was now evident to everyone that the market was broken. As the crisis unfolded, delegations from as far away as Belgium and Beijing journeyed to America's largest state to learn what had gone wrong. And plenty was going wrong. Utilities were accumulating tens of billions of dollars of losses. Governor Gray Davis announced that the state was living through an "energy nightmare," produced by "price gouging" by "out-of-state profiteers" who were holding California "hostage." He earnestly appealed to Californians to save electric power by putting their computers "on sleep mode" when not in use. He also threatened that the state would seize ownership of generating plants and go into the business of building power plants itself. The merchant generators, he declared, "have brought the state to the very brink of blackouts."[11]

It was not just electricity that was in short supply. So was the political leadership and will to bring people together and adjust what has been described as the "extremely complex and untested system" that had just been put in place. One obvious answer would have been to permit price signals to work and allow at least some moderate increase in the retail rates paid by homeowners. Davis himself recognized that reality. "Believe me," he said at one point, "if I wanted to raise rates, I could solve this problem in 20 minutes." But he was adamant. He would not do that.

Instead he blamed everyone else, ranging from the utilities to the federal government. But, by far, his greatest wrath was reserved for companies headquartered out of state, particularly those in Texas, that had bought many of the generating plants and that were trading power. They were, he said, "pirate generators" out for "plunder."[12]

This was not an environment conducive to collaboration and solutions. The crisis worsened. Spot prices for electricity were, on average, ten times what they had been a year earlier. State regulators began to ration power physically, which meant rolling blackouts. Meanwhile, as wholesale power prices went up, the financial positions of the states' utilities became even more dire. Because of that iron curtain between the deregulated wholesale market and the regulated retail side, utilities were buying wholesale power for as much as $600 per kilowatt hour but were able to sell it to retail customers at a regulated rate of only about $60 per kilowatt hour. As one analyst put it, "The more electricity they sold, the more money they lost."[13]

The state was in an uproar; its economy, disrupted. In April 2001, after listening to Governor Davis threaten the utilities with expropriation, the management of PG&E, the state's largest utility, serving Northern California, decided that it had no choice but to file for bankruptcy protection. San Diego Gas & Electric teetered on the edge of bankruptcy. The management of one of the state's major utilities hurriedly put together an analysis of urban disruption to try to prepare for the distress and social breakdown—and potential mayhem—that could result if the blackouts really got out of hand. They foresaw the possibility of riots, looting, and rampant vandalism, and feared for the physical safety of California's citizens.

But Governor Gray Davis was still dead set against the one thing that would have immediately ameliorated the situation—letting retail prices rise. Instead he had the state step in and negotiate, of all things, long-term contracts, as far out as twenty years. Here the state demonstrated a stunning lack of commercial acumen—buying at the top of the market, committing $40 billion for electricity that would probably be worth only $20 billion in the years to come. With this the state transferred the financial crisis of the utilities to its own books, transforming California's projected budget surplus of $8 billion into a multibillion-dollar state deficit.[14]

"CRISIS BY DESIGN"

Many joined Davis in fingering the power marketers and merchant generators as the perpetrators of the crisis. They were charged with engaging in various trading and bidding strategies that took advantage of the crisis and with taking plants off-line to push up prices. But a Federal Energy Regulatory Commission review concluded that it "did not discover any evidence suggesting that" merchant generators were scheduling maintenance or incurring outages in an effort to influence prices. Rather the companies appeared to have taken whatever steps were necessary to bring the generating facilities back on line as soon as possible. Moreover, it turned out that publicly owned municipal power companies, led by the Los Angeles Department of Water and Power, were among those selling the highest-priced electric power.[15]

Postcrisis investigations revealed rapacious behavior on the part of some of the energy traders, who were middlemen between generators and utilities. This was particularly true of those from Enron, who wielded trading strategies with such vivid names as "Fat Boy," "Ricochet," and "Death Star." Phone records captured their inflammatory conversations as they pursued their trading strategies through the crisis. The records also indicated that at least some of them were deliberately manipulating the movement of electricity supplies in and out of the state to try to drive up prices. Subsequently three traders admitted to such and pleaded guilty to conspiracy to commit wire fraud. By then, Enron itself was long gone. It was done in by a combination of factors: almost $40 billion of debt and obligations that it could not fund, accounting ruses and tricks that hid its true financial position and that depended upon a high stock price to avoid coming undone, a propensity to woefully overspend on investments and then not manage them well, and personal enrichment. When Enron filed for Chapter 11 in December 2001, it was the largest bankruptcy in American history.[16]

What was the impact of the traders on the crisis? One of the leading scholars on the topic, James Sweeney of Stanford University, concluded that the "amount and use of market power is unknown but subject to massive debate." But the ability to wield market power in a very tight market, he added, would have greatly decreased had the state permitted retail prices to go up and allowed utilities to enter into long-term contracts. Trading in electric power goes on every day across the country without a crisis. That the traders sought to take advantage and make money out of the political and regulatory debacle in California is clear. But that they were not the fundamental reason for the crisis is also clear. The causes reside in the way the power market restructuring was designed in the face of shifting supply and demand.[17]

Indeed, what unfolded in California was what has been called a "crisis by design."

By the summer of 2001 the crisis was easing. The state authorities had finally succumbed to economic reality and allowed retail prices to rise some. The expected happened: consumers reduced their consumption. In addition, the weather moderated compared with the previous year, and new electricity-generating capacity started to enter the system.

But it was not until November of 2003 that Governor Davis officially pronounced the crisis over. By then so was his own political career. The state's voters had just turned him out of office in a special election—only the second governor in the history of the United States to be so dismissed. His successor was Arnold Schwarzenegger.

The Terminator became the Governator. His inauguration was a global event, attended by 650 journalists. Schwarzenegger inherited a $25 billion deficit, much of it the direct and indirect result of the power debacle. "California is in a crisis," he said after he took the oath of office. "We have the worst credit rating in the country." But, recalling his days of championship weight lifting, he declared with fortitude, "We are always stronger than we know."

Gray Davis offered his own explanation for what had gone wrong: "I was slow to act during the energy crisis." As he left office, he ruefully offered a lasting truism: "It's a bummer to govern in bad times."[18]

IN THE AFTERMATH

Almost a decade after the California crisis first began, the chairman of the Federal Energy Regulatory Commission offered his own judgment: "The California crisis was not a failure of markets," he said. "It was a failure of regulation."[19]

But still, in the rest of the country, in the aftermath of the California electricity crisis, the brakes were slammed on on the movement toward deregulation. The result was to leave the United States with an "unintended hybrid" system. A map of the country reveals a patchwork among the states. About half of the utilities in the country are traditionally regulated, and half are subject to varying degrees of market competition. The utilities in the latter category own only small amounts of generation of their own within their service territories, or none at all. They are in the wires business—transmission and distribution—and thus buy electricity from generators. Yet underlining the hybrid nature of the system, several utilities today hold a portfolio of power plants, some operating in regulated markets and others operating in competitive markets.[20] The markets open to retail competition are clustered in the Northeast, the Midwest, and Texas, while the Southeast is characterized by traditional regulation.

At the same time, at the wholesale level competitive markets for electricity have been expanding apace over the past decade. Even as California's system flopped, other markets demonstrated what a well-designed power market actually looks like. The PJM Interconnection, which stretches from Pennsylvania and Washington, D.C., all the way to Chicago and includes all or parts of fifteen states, is one such market. It is the largest competitive power market in the world, serving 51 million people. PJM has deep roots, going back to a power pool that was established between Pennsylvania and New Jersey in 1927 to bring greater stability in electricity supply to the region. Today PJM operates both the high-voltage transmission system in its region and a competitive wholesale market, bringing buyers and sellers together on a real-time basis.

As for California, the state has kept its wholesale electricity markets open to competition. It now permits long-term contracts. In 2009, after several years of work, the state's Independent System Operator (ISO) introduced a new market design. It incorporated experience from PJM and other systems as well as the painful lessons from what Mason Willrich, the chairman of the ISO, called the "flawed, flawed market" that had been put in place in California in the 1990s. This new design was intended to better reflect the true cost of electricity, including the cost of transmission congestion in the grid, and, with appropriate market monitoring, deliver the benefits of competition, rather than design a crisis.[21]

The major question today for electric power is no longer market design—regulation versus deregulation. Rather, it is fuel choice. Whatever the setup in different parts of the country, the United States faces the same question about the future of its electricity supply as do many other countries: What kind of generation to build? This struggle over fuel choice is not just about meeting today's needs, but also about how to meet expected growth in demand—and new environmental objectives. Coal, nuclear power, and natural gas will all be part of the picture, both in the United States and around the world. Each, however, comes with its own constraints.

20

FUEL CHOICE

The prospects for electric power in the twenty-first century can be summarized in a single word: growth. Electricity consumption, both worldwide and in the United States, has doubled since 1980. It is expected, on a global basis, to about double again by 2030. And the absolute amount of the doubling this time will be so much larger, as it is off a much larger base. An increase on such a scale is both enormous and expensive. The cost for building the new capacity to accommodate this growth between now and 2030 is currently estimated at $14 trillion—and is rising. But that expansion is what will be required to support what could be by then a $130 trillion world economy.[1]

Such very big numbers generate very big questions—and a fierce battle. What kind of power plants to construct and, then, how to get them built? The crux of the matter is fuel choice. Making those choices involves a complex argument over energy security and physical safety, economics, environment, carbon and climate change, values and public policy, and over the basic requirement of reliability—keeping on not just the lights but everything else in this digital age. The centrality of electricity makes the matter of fuel choice and meeting future power needs one of the most fundamental issues for the global economy.

In the developing world, rising incomes and urbanization are driving demand. China literally doubled its electric power system between 2006 and 2010, and is likely to double it again in just a few years. India's power consumption is expected to increase fivefold between 2010 and 2030. The challenge for developing countries is to increase reliability, ensure that power supplies keep up with economic growth, and avoid shortfalls that constrain growth. It is also to deliver electricity to the 1.6 billion people who have no access at all to electricity but instead burn kerosene or scrounge for wood or collect dung. Billions more receive electric power only part of every day, interrupted by shortages and blackouts, taking a toll on both daily life and economic growth.

In the developed world, increasing consumption is driven by the ever-expanding role of computers, servers, and high-tech electronics. This process is so increasingly pervasive as to be taken for granted. To take a simple example, writing a book three decades ago was done on a manual typewriter, using carbon paper for copies; and research meant trips to the library and wandering through the stacks. Now the book is written on a computer, multiple drafts are produced on an electronic printer, much of the research is done over the Internet, and the final product is increasingly as likely to be read electronically as on the printed page.

In the United States, electricity consumption is expected to rise at about 1.4 percent per year. That sounds modest when compared with some developing countries today—or to the almost 10 percent growth in the 1950s in the United States when Ronald Reagan was extolling the "all-electric home." But over 20 years, it means an absolute growth in demand of about a third. That is equivalent to about 150 new nuclear reactors or almost 300 new standard-size coal-fired plants. And every single new facility means a choice over fuels—and a wrangle over what to do.

MAKING POWER

Electricity is flexible not only in what it can be used for but also in terms of how it can be made. It is not a primary energy resource in itself, unlike oil or natural gas or coal. Rather it is a product generated by converting other resources. And it is very versatile in the making. Electricity can be made from coal, oil, natural gas, and uranium; from falling or flowing water; from the blowing wind and the shining sun. Even from garbage and old tires.[2]

Electric power is a classically long-term business. A power plant built today may be operating 60 to 70 years from now. It is also a big-ticket business—in fact, it is the most capital-intensive major industry in the United States. Fully 10 percent of all capital investment in the United States is embedded in the power plants, transmission lines, substations, poles, and wires that altogether make up the power infrastructure. A new coal plant may cost as much as $3 billion, assuming it can be built in the face of environmental opposition and uncertainty about carbon regulation. A new nuclear power plant may be double that—$6 billion or $7 billion or even more. Assuming the nuclear plant can make its way through the permitting process, it can take a decade or two to site and build, and its lifetime may ultimately extend into the next century.

Yet the rules, the politics, and the expectations keep changing, creating what economist Lawrence Makovich calls "the quandary." The business itself is still subject to alternating currents of public policy—and dramatic swings in markets and popular opinion—that lead to major and abrupt changes in direction. The focus on climate change grows more intense. So does antipathy to building new plants. And it is not just the prospect of new coal or nuclear plants that engenders environmental opposition. Wind turbines and new transmission lines can also raise the ire of local publics.

How, in such circumstances, to meet the needs and close the gap between public expectations and what can actually be built? Both wind and solar still have to prove themselves on a systemic scale. (To each of these we will return later.) Efficiency and the smart grid could reduce or flatten out the growth curves.

The place to start is with the current mix. In the United States, coal's share, once almost 55 percent, has declined somewhat to about 45 percent of all electric-power generation. Natural gas is next, at 23 percent and rising; and nuclear, at 20 percent. Hydropower is 7 percent; wind is almost 2 percent; and solar does not register. Over the decades, oil has been squeezed down from over 15 percent to just 1 percent. That is why, despite what is often said, increased renewable or nuclear power would have very little impact on oil use unless accompanied by very widespread adoption of electric cars that plug into the electric grid.

The other major developed regions are somewhat less reliant on coal. In Europe, nuclear, coal, and natural gas are all tied at 25 percent each. Hydro

THE FUEL MIX
Electricity generation in 2009 by fuel type, in millions of gigawatt-hours

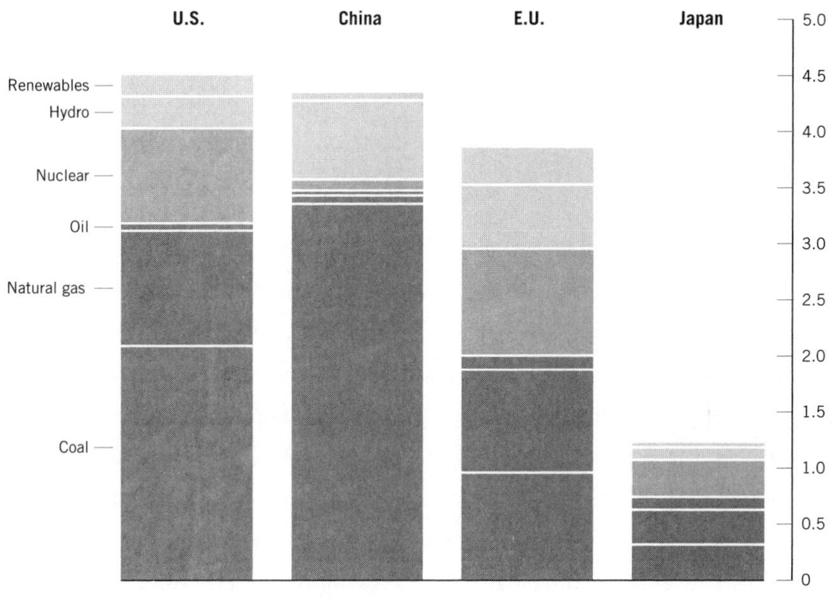

Source: IHS CERA

is 15 percent. Wind and oil are virtually neck and neck, at 4 and 3 percent respectively. Japan is 28 percent coal and 28 percent nuclear, followed by natural gas at 26 percent. Oil is 8 percent; hydro, 8 percent. Wind is negligible. In all three regions, solar has yet at this point to appear in any statistically significant way.

China and India, the world's most populous countries, rank first and third, respectively, in coal consumption, with the United States placing second. In China about 80 percent of electricity is produced from coal, while this figure is 69 percent for India. Hydropower accounts for 16 percent of electricity production in China and 13 percent in India.[3]

The choices on fuel mix are determined by the constraints and endowments of region and geography. Thus, over 80 percent of Brazil's electricity is hydropower. The choices are also shaped by technology, economics, availability, and the three *P*s—policy, politics, and public opinion.

When it is all added up, however, on a global basis, a triumvirate of sources—coal, nuclear, and natural gas—will remain dominant at least for another two decades. As one looks further out in the years ahead, however, renewables grow, and the mix becomes less clear—and much more subject to contention.

COAL AND CARBON

Today 40 percent of the world's electricity is generated from coal. Coal is abundant. The United States holds over 25 percent of known world reserves, putting it in the same position in terms of coal reserves as Saudi Arabia with respect to oil reserves. A new generation of ultra-supercritical power plants—operating under higher temperatures and pressures—are coming into the fleet. They are much more environmentally benign than the plants that would have been built a generation ago, and because of their greater efficiency they can emit 40 percent less CO_2 for the same amount of power as a plant built a couple of decades previously. Today most scenarios have coal use growing on a global basis.

Between 1975 and 1990 the output of coal-generated electricity literally doubled in the United States. In those years, government policies restricted alternatives, and coal became the reliable, buildable generation source. Policies also promoted coal as a secure energy source and one not subject to political disruption. For many countries, that is still the case. But not in the United States and Europe, where carbon emissions are a major issue. Based on the chemical composition of coal and natural gas, and the greater efficiency of a combined-cycle gas turbine, coal produces more than twice as much CO_2 per unit of electricity as does natural gas.

In 2011 about 25 coal-fired plants were under construction in the United States. But political and regulatory opposition to coal on grounds of global warming has mounted to a level that makes it difficult to launch new conventional coal plants. Permits for coal projects already under construction are being challenged, and a number of new coal power projects have been canceled or delayed in the United States—even after entering advanced stages of development. Some environmental groups have made opposition to building new coal plants a top priority.[4]

At the same time, concerns about the health impact of emissions, aside from CO_2, and water usage are leading to new regulations. These new rules will significantly increase the operating costs of existing coal plants. The expected price tag for compliance with such new environmental regulations will likely accelerate the retirement of a number of U.S. coal plants, though the pace is the subject of much debate. These new environmental requirements create a formidable gauntlet for any proposed new plant to run in order to make it through the regulatory approval process.[5]

CAPTURING THE CARBON

What then can be done to reconcile coal and carbon? That challenge preoccupies much of the power industry. Over the last 20 years—pushed by regulation and facilitated by the use of markets—the power industry and the equipment manufacturers that serve it have done a remarkable job in eliminating pollution. Some 99.9 percent of particulates, 99 percent of sulfur dioxide (SO_2), and 95 percent of nitrogen oxides (NOx) emissions have been banished by new coal plants. But the amount of carbon, embedded in the carbon dioxide emitted by burning coal, is an altogether different and a much more intractable problem.[6]

The most prominent answer today is carbon capture and sequestration (or storage), better known by the shorthand CCS. To "sequester" something is to isolate it or set it apart; the concept here is to keep carbon out of the atmosphere by capturing it and burying it underground. "CCS is the critical future technology option for reducing CO_2 emissions while keeping coal's use above today's level," said the MIT study *The Future of Coal.*

CO_2 can be captured in several ways, either before or after the coal is burned. One of the various methods, the only one that could likely be adapted to an existing coal plant, is capturing the CO_2 after burning the coal. For the others it would be so expensive and complicated that it would be cheaper just to scrap the existing plant and build a new one.

However it is separated out, the captured CO_2 is compressed into a "supercritical phase" that behaves like a liquid and is transported by pipeline to a site where it can be safely buried in a secure underground geological formation. The CO_2 would be trapped, locked in, the key thrown away, presumably forever.

In principle, the technology is doable. After all, gases are currently already captured at various kinds of process facilities. CO_2 is already transported by pipeline and pumped into old oil and gas fields to help boost production. But when all is said and done, those analogies are limited—different purpose, different geological conditions, not monitored in the way that would be required, and on a much smaller scale.

The proposed system for CCS is expensive and it is complex, whether one is talking about technology or politics and the complicated regulatory maze at the federal and state levels.

"BIG CARBON"

And the scale here would be very, very large. It would really be like creating a parallel universe, a new energy industry, but one that works in reverse. Instead of extracting resources from the ground, transporting and transforming them, and then burning them, the "Big Carbon" industry would nab the spent resource of CO_2 before it gets into the atmosphere, and transform and transport it, and eventually put it back into the ground. This would truly be a round-trip.

Indeed, this new CCS industry would be similar in scale to that of existing energy industries. If just 60 percent of the CO_2 produced by today's coal-fired power plants in the United States were captured and compressed into a liquid, transported, and injected into the storage site, the daily volume of liquids so handled would be about equal to the 19 million barrels of oil that the United States consumes every day. It is sobering to realize that 150 years and trillions of dollars were required to build that existing system for oil.

Though CO_2 is a normal part of the natural environment, at very high levels of concentration it is poisonous. The scientific consensus is that the CO_2 could be stored with little or no leakage. "Geological carbon sequestration is likely to be safe, effective, and competitive with many other options on an economic basis," in the words of the MIT report. But it adds: "Many years of development and demonstration will be required to prepare [CCS] for successful, large-scale adoption." What happens if there is a leak? Who is legally responsible to fix it? Who is legally liable? Indeed, who owns the CO_2? Who manages it and monitors it—and how? What is the reaction of people who live above the storage? Who writes all the legal and regulatory rules that need to be created? And, fundamentally, will public acceptance, if not outright embrace, be sufficient to build and operate a vast CCS system?[7]

Then there is, of course, cost. Estimates today, based on experimental projects, suggest that CCS could raise the price of coal-fired electricity by 80 to 100 percent. That can work if a significant price is put on carbon either through a cap-and-trade system or a tax. Such a carbon charge would push up the cost of conventional coal generation without carbon capture, making coal-fired electricity with CCS competitive with conventional coal generation.

Still there is nothing yet close to a large-scale plug-and-play-type system for managing carbon. A few pilot projects integrating CCS with existing power plants are now under way. "The pace is insufficient," said Professor John Deutch of MIT. It will take billions of R&D dollars and several large-scale demonstration projects and a decade and a half or more to get to the point where CCS starts to become commercial. It is an engineering challenge—"heavy-duty, large-scale process engineering . . . relentlessly squeezing cost and performance improvements out of large-scale chemical engineering facilities."[8]

If CCS is still in the future in commercial terms, will coal plants get built in the interim? They may be designed to be "capture ready," although it's not clear what kind of technology and system they should be ready for. Still, CCS will likely end up part of the solution to carbon in electric power.

In the meantime, the innovation imperative for clean coal will be very strong. Perhaps some other technologies will be developed that will offer a different solution to carbon—and perhaps cheaper and less complex. Or perhaps ways will be found to transform the waste product created from burning coal into something itself of value and use. In other words, transform CO_2 from a problem into a valuable commodity. The incentive is certainly there.

THE RETURN OF NUCLEAR

In a carbon-conscious world, nuclear power's great advantages are not only the traditional ones of fuel diversification and self-sufficiency. It is also the only large-scale, well-established, broadly deployable source of electric generation currently available that is carbon free.

Nuclear power continues to make up about 20 percent of total U.S. electric generation, as in the 1980s. But how can that be possible? United States electricity consumption has virtually doubled since 1980; yet no new nuclear plants have been started in more than three decades, and the United States has about the same number of operating nuclear units today as in the middle 1980s. How could nuclear power hold on to its 20 percent share of this much larger output?

The way that nuclear has maintained its market share is through dramatic improvements in operations. In the mid-1980s, operating problems took plants off-line so that, on an annual basis, they operated at only about 55 percent of their rated total generating capacity. Today, as the result of several decades of experience and an intense focus on performance—including recruitment of those veterans from Rickover's nuclear navy—nuclear plants in the United States operate at over 90 percent of capacity. That improvement in operating efficiency is so significant in its impact that it can almost be seen as a new source in electric power itself. It is as though the nuclear fleet were doubled without actually building any new plants.

A NEW LEASE ON LIFE

In addition to its much-improved operating and economic record, U.S. nuclear power has received another very important boost, without which it would indeed have begun to fade away. Nuclear power plants require a license to operate. This process involved years of applications and review and challenges. (It is estimated that the cost of applying for a new nuclear license today is as much as half a billion dollars.) The operating licenses—granted by the NRC, the Nuclear Regulatory Commission (and before that by its predecessor, the Atomic Energy Commission)—lasted 40 years. That length of time was based, as the NRC puts it, "on economic and antitrust considerations, not technical limitations." Whatever happened at the end of those 40-year terms would be a turning point for nuclear power, one way or the other, and would determine if nuclear power had any future in the United States.

In 1995 Shirley Ann Jackson, a physicist from Bell Labs, became the chair of the Nuclear Regulatory Commission. Licensing was at the top of her agenda. The end of the 40 years was starting to come into view for many plants, and with that the specter that the nuclear fleet would have to be shut down and decommissioned—unless the NRC extended their licenses for another twenty years. And could it be done in time?

"Some components in plants do wear out, and they need to replaced," Jackson later said. "If a plant is coming closer to the end of its licensing period, there is less incentive to invest, which could actually lead to premature shutdown of plants. To put it simply, we were potentially going to lose a significant amount of electricity."[9]

The operating record of the nuclear industry had clearly improved, and substantially so. In fact, companies were coming to the commission to request permission for power upgrades, above what had been their maximum output, because of their increased efficiency. In support of license extension, the NRC launched a crucial new initiative to update the safety system that governed the industry, using new tools and capabilities.

To date, the NRC has given extensions to about half of the 104 commercial reactors in the United States. Without those extensions, nuclear power plants in the United States would be in the process of shutting down today. Even with extensions, there is still, in view of the growth ahead, the question of maintaining the 20 percent nuclear share of electricity. Part of that is being achieved by upgrading the permitted capacity of existing plants. But new plants will be needed as well.[10]

"WE ARE GOING TO RESTART"

In February 2010 the Obama administration announced loan guarantees—to the Southern Company and its partners—to build the first two new nuclear plants in the United States in many decades. It did so under the Energy Policy Act of 2005, which provides not only federal loan guarantees but also tax incentives for the first six gigawatts of nuclear capacity to come online by 2020. The units are going to be built at the existing Vogtle plant in Georgia. "We are going to restart the nuclear industry in this country," pledged the White House energy "czar." The first six projects are also eligible for several hundred millions of dollars of federal funds to compensate them for any "breakdown in the regulatory process" or litigation. This innovative provision was introduced to offset the way in which the regulatory processes and litigation drag on for decades, dramatically driving up costs. In effect, the federal government is insuring the developers against actions by other parts of the government that cause inordinate, expensive delays.[11]

This set of policies recharged the prospects for nuclear power in the United States. Some 30 new reactors were proposed, 20 of them with specific sites and reactor types. All of the 20 would be built on existing nuclear sites, alongside currently operating plants. Subsequently, many of these proposals faded away in view of the still-challenging regulatory and cost environment.

One critical objective in the new designs is to incorporate more passive safety features. Another is to standardize the reactor designs. "One of the greatest missed opportunities with our current fleet of reactors was the failure to standardize around a limited number of designs," said Gregory Jackzo, the current chairman of the NRC. "That is not an efficient approach from a regulatory standpoint or an operational standpoint."[12]

One potential solution is a new variety of small and medium reactors—or SMRs, as they are known. Because of their size they should in principle be easier to site, and their simplified designs—and use of modular units—should bring down costs and shorten construction times. Indeed, the idea is to achieve economies of scale not by size, as was traditionally the case with reactors, but by manufacturing SMRs modularly and in greater volume. At the same time, SMRs would reduce the financial risk and complexity that come with the development and construction of large reactors.[13] Yet it will likely take years for SMRs to be realized technically and for their economic viability to be established.

"DEEP GEOLOGIC STORAGE"

A perennial uncertainty is how to handle nuclear waste at the end of the fuel cycle. In the United States, despite the expenditure of many billions of dollars and two decades of study, the development of a deep underground repository in Yucca Mountain in Nevada—first proposed in 1987—remained stalemated. In 2010 the Obama administration officially pulled the plug on Yucca Mountain. In France, used nuclear fuel is reprocessed; that is, the waste is treated to recover uranium and plutonium, which can be reused. The used fuel that is left over is highly radioactive waste that is vitrified—essentially turned into glass—and stored for later disposal.

Nuclear waste has, for many years, seemed an almost insoluble problem, at least politically in the United States. But when seen in relative terms, the problem of nuclear waste starts to look different. The physical amount of nuclear waste that would have to be stored is only a tiny fraction of the amount of carbon waste that would have to be managed and injected underground with a major carbon-storage program. All the nuclear waste generated by the entire civilian nuclear program would fill no more than a single football field to the height of ten yards. By comparison, the output of CO_2 from a single coal plant, put into compressed form, would require about 600 football fields—and that would be just one year's output.

Moreover, thinking has changed about the criterion that was established for "deep geologic storage"—10,000 years risk-free underground. Specifically, that requirement means that the people living near such storage would receive no more than 15 millirem of radiation a year for the next 10,000 years—equivalent to the amount of radiation that one receives in three round-trip transcontinental flights. But 10,000 years is a very long time. Going backward, it predates the rise of human civilization by several thousand years.

Is there not a different way to handle the problem? As it is, the nuclear waste, when first generated, is stored for several years in onsite pools while it cools off. A consensus is developing that the better course is to store it in specified, controlled sites, in concrete casks, with a timeframe of 100 years that would provide time to find longer-term solutions—and perhaps find safe ways to use the fuel again.

But waste ties into another, more intractable issue.

PROLIFERATION

In October 2003 a German freighter named the *BBC China* picked up its cargo in Dubai, in the Persian Gulf, and then made its way through the Strait of Hormuz into the Suez Canal on the way into the Mediterranean and its destination, the Libyan capital of Tripoli. The voyage appeared uneventful. But the ship was being carefully monitored. Partway through the canal, the captain was abruptly ordered to change direction and head toward a port in southern Italy. A search there revealed that the ship was clandestinely carrying equipment for making a nuclear bomb.

The interdiction actually speeded up a process that had begun earlier in the year and that would, by the end of 2003, lead Libya to begin to normalize relations with the United States and Britain, and reengage, with the global economy (until civil war erupted in Libya in 2011). In the course of so doing, Libya renounced its pursuit of weapons of mass destruction, specifically nuclear weapons, and turned over the equipment it had already received, along with detailed plans it had acquired about how to make an atomic bomb. It also paid compensation to the families on the Pan Am passenger jet that was blown up over Lockerbie, Scotland.[14]

The handwritten notations on the plans made abundantly clear where the nuclear know-how had come from. A network run by A. Q. Khan had promised a full nuclear weapons system to the Libyans for $100 million. Known as the father of Pakistan's atomic bomb and celebrated as a national hero in Pakistan, Khan had stolen the designs for centrifuges while working for a company in the Netherlands. After returning to Pakistan, he had supervised the acquisition from a global gray market of the equipment and additional know-how that culminated in 1998 in Pakistan's first atomic weapons test and turned it into a nuclear-weapons state. But as the years had gone on, Khan had also turned himself into the world's preeminent serial proliferator, with a network that could sell weapons capability to whoever would buy it. Khan's international network played a primary role in helping both Iran and North Korea in their quest for nuclear weapons. And Khan and his network were very open about advertising their capabilities at symposia in Islamabad and even taking promotional booths at international military trade shows.

After the interception of the *BBC China,* an embarrassed Pakistani government sought to distance itself from Khan. He was arrested and compelled to go on television to apologize—after a fashion. "It pains me to realize in retrospect that my entire life achievements of providing foolproof national security to my nation could have been placed in serious jeopardy on account of my activities which were based on good faith but on errors of judgment," he said. He was put under house arrest, but then after a few years was pardoned.[15]

Khan's grim specter haunts the global nuclear economy. For he graphically demonstrated not only the existence of a covert global marketplace for nuclear weapons capability but also how the development of nuclear power can also be a mechanism, as well as a convenient cloak, for developing nuclear weapons.

When it comes to proliferation, civilian nuclear power can bridge into nuclear weapons at two key points. The first is during the enrichment process, where the centrifuges can take the uranium up to the 90 percent concentration of the U-235 isotope necessary for an atomic bomb. That appears to be the route Iran is taking. The other point of risk occurs with the reprocessing of spent fuel. Reprocessing substantially reduces the amount of high-level waste that has to be stored. It involves extracting plutonium from the spent fuel, which can then be reused as a fuel in reactors. However, plutonium is also a weapons-grade material, and it can be diverted to build a nuclear device, as India did in the 1970s, or it can be stolen by those who want to make their own atomic bomb.

The great argument in favor of reprocessing is that it gets more usage out of a given amount of uranium and thus extends the fuel supply. The counterargument is that it expands the dangers of proliferation and terrorism. The risks provide the rationale for avoiding reprocessing and instead keeping spent fuel in interim storage in order to leave time for better technological answers over the next century. Moreover, there is no shortage of natural uranium.

Overall, it is clear that a global expansion of nuclear power will require a stronger antiproliferation regime. The Nuclear Non-Proliferation Treaty, implemented by the International Atomic Energy Agency, is built on safeguards and inspections, but the advance of Iran's nuclear weapons program demonstrates the need for improving the system. But it is also clear that negotiating a new regime will be extremely difficult.

Safety would always be a fundamental concern. It was recognized that a nuclear accident somewhere in the world or a successful terrorist breach of a nuclear power plant could once again arouse public opposition and stall nuclear power development. The latest generation of nuclear reactors aims to enhance safety with simpler designs and even passive safety features. They are also intended to reduce risks of nuclear proliferation and to downsize the amount of spent fuel that needs to be stored. The next generation of reactors are intended to carry these objectives further.

NUCLEAR RENAISSANCE

Today nuclear power represents 15 percent of total world electricity. A good deal of new capacity has come on line since the beginning of the century—just not in the United States and Europe. Between 2000 and 2010, 39 nuclear power plants went into operation. Most of those were in Asia. Indeed, about four fifths of the 60 units currently under construction are in just four countries—China, India, South Korea, and Russia. China embarked on a rapid buildup to more than quadruple its nuclear power capacity by 2020 and aims to have almost as many nuclear plants by then as does the United States. Both India and South Korea are also targeting substantial growth.[16]

Nuclear power is also on the agenda for other countries. In December 2009 the United Arab Emirates, facing rapidly rising demand for electricity and concerned about shortages of natural gas for electric generation, awarded to a South Korean consortium a $20 billion contract to build four nuclear reactors. Cost was not the only reason. It was also because South Korean companies had built more nuclear reactors in the last several years than any other country. The UAE expects the reactors to start becoming operational in 2017.[17]

This expansion became known as the "nuclear renaissance." Even in Europe, the opposition that had blocked nuclear power since the rise of the Green political parties and the days of Chernobyl seemed to be ebbing away. Finland is building a new reactor, its fifth, on an island in the Baltic Sea, although its cost overruns have become a subject of great controversy. Nevertheless, Finland has said it will go ahead with two new reactors. In Britain, climate change and dwindling supplies of North Sea natural gas opened a public discussion about building up to ten new nuclear power plants. The coalition government, led by Conservative David Cameron, reaffirmed the previous government's commitment to nuclear power, despite the opposition of its Liberal Democrats junior coalition partner, which has a traditional European-Green orientation. In Sweden, public opinion now ranks CO_2 as a bigger threat than radioactive waste. Sweden has shut down two nuclear plants, but ten are still operating, and, in fact, are being upgraded in terms of capacity. While "decommissioning" is still formally on the books, in reality, nothing of the sort is likely to happen. As a senior Swedish official put it, "decommissioning is still an official policy." "But," he added, "any further decommissionings are as likely in 30 years—or 300 years—as in three years."[18]

Even Germany seemed set for a turnaround. In 1999 in Germany, the Social Democratic–Green coalition decided to "phase out" the country's 17 reactors. More than a decade later, Germany remained officially committed to the phase-out of nuclear power, which currently supplies over a quarter of its electricity. But Christian Democrat Chancellor Angela Merkel conveyed her strong support for nuclear generation and called the phaseout "absolutely wrong." In 2010 a new law extended the life of Germany's nuclear reactors by an average of twelve years, although opposition parties vowed to challenge the extension in court.[19] But the chancellor strongly reaffirmed her conviction that nuclear power needed to be part of the power mix.

France is building one massive new reactor. France accounts for about half of Europe's total nuclear power–generating capacity. And, as it turns out, nuclear power is under some circumstances just too good a deal to pass up. Italy, like Germany, has a moratorium on new nuclear power. Despite their official opposition, both countries import a good deal of nuclear-generated electricity from the world's largest exporter of electricity—France.[20]

In addition to France, the other major industrial country with a strong commitment to nuclear power was Japan. It targeted 40 percent of its electricity to be nuclear by 2020 and then aimed to go even further and derive half of its electricity from nuclear in 2030. It was a determined national commitment.

That too was part of the nuclear renaissance.

FUKUSHIMA DAIICHI

Then came the earthquake. The collision between two tectonic plates off the coast of Japan on March 11, 2011, set off the most powerful earthquake ever registered in Japan and a tsunami on a scale never imagined. The giant wave overwhelmed the sea defenses along Japan's northeast coast, taking a terrible toll in human life.

Certainly a wave so huge had never been imagined when the Fukushima Daiichi nuclear station had begun operating four decades earlier. The complex was little damaged by the earthquake itself. As soon as the earthquake struck, the reactors "scrammed"—shut down automatically—as they were supposed to. Along with much of the power in the region, the electricity that supplied the station was knocked out, putting the complex into a precarious situation called "station blackout." The response to that point was according to plan. The backup power system was supposed to kick in, but the tsunami had been much higher than the sea wall, and it flooded the station, including the backup generator, so that it could not operate. That meant no lights in the control room. No readings on the controls. No ability to operate equipment. And, most crucially, no way to keep the pumps working that delivered water to the reactors.

The backup power was the safety margin. When hurricanes Katrina and Rita knocked out the electric grid along the U.S. Gulf coast in 2005, the backup diesel-powered electricity kept the nuclear plants in proper operating condition until the external power could be restored. But after the tsunami, without the power to keep the pumps working, the reactors were deprived of the critical coolant they needed to moderate the heat generated by the chain reactions.

That loss of coolant was what set off the nuclear accident, which unfolded over weeks: explosions of hydrogen, roofs blown off the containment structures, venting and spread of radiation, fires, and, most critically, the partial meltdown of the nuclear cores. Workers, suited up against the radiation, working only by flashlight and listening for hydrogen explosions, risked their lives struggling to bring water into the reactors, drain out radioactive water, get the emergency power back on, and enable the control equipment to start working again. Thousands of people in the area were evacuated. As the weeks went on, the accident, originally rated as a 4, was raised to a 5 and then a 7, the highest level, the same assigned to the Chernobyl accident a quarter century earlier, although the actual effects in terms of radiation release at Fukushima Daiichi appeared to be much lower. Still, the extent of the accident was such that it was estimated that it would take six to nine months to reach what was called a "cold shutdown." Some or all of the reactors would be damaged beyond repair and would be complete write-offs.

What was also damaged was the global prospect for nuclear power. The structural integrity of the complex had held up well in the earthquake. The accident was the result of an immense act of nature—and what proved to be poor decisions in understanding the potential size of a tsunami, protecting the site, and in positioning the backup power system. If the plant had not been flooded, the accident would almost certainly not have occurred. In addition, the Japanese governmental system was overwhelmed trying to deal with the nuclear accident. As a government report on the accident put it, "Consistent preparation for severe accidents was insufficient."

But the fact that it did occur, and the difficulties—and time required—to get it under control, shook the structure of confidence of governments and publics around the world about nuclear power that had been built up in the quarter century since Chernobyl.

Japan itself faced what was estimated as a $300 billion cost to recover from the earthquake and the tsunami, the most expensive price tag on any natural disaster ever. The credibility of the nuclear industry was gravely injured. But nuclear power would continue to be part of Japan's energy mix, although siting new plants will likely be even more difficult for some years, and there will be much closer scrutiny of existing plants and operations. The goal of 50 percent nuclear almost certainly will be abandoned, with greater reliance placed instead on imported LNG, increased emphasis on efficiency and renewables, particularly solar and possibly geothermal, and a stepped-up research effort.

The most dramatic turnaround was in Germany. Three days after the accident, German Chancellor Merkel disavowed the nuclear option. She ordered the closing of seven nuclear power plants at least temporarily and withdrew her support for life extension for existing plants. The accident in Japan "had changed everything in Germany," she said. "We all want to exit nuclear power as soon as possible and make the switch to supplying via renewable energy."[21] Several weeks later, her government made it official, ordering the closing of all the German nuclear plants by 2022.

The European Union called for "stress tests" for all nuclear reactors. Other countries were more muted in their reactions. Britain said it would continue to allow work to move ahead on new nuclear plants. France reaffirmed its deep commitment to nuclear power but launched a wide-ranging safety check.

China has the most aggressive nuclear-development program in the world. Following the accident, Beijing ordered a temporary suspension in nuclear project approvals. This strengthened central government authority over nuclear development. Beijing had already been concerned about safety and execution in the breakneck speed at which provinces were moving ahead. This will likely lead to a switch to more third-generation plants, which have more built-in safety features. Nevertheless, China is likely to remain on course to add as many as 60 to 70 new nuclear plants by 2020, which would give it a nuclear fleet rivaling that of the United States in size.

In the United States, the Nuclear Regulatory Commission launched a safety review. But also in the weeks following the accident, the NRC extended the license of one nuclear plant and gave approval to the next stage of the development of the new nuclear units in Georgia. The Obama administration said it would continue to support nuclear power as it sought to incorporate lessons learned from the accident into regulations. But, within the industry, the disaster at Fukushima was causing a rethink of plans. A month after the accident, NRG, a large power-generating company, announced it was backing out of plans to build the largest nuclear project in the United States. "Look at our situation," said David Crane, CEO of NRG. "We responded to the [federal] inducements back in 2005." But, he continued, "you couldn't move it forward. Nothing was going to happen except we were going to continue to spend money, month after month, which we have been doing for five years."[22]

Fukushima Daiichi demonstrated again the impact that a nuclear accident can have around the world. While it did not stop nuclear power in its tracks, "nuclear renaissance" is not a term likely to be heard in the years immediately ahead. One consequence will be to tilt development of new plants to more advanced designs, which incorporate passive safety features so that, for instance, cooling in an emergency would not require electricity from backup diesel generators. Many countries will still choose to include nuclear power in their energy mix for a variety of reasons—extending from zero carbon to energy independence, to the need for base-load power, to avoiding brownouts and blackouts with all the costs that they bring. But economics will also count, and in the United States, even before Fukushima Daiichi, something else was making the competitive prospects for nuclear power more challenging. Thus was the surge of inexpensive unconventional natural gas.

POWER AND THE SHALE GALE

Natural gas is the other obvious fuel choice. The breakthroughs in unconventional gas—specifically the shale gale—hold out the prospect that very large volumes will come to market at relatively low cost. That is changing the choices and calculations for electric power. John Rowe is the CEO of Exelon, which has the largest nuclear fleet in the country. But the arrival of shale gas has changed his calculations. "Inexpensive natural gas produces cheaper, clean electricity," he said. "Cheap gas will get you if you bet against it." This shift in perspective and expectations could lead to the building of a significant amount of new natural gas generation.[23]

That possibility may remind some of the dash for gas in the late 1990s that ran right into the wall of tight supplies and rising prices and ended in distress and bankruptcies. But now the arrival of unconventional gas portends low prices and abundant supplies for many decades or even a century or more. What is also different from a decade ago is that there now exists an urgency to find lower-carbon solutions. Natural gas has also gained a new role—as the enabler of renewables, which are not always available when one wants them, or needs them most. Gas-fired generation would swing into action when the wind dies down and the sun doesn't shine.

BUT HOW MUCH?

For all these reasons it is virtually inevitable that an increasing share of power generation will be fueled by natural gas. But how much? Some argue that the natural gas capacity that is already in place can be used to replace more carbon-intensive coal. A good part of that natural gas capacity needs to be kept available as a "peaking" or surge capacity to balance the overall power flows when demand increases, whether at six in the evening when people get home from work and switch everything on, or when a heat wave causes a sudden increase in air-conditioning use. Without this kind of flexibility, the stability of the overall transmission system would fall apart, leading to brownouts and potentially catastrophic blackouts.

But what about building only natural gas facilities for new capacity? That is not likely. A utility is looking out many decades because of the large capital costs and because of the long life of a unit being built today. It is too risky to overcommit to one approach when technology, expected fuel costs, regulation, public opinion, and ranking of risks can change sometimes with abrupt speed.

Diversification is the basic strategy for protecting against uncertainty and unexpected change. Moreover, while natural gas is lower in carbon, it is not carbon free. So natural gas can help reduce emissions substantially in the short and medium term, but even it could be under pressure in a couple of decades—unless carbon capture and storage works for natural gas as well as coal-fired generation.

Still, gas usage in the U.S. power sector could increase substantially—and all the more so if power demand surges and if efficiency and renewables do not deliver on what is expected and utilities thus need to do something quickly. Gas-fired capacity is the most likely default option. This is true not only in the United States. It is also likely that natural gas–fired generation will grow significantly in Europe and in China and India if unconventional gas development succeeds in those countries.

For many years to come, the power industry will be struggling with the question of what to build and what to shut down and its overarching quandary of fuel choice.

But the decisions about fuel choice will be based not only on energy considerations but also on what has come to loom increasingly large—the climate agenda. It may seem that this concern about climate is a recent development. In fact, the focus on the atmosphere and how it works has been building for a very long time.

PART FOUR

. . .

Climate and Carbon

21

GLACIAL CHANGE

On the morning of August 17, 1856, as the first sunlight revealed the pure white cone of a distant peak, John Tyndall left the hotel not far from the little resort town of Interlaken in Switzerland and set out by himself, making his way through a gorge toward a mountain. He finally reached his destination, the edge of a glacier. He was overcome by what he encountered—"a savage magnificence such as I had not previously beheld." And then, sweating with great exertion but propelled by a growing rapture, he worked his way up onto the glacier itself. He was totally alone in the white emptiness.

The sheer isolation on the ice stunned him. The silence was broken only intermittently, by the "gusts of the wind, or by the weird rattle of the debris which fell at intervals from the melting ice." Suddenly, a giant cascading roar shook the sky. He froze with fear. He then realized what it was—an avalanche. He fixed his eyes "upon a white slope some thousands of feet above" and watched, transfixed, as the distant ice gave way and tumbled down. Once again, it was eerily quiet. But then, a moment later, another thundering avalanche shook the sky.[1]

"A SENTIMENT OF WONDER"

It had been seven years earlier, in 1849, that Tyndall had caught his first glimpse of a glacier. This occurred on his first visit to Switzerland, while he was still doing graduate studies in chemistry in Germany. But it was not until this trip in 1856 that Tyndall—by then already launched on a course that would eventually rank him as one of the great British scientists of the nineteenth century—came back to Switzerland for the specific purpose of studying glaciers. The consequences would ultimately have a decisive impact on the understanding of climate.

Over those weeks that followed his arrival in Interlaken in 1856, Tyndall was overwhelmed again and again by what he beheld—the vastness of the ice, massive and monumental and deeply mysterious. He felt, he said, a "sentiment of wonder approaching to awe." The glaciers captured his imagination. They also became an obsession, repeatedly drawing him back to Switzerland, to scale them, to explore them, to try to understand them—and to risk his life on them.

Born in Ireland, the son of a constable and sometime shoemaker, Tyndall had originally come to England to work as a surveyor. But in 1848, distressed at his inability to get a proper scientific education in Britain, he took all his savings, such as they were, and set off for Germany to study with the chemist Robert Bunsen (of Bunsen burner fame). There he assimilated to his core what he called "the language of experiment." Returning to Britain, he would gain recognition for his scientific work, and then go on to establish himself as a towering figure at the Royal Institution. Among his many accomplishments, he would provide the answer to the basic question of why the sky is blue.[2]

Yet it was to Switzerland that he returned, sometimes almost yearly, to trek through the high altitudes, investigate the terrain, and, yoking on ropes, claw his way up the sides of mountains and on to his beloved glaciers. One year he almost ascended to the top of the Matterhorn, which would have made him the first man to surmount it. But then a sudden violent storm erupted, and his guides held him back from risking the last few hundred feet.

Tyndall grasped something fundamental about the glaciers. They were not stationary. They were not frozen in time. They moved. He described one valley where he "observed upon the rocks and mountains the action of ancient glaciers which once filled the valley to the height of more than a thousand feet above its present level." But now the glaciers were gone. That, thereafter, became one of his principal scientific preoccupations—how glaciers moved and migrated, how they grew and how they shrank.[3]

Tyndall's fascination with glaciers was rooted in the conviction held by a handful of nineteenth-century scientists that Swiss glaciers were the key to determining whether there had once been an Ice Age. And, if so, why it had ended? And, more frightening, might it come back? That in turn led Tyndall to ask questions about temperature and about that narrow belt of gases that girds the world—the atmosphere. His quest for answers would lead him to a fundamental breakthrough that would explain how the atmosphere works. For this Tyndall ranks as one of the key links in the chain of scientists stretching from the late eighteenth century until today who are responsible for providing the modern understanding of climate.

But how did climate change go from a subject of scientific inquiry, which engaged a few scientists like Tyndall, which to one of the dominating energy issues of our age? That is a question profoundly important to the energy future.

THE NEW ENERGY QUESTION

Traditionally, energy issues have revolved around questions about price, availability, security—and pollution. The picture has been further complicated by the decisions governments make about the distribution of energy and money and access to resources, and by the risks of geopolitical clash over those resources.

But now energy policies of all kinds are being reshaped by the issue of climate change and global warming. In response, some seek to transform, radically, the energy system in order to drastically reduce the amount of carbon dioxide and other greenhouse gases that are released when coal, oil, and natural gas—and wood and other combustibles—are burned to generate energy.

This is an awesome challenge. For today over 80 percent of America's energy—and that of the world—is supplied by the combustion of fossil fuels. Put simply: the industrial civilization that has evolved over two and a half centuries rests on a hydrocarbon foundation.

THE RISE OF CARBON

Carbon dioxide (CO_2) and other greenhouse gases, like methane and nitrous oxide, are part of the 62-mile-high blanket of gases that make up the atmosphere. It is all that separates us from the emptiness of outer space. About 98 percent of the atmosphere is composed of just two elements, oxygen and nitrogen. While carbon dioxide and the other greenhouse gases are minute in their concentrations, they play an essential role. They are the balancers. The short-wave ultraviolet radiation of sunlight passes unhindered through all the atmospheric gases on the way to the earth's surface. The earth in turn sends this heat back into the sky—but not in the same form in which it was received. For as the earth remits this heat and sends it back toward the sky, the planet's mass transforms some of the short-wave radiation into longer-wave infrared radiation.

Without CO_2 and the other greenhouse gases, the departing infrared rays would flow back into the vastness of space, and the air would freeze at night, leaving the earth a cold and lifeless place. But owing to their molecular structure, the greenhouse gases, including water vapor, prevent that. They trap some of the heat represented in the form of infrared rays and redistribute it throughout the atmosphere. This balance of greenhouse gases keeps temperatures within a band, not too hot or too cold, and thus making the earth habitable, and more than that—hospitable to life.

But balance is the issue that is at the heart of climate change. If the concentrations of CO_2 and other greenhouse gases grow too large, too much heat will be retained. The world within the atmospheric greenhouse will grow too hot, with the possibility of violent change in climate, which will drastically affect life on the planet. A rise of just two or three degrees in the average temperature, it is feared, is all that is required to wreak havoc.

The carbon levels are captured on graphs. They show a rising line, the elevated concentrations of carbon since the beginning of the Industrial Revolution. Most of the carbon in the atmosphere is the result of natural processes. But by burning fuels, humanity is generating an increasing proportion of carbon.

Humanity's share is growing for two basic reasons. The first is population. The world's population has almost tripled since 1950. The equation is very simple: more people use more energy—which leads to more carbon emissions. The second is rising incomes. World GDP has also tripled since 1950, and energy use rises as incomes rise. People whose parents were cold and bundled up with extra garments now have heat. People whose parents sweltered in muggy tropical climates now have air-conditioning. People whose grandparents rarely left their towns or villages now travel around the world. Goods that were not even imagined two generations ago are now manufactured in one part of the planet and transported over oceans and continents to customers all over the globe. In order to make all that possible, carbon that was buried underground millions of years ago is unearthed, embedded in fuels and brought up to the earth's surface, and then released into the atmosphere by combustion.

There are other major sources of emissions. Large-scale deforestation—burning forests—releases carbon, while at the same time eliminating sinks (that is, the forests) that had served to capture and store carbon. Likewise, global poverty contributes to global warming, because poor people scrounge for biomass and burn it, sending black soot into the sky. The world's herds of livestock release methane and nitrous oxide. Rice cultivation is another big source of methane. Yet by far, CO_2 is the most significant greenhouse gas volumetrically.

Scientists have taken to calling this release of CO_2 the "experiment." Once it was said in neutral tones—Tyndall's "language of experiment"—and was shaped by curiosity, not by alarm. Now it is spoken in dire tones. For these scientists warn that mankind is experimenting with the atmosphere in a manner that could irrevocably change the climate in potentially apocalyptic ways—melting the ice caps, burying great swaths of the world's populated coastlines under water, transforming fertile areas into dying deserts, obliterating species, unleashing violent storms that cause great human suffering—along with devastating economic repercussions so vast that no insurance premium could possibly be large enough.

Some scientists disagree. They say that the mechanisms are not obvious, that the climate has always changed, that most of the CO_2 is released by natural processes, and that the rise of CO_2 in the atmosphere may not be a cause of climate change but the result of other factors, such as solar turbulence or wobbles in the earth's orbit. They are the minority.

WHY NOT TOO HOT OR TOO COLD?

The subject here is not weather, but rather climate. Weather is what happens day by day, the daily fluctuations reported each morning by the affable television weather anchors. Climate is something much bigger and more far-reaching. It is also much more abstract, not something that will be experienced on a daily basis, but something that unfolds over decades or even a century.

How is it that something so complex—and indeed so abstract, something that is inferred rather than touched—could come to so dominate the future of energy and how people live, and become one of the main issues in the politics among nations? That is the story that follows here.

It is striking to see how glaciers and their advance and retreat have been the constant, the leitmotiv, indeed, even central actors, in the study of climate change from the very beginning of the scientific investigations all the way up to the contemporary images of blocks of melting Antarctic ice tumbling into sea. Today glaciers serve as Cassandras for climate. But they are also living history—time machines that enable us to be in the present and yet, at the same moment, go back 20,000 years into the past.

A series of related puzzles converged in the late eighteenth and nineteenth centuries to provide the intellectual origins of thinking on climate change. One was the determinants of the earth's temperature. Why, to put it simply, was life possible on earth? That is, why did the planet not become burningly hot when the sun shone and then freezingly cold at night? Another was the suspicion—and the fear—that the current era of moderate temperatures had been preceded by something different and more extreme, something that haunted thinking about mankind's past: what came to be known as the Ice Age.

These puzzles led to two arresting questions: What could have made the climate change? And could glaciers return, like some immense, fearsome primordial beasts, crushing everything in their paths, smashing and obliterating human civilization as they advanced?

The story begins in the Swiss Alps and its glaciers, more than half a century before John Tyndall first laid eyes upon them.

THE ALPINE "HOT BOX"

Horace Bénédict de Saussure was a scientist, a professor at the Academy of Geneva. He was also an Alpinist, a mountain climber and explorer who devoted his life to trying to understand the natural world in Switzerland's high peaks. To describe his vocation in his classic work, *Voyages dans les Alpes,* he invented the word "geology." Saussure was fascinated by heat and altitude, and built devices to measure temperatures at the tops of mountains and the bottoms of lakes.[4]

But a question troubled Saussure as he traipsed through the Swiss mountains. Why, he asked, did not all the earth's heat escape into space at night? To try to find an answer, he built in the 1770s what became known as his "hot box"—sort of mini greenhouse. The sides and bottom were covered with darkened cork. The top was glass. As heat and light flowed into the box, it was trapped, and the temperature inside would rise. Perhaps, he mused, the atmosphere did the same thing as the glass. Perhaps the atmosphere was a lid over the earth's surface, a giant greenhouse, letting the light in but retaining some of the heat, keeping the earth warm even when the sun had disappeared from the sky.

The French mathematician Joseph Fourier—a friend of Napoléon's and a sometime governor of Egypt—was fascinated by the experiments of Saussure, whom he admiringly described as "the celebrated voyager." Fourier, who devoted much research to heat flows, was convinced that Saussure was right. The atmosphere, Fourier thought, had to function as some sort of top or lid, retaining heat. Otherwise, the earth's temperature at night would be well below freezing.

But how to prove it? In the 1820s Fourier set out to do the mathematics. But the work was daunting and extremely inexact, and his inability to work out the calculations left him deeply frustrated. "It is difficult to know up to what point the atmosphere influences the average temperature of the globe," he lamented, for he could find "no regular mathematical theory" to explain it. With that, he figuratively threw up his hands, leaving the problem to others.[5]

Over the decades, a few other scientists, harking back to Saussure and Fourier, and especially to Saussure's hot box, began to speak about a "hot-house," or "greenhouse," effect as a metaphor to describe how the atmosphere traps heat. But how exactly did it work? And why?

"GREAT SHEETS OF ICE"

The Swiss scientist Louis Agassiz was also obsessed with glaciers—indeed so obsessed that he put aside his research on fossils of extinct fish in order to probe the workings of glaciers. He even built a hut on the Aar glacier and moved into it so that he might more closely monitor the glacier's movement.

In 1837, more than a decade before John Tyndall first caught sight of a glacier, Agassiz propounded a revolutionary, even shocking idea. There had once been something before the present age, he declared. That "before" was an ice age, when much of Europe must have been covered by massive glaciers, "great sheets of ice resembling those now in Greenland." That was an age, he said, when a "Siberian Winter" gripped the world throughout the year, a time when "death enveloped all nature in a shroud."

The ice, Agassiz maintained, came about due to a sudden, mysterious drop in temperature that was part of a cyclical pattern stretching back to the beginning of earth's history. As the glaciers had retreated to the north, they had left behind in their wake the valleys and mountains and gorges and lakes and fjords and boulders and gravel that documented their movement.

Agassiz's bold assertion was met with great skepticism. One colleague advised him, for his own good, to give up on glaciers and instead stick to his "beloved fossil fishes."

Agassiz would not be swayed. His continuing research provided further evidence on the movement of glaciers, or what he called "God's great plough." He later migrated to the United States, where he became a professor at Harvard University. He organized an expedition to the Great Lakes that demonstrated that they had been sculpted into the earth's surface by the advance and retreat of glaciers—yet more evidence of an ice age. By proving that the earth had lived through different ages in terms of temperature, Agassiz was the real inventor of the idea of climate.[6]

THE ATMOSPHERE: "AS A DAM BUILT ACROSS A RIVER"

John Tyndall built his own research on the work of these predecessors. His keen interest in the migration of glaciers across Europe led him to seek to understand whether and how the atmosphere could trap heat. If he could make sense of that, he could begin to understand how the climate could change, a process that was embodied in the glaciers that obsessed him.

To find the answer, Tyndall built a new machine in his basement laboratory in the Royal Institution on Albemarle Street in London. This was his spectrophotometer, a device that enabled him to measure whether gases could trap heat and light. If the gases were transparent, they would not trap heat, and he would have to find some other explanation. He first experimented with the most plentiful atmospheric gases, nitrogen and oxygen. To his disappointment, they were transparent, and the light passed right through them.

What else could he test? The answer was right there in his laboratory—coal gas—otherwise known as town gas. This was a carbon-bearing gas, primarily methane made by heating coal, that was pumped into his laboratory by the local London lighting company to burn in order to provide illumination—pre-electricity. When Tyndall put the coal gas into the spectrophotometer, he found that the gas, though invisible to the eye, was opaque to light; it darkened. Here was his proof. It was trapping infrared light. He then tried water and carbon dioxide. They too were opaque. That meant that they too trapped heat.

By this point, Tyndall was close to collapse from continual ten-hour days in the laboratory and from his inhalation of fumes—of "gases not natural even to the atmosphere of London." But that did not matter. He was elated. "Experimented all day," he wrote in his journal on May 18, 1859, adding joyously, "The subject is completely in my hands!" Just three weeks later, he delivered a public lecture at the Royal Institution—with Prince Albert, the Prince Consort of Queen Victoria, in the chair—demonstrating and explaining his discovery and its significance. There on Albemarle Street, just off Piccadilly, was "the first public, experimentally based account" of the greenhouse effect.[7]

"As a dam built across a river causes a local deepening of the stream, so our atmosphere, thrown as a barrier across the terrestrial (infrared) rays, produces a local heightening of the temperature at the Earth's surface," said Tyndall. "Without the atmosphere, you would assuredly destroy every plant capable of being destroyed by a freezing temperature. . . . The atmosphere admits of the entrance of the solar heat, but checks its exit; the result is a tendency to accumulate heat at the surface of the planet."

What Tyndall had done in his basement laboratory was to provide the explanation for the greenhouse effect, for how climate worked, and for how, in his words, "every variation" of the constituents of the atmosphere "must produce a change of climate." He gave particular credit to Saussure and Fourier. Here also was a confirmation for Louis Agassiz's theory of the Ice Age. For variations in the balance of gases in the atmosphere "may have produced all the mutations of climate which the researches of geologists reveal."

Tyndall went on to make other important contributions to science and gained great renown. Until late in life, he would also regularly return to Switzerland to take in the glaciers and climb the peaks. After a life as a mountaineer, undertaking many dangerous and daring mountain expeditions, including a number of near fatal accidents, Tyndall died in 1893, at age 73, under more prosaic circumstances. His wife had accidentally administered an overdose of sleep nostrum to relieve his intolerable insomnia. As he slipped away, he murmured, "My poor darling, you have killed your John."[8]

ARRHENIUS: THE GREAT BENEFIT OF A WARMING CLIMATE

The year after Tyndall's death, in 1894, a Swedish chemist named Svante Arrhenius picked up the story. Arrhenius was curious as to what effects increasing or decreasing levels of carbon dioxide—or carbonic acid, as it was called at the time—would have on the climate. He too wanted to weigh in on the mechanisms of the ice ages, the advance and retreat of glaciers, and what he called "some points in geological climatology."

Arrhenius's own academic career was not smooth. He had difficulty getting his Ph.D. accepted at the University of Uppsala. But now, more established in Stockholm, he found his interest in carbon and the ice age stoked in a scientific seminar that met on Saturdays. Melancholic over his divorce and loss of custody of his son, and with much time on his hands, Arrehenius threw himself into month after month of tedious calculations, sometimes working 14 hours a day, proceeding latitude by latitude, trying by hand to calculate the effects of changes in carbon.

After a year, Arrhenius had the results. Invoking Tyndall and Fourier, he said, "A great deal has been written on the influence of the absorption of the atmosphere upon the climate." His calculations showed that cutting atmospheric carbon in half would lower the world's temperature by about four to five degrees centigrade. Additional work indicated that a doubling of carbon dioxide would increase temperatures by five to six degrees centigrade. Arrhenius did not have the benefit of supercomputers and advanced computation; he arrived at the above prediction after a tediously huge number of calculations by hand. Nonetheless, his results are in the range of contemporary models.[9]

Even if he was the first to predict, at least to some degree, global warming, Arrhenius was certainly not worried about the possibility. He thought it would take 3,000 years for CO_2 to double in the atmosphere, and in any event that would be a good thing. He later mused that the increased CO_2 concentrations would not only prevent a new ice age but would actively allow mankind to "enjoy ages with more equable and better climates," especially in "the colder regions of the earth," and that would "bring forth much more abundant crops than at present for the benefit of rapidly propagating mankind." And that did not sound at all bad to a lonely Swedish chemist who knew all too well what it was like to live, year after year, through long, dark, cold winters.[10]

"My grandfather rang a bell, indeed, and people became extremely interested in it at that time," said his grandson Gustaf Arrhenius, himself a distinguished chemist. "There was a great flurry of interest in it, but not because of the menace, but because it would be so great. He felt that it would be marvelous to have an improved climate in the 'northern climes.' And, in addition, the carbon dioxide would stimulate growth of crops—they would grow better. So he and the people at the time were only sad that in his calculations it would take [so long] to have the marked effect."[11]

In time, however, attention drifted away from the subject of carbon and climate. Arrhenius himself turned to a number of other topics. In 1903 he was awarded the Nobel Prize in chemistry—not bad for someone whose Ph.D., which initiated the research for which he won the prize, was almost rejected.

In the decades that followed, the world became much more industrialized. Coal was king, both for electric generation and factories, which meant more "carbonic acid"—CO_2—going into the air. But there was little attention to climate.

In the Depression years of the early 1930s, drought struck the American

Midwest. Poor cultivation techniques had left the topsoil loose and exposed, and winds swept it up into great dust storms, sometimes so intense as to block out the sun, leaving the land barren. The economic devastation drove hundreds of thousands of farm families to pack their belongings on their Model Ts, and, like the fictional Joad family in John Steinbeck's *Grapes of Wrath,* living in a "dust-blanketed land," take to the roads and head to California as migrant refugees from the Dust Bowl.[12]

But those droughts were "weather," not "climate." No one talked about climate for decades. Or almost no one.

THE EFFECT OF GUY CALLENDAR: CALCULATING CARBON

In 1938 an amateur meteorologist stood up to deliver a paper to the Royal Meteorological Society in London. Guy Stewart Callendar was not a professional scientist, but rather a steam engineer. The paper he was about to present would restate Arrhenius's argument with new documentation. Callendar began by admitting that the CO_2 theory had had a "chequered history." But not for him. He was obsessed with carbon dioxide and its impact on climate; he spent all his spare time collecting and analyzing data on weather patterns and carbon emissions. Amateur though he was, he had more systematically and fully collected the data than anyone else. His work bore out Arrhenius. The results seemed to show that CO_2 was indeed increasing in the atmosphere and that would lead to a change in the climate—more specifically, global warming.[13]

While Callendar found this obsessively interesting, he, like Arrhenius, was hardly worried. He too thought this would make for a better, more pleasant world—"beneficial to mankind"—providing, among other things, a boon for agriculture. And there was a great bonus. "The return of the deadly glaciers should be delayed indefinitely."[14]

But Callendar was an amateur, and the professionals in attendance that night at the Royal Meteorological Society did not take him very seriously. After all, he was a steam engineer.

Yet what Callendar described—the role of CO_2 in climate change—eventually became known as the Callendar Effect. "His claims rescued the idea of global warming from obscurity and thrust it into the marketplace of ideas," wrote one historian. But it was only a temporary recovery. For over a number of years thereafter the idea was roundly dismissed. In 1951 a prominent climatologist observed that the CO_2 theory of climate change "was never widely accepted and was abandoned." No one seemed to take it very seriously.[15]

22

THE AGE OF DISCOVERY

Quite late in his life, Roger Revelle ruminated on his career in science. "I'm not a very good scientist," he said. But then he added, "I've got a lot of imagination." One of the things that had captured his imagination, and held it for many decades, was carbon dioxide. And that preoccupation would turn out to be profoundly important not only for the understanding of climate, but also for the future of energy.

Revelle was, however, more than a little self-deprecating. For he had made the remark in conjunction with being awarded the National Science Medal, the country's highest scientific honor, by President George H. W. Bush in 1990 in recognition of his far-reaching impact on science.

In addition to being a scientist, Revelle, a man of imposing stature and dominating personality, was also a naturalist, an explorer of the seas, an institution builder, and one of the inventors of the connection between basic research and government policy. He came equipped to his subjects with considerable curiosity abetted by what academic opponents derided as "impetuous enthusiasm and crusading spirit."[1]

In presenting the award to Revelle, President George H. W. Bush singled out his "work in carbon dioxide and climate modification" as the first of his accomplishments, ahead of his other achievements in "oceanographic exploration presaging plate tectonics, the biological effects of radiation in the marine environment, and studies of human population growth and food supply."

Revelle had launched his career with research expeditions into the unexplored deep waters of the Pacific. But, as it turned out, what he had set in motion in terms of research into carbon's role in the atmosphere and man's impact on that balance would also be of great—indeed, monumental—importance. And that grand scientific expedition, unfolding over decades, enlisting ever-greater computing power, traversing oceans and glaciers, mountaintops, the depths of the seas, and even outer space, is what put climate change and the heretofore unknown subject of global warming firmly on the political map.

Or, as Revelle put it, explaining the reasons he had received the National Science Medal, "I got it for being the grandfather of the greenhouse effect."[2]

Revelle started off to be a geologist, but a fear of heights made him shy away from climbing up the sides of mountains, and he turned instead to the study of the depths of the oceans. He was one of the people who transformed oceanography from a game for wealthy amateurs into a major science. During World War II he was the U.S. Navy's chief oceanographer. After the war he was one of the leaders in creating the Office of Naval Research, which supported much of the basic postwar scientific research in American universities—funding almost anything "that could, by the most extreme stretch of the imagination, serve national defense interests." The Office of Naval Research, with Revelle's prodding, was also the progenitor for what became the National Science Foundation. Revelle transformed Scripps Institution of Oceanography in La Jolla, California, north of San Diego, from a small research outpost, with one boat, into a formidable research institution, armed with a flotilla of ships that continually pushed out the frontiers of oceanic knowledge. He also made it into a "top carbon-cycle research center in the U.S."[3]

Revelle organized and led historic expeditions after World War II that sailed for months and months into the then-unknown waters of the Mid- and South Pacific, exploring some of the deepest waters in the world. He recalled those expeditions as "one of the greatest periods of exploration of the earth . . . Every time you went to sea, you made unexpected discoveries. It was revolutionary. Nothing that we expected was true. Everything we didn't expect was true." At the time, most geological textbooks said that the deep-sea floor was a "flat and featureless plain." Instead Revelle and his fellow explorers found deep trenches in the sea floor and identified the huge, heretofore unknown deep-sea Mid-Pacific Mountain Range. These discoveries were critical to the now-dominant plate tectonics theory of the movement of the continents and the earth's surface. Revelle was the driving force in the establishment of the University of California at San Diego. At the same time, he helped build the cultural life of San Diego. For, he asked, how could first-rate academics be attracted to a city whose "best-known cultural attraction" was a zoo? He went on to help shape the field of population studies and worked on economic development in the third world.

Amid all of this he also launched the modern study of climate change.

What first caught Revelle's interest in CO_2 was something that he had learned as an undergraduate at Pomona College—that the oceans contained 60 times more CO_2 than the atmosphere. His 1936 Ph.D. argued that the ocean absorbed most of the CO_2 that came from people burning fuel. Accordingly, human activity that released carbon would have very little, if any effect at all, on climate because the ocean, as a giant sink, would capture most of it. That was the dominant view over the next several decades.[4]

"A LARGE-SCALE GEOPHYSICAL EXPERIMENT"

Over the years, Revelle had given some intermittent thought to the Callendar Effect—the argument made by Guy Callendar that increasing CO_2 concentrations would raise the earth's temperatures. His response, based upon his own research going back to his Ph.D., was that Callendar was probably wrong, that Callendar didn't understand that the ocean would absorb CO_2 from the atmosphere. But by the mid-1950s Revelle was beginning to change his mind. The reason emerged from his research on nuclear weapons tests in the Pacific.

After World War II, the Navy enlisted Revelle to help understand the oceanographic effects of those tests. Revelle's assignment was to devise techniques to measure the waves and water pressure from the explosions. This would enable him to track radioactive diffusion through ocean currents. In the course of this work, Revelle's team discovered "sharp, sudden" variations in water temperatures at different depths. This was the startling insight—the ocean worked differently from what they had thought. In Revelle's words, the ocean was "a deck of cards." Revelle concluded that "the ocean is stratified with a lid of warm water on the cold, and the mixing between them is limited." That constrained the ability of the ocean to accept CO_2.[5] It was this period, in the mid-1950s, that Revelle, collaborating with a colleague, Hans Suess, wrote an article that captured this insight and would turn out to be a landmark in climate thinking.

The title made clear what the article was all about: "Carbon Dioxide Exchange Between Atmosphere and Ocean and the Question of an Increase in Atmospheric CO_2 During the Past Decades." Their paper invoked both Arrhenius and Callendar. Yet the article itself reflected ambiguity. Part of it suggested that the oceans would absorb most of the carbon, just as Revelle's Ph.D. had argued, meaning that there would be no global warming triggered by carbon. Yet another paragraph suggested the opposite; that, while the ocean would absorb CO_2, much of that was only on a temporary basis, owing to the chemistry of sea water, and the lack of interchange between warmer and cooler levels, and that the CO_2 would seep back into the atmosphere. In other words, on a net basis, the ocean absorbed much less CO_2 than expected. If not in the ocean, there was only one place for the carbon to go, and that was back into the atmosphere. That meant that atmospheric concentration of CO_2 was destined, inevitably, to rise. The latter assertion was a late addition by Revelle, literally typed on a different kind of paper and then taped onto the original manuscript.

Before sending off the article, Revelle appended a further last-minute thought: The buildup of CO_2 "may become significant during future decades if industrial fuel combustion continues to rise exponentially," he wrote. "Human beings are now carrying out a large scale geophysical experiment of a kind that could not have happened in the past nor be reproduced in the future." This last sentence would reverberate down through the years in ways that Revelle could not have imagined. Indeed, it would go on to achieve prophetic status—"quoted more than any other statement in the history of global warming."[6]

Yet it was less a warning and more like a reflection. For Revelle was not worried. Like Svante Arrhenius who had tried 60 years earlier to quantify the effect of CO_2 on the atmosphere, Revelle did not foresee that increased concentrations would be dangerous. Rather, it was a very interesting scientific question.

"Roger wasn't alarmed at all," recalled one of his colleagues. "He liked great geophysical experiments. He thought that this would be a grand experiment . . . to study the effect on the ocean of the increase of carbon dioxide in the atmosphere and the mixing between the ocean reservoirs." (Even a decade later, in 1966, Revelle was arguing that "our attitude" toward rising carbon dioxide in the atmosphere "brought about by our own actions should probably contain more curiosity than apprehension.")[7]

At the time, Revelle was deeply involved in planning for an unprecedented global study of how the earth worked that might answer some of the climate questions. This was the IGY—the International Geophysical Year.[8]

THE UNEXPECTED IMPACT OF THE INTERNATIONAL GEOPHYSICAL YEAR

The International Geophysical Year (IGY) was born out of the idea of using the new technological capabilities stimulated in World War II and after—ranging from rockets and radar to the first computers—to explore heretofore inaccessible places where "metal loses its strength, rubber breaks, and diesel fluid becomes viscous like honey," and thus generate much greater, deeper insight into how the earth worked and its interaction with the sun. It bloomed into a cross-disciplinary network of several thousand scientists from more than 70 countries. The earth's processes—from its core and the seabed floor to the outer reaches of the atmosphere—would be mapped and measured in thousands of experiments coordinated on a global basis and conducted in a much more sophisticated and consistent way than ever before. Some of these experiments would involve Herculean physical feats of technology and endurance.[9]

The IGY was a sort of extended leap year, for it actually ran from July 1957 through December 1958, a period chosen to coincide with a fever point of solar activity. This global exploration brought forth an extraordinary body of new knowledge on everything from the flows of the deep waters of the oceans and the nature of the sea floor to the intense high-altitude radiation that girdles the earth. Glaciers constituted one of the major topics, continuing the fascination they held for scientists going back to Saussure and Tyndall.

"OKAY, LET'S GO": THE STRATEGIC IMPORTANCE OF WEATHER

Then there was the weather. The IGY brought an unprecedented concentration of scientific talent to bear on better understanding weather. In addition to scientific curiosity there were also important strategic considerations. The Second World War had scarcely ended a decade earlier, and time again during that conflict, weather had proved of decisive importance on the battlefield. In western Russia, winter's icy grip—what Russians called General Winter—decimated the Nazi armies as they besieged Leningrad and assaulted Stalingrad.

But nothing had so forcefully underlined the strategic importance of better comprehension of the weather than D-Day, the invasion of Normandy in June 1944. The "Longest Day," as it was called, had been preceded by the "longest hours"—hours and hours of soul-wrenching stress, uncertainty, and fear in the headquarters along the southern coast of England, as indecisive hourly briefings followed indecisive hourly briefings, with the "go/no go" decision held hostage to a single factor: the weather.

"The weather in this country is practically unpredictable," the commander in chief Dwight Eisenhower had complained while anxiously waiting for the next briefing. The forecasts were for very bad weather. How could 175,000 men be put at risk in such dreadful circumstances? At best, the reliability of the weather forecasts went out no more than two days; the stormy weather over the English Channel reduced the reliability to 12 hours. So uncertain was the weather that at the last moment the invasion scheduled for June 5 was postponed, and ships that had already set sail were called back just in time before the Germans could detect them.

Finally, on the morning of June 5, the chief meteorologist said, "I'll give you some good news." The forecasts indicated that a brief break of sorts in the weather was at hand. Eisenhower sat silently for 30 or 40 seconds, in his mind balancing success against failure and the risk of making a bad decision. Finally, he stood up and gave the order, "Okay, let's go." With that was launched into the barely marginal weather of June 6, 1944, the greatest armada in the history of the world. Fortunately, the German weather forecasters did not see the break and assured the German commander, Erwin Rommel, that he did not have to worry about an invasion.[10]

A decade later, knowing better than anyone else the strategic importance of improved weather knowledge, Eisenhower, now president, gave the "let's go" order for the International Geophysical Year.

The IGY was designed to deepen knowledge not only about weather but also climate. As Roger Revelle wrote, among the "main objectives of the International Geophysical Year" was to gain a deeper understanding of climate change—what had triggered the coming and retreat of the Ice Age, that "dark age of snow and ice"—and the ability to predict future climate change.

Researchers did indeed discover and confirm some of the planet's most important regulatory cycles that affected climate, including the impact of ocean and air currents in transmitting heat. But other elements also shaped the climactic system, including, some suspected, greenhouse gases. One of the organizers speculated that the earth might be "approaching a man-made warm period, simply because we are belching carbon dioxide into the air from our factories at a present rate of several billion tons a year!"[11]

THE MEETING AT WOODS HOLE

Roger Revelle, who headed the oceanography panel for the IGY, wanted to make sure the impact of carbon dioxide was, in his words, "adequately documented in the course of the IGY." With that in mind, Revelle sat down with three other scientists at the Woods Hole Oceanographic Institution, in Massachusetts, to plot out a global research agenda for part of the IGY. Gustaf Arrhenius, the grandson of the Swedish Nobel Prize winner Svante Arrhenius, remembered this discussion at Woods Hole as "an historic event when we got together." They decided that one of the objectives of the International Geophysical Year should be to actually measure what Arrhenius's grandfather had tried to calculate more than half a century earlier—the impact of CO_2 on the atmosphere.[12]

But was it possible to get decent readings of CO_2? Someone at that Woods Hole meeting had heard about "a promising young man," a researcher at the

California Institute of Technology who was working on measuring CO_2. Perhaps they could get him to Scripps.

KEELING AND HIS CURVE

The one thing that Charles David Keeling did not want to study was economics. His father was an economist, he had grown up in a household in which economics was a constant topic, and he would go to great lengths to avoid studying economics. At the University of Illinois he dropped his chemistry major because it had an economics requirement and ended up majoring in liberal arts. Still, he managed to get himself into the Ph.D. program in chemistry at Northwestern. While laboring away on his chemistry he came across a book, *Glacial Geology and the Pleistocene Epoch,* that had a major impact on him. "I imagined climbing mountains while measuring the physical properties of glaciers," he recalled. As with John Tyndall, glaciers captivated him, and he spent a summer hiking and climbing in the "glacier-decked" Cascade Mountains of Washington State. He ended up supplementing his chemistry work with geology.[13]

For his postdoctoral work, Keeling wanted to find a way to combine his love of chemistry and geology. A new geochemistry program at the California Institute of Technology provided the answer. He would focus on carbon. Using a device he designed, Keeling stationed himself atop one of the Caltech buildings and got busy measuring CO_2 in the air. But local pollution made the readings highly erratic. Seeking purer air, Keeling decamped for the wild sea-swept beauty of Big Sur, along the Northern California coast. He loved being in the outdoors, he said, even if, in order to take measurements, "I had to get out of a sleeping bag several times a night."[14]

But Big Sur did not work either; CO_2 levels in forests fluctuated through daily cycles. For a true reading on carbon dioxide levels, he needed to measure the levels with a stable "atmospheric background." For that he needed funding.

It was just about that time that Revelle reached out to Keeling and offered him a place at Scripps, along with research money. Revelle recognized that there was a certain risk but thought Keeling's obsessiveness was a clear plus. "He wants, in his belly, to measure carbon dioxide, to measure it every possible way, and to understand everything there is to know about carbon dioxide," Revelle was later to say. "But that's all he's interested in. He's never been interested in anything else."

Keeling got to work, devoting all his scientific energies, as he put it, to "the pursuit of the carbon dioxide molecule in all its ramifications." At that time it was all in the name of science. "There was no sense of peril then," recalled Keeling. "Just a keen interest in gaining knowledge."[15]

The Weather Bureau provided Keeling with the "where"—its new meteorological observatory in Hawaii, 11,135 feet up, near the top of the volcanic peak Mauna Loa. Here was the pure air, untroubled either by urban pollution or the daily cycles of forest vegetation, that would provide the stable atmospheric background Keeling needed. Another of his measuring devices was dispatched to the Little America station in Antarctica.

The cumulative results from the station atop Mauna Lao would prove something startling. In 1938 Guy Callendar may have been pooh-poohed by the professional meteorologists when he delivered his paper in London. But Keeling would prove him right. There really was a Callendar Effect. For, over the years, Keeling's pioneering research established a clear trend: Atmospheric CO_2 levels were increasing. In 1959 the average concentration was 316 parts per million. By 1970 it had risen to 325 parts per million, and by 1990 it would reach 354 parts. Fitted on a graph, this rising line became known as the Keeling Curve. Based upon the trend that Keeling had identified, the carbon dioxide in the atmosphere would double around the middle of the twenty-first century. But what could increasing carbon mean for climate?

The International Geophysical Year provided a kind of an answer, if at least by analogy. Until then the planet Venus had been the province of magazines like *Astounding Science Fiction.* But now scientists began to understand from the IGY study of Venus what the greenhouse effect could mean in its most extreme form. With higher concentrations of greenhouse gases in its atmosphere, the surface of Venus was hellishly hot, with temperatures as high as 870°F. Venus would eventually become a metaphor for climate change run amuck.[16]

Year after year, Keeling pursued his measurements, working doggedly with his small team, improving the accuracy, meticulous in details, building up the register of atmospheric carbon. Revelle was to look back on Keeling's work as "one of the most beautiful and important sets of geochemical measurements ever made, a beautiful record." At Scripps, Keeling was known for his obsessional interest in his subject. Once the chemist Gustaf Arrhenius was rushing his pregnant wife, who was going into labor, to the hospital. Keeling flagged the car down on the Scripps campus and launched into an intricate discussion of some challenge of carbon dioxide measurement. Finally, after his wife signaled that she was not going to be able to hang on much longer, Arrhenius interrupted. "I'm sorry," he said. "We're going to have a baby now." He added, "In a few minutes." At that point, Keeling finally realized what was going on and waved them off.[17]

Keeling's work marked a great transition in climate science. Estimating carbon in the atmosphere was no longer a backward-looking matter aimed at explaining the mystery of the ice ages and the advance and retreat of glaciers in past millennia. It was instead becoming a subject about the future. By 1969 Keeling was confident enough to warn of risks from rising carbon. In 30 years, he said, "if present trends are any sign, mankind's world, I judge, will be in greater immediate danger than it is today."

As a result of Charles Keeling's work on atmospheric carbon, the little-known Callendar Effect gave way to the highly influential Keeling Curve. Keeling's work became the foundation for the modern debate over climate change and for the current drive to transform the energy system. Indeed, Keeling's Curve became "the central icon of the greenhouse effect"—its likeness engraved into the wall of the National Academy of Sciences in Washington, D.C.[18]

"GLOBAL COOLING": THE NEXT ICE AGE?

During these years concern was rising about climate change, but for a variety of reasons. Some in the national security community worried about climate change as a strategic threat: they feared the Soviet Union would alter the climate, either intentionally for military advantage or accidentally, as a result of diverting rivers or such "hare-brained" ideas as the proposal to dam the Bering Straits.[19]

The implications of Keeling's work on carbon were beginning to seep into the policy community. A 1965 report on "environmental pollution" from

442

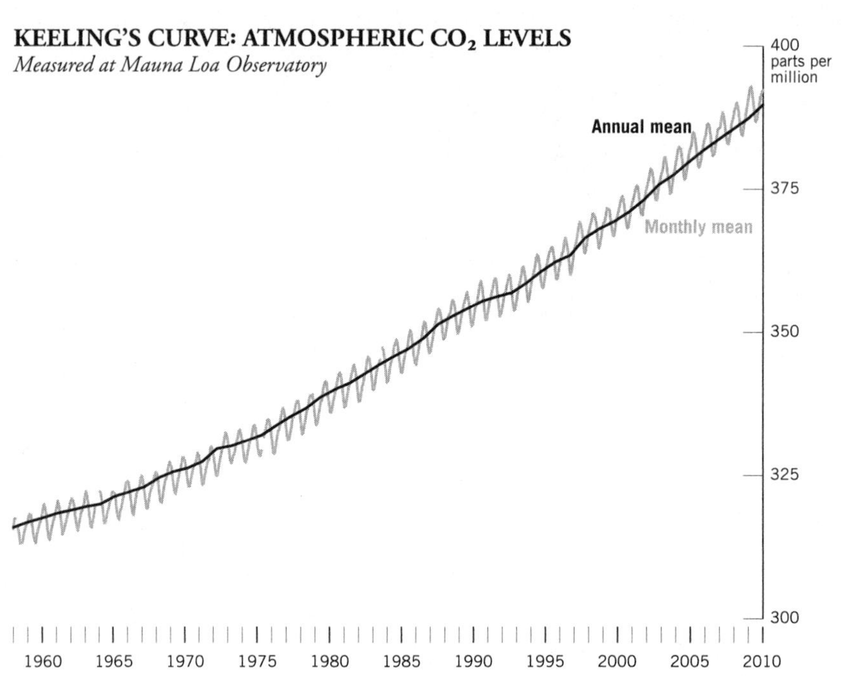

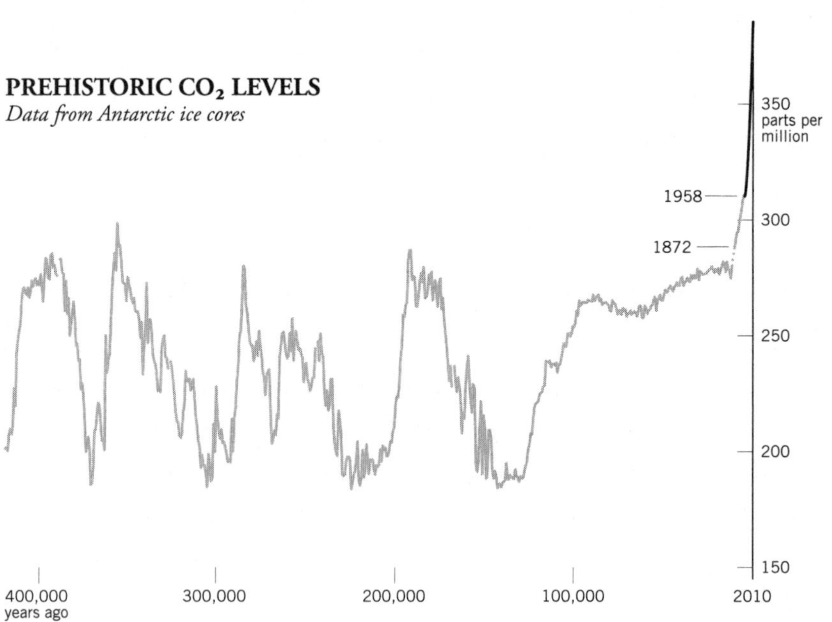

Source: NOAA Earth System Research Laboratory, Carbon Dioxide Information Analysis Center

President Lyndon Johnson's Science Advisory Committee included a 22-page appendix written by, among others, Revelle and Keeling. It reiterated the argument that "by burning fossil fuels humanity is unwittingly conducting a vast geophysical experiment" that almost certainly would change temperatures.

In 1969, picking up on this and other research, Nixon White House adviser (and later senator) Daniel Patrick Moynihan wrote a memo arguing that the new Nixon administration "really ought to get involved" with climate change as an issue. "This very clearly *is* a problem" and "one that can seize the imagination of persons normally indifferent to projects of apocalyptic change." The research, he said, indicated that increasing CO_2 in the atmosphere could raise the average temperature by seven degrees by 2000 and sea levels by ten feet. "Good-bye New York," he said. "Good-bye Washington, for that matter." He had one piece of good news, however: "We have no data on Seattle."

Yet these early statements notwithstanding, at least as much of the discussion was about global cooling as about global warming. As the deputy director of the Office of Science and Technology wrote back to Moynihan, "The more I get into this, the more I find two classes of doom-sayers, with, of course, the silent majority in between. One group says we will turn into snow-tripping mastodons . . . and the other says we will have to grow gills to survive the increased ocean level due to the temperature rise from CO_2."[20]

Fears were growing that the glaciers would return, the same fears that had animated Louis Agassiz and other scientists a century earlier. Already, at the end of the 1950s, Betty Friedan—later famous for writing *The Feminine Mystique*—popularized these theories in an article on "The Coming Ice Age." "If man finds no way to switch the glacial thermostat and avoid a new ice age," she said, "there may well be a real estate boom in the Sahara." By the early 1970s the CIA was investigating the geopolitical impact of global cooling, including the "megadeaths and social upheaval" that would ensue. In 1972 *Science* magazine reported that earth scientists meeting at Brown University had concluded that "the present cooling is especially demonstrable" and that "global cooling and related rapid changes of environment, substantially exceeding the fluctuations experienced by man in historical times must be expected." Around the same time, a number of scientists who had participated in a Defense Department climate analysis wrote to President Nixon that the government needed to study the risk that a new glacial period was coming. Others warned that the increasing concentrations of aerosols in the atmosphere could be "sufficient to trigger an ice age." The U.S. National Science Board reported a few years later that the last two or three decades had recorded a cooling trend. It was not a one-sided argument by any means, as is clear from the pages of *Science*. In 1975 one scientist blasted the "complacency" of those who focused on the falling temperatures "over the past several decades," which was leading them to "discount the warming effect of the CO_2 produced by the burning of chemical fuels."[21]

The increasing interest in climate change meant that money was beginning to flow into climate study. The reason was clear. "The propelling concern for climate research," as two students of the era have observed, "was the possibility of climate *cooling,* rather than climate warming."[22]

The same concerns were reflected in public discussion. "The central fact is that after three quarters of a century of extraordinarily mild conditions, the earth's climate seems to be cooling down," wrote *Newsweek* in 1975. While meteorologists argued about the "causes" and "extent," they were "almost unanimous" in seeing a cooling trend that could lead to another "little ice age," as between 1600 and 1900, or even another "great Ice Age." In 1976 *National Geographic* gave equal weighting to the question as to whether the earth was "cooling off" or warming "irreversibly." The same year *Time* magazine was reporting, "Climatologists still disagree on whether earth's long-range outlook is another Ice Age, which could bring mass starvation and fuel shortages, or a warming trend, which could melt the polar icecaps and flood coastal cities."[23]

By the early 1980s, discussion about global cooling had taken a new form—the harsh "nuclear winter," the extreme cooling that could be set off by a nuclear war between the United States and the Soviet Union. This would be the result of the vast smoke and dust clouds triggered by the atomic explosions, which would cut off sunlight and darken the earth, lead to "subfreezing temperatures" even in summer, and "pose a serious threat to human survivors." The best-known proponent of the threat of nuclear winter was Carl Sagan, who as a young man had achieved fame among astronomers for identifying the extreme greenhouse atmosphere of Venus, and then went on to achieve much greater fame as host of the PBS television series *Cosmos* (and his much imitated refrain about "billions and billions of stars").[24]

Notwithstanding the fear of nuclear winter, by the end of the 1970s and the early 1980s, a notable shift in the climate of climate change research was clear—from cooling to warming. Keeling's Curve was beginning to flow into a larger realm of scientific research, ranging from direct observations in the air, on land, and on sea, to what would prove most crucial indeed: advances in modeling climate in computer simulations.

MODELING THE CLIMATE

Specifically, two technological advances were broadening the scientific base for understanding climate. One was satellites. The first U.S. weather satellite was launched in 1960, opening the doors not only to a much more holistic view of the earth but also to a much greater and continually growing flow of data. Initially this fueled work on a subject that gained some attention and government funding—"advertant" (that is, intentional) weather modification, aimed at such things as moderating storms and increasing rain in dry parts of the world. Already in 1961 President John F. Kennedy, addressing the United Nations, was calling for "cooperative efforts between all nations in weather prediction and eventually in weather control." The topic of weather modification passed from the scene, but the contribution of satellites to vastly improved understanding of weather continued to grow.

The second advance was the invention of, and extraordinary development in, computing power, which in turn made possible the new discipline of climate modeling. The advent of the computer, in historical terms, owes much to a chance meeting on a railroad platform near the army's Aberdeen Proving Ground in Maryland during World War II. A young mathematician caught sight of a world-famous figure—at least world famous in the worlds of science and mathematics. His name was John von Neumann. "With considerable temerity" the mathematician, Herman Goldfine, started a conversation. To Goldfine's surprise, von Neumann, despite his towering reputation, was quite friendly. But when Goldfine told von Neumann that he was helping develop "an electronic computer capable of 333 multiplications per second," the conversation abruptly changed "from one of relaxed good humor to one more like the oral examination for the doctor's degree in mathematics."[25]

John von Neumann—born János Neumann in Budapest—had emigrated to the United States in 1930 to become, along with Albert Einstein, one of the first faculty members at Princeton's Institute for Advanced Study. Von Neumann would prove to be one of the most extraordinary and creative figures of the twentieth century, not only one of the century's greatest mathematicians but also an outstanding physicist and, almost as a sideline, one of the most influential figures in modern economics (he invented game theory and is said to have "changed the very way economic analysis is done"). Not only that, he is often described as the "father of the computer" as well as the inventor of nuclear deterrence. (In 1956, near the end of his life, gathered around his bed in Walter Reed Hospital were the secretary of defense and his deputies, the secretaries of the army, navy, and air force, and all the joint chiefs of staff, all there for his "last words of advice and wisdom.") He also fathered the modern mathematical analysis of climate modeling that became the basic tool for diagnosing global warming. He accomplished all this before he died in 1957, at the age of fifty-three.[26]

Von Neumann had an extraordinary ability to do complex calculations in his head at lightning speed. Once, as a six-year-old, he saw his mother staring off into space, daydreaming, and he asked her, "What are you calculating?" As an adult he let his subconscious work on mathematical problems in his sleep and woke up at 3:00 a.m. with the answer. At the same time, he had the ability to look at things in a wholly new manner. The mathematician Stanislaw Ulam emphasized how much analogies figured in von Neumann's thought processes. One of his closest friends, Ulam would exchange both mathematical insights and intricate Yiddish jokes with him. Ulam would tease von Neumann for being too practical, for trying to apply mathematics to all sorts of problems. Once he told von Neumann, "When it comes to the application of mathematics to dentistry, maybe you'll stop."

The economist Paul Samuelson said von Neumann had "the fastest mind" he had ever encountered. The head of Britain's National Physical Laboratory called him "the cleverest man in the world." A peer summed up what many who worked with him thought: "Unquestionably the nearest thing to a genius I have ever encountered."[27]

That chance meeting on the Aberdeen railroad platform in August 1944 would propel von Neumann to become the "father of computing." Until then, computers were not machines but a job classification: "computers" were people who did the tiresome but essential calculations needed for surveying or for calculating the tides or the movements of heavenly bodies. But von Neumann had been questing after something like a mechanical computer in order to handle the immense computational challenge he and his colleagues had faced while working on the atomic bomb during World War II. At the secret Los Alamos, as they struggled to figure out how to transform the theoretical concept of a chain reaction into a fearsome weapon, they had "invented modern mathematical modeling." But they needed the machines to make it practical.[28]

Immediately after the encounter on that station platform, von Neumann used his authority as a top-flight scientific adviser to the war effort to jump into this nascent and obscure computer project and promote its development. By June 1945 he had written a 101-page paper that became "the technological basis for the worldwide computer industry." He started designing and building a new prototype computer in Princeton at the Institute for Advanced Study.

But to what to apply this new tool? Van Neumann identified "the first great scientific subject" for which he wanted to use this newly discovered computer power: "the phenomena of turbulence," or, put more simply, forecasting the weather. He recognized the similarities between simulating atomic explosions and making weather predictions; both were nonlinear problems in fluid dynamics that needed vast amount of computation at breakneck speed.[29]

The complexity of the weather cried out for the rigorous mathematical analysis that von Neumann loved and that only the computer made possible. The strategic significance made it urgent. The intellectual challenge appealed to him. He feared that the Soviets might add weather modification to their arsenal and wage "climatological warfare" against the United States. He himself gave some favorable thought to using better knowledge of the weather to "jiggle the earth," as he put it—that is, modify the weather and create a warmer semitropical climate around the world. Frankly, he thought, people would like that.

In seeking support for funding for the navy computing and climate studies, he argued that high-speed computing "would make weather predictions a week or more ahead practical." He thereafter supervised the building of MANIAC—for Mathematical Analyzer, Numerical Integrator and Computer. The *New York Times* would call it a "giant electronic brain."[30]

By 1948 the Numerical Meteorology Project was up and running. A new recruit, Jule Charney, a mathematician and meteorologist, took the lead in figuring out the mathematical formulas to conjoin climate modeling with the advances in computing. What they were trying to do was express the physical laws governing the dynamics of heat and moisture in the atmosphere in a series of mathematical algorithms that could be solved by a computer as they unfolded over time. By the early 1950s Charney and the group were producing its first computer simulations of climate. By the 1960s the Princeton initiative had morphed into the GFDL—Geophysical Fluid Dynamics Laboratory, now part of the National Oceanic and Atmospheric Administration—which became one of the leaders in developing climate-change models.[31]

Von Neumann's quest to understand stratospheric circulation and atmospheric turbulence was giving rise to increasingly sophisticated simulations of how the global atmosphere worked—the patterns and flows by which the air moved around the world. These became known as general circulation models. They had to be global because the earth had only one atmosphere. The modelers were constantly striving to make their models more and more realistic, which meant more and more complex, in order to better understand how the world worked.

Climate modeling was very difficult, taxing, and definitely pioneering. "The computer was so feeble at the time," recalled Syukuro Manabe, recruited to the GFDL from the meteorology faculty at Tokyo University and one of the most formidable of all the climate modelers. "If we put everything into the model at once, the computer couldn't handle it. I was there and was watching the model blow up all the time."

But already in 1967 Syukuro Manabe and Richard Wetherald, members of the Princeton lab, were hypothesizing, in what became a famous paper, that a doubling of CO_2 would increase global temperatures by three to four degrees. They backed into the subject by accident. "I wanted to see how sensitive the model is to cloudiness, water vapor, ozone, and to CO_2," said Manabe. "So I was changing greenhouse gases, clouds . . . playing and enjoying myself. I realized that CO_2 is important, as it turned out, I changed the right variable and hit the jackpot," he continued. "At that time, no one cared about global warming . . . Some people thought maybe an ice age is coming."

Notwithstanding his conviction that "probably this is the best paper I wrote in my whole career," Manabe led further breakthroughs on modeling in the mid-1970s. Over the years data from satellites provided a benchmark against which to test the accuracy of the ever-more-complex models. And yet that 1967 hypothesis—that a doubling of CO_2 would bring a three-to-four-degree increase in the average global temperature—would become a constant in the debate over global warming. And a fuse.[32]

"BOY, IF THIS IS TRUE": THE RISE OF CLIMATE ACTIVISM

The widening body of global-warming research started to connect with what would turn out to be the first generation of climate activists. For them, the focus was not scientific experiment but political action.

In 1973, on the Old Campus at Yale University, botanist George Woodwell delivered a global warming lecture. One of the people in the audience was an undergraduate named Fred Krupp. "Boy, if this is true," Krupp remembers saying to himself, "we're in a lot of trouble." Krupp would become the president of the Environmental Defense Fund eleven years later, at age 30, and from there one of the foremost policy proponents for reducing carbon emissions.[33]

A few years later, in 1978, in Washington, D.C., Rafe Pomerance, president of the environmental group Friends of the Earth, was reading an environmental study when one sentence caught his eye: increasing coal use could warm the earth. "This can't be true," Pomerance thought. He started researching the subject, and he soon caught up with a scientist named Gordon MacDonald, who had been a member of Richard Nixon's Council on Environmental Quality. After a two-hour discussion with MacDonald, Pomerance said, "If I set up briefings around town, will you do them?" MacDonald agreed, and they started making the rounds in Washington, D.C.

The president of the National Academy of Sciences, impressed by the briefing, set up a special task force under Jule Charney. Charney had moved from Princeton to MIT where, arguably, he had become America's most prominent meteorologist. Issuing its report in 1979, the Charney Committee declared that the risk was very real. A few other influential studies came to similar conclusions, including one by the JASON committee, a panel of leading physicists and other scientists that advised the Department of Defense and other government agencies. It concluded that there was "incontrovertible evidence that the atmosphere is indeed changing and that we ourselves contribute to that change." The scientists added that the ocean, "the great and ponderous flywheel of the global climate system," was likely to slow observable climate change. The "JASONs," as they were sometimes called, said that "a wait-and-see policy may mean waiting until it is too late."[34]

The campaign "around town" led to highly attended Senate hearings in April 1980. The star of the hearing was Keeling's Curve. After looking at a map presented by one witness that showed the East Coast of the United States inundated by rising sea waters, the committee chair, Senator Paul Tsongas from Massachusetts, commented with rising irony: "It means good-bye Miami, Corpus Christi . . . good-bye Boston, good-bye New Orleans, good-bye Charleston. . . . On the bright side, it means we can enjoy boating at the foot of the Capitol and fishing on the South Lawn."[35]

One of the recipients of the MacDonald-Pomerance briefings was Gus Speth, chairman of the U.S. Council on Environmental Quality. Speth asked for a report short enough for policymakers. The authors were those at the forefront of global-warming study—Charles Keeling, Roger Revelle, George Woodwell, and Gordon MacDonald. They warned of "significant warming of world climates over the next decades unless mitigating steps are taken immediately." In contrast to Arrhenius and Callendar, who had seen virtue in a warm climate, they were emphatic: "There appear to be very few clear advantages for man in such short-term alterations in climate." They offered a four-point program: acknowledgment of the problem, energy conservation, reforestation—and lower carbon fuels. That last meant using natural gas instead of coal.[36]

Speth took the report to the White House and the Department of Energy. The reception was frosty. For at that moment the Carter administration—reeling from second oil shock, the Iranian Revolution, and natural gas shortages—was restricting natural gas use and promoting more coal.

Speth did not give up. He made the issue central to the 1981 annual report from the Council on Environmental Quality. But that was the end of the road, at least for the time being. For Jimmy Carter had already been defeated by Ronald Reagan in November 1980.[37] But some environmental groups were beginning to take up climate as a core issue.

Under the Reagan administration, government money for climate research was reduced. No one knew this better than Charles Keeling. Though his funding was often precarious, the integrity of the carbon-monitoring project at

Mauna Loa in Hawaii was preserved. Overall, though constrained, scientific research on climate did continue.

A key breakthrough in the science of climate change occurred in the 1980s with the recovery of ice cores, extracted from deep under the earth's surface both in Greenland and at Vostok, the Russian research station in Antarctica that was so remote it could be resupplied only once a year. These ice cores were truly time machines. They provided crucial evidence to the theory of climate change. For the tiny air bubbles trapped in these cores preserved the atmosphere as it had been thousands of years ago, and could be dated through radiocarbon analysis. Painstaking study seemed to make one thing very clear: that carbon concentrations had been lower in the preindustrial age—275 to 280 parts per million compared with 325 parts in 1970 and 354 parts in 1990.[38]

REVELLE'S EXILE

When the new campus of the University of California was established in San Diego, Roger Revelle, the head of the Scripps Institution of Oceanography and the mentor of Charles Keeling, seemed the inevitable choice to be its first chancellor. He had been the new campus's leading champion, and his heart was set on the chancellorship. But Revelle had powerful enemies, one of whom, a powerful regent of the university, blocked his appointment. It was probably the biggest disappointment of Revelle's professional career. He did not want to stay around and instead decided to go into what one of his friends called "exile."

This particular exile was hardly unpleasant, for he took up a professorship at Harvard, teaching a popular course—Natural Sciences 118: Human Populations and Natural Resources, otherwise known as Pops and Rocks.[39]

"By bringing fossil fuels to the surface and burning them, human beings are simply returning the carbon and oxygen to their original state," he told students in the autumn of 1968. "Within a few short generations we are consuming materials that were formed and concentrated over geologic eras. There was probably never more CO_2 in the air at any time in the past billion years than today." Burning of fossil over the next few generations, he said, would add vast amounts of additional CO_2 to the atmosphere. The results would likely be increases in temperature and "significant effect on the earth's climate."

Yet Revelle, thinking about the overall system, also spoke about he called the "complicating factors"—the possible offsets. Higher temperatures, for instance, would increase evaporation of water, and thus increase cloudiness "which in turn will reduce the amount of incoming solar energy, and tend to lower the temperature."

His conclusion was similar to that of his 1957 paper: "We can think of the increase of atmospheric carbon dioxide as a gigantic, unintentional experiment being conducted by human beings all over the world, that may give us greater insight into the processes determining climate."[40]

Revelle was a compelling teacher who presented a distinctly global view of environmental issues. Among those in Pops and Rocks was a student named Albert Gore Jr., the son of Senator Albert Gore of Tennessee. If Revelle's impact on Keeling and research into carbon concentrations was to have decisive impact on the science of climate, then his lectures to the class, which included Al Gore, would also have a profound impact on the politics of climate. "A great teacher of mine at Harvard, Dr. Roger Revelle, opened my eyes to the problem of global warming," Gore wrote much later. "The implications of his words were startling . . . Like all great teachers, he influenced the rest of my life."

That was in the late 1960s. Two decades later, in the late 1980s, Gore and others in Congress were determined to make climate change into a political issue. As he and seven other senators put it in a letter in 1986, research on the impact of CO_2 on climate change had left them "deeply disturbed." They wanted not only more research. They wanted to see some true action.[41]

23

THE ROAD TO RIO

That particular day—June 23, 1988—was very much a Washington summer day, for it was not only hot, very hot—with the temperature getting up over 100 degrees—but also muggy, almost unbearably so. Moreover, it followed months of high temperatures, and half the counties in the United States were officially suffering from drought. "For the Midwest," it was reported, "drought has become a way of life." All this meant that the media would be intensely interested in anything to do with weather. In short, June 23 was a perfect day for a Senate hearing on global warming.

The hearings that ensued would mark the emergence of climate change as a political issue. The chairman that day was Senator Tim Wirth of Colorado. Half a year earlier, in January 1988, Wirth had ruminated with his aides about finding a very warm day for a climate-change hearing. What would likely be the hottest day of the year, he had asked. One of them had calculated that late June was a good bet. (To double-check, the aide had called an economist at Harvard, who, somewhat startled, said that he had no expertise on that subject, but, thinking quickly, helpfully recommended that the aide consult the *Farmer's Almanac*.)[1]

Ever since, there has been a legend that the windows were left open the night before and the air-conditioning was turned off, to make certain that the hearing room would be sweltering. Wirth himself did later refer to some artful "stagecraft." As it turned out, the room *was* sweltering, and sweat would glisten on the foreheads of the witnesses. Ensuring that the room would be very hot were the lights that went with two solid banks of television cameras. "Having a hearing is educational," Wirth would say, quoting a political proverb. "Having a hearing with a television camera is useful; having a hearing with two rows of television cameras is heaven." For the ethereal issue of climate change, that day counted as heavenly.[2]

"The scientific evidence is compelling," said Wirth, as he opened the hearings. "Now the Congress must begin to consider how we are going to slow or halt that trend." The lineup of witnesses featured some of the strongest voices on climate change. But the most dramatic message came from the leadoff witness. Climate change was no longer an "academic" issue, said James Hansen, an atmospheric physicist and director of NASA's Goddard Institute for Space Studies in New York City. A leading climate modeler, Hansen had already become prominent as one of the most apocalyptic in his predictions. And now, wiping the sweat from his forehead in the sweltering room made even hotter by the television lights, Hansen told the senators, the long-awaited "signal" on climate change was now here. Temperatures were indeed rising, just as his computer models had predicted. "We can ascribe with a high degree of confidence a cause-and-effect relationship between the greenhouse effect and observed warming," he said. Afterward he summarized his testimony to the *New York Times* more simply: "It is time to stop waffling." The story about his testimony and the hearing ran on the *Times'* front page.[3]

As another witness, Syukuro Manabe, one of the fathers of climate modeling, recalled, "They weren't too impressed by this Japanese guy who had this accent; whereas Jim Hansen made a bombshell impression."

The hearing "became a huge event," said Wirth. "A lot of people had never seen anything like this before. It got an inordinate amount of attention for a Senate hearing." One scientist summed up the impact this way: "I've never seen an environmental issue move so quickly, shifting from science to the policy realm almost overnight."[4]

Wirth's hearings demonstrated an increasing interaction between scientists and policymakers. That was accompanied by rapidly increasing cross-border research and network building on atmospheric subjects among scientists around the world. Roger Revelle, who had been there from the beginning of the modern effort, looked at the change with a certain wry amusement. "During the last ten years the literature on the greenhouse effect has proliferated beyond belief," he noted in 1988. "What started out as a cottage industry with David Keeling as the principal worker has now become a major operation, with a cast of thousands."[5]

The emergence of a global scientific network on climate change had already become clearly evident in 1985, three years before Wirth's hearings, when a group of scientists met at Villach, in the Austrian Alps. Convinced by the range of evidence, from supercomputer models to what had been learned about the lower carbon levels in the ice ages, they thought that climate change was neither far off nor would it be beneficent. They also concluded that "understanding of the greenhouse question is sufficiently developed that scientists and policymakers should begin an active collaboration." Their five-hundred-page report called for an international agreement to control carbon.[6]

THE HOLE IN THE OZONE: THE ROLE MODEL

In 1987 a conference convened in Montreal that was also aimed at an atmospheric threat. Out of it came a new international agreement that would have seemed unachievable only a few years earlier. It provided a powerful precedent for environmental collaboration on a global scale.

Greenhouse gases include not only carbon dioxide but also methane and nitrous oxide, as well as a group of man-made gases called chlorofluorocarbons (CFCs) that were first developed in the late 1920s. Though in much smaller concentrations in the atmosphere, chlorofluorocarbons are potent in trapping heat; indeed, it was estimated, ten thousand times more potent, molecule to molecule, than CO_2. The use of CFCs had multiplied over the years, from propellants in aerosol cans to coolant in refrigerators.

In 1985 researchers from the British Antarctic Survey, using satellite data from NASA, saw something that stunned them: a "hole" was opening up in the ozone over Antarctica. The chlorofluorocarbons were eating at the ozone, literally thinning out and depleting the layer in the atmosphere.

The threat was immediate. Ozone absorbed what would otherwise be deadly concentrations of ultraviolet radiation. The loss of ozone threatened massive epidemics of skin cancer around the world as well as devastating effects on animal and plant life on earth. Such was the fear that in record time—by 1987—some twenty-four countries signed on to the Montreal Protocol, which would restrict chlorofluorocarbons.

The Montreal Protocol had a direct impact on the climate-change movement. It acknowledged that increasing concentrations of greenhouse gases were dangerous. It dramatically underlined the acceptance of the notion that human activity imposes damage on the earth's atmosphere. And it demonstrated that countries could come together quickly and agreed to eliminate a common environmental threat. To climate activists, all of that seemed to be a dress rehearsal for what should happen with global warming. There was one striking difference, however. The relevant universe was so much smaller. Fewer than forty companies manufactured chlorofluorocarbons, and just two had half the market. But the whole world burned fossil fuels. Nevertheless, global warming, with all its complexity, was by the summer of 1988 entering the political arena. And a Montreal Protocol approach looked like the most likely template.[7]

JAMES HANSEN'S "VENUS SYNDROME"

Those hearings on that hot day in June 1988 turned James Hansen into a scientific celebrity and a figure who would have much impact on the climate debate thereafter.

To many in the political arena and the public, Hansen became the voice of science on climate, which created discomfort for other climate scientists who thought that he was too categoric. *Science,* the magazine of the American Association for the Advancement of Science, summed up the issue in an article titled "Hansen vs. the World on the Greenhouse Threat" by reporting "what bothers . . . his colleagues" is that he "fails to hedge his conclusions with appropriate qualifiers that reflect the imprecise science of climate modeling."[8]

A few weeks after his hearing, Senator Tim Wirth wrote to Roger Revelle soliciting his views. The message he got back was quite different from what he had heard from Hansen and others in the hearing room. Indeed, it was a word of caution. "We must be careful not to arouse too much alarm until the rate and amount of warming becomes clearer," said Revelle. "It is not yet obvious that this summer's hot weather and drought are the result of a global climactic change or simply an example of the uncertainties of climate variability." Revelle added, "My own view is that we had better wait another ten years before making confident predictions." Revelle wrote to another congressman that it might actually be twenty years before humans understood the negative and positive implications of the greenhouse effect. He believed humans should "take whatever actions would be desirable whether or not the greenhouse effect materializes." His list included a much larger role for nuclear power and launching a major program to expand forests, because the trees would capture and sequester what would otherwise be additional carbon in the air. "It is possible," he said in his letter to Wirth, "that such expansion could reduce carbon dioxide emissions very drastically, to a quite safe level."[9]

Hansen and Revelle came to the subject from different backgrounds and perspectives. Revelle started as a geologist, but Hansen had found his way into the climate studies via an interplanetary course through outer space. Hansen had written his physics Ph.D. on the atmosphere of Venus and was working on a Venus orbiter space vehicle shot in 1976 when a postgraduate student asked his help on calculating the atmospheric effects of some of the greenhouse gases. "I was captivated by this greenhouse problem," Hansen later explained. He shifted his research to the earth's atmosphere and to modeling it, although continuing his work on the other planets in the solar system.

Decades of science fiction writers had imagined life on earth's nearest neighbors. But telescopic observation and unmanned space vehicles had established that the atmospheres of Mars or Venus ensured that life in any form that humans would recognize was most unlikely. Mars, with a very thin atmosphere, was freezingly cold. Venus, with an atmosphere super rich in CO_2, was hellishly hot—almost 900°F on the surface. This space research informed understanding of the earth's climate. "Clearly a great deal stands to be gained by simultaneous studies of the earth's climate and the climate on other planets," Hansen and colleagues had written in 1978. Indeed, he was to say decades later, the differences in Mars's and Venus's atmospheres "provided the best proof at the time of the reality of the greenhouse effect." Venus came to play an even more direct role. It became, because of its CO_2-soggy atmosphere and burningly hot temperatures on the ground, the metaphor for an irreversible "runaway greenhouse effect," what Hansen would dub the "Venus Syndrome." It would prove to be a metaphor of great—and persuasive—power.[10]

THE HOT SUMMER OF 1988 AND THE "WHITE HOUSE EFFECT"

Just a few days after the Wirth hearings, the World Conference on a Changing Atmosphere convened in Toronto. It was the first time that large numbers of scientists, policymakers, politicians, and activists had gotten together to discuss climate change, and they did so with great urgency and sense of mission. The conference called for the world community to adopt coordinated policies to dramatically reduce CO_2 emissions.[11]

The hot weather led to much greater attention to the Toronto conference, as with the Wirth hearings, than would otherwise have been the case.

Although climate change was a longer-term phenomenon, the signal that James Hansen had identified seemed to reverberate over the rest of the summer of 1988 in an almost Biblical unfolding of weather-related plagues: intense heat waves, widespread droughts, impaired harvests, blazing forest fires in the West, navigation troubles on rivers as water levels fell. The electricity supply was balanced precariously, straining to meet the surging demand for air-conditioning.

All of this contributed to an increasingly pervasive anxiety that the environment was degrading.

That anxiety was captured in Boston Harbor on the first day of September. The Democratic governor of Massachusetts, Michael Dukakis, was well ahead in the polls against Vice President George H. W. Bush in the 1988 race to succeed Ronald Reagan. Dukakis was campaigning as an environmentalist, and Bush wanted to take him on in his home territory and on his core issues. So Bush boarded an excursion boat to cruise around Boston Harbor. Accompanied by a gaggle of reporters and cameras, he delighted in pointing out the vast amount of garbage floating in the harbor, which he attributed to the lapses of Dukakis's governorship. (Dukakis would reply that the garbage was the fault of the Reagan administration for foot dragging on promised cleanup funds.) Presenting himself as a "Teddy Roosevelt Republican," Bush promised to be an Environmental President. Among his pledges was the noteworthy statement that "those who think we are powerless to do anything about the 'greenhouse effect' are forgetting about 'the White House effect.'" And the president added, "I intend to do something about it." For the first time, a potential president had made greenhouse gases and climate change a campaign issue—and he had promised international collaboration to address it.[12]

The heat was headline news. But then heat waves and droughts had always been news. *Time* magazine, August 1923: "Another heat wave has struck Europe. So hot has it been in the Alps that the great glaciers have been melting and causing avalanches." *Time,* June 1934: "Down upon a third of the U.S. poured a blistering sun . . . broiling, baking, burning . . . Not only was the Midwest as hot as the hinges of Hell. It was also tinder dry." *Time,* June 1939: "It was so hot" in London "that ten extra waiters were engaged to serve cooling drinks to perspiring legislator in the House of Commons terrace restaurant . . . The asphalt on Berlin's Via Triumphalis was so soft that no tanks or cars with caterpillar treads were allowed on the avenue." *Time,* August 1955: "In the Eastern U.S., the dreadful summer of 1955 will be remembered for a long time to come . . . the region was withered by drought and a heat wave, the worst on record."[13]

But now, from the late 1980s onward, when people wrote about heat waves and droughts, it was not only about their severity and the disruptions and distress they caused, but also about links to carbon dioxide and climate change, and as alarm bells for global warming. In the months that followed, major stories on global warming ran in *Time* and *Newsweek,* the major business magazines, and even in *Sports Illustrated,* whose story was headlined "A Climate for Death." Global warming had at last found a place in the national consciousness.

Yet as the hot summer of 1988 faded, so did the sense of urgency. Just a couple of days after Bush's harbor cruise, a science writer at the *New York Times* sought to sum up the hot summer of 1988. James Hansen's "signal," the writer concluded, was not so crystal clear as it might have sounded in the hearing room on June 23. The heat-wave summer of 1988 had turned out to be not the hottest, but only the eleventh hottest in the 58 years that records had been kept. The worst drought was not 1988, but in the Dust Bowl days of 1934, when the upper Midwest was dubbed "the new U.S. Sahara." The reporter quoted a climate scientist who said, "In the short term, I don't see any major climate shift in the offing, and I don't feel we should be packing our bags to move to Manitoba just yet." When climate change was raised that same month at the U.N. General Assembly, one delegate said that it "still seemed like science fiction to many people."[14]

MRS. THATCHER

But one more important, and perhaps surprising, voice on climate change was still to be heard that September. It was that of the first leader of a major industrial nation to deliver a policy address focused on the subject—Britain's Conservative prime minister Margaret Thatcher. She was quite taken with the subject, for she was a scientist as a well as politician. With an Oxford degree in chemistry, she had worked for a few years as a research chemist for the J. Lyons food company until deciding that she was more interested in the art of politics than the molecular workings of glycerides monolayers—otherwise known as cake frostings. But her scientific training provided a framework for her to grasp quickly the issues surrounding climate change.

There was also a political element. Two years earlier she had been locked in a battle to the death with the left-wing coal miners' union, which had sought to cut off the delivery of coal, thus disrupting the nation's electricity supply and shutting down the country. That struggle was one of the defining moments in her 12 years as prime minister, and her victory broke the stalemate in industrial relations that had been driving Britain into chronic paralysis and economic decline. Replacing coal in electric generation with less-carbon-intensive natural gas from the North Sea would ensure that the coal miners' union would never again be strong enough to put a hammer lock on the nation's energy supply and bring its economy to a standstill.[15]

On September 27, 1988, Thatcher delivered an address to the Royal Society in Fishmongers' Hall in London in which climate change figured large. Thatcher had assumed that her speech, sounding the tocsin about climate change, would generate much attention. In practical terms, she had counted on that interest to ensure the presence of a bevy of television cameras, so that their bright lights could provide the illumination she needed to read her speech amid the pervasive gloom of the Fishmongers' Hall. But, to her disappointment, there was little media interest and, to her horror, no television cameras—not a single one. In fact, it was so dark that she was unable to read her speech at all—until, finally, a candelabra was passed up the table.

"For generations, we have assumed that the efforts of mankind would leave the fundamental equilibrium of the world's systems and atmosphere stable," she said when finally able to begin her speech. "But it is possible that with all these enormous changes (population, agriculture, use of fossil fuels) concentrated into such a short period of time, we have unwittingly begun a massive experiment with the systems of this planet itself." Although one could not yet be certain, she warned, "we have no laboratory in which to carry out controlled experiments." As not enough was yet known to make decisions, intensive programs of research and a good deal of "good science" were needed. As good as her word, she upped the British government's spending on climate research.

But the absence of television cameras certainly indicated that climate change was not yet an issue that would light up the public's imagination.[16]

THE IPCC AND THE "INDISPENSABLE MAN"

But before the year was out, and far from the glare of public attention, the decisive step would be taken that would frame how the world sees climate change today. In November 1988 a group of scientists met in Geneva to inaugurate the IPCC, the Intergovernmental Panel on Climate Change. This launch might have been lost in the alphabet soup of international agencies, conferences, and programs, but over the course of the next two decades, it would rise out of obscurity to shape the international discourse on this issue. The IPCC drew its legitimacy from two international organizations, the World Meteorological Organization and the United Nations Development Program. But the IPCC itself was not an organization in any familiar sense. Rather it was a self-regulating, self-governing organism, a coordinated network of research scientists who worked across borders, facilitated by cheaper and better communications.

There was certainly a "coordinator in chief"—a Swedish meteorologist named Bert Bolin. If one man was at the center of the growing international climate work, and would be there for almost half a century, year in and year out, it was Bolin—the "indispensable man" of climate research. Bolin was convener, keynoter, conference chair, editor, writer, adjudicator, balancer, scientific statesman, and international policy entrepreneur. He had started as a mathematician focused on atmospheric circulation. In the 1950s he had worked at Princeton with John von Neumann and Jule Charney, helping to write equations for those first computerized weather predictions. Back home in Sweden he had switched to geochemistry and become expert on carbon dioxide and the carbon cycle. As one research committee and conference begat another, which in turn begat another, which begat still another, the list of acronyms grew ever longer—and longer. Bolin seemed not only to be part of virtually all of them, but he also had no trouble keeping straight the otherwise incomprehensible jargon. As he wrote with great fluidity in his quasi-memoir, "As chairman of the CAS I submitted to ICSU a report for careful and urgent consideration by IUGG and ICSU and transmitted it to WMO which cosponsored the study conference and necessarily had to play an important role in the future planning and organization of GARP."[17]

Although plans for the IPCC were formally hatched in the spring of 1988, Hansen's testimony and the Toronto Conference alarmed Bolin. He believed that the evidence had to be carefully evaluated, and that policy should not get ahead of what was known. As Bolin, the artful consensus builder, expressed it, "An intense debate amongst scientists followed" Hansen's testimony, "and most of them disagreed strongly with Hansen's statement. The data showing the global increase of temperature had not been scrutinized and there was insufficient evidence that extreme events had become more common. This was to me a clear warning of how chaotic a debate between scientists and the public might become, if a much more stringent approach to the assessment of available knowledge was not instituted." He was similarly worried about the "unrealistic ad-hoc recommendation" about cutting carbon coming out of the Toronto conference. As he put it with a certain understatement, "The need for another, more trustworthy, assessment was very obvious."

Through workshops, papers, dialogue, reviews—and more reviews and still more reviews—the IPCC would seek to understand what was known about climate in all its manifestations, and what was uncertain. The days of the Tyndalls and the Keelings—individual atmospheric scientists, working on their own—were over. Science was now a multifaceted, cross-disciplinary, multinational enterprise. Yet when it came to climate, Bert Bolin was at the center of it all.

The fuse for the first IPCC report was short. It had to be ready by 1990, in time for the United Nations General Assembly. One of the preparatory meetings, held in Washington, D.C., was opened by James Baker, giving his very first speech as secretary of state. In it he called for a "no regrets" policy on climate change—which meant that the international community, even if not sure, should take actions that would be prudential in case the risks turned out to be real. Bolin was happy to hear Baker's speech but thought it was "premature to rush into an action program."[18]

SHOOT-OUT AT SUNDSVALL

All sorts of obstacles stood in the way of getting the work done. In late August 1990, as the deadline for preparation of the report for the U.N. General Assembly approached, scientists and policymakers met in the northern Swedish town of Sundsvall. A week of acrimonious negotiations ensued, with enormous frustrating arguments even about individual words. What, for instance, did "safe" really mean? By Friday afternoon there was still no agreement. And without agreement they could not go to the United Nations General Assembly with concrete recommendations.

Then came the epic crisis that threatened to scuttle the entire IPCC process: At 6:00 p.m. the U.N. translators walked off the job. They had come to the end of their working day and they were not going to work overtime. This was nonnegotiable. Those were their work rules. But without translators the delegates could not communicate among themselves, the meeting could not go on, there would be no report to the General Assembly and no resolution on climate change. But then the French chairman of the session, who had insisted on speaking French all week, made a huge concession. He agreed to switch to English, in which, it turned out, he was exceedingly fluent.

The discussions and debates now continued in English, and progress was laboriously made. But the chief Russian delegate sat silent, angrily scowling, wreathed in cigarette smoke. Without his assent, there would be no final report, and he gave no sign of coming on board.

Finally one of the scientists from the American delegation who happened to speak Russian approached the scientist. He made a stunning discovery. The Russian did not speak English, and he was certainly not going to sign on to something he did not understand. The American scientist turned himself into a translator, and the Russian finally agreed to the document. Thus consensus was wrought. The IPCC was rescued—just in time.[19]

So it was that, in October 1990, the IPCC was able to deliver its First Assessment Report to the United Nations. It answered the fundamental question by stating unequivocally: The earth was warming. But was it man-made? The warming, it said, was "broadly consistent with the predictions of climate models" regarding "larger man-made greenhouse warming." But the problem was that it was also broadly consistent with "natural climate variability." It would take another "decade or more" for "the unequivocal detection of the enhanced greenhouse effect from observations." So, said Bert Bolin's first IPCC, it was too soon to say whether man was causing the warming.

But that left a very big risk on the table. "By the time that question was clarified," said Bolin, "the commitment to future climate change will be considerably larger than today"—and it would be that much harder to deal with.[20]

GETTING READY FOR RIO

In response to the first IPCC report, the United Nations General Assembly had called for an international agreement—a "convention"—to limit greenhouse gases, primarily CO_2. It was supposed to be ready for a future Earth Summit, officially known as the United Nations Conference on Environment and Development, which would be held in Rio. What was to ensue was a complex, highly contentious international negotiating process that proved to be a cliffhanger until the very end.

For the first time, developing nations were seriously involved in climate discussions. But the last thing they wanted was limits on carbon emissions that would constrain their energy use and thus economic growth. Industrial nations were responsible for most of the human-released carbon in the atmosphere; they had been burning coal, oil, and natural gas for a very long time. It was their carbon; they were responsible for the problem, and they should be the ones to pay for fixing it. Why should the developing countries be denied their chance to grow? The developing nations vehemently opposed putting another issue on the agenda—deforestation, which also releases copious CO_2. That too could constrain their freedom of action and development.

The developed nations were bitterly split. Many—principally European—sought specific timetables and targets to reduce emissions. In their view there was no time to waste. Others wanted to proceed, but more slowly, with more caveats, and not with specific targets. There was much too much uncertainty, and they certainly did not want, especially during the recession years of the early 1990s, to put their own economic prospects at further risk.

The latter was the position of the United States—more or less. For the Bush administration itself was divided on the issue. Climate change had moved from science to the world of policy. The struggle within the Bush administration would become a paradigm for the climate debate over the decades that followed.

TO GO OR NOT TO GO

Would he, or wouldn't he? That was the question. Would President George H. W. Bush go to the Earth Summit in Rio de Janeiro in June 1992? Or would he stay home? As he had promised, he had brought greenhouse gases into the White House. But the "White House effect" was not quite what had been intended. For those gases had inflamed a torrid battle within his administration.

William Reilly, the administrator of the Environmental Protection Agency, the EPA, had been worrying about climate change for a decade, going back to his days as head of the Conservation Foundation and the World Wildlife Fund. He strongly argued for targets and, even more strongly, argued that Bush had to go to Rio. For him, Bush's 1988 promise to bring greenhouse gases into the White House was "highly significant." The president had said it; it was administration policy; and, as Reilly put it, "I dined out on it all the time."

Others in the administration, however, told the president that carbon restrictions would put the economy, already in recession, at "enormous risk." The chairman of the Council of Economic Advisers warned that the president might be making a "bet your economy" decision. This was the beginning of what continues today as the debate over the costs of adapting to climate change. The opponents of Bush's going emphasized the uncertainty and lack of sufficient evidence of temperature change to support the global-warming thesis. Sophisticated computer models were, in the eyes of the critics within the administration, still just models. Moreover, the IPCC itself had said human agency was not yet proved, and so how could targets be imposed? Some also saw the climate issue as a shift in tone from "red" to "green" in the opposition to capitalism and the market system—or, as one critic put it, "a green tree with red roots."[21]

The leading opponent within the administration was John Sununu, the White House chief of staff. During his three terms as governor of New Hampshire, Sununu had battled antinuclear activists over the Seabrook nuclear power plant, in what has been described as "one of the country's bitterest nuclear power fights." He now regarded the climate change activists as part of the same "anti-growth, anti-development crowd." Indeed, to him they were cut from the same mold as the1972 Club of Rome Report, whose model-driven scenarios had famously—and wrongly—predicted that economic growth would soon be snuffed out by overpopulation and shortages of natural resources.

Sununu was also a Ph.D. in engineering from MIT. "I made a living out of models before I went into politics, and you can get whatever results you want," he later said. "If people think these models have any validity, they are out of their minds." He questioned the feedbacks and observed that the failure to include the oceans in the models at the time was a serious shortcoming. Sununu supported substantial increases in funding for climate research but took the lead in the administration challenging the premise of climate change—and argued most vigorously against Bush's going to Rio.[22]

Climate change was far from the biggest and most urgent issue for the administration. Much of Bush's tenure was dominated by an epochal crises—the fall of communism in Eastern Europe and the collapse of the Soviet Union, and then Iraq's invasion of Kuwait and the Gulf War. Bush and his team demonstrated enormous skill in negotiating their way through these crises, working with allies, and building coalitions. The Gulf War ended in March 1991; the Soviet Union dissolved itself in December 1991.

But allies mattered to Bush and he was under pressure from the Europeans. Prime Minister Thatcher insisted that her cabinet sit through a day-long tutorial on climate change. The European Community's environmental commissioner publicly denounced Bush for his "hostility" to specific targets and timetables on emissions. The Germans argued that the United States needed "to accept the stabilization commitment."[23]

"A MAJOR HARANGUE DOWN THERE"

But now Rio was getting very close. The indecision about the president's plans had become palpable.

"Wouldn't it be difficult for you, having sold yourself as an environmental president, not to go?" a reporter asked at a press conference.

"I think it could work out either way," the president replied. "What I want to do is see if we can't hammer out consensus so you have a meeting that is viewed as positive instead of a major harangue down there."[24]

Finally, in April 1992, agreement was reached on a greenhouse gas convention. It called for a stabilization of greenhouse gases, though without targets.

The United States could accept this agreement. Bush would go to Rio. There were other compelling reasons as well. Bush saw himself as an environmentalist, and wanted to be seen as a Teddy Roosevelt Republican. He also recognized that the leaders of those key allied countries with whom he had worked so closely—on the fall of communism and the collapse of the Soviet Union, and then in the Gulf War coalition—would be in Rio, and he did not want to let them down. And then there were domestic politics. Just a little over a year earlier, in March 1991, in the aftermath of the Gulf War, Bush held an extraordinary—indeed, stratospheric—90 percent approval rating in the polls. But as the nation sunk deeper into a recession, Bush's poll numbers plummeted, and he was no longer the decisive war leader but increasingly portrayed as just "out of touch."

In the spring of 1992, as Rio approached, and with the November election not that far off, Bush was being pummeled every day by his two putative opponents: the data-processing billionaire Ross Perot, running as an independent, and the badly trailing Democratic candidate, Arkansas governor Bill Clinton. The daily barrages included a constant fusillade of criticism on his environmental policies. Bush was guilty, Clinton declared, of "grievous errors" on the environment and for being the "lone holdout to environmental progress." Were Bush not to go to Rio, the onslaught would only be worse, and his claim to be a Teddy Roosevelt Republican would be totally for naught.[25]

One other thing had changed. The leading opponent of his going to Rio—White House Chief of Staff John Sununu—had left the administration.

"THE DIPLOMATIC FREE-FOR-ALL"

And so Bush went, heading into a Rio Summit that was described at the time as a "fractious 12 days of diplomatic free-for-all." It was also a monstrous event: more than 160 heads of state and governments and international organizations; 10,000 other government officials; and another 25,000 people—activists, NGOs, business leaders, and journalists. Many of the NGOs were an integral part of the negotiating process in a way that had never happened before; others were holding their own parallel earth summit. Still others were out protesting; some activists hung a huge banner on the iconic Sugar Loaf Mountain that overlooks Rio denouncing the conference as a sellout.

There were certainly no shortages of harangues. Judged solely by the applause and excitement, the most popular head of state was Fidel Castro. The Cuban leader demonstrated his mastery of haranguing, whipping himself and his audiences into a fury as he denounced capitalism and consumerism as the scourge of the environment. This was despite the enormous and grim environmental degradation just then being revealed, with the fall of the Iron Curtain, in the ex-communist lands of Eastern Europe and the former Soviet Union.

For his part, George Bush tried to respond to the harangues. "America's position on environmental protection is second to none," he shot back, "so I did not come here to apologize." It was to little avail, for he was typecast, as the *New York Times* put it, as "the Darth Vader of the Rio meeting." And it was not just him. When William Reilly, the leading advocate for a climate treaty in the U.S. government, landed in Rio, he was greeted by his photo in a newspaper under the headline "Arch Fiend Arrives in Rio."[26]

On the second to last day of the Earth Summit, amid all the hullabaloo, the United Nations Framework Convention on Climate Change was signed. The very first signatory was George H. W. Bush, on behalf of the United States. Some 153 other leaders signed on. A few months later, the U.S. Senate approved the convention, making the United States the first industrial nation to fully ratify it. Climate change was now embodied as a global priority in an international agreement adhered to by virtually all the world's countries.

WHAT THE FRAMEWORK CONVENTION SET IN MOTION

The Framework Convention's ultimate objective was far-reaching, perhaps more far-reaching than many signatories realized. The goal was "the stabilization of greenhouse gas concentrations in the atmosphere at a level that would prevent dangerous anthropogenic interference with the climate system." The phrase "dangerous anthropogenic interference" became a famous and much-quoted piece of jargon. "Anthropogenic" was a Latinate way to refer to mankind itself. The convention centered attention on the release of greenhouse gases as the result of human activity—principally burning coal, oil, and natural gas, along with the cutting down of forests.[27]

As part of the agreement, the developed countries took on commitments to control their emissions; the developing countries had no obligations other than monitoring. In addition, the developed countries agreed to "provide new and additional financial resources" to help developing countries reduce their emissions. The concept of "joint implementation"—countries' encouraging companies within their borders to work with similar groups in other countries—was introduced. Overall, the convention emphasized that dealing with climate change would be a process that would extend over many years, even decades. And its execution demonstrated that the character of international negotiation was changing—that nongovernmental organizations were now sanctioned as part of the process, with their own more-or-less guaranteed seats at the table.

The U.S. administration's own experts had calculated that the United States could manage to hold emissions by 2000 at 1990 levels through new energy-efficiency programs and new environmental technologies. "That was just wrong," Reilly later said. "We did not anticipate the fabulous economic growth that the United States would experience in the 1990s. Emissions actually rose 11 percent in the 1990s. On the other hand, if there had been targets, that would have enabled policies that would have led us to be more efficient."[28]

. . .

As it was, the Framework Convention on Climate Change—the agreement that came out of Rio—was remarkable. Not because of its targets, for it had none save the "aim" to reduce emissions in 2000 to 1990 levels, but because it existed at all. Four years earlier, climate change had not even been on the political agenda in the United States, nor on that of many other countries. Yet in less than half a decade, what heretofore had been an obscure scientific preoccupation had been turned into something that the international community had gone on record promulgating as an urgent and fundamental challenge to humanity and to the planet's well-being.

The road to Rio was actually quite long; it had begun more than two centuries earlier, in the Swiss Alps. But what had started as an obsession by a handful of researchers with the past, with glaciers and the mysteries of the Ice Age, was now set to become a dominating energy issue for the future.

24

MAKING A MARKET

The idea was reprehensible—morally reprehensible. Create a market in pollution? Trade "allowances" that give companies the right to sell their pollution like a commodity? Put a market price on environmental degradation? Unbelievable!

That was the response of many environmental organizations, academics, and many others to a revolutionary idea: using the mechanisms of the marketplace—buying and selling—to solve environmental problems.

One prominent political theorist put the objections in philosophical terms: "Turning pollution into a commodity to be bought and sold," he declared, does the grave disservice of removing "the moral stigma that is properly associated" with pollution. The head of a major environmental organization was more blunt. "Economics," he said, "is an advanced form of brain disease."[1]

That may have been the common reaction in the late 1980s and into the 1990s when the battle over using markets to curb pollution was at its fiercest. This particular form of "brain disease" arose from the world of ideas, from a debate among economists about how to subject pollution to the laws of economics. Then, intrigued by its possibilities, and at the same irate with the rigidities of conventional regulation and frustrated by inaction, a small group of "policy entrepreneurs"—economists, environmental activists, and officials—seized upon the idea of using the market to address climate change. Instead of an abomination, it came to be seen as the "better" way to take on the challenge of climate change—and, indeed, as the essential tool. They eventually called it cap and trade.

The ambitions held for it were breathtakingly large; it was intended to do nothing less than remake the world's energy marketplace and the character of energy in every person's life and thus many of the daily choices that we make. How did this come about? It goes back to what John Maynard Keynes called the "academic scribblers"—those who come to influence subsequent politicians and lawmakers and "practical men" in general—none of whom have any idea that they are channeling thinkers they had never heard of in the first place.

THE "SCRIBBLER IN CHIEF"

In this case, there was even a "scribbler in chief"—Ronald Coase. Yet Coase would have seemed a most unlikely candidate for this post. Born in 1910, he suffered as a child from "weakness" in his legs, thought to be polio, as a result of which he had initially been put into classes for physically and mentally handicapped children. He managed to learn to read only by studying the labels on bottles of medicine. But, at age 11, his father, a postal worker, took him to a phrenologist, who, seeking to bolster his confidence, said, "You may be inclined to underrate your abilities." It was good advice. The next year, Coase managed to switch into a regular educational track. He made up for lost time and ended up with a Ph.D. from the London School of Economics. In 1951, he emigrated to the United States.[2]

Four decades later, in 1991, at age 81, he received the Nobel Prize in economics, mostly for two enormously influential articles. For the work of a Nobel Prize winner in economics, both articles were strikingly devoid of any mathematics save simple arithmetic. But they were very powerful in their arguments. In one, "The Nature of the Firm" published in 1937, Coase took on a very basic question—why do people coalesce into companies in a market economy rather than remain as freelancers in a sea of the self-employed? The answer, he said, was "transaction costs"—costs are lower within companies, things are easier to get done, and efficiency is higher.

The second article, the result of a friendly debate with Milton Friedman, was "The Problem of Social Costs." Published in *The Journal of Law and Economics*, it ended up one of the most cited articles in the history of economics. Over time, it became the foundation for the idea of using markets to solve environmental problems. Coase's thinking was much influenced by his studies of state-owned industries and regulation, and what he saw as their gross inefficiencies. Coase argued that markets and pricing systems could provide better solutions than direct government intervention and control. To make his argument, he homed in on externalities, or what he called "harmful effects"—in this particular instance, the unwanted pollution that is consequent from economic activity.

This question of externalities—undesirable side effects or consequences—is something with which economists have long struggled. Early in the twentieth century, the economist Arthur Pigou had argued, with great influence, that the way to deal with externalities, which are not reflected in the price of a good, was for the government to intervene and place a tax on the externality. Think of it as a sort of sin tax. A one-dollar tax per pack of cigarettes or a fifty-cent carbon tax on gasoline would be examples of Pigovian taxes. But Coase was sure that Pigou was all wrong, that he was placing far too much faith in the wisdom of government and that he failed to understand the role of property.

Coase's examples focused on legal issues involving pollution, some going back to the Middle Ages. What happens if the "conies"—another term for domesticated rabbits—that a medieval landlord was raising on his estate for fur and food were instead to start burrowing into the estate of his neighbor, and then proceed to breed and multiply wantonly, thus despoiling the neighbor's estate? What about "smoke nuisance" from a neighbor's burning of coal? These were questions of property rights and relative values that the contesting neighbors would put on them. The way to solve these questions, Coase argued, would not be through a regulation or a tax, but through the marketplace. "All solutions have costs," Coase wrote. "Direct governmental regulation will not necessarily give better results than leaving the problem to be solved by the market or the firm."[3]

Coase never talked about actually *trading* pollution rights, but the idea is inherent in what he wrote. His ideas would be taken up and specifically applied to environmental issues by others. In *Pollution, Property & Prices,* published in

1968, the Canadian economist John Dales argued that the best way to clean up pollution in the Great Lakes was with a "market in pollution rights." Dales made his arguments in English; David Montgomery, writing a Ph.D. at Harvard a few years later, made parallel arguments in equations. But both came to the same point: Would it not be preferable, more efficient, and less costly, they asked, if emissions could be traded as though property, or at least quasi-property, just as you could trade currencies or oil, or stocks and bonds, or real estate?[4]

"THE WAR ON POLLUTION"

In the late 1960s and early 1970s, economists were turning their attention to pollution, which was rising on the political agenda. In 1970 President Richard Nixon established the U.S. Environmental Protection Agency to lead, in his words, the nation's "war on pollution." This marked the opening of an era of much more intense environmental regulation. That regulation generally took the form of administrative control and micromanagement, with detailed standards, mandates, and requirements, down to nitty-gritty prescriptions for specific technologies and tightly policed compliance—for instance, setting the maximum of so many pounds of emission per hour per machine. This approach became known as "command-and-control" regulation, a phrase suggestive of the centrally planned, highly inefficient "command economies" of the Soviet Union and its satellites.

But, starting later in the 1970s, some very modest experimentation with more market-based approaches began in the United States at the federal level, and in a couple of states.[5]

"OLD ENOUGH TO REMEMBER"

In the early 1980s, the decision was made to phase out lead from gasoline because of its toxicity. "Knocking" had chronically afflicted the early auto engines, sometimes so loudly that it was impossible to ignore, and often doing great damage to the engines. Years of research finally eliminated knocking in the 1920s with the introduction of tetraethyl lead as an additive. As late as

1963, tetraethyl lead was hailed as "undoubtedly one of the most remarkable innovations of the twentieth century."[6]

Yet less than two decades later, there was consensus that lead was a menace to human health and that, whatever its value to engines, it had to go. During the Reagan administration, a substantial part of one cabinet meeting was devoted to the question of how to get lead out of gasoline. As the discussion proceeded, President Reagan shook his head and recalled that, when he was a teenager, the introduction of tetraethyl lead had been celebrated as one of the greatest advances in motor fuels and auto performance ever. As he looked around the cabinet table, Reagan encountered only blank, uncomprehending looks. He shrugged. "Oh, well," he said," I guess I am the only person old enough to remember this."[7]

Under the lead phaseout, refiners—instead of being given detailed requirements—were allowed to trade lead "permits" among themselves, providing an economic incentive for those that could get rid of lead more quickly than under a mandate system to do so. This was a market-based solution. The lead program proved much more successful than expected. By 1987—that is, within five years—lead was gone from gasoline, and the cost proved much lower than anticipated. The road to future pollution reduction seemed to be paved with lead. Maybe there was something to this market approach, after all.[8]

In the presidential election year of 1988, two senators took on a self-assigned mandate—to inject vigorous "new thinking" about the environment into the campaign. Tim Wirth, who had chaired the June 1988 global-warming hearings, was a liberal Democrat, and John Heinz, a moderate Republican. They had been at the forefront of environmental issues in their respective parties. The two senators organized what became known as Project 88. As project director, they hired a young Harvard economics professor named Robert Stavins. "They wanted new ideas," said Stavins. "They hired an economist, and so they got economic ideas."[9]

Project 88 identified a host of environmental and energy problems for which "harnessing market forces" would be a major step forward. "Economic-incentive systems" would deliver quicker, better results for much less money than the "dictated technological solutions" of command-and-control. Climate change was on the target list.[10]

THE ACID TEST OF ACID RAIN

Project 88 may have put the idea of using prices and markets out there. But now, with the 1988 election over, an acid test was at hand. It happened to involve "acid rain." The story about acid rain, and how it was dealt with, has become a central, often-cited narrative for those promoting market-oriented climate change policies today.

"Acid rain" was the evocative term applied to the effects of the sulfur dioxide, SO_2, which, when emitted by coal-burning power plants, reacts in the atmosphere to become sulfuric acid. It was a major issue in parts of Europe, where, among other things, it was said to have damaged half the trees in the Black Forest in Germany.

It was ranked, by far, the major air pollution issue in the northeast United States and eastern Canada. This was not the familiar matter of local pollution, which could be addressed with local standards. The tall chimneys of coal-burning Midwest utilities sent the SO_2 high into the atmosphere where it migrated across state and national borders, damaging forests and acidifying lakes, killing fish, and corroding buildings. By the end of Ronald Reagan's term, more than 70 different acid rain bills had been introduced in Congress. Whatever their many differences, they all shared one striking characteristic—none had become law. The issue had become so corrosive with Canada that its prime minister had, with a certain acid humor, jokingly threatened to declare war on the United States over acid rain. But during the 1980 campaign, both Michael Dukakis and George H. W. Bush had categorically pledged to reduce SO_2.[11]

Shortly after George H. W. Bush's victory, C. Boyden Gray, the new president's White House counsel, invited Robert Stavins down from Harvard to talk about how to implement a market based-approach to acid rain. Boyden Gray had read the Project 88 report, and he was very interested in applying market principles to environmental questions to reduce compliance costs. During the Reagan administration, Gray had worked on the lead phasedown. In addition to the work of economists, Gray was also influenced by legal scholars working on structuring markets for pollution reductions, most notably Bruce Ackerman and Richard Stewart, who was a former chairman of the board of the Environmental Defense Fund.[12]

"LEAST-COST SOLUTIONS"

Boyden Gray built a small team of advisers, which included Robert Grady from the Office of Management and Budget, and an economist on the Council of Economic Advisers, Robert Hahn, whose California Institute of Technology Ph.D. was about market-based solutions to Los Angeles' smog. Gray's team was united in its determination to design a lower-cost system by creating market-based system in which utilities could trade emissions. "One quarter of U.S. regulatory costs were from the Clean Air Act," Gray later recalled. "The best way to lower costs to the American people was by lowering compliance costs."

But how to do it—and how to sell it politically?

Gray had read an article by Fred Krupp, in the *Wall Street Journal,* in which Krupp, the president of the Environmental Defense Fund, had advocated using markets to help solve water issues in the West. Now, he brought Krupp into the acid rain discussions. Gray told Krupp that if EDF could draft something that had a reasonable chance of making its way through the Congress, he would present it to the president. Krupp in turn brought in two of his colleagues, a lawyer named Joseph Goffman and Daniel Dudek, an economist who was an evangelist for the market-based approach.

But the opposition was fierce. There had been a decade-long stalemate on cleaning up acid rain because of a coal versus coal battle between the congressional delegations representing Appalachia and the Middle West (where high sulfur coal was produced by unionized miners), and the West (where low sulfur coal was produced by non-union miners). Moreover, except for EDF, just about every major environmental organization was resolutely opposed to emissions trading. They thought that emissions trading—a "license to pollute"—was perverse, heretical, immoral, and totally unacceptable. The environment should not be "for sale."[13]

There was another important opponent—the bureaucracy itself. As John Schmitz, Boyden Gray's deputy, recalled, the Environmental Protection Agency "was not enthusiastic. They had already pulled the map out of all the big plants in the Midwest and knew what technology they wanted on each of those power plants. . . . We were arguing a totally different concept—let the market decide that." But letting the market decide would shift "decision-making from the bureaucracy to the private sector." Instead of making the technical decisions, and ordering compliance, the agency officials would become more like market monitors.[14]

Gray and his team were convinced that a market-based solution would allow much wider latitude for innovation. The fundamental difference from the command-and-control approach was that the proposed legislation would specify performance and outcomes, rather than ordain specific technologies and processes. It would, as Goffman and Dudek of EDF wrote, "harness the complex, widely dispersed and ever-changing information needed" to get the best—and "least-cost"—outcomes.[15]

In a lesson of lasting importance, the acid rain legislation would demonstrate what could be achieved with bipartisan collaboration. This was a flagship issue not only for the Republican president but also the Democratic Senate Majority Leader, George Mitchell. Still the struggle was intense before a bill could work its way through Congress.

"THE GRAND POLICY EXPERIMENT"

On November 15, 1990, George H. W. Bush signed the Clean Air Amendments into law. Title IV established an emissions trading system to reduce acid rain. It was a great victory for something that had been considered beyond-the-pale just a year earlier. Shrinking the caps over time, that is, reducing the total number of allowances or permits year by year, would have the effect of making the permits scarcer and thus more expensive, increasing the incentive to reduce emissions. Many called this system allowance trading. Others, more optimistically, called it the "Grand Policy Experiment."[16]

After a slow start, the buying and selling of allowances became standard practice among utilities. The results in the years since have been very impressive. Emissions trading delivered much larger reductions, at much lower costs, and much more speedily, than what would have been anticipated with a regulatory system. By 2008, emissions had fallen from the 1980 level by almost 60 percent. As a bonus, the rapid reduction in emissions meant less lung disease and thus significant savings on health care.[17]

The impact on thinking about how to solve environmental problems was enormous. "We are unaware of any other U.S. environmental program that has achieved this much," concluded a group of MIT researchers, "and we find it impossible to believe that any feasible alternative command-and-control program could have done nearly as well." Coase's theorem worked; markets were vindicated. Within a decade, a market-based approach to pollution had gone from immorality and heresy to almost accepted wisdom. The experience would decisively shape the policy responses in the ensuing debate over how to deal with climate change. Overall, the evidence on SO_2 was so powerful that it was invoked again and again in the struggles over climate change policy.

Allowance trading had also acquired a new name—cap and trade.

The fact that the SO_2 program provided credibility for cap and trade for climate change was not exactly accidental. For the proponents saw the 1990 program as a "demonstration model" for what was coming to be their prime issue—climate change. And the success of the acid rain program became a touchstone for the growing number of environmental organizations that were working Capitol Hill to promote climate change policies. "We were going to wrap up clean air in a couple of years, we hoped, and then start gearing up to do climate in the 1990s," recalled Joseph Goffman.

"We used that conviction to keep up our morale," he added.[18]

"A DISCERNIBLE HUMAN INFLUENCE ON CLIMATE"

In the early 1990s, as the SO_2 market was getting going, the IPCC was busy preparing its next every-half-decade "assessment" of where the science was on climate change. Once again the process was unfolding—pulling together research, examining it, challenging it, making sense of it, arguing about it, all across the world's time zones. This time the "bulk reports" that constituted the Second Assessment Report would total two thousand pages and would reference ten thousand scientific papers.

Once again, the process was under the steady, cautious hand of the Swedish meteorologist Bert Bolin, and once again, he wanted to be very careful and make sure that the conclusions did not outrun what could be known. "It was still difficult," he said, "to tell how trustworthy projections of future changes might be." He worried about misunderstandings. For instance, the use of the word *prediction*—when talking about climate change issues to the public or politicians—could "transmit a false impression of a capability that in reality is quite limited."

Bolin had to stand his ground. Some of the scientists wanted to declare that "appreciable human influence" on climate was now clear. It was not clear, however, to Bolin. On his motion, "appreciable" was replaced with the word "discernible." And thus the second IPCC report, in 1995, declared, "The balance of evidence suggests that there is a discernible human influence on global climate." As it was, that sentence became famous. So did the report's "best estimated" judgment that, on current tracks, global temperatures would rise two degrees centigrade by 2100.

"It's Official," headlined *Science* magazine, reporting on the IPCC. "First Glimmer of Greenhouse Warming Seen." It announced that the report had identified the "newly perceived fingerprint of human-induced climate change."[19]

DEVELOPED VERSUS DEVELOPING COUNTRIES

The IPCC may have gone up several steps in confidence, as well as visibility; but that, in turn, also meant that it was becoming more controversial. The first point of contention was the renewal of the "North-South" face-off between developed and developing nations. Some 75 percent of total accumulated emissions of CO_2 between 1860 and 1990 had come from the industrialized nations. But they had only 20 percent of world population. As carbon limits seemed to take on greater likelihood, the developing countries became more vociferous in opposing limits on their use of hydrocarbons and the constraints such limits could impose on their economic growth. Bolin received an angry letter from China about the impact of proposed restrictions on developing countries. "We feel sorry for such a scientific assessment lacking fairness and equity," the Chinese declared. Some editing was made in the report to make them feel less sorry.

This clash between developed and developing nations was a dominant issue when national delegations convened in Berlin in 1995 to follow up on Rio and work out a "mandate" that would serve as the basis for the upcoming conference in Kyoto. The chairman of the Berlin meeting was Angela Merkel. Just a few years earlier, she had been working as a physical chemist in communist East

Germany with no expectations of any career change. But the abrupt German reunification in 1990 had catapulted her into politics and, quite quickly, into the leadership of the Christian Democratic Party. Now, just half a decade after the fall of the Berlin Wall, she was environment minister of unified Germany. In her opening remarks to the Berlin conference, she stressed the importance of the industrialized countries being "the first to prove that we are bearing our responsibility in protecting the global climate."[20]

That was the thrust of the outcome. The Berlin Mandate concluded that while the industrial nations would take on specific targets in the next phase of global climate regulation, the developing countries would be spared such obligations. That "differentiated responsibility" would come to be an ever more important battlefield in the global politics of climate change.

RISING STAKES—AND RISING CLASH

The second point of contention was what Bolin called the polarization over the IPCC process itself. As climate change gained traction as a political issue, the implications of what was embodied in the IPCC's assessments became starker. For, if acted upon in the way some suggested, they would require a radical change in the energy foundations of the world economy, with potentially significant impacts—so some argued—on economic growth and well-being. Critics from the science community and from energy-producing and energy-consuming industries argued—and continue to argue—that there was much greater uncertainty about the science of climate change and the relative impacts of natural and human forces than the IPCC had allowed. They said that the syntheses and summaries projected a consensus that was not borne out by the myriad research on which it was founded. Some challenged the scientific objectivity of leading participants and, indeed, the legitimacy of the entire process. And some went even further, arguing that increased CO_2 would actually be beneficent, for it would mean richer harvests and a lusher, more florid world. Some simply questioned how the human share of total CO_2 emissions could be so decisive in the global climate system.

In turn, participants in the IPCC dismissed the critics as ignorant charlatans, industry hacks, and practitioners of "junk science." The ever-careful Bolin did not hide his disdain and exasperation when he denounced "the almost always scientifically inadequate approaches in the shallow analyses by skeptics who lacked the scientific knowledge to deal with the climate change issue." In due course, the "skeptics" would be further dismissed as "climate deniers." Some, like Richard Lindzen, a professor of meteorology at MIT who is often described as a climate denier, while praising the scientific work in the IPCC, continue to argue that the "iconic claim" of human responsibility cannot be substantiated and that key factors in climate, like the role of clouds, are very poorly understood. As Bert Bolin wrote in 2007, the focus of Lindzen's research was "a legitimate scientific approach," elsewhere adding, "We all know that projections into the future cannot be checked against observations and some basic processes and secondary feedback may still be poorly described."[21]

To be sure, little of this debate would have ever happened had not the IPCC continued to gain in credibility and impact as the arbiter of climate change and its risks. Its second assessment set the framework for what came next—a huge international conference that was to work out the game plan for implementing the pledges made in the United Nations Framework Convention on Climate Change at the Rio de Janeiro Earth Summit in 1992. The location—the ancient Japanese capital of Kyoto—would become synonymous with global climate change policy. "Kyoto" would come to represent the transition of climate change from a subject of international discussion among a narrow range of officials, scientists, and interested parties into a global political issue.

BATTLES AT KYOTO

In the autumn of 1997, Stuart Eizenstat, Undersecretary of State for Economic, Business and Agricultural Affairs, found himself on a few weeks notice drafted to lead the U.S. delegation to the Kyoto conference. Intense, focused, and very logical, with a tremendous ability to master a brief, Eizenstat was known as a consummate problem solver and master negotiator. But, in taking the Kyoto brief, he found himself launched into what he would later describe as "the most complex, difficult, and draining" negotiation he had ever encountered.

The meeting at Kyoto's International Conference Center, set on a lake, among the gardens and hills of what had been for a thousand years Japan's capital, was convened to settle on binding targets for greenhouse gas reductions and on the mechanisms to implement it. Like Rio five years earlier, Kyoto had a circuslike quality to it—10,000 people, including officials, experts, NGOs, industry representatives, journalists—in a melee of meetings and negotiations, caucuses and huddles, plotting and arguments, and all of them constantly trading information and rumor about what was happening in this delegation or that subgroup or, most important, among the main negotiators. A number of them were awkwardly wielding, for the first time, bulky early-generation cell phones that were almost the size of shoes as they tried to keep up with all the twists and turns of negotiation and on top of every rumor.

To demonstrate environmental sensitivity, the Japanese organizers turned down the heating in the conference center. But this created a new problem as Kyoto in December was cold. To compensate, the Japanese decided to distribute blankets to the delegates. But they did not have enough blankets, and so a whole separate negotiation erupted over how many blankets would be allocated to each delegation.[22]

It was clear that countries would fall far short of the voluntary targets for national CO_2 emissions conceived at Rio. So Kyoto was going to try for mandatory, binding targets, which would be much more challenging. It was not exactly the most auspicious time. The Asian financial crisis, which would throw much of the region into an economic collapse, had started the previous July.

EUROPE VERSUS THE UNITED STATES

The first big question at Kyoto pitted the European Union against the United States, and it led to a standoff. The Europeans wanted the Americans to take deeper cuts. The United States refused. The Europeans would have an easier time beating 1990 targets than the United States owing to the luck of history: Germany had been unified in 1990, and since then, the dirty old coal plants in the formerly communist eastern Germany were being retired. And in Britain, as a result of Margaret Thatcher's victory over the left-wing coal miners' union, coal was being phased out of electric generation and replaced with natural gas from the North Sea. What broke the deadlock on this issue was the sudden arrival of Vice President Al Gore in Kyoto for all of sixteen hours.

At a pre-Kyoto meeting in his office in the West Wing, senior advisers had urged Gore not to go—not to spend his political capital on a ten-thousand-mile trip that might end in failure. But, for Gore, this was an issue to which he was deeply committed, and he went. "I was always planning to come," he said when he arrived in Kyoto. "It just took a while to get my staff on board." His speech had an electric effect on the conference, assuring the delegates that the United States was deeply engaged with climate change and that they were dealing with a "serious U.S." His appearance broke the deadlock, with the result that the United States, Europe, and Japan all ended up with roughly the same binding targets—CO_2 emissions between 6 and 8 percent lower by 2008–12 compared with 1990.[23]

DEVELOPING VERSUS DEVELOPED COUNTRIES

The second big question at Kyoto reopened the debate as to whether the developing nations would also make binding commitments about reducing emissions. Their answer was a very firm no. The Berlin Mandate had, two years earlier, exempted them. And they had no intention of budging. When Eizenstat went to meet with the delegates from the developing countries, "I received," he recalled, "about as cool a reception as I've ever gotten in any forum."[24]

If one looked backward at emissions, then the developing countries had a strong case. But, if one looked forward, the developing countries would be responsible for a growing share of CO_2 as their economies grew. But this was still a pivotal moment in the world economy, though not quite recognized at the time. The developing world, led by China, India, and Brazil, was about to embark on a period of extraordinary economic growth. But especially during the depths of the Asian financial crisis, this was hard to envision. Ten years earlier, one would not have worried at all about emissions from developing countries, particularly from a China that was only beginning to emerge from its Maoist grip. Ten years later, it would have been impossible not to focus on those emissions.

Yet without binding targets for developing countries, it would be very hard to turn an agreement at Kyoto into a treaty approved by the U.S. Senate. For, the previous July, the Senate had passed the Byrd-Hagel Resolution. This was not, as is sometimes said, a rejection of the treaty by the Senate, as it was passed months prior to the Kyoto conference. Rather, it was a strong shot across the bow—a declaration that the United States would not accept a treaty that did "serious harm" to the U.S. economy or that exempted developing countries, which, it was feared, would put U.S. industry at a competitive disadvantage. "We could see that China would eventually overtake the United States in greenhouse gases," Hagel later recalled, and thus should not be exempted from binding targets. The Senate adopted the Byrd-Hagel Resolution by a 95-to-0 vote. That was pretty categoric.[25]

But at Kyoto there was no give, and no reason that the developing countries would give. The closest thing to a compromise was the establishment of the "Clean Development Mechanism," under which companies from developed countries could invest in "clean energy" projects in developing countries. But the inability to get the developing countries—whose emissions were on a fast-growth track—into a binding system would doom the Kyoto Protocol as far as the U.S. Senate was concerned. And the United States could not accede to the treaty without Senate ratification.

"COST, COST, AND COST"

The third big question at Kyoto was how to implement reductions. The Europeans wanted mandates and direct intervention. They called it policies and measures, but they meant command-and-control. The United States was committed to a trading system along the lines of acid rain (although creating a trading system for about one thousand coal-fired units in the United States was much less daunting than doing the same for the world's consumption of fossil fuels). To this, the Europeans were adamantly opposed. They were inherently more suspicious of markets. They thought emissions trading might be an academic experiment foisted off by some professors. Or even a trick. And for many of them, the notion of selling pollution credits seemed akin to immorality, just as it had to some environmental groups during the 1990 Clean Air fight. And so the Europeans denounced the very idea of selling emission rights—what they dismissed as "hot air."

Bolstered by the success of the SO_2 program, policymakers in the Clinton administration became convinced that this was the only way to go. As Eizenstat put it, "There were three issues—cost, cost, and cost." And the cost of mitigating climate change without a market system would be far too expensive for any economy to bear.[26]

But the trading issue was proving intractable. The deadline for the conference's conclusion was getting very close, and still there was no agreement. Everyone was exhausted, and time was just about up. In fact, it was now overtime. The ventilation system had been turned off, the translators had left, and the delegates could already hear the banging of carpenters beginning to prepare the next conference.

The chairman asked Eizenstat and his antagonist, the chief European negotiator, Britain's deputy prime minister John Prescott, to go with him into an adjacent green room. The conference at this point was down to the issue of emissions trading. Prescott adamantly held to the European position, insisting that trading be no more than "supplementary," a secondary tool. Eizenstat said that the United States would not budge, and it was not bluffing.

"It's very simple, John," he said. "We're not going to sign, we are not going to do it. All of this time over 15 days will be wasted. Do you really want to go back to Europe with no agreement?"

"Or," he added, "we can have an historic agreement."

Prescott recognized that Eizenstat would not budge, and reluctantly agreed to the central role of trading. With that, the Kyoto Protocol was effectively done and negotiated, the carpenters could continue, and the follow-on conference could move into the hall.[27]

And that it is how, in the little green room on the last day in Kyoto, "markets" became embedded in climate change. Ronald Coase's theorem, and John Dales's refining of it into a "market for pollution rights," had become international policy. And, if one were looking for confirmation of Keynes's theory about the impact of "scribblers" on people who had never heard of them, then Kyoto—including the deal made in the green room—was a prime example.

HOW REALISTIC?

The agreement at Kyoto, Bert Bolin later wrote, marked "the first steps toward actually creating a political regime for preventing a human-induced climate change." But there was a problem with it. As Bolin added, "At the time of its adoption it was already politically unrealistic."[28]

The Kyoto Protocol would be a treaty, which meant, for the United States, that it would require 67 votes in the Senate. But then there was the Byrd-Hagel Resolution, which said that any climate agreement should maintain U.S. competitiveness and that all the major emitters should be included—including the developing world. But Kyoto did not include them. And that would be a fatal flaw for a treaty trying to make its way through the U.S. Senate. "There was no detectable effort in the administration or the Senate to put something together," recalled one player. It never submitted the treaty for ratification.

"I was surprised," said Chuck Hagel, whose Senate subcommittee would have had jurisdiction. "I thought they would."[29]

But the Clinton administration could count votes.

25

ON THE GLOBAL AGENDA

In 2005 the leaders of the G8 countries convened for their biannual summit at the venerable Gleneagles Hotel in Scotland, home to one of the world's most-fabled golf courses. The host was British prime minister Tony Blair. In the face of considerable domestic opposition, Blair had aligned himself with George Bush in the war on terror and the Iraq invasion of March 2003. But on climate change he was in the lead, and he had put it at the top of the agenda for Gleneagles, somewhat to the consternation of the Bush administration.

Blair was in an exultant mood; he had just learned that London had won out over Paris and Madrid for the 2012 Olympics. But on the second of the two days of summitry, when the presidents and prime ministers assembled around the table to talk about climate change, Blair himself was absent. The day before, during a meeting with China's president, an aide had passed Blair a note. Blair abruptly excused himself and hurried back to London. During the morning rush hour, four Islamic jihadists born in Britain, but at least three of them trained at terror camps in Pakistan, had detonated bombs in the London transport system, setting off infernos in the Underground and blowing up a red double-decker bus. The normality of the morning commute was transformed to horror—some 52 people killed and another 700 injured. The capital was in gridlock and shock, and on very high alert for the next attack.[1]

Back at Gleneagles, the summit on climate, which had been Blair's highest priority, went on, despite the absent prime minister. Aside from the leaders, one of the other few people in the room was an economist named Nicholas Stern, who had prepared a report on Africa that was going to follow the climate change dialogue. As he looked around during the discussion on climate, Stern was struck by what seemed to him the body language of the leaders in the room, which communicated skepticism and a lack of urgency and interest. Some, Stern thought, "looked distinctly bored."[2]

Yet within the next few years, climate change would rise to the top of the global agenda and rank with the economy and terrorism as one of the foremost subjects for international discussion and negotiations. New climate change policies were intended to make a profound transformation of the energy foundations that support the world economy—a transformation as far-reaching as that when civilization moved from wood to coal and then on to oil and natural gas. Indeed, so thorough a change would mean a transformation of the world economy itself.

The general objective is to reduce CO_2 emissions substantially—in some formulations by more than 80 percent over the next few decades. But climate is hardly simple to address. Indeed, it is perplexing in a world in which hydrocarbons—oil, natural gas, and coal—provide over 80 percent of today's total energy, and overall energy demand is expected to increase by as much as 40 percent over the next two decades. In short, making any such change is more than challenging.

THE "K" WORD

During the 2000 U.S. presidential campaign, not much had been said about environmental issues. "The environment was not even an issue in 2000," recalled an environmental adviser to the Bush campaign. "The interest level was zippo." Al Gore had of course talked about Kyoto but hardly focused on it. Gore's opponent, George W. Bush, had, as Texas governor during the 1990s, made himself the "governor of wind," initiating the ambitious development of renewable wind power in Texas. During the 2000 campaign, he had declared that "global warming needs to be taken seriously" and had called for mandatory reductions on "four main pollutants," of which carbon dioxide was the fourth.

Though not plentiful, such comments suggested that Bush, if elected, would want to address climate.

That was certainly the way it was interpreted after the election by two of his top appointments. In a memo to Bush in March 2001, Christine Todd Whitman, the new administrator of the Environmental Protection Agency and the former governor of New Jersey, said, "I would strongly recommend that you continue to recognize that global warming is a real, and serious issue." She added, "We need to appear engaged and shift the discussion from the focus on the 'K' word"—as in Kyoto—"to action." The new treasury secretary, Paul O'Neill, in his former position as CEO of Alcoa, had featured climate change as an issue in his annual letter to shareholders. At a cabinet meeting at the beginning of the administration, he went around the room, handing out a pamphlet he had written on dealing with climate change. Some of those in the room thought it was a little puzzling to see the secretary of treasury distributing a corporate pamphlet warning of the risks from global warming at a cabinet meeting. But O'Neill was an industrialist accustomed to speaking what was on his mind. O'Neill wrote a memo to Bush saying that the administration should get organized to prepare options "for amending or replacing the Kyoto treaty . . . with a plan that is grounded in science."

But that was not to be. On March 13, 2001, EPA administrator Christy Whitman went to see President Bush to urge his support for Kyoto. The reception was not what she had expected. The president said he had already made up his mind about Kyoto and then went on to tell her about the contents of a letter he was sending to a group of senators. In it, Bush declared that while the administration "takes the issue of climate change very seriously," it was resolutely opposed to the Kyoto Protocol, and would not go forward with it, because it did not include 80 percent of the world's population and was an "unfair and ineffective means of addressing global climate change concerns." He also cited concerns that caps on carbon dioxide would promote a shift from coal to natural gas in electricity generation at a time when California's energy shortage looked like a precursor to a national natural gas shortage.[3]

It appeared to many as though the Bush administration had shut down on climate change. What seemed to be the attitude of the Bush administration was captured at a ceremony at the State Department in May 2001, when Secretary of State Colin Powell swore in Paula Dobriansky as Undersecretary of State.

Going through her list of responsibilities, he came to climate change. At that point, he paused, and with a small, almost embarrassed grin, laughed, and jokingly put his hand over his mouth as if he had said something slightly naughty.

TWENTY-ONE QUESTIONS

Climate change faded in the face of the recession of 2001. Then it lost whatever salience it had with the body politic with the September 11, 2001, attacks on the World Trade Center and the Pentagon. Yet for a narrow but key segment of the public, it was not only a highly charged but also highly symbolic issue. For some, the bitterness over the outcome of the 2000 election made the Kyoto Protocol—so vividly identified with Al Gore—a litmus issue. The rejection of Kyoto by the Bush administration energized the environmental community and many of the administration's opponents. It also stirred a storm of opposition and criticism in Europe. "I remember going to Europe in 2001, and people were screaming at us that the administration was going to ignore Kyoto," recalled Don Evans, commerce secretary at the time.

Yet things were hardly shut down. The United States was spending half of the world's total budget for climate change research, a sum that would rise under Bush. But the spending, inherited from the Clinton administration, had also been spread in a confusing mélange across thirteen different agencies. "All in all it was about five and a half billion dollars, and no one's talking to the other people," said Evans, who oversaw the main agency working on climate research. "One thing we could do was prioritize—what do we need to know and what information do we have to have to make reasonable policies."[4]

For this purpose, Evans turned to James Mahoney to take the position of Assistant Secretary of Commerce for Oceans and Atmosphere and Deputy Administrator of the National Oceanic and Atmospheric Administration. Mahoney was a climate modeler by academic training. He had a Ph.D. in fluid mechanics from MIT, where a mentor had been Jule Charney, one of the fathers of climate modeling. Mahoney had served as president of the American Meteorological Society and editor of the *Journal of Applied Meteorology*.

Mahoney's job was to organize and focus about $2 billion of the government's research effort into a coordinated Climate Change Science Program.

"If you are going to coordinate thousands of scientists, you need a framework, key questions," he later explained. The research was organized around 21 questions. They covered a wide range of topics, such as: What happens to climate in the lower atmosphere? What is the history of climate variability in the Arctic and high latitudes? The strengths and weaknesses of climate models? The risks of "abrupt climate change"? And, getting closer to policy, how to incorporate "scientific uncertainty in decision-making"? As part of the review, the administration commissioned two studies by the National Academy of Sciences on climate change. In parallel, a second, $3 billion Climate Science Technology Program was brought together under the Department of Energy.

But there were big battles within the administration from the beginning, for as Mahoney put it, there were deep divisions and thus two faces to the climate program. One was "that we have to get the science right. But the other not-spoken message was 'how many years will it take to get the science right?' The implication was that we didn't have to do anything in the meantime.

"The Holy Grail of the science effort was a unified systems model of the earth," Mahoney said. "But turn the corner and there is a whole rich tradition of decision making under uncertainty—decision analysis and policy development," he said. "But there was very strong opposition to going there. There were major scientific questions, and a lot were being answered, but there will always be a lot of uncertainty with a whole earth system. You never know."[5]

THE FOOT-AND-MOUTH PANIC

With the United States focusing on what the Bush administration generally described as the need for more research, the international advocacy on climate change would pass into the hands of Britain and, specifically, the government of Prime Minister Tony Blair. But it might not have happened in quite the way it did were it not for the outbreak of an epidemic among farm animals in Britain.

In October 2000 David King, a Cambridge University chemistry professor, became science adviser to Blair. In his new job, King was initially focused on mapping out a low-carbon future. But in February 2001 the biggest outbreak of foot-and-mouth disease in world history erupted in Britain. As the country's herds of cows and sheep were culled and burned, the nation was transfixed by the plumes of smoke that rose up from their pyres and spread across the countryside. All other science-oriented issues became secondary. Over the next six months, King emerged as the government's point man for analyzing and managing the epidemic. The skill with which King directed the campaign brought him close to the prime minister and built a deep personal credibility. His participation, said Blair, was a "masterstroke" and of "priceless value."[6]

That prominence took on particular significance when in 2002 King delivered the Zuckerman Lecture, the most influential platform for discussing science policy in Britain. King's topic was "The Science of Climate Change: Adapt, Mitigate or Ignore?" He clearly did not intend it to be ignored. He warned that in a business-as-usual case, rising levels of carbon would result in, among other things, "the eventual loss of global ice and hence also of our coastal cities."

The lecture crystallized policy in the UK. After a cabinet meeting, Blair said to King, "David, what you have to do is get around the world, and persuade the rest of the world. Britain cannot solve this issue by itself." Before he wound up his time as science adviser in 2007, King would have given at least 500 lectures on climate change in Britain and around the world.

In January 2004, in advance of a speech in the United States, King published an article in *Science* attacking the Bush administration for inaction on climate change. He also wrote that "climate change is the most serious problem that we are facing—more serious even than the threat of terrorism."

This greatly irritated the Bush administration, which, in partnership with Britain, had launched the Iraq war just ten months earlier as the linchpin of the war on terror. The American ire was conveyed to Blair, who himself was quite put out, since he had staked his foreign policy on his relationship with George W. Bush. Moreover, week after week, during the prime minister's weekly Question Time in Parliament, Blair was tormented by a Liberal Democrat MP who kept asking him whether he agreed or disagreed with his science adviser that climate change was a bigger threat than terrorism.

Despite the controversy, King pushed on. The threats of rising ocean and river levels from climate change would inevitably preoccupy an island nation. King's office produced a report predicting that global warming might cause the dire floods that were expected only every hundred years—the so-called hundred-year floods—to now occur every three years. Soon Britain was spending half a billion pounds a year to shore up its coastal and inland defenses against floods and rising sea levels.[7]

Blair decided to make the issue of climate change the centerpiece on the agenda at the G8 meeting in Gleneagles. And it was not just the G8 leaders who were involved, for the meeting had been expanded to include the leaders of China, India, Brazil, South Africa, and Mexico.

Despite the disruption of the London bombings, the Gleneagles Summit firmly established climate change in the framework of world affairs. It was now a major issue for world leaders, along with the other big issues on the international agenda.

MAKING A MARKET IN CARBON

The Kyoto Protocol had to be ratified by 55 countries to go into effect. In February 2005, just a few months before the Gleneagles Summit, Russia, with the signature of Vladimir Putin, became the fifty-fifth country to sign on to Kyoto. It was not that Putin was convinced of the risks from climate change; in fact, he had mused that a few degrees greater warmth would be welcomed in Siberia and would help Russian agriculture—and reduce the need for fur hats and fur coats. The Russian signature was seen as a trade in Russia's quest for membership in the World Trade Organization. Additionally, Russia, with its reduced industrial output, could earn substantial revenues from selling "hot air" in the form of carbon credits.[8]

So Kyoto was now in business. But how to establish the actual markets for clearing trades in carbon? As it turned out, work on a prototype had been going on for over a decade.

Among those at the 1992 Rio Earth Summit conference was Richard Sandor, an economist, consultant, and part-time professor at Northwestern University. Sandor had a knack for creating markets where there were none before. In the 1970s he had been one of the inventors of the business of trading interest-rate futures, initially an alien concept but now measured in trillions of dollars a day. Some of his ideas did not work out so well; he had once written an article on the futures market in plywood. In 1992 Sandor had gone to Rio to talk about creating financial markets and on how to set up such markets for emissions.

After listening in on other sessions, he was "persuaded by the gambler's ruin," he said. "No matter how good the odds, never make a bet that could ruin you if it goes against you. Why take the risks on climate change if it could end in catastrophe?"

As he sat one afternoon on the famed beach at Ipanema, he reflected on how to design a carbon market. "This can be done," he said to himself.

Sandor came back to Chicago determined to set up an exchange to trade carbons, what eventually became known as the Chicago Climate Exchange. The first decade was not easy. The venture almost ran out of money. Finally, he found an outside investor, a Jesuit group from Northern California, which put in $1.5 million—just enough to see them through an IPO. Sandor managed to get 14 participants, mostly companies, but also the city of Chicago, to set up an exchange to trade carbon among themselves. The experience demonstrated that a contract for trading carbon could be written—and that it would work. But this was really a practice, a prototype. The United States was not going to sign on to Kyoto. In a quest for a more sustainable business, Sandor created a sister venture called the European Climate Exchange. That made sense. For the action on climate change was now in Europe.

Indeed, nowhere else was Kyoto, and its principles, so strongly supported as within the European Union. At Kyoto, the EU may have vehemently opposed trading; but thereafter, ironically, the EU fervently embraced the concept of trading. In 2003 Brussels formally established a cap-and-trade system called the European Union's Emissions Trading Scheme, otherwise known as the ETS. In its first phase, meant to run between 2005 and 2007, prices for carbon moved with unexpected and astonishing volatility. But during those years the machinery was put into place—the exchanges, brokers, trading desks in companies, and a financial infrastructure—to support the ETS, centered in London. Meanwhile, Sandor's Climate Exchange, the parent company, set up another joint venture in China, this with the Chinese National Petroleum Corporation, in the city of Tianjin, ninety miles from Beijing.

In 2008 the European Union adopted a very ambitious goal: to reduce by 2020 global greenhouse emissions, primarily CO_2, by 20 percent, from 1990 levels. Trying to achieve that would ensure that carbon trading would become a very big business. How big? "Carbon markets are potentially the biggest commodity markets in the world, bigger than crude oil," said Sandor. It was simple arithmetic. "After all," he added, "carbon is released not only by oil, but also by coal and natural gas and other processes."[9]

In 2010 Sandor's Chicago Exchange PLC, the parent of both the Chicago and European exchanges, was bought by the Intercontinental Exchange, the major global rival to the NYMEX for oil trading. The price was $600 million.

THE POWER OF IMAGES

In the meantime, despite appearances, the political terrain in the United States was already changing. In 2003 Republican senator John McCain and Democratic senator Joseph Lieberman had introduced a cap-and-trade bill in the U.S. Senate. It garnered a surprising 43 votes. Yet it did not have wide resonance and still seemed somewhat abstract.

What was not abstract was what happened in 2005, when the devastating hurricanes Katrina and Rita struck the Gulf Coast of the United States. The media image of the hurricanes' devastation—the desperate people in the Superdome and the refugees fleeing the submerged city—all this provided a grim metaphor for the storms and the ensuing destruction and chaos that could become more common with an increasingly more aggrieved climate.

The next year a different kind of media education took place. It was a rather unlikely movie, *An Inconvenient Truth*—a documentary, more precisely; the setting to film of a slide show that former vice president Al Gore had been showing around since 1990. He had been reluctant to turn his slide show into a film, but the producers were persuasive. The film played to packed theaters, and it had an extraordinary impact on the public dialogue. Some of the footage was overpowering, most notably the melting glaciers and the giant sheets of ice falling into the sea—the very kind of imagery that would have riveted John Tyndall and the other nineteenth-century pioneers of climate change research. *An Inconvenient Truth* became a global cinematic event. The British government had it distributed to secondary schools. And in February 2007 it won an Academy Award—a mighty achievement for a film that started as a slide show.

That same month, February 2007, the IPCC began releasing its fourth assessment. Its most sophisticated calculations had been done on the supercomputers of the U.S. Department of Energy, the only computers in the world capable of handling the problems. This new IPCC report was the starkest yet. One of its consistent themes was how much the science had advanced since the third report, in 2001. It was "very likely"—over 90 percent probability—that humanity was responsible for climate change.

But all this was only a prelude to the looming threat—a doubling of CO_2 would likely lead to a temperature increase of 2°C to 4.5°C (3.6°F to 8.1°F). But "values substantially higher than 4.5°C cannot be excluded," it ominously added. The report itself, if not its summary for policymakers, did identify a number of "key uncertainties"; for instance, "Large uncertainties remain about how clouds might respond to global climate change." But overall, the confidence and definitiveness were much greater than in the previous reports.

Moreover, an even more alarming specter threaded throughout the report—that of "abrupt climate change." The consequences, said the IPCC, could be devastating—no time to adapt, no time to mitigate. The images of thousands and thousands desperately fleeing from Hurricane Katrina could be replicated on a much larger scale in Bangladesh or coastal China—or Florida.[10]

The IPCC report had been preceded by a few months by another influential study, *The Stern Review of the Economics of Climate Change.* A couple of weeks after the Gleneagles Summit, the British government had asked economist Nicholas Stern to lead a team tackling climate change. The resulting thousand-page report argued that the costs of inaction on climate change would be enormous and that the costs of mitigating climate change would not be prohibitive by comparison. Stern declared, in economists' language, that climate change was the biggest "market failure" of all time.

The impact of the Stern report was far greater than anyone had anticipated. With a certain degree of understatement, the *Economist* summed up the reaction thusly: "Rarely has a report with so many charts and equations in it caused such a stir."[11]

The report set off a furious row among economists. Critics argued that Stern's discount rate—the value of a dollar in the year 2100 as opposed to in 2006—was much too low, and that it was this choice of discount rates that drove the policy conclusions. Other economists who privately disagreed with the analysis felt peer pressure not to go public with any criticism. Stern's rejoinder was that the critics did not understand that this was not a normal economic situation and that they failed "to appreciate the magnitude of the risks that the science was identifying." But whatever the argument among professional economists, the report's impact on policymakers, politicians, and the environmental activists, particularly in Europe, was very significant. It filled what turned out to have been a vacuum. For it built out an economic structure to complement the expanding edifice of the IPCC studies.[12]

GREEN CREDENTIALS

Companies were starting to demonstrate green credentials. For some that meant focusing on climate change, and figuring out how to adapt their businesses to a coming age of carbon regulation. John Houghton, formerly head of the UK Meteorological Office, was the coleader of the scientific assessment of the first three IPCC reports. In the mid-1990s he started a dialogue with BP. At one point he went to the BP office in London to meet with a group of senior executives. One way or the other, the same question kept coming up. "Could you prove it?" No, Houghton said. It could never be conclusive. But the evidence was overwhelmingly convincing.

One who was certainly convinced was John Browne, then the chief executive of BP. Much influenced by the IPCC reports, Browne decided that BP should take climate change seriously and act on it. In May 1997 he delivered a speech at Stanford University. "It would be unwise and potentially dangerous to ignore the mounting concern," he said. "We must now focus on what can and should be done, not because we can be certain climate change is happening, but because the possibility can't be ignored."[13]

This was the first time that a major figure in the oil industry—and possibly in the whole energy industry—had so publicly and personally taken that position. Others in the industry said that "BP is going green," which seemed to be borne out when the company expanded its logo to mean not only British Petroleum but also the slightly mysterious "Beyond Petroleum." The speech triggered initiatives within the company: reducing CO_2 emissions, developing alternative energy, establishing an internal BP CO_2 trading system. It also set off an argument with Royal Dutch Shell, which, pointing to its most recent annual report, said that it had been the first international oil company to identify climate change as a risk.

Meanwhile, most of the American energy companies remained aligned with the Global Climate Coalition, which continued to challenge the IPCC scientific view and to lobby against climate change initiatives. The coalition argued that "radical reductions in the United States could cause "severe unemployment, decreased competitiveness of U.S. goods, and other grave economic disruptions."

By the beginning of the new century, climate change was gaining attention on corporate agendas. General Electric's businesses run the gamut from gas turbines to nuclear reactors and locomotives to lightbulbs. It had also recently acquired a wind-turbine business. In 2004 GE's CEO, Jeff Immelt, convened, at the company's educational campus at Croton-on-Hudson, New York, a meeting of electric-utility executives and environmentalists to discuss major energy issues. Over the preceding year Immelt had been hearing a recurrent refrain from his own senior executives: that customers were talking more about wanting "clean" or environmentally enhancing solutions. He called the Croton meeting to try to sort out thematically what was happening, and what was changing.

The conference was organized as pretty much of a free-for-all teach-in. Immelt himself sat in one of the upper rows in the tiered classroom, jumping into the discussion. While the "environment" was its overall topic, climate clearly moved to the front of the discussions in the lecture hall. That day helped set the stage for GE's launch of a wide-ranging "eco-imagination" campaign and accelerated a refocusing of much of GE's business around these themes.

The corporate lineup was definitely changing. A large number of companies made a focus on the environment part of their corporate strategies. In 2007 nine leading industrial companies and utilities, including both BP and General Electric, along with four environmental organizations, converged to form the U.S. Climate Action Partnership—USCAP—to promote climate legislation. By 2009 the membership had grown to twenty-five companies. Meanwhile, the Global Climate Coalition, which had opposed any climate regulation, dissolved itself in the face of defections and dissension among its members.[14]

THE NOBEL PRIZE

Nothing else so truly epitomized the accession of climate change as a global issue than what happened in Oslo City Hall on December 10, 2007. On that day, a committee of the Norwegian parliament awarded the Nobel Peace Prize jointly to Al Gore and to the Intergovernmental Panel on Climate Change, the IPCC.

"We must begin by making the common rescue of the global environment the central organizing principle of the world community," said Gore in his acceptance speech. The world, he declared, faced "a planetary emergency."[15]

Gore, of course, was eminently recognizable in the photographs from Oslo. But who was that other person, standing next to him, somewhat incongruous in a Nehru jacket, with his long black hair merging into a black-and-white beard who described himself as "the bearded face of the IPCC"?

This was Rajendra Pachauri, an Indian economist and engineer who was accepting the award on behalf of the IPCC because he was its chairman. Pachauri coordinated a complex international network that involved the work of 450 lead authors, 2,500 scientific expert reviewers, and 800 contributing authors, representing altogether 113 countries—along with the representatives of those governments, all of whom had to acquiesce at least to the overall summary.

Pachauri's role also clearly indicated a growing engagement by the developing countries. After an undergraduate degree from the Indian Railways Institute of Mechanical & Electrical Engineering, Pachauri had begun his career as an engineer, designing diesel locomotives. But then, earning Ph.D.s in both engineering and economics at North Carolina State University, he had switched to energy economics. In 1982 he had become director of TERI, one of India's leading research institutions.

Not long after, he had begun to investigate climate change. In 1988 he was elected head of the International Association for Energy Economics. "The greenhouse effect is no longer an abstract theory," he had declared in his 1988 inaugural address. "We can postpone a deeper interest in this subject only at the risk of a continuing insularity and myopia." His remarks were greeted with incomprehension—and worse. "People thought I had lost my mind," Pachauri later said. In the years that followed, he became one of the most prominent advisers on environmental issues to the Indian government and increasingly active internationally on climate change.

The Nobel Prize, he said, "has certainly raised the alarm." It also greatly broadened the recognition of the IPCC and solidified its international role. Shortly after receiving the award, he told an energy conference in Houston that the IPCC's warning is "not based on theories and suppositions. It's based on analysis of actual data which is now so extensive and overwhelming that it leaves no room for doubt."[16]

MASSACHUSETTS VERSUS EPA: THE SUPREME COURT STEPS IN

The political landscape in the United States was changing as well. A number of states adopted state-wide emission targets. Various groups of states established regional cap-and-trade programs. To top off such initiatives, California adopted Assembly Bill 32, which required the state to return to 1990 emission levels by 2020.

In 2006 the Democrats captured control of both the Senate and the House of Representatives, for the first time in twelve years. With this came a Democratic leadership determined to pass climate change legislation. Nancy Pelosi, the new Speaker of the House and the first woman Speaker ever, announced that climate change was her "flagship issue." And to drive home the point she established a special new Select Committee on Energy Independence and Global Warming.[17]

Just a few months later, in the spring of 2007, the legal terrain also changed, and decisively so.

Years earlier, in 1998, Carol Browner, Bill Clinton's Environmental Protection administrator (and later Barak Obama's White House czar for energy and the environment), was jousting in a congressional hearing with Tom Delay, the then Republican Majority Leader. You are trying to regulate greenhouse gases, Delay insisted. No, Browner replied, we're only studying them. This went on for a while, until Delay challenged her flat out. "Do you think that the Clean Air Act allows you to regulate the emissions of carbon dioxide?" he asked Browner.

"I think we are granted broad authority under the Clean Air Act to," Browner responded.

"Would you get me a legal opinion on that?" DeLay retorted.

"Certainly," said Browner.

Later Browner recalled: "And so I went back, and the lawyers took a look and they wrote a memo saying 'we probably do.' "

In 2001 the incoming Bush administration resolutely did not agree. It concluded that this interpretation could not possibly be right. Greenhouse gases were never even mentioned in the original Clean Air Act. Carbon dioxide "is not a 'pollutant' under the Clean Air Act," Bush had said with some finality in 2001. And that seemed to be the end of it.[18]

But as it turned out that was not the end. For that memo was then taken up and put to use by various plaintiffs, including the state of Massachusetts, which sued the EPA for not regulating greenhouse gases—specifically CO_2—coming out of automobile tailpipes. Though the court of appeals ruled against them, the U.S. Supreme Court agreed to hear the case.

The oral arguments took place at the end of November 2006. The assistant attorney general of Massachusetts argued that the EPA's failure to regulate CO_2 emissions from new autos would contribute to global warming, which would cause sea levels to rise, submerging the state's coastal regions. The Bush administration countered that the Clean Air Act did not give the EPA authority to regulate CO_2 and that Massachusetts had no legal standing to be bringing the case because climate change was a global issue and Massachusetts was only one of 50 states.

The exchanges with the justices were spirited. The Massachusetts assistant attorney general tartly told Justice Antonin Scalia that the eminent justice had confused the stratosphere with the troposphere. Justice Stephen Breyer said that while one could not prove that regulating tailpipe emissions by themselves would be sufficient, combine that with other measures, "each of which has an impact, and lo and behold, Cape Cod is saved."

On April 2, 2007, the Supreme Court delivered its opinion in what has been called "the most important environmental ruling of all times." In a split 5–4 decision, the Court declared that Massachusetts had standing to bring the suit because of the costly storms and the loss of coastal shore that would result from climate change and that the "risk of harm" to Massachusetts was "both actual and imminent."

And in the heart of its opinion, the Court said that CO_2—even though it was produced not only by burning hydrocarbons but by breathing animals—was indeed a pollutant that "may reasonably be anticipated to endanger public health and welfare." And just to be sure not to leave any doubt as to how it felt, the majority added that the EPA's current stance of nonregulation was "arbitrary" and "capricious" and "not in accordance with the law."[19]

The consequences were enormous; for it meant that if the U.S. Congress did not legislate regulation of carbon, the EPA had the authority—and requirement—to wield its regulatory machinery to achieve the same end by making an "endangerment finding." Two out of three of the branches of the federal government were now determined that the government should move quickly to control CO_2.

The Bush administration had to figure out how to respond to the Court's decision. Around this time, the answers were starting to emerge from the 21 different research programs from James Mahoney's Climate Change Science Program. "The preponderance of results indicated a real problem," recalled Samuel Bodman, then Secretary of Energy. "But dealing with it is a bear." Meanwhile, internationally, British prime minister Tony Blair and German chancellor Angela Merkel were continuing to press Bush on the issue.

For all these reasons, climate change was clearly back on the political agenda of the administration. In his 2007 State of the Union Address, Bush declared that the United States should "confront the serious challenge of global climate change." But it certainly would not go the cumbersome route of Kyoto and the United Nations. Instead it sought to go down a different path; it brought together a new grouping of seventeen nations that produced the bulk of the world's man-induced CO_2 emissions. The Bush administration came up with a name for this new group: the Major Emitters.

"However, when we sent out the invitations," said then Undersecretary of State Paula Dobriansky, "the message came back from the other countries that they didn't really like being called 'emitters.' "[20]

It was a reasonable call. After all, "emitters" was, Understandably, considered somewhat negative by those convened. The Major Emitters became the "Major Economies," which came together at the State Department in September 2007. These were the countries that, collectively, represented 80 percent of world GDP, consumed 80 percent of world energy, and produced 80 percent of the world's CO_2. And, therefore, they were the countries that could have the most impact. Moreover, with countries like China, India, and Brazil included, this new grouping provided a way to manage the contentious divide between developed and developing countries.

This was quite a different position from that at the beginning of the Bush administration seven years earlier. But the administration's time was running out.

26

IN SEARCH OF CONSENSUS

The weekend after Barak Obama's inauguration, phone and e-mail invitations were hurriedly circulated around Washington for his first speech at the White House that following Monday. Those lining up early that chilly morning at the East Gate of the White House, many of them still in the post-inauguration euphoria, thought they were going to an energy event. Yet proceedings in the East Room were really about climate change, the issue that would now define energy policy.

"The days of Washington dragging its heels are over," said the new president. He added that "America will not be held hostage" to "a warming planet." The president's priority was clear. And with the president aligned, the House leadership set out to make cap and trade the law of the land.[1]

The enterprise was in the hands of Henry Waxman, chairman of the Energy and Commerce Committee, and Edward Markey, chairman of the Select Committee on Energy Independence and Global Warming that Speaker Nancy Pelosi had set up two years earlier.

For Markey, also chairman of the Subcommittee on Energy, climate change had been on his agenda for most of his 33 years in Congress. On the wall of his office, catty-cornered from a large solar panel, hangs a framed front page of the now-defunct *Washington Star* newspaper from November 7, 1976. The right-hand lead is headlined "Natural Gas Supply Cut Is Projected." The left-hand lead is an interview with a professor from the University of Pennsylvania, warning of coming world crises—one of them being a "world change in climate"—perhaps caused by manmade CO_2, but perhaps, the professor allowed, by the natural workings of the glacial cycle.

And in the middle of the page is a photograph of a mop-haired 30-year-old Markey making his first trip ever in his life to Washington, D.C., to take up his seat as a newly elected congressman. Under the headline "A New Mr. Smith Comes to Washington," the story compared him with the "idealistic hayseed" freshman played by Jimmy Stewart, who shakes up the nation's capital in Frank Capra's 1939 classic film. "I've got a few things I want to say to this body," the Jimmy Stewart character says at the climax of the movie. This new "Mr. Smith," Ed Markey, had, over his 33 years in Congress, quite a few things to say as well on a number of different subjects—on everything from financial derivates to nuclear power safety and proliferation to telecommunications deregulation. But energy preoccupied him. At the 1980 Democratic convention, he had called, in a prime-time speech, for the United States to be "a truly solar society" by 2030. He had written the first national efficiency standards for appliances in 1987 and had continued to work for his "solar/wind future"—albeit not with anywhere near the impact he wanted. Now in 2009, with Barak Obama in the White House and the Democrats in power in Congress, he was, in concert with Waxman, in a position to push cap and trade, and thus reshape the fundamental economics of a substantial part of the entire U.S. economy.

CARROTS AND STICKS

But how did one go about reshaping so much of the economy—energy, auto and transportation, buildings, manufacturing, and all the rest? Waxman and Markey had a two-part strategy. The first part was to bring people on board with the inducements that cap and trade had in terms of handing out allowances for free to specific industries, rather than auctioning off the allowances. That was the carrot. And those carrots were measured in billions of dollars of value.

The second part of the strategy was the stick—the Environmental Protection Agency. As Markey put it, "It was legislation versus regulation." If there was no legislation, then the EPA, under the Supreme Court ruling, would go back in time to the pre–Clean Air Act era and begin to regulate carbon dioxide, command-and-control style. And unlike the Congress, the EPA would not be able to offer any inducements or mitigation. No carrots at all. Only the stick. Or, as the CEO of one electric utility described it, "the bayonet."

And so they built a considerable coalition. The Clean Air Act Amendments of 1990 and the resulting SO_2 reductions constituted the model for what they were trying to do on cap and trade. That was the narrative for what they said would happen with cap and trade—faster achievement, lower costs, bigger impact. But Markey had another narrative in mind as well: the way in which the digital revolution was transforming the American economy. He had championed legislation that had helped to make the digital revolution possible by promoting competition in the cable and phone industries. "We took down all the barriers," he said. "Everybody could do everything. We created a broadband digital revolution." When Bill Clinton signed the Telecommunications Act in 1996, not a single home in America had broadband. And now it's all been transformed. "The job of government is to create conditions for paranoia-inducing Darwinian market competition, and you will have capitalism that is flourishing, and then government can get out of the way," Markey continued. "If we incentivize, we will unleash innovation."[2]

And if the broadband revolution had created what he estimates to be almost a trillion dollars of new value, then, by his calculation, a similar ruthless Darwinian climate-change-stimulated competition in the much larger energy sector should stimulate whole new industries and create several trillion dollars of new value.

As the bill made its way through committee and markup, it grew from six hundred pages to over fourteen hundred pages. Its goal was to reduce carbon dioxide emissions by an extraordinary 83 percent by 2050 from 2005 levels, which meant that, going forward, energy investment in the United States would have one central focus—carbon reduction. Unless some form of carbon sequestration could be economically developed on a large scale, oil, natural gas, and coal would mostly disappear. And all the things that depend on these fuels would change. This was not the energy system that Americans—and the American economy—now knew. The carrot was very large: As a result of all the horse trading and pragmatism, over $2.3 trillion of allowances would be awarded to various sectors in the economy. Moreover, the bill would largely withdraw the authority of the EPA to regulate carbon dioxide under the Clean Air Act Amendments of 1990. The bayonet would be withdrawn.

Some argued that it could not happen that fast, that the energy sector is more complex, more capital-intensive, more long-term, and thus much slower to change than telecommunications. They doubted that the technologies would be there in scale—and in time. Carbon capture and sequestration had a long way to go before it was proved. Many wondered about the complexity and scale of cap and trade, and thought a tax was so much simpler and more direct. Others said that, in any event, cap and trade was simply a tax disguised in a complex garb, and they took to calling it "cap and tax." They argued that vast disruptions would ensue. And that the costs were being woefully underestimated. The Midwest, with its coal-fired electricity, would be hit hard. So would agriculture.

Here the Congress was going to create a vast new market in carbon—bigger than any other market—in the very year that the Great Recession had bred such deep distrust of markets. Carbon would become an "asset," a "currency." Cap and trade, critics warned, would not be a boon to the environment but to Wall Street and all the others who would figure out how to trade—and game—the carbon markets, at a time when the repute of financial markets and financial institutions had fallen markedly.

On the evening of June 26, 2009, the bill passed, 219–212. Forty-four Democrats voted no, eight Republicans voted yes. Still, there would be no new legislation without the U.S. Senate. Nothing would happen unless a bill got through the Senate.

CHINA: "WIN-WIN"

In 2007, by some measures, China's carbon dioxide emissions exceeded those of the United States. By 2030 its CO_2 output, if unchecked, could, some said, exceed that of the member countries of the entire Organisation for Economic Co-operation and Development (OECD) combined. China was also facing increasing international criticism over this increase.

Beijing replied to this in three ways. First, it noted that its energy use and CO_2 emissions—when measured on a per capita basis—are only a small fraction of that of the United States and Europe. Second, it emphasized that China is still a relatively poor nation making a transition that Europe and North America—and Japan—made decades ago, and it should not be denied the same opportunities and standards of living as the developed countries. In so doing, it distinguished between the "luxury emissions" of the developed world and the "survival emissions" of developing countries. Third, it pointed out that one reason that its energy use—and emissions—are going up so rapidly is that Europe and North America have in effect outsourced a significant part of their energy-intensive production to China, as their own economies continue to shift to services and consumption. As the former chairman of China's National Development and Reform Commission expressed it, "A considerable amount of the increase in China's energy consumption is a 'substitute' for energy consumption in other countries and regions."[3]

Internationally, there would be no international climate change regime without China. But China's own position was evolving. In 2006 the government released a National Assessment of Climate Change. It was the culmination of a four-year study, involving twenty government departments, that very much reflected the framework of the IPCC. It also represented a process of education for the country's top leadership, which was briefed on the risks.

The day before World Environment Day, 2007, the government released its first "national strategy on climate change," which warned that "the trend of climate change in China will further intensify in the future." It reinforced the emphasis on conservation and energy efficiency, as well as on changing the fuel balance, protecting the ecosystem, restoring forests to 20 percent of total land, and developing world-class energy technologies. New natural gas resources and imported LNG would replace open coal burning in Beijing, Shanghai, and other cities with natural gas networks.

China's stance toward climate change shifted for both scientific and practical reasons. Droughts and floods highlighted the risks of climate change. Chinese scientists and the country's leadership have become preoccupied with what global warming would do in the west, to the "water tower of Asia"—the glaciers and snow mass in the Himalayas and the Tibetan plateau that feed China's great rivers—and the impact on the country's water supplies. In the east, rising sea levels would threaten the low-lying coastal regions that generate so much of the nation's GDP and economic growth. Droughts, desertification, extreme weather, and instability in agricultural production—all these would be possible consequences.

But the domestic usefulness of the issue should not be underestimated. For climate change provides a very useful envelope for addressing the critical and all-too-immediate local and regional air and water pollution that affect so much of the country and that are an increasingly grave domestic political issue. It also becomes a very convenient tool for driving greater efficiency in the economy and, specifically, in energy use.

There are other practical aspects. China is deeply embedded in the global mesh of international trade and finance; indeed, it is that engagement that has been the foundation of its growth since 1979. Climate change is an issue that China encounters, it seems, at almost every economic conference. Threats of trade restriction from its major trading partners in retaliation for not reducing emissions cause considerable alarm. Vocal constituencies in the United States and other countries call for the imposition of border taxes or border adjustments on countries, preeminently China, that do not sign on to a specified international climate regime. Some of this sentiment is protectionism in disguise—somewhat off target since the bulk of China's exports are low carbon in their intensity. But the Chinese leadership hardly wants to be the country accused of standing in the way of global cooperation on climate, let alone bear the potential costs. China concluded that its embrace of climate change policies would be a key element in its overall relations with the United States and Europe, and in mitigating political and trade tensions. President Hu Jintao summed it up in the autumn of 2009, with a resounding call at the United Nations for a "win-win" approach on climate change between developed and developing countries.[4]

INDIA: "THE CLIMATE AGNOSTIC"

India and China are often lumped together as though they share the same perspective. They do share a deep common interest in the Himalayan water tower that supplies their rivers. But India's overall position is quite different. While it uses coal to produce most of its electricity and also burns a great deal of biomass, India produces only about 5 percent of the world's CO_2 compared with China's

23 percent, which makes sense as India's economy is only about one quarter the size of China's. India's traditional approach to international climate change negotiations was to reiterate even more strongly that it is a developing country with much poverty and that it and its economic growth should not be penalized for emissions that industrial countries have been putting into the atmosphere for over two centuries. Moreover, in the words of Environment minister Jairam Ramesh, it was the "kiss of death" for an Indian politician to be seen agreeing with the United States or the European Union on climate change policy.

But as India becomes more integrated into the world economy, the perspective is changing. When Prime Minister Manmohan Singh appointed Ramesh to the Environment ministry, he instructed him, "India has not caused the problem of global warming. But try and make sure that India is part of the solution."

Thereafter the tone changed. "The most vulnerable country in the world to climate change is India," Ramesh said in a parliamentary debate. "We are dependent on monsoons . . . they are the lifeline of our country . . . We are depressed when the monsoons fail and happy when the monsoons are good . . . The uncertainty caused by climate change on the monsoons is of first and overriding priority for India."

The second point of vulnerability was the state of the glaciers. "What happens to the Himalayan glaciers will determine the water security of our country." But he went on to say that it was a matter of great uncertainty as to whether the glaciers are receding as a result of global warming or from "the natural process of cyclical change."

For an environment minister, Ramesh offered an unusual perspective: "The climate world is divided into three," he said. "The climate atheists, the climate agnostics, and the climate evangelicals. I'm a climate agnostic." To Ramesh, in his words, the "bread and butter" local issues of water and air pollution loom "more important and more urgent than climate change."[5]

After World War II, the powers that were trying to negotiate a postwar settlement—the United States, Britain, France, and the Soviet Union—became known as the Big Four. There is a new Big Four when it comes to negotiating an international climate regime—the United States, the European Union, China, and India, with Brazil as an increasingly important interlocutor. That became clear at the Copenhagen climate conference in December 2009.

"HOPENHAGEN"

The Copenhagen conference—otherwise known as COP 15—was intended to be the successor to Kyoto, and expectations for a new global agreement were high. Billions of dollars had been spent on climate research in the 12 years since Kyoto. There was now much greater consensus among governments and in the media on climate change. The United States had a new president who was building his energy policy around climate change; the U.S. House of Representatives had passed a cap-and-trade bill; the European Union was completely on board; and China and India, along with other developing countries, had moved along toward internalizing climate as an issue. No wonder that in the run-up to the Copenhagen conference, it had been nicknamed "Hopenhagen."

A total of 113 heads of state or government attended Copenhagen, and just ferrying around all the delegations turned into a logistical nightmare when there were tens of thousands NGO activists who were also trying to get around town. The conference hall itself could accommodate 15,000 people; 40,000 tried to sign up; and eventually 27,000 got accredited.

Despite all the preparation, there was no agreement in advance on the basic issues. It was clear that the United States could not agree at Copenhagen to a legally binding treaty since the Senate had not yet passed climate legislation. It was no less clear that the major developing nations would not agree to be treated the same as the developed countries. But if they were not, then it would be much more difficult to get the U.S. Senate to agree to a climate bill.

The combination of the number of delegations, the overall size of the crowd, and the sharp disagreement on the basic questions—all these led to a chaotic conference that was, as the days went by, becoming more and more frustrating for all involved. It was possible that there would be no agreement at all.

Barack Obama flew in early one morning toward the end of the conference, with the intention of leaving later in the day. Shortly after his arrival, he was told by Secretary of State Hillary Clinton, "Copenhagen was the worst meeting I've been to since eighth-grade student council."

After sitting in a confusing meeting with a group of leaders, Obama turned to his own staff and said he wanted, urgently, to see Premier Wen Jiabao of China. Unfortunately, he was told, the premier was on his way to the airport.

But then, no: word came back that Wen was still somewhere in the conference center. Obama and his aides started off at a fast pace to find him. Time was short, for Obama himself was scheduled to leave in a couple of hours, hoping to beat a blizzard that was bearing down on Washington.

At the end of a long corridor, Obama came upon a surprised security guard outside the conference room that was the office of the Chinese delegation. Despite the guard's panicked efforts, Obama brushed right passed him and burst into the room. Not only was Wen there but, to Obama's surprise, he found that so were the other members of what was now known as the BASIC group—President Luiz Inácio Lula da Silva of Brazil, President Jacob Zuma of South Africa, and Prime Minister Manmohan Singh of India—huddling to find a common position. For their part, they were no less taken aback by the sudden, unexpected appearance of the president of the United States. But they were hardly going to turn Obama away. He took a seat next to Lula and across from Wen. Wen, overcoming his surprise, passed over to Obama the draft they were working on. The president read it quickly and said it was good. But, he said, he had a "couple of points" to add.

Thereupon followed a drafting session with Obama more or less in the role of scribe. At one point the chief Chinese climate negotiator wanted to strenuously disagree with Obama, but Wen instructed that this interjection not be translated.

Finally, after much give-and-take, some of it heated, they came to an agreement. There would be no treaty and no legally binding targets. Instead developed and developing countries would adopt parallel nonbinding pledges to reduce their emissions. That would be accompanied by a parallel understanding that the "mitigation actions" undertaken by developing countries be "subject to international measurement, reporting and verification." The agreement also crystallized the prime objective of preventing temperatures from rising more than 2°C (3.6°F). The BASIC leaders tossed it to Obama to secure approval from European leaders, Chancellor Angela Merkel of Germany, President Nicolas Sarkozy of France, and Prime Minister Gordon Brown of the UK. The Europeans did so, but only reluctantly, as they wanted something much stronger. Obama then took off, beating the snowstorm back to Washington. Back in Copenhagen the strom still raged. The agreement was "rated" by the entire conference, though with no great enthusiasm and indeed with some irritation on the part of many of the delegations. It was not adopted.

The Copenhagen Agreement was not a ringing international compact but rather more of a holding action; the outcome drove home that the United Nations was too big and unwieldy to hammer out a climate action plan. The answer has now to be sought in what has been described as the "variable geometry" of international relations—bringing together those who share interests in a specific problem and have the ability to act on it. In this case, the "variable geometry" would involve a much smaller number of nations but those who represented the largest part of GDP would—and the largest share of emissions. That meant going back to the Major Economies; that is, back to what had originally been called the Major Emitters when George W. Bush had begun to assemble them in Washington, D.C., in 2007 in search of a more workable alternative to the United Nations for negotiating on climate change.[6]

Copenhagen was not the only disappointment for those who had hoped for major progress on a climate regime. A second disappointment was what didn't happen in the U.S. Congress. In contrast to the House of Representatives, it was much more difficult to get a climate bill through the U.S. Senate. Part of the reason was mathematics. A quarter of the total votes in the House of Representatives for Waxman-Markey had come from the more liberal states of New York and California, owing to their populations. But in the Senate, those two states had only two votes each. Moreover, in the Senate, rules meant that passage would require 60 out of 100 votes. Senators from coal-burning states and energy-producing states were not enthusiastic. Given the deep recession and the slow recovery, many senators were concerned about the economic impact of a climate bill. And given the meltdown on Wall Street, some were hardly enthusiastic about creating a vast new financial market in trading carbon. After the Republicans won the House of Representatives in 2010, a climate legislation became even less likely.

"THE HEALTH OF THE HIMALYAS"

More or less concurrent with Copenhagen was a chipping away of the credibility of the IPCC itself. In what became known as climategate, somebody hacked into the e-mails of the Climatic Research Unit at the University of East Anglia in England, which was one of the main research centers supporting climate research and the work of the IPCC. To many climate scientists and activists, the e-mails were being taken out of context and grossly misconstrued. But the way others read the e-mails was that some prominent scientists had turned to "tricks" to come out with the results they had wanted and went out of their way to denigrate and isolate those who might disagree. The particular trick that aroused the most controversy was the blending of data sets that did not agree with one another in a way that more clearly produced an upward graph of rising temperatures. Several subsequent investigations, while offering some criticisms, generally exonerated the researchers involved, saying that they did not deviate from "accepted practices within the academic community" in their handling of the data.[7]

However, a great controversy had been stirred, and the fourth IPCC report, issued in 2007, became a target. The father of the IPCC, Bert Bolin, had laid down the principles of great care and not going beyond the evidence. But the "indispensable man" in coordinating climate research had passed away in 2007. And now it was noted that in the newest IPCC report, the summary for policymakers was much more categoric than the overall report. Moreover, some errors became evident. The source for the report on melting in the Andes was a hiking magazine based on interviews with mountain guides. But the biggest controversy erupted over the dramatic assertion that the Himalayan glaciers, including the one that fed the river Ganges, were melting so fast that they could disappear by 2035 "if not sooner." It was among the starkest predictions in the entire fourth IPCC report.

India's Environment Ministry commissioned a study by Indian scientists that challenged the assertion. It said that while there was melting among many glaciers, one glacier was actually advancing. "Himalayan glaciers are retreating," said the scientist who wrote the report. "But it is nothing out of the ordinary." In what was considered one of the striking comments, the minister's report said that the Gangotri glacier, which feeds the river Ganges, receded fastest in 1977 and today is "practically at a standstill."

The Indian government's study stirred a storm of protest. Rajendra Pachauri, the chairman of the IPCC, dismissed it as "arrogant" and "voodoo science" of the ilk associated with "climate change deniers and school boy science." But then it emerged that the 2035 date was itself not the result of careful research but rather the product of a phone interview with an Indian scientist in 1999 by an English science magazine. The assertion had then been picked up in a report by an environmental group and then was "copied straight into the IPCC impacts assessment."

"The health of the Himalayan glaciers is a cause for concern," said Jairam Ramesh, India's Environment minister. "But the alarmist concern of the IPCC that these would disappear by 2035 is not based on an iota of scientific evidence." And the scientist who had given the 1999 telephone interview now said that his comments were "speculative" and that he had not given a date. He also said that he was not an "astrologer." He did, however, emphasize that the glaciers were in a "pathetic state."

In due course, the IPCC made a correction and apologized.

Subsequent reports bolstered the IPCC in its overall scope and mission, but some damage had been done to the process, and the result was to suggest a wider band of uncertainty than had been thought prior to autumn of 2009. And, at least for a time, public-opinion polls globally showed declining interest in global warming and reduced urgency and support for climate change policies.[8]

"EXTREME WEATHER"

Like the weather itself, public opinion on climate is variable. But in the summer of 2010, the traditional distinction broke down in the minds of policymakers and the public between the short-term, highly variable fluctuations of weather and the long-term trends of climate, which unfold over decades and centuries and millennia. Some political leaders began to shift from the risks of climate change to the dangers of climate disruption. Extreme weather struck simultaneously around the world. Drought hit parts of the United States, torrential rains poured down on others, while the East Coast sweltered from unusually hot days that tried both tempers and the limits of the power system. Over Pakistan and western China, huge storms loosed massive flooding of a kind no one could remember. In Pakistan alone, this displaced 20 million people, all grasping for food, water, and shelter. Day after day large parts of Russia were burned by the sun. Temperatures were consistently over 100 degrees, and fires raged, creating storms of smoke that choked Moscow and turned Red Square, even from a few hundred feet away, into a ghostly silhouette. A third of Russia's wheat crop was ruined, leading to a ban on grain exports and sending wheat prices spiking on the world market. "Our country has not experienced such a heat wave in the last 50 or 100 years," said President Dmitry Medvedev. "Unfortunately, what is happening now . . . is evidence of the global climate change, because we have never in our history faced such weather conditions in the past. This means that we need to change the way we work, change the methods that we used in the past."

"Everyone is talking about climate change now," he added.

That included Prime Minister Vladimir Putin, who had previously said that climate change would mean that Russians would need to buy fewer fur coats. On a visit to a scientific research station in northern Russia in August 2010, he said, "The climate is changing. This year we have come to understand this when we faced events that resulted in fires." Nonetheless, Putin said he was still waiting for an answer to the question of whether climate change is the result of human activity or of "the Earth living its own life and breathing."[9]

MAKING THE PLEDGE AT CANCÚN

After the disappointment and, to some, the debacle at Copenhagen, the next major meeting a year later at Cancún seemed to get climate regulations back on track. Yet what was described as the relative success of Cancún was a function, at least in part, of much lower expectations.

Some 193 nations signed on to the accord at Cancún, which offered—after a year of torturous negotiation—what the United States, the European Union, and the BASIC countries had agreed to in Copenhagen. A central element of the agreement was the adoption of specific pledges by countries for emissions reductions. The agreement also established a process of monitoring and verification. Under this system, mitigation efforts undertaken with domestic resources would be monitored domestically, while those taken with the help of international resources would be monitored internationally. To boost transparency of domestic actions, a system of international consultations and analysis every two years was agreed to. As part of it, information will be shared in an international forum that includes technical experts. Reconfirmation of the long-held goal of keeping temperature rises to within two degrees Celsius—though one regarded by many as overly optimistic—was another key element of the Cancún agreement.

But Cancún left much still up in the air. Most significantly, Cancún kicked down the road the question of whether to renew for another term the Kyoto Protocol, due to expire in 2012. While the sharp differentiation between the responsibilities of developed and developing countries set out in Kyoto was increasingly seen by developed countries as untenable, developing countries still generally hold fast to this concept. One possibility was to replace the Kyoto agreement with an agreement that was acceptable to both developed and developing countries. This would likely mean an agreement that does distinguish between the two groups in terms of historical emissions, but that acknowledges the reality that the largest emitters now come from both sets of countries, and that there should be a more equitable sharing of burdens. In short, much has to be done to shape a new framework.

IT'S UP TO THE EPA

For its part, the United States pledged under the Cancún agreement to reduce emissions by 17 percent by 2020 compared with 2005 levels. The likelihood of near-term legislative action ended when cap-and-trade stalled in the Senate. With the legislative avenue blocked, the Obama administration shifted from the carrot to the stick—or as some said, the bayonet—and pushed ahead with regulatory action. That meant that the action was with EPA. In 2009 the agency, bolstered by the 2007 *Massachusetts v. EPA* decision, issued an "endangerment" finding that greenhouse gas emissions threatened the public health and welfare, and thus falls under the agency's purview to regulate under the Clean Air Act.

After making this endangerment finding, the EPA embarked on a years-long process of issuing standards emissions. The standards would cover both mobile sources of emissions—autos and trucks—and stationary sources of emissions—power plants and refineries. For mobile emissions, these standards took the form of higher fuel-economy standards, and these standards were issued jointly in 2010 by the EPA and the Department of Transportation.

In January 2011 the EPA took an initial step to regulate emissions from stationary sources of CO_2 when it issued permitting requirements. Under these requirements, each time a power plant or refinery is built, or a major renovation to an existing one is made, the owners of the facility must use the best available technology to control emissions. In the next leg of regulation, the EPA was planning to roll out performance standards for power plants and refineries over a number of years. Such standards are potentially much further reaching than the permitting requirements. While not yet settled on, they are likely to require that such facilities limit the amount of carbon dioxide they emit as a measure of the amount of electricity they produce.

But the EPA's subsequent move to regulate emissions from stationary sources provoked a backlash. Resistance to the EPA's regulation of greenhouse gas turned into resistance to the EPA itself in Congress and in the states. Opponents to regulation of CO_2 emissions argued that the EPA was overstepping its bounds, that the rules would harm the economy, and that the agency was going against the will of the people. The Republican majority talked of denying the EPA money to run its CO_2 programs. More than a dozen states went on to court to challenge the EPA greenhouse gas regulations. Texas governor Rick Perry went so far as to refuse to comply with EPA CO_2 orders. "Our dispute with the EPA in particular," said Perry, "illustrates how Washington's command-and-control environmental bureaucracy is destroying federalism and individuals' ability to make their own economic decisions."

On Capitol Hill, Representative Fred Upton, Chairman of the House Energy and Commerce Committee, said, "We will not allow the administration to regulate what they have been unable to legislate." He recommended to EPA administrator Lisa Jackson that, since she would be called so often to testify, she should get her own parking place on Capitol Hill.

The outcome of the battle over CO_2 regulation will depend on the makeup of the U.S. Congress over the next half decade and the disposition of the counts. It will also be a critical factor in determining whether there is an international regime for climate change and what shape it takes.[10]

THE LEGACY OF THE GLACIERS

The issue of climate change has been transformed almost unrecognizably since it was first broached by a few scientists and naturalists in earlier centuries. They were curious about where the glaciers had come from and what happened to them. Had there once been a much colder world, an ice age? And could the glaciers return and crush human civilization? And they asked about the atmosphere. Why was it not boiling hot during the day and freezing cold at night? Did the atmosphere serve as a blanket to separate earth from outer space—and thus provide a lease for life to flourish on this planet?

John Tyndall, as he trekked through the Alps in the mid-nineteenth century, was overcome by the "savage magnificence" of the glaciers he saw, and the vast, overwhelming masses of ice filled him with "wonder" that turned into "awe." It was that awe that led him to learn how the atmosphere retained some of the heat from the sun and then stabilized temperatures.

It was in 1958 that Charles Keeling first climbed up to the meteorological observatory on Mauna Loa in Hawaii to begin his lonely research. That year his readings indicated that the atmosphere was about 315 parts per million composed of CO_2. Half a century later, the atmosphere's level of carbon concentration is at about 387 parts per million. Climate change has become the research subject for thousands and thousands of scientists and the recipient of many tens of billions of research dollars. It has also become the focus of policy and politicians. The general objective is to keep concentrations from going over 450 parts per million in order to avoid the worst effects of climate change. As it is, some warn that rising carbon levels may already hold out the risk of an "iceless world" and that humanity is heading toward an iceless age.

Others say that the bounds of uncertainty are wider, the knowledge of how climate works is less developed, and that fluctuations have always characterized the weather. Some also believe that the target of 450 parts per million is unrealistic, as is the possibility for a speedy transition from fossil fuels, which together currently provide about 80 percent of the world's total energy.

Yet whatever the debates over science and policy, the elevation of climate change and the effort to regulate CO_2 are transforming energy policy and markets, stimulating investment, and starting a torrent of technological research. All this is giving a great new boost to the drive for greater energy efficiency, low-carbon or even carbon-free energy—and for the rebirth of renewables.

PART FIVE

...

New Energies

27

REBIRTH OF RENEWABLES

It was the first and only press conference ever held on top of the White House. On June 20, 1979, President Carter, along with his wife, Rosalynn, tramped up onto the roof, entourage and press in tow, in order to dedicate a solar hot water–heater system. "No one can ever embargo the sun," Carter declared. He put the system's cost at $28,000 but quickly added that the investment would pay for itself in seven to ten years, given high energy prices. "A generation from now," he said, this solar heater could be "a small part of one of the greatest and most exciting adventures ever undertaken by the American people . . . harnessing the power of the sun." Or, he said, it could be "a curiosity, a museum piece."

And there, standing on the White House roof, he set a grand goal: that the United States would get 20 percent of its energy from solar by the year 2000. He promised to spend $1 billion over the next year to get the initiative going.[1]

By the time of Carter's 1979 press conference, the idea that the world needed to transition to what was then called solar energy (and later renewables) had already become a clear trend in energy thinking. The Arab oil embargo earlier that decade, and the then unfolding Iranian Revolution, brought not only disruption in petroleum supplies but also grave fears about the future of world oil. All that combined with a sharpening environmental consciousness to make solar and renewable energy the natural solution. It was clean and it provided stability. And it would never run out. In Washington, incentives were wheeled into place to jump-start a renewable industry. Research dollars started to flow. Technologists, big companies, small companies, entrepreneurs, activists, and enthusiasts were all getting into the solar game.

But nothing like 20 percent happened. Instead what followed this initial burst of enthusiasm were decades of disappointment, disillusionment, bankruptcies, and sheer stagnation. It was only in the late 1990s that the industry, by then established in Japan and Germany with strong government support, began to revive in the United States, and only around 2004–5 that it started to gain real scale. Even as late as 2010, renewables accounted for only 8 percent of the U.S. energy supply—about the same share it had in 1980. Remove two items—hydropower (which has been constant for many years) and biomass (primarily ethanol)—and renewables in 2009 constituted less than 1.5 percent of the total U.S. energy supply. Much the same holds true around the world.

Yet today renewables are reenergized to become a growing part of energy supply, embraced as a key solution to the triple challenges of energy supply, security, and climate change. China's President Hu Jintao said that China must "seize preemptive opportunities in the new round of the global energy revolution." The European Union has gone further, with a 20 percent renewable goal for 2020. "I want us to be the greenest government ever," declared British prime minister David Cameron, promising "the most dramatic change in our energy policy since the advent of nuclear energy." In 2011, German Chancellor Angela Merkel set a new target for Germany—to move renewables' share of electricity from 17 percent in 2011 to 35 percent by 2020.

More than any other president before him, Barack Obama has invested his administration in remaking the energy system and driving it toward a renewable foundation. Indeed, he has raised the stakes in renewable energy to the level of national destiny. "The nation that leads the world in creating new energy sources," he said, "will be the nation that leads the twenty-first-century global economy." Both companies and investors now see renewables as a large and growing part of the huge global energy market.[2]

Yet reaching the higher targets will be no easy achievement given the scale and complexity of the energy system that supplies the world's economy. Today it is still at the level of policy and politics where the future of renewables is primarily determined. They are, mostly, not competitive with conventional energy, although costs have come down substantially over the years. A global price on carbon, whether in the form of a carbon tax or a cap-and-trade system, would further augment the competitive economics of renewables against conventional energy.

Still, renewables are set, after a twenty-five-year hiatus, to become a significant and growing part of the energy mix. It is almost as though a time chasm has closed, compressing the decades and conjoining the late 1970s with the second decade of the twenty-first century.

WHAT DOES "RENEWABLES" MEAN?

The idea of "renewables"—an inexhaustible and environmentally friendly energy source—is deeply appealing. But what are renewables? Parse the word "renewables," and one finds a series of disparate technologies:

1. *Wind*—the fastest growing, which powers technologically sophisticated machines, clustered in "farms," that generate electricity.
2. *Direct sunlight*—captured either by photovoltaic cells (PVs) or by mirrors or other technologies that concentrate the light and transform its energy into electric current.
3. *Biofuels*—ethanol, biodiesel, and advanced biofuels (made of algae, cellulose, or other feedstock), all of which substitute for gasoline, diesel, or potentially jet fuel.
4. *Biomass*—wood or other plant material palletized or otherwise treated and burned in a power plant; also wood or dung that people in developing countries burn for heating and cooking.
5. *Geothermal*—either hot water or hot steam that is pumped from beneath the ground to the surface to drive an electricity-producing turbine.
6. *Hydropower*—falling or pressurized water that drives turbines; dams are increasingly criticized on environmental grounds and thus are hard to build in many countries.
7. *Passive solar*—now also known as green buildings, which take advantage of the natural habitat to reduce energy consumption, and which often overlaps with energy efficiency.

There are other technologies, including tidal power. Garbage-to-energy might count as well, if one thinks of garbage as a renewable resource. But those listed above are where most of the effort is focused. What unifies these varied technologies as renewables? They are not based upon finite resources; they are widely distributed; they do not add, at least in theory, to carbon, and thus have a much more restricted carbon footprint.

One other technology needs to be added to the list: batteries for electric cars. These are not strictly renewable in the same way but fall within the same framework. They could count as renewable if the electricity by which they are recharged happens to be the product of wind or sunlight.

EARTH DAY

In 1951 the Paley Commission, appointed by President Harry Truman to investigate raw material shortages during the Korean War, warned against future oil shortfalls and dependence on Middle Eastern oil. "Direct utilization of solar energy," it declared, "is perhaps the most important contribution technology can make to the solution of the materials shortage." In 1955 President Eisenhower issued what has been described as "the first Presidential message on solar energy development," praising what he called "movement toward a fuller use of virtually unlimited energy of the sun." But not much at all happened for the next decade and a half.[3]

But then a single day, April 22, 1970—Earth Day—crystallized a new environmental consciousness in America and established its political potency.

Denis Hayes, a graduate student at Harvard's Kennedy School of Government, had taken a year off to create Earth Day. It turned into a coast-to-coast "happening" aimed at mobilizing the national consciousness. An estimated 20 million Americans joined in. They demonstrated and marched; they attended symposia and teach-ins; they protested outside polluting factories; they dragged tires and old appliances out of rivers; they buried autos to campaign against smog. The main targets of Earth Day were dirty air, polluted rivers and seas, toxic waste, chemical pesticides, strip mining, noise, oil spills, and overpopulation (a popular button, aimed at prospective parents, was "Stop at Two"). Congress shut down so that members could go back home. ("Everyone I've talked to," commented one congressman, "is making a speech somewhere.")

After Earth Day the nation simply thought differently than it had before. A few months later, the first Clean Air Act was passed, and President Richard Nixon established the Environmental Protection Agency (EPA). *Time* magazine crowned "The Environment" as the "Issue of the Year."

Yet what is striking in retrospect is what was omitted. While aspects of energy production and consumption (for example, smog) were among the targets, energy itself was not part of the agenda on that April day in 1970. "People spoke of oil, gas, coal, nuclear, and hydro," Denis Hayes recalled. "But there was no discussion of 'energy.' "[4]

Until the 1973 oil embargo, the energy business was just that—a business—or, actually, several different businesses. From 1973 on, energy became everybody's business.

"YOU WILL LEARN"

In Washington, energy suddenly went from being a nonissue to being the number one issue. The reasons were the 1973 oil embargo, skyrocketing gasoline prices, and long lines at the gasoline pump. Jacob Javits, a senator from New York, was one of the most prominent of what were called "liberal Republicans." In late 1973, shortly after the first oil embargo, Javits found himself sitting for 90 minutes in a gas line at a Washington, D.C., service station, fuming while he waited to fill his car. Once back on Capitol Hill, he stormed into his office, demanding to know who on his staff did energy. The answer was nobody. His frustration rising, the senator sent for a young staffer named Scott Sklar. Without even looking up, Javits informed Sklar that he would now be the senator's "energy" aide. Sklar protested, though politely, that he was hardly prepared—he had done his graduate degree on Chinese-Russian relations and worked on military issues. To underline the point, he walked over to the hall and flipped the light switch on and off. "I have no idea where this stuff comes from, Senator," said Sklar.

Javits laughed. "Son, you will learn."[5]

In 1974 the first of several solar energy bills went into law, and federal research appropriation jumped substantially. Not coincidentally, that was more or less when the modern renewables energy industry was really born, although at the time, "solar" was the umbrella term for most renewables. In 1975, the second year of the Gerald Ford presidency, some five thousand people came to Washington, D.C., to participate in a solar energy industry conference. "Solar power has suddenly become respectable," the *New York Times* declared that year, adding, "Only a few years ago, it was treated in the United States as a subject for eco-freaks."

By the mid-1970s the environmental movement was focusing in on energy; it was organizing against nuclear power, and it embraced solar as the answer. One of the major intellectual protagonists was Amory Lovins, an American who had studied physics at Oxford and worked for Friends of the Earth. Lovins wrote an influential article for *Foreign Affairs* on what he called the "soft path." He argued that energy efficiency and renewables would be more productive and much less costly than the "hard path" of oil, gas, coal, and nuclear. In 1977, the founder of Earth Day, Denis Hayes, published his own book, *Rays of Hope: The Transition to a Post-Petroleum World*. By coincidence, its publication date was perfectly timed: New York City was hit just then by a massive power blackout.[6]

But the most important single boost for renewable energy was the arrival in January 1977 of a new man in Washington.

THE "MORAL EQUIVALENT OF WAR"

Jimmy Carter worried about the dangers of dependency on foreign oil and the risks of another energy crisis. Indeed, he saw energy as the great challenge for his new administration, and he looked to coal and energy conservation as the two principal answers. Reinforcing his fears about energy insecurity, the CIA had just completed a study warning that world oil supplies would start to decline within a decade. Less than two weeks after his inauguration in 1977, Jimmy Carter sat down next to a fireplace for his first "fireside chat" from the White House, wearing what would become an iconic sweater—beige with buttons down the middle. He told the American people that "one of our most urgent projects is to develop a national energy policy." The speech was well received.

Two months later, speaking from the Oval Office, Carter warned the

American people that he would be holding "an unpleasant talk with you" about "the greatest challenge that our country will face during our lifetime" with "the exception of preventing war." The energy problem, he explained, will "get progressively worse through the rest of this century . . . We are now running out of oil and gas, we must prepare for a . . . change—to strict conservation and to a renewed use of coal" along with "permanent renewable energy sources like solar power." This "difficult effort," he concluded, was nothing less than the "moral equivalent of war"—forever memorialized by its initials: MEOW.

Whatever the specifics about supply-and-demand, Carter laid out the long-term energy challenge for the United States and the world community. The United States, he made clear, was now, fatefully, tied into a world market.

"I gave the energy message on television and think it came out all right," Carter wrote in his diary. But the speech was not well received. Its brittle tone and pessimism, its emphasis on sacrifice and moral failing, and its expectation of permanent scarcity—all these left a very mixed legacy. Many decades later a senior energy adviser walking through the Old Executive Office Building, next to the White House, observed, "These halls are still haunted by Jimmy Carter's sweater."[7]

Carter put James Schlesinger, formerly director of central intelligence and secretary of defense under Nixon and Ford, in charge of a 90-day crash program to develop a national energy plan. Schlesinger, a master of the complexities of bureaucracy, combined 50 government agencies concerned with energy into a single new organization, the Department of Energy.

Support for solar continued to build, and the Carter administration moved with it. As Schlesinger summarized it, "Solar has captured the public imagination." It was in these years that the Carter administration and Congress laid down the baseboards for today's renewables industry. They did so with tax incentives, grants, regulations, a solar bank, and R&D funding. The administration also established a new national research laboratory devoted to solar energy—the Solar Energy Research Institute—in Golden, Colorado, in the foothills of the Rockies. To head it, Energy Secretary Schlesinger chose, of all people, Denis Hayes, who had been criticizing the Carter administration for not moving fast enough on solar. But Schlesinger had a reasonable theory: if a nuclear proponent headed the nuclear program, and a coal proponent the coal program, then why not a renewables advocate to head the renewables program?[8]

"PURPA MACHINES"

One other policy would prove of critical importance. It is one that has already been cited: Section 210 of the Public Utility Regulatory Policies Act of 1978, otherwise known as PURPA. This may have been obscure at the time, but it turned out to be one of the main foundations on which the renewable industry was born.

Electric utilities were required to contract to buy the power output from what were called qualifying facilities, or QFs. These facilities were mostly meant to be cogeneration projects or small renewable facilities, such as a small dam or wind turbines. The rate that the utilities would pay the owner of the QF was set on a state-by-state basis by the slightly arcane notion of "avoided cost." That is, the utility would guarantee to buy the electric output at what was calculated to be the cost of theoretical oil supplies at some point in the future, plus the high costs of building theoretical new power plants—again against some point in the future. The costs that were avoided were often set at the peak of the market and sometimes, especially in the case of a place like California, on very generous terms. A guaranteed market with guaranteed high prices certainly provides the incentives to get people moving and help jump-start an industry. It worked here. In time, however, many of these facilities became known as "PURPA machines," as they would never have been economic had it not been for what turned out to be those excessively high estimates of the avoided costs.

In addition to creating a market, these PURPA machines had another consequence. By requiring utilities to purchase power from these units, which were not owned by the utilities, the government was taking the first step to erode the natural monopoly that had characterized the power business for more than seventy years. This would give a further boost to renewable energy.

There was in those years much debate over solar policy and the nature of incentives. Some argued that systems had been overdesigned and were too expensive and too complex. "We've built a Cadillac when people want a Volkswagen," complained one critic, George Tenet, the promotion manager of the Solar Energy Industries Association (and many years later the head of the CIA). Yet the momentum continued to build. By 1980 over a thousand companies belonged to the Solar Energy Industries Association. Some of them were start-ups but some were large companies, ranging from Grumman, Boeing, and Alcoa to General Motors and Exxon.[9]

GOOD-BYE SUNSHINE

That shining moment did not last. As quickly as it had emerged, the solar energy industry seemed to fold. The Iranian Revolution led to chaos in the oil market, rapid increases in prices, new gas lines, and a second oil shock, and the Carter administration started to come unwound. In July 1979, just a few weeks after announcing the bold solar goal atop the White House, President Carter delivered what became known as the "malaise speech," warning that the nation faced a crisis of confidence and a "crisis of the American spirit." His own response was to fire much of his cabinet and announce that he was now putting most of his energy chips, and billions of dollars, into synfuels—liquids made either from coal or oil shale—as the way out of the energy crisis.

Confidence was not restored. In November 1980 Ronald Reagan defeated Jimmy Carter for the presidency. Carter's renewables policies went down with him.

"I really believe that the effort I made over those four years was the maximum that a human being could do," Carter said many years later. "I'm not bragging on myself... I made eight or nine speeches on energy, until people got sick of it." His advisers, Carter added, said, "'Look, don't talk about energy anymore, Mr. President. You're hitting your head against a stone wall.'" The political cost in Carter's own estimation proved to be very high. "It sapped away a substantial portion of my domestic influence."

Reflecting on his experience, Carter summed it up this way: "It was like gnawing on a rock."[10]

"PRODUCTION, PRODUCTION, PRODUCTION"

If Jimmy Carter was the energy pessimist, prophesying about the great dangers ahead and warning Americans to change their ways, Ronald Reagan was the opposite, the sunny optimist, the beacon of self-confidence, the proponent of a new "morning in America."

The Reagan administration, which came into office in 1981, was determined to let market principles and price signals shape the energy marketplace. It was also responding to the distortions, bureaucratic nightmare, and endless litigation that resulted from the oil and natural gas price controls that Richard Nixon had hurriedly put in place a decade earlier. The Carter administration, paying a considerable political price, had already initiated price deregulation that would unfold on a schedule. But the Reagan administration moved swiftly to terminate the system altogether.

Although there was some continuity on the issue of price controls, renewable energy was an entirely different story. It had become a political divide—indeed, an ideological test—and, as such, represented a major discontinuity between the two administrations. The difference was made abundantly clear at the outset of the Reagan administration by Michael Halbouty, the head of the energy transition team and successful Texas wildcatter, as well as the developer of the sprawling Galleria shopping center and hotel complex in Houston. To a visitor at the Department of Energy, Halbouty announced that he could sum up the energy policy of the Reagan administration in just three words—"Production, production, and production"—as in domestic production of oil and natural gas.

Renewables had little place in that paradigm, and they quickly fell by the wayside. As far as the Reaganites were concerned, renewables were much too identified with the Carter administration and its travails and, even worse, with California Governor Jerry Brown. He was not only Reagan's successor as governor, but was seen as the very embodiment of the anti-Reagan liberal. Nicknamed "Governor Moonbeam," he had become the nation's most vigorous champion of power from wind and the sun.

There were also practical problems. These were new technologies; there was hype, and there were things to criticize. Many of the PURPA machines were never going to be economic—indeed, some were highly uneconomic, miniature white elephants. Some never functioned properly. Under Reagan, the funding and incentives for renewables were slashed or eliminated altogether. (So was the Carter administration's multibillion-dollar program in synthetic fuels.) Denis Hayes, the director of the Solar Energy Research Institute, was abruptly summoned to the Denver airport to meet the head of the organization that oversaw the institute. Hayes was told that his budget was being slashed and 40 percent of the staff would be fired immediately. Hayes resigned on the spot.[11]

But solar and other renewables would have in any event faced a much rockier road because of the marketplace. The sky-high interest rates and deep recession of the early 1980s, the consequences of the battle against inflation, would have slowed solar sales, mostly rooftop water heaters, in any event, as people stopped spending and real estate went into a bust.

Solar just lost its luster as a business. In 1981 Exxon sold its solar thermal business. "Our view of solar had changed," recalled A. L. Shrier, the president of the Exxon unit at the time. "It was going to take longer and would be harder to make it widespread. We didn't see the costs coming down or the technology developing fast enough." With Reagan elected, it was also clear that the heady Carter objective of 20 percent solar by the end of the century was gone. Most other large companies came to the same conclusion.[12]

In 1986, in the face of a large oversupply of oil on the world market, oil prices plummeted from a high of $34 a barrel to as little as $10 a barrel. That completely knocked the economic legs out from under the nascent solar industry. Price, it turned out, mattered enormously, and solar, as it was then, just could not compete. A solar architect who had thought he was "battling" OPEC found instead that his business was on the ropes without the support—and expectation—of relatively high energy prices.

THE EPITAPH?

In 1986, the same year as the price collapse, the solar hot water system on the roof of the White House sprung a leak. Instead of being repaired, the system was dismantled. Its designer would later explain that White House Chief of Staff Donald Regan "felt that the equipment was just a joke, and he had it taken down." The disassembled equipment was eventually shipped off as surplus government property to a college in Maine, which used it to produce hot water for its cafeteria. Eventually the system outlived its usefulness on campus. In 2006 it was dismantled again, and part of it was packed up and shipped to Atlanta where—as Carter had speculated at his rooftop press conference twenty-seven years earlier—it ended up a museum exhibit. And, where else, but in the Carter Presidential Library.

The "rays of hope" for solar power dimmed, at least in the United States, into a very faint glow. Or, as the *New York Times* put it, "The promise of renewable power has become a distant hope." Companies went bankrupt or disappeared altogether. Activists and entrepreneurs moved on into other fields. The

Economist described this once buoyant solar industry as "a commercial graveyard for ecologically minded dreamers." Within the nascent renewables industry, the decades of the 1980s and 1990s were to be recalled as the Valley of Death—companies struggled just to stay alive.

By this time, Scott Sklar, the former aide to Senator Javits, was head of the Solar Energy Industries Association, and the solar industry's chief lobbyist in Washington. He remembered all too well the mood in those times.

"We were really morose," he said.[13]

JAPAN: STAYING ALIVE

The end of the "solar dream" in the United States would pretty much have seemed to mean the end of the road for renewables. If the United States, the global leader in technology and R&D, had more or less given up on renewables, who else would stick with it? The answer was Japan.

In the early 1970s, Kotaro Ikeguchi was a rising young official in MITI, Japan's powerful Ministry of International Trade and Industry. Assigned to a department dealing with energy and mining, he became alarmed that Japan had become dangerously overreliant on Middle East oil and was oblivious to the risks. The consequences of a cutoff of supply could be disastrous.

But Ikeguchi could not stir much interest. For Japan's high-speed economic growth in the 1960s and early 1970s had been fueled by Middle Eastern oil, and there was little expectation that would change.

So as an outlet for his anxieties, Ikeguchi decided to write a novel that might wake up both officialdom and the public to Japan's vulnerability. His imaginary crisis was a Middle Eastern war that resulted in a cutoff of imports. His hero? By coincidence, it was a spry, incisive, but very pragmatic MITI bureaucrat with an understanding of Japan's precarious energy dependence. Since he was a working bureaucrat, he needed a pen name. He came up with "Taichi Sakaiya," which means, loosely, "Big Man on the Roof of the World."

But before he could find a publisher, reality intruded. His fiction became nonfiction. With the 1973 oil crisis, the Japanese suddenly feared that their whole edifice of economic growth might collapse. Ikeguchi decided it would

John Tyndall, great nineteenth-century scientist and avid mountaineer, answered the question "Why is the sky blue?" His obsession with Swiss glaciers led to his discovery of how the atmosphere retains heat—the "greenhouse effect."

Beginning in 1837, Louis Agassiz encamped on Swiss glaciers to research his theory that an ice age had once gripped Europe. His work proved that climate changes.

Guy Callendar, an iconoclastic steam engineer, was derided by professional meteorologists in 1938 when he argued that CO_2 in the atmosphere could affect global temperatures.

Roger Revelle (left and above leaning over the rail) sailed the seas in a modern age of discovery, mapping the ocean floor. He helped transform understanding of the atmosphere and charted the study of climate change, warning "human beings are now carrying out a large scale geophysical experiment."

Charles David Keeling, atop a volcano in Hawaii where he tracked carbon in the atmosphere. He wanted "in his belly, to measure carbon dioxide, to measure it every possible way." He produced the Keeling Curve, showing rising atmospheric levels of carbon.

In the 1890s, Svante Arrhenius calculated the impact of increased carbon on temperatures. His handwritten models were within the range of those generated by modern supercomputers. Celebrated as the father of climate modeling, he welcomed global warming as it would "bring forth much more abundant crops."

Dwight Eisenhower, Allied Supreme Commander in Europe, met with troops on the eve of the D-Day landing in Normandy, in June 1944. The "practically unpredictable" weather forced him to postpone D-Day. Later, as president, he promoted research to help better predict weather.

John von Neumann stands beside a computer he built in the early 1950s. One of the great geniuses of the twentieth century, he did revolutionary work in mathematics, physics, and economics. He was the father of the computer, which he used to model nuclear reactions and the weather.

It was no coincidence that Senator Tim Wirth's hearings on global warming fell on June 23, 1988, one of the hottest days of the year. Star witness James Hansen (right) "made a bombshell impression" said pioneering climate modeler Syukuro Manabe (left).

Margaret Thatcher was a food chemist before politics. As prime minister of Britain, she was the first major world leader to give a speech on climate change.

The "indispensable man," Swedish scientist Bert Bolin, established the framework for international collaboration on climate science.

Running for president in 1988, George H. W. Bush promised to counter the greenhouse effect with the "White House effect." But Bush (center) and his EPA administrator, William Reilly (right), were attacked as "Darth Vader" and "Arch Fiend" at the Rio Earth Summit in 1992.

"Academic scribbler in chief" Ronald Coase won the Nobel Prize in Economics and showed how markets could solve environmental problems.

At the Democratic National Convention in 1980, Congressman Ed Markey called for the United States to become a "truly solar society" by 2030.

In 2007, Al Gore and Rajendra Pachauri received the Nobel Peace Prize for their work on climate change. Pachauri accepted not for himself, but as what he called "the bearded face of the IPCC."

The U.S. Supreme Court hears arguments that led to its April 2007 ruling that carbon dioxide is a pollutant. Justice Stephen Breyer (far left) reasoned that controlling carbon could avert global warming and "lo and behold Cape Cod is safe."

The first president to push renewable energy, Jimmy Carter unveiled a solar water heater on the White House roof in June 1979. It would, he said, launch "one of the greatest and most exciting adventures undertaken by the American people," or end up as "a museum piece." It ended up a museum piece.

When gasoline ran short during the oil crises of the 1970s, fuming motorists lined up to get whatever they could.

In 1970, grad student Denis Hayes organized Earth Day, a coast-to-coast "happening" that mobilized environmental activism for a generation.

The Japanese novelist-bureaucrat Taichi Sakaiya wrote the novel *Yudan!* about an oil crisis that paralyzes Japan. After the oil shocks of the 1970s he set up a new bureaucracy to promote renewable energy.

Governor Jerry Brown, addressing a renewable energy hearing in 1979, kick-started wind power in California.

California's flawed deregulation created an electric power crisis in 2000, causing great pain for both the state and Governor Gray Davis. "It's a bummer to govern in bad times," Davis said after being driven from office.

Once again governor, 37 years after first elected, Jerry Brown signed legislation that mandated one third of California electricity come from renewable energy by 2020.

General Georges Doriot on the cover of *BusinessWeek* in 1949 (below) and teaching his famous course "Manufacuring" at the Harvard Business School (right). During World War II, he spearheaded innovation for the army. After the war, he created the industry of venture capital.

The name Sand Hill Road is synonymous with venture capital. The engine of Silicon Valley, venture capital only moved into energy in a big way in the mid-2000s.

Nancy Floyd was one of the early clean energy venture capitalists. Raising her first fund in the 1990s was "like pushing a boulder up the hill."

In ten weeks in 1905, while working in the Swiss patent office, Albert Einstein wrote five papers that changed the world. One unlocked the potential of nuclear energy. Another laid the basis for photovoltaics—solar-powered electricity.

"VAST POWER OF THE SUN IS TAPPED BY BATTERY USING SAND INGREDIENT"

—*New York Times*, April 26, 1954

In 1953 scientists at Bell Labs in New Jersey stumbled upon silicon's photovoltaic potential. In April 1954, they unveiled solar cells "capable of producing useful amounts of power."

Solar cells proved their worth in 1958 in the space race with the Soviet Union. When the batteries on America's Vanguard satellite ran out, its solar cells continued to generate power—and did so for years thereafter.

In 1998, longtime solar advocate Scott Sklar presented President Bill Clinton with a solar roof shingle.

A power tower uses fields of mirrors to concentrate sunlight to generate superheated steam and drive a turbine that produces electricity.

Yak herders in Mongolia welcome electricity from solar cells. Photovoltaics provide power to parts of the world not connected to the grid.

Zhengrong Shi returned to China from Australia to found Suntech Power, which became the world's largest photovoltaics manufacturer.

In 1887, the first large windmill for electrical generation was built in the backyard of a mansion on "millionaire's row" in Cleveland.

James Dehlsen at Victory Garden, his wind farm on Tehachapi Pass in Southern California, in 1986. Combining sturdy Danish hardware and California's incentives with his own grit, Dehlsen helped found the modern wind industry.

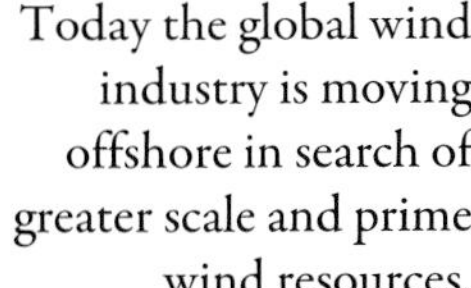

Today the global wind industry is moving offshore in search of greater scale and prime wind resources.

THE CHATTANOOGA TIMES: CHATTANOOGA, TENN., TUESI

BELIEVE IT OR NOT — By Riple

"WHILE WALKING IN A FOG"—

WILLIS H. CARRIER, Syracuse, N.Y.
HIT UPON THE IDEA OF MODERN AIR CONDITIONING BY PRODUCING FOG ARTIFICIALLY AND REMOVING ALL FREE MOISTURE.

Copr. 1939, King Features Syndicate, Inc., World rights reserved

Willis Carrier (left) hit upon the idea for air-conditioning on a foggy railway platform. By the 1930s, air-conditioning was being installed in movie theaters, department stores, the U.S. Congress—and even on a bus traveling between Baghdad and Damascus (below).

Lee Kuan Yew, the founder of modern Singapore, called air-conditioning "the most important invention of the twentieth century."

Kroon Hall, which opened in 2009, is the ultra-energy efficient building of Yale University's School of Forestry & Environmental Studies. It uses half the energy of a comparable building.

"Jieneng! Jianpai!"
"Save energy! Cut emissions!"
is now a national slogan across China.

Promoting alcohol fuels in 1977, Senator Birch Bayh poured a bottle of vodka into an antique car on the grounds of the Capitol.

In 1979, hard-pressed farmers descended on Washington in a "tractorcade" of several thousand tractors, demanding a national commitment to "gasohol"—now known as ethanol.

In 2011, ethanol made up almost 10 percent of U.S. gasoline supply by volume.

Sugarcane arrives at a refinery in Brazil, where it is processed into either ethanol or sugar. Ethanol now provides more auto fuel than gasoline in Brazil.

In the 1950s, smog repeatedly attacked Los Angeles, burning eyes, searing lungs, and making breathing a health hazard. In 1954, even members of the local Optimists Club donned gas masks in protest.

Arie Haagen-Smit, a chemist at the California Institute of Technology, solved the riddle of smog—it was largely due to auto emissions. He later chaired the California Air Resources Board, today the regulatory force behind the electric car.

In 1896, Thomas Edison (center) told the young Henry Ford (center left) that he should stick with gasoline and the internal combustion engine. Edison later changed his mind and spent years trying to develop a battery for electric vehicles.

At the beginning of the twentieth century electric cars were more numerous than gasoline-powered cars.

A century later, the electric car returned, fueled by environmental concerns and government policy. In 2010, Carlos Ghosn, CEO of both Nissan and Renault, plugged in an all-electric LEAF.

Toyota's first import to the United States in 1957, the Toyopet, was known for neither its style nor its quality. Over the years that changed. Its hybrid Prius set the standard for hip green technology—including for George Clooney (above right) at the 2006 Academy Awards.

President Barack Obama went for a spin in America's first plug-in hybrid, the Chevy Volt. He said that he had driven only "about 12 inches" because the Secret Service doesn't "let me drive much these days."

Tesla's electric Roadster proved that an electric car could also be a super car. But the company is betting on an all-electric luxury sedan—the Model S. It is still too early to see the road ahead for the electric car.

be inappropriate to publish his novel while the Japanese people were suffering through a real energy shortage, and he put it into a drawer.

Like his fictional hero, Ikeguchi was drafted to help formulate Japan's response to a real energy crisis. He was tapped to head Japan's Sunshine Project, the all-out national initiative to find a way to reduce Japan's dependence on Middle Eastern oil. He parceled out grants, hammered out industry research partnerships on a wide variety of technological ventures, and pushed through bureaucratic changes in government research institutes.[14]

THE "BUREAUCRAT-NOVELIST"

After the first oil crisis eased, Ikeguchi pulled his manuscript out of the drawer and in 1975 published it as *Yudan!* The title can be translated as "Cut Off!" or more evocatively, "Starvation in Winter!" It became a huge best-seller—over a million copies. Ikeguchi became famous. Thereafter he was much better known by his pen name Taichi Sakaiya. Highly prolific, he continued to publish books, ranging from an enormously influential treatise called *The Knowledge-Value Revolution,* which presaged today's information economy, to a four-volume historical novel on Genghis Khan. One Japanese publication described his "unique position" as "bureaucrat-novelist." When the second oil crisis hit in 1979, he was recruited to establish an entire new bureaucracy—the New Energy and Industrial Technology Development Organization, NEDO. With a dedicated budget and staff, NEDO continued to propel Japanese research on renewables, even when the rest of the world, including the United States it seemed, had lost interest.

"I thought that the age of oil was over," recalled Sakaiya. "It was the age of the knowledge revolution."[15]

After a flirtation with geothermal—partly abandoned because many of these resources were in environmentally sensitive areas—MITI turned to solar energy. Japan's experience with semiconductors was applicable to the manufacture of solar cells, as silicon was the main building block for both. It appeared to the Japanese government that there was some chance of making solar photovoltaics competitive as a source of primary energy if costs could be cut massively.

The solar market took off, fueled by large government subsidies that helped consumers purchase solar panels, along with the most expensive domestic electricity rates in the world, plummeting costs, efficiencies of scale, and increased competition. Led by such companies as Sharp, Kyocera, and Sanyo, Japan was by the beginning of this century the world's dominant solar manufacturer.

The original MITI vision that Taichi Sakaiya had articulated—of creating a new knowledge-based industry with strong export potential—seemed to be on the cusp of realization. But by then the renewable mandate was passing to another country.

FEEDING INTO GERMANY

It was drilled into the East German guards at the Berlin Wall that their prime mission, above all else, was to keep their fellow citizens from crossing from communist East Berlin into democratic West Berlin. Over the course of 1989 they had become increasingly jumpy. The Soviet grip on Eastern Europe was weakening, and the Berlin Wall was the front line in the East-West stand-off. Any East German attempting to breach the wall risked being shot dead on the spot by the border guards.

But on the night of November 9, 1989, after an ambiguous message by the East German leadership during a televised press conference, hundreds of thousands of East Berliners surged toward the wall, expecting it to come down, demanding that it be opened. Confused and uncertain, the guards hesitated, but finally did allow the wall to open, changing the course of history. People poured across the border. The division of Germany was over, as soon would be the Cold War itself.

Thereafter, the entire nation was to be preoccupied with reunification—the difficult incorporation of a ramshackle, dilapidated East Germany into a West Germany that had a vastly higher standard of living. Unification would end up a trillion-dollar-plus project.

As their part in reunification, the West German electric utilities focused on integrating East Germany's power system and modernizing its generation, which was based on a type of coal called lignite. While they were preoccupied with the East, a diverse coalition representing a new kind of movement was stealthily promoting a renewable energy law whose adoption was "almost accidental." And so, as it turned out, the opening of the Berlin Wall also opened a door that turned Germany into the world's leader in renewable energy for a decade, and as such, did much to lay the basis for today's global renewable energy industry.[16]

At the tip point of this environmental coalition was the Green Party. The Greens had emerged in the late 1970s to protest the environmental degradation that had come with Germany's economic miracle—polluted rivers, dirty air, and later, of special significance, ecological damage to forests. One thing that unified the entire movement was opposition to nuclear power. The movement also encompassed a New Left, anticapitalist, anti-American strain.

Indeed, what really mobilized the Green movement and helped turn it into a political party was, in the early 1980s, the proposed deployment of new nuclear weapons in Europe and then American missiles in Germany, which were intended to counterbalance new Soviet missiles. Ronald Reagan became the perfect foil, and vast anti-Reagan and anti-American demonstrations across Germany established the Greens as a real political force.

In April 1986 came the terrible nuclear accident at Chernobyl. The winds blew westerly from Soviet Ukraine, carrying radiation toward Central Europe, stirring alarm and even panic, and fueling antinuclear activism in Germany and other countries. This fueled lasting antinuclear opposition across the German political spectrum. Former German Chancellor Gerhard Schroeder recalled that the real turning point in coalescing opposition to nuclear power was in 1986. "For me, it was the catastrophe at Chernobyl," he said. "Mothers of young children kept them inside and did not send them to kindergarten. You need the support of society, and we had it." In the aftermath of the accident, the Greens gained great credibility, and, in 1990, for the first time, they won seats in the Bundestag.

Renewable energy was at the top of their agenda. But they were not alone. The environment leader for the Social Democrats was Hermann Scheer, a former researcher on the nuclear fuel cycle, and many years later to be celebrated by *Time* magazine as a "solar crusader" of the "Green Century." He opposed nuclear power on the grounds that the world should not depend on "an electricity source which cannot be allowed to make a major failure." His aim became "to introduce a new paradigm into the energy policy," beginning with a new type of energy law.

In the late 1980s a few cities began to experiment with what would become known as the feed-in law—or "feed-in tariff"—which ranks with PURPA for its central importance in creating the economic basis for the modern renewables industry. Germany's feed-in tariff gave the renewables industry its first commercial scale, bigger than in Japan. The feed-in tariffs set prices that subsidized renewable generators.

One of the pioneers in the town of Hamelburg was a high school physics teacher named Hans-Josef Fell, who had been convinced by the 1972 Club of Rome study *Limits to Growth* that the world would soon start running out of resources. "Most people thought the feed-in tariffs were much too expensive, and that a crash would happen," said Fell. "Our argument was that you needed a market. You needed private capital."

In 1990 Fell and the other Greens won election to the Bundestag. They collaborated with Scheer and his faction of the Social Democrats to broaden the feed-in tariffs. To do so, they formed an unlikely alliance with conservative members of the Bundestag, who represented small hydro generators in Bavaria that were frustrated that they could not sell their power into the grid. Scheer and Fell took advantage of the general preoccupation of unification with the East to maneuver their plans into law.

"The German utilities were totally concentrated on East Germany," said Scheer. "They could not imagine how our program could succeed, and they did not take it seriously. They started to organize, but they were too late."

This feed-in tariff was notable not only for what it did for the renewable industry. It was also the very last law of the West German parliament, before unification came into force on January 1, 1991. "And yes," said Scheer, "it was, indirectly, the result of the fall of the Berlin Wall."[17]

The Feed-In Law of 1991 borrowed from America, specifically PURPA. Its model required German utilities to buy electricity from renewable generators at higher fixed rates—or very much higher fixed rates—and then subsidize those rates by spreading them across the system so that the costs blended into the overall price. In this way, the otherwise uncompetitive renewable energy would be fed into the grid, and the renewable producers could make a profit.

By 1993 wind turbines were going up across Germany. In 1998 national elections took the Greens from opposition and sent them into a new ruling Red-Green coalition government with the Social Democrats. Renewables, at the insistence of the Greens, were a key part of the coalition agreement. "I have to say that the Green Party pushed the Social Democrats to see that this was a need," said Schroeder, who became chancellor in the new coalition. "It was a ten-year discussion."

In turn, the coalition pushed through the more aggressive Renewable Energy Law in 2000. The rates varied according to the technology. Photovoltaics received the most preferential feed-in rates, as much as seven times that of conventional electricity. Again, the costs were spread out across the entire system, with power companies passing on the extra costs to customers.

"With the law supporting the use of renewable energy," said Schroeder, "we forced the electricity companies to accept renewable energies. That was the main step."[18]

Two years later the governing coalition—reaching back to the origins of the Greens and the impact of Chernobyl—adopted a program to phase out all nuclear power, currently providing over a quarter of Germany's total electricity. This provided a further urgency to the development of renewables.

Wind, with over 90 percent of the new renewable capacity, has been by far the biggest winner from the feed-in laws. But Germany also became the world's biggest market for photovoltaics. The feed-in tariffs, said one solar executive, have "basically been a turbocharger." The development of high feed-in tariffs in other countries, notably Spain, has similarly stimulated very significant renewable development.[19]

Critics said that the subsidies in the feed-in tariffs were excessive and that as the volume of subsidized renewables increases, the costs would eventually lead to a consumer backlash. They also argued that paying different rates for different forms of renewable power, and even different subrates for different versions of the same technology, was economically irrational. Indeed, some backlash exactly along those lines was to occur.

Spain instituted particularly generous subsidies for renewables. Eventually, however, the program spun wildly out of control. Far more capacity was built than was targeted, costing the government much more than it ever intended. In the end, the financial burden was simply too much for an overburdened government. In 2008 Spain substantially reduced its feed-in tariffs, and did so again in 2010 amid fiscal austerity brought on by excessive government debt.

However, the feed-in laws did bring renewable power on much faster than some might have imagined. "No one forecast in 2000 what would happen," said Hans-Josef Fell. Subsidies of this magnitude and a guaranteed market provided very powerful incentives. In 2009 renewables' share of German electricity consumption reached 14 percent, exceeding its 2010 goal, and the government raised the renewable electricity target for the year 2020.

Germany's feed-in laws also proved popular outside Germany—indeed, wildly popular. This was particularly true in China, as German feed-in tariffs turned Germany into one of the biggest export markets for China's fast-growing photovoltaic industry.[20]

FROM "SOLAR" TO "RENEWABLES": RECOVERY AND REBRANDING

In the early 1990s life began to creep back into the American solar industry. Environmentalism was already firmly established as a political force. The twentieth anniversary of the first Earth Day was marked by Earth Day 1990. Organized with a budget 25 times bigger than the first one, it included events in 3,600 U.S. communities and 140 other countries and mobilized upward of 200 million people for a day of activities around the world. Of more immediate impact was the passage of the Clean Air Amendments of 1990, which gave a major boost to environmental concerns. The administration of George H. W. Bush also restored some of the tax incentives for renewable energy. Solar was once again part of the portfolio.

"Solar" also got rebranded. Around this time, "solar energy" gave way to "renewable energy" as the all-encompassing term. "It was a response to the visceral antisolar rhetoric of the Reagan years," said Scott Sklar, who at the time headed the Solar Energies Industry Association. "Specific industries tried to rename themselves so as not to have a target on their heads." The wind industry wanted its own identity. So did geothermal and ethanol. None of them fit very comfortably under the heading of "solar." But they were all comfortable under the umbrella of "renewables." The Bush administration not only put additional money into the Solar Energy Research Institute but also participated in the general rebranding, rechristening it the National Renewable Energy Laboratory, NREL.

The welcome was even warmer under the Clinton administration. On a hot summer day, Bill Clinton was slated to give a speech on the White House lawn announcing an environmental initiative. Among those invited was Scott Sklar in his capacity as head of the solar trade association. Since it was hot and Sklar is bald—and something of a solar showman—Sklar decided to wear an unusual hat, a cross between a pith helmet and a beanie, with a solar-powered fan. It was only with some difficulty that he was able to persuade the White House guards to let him in. When Clinton caught sight of this odd contraption on the head of one of the guests in the crowd, it caught his interest. The president, to the distress of his staff, made his way over and asked Sklar what it was. Sklar explained. The president said he should have been wearing one too. He pulled out a business card and gave it to Sklar, telling him that if he had any other things like that, he should make a point to drop by the White House.[21]

THE STATES AS LABORATORIES

One of the most important reasons for the rebirth of renewables took place at the state level, bearing out the famous adage of Supreme Court Justice Louis Brandeis that states can serve as the laboratories of democracy. Without a particular innovation introduced by individual states—what are called renewable portfolio standards—it is doubtful that renewable energy in the United States would have seen the growth it has experienced since the new century began.

These standards—nicknamed RPS—require that utilities' generation portfolios include a certain amount of renewables by a specified date. The first small steps were in Iowa and Minnesota. But it was not until the late 1990s and early years of this century that a number of states imposed renewable standards. In many of the states, these portfolios were largely driven by the growing concern about climate change.

That was not the case in Texas. In fact, climate change was deliberately not part of the discussion there at all. The main reasons were anxieties about the adequacy of electric power, a desire for diversity, and mounting worries about poor air quality in a number of cities. The RPS was signed into law by Texas Governor George W. Bush in 1999. The RPS provision turned out to be wildly successful in stimulating wind development, more so than anyone had imagined, setting off what became known as the Texas Wind Rush. The state had excellent wind resources, the requirements encouraged scale, and federal tax credits helped make wind economically competitive. (Indeed, so much wind was developed that, later, the costs of new transmission capacity would become a major issue.)

By 2011 29 states and Washington, D.C., had renewable portfolio standards in place, and most of the new capacity came on line in the RPS states. The results have been disproportionately weighted to wind. Some of the states have very significant targets: New York at 29 percent by 2015. Illinois, Oregon, and Minnesota all are aiming at 25 percent by 2025. In 2011 Jerry Brown, back as governor of California, signed an ambitious bill lifting the state's requirement from 20 percent, by 2020, to 33 percent. "You can't be afraid to be called a moonbeam, weird, deviant, interesting, unexpected," Governor Brown said as he signed the bill. As he put it, "I didn't get my name 'Governor Moonbeam' for nothing."

These standards will continue to be a major driver for renewable power in the United States. They also provide the mechanism for folding higher-cost renewable energy into the overall power portfolio, although some foresee a reaction to rate shock on the part of consumers owing to the higher costs of renewables.[22]

CLEANTECH

The rising prices for energy, beginning around 2003 and 2004, helped propel accelerated growth of, and support for, renewables in the United States. It also, at least for a time, narrowed the cost gap between renewable and conventional energy. Climate change became a much more explicit part of energy policy. As a result of all these factors, investment in renewables increased dramatically. As venture capital began investing in the sector, renewables gained yet another new name—"cleantech." And providing confirmation that renewables were moving into the mainstream, investment banks established "clean energy" teams and began to distribute cleantech research.[23]

But as the Great Recession of 2008 broke, it hit renewables hard. Financing became increasingly difficult to arrange. Moreover, even with the subsequent rebound in prices from the lows of late 2008, renewables were still at a competitive disadvantage.

This time, however, unlike the 1980s, there was no Valley of Death for the renewable industry. Renewables were now a much bigger industry with a strong constituency, it was international, and it had continuing policy support, including in the United States, energy legislation in 2005 and 2007. By now, renewables really were a global business.[24]

THE "THREE DENCHI BROTHERS"

Japan continued to be preoccupied with its high dependence on energy imports, and more than any other country. MITI—now the Ministry of Economy, Trade and Industry, or METI—continues to play an important role in steering Japan's industrial policy. It has promoted a very distinctive agenda for renewables. It is the "three Denchi brothers"—or *San Denchi Kyodai,* as Takayuki Ueda, a vice minister at METI, called them.

In Japan, fuel cells, solar cells, and batteries are all referred to as "batteries." METI sees these three technologies as pivotal to its triple mandates of ensuring Japan's industrial competitiveness, improving energy security through diversification, and tackling the problem of climate change. For each of these devices, new materials and fabrication techniques will be required to improve efficiency and reduce cost. "One day we will reach a point where all our electricity generation is renewables," says Ueda.

Japanese companies are laboring methodically to realize this dream, but they are also counting on another METI assumption—that, as Ueda said, cutting emissions by 80 percent will be "almost impossible without those three technologies. The three denchi brothers are very important not only for Japan, but for the world."[25]

GREEN DRAGON

China has over the last years embraced renewables with a fervor that has pushed it into the lead as a market, as a manufacturer—and as a competitor. In 1973 China had already introduced an agricultural law that called for solar and wind energy. In 1988 the first wind-power project was hooked up to the grid in the far west. Yet for many years renewables were largely considered antipoverty measures for the benefit of the rural poor. By the turn of the century, renewables were starting to get more serious attention. China also recognized that if it was going to be a player in renewables, it needed to put a priority on acquiring technology and know-how—and on supporting entrepreneurs.[26]

The decisive change came with the Renewable Energy Law of 2005, which jump-started renewables in China. A host of factors had suddenly raised the salience of renewables. Rapid economic growth, particularly for heavy industry, was leading to even more rapid growth in energy consumption. The country had been going through its internal energy crisis, with electricity demand outrunning the availability of coal and electricity, resulting in bottlenecks in supply and brownouts in power. Energy security had become an urgent issue for the top leadership because of growing oil imports and rising oil prices. China would soon start becoming an importer of coal as well. "Based on our current consumption, our fossil energy reserve could not support our economy," said the chief engineer of China's National Energy Administration. "We were too large now. So China made the decision to accelerate new and renewable technologies. We need to have the golden momentum of economic growth and the green momentum of clean energy." The "clean" part was very important. Pollution was a pervasive problem throughout the country. Climate change, emissions from burning coal in particular, was becoming an ever more contentious international issue. And it looked as though renewables would become a global growth industry, and China wanted to be at the forefront.[27]

The 2005 Renewable Energy Law was followed in 2007 by the Medium- and Long-Term Development Plan for Renewable Energy, which set out specific targets and called for renewables to reach 15 percent of total energy by 2020. With these policies, bolstered by the government's massive stimulus spending during the global financial crisis, China's renewable energy moved into high gear. Wind capacity doubled each year between 2005 and 2009.[28]

China also used its renewables push to promote the cleantech industry, which it had identified as a key growth industry for the twenty-first century. "We will accelerate the development of a low-carbon economy and green economy so as to gain an advantageous position in the international industrial competition," said China's Premier Wen Jiabao. As low-cost manufacturers, and bolstered by strong national and local government support, including attractive financing from state-owned banks, Chinese companies have come to dominate the solar panel market and have made significant inroads into the wind-turbine industry. One reason for the latter was China's decision to insist that 50 percent, and then 70 percent, of the components for domestic wind installations had to be made in China. Although the requirement ended in 2009, this policy gave Chinese wind-turbine suppliers time to expand the scale and sophistication of their operations and building on China's comparative advantage in manufacturing costs, to be more competitive with foreign companies at home and abroad.[29]

Yet even with China's strong support for its renewables industry, the country's push to boost renewables faces challenges. Hydropower has by far the largest share of any of the renewables, and will likely continue to have such. Though wind and solar are growing at a much faster rate than hydropower, they may together account for just 5 percent of China's total electricity generation in 2020. Even as China's renewable generating capacity rapidly expands, so too does its fossil fuel capacity, for China must rapidly expand its electricity capacity to meet a 10 percent annual growth in power demand. This puts a premium on projects that can supply a large amount of power—which still points to coal. It also explains why China is putting a lot of funding into research on clean coal.[30]

The commitment to renewables will grow stronger. But it will be in the framework of what Chinese government planners call an "emerging energy policy" that encourages not just renewables but more broadly any fuel that is not coal or oil, including nuclear and natural gas. The 12th Five Year Plan, adopted in 2011, emphasizes this policy. Of the seven Strategic Emerging Sectors identified by the plan, three are energy focused: energy conservation and environmental protection; new energy; and new energy vehicles. As it is, however, in a few short years China has become both the biggest market for wind in the world and the largest manufacturer and exporter of solar cells.

"NO AREA'S MORE RIPE"

With the Obama administration, the push for renewable energy became the top energy priority. The administration responded to the financial crisis and ensuing recession with a massive economic stimulus program, a significant part of which was aimed at renewables and cleantech. Other countries rushed to support their own faltering economies through fiscal stimulus—or government spending—and that also included building up their renewable energy sectors.

In the United States, the energy stimulus was sometimes described as the largest energy bill ever passed. Renewable energy became a significant theme of the recovery. The promise of green jobs and cleantech jobs was a major component in the promotion of the stimulus package. Even more than Jimmy Carter, Obama focused on transforming America's energy system. "We need to encourage American innovation," Obama told Congress in his 2010 State of the Union Address. "And no area's more ripe for such innovation than energy."[31]

The scale of renewable energy can be measured in terms of dollars. Total global investment in renewable energy capacity reached $150 billion in 2009, about four times what it had been just four years earlier. Renewables are currently only about three percent of the world's total installed electric capacity. But they accounted for almost 50 percent of the new capacity added in 2007–9. In short, renewables are becoming a substantial business. But it did take longer than might have been imagined since the first time renewables were born.[32]

"The world right now in terms of renewables is about where I expected it to be in 1985," somewhat ruefully said Denis Hayes, who created the first Earth Day on a shoestring in 1970 and then became the director of the Solar Energy Research Institute. "We weren't in error about what it would take to get there, but in error about the political process that we counted on to facilitate it."[33]

Yet, one must add, it has also taken decades for the technologies to develop and mature. Moreover, the questions about scale and cost are still being answered.

Still, when it comes to renewables, the time chasm has been closed. No longer is there a great ideological divide over renewables. It is a business, it is popular, and it is international. And solar energy has come back to the White House. It first came back in a small way, and quietly, in 2003, with the installation of solar cells on a little building on the White House grounds called the Pony Shed. In 2010 the Obama administration announced that solar panels and a solar water heater would be reinstalled on the roof of the White House residence—from where Jimmy Carter's solar hot water heater had been removed in 1986.[34]

If a transition to renewables is really made on a large scale, it will rival the importance of the world's transition to reliance on oil in the twentieth century, whether seen from a geopolitical or economic or environmental perspective. However, it will likely be a long road. Historically, energy transitions have occurred over many decades.

Thus even with rapid growth, renewables in 2030 are likely to still be far from being a dominant energy resource. Their actual role and market share will be determined by the interplay of policy, economics, and innovation. There is not a single scenario for the future of renewables. Rather it is a narrative of very different technologies, each with its own story and its own distinctive prospects. And its own challenges.

28

SCIENCE EXPERIMENT

Certain streets are iconic onto themselves. Merely mentioning their name tells a story and evokes an entire culture: Wall Street. Pennsylvania Avenue. The Champs-Élysées. Whitehall. And, of course, Rodeo Drive.

And then there is Sand Hill Road, which slides down the western edge of Stanford University in Palo Alto, California. On one side of the road is Stanford's Linear Accelerator, used for advanced nuclear experiments. On the other, partly hidden by leafy trees, is a series of mostly three- or four-story buildings that discreetly descend the hillside.

The name Sand Hill may not be as widely resonant as those other streets, but to those who do know it, Sand Hill Road is synonymous with Silicon Valley and the innovation and technology that are changing the world. For it is on Sand Hill Road that are headquartered many VCs—venture capitalists—that are the ignition switch for new business formation, formerly mainly for Silicon Valley but now for the whole world. Continue down along Sand Hill and up on University Avenue and you will find scores more of the VCs. Whatever their size, they generally raise a series of investment funds from pension funds, university endowments, foundations, and high-net-worth families, and then disburse that money to people starting up companies. The ultimate objective is to deliver to their investors within five or six years—or sooner—a return that is a multiple on their original commitment.

The VCs made their names, and the returns for their investors, primarily in tech; that is, information technology, computers, software, communications—and biotech. But in recent years many of these firms have decided that the next frontier for venture capital investing is not necessarily in those categories, although they will certainly continue to do all of the above and often with great enthusiasm. The new frontier is "cleantech."

THE GREAT BUBBLING

These VCs are hardly alone. Today there is a "great bubbling" in the broth of energy innovation as has never occurred before. And it is happening all across the energy spectrum—conventional energy, renewables, alternatives, efficiency. Indeed, the energy industry has never seen such a focus on innovation and technological change. But who will be the agents of change? Where will the breakthroughs come from? Who will push them from the lab into the marketplace? And how many of them will actually make that transition?

Energy has always been a business of science and technology. That is certainly true of many of the established energy companies. The oil and gas industry is dominated by swaths of engineers, many of whom have master's degrees and Ph.D.s. But the technological advances within the overall energy industry, as significant as they are, have largely been focused on traditional fuels—oil, natural gas, coal, and nuclear power. These advances are part of a process of continual improvement, pushing out technological frontiers. Sometimes they can be breakthroughs that can dramatically change the supply outlook.

The traditional energy companies are also involved in developing alternatives. Though largely forgotten, the major oil companies were early on among the main players in the development of photovoltaics in the United States. Today some of them are major players in wind. But their main alternative focus is on advanced biofuels, which could flow through pipelines and pumps and into automobile engines and thus be relatively compatible with existing infrastructure.

Venture capitalists may be looking for these kinds of innovations. But they are also seeking what Professor Clay Christensen of Harvard Business School calls "disruptive technologies" that change the game. The great ambition is to find, fund, develop—and then exit—the "Googles" of energy, although they would be happy with a decent though something less than Google-type return on their investment. They are largely not trying to create new technologies themselves so much as to find, finance, and guide the innovators with the ideas and the start-ups that embody new technology and channel them into the marketplace.[1]

NOT MERELY "GOOD SCIENCE"

But from where do the new technologies themselves come? Energy change is most likely to be developed from basic science and research and development, and will be the work of scientists and engineers—and creative and persevering and sometimes stubborn and iconoclastic innovators.

The private sector was a major player in basic R&D in the postwar decades. Until the 1980s, large corporate labs—Bell Labs, Westinghouse, RCA, and General Electric—were committed to basic research. Young physicists often saw jobs at these labs as being even better for basic research than a university faculty. "Bell Labs management supplied us with funding, shielded us from extraneous bureaucracy, and urged us not to be satisfied doing merely good science," recalled U.S. Energy Secretary Steven Chu, who spent nine years at Bell Labs.[2]

Out of the 16,000 people at Bell Labs in its heyday, a little over a thousand did basic science research—"doing something just because you wanted to understand it better," said John Tully, professor of chemistry at Yale, who spent 25 years at Bell Labs. "One of the key things was excitement. It was really contagious." The process was made much easier because "funding was automatic. You didn't have to put out a lot of paper as you do when a grant is running down and you have to apply for a new grant."

However, with the breakup of the original AT&T in the 1980s and the increasing pressure of quarterly performance from the investment community, the "headlights" for corporate research have been foreshortened. Basic research was seen as less relevant to the pressing near-term needs of most companies. Or, as former Undersecretary of Energy Raymond Orbach put it, the "patience scale was diminished" in the private sector. Over time, most of the big corporate labs disappeared. Bell Labs was progressively slimmed down. "You had to justify your work over shorter time periods," said Tully. In 2008 Bell Labs' new owner, Alcatel-Lucent, said it was going out of the basic research business altogether.[3]

With the decline in corporate research, the basic science and R&D endeavor has increasingly been driven by what has over the last 70 years been the largest engine of scientific advance, and the biggest funder—the U.S. government.

THE PRIME DRIVER

If there is one thing that venture capital is clearly not about, it is scientific experimentation. Yet those "science experiments" are essential to progress. "Experiment" is what Energy Secretary Steve Chu, at his Nobel award ceremony, called "the ultimate arbitrator"; for research and development is the foundation, crucial to everything else. For the most part, the government is today the primary generator of basic R&D in the United States, not only for energy but, with the exception of pharmaceuticals, for most everything else as well.[4]

The federal government's role in stimulating innovation, going back to the beginning of the republic, was often directly for national defense. In 1794 George Washington, unhappy with the performance of muskets, established a group of national armories, thus launching what was the first R&D initiative by the U.S. government. The objective was to replace rifles that were laboriously handmade by individual craftsmen with ones that were produced with interchangeable parts, thus greatly simplifying and speeding up the manufacturing of rifles. This innovation in interchangeable parts became known as the American system of manufacturing and was critical to America's rise as an industrial power.[5]

But it was only after World War II that the government took on a much broader responsibility for supporting basic research and the whole R&D system.

THE PUBLIC GOOD

Spending on R&D has generally been recognized as a government responsibility because it is a public good. Beyond what the private investor can expect, R&D provides benefits in the form of higher economic growth, improved quality of life, and national security. When receiving the Nobel Prize in economics, MIT economist Robert Solow emphasized the central importance of innovation—the transfer of technology "from laboratory to factory"—to economic growth.

Energy R&D is required to meet the more specific challenges of energy supply, usage, security, environmental impact—and, increasingly, climate change. The time horizons for energy innovation are often far longer than can be sustained either by companies, under quarterly-profit pressure, or by investment funds, which aim to exit an investment within five years. For instance, it took four decades and four generations of technology to get the scrubbers right for removing SO_2 from coal plants. It took 15 years of research and demonstration before coal bed methane became viable. Such long-term horizons make volatility, uncertainty, and stop-and-go in funding so disruptive and so expensive in terms of lost opportunity.[6]

The U.S. Department of Energy supports a sprawling R&D enterprise that extends from national laboratories like Los Alamos and Oak Ridge and the National Renewable Energy Laboratory to university scientists, private contractors, and companies. The DOE's 17 national laboratories alone employ over 12,000 Ph.D. scientists full time, making it the largest employer of scientists in the world. Overall the DOE is also the "ministry of science" for the physical sciences, supporting almost half of all the physical sciences research in the United States, including over time the work of 111 Nobel Prize winners.[7]

The level of U.S. government spending on energy R&D has fluctuated often in rough parallel with oil prices. Funding spiked during the Carter years, around the second oil shock, and then declined in the 1980s as energy prices came down. In the aftermath of the 1991 Gulf War, worries about energy security ebbed away. Thereafter, in the 1990s, as a report on energy R&D observed at the time, the national preoccupation was "on how to cut programs to reduce the federal deficit." Indeed, the low point for DOE R&D was in 1998, when oil prices collapsed. Spending started to go up again with the new century. But energy R&D funding has remained low when measured against the energy and security challenges and the need for innovation. The total annual energy R&D spending in 2008 was equivalent to two weeks' spending on the Iraq War.[8]

ENTER THE VENTURE CAPITALISTS

Until four or five years ago, venture capitalists did not even know, in the words of one of its practitioners, "how to spell the word 'energy.'" But it has certainly been playing a transformative role in capitalism and markets since the middle of the twentieth century.

Some like to say that venture capital—putting money into start-ups, betting on entrepreneurs and innovators—goes back much further. "Queen Isabella of Spain was one of the early venture capitalists when she backed Columbus," said William Draper III, a veteran venture capitalist. She put her faith in a management team led by Christopher Columbus. "What she did was look into Columbus's eyes and say that this guy might really sail off to some land and bring back some jewels." J. P. Morgan's funding of Thomas Edison's electricity start-up in the 1870s and 1880s certainly qualifies as proto–venture capital.

The outlines of modern venture capital emerged just before World War II. The portfolio of one of the innovators, J. H. Whitney and Co., ranged from Minute Maid orange juice and Technicolor to the financing for the film *Gone With the Wind*. According to legend, a partner at J. H. Whitney came up with the initial name for this new type of investing—"private adventure capital." But that just didn't ring quite right; it sounded overly risk-oriented, even a little reckless. What responsible fiduciaries want to embark on an "adventure" using the moneys entrusted to them for prudent management? So later it got shortened, for simplicity and for probity, to "venture capital."[9]

GEORGES DORIOT: PROPHET OF THE "START-UP NATION"

Yet the real birth of modern technology-focused venture capital investing can be attributed to one man, a stern but charismatic professor at Harvard Business School—Georges Doriot, otherwise known as General Doriot. The son of one of the founders of the Peugeot automobile company, Doriot emigrated from France just after World War I and enrolled at the recently established Harvard Business School. He would remain on as a professor there for 41 years.

Doriot taught what eventually became a famous second-year course, simply called Manufacturing. Unlike the classic Harvard Business School case method, that class was "all Doriot"—all lecture, on all aspects of running businesses. Given to aphorisms and oracular advice, Doriot would tell his students that the first thing that they should read each morning in the *New York Times* were the obituaries, in order to learn from the lives of "great men." He even delivered a lecture to what were then all-male classes on how to properly pick a wife.

World War II turned Doriot into a pioneering venture capitalist—for the war effort. He became head of research and development for the Quartermaster Corp, charged "to identify the unmet needs of soldiers and oversee the development of new products to fill those needs." Doriot directed the development of everything from rain-repellant garments and combat boots that soldiers needed to trudge across Europe, to K-ration compact food, to what became known as Doron (after Doriot)—bullet-resistant plastic armor that was developed just in time for Marines to use in the Pacific. He also played a key role in the development of synthetic rubber, which became an urgent need when the Japanese captured the rubber-producing lands of Southeast Asia. All this taught him a basic lesson: that modern warfare, as he put it, "is in reality applied science."[10] He would apply that same lesson later, after the war, to the private sector.

In 1945, with the war over, Doriot—now General Doriot—returned to Harvard. Drawing on his wartime experiences, Doriot launched the pioneering ARD—American Research and Development. Doriot, as a colleague of his later remarked, was "the first one to believe there was a future of financing entrepreneurs in an organized way." Or as Doriot said, his job as a venture capitalist was to interface between, on the one side, large companies with resources but an inability to nurture innovation and, on the other, academics and inventors with creative ideas but no funds who were "trying desperately to become poor businessmen."

Though Doriot himself was deeply embedded in Harvard, much of what ARD did under his aegis was to commercialize technologies nurtured down the Charles River at the Massachusetts Institute of Technology. MIT, unlike some other universities, was not shy about connecting its laboratories and classrooms directly to the marketplace. In fact, it was part of its mission, in contrast to most of the Ivy League universities, which were founded as divinity schools; MIT was established, in the words of its founding charter of 1861, to promote the "practical application of science in connection with . . . commerce."

Though rather autocratic in his own management, Doriot attracted a number of talented colleagues, including a young MIT Ph.D., Samuel Bodman, who years later would serve as U.S. secretary of energy. "Georges Doriot was a man of very different personalities," recalled Bodman. "On the one hand, he was engaging, gracious, and brilliant. On the other hand, he was dominating intellectually and had the capability to treat people in a less than positive fashion."

This nascent enterprise of venture capital was not an easy business. "Never go into venture capital if you want a peaceful life!" was one of Doriot's aphorisms. Every business, no matter how successful ultimately, seemed to go through at least one or two crises or disasters that involved, as Doriot put it, telephone calls "at two o'clock in the morning to tell you about a new human accident."

By the 1960s the community around greater Cambridge, Massachusetts (yes, including Harvard), radiating out to the north and the west along Route 128, had become the nation's first great incubator for new technology.

ARD strayed into energy only a couple of times, one of them in an oil production company called Zapata Off-Shore, founded by a recent Yale graduate named George H. W. Bush. But these were the exceptions. "Energy was too much money," recalled Bodman. "That's why it never happened. Energy was looked at as the province of big companies. The idea of a small company making its way was kind of preposterous."[11]

GO WEST

But if Doriot's ARD laid out the model, a still-greater center of venture capital was to grow up elsewhere. The place was Stanford University, and it was the doing of Frederick Terman, Stanford's dean of engineering and later its provost. Having done his Ph.D. at MIT, Terman recognized the value of linking a research university to the marketplace, and he was determined to create a high-tech industry amid all those fruit orchards around Stanford's 8,000-acre campus in the Santa Clara Valley. Thus did "Valley of Heart's Delight" turn into Silicon Valley. Among other things, Terman established the Stanford Industrial Park to tie the university to business. It was through Terman that a couple of Stanford graduates got to know one another—one named William Hewlett and the other, David Packard. Out of which came Hewlett-Packard, eventually HP, the largest computer company in the world.[12]

From Terman's vision emerged the distinctive and highly interconnected ecosystem of Silicon Valley that encompasses Stanford and the University of California at Berkeley; the venture capitalists of Sand Hill Road and University

Avenue and San Francisco; and the scientists and engineers and entrepreneurs who surround them. One of the first venture capital firms that shaped the Silicon Valley system was Kleiner Perkins (later Kleiner Perkins Caufield & Byers), which was founded in 1972. The original partners were Eugene Kleiner, who had fled Vienna with his family to escape the Nazis and later joined an early Silicon Valley start-up, and Tom Perkins, an MIT engineering and Harvard Business School graduate and a Hewlett-Packard veteran, who had been a student in Georges Doriot's Manufacturing class at the Harvard Business School.

Kleiner Perkins set out to further refine the VC business model into something different from traditional finance, and also different from traditional R&D. That meant direct engagement in everything, from management and strategy to honing technology to recruiting talent. This became a general business model for the venture capital business. In some cases it included conceptualizing needs and technologies to meet the needs, and then finding the technologists and entrepreneurs to implement the ideas. The whole process was characterized by an urgency about getting to market. The quickest way back then to shoot down a proposed venture capital investment for a new start-up was to describe it as "a science experiment." It still is today. Venture capitalists will, as they say, "crawl university laboratories," but they usually go to great lengths to avoid anything that smacks of science experiments. This stance is what so sharply differentiates venture capital from actual R&D. For R&D is all about the experiment.[13]

From Genetech, Apple Computer, and Adobe to Google, eBay, YouTube, and Facebook—all these are the progeny of this Silicon Valley ecosystem, along with many more whose names may not be so well known but whose technologies do much to make the modern world work.

"CAREER SUICIDE"

But for many years, energy was of little interest to venture capital. That was for Bell Labs and other large-scale laboratories in established companies, national labs, research institutes, and universities. But definitely not for venture capital.

One of the few exceptions among the venture capitalists was Nancy Floyd. She set out to start what became one of the very first VC firms focused on energy. The basic reason, she explained, was because of "my somewhat disjointed career." She had been an electric-power regulator in Vermont and then an early wind developer in California, climbing up into the Altamont Pass wearing rattlesnake guards. After the breakup of the AT&T phone monopoly in the early 1980s, she helped start a telecommunications company that was later sold to IBM. "I had seen the role that technology could play in disrupting a previously regulated industry," she recalled.

In the 1990s the deregulation of the electric power industry seemed to offer similar opportunities, and in 1994 she decided to set up a venture capital firm, Nth Power, to exploit those new opportunities. The world was definitely not waiting, either for her or for Nth Power. She spent the next three years on the road, visiting hundreds of investors around the world—as it turned out, highly uninterested investors. With her funds running low, Floyd started staying in $39-a-night hotels, which wasn't easy for her. For, as she put it, "I'm not a $39-a-night-type gal."

But she hung on with what she later called the "common trait of all successful entrepreneurs"—tenacity—and by 1997 she had raised her first fund from just a handful of investors. Things did not get much easier. The first few years were "like pushing a boulder up the hill."[14]

Another early energy investor was Ira Ehrenpreis, a partner at Technology Partners. Ehrenpreis made his first investment in an energy technology company in the late 1990s. "I spent most of my time in the IT world, governed by Moore's Law, where every 18 months products are leapfrogged by the next generation," said Ehrenpreis. "Then, as chairman of this energy company, I'd interface with the utilities, and learned that the lens of innovation that they looked through was decades."

Ehrenpreis also felt pretty lonely in the field. "My venture brethren thought I'd lost my sense of reason," he recalled. "Closer friends worried that I was committing career suicide."[15]

THE $6 TRILLION OPPORTUNITY

But now Nancy Floyd and Ira Ehrenpreis are seen as pioneers. For around 2003 and 2004, the VC community discovered energy and cleantech. Rising energy prices was one reason. But there were others. "It was a combination of energy independence for the United States, the priority to address global warming, and the fact that we had technology that we just didn't have in 1979," is how Ray Lane, a partner at Kleiner Perkins, explained his firm's move into the industry. The sheer scale of the opportunity was very compelling. In its analysis, Kleiner Perkins estimated that the total annual information technology market was $1 trillion a year, while that for energy was $6 trillion.

The entry of venture capital into cleantech has gone from the trickle to the veritable flood. Investment in the U.S. cleantech industry went from $286 million in 2001 to $3.7 billion in 2010—a rise of more than ten times. In 2010 cleantech represented 17 percent of total VC investment in the United States.[16]

"MIT IS DOING ENERGY"

Robert Metcalfe is one the legends of the information technology business. He invented the Ethernet, which makes possible the LANs—local area networks—that link computers in offices and homes. He was also on the board of the company that developed PowerPoint, the inescapable tool of most presentations. He has been awarded the U.S. National Medal of Technology. An MIT graduate, he had returned from Silicon Valley to join Polaris, a Boston venture capital firm.

On May 6, 2005, Metcalfe attended the inauguration of Susan Hockfield, a neurobiologist, as the sixteenth president of MIT. At the ceremony, held in Killian Hall, which looks out toward the Charles River, he heard Hockfield declare that it was the university's "institutional responsibility" to address energy issues across every department. To a venture capitalist who was highly attuned, Doriot-style, to the research trends on the MIT campus, that was about as clear a signal as you could get. He went back to his office that afternoon. "Susan Hockfield said MIT is doing energy," he told his colleagues, "and we're now doing energy." Polaris subsequently became an early cleantech investor.

But will the bubbling of innovation activity produce those "disruptive technologies"? Or will it, at least, generate new companies that will have a substantial impact on the energy mix? Vinod Khosla, a prominent cleantech venture capitalist has said that venture capital will do to energy what it did to the old IBM-dominated computer industry and the old AT&T-dominated

phone business: undermine the established companies, redefine the business model, and spawn a host of major new competitors. (To be sure, the U.S. Justice Department helped that "undermining" with its far-reaching antitrust cases against both companies.)

Others have a different perspective. Robert Metcalfe sees the possibility of a green tech and global-warming bubble that will end with a crash. But from a big-picture perspective, that will accelerate the development of new technologies. "Bubbles accelerate innovation," said Metcalfe. And one spin-off from innovation is "surprises."[17]

Actual experience has been mixed. There have been some strategic sales and some high-profile IPOs that rival Internet or information-technology start-ups. But the general learning for members of the venture community is that energy is a harder road than they had thought from their experience in other sectors. It is a learning in which the entrepreneurs have shared.

Energy, at least energy production, is different in terms of time, money, and scale. "I see few similarities between the digital world and the energy world," said Ray Lane. "There is no Moore's Law. In fact, there are different laws like thermodynamics, physical relationships, chemical reactions, and biological systems. It is a policy-influenced, low-cost, mature, capital-intensive industry, which investors must understand. I recommend leaving most of the digital lessons learned at home." Energy has much longer lead times; it needs much more capital than the typical IT or software start-up, and then requires several subsequent rounds of big capital injections, and its scale is much bigger. Projects need to proved and then proved again at every stage. They may have to cope with unanticipated delays and substantial cost increases. And then the products have to be sold to industries that are often very cautious about new technologies because of the costs and risks of something going wrong in energy production or distribution in a complex system. Moreover, energy-production facilities tend to have long lives and are not going to be quickly turned over. Consumers may change their computers every three years or their cell phones every two years; electric utilities will continue to operate power plants for 50 or 60 years.

In short, everything seems to take longer. Significant changes in energy do not necessarily happen in the three- to five-year time span that suits the metabolism of venture capital. As Steven Koonin, undersecretary of energy for science and the former provost of Caltech, observed, "Even accelerated energy transformation will take decades." Adding to the challenge is the complexity of systems integration. Combining three or four dozen different technologies for a smart grid system is far more difficult—and time consuming—than coming up with a new iPhone app.

Because energy involves the distribution of vital necessities, it is enmeshed in a great network of regulation, and the issues around it are often contentious. As a result, it generates a high degree of "political interest," observed Professor Ernest Moniz, head of the Energy Initiative at MIT and a former undersecretary of energy. "This has enormous significance for what it takes to innovate and then introduce and scale new technologies."[18]

Of course, a Google of energy may happen. It may even be happening right now but might not be recognized for five years. After all, how many people had heard of Google in 1998? But energy is different, very different. Google was helping to create a new industry—search—but not to take away market share from incumbent commodity suppliers, on which the entire economy depends.

"THE ONLY WAY TO BREAK OUT"

In 2009 the Obama administration came in determined to take energy R&D spending to levels that had never before been seen. Barack Obama underlined the emphasis on innovation when he appointed Steven Chu, then heading the Lawrence Berkeley national lab, as energy secretary. Chu had received his Nobel Prize in physics for work he had done on lasers.

The Obama administration's emergency stimulus package put tens of billions of dollars into energy and efficiency. The stimulus was further bolstered by tax incentives meant to encourage investment in clean energy. This also meant a big, if temporary, step-up in R&D spending.

Much of the spending was directed toward climate change, but Chu has called attention to the difficulties of moving beyond the current energy system. The answer was not merely to develop low-carbon energy sources but such sources that met the test of the competitive marketplace. That required more rapid development of new technologies. And "a theory of the innovation chain" governed the whole enterprise. It proceeds along a path, from knowledge creation—basic science to the lab bench and experimentation—to prototypes and demonstrations to commercialization and finally into the marketplace. The cast of characters in this enterprise ranges from theoretical physicists to entrepreneurs and venture capitalists to large companies and, of course, the final arbiters, consumers.

But as the President's Council of Advisors on Science and Technology has emphasized, this in not a linear process; it is not that something gets invented and then pushed out the door. Rather it is highly interactive among the stages, with the essential feedback generated by the "learning by doing" and the "learning by using." The government's role was, in the words of Matthew Rogers, DOE's point person for the stimulus program, to "accelerate the rate at which ideas move from one end of the chain to the other. People think of clean energy as high-cost energy. The only way to break out of that is to innovate our way out of it." That would mean, as General Doriot said during World War II, putting "applied science" to work.

This new innovation agenda ended up being organized around ten priorities, ranging from vehicle batteries and solar energy to biofuels, carbon capture and storage, and grid-scale storage of electricity. In each area, the objective was to achieve, eventually, much-improved performance and lower cost. And in each area support went to five or ten different projects, with the idea that they would be competing against one another, which would lead to higher probability of success. It was just not possible to know in advance which would succeed and which would not. That is the nature of R&D and innovation. "Investing in R&D is rolling the dice," said Chu. "We expect failures, but we expect home runs."[19]

There were three specific initiatives. First, about 50 Energy Frontier Research Centers were established at universities and national labs to tackle grand challenges in energy. Second and larger are new research hubs, which are meant to take on basic questions and encompass most of the innovation chain, from the basic research to the point when the know-how can be passed to the marketplace.

The third initiative, developed in Congress and then implemented by the Obama administration, is ARPA-E, the Advanced Research Projects Agency for Energy. It was modeled on the Defense Advanced Research Projects Agency, DARPA, the organization within the Department of Defense charged with identifying major new needs and challenges and the "far-out ideas," and funding them on a multiyear basis. Many of the most important advances in computing trace back to DARPA, along with GPS and the Internet. Of course, even with the Internet, it took almost three decades from the first identification of the problem to the beginning of its massive impact.

The current level of federal energy R&D is about $5 billion a year, which, as a percentage of GDP, is considerably lower than the GDPs of Japan, South Korea, France, and China. With the renewed focus on federal spending and deficits, energy R&D spending is once again, as in the 1990s, a target for cuts. That would have real costs. But if funding and focus are consistently maintained over the years, the consequences could be significant. And could well provide surprising solutions.[20]

THE NATURE OF THE EXPERIMENT

One of the commandments of venture capital is "Thou shall not do science experiments." Yet venture capital is indeed, along with everybody else in the sprawling energy-research enterprise, part of a very large experiment that is seeking to answer an enormous question: Can today's $65 trillion world economy be sure it will have the energy it needs to be a $130 trillion economy in two decades? And to what degree can such an economy, which depends on carbon fuels for 80 percent of its energy, move to other diverse energy sources? The answers are far from obvious.

This experiment is definitely not something just for the future. It has already begun. It takes a variety of forms today—among them, capturing the wind, harnessing the energy that is being created by the giant nuclear fusion furnace of the sun, harvesting energy from the richness of the soil, improving efficiency wherever we use energy, and remaking the vehicles that carry us all about.

29

ALCHEMY OF SHINING LIGHT

Albert Einstein possessed a power of mind that would do nothing less than forge a new understanding of the universe. In the summer of 1900, he had a more immediate problem. Diploma in hand, he really needed to find a job. He had hoped for a university position, but it was not to be. None of Einstein's professors would give him a positive recommendation, in part due to a mediocre diploma essay as well as his reputation for being, as one of his professors put it, a "lazy dog." Yet whatever his supposed sloth, this rebellious student had not only extraordinary gifts for mathematics and physics but also the capability to marshal them with momentous results. But that was not enough to get him employed.

While hunting for a job, Einstein tried to support himself by doing some private tutoring in math and physics. He even advertised in a local paper, offering prospective students free trial lessons for what he billed as "exceedingly thorough" services. His family, its finances stretched, could not provide much financial assistance, but they were clearly worried about him. Unbeknownst to Albert, his father, Hermann, went so far as to write a chemistry professor asking for help. "My son," he said, "feels deeply unhappy & each day the thought gains strength in him that his career has been derailed & he cannot find a connection any longer. He is moreover depressed at the thought that he is a burden to us, who are not very well off."

But then Einstein had a lucky break. He landed a job at the Swiss patent office in Bern. In June 1902 he reported for work at the patent office in the new Postal and Telegraph Building, near the railway station. Examining patent applications was not very taxing work for the intellectually curious young physicist, but most important, it would provide him the security he needed—and the time.

The patent office was actually a good fit for Einstein. He was interested in the practical as well as theoretical, particularly when it came to electricity. After all, his father was an engineer. Hermann and his youngest brother, Jakob, ran an electric generation company in Munich. Part of the first generation of entrepreneurs building on Edison's revolution in electric power, they were at the forefront of the high tech of the day. They competed with companies like Siemens for contracts to illuminate the towns and cities of Europe. Unfortunately, Hermann and Jakob Einstein lost out on a contract to light the Munich city center and were never really able to make a go of their business. But at least Hermann Einstein no longer had to worry about his son's job prospects.[1]

TEN WEEKS THAT SHOOK THE WORLD

Ensconced at the patent office and with time on his hands, Einstein eventually went to work on a pent-up store of problems that were filling his mind. Over a period of just ten weeks in the summer of 1905, in an astonishing burst of creativity and analysis, he would turn out five papers that would transform the understanding of the universe and change the world in which we live. One of them was called "Does the Inertia of a Body Depend upon Its Energy Content?" This was the paper with perhaps the most famous equation ever: $e=mc^2$. That paper laid the theoretical foundations for both exploiting the terrifying potential of nuclear reactions in the atomic bomb and harnessing nuclear reactions for peaceful power.

One of the other papers had the obscure title "On a Heuristic Point of View Concerning the Production and Transformation of Light." This paper, Einstein wrote to a friend, "deals with radiation and the energy properties of light and is very revolutionary." In the paper, Einstein proposed the hypothesis that matter and radiation can interact only by way of the exchange of independent "quanta" of energy. He demonstrated that this hypothesis explains a number of phenomena, including what he called the "photoelectric effect."[2]

In so doing, the paper provided the theoretical foundations for what, more than a century later, is the rapidly growing photovoltaics industry, an industry that many see as the ultimate future for renewables. The significance of that paper from the summer of 1905 was summed up succinctly more than a century later by one of the leading technologists in the industry today.

"Einstein," he said, "explained it all."[3]

SOLAR CELLS

Today, while wind has captured much more investment, no part of the renewable industry is attracting as much research focus as the quest to directly harness the power of the sun—especially photovoltaic cells, or PV, otherwise known as solar cells.

In many ways solar cells represent the purest ideal for renewable technologies. Sunlight is an abundant resource in almost all corners of the earth. Once the cells are made, there are no complex industrial facilities to operate. Cells—a basic system that can go on the roof of a house—can be installed in a matter of hours. They don't necessarily even need any transmission lines. Just the direct conversion of sunlight into electricity.

This transformation may sound like the type of feat that alchemists in the Middle Ages claimed to accomplish—the "great work" of transmuting base metals into gold. But unlike the magic of the Middle Age wizards, this modern alchemy is real: light penetrates a surface and emerges as electricity. It is fundamental physics. That was Einstein's great insight.

Though the market for PV has seen enormous growth since the mid-2000s, it is still much smaller than that of wind. Yet nothing else across the renewables spectrum generates such high expectations as the potential of directly harnessing the power of the sun—especially for PV. And with good reason. It saves hundreds of millions of years—about the time it can take for organic matter to be transformed into fossil fuels. There is conviction that, in the words of MIT physicist Ernest Moniz, solar energy will eventually be the "tallest pole in the tent"—the ultimate source of electric power. But when? And will photovoltaics

FROM LIGHT TO ELECTRICITY
Generalized diagram of a solar photovoltaic cell

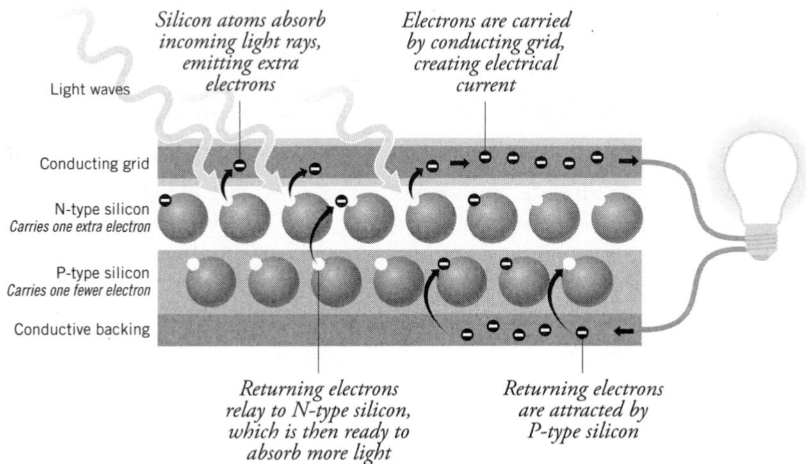

Source: U.S. Department of Energy

fundamentally transform our entire electric power system? Will this system shift from a network of generating stations and wires to one where every house and office building is a mini–power plant, generating its own electricity, without coal, natural gas, nuclear power, or even wind? Or will, instead, a new kind of power plant become commonplace, where the dispatched electricity is generated from solar panels?[4]

Whatever the path, one obstacle that stands in the way is scale. To get to scale—to proliferate across the rooftops of the world—requires the conquest of costs. And that depends upon further innovation. Costs may be coming down, but they are still higher than competitive sources of generation. Mass production has not yet brought costs down to what is required for true scale.

Where PV are competitive is where there is no established infrastructure of wires delivering electricity, such as in outer space or remote jungle villages, and they may also be competitive when power prices are high and the solar resources are strong. Otherwise they need significant government support and subsidies. In Germany, the country that did much to transform solar cells from a small niche into a substantial business, those price supports have been at levels as much as five times the cost of conventional electricity. But the whole weight of the industry is concentrated on that single goal—bringing costs down further.

"THOROUGH INVESTIGATION"

Well before Einstein had put pen to paper in 1905, earlier scientists and engineers had already observed the photoelectric effect—that in some circumstances light could produce an electric charge—but they just could not explain it. A few scientists and engineers worked with the element selenium, producing electric current by exposure to sunlight, and even candlelight. Werner Siemens, the founder of the Siemens engineering company, proclaimed that "the direct conversion" of the "energy of light into electrical energy was an entirely new physical phenomenon" that required "thorough investigation." It was left to Einstein to explain the why.[5]

Until that time, physicists insisted that light was a wave moving through the ether—an invisible substance that supposedly suffused the universe. Einstein thought otherwise. Light, he said in his paper on the photovoltaic effect, was made up of tiny particles called quanta, also known as photons, that moved at 186,000 miles per second and were indivisible.

It was this paper that established the science that explained photovoltaic reactions. When sunlight descends on solar photovoltaic cells, the photons are absorbed. They dislodge and displace electrons within the semiconductor. These loose electrons flow out of the silicon along minute channels—almost like water flowing through a canal—as electric current. The photons are one form of energy, and the elections another form.

Einstein received the Nobel Prize in 1922 not for the paper that laid the basis for nuclear energy, but rather for this paper on photons and quantum mechanics—for "his discovery of the law of photoelectric effect," in the words of the award.[6]

But theory is one thing. It would take a half century after Einstein's paper for the real breakthrough in putting the theory to practical use. That feat occurred in 1953 at AT&T's Bell Labs, in New Jersey. There two scientists, Gerald Pearson and Calvin Fuller, were trying to develop an improved transistor for communications, a device that also happened to have been invented a few years earlier at Bell Labs. But now Pearson and Fuller discovered, to their surprise, that silicon panels that were doped—that is, contaminated with a deliberately introduced impurity, in this case gallium—achieved the alchemic reaction described in Einstein's paper. The light was transmutated into electricity.

A year later, after much further experimentation, the Bell Labs scientists unveiled "the first solar cells capable of producing useful amounts of power." To dramatize their discovery when they presented it to the National Academy of Sciences in 1954, they used the solar cells to power a small radio transmitter. But that would only be the beginning. Bell Labs declared that these new solar cells would "profoundly influence the art of living." "Vast Power of the Sun Is Tapped by Battery Using Sand Ingredient," trumpeted the *New York Times,* which reported that this invention "may mark the beginning of a new era" and "the realization of one of mankind's most cherished dreams—the harnessing of the almost limitless energy of the sun for the uses of civilization." Yet the initial step along the commercial path was more down to earth: providing power for rural telephone lines near Americus, Georgia.[7]

However, these photovoltaic cells were not very efficient, and they were very costly. Aside from rural phone lines, where could they find any use at all?

THE RACE INTO SPACE

In October 1957 a Soviet rocket roared into space carrying Sputnik, the first man-made satellite. Sputnik—which in Russian translates to "traveling companion"—caught the United States off guard. Hoisting it into orbit was seen as a political and military victory of the first order for the Soviet Union—and a strategic catastrophe for the United States. The Soviets had not only bested the United States on the frontier of science but, worse, had shattered Americans' sense of invulnerability. No longer was the United States protected by two vast oceans, not when Soviet armor could circle above it, in outer space.

For the Soviet leader, Nikita Khrushchev, Sputnik was a way to project an image of strength and to disguise what he knew were the country's weaknesses. But that is not the way it was seen in the United States. The Soviet success ignited what has been described as a "near-hysterical reaction" on the part of "the American press, politicians, and public." "Whoever controls space will control the world," declared Senate Majority Leader Lyndon Johnson. Physicist Edward Teller, known as "the father of the hydrogen bomb," warned President Eisenhower at a White House meeting that Sputnik was a greater defeat for the

United States than Pearl Harbor. A high-powered national commission urged the administration to build enough nuclear fall-out shelters to house every single American. Legislation was rushed through Congress to subsidize the study of foreign language on college campuses in the name of national defense.

At the same time, the government launched a number of programs that would drive American technology with far-reaching impact. It was in 1958 that the Defense Department created what became DARPA, the Defense Advanced Research Projects Agency. That same year, NASA, the National Aeronautics and Space Administration, was established. Government funding for research and science in general surged.

In the face of the Sputnik challenge, the calmest man in America, it seemed, was President Eisenhower himself. "As far as the satellite itself is concerned," he said five days after its launch, "that does not raise my apprehension, not one iota." He was concerned, in a recession year, to keep the budgetary expenditures from going, as he put it, "hog wild." He shunted aside proposals for nuclear-powered airplanes and also for a nuclear-powered spaceship that would fly to the moon, explaining, "I'd like to know what's on the other side of the moon, but I won't pay to find out this year."

One reason for his calm was that he knew that the United States had its own missile and satellite program—in fact, several competing ones, from the different military services.

Whatever his reassuring words to the public, Eisenhower clearly understood that the single most important thing to do was get a satellite up—and get it up quickly. On the first try, in December 1957, the rocket blew up only two seconds after takeoff, and the satellite was destroyed in a highly embarrassing ball of fire. The failed American satellite was immortalized as "Kaputnik." A second satellite, Explorer I, was, however, successfully lofted into orbit in January 1958. This satellite, though, was very unadorned, even primitive. The need remained to get up a satellite that would be taken seriously.[8] And that meant accelerating the Vanguard program, which was to put into orbit a civilian research satellite to support the 1958 International Geophysical Year.

But the Vanguard program ignited a critical and acerbic internal battle. How to power the Vanguard satellite once it was in orbit? On this crucial question, the navy, which was responsible for the Vanguard, wanted to use traditional chemical batteries. But on the flank emerged an unlikely adversary in the form of a German scientist named Hans Ziegler, who had been brought to the United States by the U.S. military after World War II. Ziegler had become an American citizen and was working on communications for the military. When Ziegler visited Bell Labs in New Jersey soon after the invention of the silicon-based photovoltaics, he was instantly smitten by the new technology. He believed that man's ultimate source of energy was destined to be the sun and relentlessly lobbied the armed forces and Congress to "give mankind the benefit of this invention at the earliest possible time."

The navy, however, had no intention of entrusting the power source of its first satellite to what it described as an unproved "unconventional and not fully established" new invention. But Ziegler convinced a critical government panel that the chemical batteries on Vanguard would last only a few weeks while the experiments aboard Vanguard would "have enormously greater value if they can be kept operating for several months more."

In the end, Ziegler managed to muscle solar panels onto the Vanguard vehicle, which was launched in March 1958. The orbiting Vanguard helped restore confidence in America's scientific preeminence.

Vanguard was also the great break that established the credibility for solar cells. How big the break was made clear in a *New York Times* headline nineteen days after launch: "Vanguard Radio Fails to Report/Chemical Battery Exhausted/Solar Unit Functioning." A year later Ziegler and his colleagues in the signal corps clinked glasses when the orbiting solar cells were still producing current. Indeed, high above the earth's atmosphere, the cells would produce sustained electricity over a number of years. Here in the emptiness of outer space was the real-life demonstration for Albert Einstein's paper "On a Heuristic Point of View Concerning the Production and Transformation of Light."

From then on, solar cells became standard on satellites, which was their first major market. Hans Ziegler's ambitions for the technology were still grander. He saw it as "an important source of electrical power" and envisioned "the roofs of all our buildings in cities and towns equipped with solar [cells]." Alas, the cells were still expensive—enormously expensive. And that meant that they were, for the most part, really competitive only in one place: outer space.[9]

DOWN TO EARTH

A key moment in the journey of photovoltaics down to earth can be dated very precisely: August 1, 1973. That was the day that a start-up company called Solarex opened its doors in Rockville, Maryland, outside Washington, D.C. It was founded by two refugees from communist Hungary—Joseph Lindmayer, a brilliant physicist, and Peter Varadi, a very talented chemist. Both had managed to escape from Hungary during the 1956 revolution against Soviet rule.

Lindmayer and Varadi met twelve years later, in 1968, when both started working at Comsat, the quasi-private company that owned the commercial satellites that the U.S. government put into orbit. Lindmayer ran Comsat's physics laboratory; Varadi, the chemistry lab. Improving the efficiency and reliability of PVs was one of Lindmayer's prime objectives. Over espresso coffee (what was then considered an exotic European beverage) the two continentals would talk about photovoltaics and muse on their possible applicability to electric generation on earth. But they recognized that the way in which solar cells were manufactured for space—under vacuum conditions to assure very high performance—made them far too expensive for terrestrial use. Lindmayer began turning the problem over and over in his mind. He also began experimenting with totally different approaches in the basement of his house in Bethesda, Maryland. He started to visualize a pathway, which he and Varadi talked through. There is also a legend that he used Coca-Cola to dope his early solar cells in his kitchen oven.

They submitted a proposal to Comsat's management to start producing terrestrial solar cells, for ground use. But the retired air force generals running Comsat turned down the proposal, saying it had nothing to do with their mission, which was in outer space.

Why not, the two scientists asked each other, start their own company? Not that they had any idea what to do. They knew nothing about business. They were refugees who had secure jobs. "We pondered why well-paid scientists would get into such a hare-brain idea when there is no technology, no product, no market, and we have no money," Varadi later said.

Nevertheless, they managed to cobble together funding from friends and family. They also needed a name. Lindmayer did not care what the name was so long as the name ended in *X*. And thus Solarex was born.

Two decisive things happened in the first few months of the company's history. A few weeks after Solarex opened its doors, their former employer, Comsat, sued them for stealing intellectual property. After touring the facility, the Comsat people reluctantly came to the conclusion that Lindmayer had invented an entirely different process. They dropped the suit. Then, eleven weeks after they started the company, the world abruptly changed. The Arab oil embargo ignited the 1973 oil crisis.

"I could tell you that we foresaw the oil crisis and that was the reason that we planned to open the company," Varadi later said. "But that would be a lie. We had absolutely no inkling that there would be an oil crisis." But, he added, "The oil crisis had a very profound effect on us. We realized what an incredible business we got ourselves involved in."

The two scientists divided up the work. Lindmayer would run the technology and science. Varadi volunteered that "since as of that time I had not received the Nobel Prize in chemistry, I should get out of chemistry and go into some other field." That field was running the business. It was not altogether easy. "We made a business plan, and it was all wrong," Varadi said. "I didn't have any business training, but I had common sense, and I have a good memory for numbers." Having just left the satellite business, he could also say with personal knowledge, "This was not rocket science." He added, "I had to sell something that people wanted to buy." And they did. Solarex was profitable within a year. It was the first commercial photovoltaic start-up.

During the 1970s Solarex faced only two major competitors. Both represented diversifications by the oil industry. One was ARCO Solar, which had announced its intention to become "the General Motors of the photovoltaic industry." The other was the Solar Power Corporation, which Exxon established in 1975 as part of its new venture company. But it was the process that Lindmayer began developing in his basement in Bethesda that became the basis for most of the PV production around the world today.[10]

Yet whatever Lindmayer's dream of competing with utilities, that was not to be. Solar cells were far too expensive. Nonetheless, there were at least a handful of potential niche markets, all remote locations where people needed electricity but had no access to the electric grid.

One early market was the U.S. government, including the weather bureau and the Bureau of Land Management, which oversees the far-flung wilderness owned by the federal government. Much of Solarex's business was in communications—powering, for instance, transmission equipment in remote mountain areas. The Coast Guard put PV on its buoys, supported by small backup batteries.

Another market was in the oil industry. It was difficult and expensive to get electricity for some purposes on pipelines or on offshore oil platforms. For the pipelines, the PV generated the electric current necessary to prevent corrosion inside the lines. On the platforms, solar cells supplied fail-safe electric current for safety signals and for the horns that warned off ships that might otherwise collide with the platforms.

A third early market was remote areas in the third world, as well as on small islands. In villages in Africa, photovoltaics provided a good alternative to diesel generators, powering everything from lightbulbs to water pumps, thanks in part to support from the World Bank.

One market, however, was wholly unanticipated. Sometimes, bizarrely, PV arrays would be stolen from oil and gas pipelines in various parts of the United States and Canada. Because they were a highly specialized commodity, they could not be readily resold without raising suspicion. Thus their value to the thieves was a mystery. Then the Royal Canadian Mounted Police cracked the case: Illegal marijuana growers had figured out that the police could track them down by identifying the big surges in electricity use that came from the lights they installed to nurture marijuana plants indoors. PV enabled the growers to detach themselves from the electric power grid and so keep their surge in electricity use—and thus their heads—down. In the end, pipeline operators were able to prevent such thefts by welding the PV arrays into much more inaccessible settings along their pipeline routes. In the meantime, however, what was known as "clandestine agriculture"—marijuana growing—became one of the big early markets for PV in California.[11]

THE RESEARCH PROGRAM

But these early markets were still very limited. The big obstacles remained cost and efficiency. Could PV costs be brought down sufficiently to make them competitive not just in remote locations, where the competitor was a diesel generator, but also where customers were connected to the grid and the competitor was the local electric utility?

In the mid-1970s the U.S. government recruited a physicist named Paul Maycock to run the solar program in what became the U.S. Department of Energy (DOE). Maycock had already become enamored with photovoltaics while working at Texas Instruments. He now quickly built up the government's program, which for the first time funded substantial amounts of solar research. It was Maycock who, out of his DOE budget, paid for the solar water heater that adorned the roof of Jimmy Carter's White House. But solar cells were the main focus. "It was proved beyond a doubt that PV could be a very reliable, cost-effective, off-grid source of electricity," recalled Maycock. The challenge was to bring the cost of PV down and the efficiencies up, so that they could compete with the grid. "We put in place a structured program for cost reduction," said Maycock. Spurred on by grants, companies large and small charged into the field, exploring different ways to increase efficiency.

But in the early 1980s, the Reagan administration came into office and sliced the solar budget by two thirds. "I had to cancel contracts all over the place," said Maycock, who soon enough left the government to devote himself to analyzing what was now a shrinking industry. The dream of a direct conversion of sunlight into electricity for anything other than remote purposes was fading with falling energy prices.[12]

As part of its general retrenchment during a time of falling oil prices and in response to the cuts in federal R&D spending, Exxon decided to close down Solar Power Corporation. ARCO had viewed solar as a hedge against high energy prices, and by the end of the 1980s, it was the world's largest producer of solar photovoltaic panels. But during this time, it also concluded that the PV business was just too small, and too peripheral to its core business of oil, gas, coal, and petrochemicals. The prospects for a solar business did not look good in the United States. In 1996 ARCO sold the business to Siemens of West Germany.

While Solarex had continued to be profitable during this period, its demand for capital kept growing along with its sales. So in the 1980s, Lindmayer and Varadi sold Solarex to another major U.S. oil company, Amoco. (After the merger of Amoco and BP, it became part of BP Solar, where it still resides today.) The investors made many multiples on their original investment—not a bad return for betting on a company run by two scientists who did not know anything about business.[13]

And that left the PV business in the United States where it had been—a small business focused on niche, remote markets—but now one with a lot less optimism about its future.

SUNSHINE PROJECT

One country, however, ensured that the prospects for photovoltaics as a scale business would remain alive after the sharp cuts to the U.S. solar program in the early 1980s: Japan. The Japanese contribution was critical. For the Japanese, the energy crisis of the 1970s was something that could not be conquered, only managed. Unlike the United States, Japan, virtually devoid of natural resources, could not even dream of energy independence. Yet dependence on a volatile world oil market made the Japanese people, in the words of a vice minister of the Ministry of International Trade and Industry, "very apprehensive."

As if to underline the point, during the second oil shock around the time of the Iranian Revolution, the government ordered the electric lights in the Ginza, famous for its late-hour nightlife, to be dimmed.

Under Taichi Sakaiya—the author, as described earlier, of the political thriller *Yudan!*—NEDO, the New Energy and Industrial Technology Development Organization, set out to nurture and develop new alternatives to oil, including the use of oil in electric generation. This was the national initiative that would drive, and subsidize, solar photovoltaic development.[14] Japan became the center of global PV development as government resources, under the Sunshine Project, flowed into research. The industry moved forward in a characteristic Japanese way, with major companies coordinating on the national strategic goal, while competing vigorously among themselves.

Soon cells produced by Japanese companies started showing up everywhere—not as household power sources, but as "batteries" slipped into applications that did not require large volumes of electric current. Electronic watches were one such device, but the best-known application was in another Sharp invention: the increasingly cheap and soon ubiquitous solar-powered calculator.[15]

By the 1990s companies like Sharp, Kyocera, and Sanyo were producing

EUROPE'S SOLAR POTENTIAL

Source: PVGIS:EC

Government policy rather than natural endowment turned Germany into Europe's solar hot spot.

rooftop photovoltaic systems that consumers purchased with significant help from government subsidies and what was called the New Sunshine Project. These subsidies—combined with some of the highest electricity rates in the world, falling costs, and efficiencies of scale—propelled Japanese solar manufacturers to the top ranks of global photovoltaic producers. One Japanese solar manufacturer after another claimed the number one spot among global photovoltaics producers. By the end of 2001, there were 77,503 "solar roofs" in Japan.

Japan had succeeded in expending PV beyond specialized applications and turning it into a real business with at least the beginnings of a mass market. In the late 1990s, an executive from an American PV company visited Japan. He toured Sharp's highly automated photovoltaic-manufacturing factory. "I was

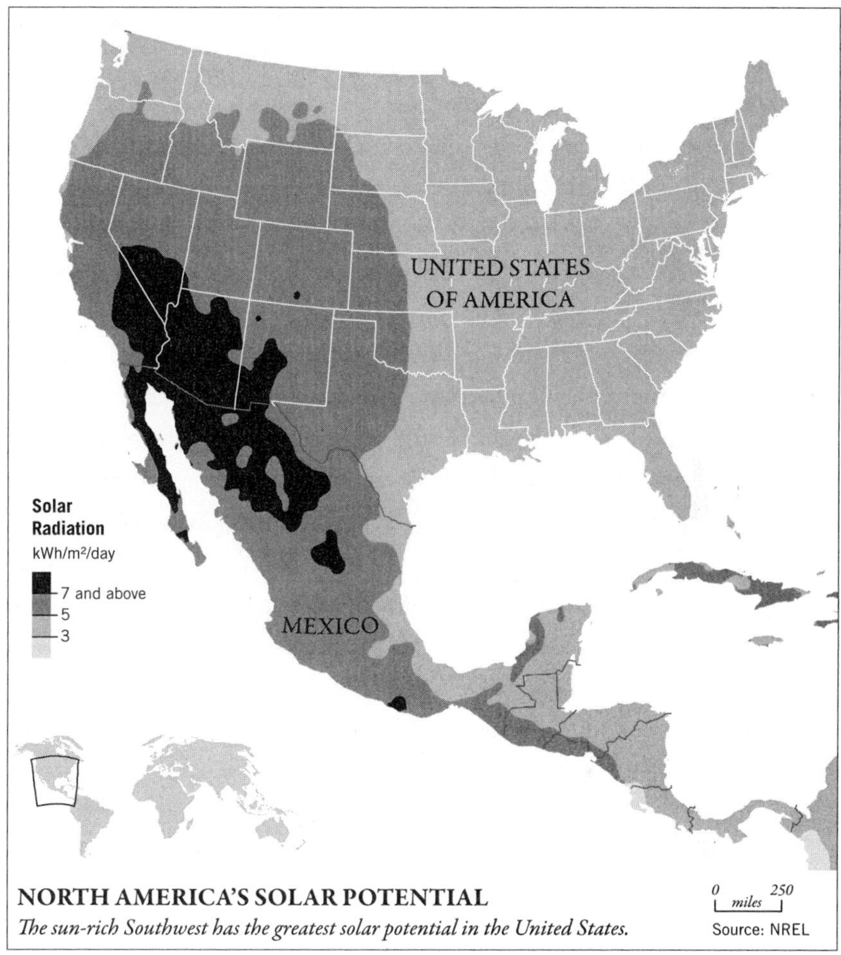

NORTH AMERICA'S SOLAR POTENTIAL

The sun-rich Southwest has the greatest solar potential in the United States.

shocked by how advanced it was," he said. "It seemed as if we were a generation behind the Japanese in manufacturing." Japan had reached the point where some solar energy in urban areas, even without subsidies, could be considered almost competitive with electricity produced by traditional generation and transmitted over the grid.[16]

Still, perspective is required. Solar represents just about 1 percent of Japanese electricity. Even if Japan's target of about 70 percent of new houses being equipped with solar cells on their roofs by 2020 is met, solar cells will still not be a regular source of electricity. As one Japanese official put it, "Solar will be significant, but not substantial."

THE GERMAN BOOM

One thing was indubitably clear: Japan had taken on the solar mantle at the beginning of the 1980s and held on to it right into the first years of the twenty-first century. "They dominated the industry by 2004," said one veteran solar executive. "What they didn't realize was that right behind them would be Germany with a much bigger program."

What drove the changes in Germany was the aforementioned feed-in tariffs, which had actually begun in the late 1980s to ensure profitability to investments in renewables production. In 1999, the same year that the newly elected coalition of Social Democrats and the Green Party set out to promote renewables and reshape Germany's energy policy, a German engineer named Reiner Lemoine approached a strategy consultant, Anton Milner, with a business plan for a new solar cell company. Renewables were coming because of pollution concerns and technological innovation, said Lemoine. While no one had made "any real money" in photovoltaics, his plan showed how it could be done—by rapidly seeking scale and aggressively driving down costs. But, added Lemoine, "We're two scientists and one engineer, and the banks won't even talk to us," he lamented. "We don't have any money and we can't pay anyone."

As Milner read the business plan that evening, he found it, somewhat to his surprise, persuasive. In fact, very persuasive. Instead of becoming a consultant, Milner joined the company and found himself the CEO of what was a very tiny venture. They were able to raise some money at the tail end of the Internet boom, and they got some German government funding by agreeing to build their factory in a depressed part of the former East Germany. By 2001 production had begun and the company was up and running, with a grand total of 19 employees. They called it Q-Cells—for high performance and high "quality." At that point the only real market in the world was the niche in Japan. But Germany's new, much strengthened feed-in tariff was going into effect just at that time. And that meant subsidies up to five times the cost of conventional electricity.

Over the next few years, Q-Cells redesigned processes and automated production, driving down costs by as much as 50 percent. In 2003 and 2004, its business—like that of all the cell manufacturers—took off. By 2007 it was the number one producer of solar photovoltaic cells in the world. "PVs could live very nicely as a subsidized niche product, and you could have a pot of money," said Milner a couple of years later. "Our job is to change that, to get PVs competitive against mainstream electricity on a nonsubsidized basis. We're not there yet."[17]

But the more difficult competition proved to be with other PV manufacturers—non-German and lower cost. As a result, Q-Cells' market share fell. So did its stock market value—from $15 billion in 2007 to about $500 million in mid-2011. This new competition was coming from the East.

CHINA ENTERS

The global solar industry's center of gravity had shifted to China, which now accounts for the largest share in the world of solar module manufacturing capacity, and more than half the world's production of crystalline silicon solar modules, the most popular type of solar module. And few individuals in the country have played a more instrumental role in developing the sector as Shi Zhengrong. Shi became a solar tycoon "by accident," as he puts it. "In our generation we didn't have the freedom to choose. We just accepted whatever was given."[18]

Shi was able to go to university in 1979 as the universities, which had been closed during the Cultural Revolution, were starting to reopen. Deng Xiaoping was just beginning his post-Mao reform. A few years later, Shi was overjoyed when he learned that he had won a stipend to do graduate work in the United States. But then he was told that, because of a bureaucratic mistake, he was going to have to go to Australia instead. "I wanted to pursue the American dream," he recalled. "I was learning American-accented English. I was a little depressed." He found himself instead at the University of New South Wales, in Sydney.

Once into his studies, he went to see Professor Martin Green in search of some extra work. Green, a legend in solar cell research, offered Shi a scholarship to work with him. After his doctorate, Shi took a job as research director for a spin-off company from Green's lab. There he compiled an impressive portfolio of patents. The young Chinese researcher took Australian citizenship and started to buy real estate. Soon enough, with three houses to his name, he assumed that his life would be in Australia.

Then, over a dim sum lunch in Sydney, he heard from a friend visiting from China that things were changing in his homeland. China was opening up to entrepreneurial business. In 2000 Shi went back to see for himself. Overwhelmed by how fast things were moving, he sat down and, in a matter of days, wrote a 200-page business plan for a China-based solar cell company. But it took him ten months to find the money. Finally, he managed to raise $6 million from a local government. With that he was able to found a company, which he named Suntech. The firm began operations in 2001, the same year as Q-Cells.

"I never thought I'd come back to China," said Shi. "I never thought I could be a businessman. I thought my career path was very clear. I would become a professor."

But now as a businessman, Shi kept his focus on "low-cost expansion" and driving down manufacturing costs. He bought used equipment and looked for the cheapest supplies. And, when it made sense, he took a step backward. He "de-automated" parts of the business, realizing that some processes would be cheaper if done by low-cost Chinese workers rather than expensive machines. "The only barrier to renewable energy is cost," he said. "To get the costs down for renewable energy is the most important thing. It is the most urgent thing. Thirty percent is technology, but 70 percent is manufacturing efficiency."

Just four years after Shi launched Suntech, he took his company public on the New York Stock Exchange. In 2010, sales were over $3 billion.

Shi's success can also be attributed to the globalization of the renewable business. For the company owed its growth not to the market in China, but to feed-in tariffs in Europe and subsidies in Japan, which created business that Suntech and other Chinese companies captured thanks to their low costs. Shi is particularly grateful to the German feed-in tariff. "I was very lucky," he said. "In 2004 Germany created the world market." Today about 95 percent of the total revenues of Suntech and Yingli Green Energy, another Chinese solar company, are derived from markets outside of China.

"There's great momentum in China," Shi said. "We used to pursue the American dream. Now everybody is pursuing the Chinese dream. And now Suntech has a host of competitors in China. The world is very competitive. If I'm not careful, I will be left behind. We have to keep innovating."[19]

China's advantages extend beyond low-cost manufacturing. Chinese incentives are aimed not just at stimulating domestic market demand, as in the

United States, Europe, and Japan, but at promoting manufacturing and exports. In consequence, non-Chinese manufacturers are shifting a growing part of their manufacturing to China in order to stay competitive. Meanwhile, the degree of support provided by Beijing and by local Chinese governments for solar manufacturing has emerged as a new trade issue between China and the West.

THIN FILM

Despite the striking shift of the solar cell industry east to China, one of the world's largest—and lowest cost—manufacturers of solar panels is a U.S. company based in Arizona, First Solar. John T. Walton—a son of Walmart's founder, Sam Walton, and an heir to the Walton fortune—was the major early backer in the late 1990s.

First Solar is able to produce solar cells at such a low cost because of an innovative manufacturing process based on thin-film technology, which it has refined over the years. Crystalline silicon, going back to Solarex, is the manufacturing technology that is most favored on an industrywide basis. Thin-film production is a mass-manufacturing process that uses nonsilicon materials. In general, thin-film cells are less efficient than crystalline silicon cells, but they can also be significantly cheaper to produce.

Indeed, First Solar has been able to drive costs so far down as to make it more competitive with some kinds of conventional generation. Reflecting the increasingly global nature of PV demand, First Solar runs production lines in factories on three continents: the original, near Toledo, Ohio; another in Germany; and the largest, in Malaysia.

First Solar has been expanding from its core business of making PVs into the business of developing solar projects. In 2009 First Solar signed a contract to undertake construction of what it has said will be the world's largest solar plant with a massive 2-gigawatt solar farm in China's Inner Mongolia Province, with a surface area of about twenty-five square miles (slightly larger than the area of Manhattan). "This is nuclear power–size scale," said Michael Ahearn, CEO of First Solar at the time of the announcement. First Solar is expected to build a factory in China to help supply solar cells for the project, which is scheduled to be completed by 2019.[20]

THE SOLAR MENU

It has been more than a century since Albert Einstein, in those weeks in the patent office in Zurich, laid out the principle of photovoltaics. But it was not until the twenty-first century that photovoltaics really began to move beyond remote locations for their viability.

With declining costs, greater capacity, and government subsidies, the annual PV market has grown from 0.6 gigawatts in 2003 to 20 gigawatts in 2010. By 2010 about 40 gigawatts of solar cells have been installed, with most of this coming in just in the last few years. In 2010, $75 billion was invested in the solar photovoltaic business worldwide. Future growth depends both on the extent of government support and the rate at which PV costs are brought down further.[21] Yet the industry's growth has been volatile, even more than other corners of the renewables sector. Sentiment of panel makers and investors, among others, has swung rapidly—in large part propelled by the introduction (or amendment or phase out) of incentives.

As the solar cell industry has grown, so too has the interest of venture capitalists in investing in it, and funding has increased dramatically. Today there is a fierce race among companies—both established companies and new VC-funded start-ups—riding a host of competing technologies, to bring down costs and improve efficiencies.[22]

The menu of technologies for PV is extensive. There are trade-offs to each of these technologies, which can be summarized as cost versus efficiency. Some types of PV are cheaper to make than others but are less efficient at converting sunlight into energy. Others are more expensive to make but do a better job at creating energy.

The menu includes solar cells in which the semiconductors are made from silicon in crystal form, or crystalline silicon. Monocrystalline and polycrystalline, the two primary types of manufacturing processes that produce this type of PV, are similar to those developed first by Solarex.

Then there are solar cells in which the semiconductor is made using a thin-film manufacturing process, in which just a very thin layer of photovoltaic material is employed. These have the potential, at least, to achieve much lower costs. One approach uses amorphous silicon, which does not need the same processing as crystalline silicon processes. However, efficiencies are low compared with other approaches. Another key thin-film technology does not use silicon at all, but rather cadmium-telluride. This process involves coating a sheet of glass with a thin film of cadmium-telluride to produce the photovoltaic effect. This is the technology that First Solar uses to make PVs. A third thin-film technology that is attracting a good deal of investment are CIGS, for Copper, Indium, Gallium di-Selinide. They can be produced in flexible materials that can, more easily, be integrated into building materials.

Scientists are working on still other innovative processes for making solar cells. Some are trying to apply nanotechnology to perfect more efficient materials that can be applied almost like an ink or a dye. One major focus of research is to develop systems that allow photovoltaics to be incorporated into roofing material and even into walls—"Building Integrated PV."

Indeed, it is a horse race among companies and technologies, all seeking the same goal. "The objective is higher efficiencies with lower costs," said David Carlson, who is the chief scientist at BP Solar. "That's what the whole game is all about." Carlson brings a unique perspective to these questions, for he actually invented amorphous thin-film silicon at RCA Labs in 1974. "I've been there when we thought that things would go especially fast. But it takes time to build the base. It's not like computers and integrated circuits where speed doubles every eighteen months because of Moore's Law," Carlson said. "Photovoltaics are more chaotic. There are more efficient ways to take advantage of sunlight, but there are many different approaches, and no clear winner. People underestimate how long entirely new approaches take. You have to build the scientific foundation, and then the engineering basis, and then the whole infrastructure."[23]

Given the stakes and intensity of the competition, the scientists and engineers working on the various approaches are competitive, convinced of the virtues of their process and disbelieving of the competitors. One venture capitalist recounted how, in a spirit of détente, he had brought together the CEOs of two of his portfolio companies, each a champion of a competing PV technology. The meeting was superficially amiable, but afterward each privately conveyed his deep conviction to their common capitalist that the other was going down a fruitless path and was surely doomed to fail.

CONCENTRATING THE SUN

Photovoltaics are not the only avenue for solar. Effort and money are also flowing into other forms of solar energy—most notably what is called concentrated solar. This process is closer to conventional electricity production. Think of these as generation plants, but where the input is not coal or natural gas or uranium, but sunlight. Concentrated solar captures light with large mirrors of various kinds and then focuses it. The heat, now much more intense, brings a fluid inside the pipes to a very high temperature, which in turn is used to vaporize water that drives a turbine and produces electricity. The first concentrated solar plant, based on an Israeli design with parabolic mirrors, went up in the Mojave Desert in 1984. But just around that time energy prices plummeted, particularly natural gas prices. The technology, and the interest, languished.

However, concentrated solar has come back to life, with a number of different new designs, including trough designs, where large banks of trough-shaped mirrors are used to concentrate energy in fluid-filled pipes; power towers, on which sunlight is focused to bring the fluid to its superhigh temperatures; and stirling engine systems, where sunlight is reflected off a dish to run a small stirling engine at the dish's center. There is also a hybrid approach to concentrated solar as well. That is to use a concentrated facility to capture the sunlight and then focus it, in much more intense form, on large arrays of photovoltaic cells. Those concentrated plants that heat a liquid have an advantage over solar cells: storage. That is, they can store the heat in molten salt and continue to operate—and generate electricity—so as to match up with peak loads.

Meanwhile, a concentrated solar project on a much grander scale has been envisioned for North Africa. The project, called Desertec, is far from generating any electricity. Yet the idea is to build huge solar farms in the Sahara Desert and transmit the power produced across the Mediterranean Sea to markets in Europe. The ambitions are huge. So is the price tag. Financing such a vast project is a major hurdle, so is the fact that concentrated solar still costs much more to produce than traditional forms of power. Uncertain politics will also be a very big hurdle.

In general, concentrated solar plants face key constraints: land, access, transmission—and cost. They can be used only in hot sunny areas. The typical design can also use substantial amounts of water, which can be a problem when the places most suited to concentrated solar projects are hot and arid.

Nonetheless, recent years have seen a land rush in the California desert for sites to build either concentrated solar plants or utility-scale arrays of solar panels. These expansive solar plants have run into what might strike some as a surprising obstacle: the opposition of environmental groups that are determined to protect the sparsely settled desert regions against development.[24]

GRID PARITY?

What many believe is now in sight, whatever the technology, is the prospect of grid parity. The concept emerged around 2000–2001. It holds that solar will eventually be able to compete head to head with electricity from the local utility and come out cheaper, or at least equal. Yet calculating grid parity is not easy, since it's not really a one-to-one comparison. Indeed, it's not altogether clear how one ought to compare a one-time investment—with free electrons thereafter—to a monthly bill from the local utility.

Calculating grid parity is complicated because the math has to account for the cost of manufacturing the solar cells, installation costs, and present and future power prices. And, of course, of critical importance is the issue of sunlight: that is, how much sunlight is delivered to that particular region in the various seasons and, thus, how many hours a year can the solar panel operate. Italy has about twice as many hours of sunlight a year as Germany, and this factor alone will affect grid parity.

There is another complication: PV are not dispatchable power that one can count on, as is the case with electricity dispatched from a power plant. Like wind, PV are intermittent. They do not generate much electricity on cloudy days or any at night. The advantage that they have over wind, however, is that they can deliver on hot, sunny days when electricity demand spikes upward, and thus can offset utilities' need to build peak capacity that is used only at times of heaviest demand.

This intermittency affects the investment requirements. A gigawatt of installed PV capacity is not the same as a gigawatt of coal or nuclear capacity because the PV installation does not operate at night or when the sun is not shining. That is why, when talking about PV, as with wind, one must distinguish between installed capacity and electricity actually generated. Tower-based concentrated solar, however, does hold out the promise of dispatchability.

Some express concern that the concept of grid parity looks only at the direct costs for the consumer and not at the total cost to the entire system—the additional investment in backup power and additional transmission investment necessitated by intermittency, as well as subsidies and incentives. The result is to add another layer of cost and complexity to the power system. The fuel—the sun (or wind)—may be free, but the full cost in some way "must be covered by the market and ultimately ratepayers," according to one study.

Grid parity is linked to another concept: net metering. This allows a power customer to deduct the amount of electricity it puts into the grid, owing to its solar generation, from the amount it receives from the grid. In some markets, where electricity prices are high, grid parity, at least looking at it from the viewpoint of the consumer, may be near, but it has not yet arrived. "All grid-connected markets are subsidized," observed Paul Maycock, who ran the government's solar program under President Carter. "If you are getting this subsidy, the market is not yet real."[25]

ALL THE ROOFS?

Hans Ziegler was the passionate proponent of photovoltaics who in 1958 championed the solar cells aboard the Vanguard satellite. When, half a century ago, he enunciated his vision that the "roofs of all of our buildings in cities and towns" would be equipped with photovoltaics, it was not only very early but also, frankly, pretty far-fetched. A half century later, that prospect, or some fraction of it, is something on which a lot of significant bets are being placed—in the United States, in Europe, and in Asia. Some of the estimates for growth, and future installed capacity, are very high. Some believe that they could be providing a substantial part of the world's electricity by the middle of the twenty-first century.

Photovoltaics may appear to offer the alchemy of shining light—turning light into electricity. But they are not magic, not when one considers the scale of the world's electric power system and the current costs of solar. Somewhat cautious, strangely enough, is one of the leading longtime advocates of solar cells. Paul Maycock is as experienced as anyone in the world with the development of photovoltaics. As he says, he has "lived, eaten, and drunk solar cells" for more than forty years, and he has been an advocate over all those years. "All of the projects we worked on in the Department of Energy in the 1970s are coming true," he says. "Just several decades later." Yet he says that he is "scared" that "people will decide that PV are *the* green option when they are really one of eight or nine green options.

"If we reach ten percent of total electricity from PVs by 2050, that will be a great achievement," Maycock added. "Theoretically we may be able to eventually get to 15 or 20 percent without a breakthrough in storage technology. But 15 percent of the world's electricity is a very big number. To reach 15 percent will require trillions of dollars of investment. For a business that is now doing sixty billion dollars a year, that is a very nice mountain to be challenged by."[26]

30

MYSTERY OF WIND

Experience had taught Philip Marlowe to pay close attention to the winds that blew in from the desert into the Los Angeles Basin.

"There was a desert wind blowing that night," he said of one particular evening. "It was one of those hot, dry Santa Anas that came down through the mountain passes and curl your hair and make your nerves jump and your skin itch. When the Santa Anas blow," added Marlowe, "anything can happen."[1]

But it probably would never have occurred to the fictional detective, nor to his creator, Raymond Chandler, that one thing that would happen was that California's winds could help jump-start a global industry.

Yet the state's gales were key to wind becoming the largest and the fastest growing source of renewable energy in the world today. In the United States, wind power has increased tenfold in ten years. In Germany, wind accounts for about 60 percent of the total renewable capacity added over the past decade.

While wind has become a big business, it is still small—only 2 percent of total electricity generated in the United States. It is also more expensive than other sources, although the cost is declining.

But hopes for the future development of wind are very high. In the United States, the Department of Energy has proposed a national target for the United States to get 20 percent of total electricity from wind by the year 2030. Another study predicts that, globally, wind could be 22 percent of total electricity supply by 2030. Are such ambitious targets doable?[2]

After all, wind runs into certain obstacles. The more successful that wind is—the more wind in the electricity system—the bigger the challenge of integrating it into the existing system. Wind does not blow all the time, and its strength varies. That makes it intermittent, which means you cannot count on it being available when you want it. As a result, wind, as with solar, is not well suited to provide the constant base-load generation. Something else needs to be available the other two thirds of the time when the wind is not blowing sufficiently. That something else requires additional investment—and added cost—for new conventional generation in order to pick up the slack. Wind's intermittency also creates new complexities for managing the overall grid and balancing the different energy sources. Moreover, wind supplies tend to be dispersed, and often distant from where people live, and thus require substantial new transmission systems to deliver the electricity.

Today's wind turbines are not simple machines—and they are very large. Yet while the power electronics, computer controls, and engineering of a modern 25-story-tall wind turbine may be complex, the basic concept is not. The energy supply—wind—is provided free of charge, courtesy of Mother Nature. Winds are generated by the spinning of planet Earth itself, by the irregularities of the Earth's surface (from mountains and valleys to oceans), and by solar radiation. For when air is heated by the sun, it expands and becomes lighter and thus rises, creating a vacuum, and other cooler air rushes in to fill the vacuum. That flow may be as gentle as a breeze or as powerful as a tempest. It is this direct impact of the sun on the temperature of air that most explicitly qualifies wind as a form of solar energy.

A traditional windmill captures the moving force of the wind—its kinetic energy—and transforms it into mechanical energy. In an electric turbine, the mechanical energy is then transformed by a generator into electricity. A large wind turbine is really a small power plant. The wind may be free, but that is not true of the system required to harness it in large volumes, put it through the grid, and deliver it to consumers. How much more will it cost? How much actual backup investment in other sources will be needed? Do these constraints put limits on what can be expected of wind? All these are subjects of debate, and all are part of the mystery of wind—the mystery of how big it can get and how large a role it can play in meeting future needs for electricity.

"THE FREE BENEFIT OF WIND"

The oldest use of wind was to fill billowing sails of ships and move them across the water, supplementing the human labor of oarsmen. On land, windmills go back a thousand years or more. They were developed to provide mechanical energy for two essential endeavors—grinding grain and water management; that is, pumping, irrigation, and drainage. This greatly reduced the need for exhausting, time-consuming human labor of pounding grain and hauling water.

By the tenth century or perhaps even earlier, primitive windmills were already working in Persia, and then spread through the Islamic world and into China. Windmills also began to appear in Europe. In medieval England, they represented an attempt by rural entrepreneurs to do an end-run around the authorities of the day. The nobility and the church jealously guarded their exclusive rights to use riverbanks for their waterwheels, which ground grain. These monopolies were a source of wealth and power. For acquiring grain from a waterwheel spared a woman the daily hours of hard work and monotony that she would otherwise expend pounding grain for her family.

In the twelfth century, in Suffolk, England, a certain fearsome Abbot Samson, from the abbey at Bury St. Edmunds, controlled the nearby riverbanks on which his watermills operated. In order to circumvent the abbot's monopoly, an elderly clergyman known to history only as Herbert built a rudimentary windmill. Abbot Samson, enraged by this challenge to his monopoly over grinding grain, ordered the windmill dismantled. Herbert replied with a ringing defense: "The free benefit of the wind ought not to be denied to any man." Alas, this battle cry of freedom only enraged Abbot Samson more. Herbert's windmill was destroyed.[3]

But technology could not be stayed. Other windmills did begin to sprout across England—indeed, thousands of them—and across Europe. Don Quixote famously charged, lance in hand, at "30 or more monstrous giants" despite the protestations from Sancho Panza that "most certainly they were windmills."

The encounter sent Cervantes' noble knight tumbling and gave rise to the adage "tilting at windmills."

Windmills became a familiar part of the natural landscape in Holland, where they were used not only for grinding grain but for draining marshes and lakes and thus opening up much land to cultivation behind newly constructed dikes. Windmills in Europe came to be used for many other industrial purposes, from crushing olives to making gunpowder to powering the bellows of blast furnaces. The widespread use of windmills, along with watermills, one historian has written, "marked the beginning of the breakdown of the traditional world in which man had to depend for power on animal or vegetable sources of power. It was the distant announcement of the Industrial Revolution." It is estimated that a quarter of Europe's total industrial energy came from wind in the centuries between 1300 and the emergence of steam and coal in the nineteenth century.[4]

THE ELECTRIFICATION OF WIND

In 1883, just a year after Edison's Pearl Street station opened, people began to wonder, could wind compete with coal in generating power? *Scientific American* wrote: "It seems incomprehensible that so ready and potent an agent should escape practical use so completely." Yes, it added, wind was "destitute of all uniformity . . . sometimes furious . . . sometimes absolutely nothing, and at all times unsteady and capricious." And it pointed to what continues to be a very key question—the problem of intermittency: "How shall we *store* the power that may come to us by day or night, Sundays and week days, gathering it at the time we do not need it and preserving it till we do. This is the problem."

"Who," asked *Scientific American,* "is the man to solve it?"

That man, it turned out, was a certain Charles Brush, one of Edison's great rivals. The Brush lights, used for outdoor lighting, had been one of the main competitors to Edison's lightbulb. By 1880 some 6,000 of his Brush lights were illuminating cities across the country. This made Brush a rich man.

In 1887, in his backyard on Euclid Avenue in Cleveland—just down the street on "Millionaires' Row" from the world's leading oil tycoon, John D. Rockefeller—Brush set out to solve the problem of wind and electricity.

He built a 60-foot windmill connected to a dynamo and a network of batteries in the basement. With this he illuminated his mansion. Brush's machine was the first time that electricity was, in a practical way, generated from the wind. While praising Brush, *Scientific American* cautioned its readers not to assume that lighting, powered by wind, "is cheap because the wind costs nothing. On the contrary, the cost of the plant is so great as to more than offset the cheapness of the motive power." Eventually Brush succumbed to temptation and hooked up his home to the centrally generated city electric system that his competitor Edison had pioneered—it was more convenient. But Brush had proved that the wind could be a source of electric power.[5]

The rapid spread of centrally generated electricity in cities and towns meant that there was no demand for wind-generated electricity. This was not true, however, for America's isolated farms and ranches.

To meet their needs engineer-entrepreneurs developed small electricity-generating windmills along with battery systems to store the power. Traditional windmills had been used for a traditional purpose, pumping water. Wind electricity could do more. It could provide farmers and ranchers—and their wives and children—with light, and reduce tiring, repetitive physical labor.

Two farm boys from North Dakota, the Jacobs brothers, took the lead. One of them, Marcellus, designed the blades by observing how the propellers worked on the small planes he had learned to fly. Their advertising trumpeted: "Wind! The Cheapest Power in the World Is Easily Available to Every Farm Home." The brothers also marketed Jacobs-branded appliances, ranging from refrigerators to waffle makers. An estimated 30,000 Jacobs wind turbines were sold, along with hundreds of thousands of turbines from other manufacturers.[6]

But Franklin Roosevelt's New Deal would eventually disconnect many of the blades turning on America's farms and ranches. As the rural electric cooperatives, backed by the new Rural Electrification Administration (REA), began to spread their wires and grids across the landscape in the late 1930s, they delivered a superior quality electricity, and over the next two decades, wind faded away as a power source for America's farmers and ranchers.

ON GRANDPA'S KNOB WITH PALMER PUTNAM

In the winter and spring of 1941, convoys of trucks carrying what would amount to 500 tons of equipment and parts, including two blades each weighing eight tons, inched their way up an arduous dirt track with almost impossible hairpin turns, to the top of a mountain called Grandpa's Knob, a dozen or so miles from the Vermont city of Rutland. All this industrial activity on this isolated mount was aimed at building a windmill that would generate 1.5 megawatts—an almost unimaginable output at the time.

Palmer Putnam, the person responsible, was the grandson of the founder of the publisher G. P. Putnam's & Sons. Though he himself served a short time as its president, Putnam's heart was in engineering. Educated at MIT, he had worked as a geologist in the Belgian Congo. Later, when he built a house on Cape Cod, Putnam found "both the winds and the electric rates surprisingly high." To Putnam the solution was obvious: wind power.[7]

Putnam assembled a first-rate team, including some of America's most prominent scientists as well as leading companies, among them General Electric, which helped with the electrical mechanisms. The quite isolated and inaccessible Grandpa's Knob was chosen because of the quality of its winds.

By the autumn of 1941, Putnam's 175-foot-tall windmill was generating electricity. Rather than powering a single farm, it fed into the grid of Central Vermont Public Service, just as a coal-fired plant would, adding its contribution to the anonymous electrons moving through the wires. This insight—that the wind system could feed into the whole grid, rather than be independent—was one of Putnam's fundamental contributions. Wind could be integrated into, rather than compete with, the existing system.[8]

Palmer's turbine worked well until the middle of World War II, when a mechanical failure shut it down. By that time, Putnam was designing amphibious landing craft for the invasion at Normandy and working on strategy for amphibious warfare in the Pacific. It was not until 1945 that the windmill could be fixed. Just a few weeks later, one of the eight-ton blades came loose, spun off, and crashed down the mountainside. That was the end. There was neither the funds to repair it nor the willpower.

Yet that abandoned 175-foot tower on Grandpa's Knob would turn out to be a beacon over the decades, for it proved what was possible. As one scientist explained to a congressional committee in 1974, Putnam's wind turbine "was really the precursor of all of the wind work that is being done today."[9]

THE MODERN INDUSTRY

By the mid-1970s, in the aftermath of the oil embargo and amid the quest for alternative energy sources, wind electricity became a serious subject. But the wind industry, as it is today, owes its birth not only to OPEC but also to two other things: the Danish farm-machinery business and California tax credits. Without their marriage, there might well not be the industry that now exists. That, however, was not the way it began.

After the 1973 oil crisis, the federal government began to fund wind energy research and development. For wind power to be credible to utilities, larger-scale machines would be necessary, and the government turned to large defense contractors. After all, if they could build jets and bombers, and helicopters and planes with propellers, then surely they could build tall towers with rotating propeller-like blades. A host of companies went to work on the problem—Boeing, McDonnell Douglas, United Technologies, General Electric, and Alcoa, among others. But these early wind machines generally performed poorly. "We tended to be blinded because windmills had been used for more than a thousand years," one government R&D manager concluded. "We thought the technology was there and all we had to do was bring it into the twentieth century."[10]

With the deep program cuts of the Reagan era, the federally funded wind power R&D program came to an end.

"CALIFORNIA WIND RUSH"

While federal R&D spending was terminated before it could be effective in promoting wind energy, other government policies—regulatory and tax—were available. First there was the aforementioned Public Utilities Regulatory Policies Act, PURPA, which required utilities to take power from small non-utility generators. And then there were the tax credits, generous tax credits. The federal government provided tax credits for wind power, and so did the state of California, even for projects that generated little or no electricity. Indeed, the person who really made the difference, and did as much as any single person to launch wind power, was California's Governor Jerry Brown. Developers also got accelerated depreciation on their wind assets, and all this made the investment almost risk-free. As a kicker, California wind developers would be paid for any electricity sold into the grid as the state's generous PURPA "avoided" rates for renewable electricity.

The result was California's extraordinary wind rush. Committed wind advocates, serious developers, skilled engineers, and practical visionaries were joined by flimflam promoters, tax shelter salesmen, and quick-buck artists. Thus was the modern wind industry born.

The frenzy gave rise to a critical innovation. Rather than depend upon a single mammoth machine, as Palmer Putnam had, smaller turbines were clustered together and connected by a computer network so that they functioned as though they were a single machine. These networked wind turbines became known as wind farms. This approach had the added value that if a few machines went down, the system would continue to function, and most of the electricity would continue to flow into the grid.

If California was, for a time, the Saudi Arabia of wind, then it had three giant wind fields with enormous wind resources. One was in the northern part of the state, the Altamont Pass, between the San Joaquin Valley and the San Francisco Bay Area. Others were in the Tehachapi Pass, south of Bakersfield, and the San Gorgonio Pass, near Palm Springs.

Developers raced to acquire sites. Many of the best locations were inaccessible and took much ingenuity, great effort, and some daring to develop. But it was only when they had started to build their machines that the developers found out how truly violent and turbulent and unpredictable those winds could be—and how daunting it would be to harness them.

The machines would be tested every day by the actual conditions under which they operated. The wind, said an engineer at the time, "beats on you all day. It never lets up. Your eyes get affected . . . You can literally lean your body into the wind, and it will suspend you." Many turbines could not stand up to the stress. Blades crumpled or flew off, towers toppled over, electronics malfunctioned. Most produced far less electricity than manufacturers had promised. Reliability and performance became a central issue.

Until the arrival of wind, the tiny community of Cabazon, ten miles west of Palm Springs, had been known mainly as the home of Hadley's, a sprawling fruit store, famous for the delicious date shakes it sold to thirsty travelers on their way back from the desert. Then, with great hope, a wind park was built in Cabazon. For Cabazon was in the San Gorgonio Pass, the juncture between the Mojave Desert and the Los Angeles Basin. The ferocious winds disabled the Cabazon turbines almost immediately. The wind machines produced virtually no electricity. Rather they were "an eyesore of broken and twisted blades."[11]

One of the most important and committed pioneers was James Dehlsen. His company, Zond, was partly named for the *zonda,* the wind that blows from the Andes down over Argentina, and for the German word that means "probe."

Along with everybody else in the California wind business, Dehlsen found that his economics depended in part upon the tax credit. And so he and his colleagues spent New Year's Eve, 1981, struggling in a raging blizzard on a dangerous ridge in the Tehachapi Pass, battling to get the balking wind turbines up before the new year in order to qualify for that year's tax credits, which would expire at midnight.

"As soon as we started turning the turbines on, they started disintegrating," he said. "The next day we picked up the pieces. We concluded that we'd better get a better technology pretty damn quick."[12]

STURDY DANES

Dehlsen decided to look for that technology in Europe and set off for Holland. A Danish engineer, Finn Hansen, whose family owned an agricultural-equipment manufacturing company, heard that Dehlsen was about to buy Dutch turbines. He hurriedly flew down to Holland in his small propeller plane, picked up Dehlsen, and flew him back to Denmark, to visit the family business, Vestas.

A few years earlier, Finn Hansen had decided to put his family company's skills to work on turbines, building on a Danish interest in wind-generated electricity going back to the end of the nineteenth century. During both world wars, Denmark overcame disruptions to its conventional energy supplies by depending upon winds coming off the sea to generate much of its electricity. After World War II, wind could no longer compete with cheap centrally generated electric power. But the oil crises of the 1970s rekindled the interest. By 1979 Vestas had built its first wind turbine. Other Danish companies were developing their own wind machines. The reborn Danish industry was rooted in agricultural machinery; in fact, a number of the original wind companies were members of the Union of Blacksmiths. The Danish designs emphasized durability, reliability, and ruggedness, characteristics much prized in farm machinery.[13]

The Danes had something else going for them, too, which proved to be of critical importance—the Risø National Laboratory, situated on a fjord 40 miles from Copenhagen. Risø had been created under the auspices of the Danish Nobel laureate physicist Niels Bohr, who had spent part of World War II at Los Alamos and was one of the fathers of the atomic bomb. After the war Bohr returned to Copenhagen, where he presided over the founding of Risø Laboratory, the purpose of which, reflecting Bohr's fervent dream, was "to further the peaceful use of atomic energy for the benefit of society."

But by the mid-1970s, support for nuclear power in Denmark had so waned that some of the members in the reactor department at Risø shifted their research over to wind. They did everything, from study the kinetic power of winds to prepare an atlas of wind resources in Denmark and then Europe. Most important, they tested turbine designs. Risø was critical to the rise of the Danish industry. So were subsidies from the Danish government. But much of the Danish market was initially composed of what has been described as "mostly long-haired activists living in collectives and alternative farmers."[14]

James Dehlsen's arrival would change that. He tramped out into the field with Hansen and examined the Vestas machines that were up and operating. They would, he decided, be able to withstand the furious winds on the ridges in California. Virtually on the spot, he put in an order for 150 turbines, far more than Vestas had produced till then. Over the decade, Zond bought almost all Vestas' output. Dehlsen did as much as anyone to create the scale market that nurtured the Danish industry. Dehlsen and the other California developers who turned to Danish companies for their more rugged wind machines did much to restore

HARNESSING WIND POWER

Generalized diagram of a wind turbine.

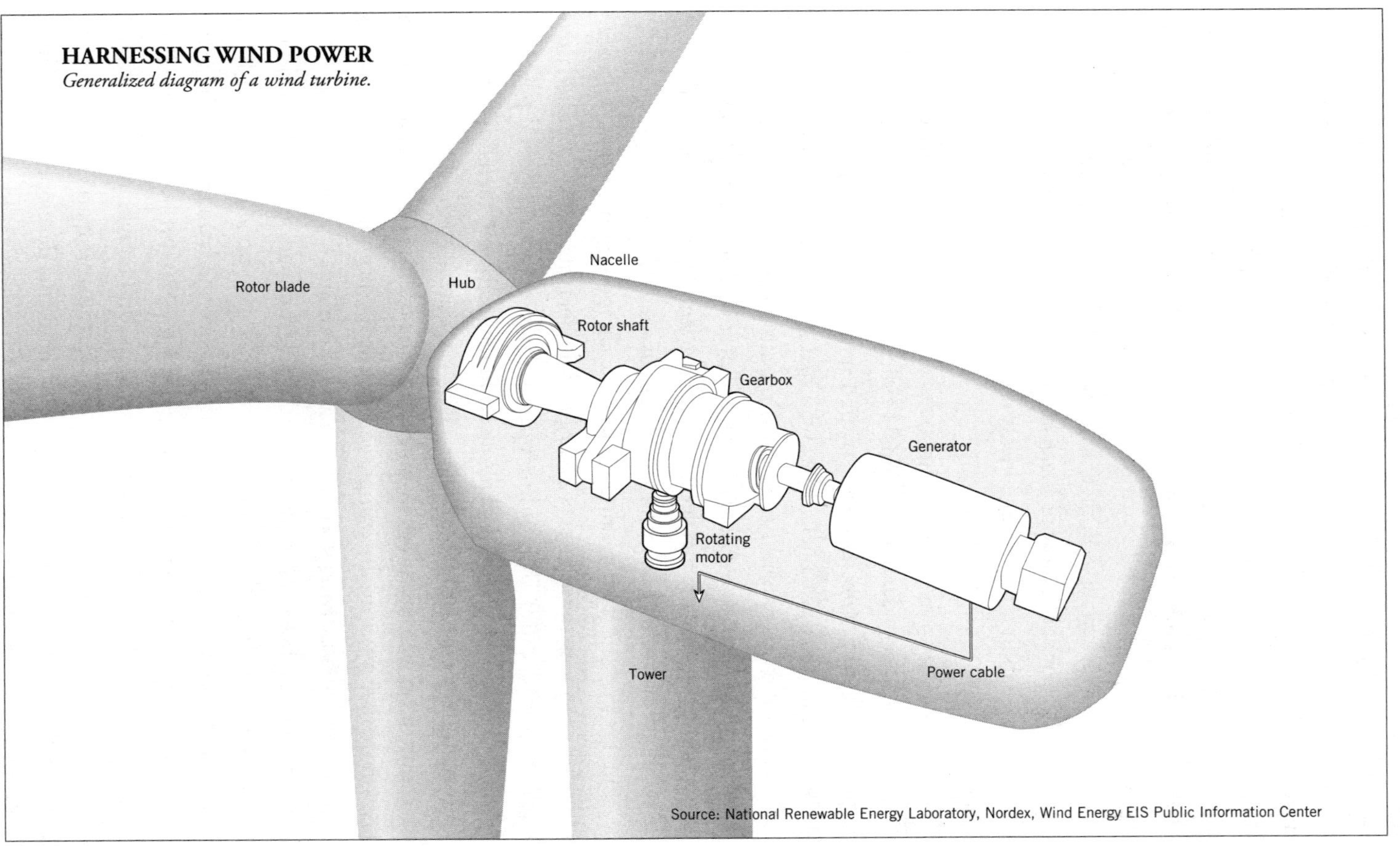

Source: National Renewable Energy Laboratory, Nordex, Wind Energy EIS Public Information Center

the tattered credibility of wind power. By 1987, 90 percent of the new machines being installed in California were made in Denmark.

This is how California became the birthplace of the modern wind industry. By the mid-1980s, 96 percent of U.S. wind investment was in California, and 90 percent of worldwide wind development was taking place in the Golden State.[15]

But difficulties emerged. The threat to birds and bats from the whirling blades galvanized opposition among environmental and animal rights activists. They kept logs of the number of raptors—birds of prey, including golden eagles—killed by colliding with the turbines in the Altamont Pass. Others rose up in opposition because of the whooshing, clanging, irritating noise, or because of what they regarded as eyesores and defacing of the natural environment, especially where wind-battered machines had collapsed or fallen apart. In the resort city of Palm Springs, many residents were outraged by the wind machines that were crowding in on their vistas. Palm Springs' mayor, the entertainer Sonny Bono (and former husband of Cher) went on the attack against proposed new wind turbines that would tower above Palm Springs in the San Gorgonio Pass. He announced that he would fly to Washington, D.C., "to do battle as Don Quixote did against windmills." However, when a budget crunch hit Palm Springs, he changed his mind and instead went to war against neighboring Desert Hot Springs, battling over which city would get to annex nearby wind farm sites in order to augment ailing property tax revenues.[16]

THE SLUMP

The boom didn't last. By the early 1990s, the California wind rush had turned into a bust. Jerry Brown was no longer governor, and the federal tax credits had expired.

Indeed, there had been enough flimflam that the tax credits themselves had become a target. "These aren't wind farms," one California congressman had fumed. "They're tax farms." With the collapse of energy prices, the rationale for wind power had also lost much of its force. Moreover, with lower prices, there were no more rich "avoided cost" contracts.[17]

The wind industry went into a deep downturn. "They are very visible, and very ugly," the *Washington Post* said of turbines in 1991, adding, "Wind power will never be more than a supplemental source of electric power." Many of the American wind companies went bankrupt, as did Vestas in Denmark. Kenetech, the publicly traded subsidiary of what had been U.S. Windpower, was the biggest and most famous of all the American wind companies. It had gone as far afield as Argentina, New Zealand, and Ukraine. Finally, in 1996, Kenetech went bankrupt too. Its collapse seemed to sound the death knell for the U.S. wind business.

"It was a really grim story," James Dehlsen remembered. "We were hanging by a thread." What kept his company, Zond, alive was the fact that it had taken a little bit of ownership in every project it had developed, which gave it a revenue stream. "We could survive until the next stage."

Dehlsen acquired a major new innovation that Kenetech had developed just before its demise: variable-speed technology. "This was the most important technical advancement in the industry since the beginning," said Dehlsen. Using advanced power electronics, variable speed enabled turbines to adjust to very low and very high wind speeds, and continue to produce steady levels of electricity, helping to contribute to the stability of the overall grid.[18]

THE RETURN OF WIND

But in the mid-1990s, just as it looked as though the wind industry was on its last legs, prospects began to improve. Innovation was increasing both the efficiency and reliability of machines. Environmental considerations were coming to the fore, and wind had the great virtue of emitting no carbon. In the aftermath of the 1991 Gulf War, there was an inevitable drive in Washington, D.C., to do "something" about energy, and that took the form of the Energy Policy Act of 1992. One of its provisions was a reintroduction of tax credits for wind power, but with an important difference. The new production tax credits for renewable power rewarded not investment in building new turbines, as had the previous credits, but instead rewarded operating time, the actual production of electricity from the turbines. Later in the 1990s, individual states started to implement renewable portfolio standards—which mandated that a certain amount of renewable generation had to be installed.

The company that actually put wind back in business in the United States was Enron, the high-flying natural gas and electric power company, which at the time was an innovator in the power sector. Robert Kelly, a West Point graduate with a Ph.D. in economics from Harvard, had come back to Houston after five years of running Enron's business in Europe. Unsure what to do next, he spent an afternoon talking to Enron's CEO, Kenneth Lay. "We were trying to decide what would be the next opportunity," said Kelly. "For some reason, we said why not take a look at renewable energy. I had the sense that something real was there. I had seen firsthand the difficulties of getting gas supply for our electricity plant in England, and there was the looming issue of global warming. Wind was also a good hedge against exploding natural gas prices." Enron bought part of Zond. Or, as Kelly put it, "We brought Zond back from the brink."[19]

A MAINSTREAM TECHNOLOGY

A few years later Enron purchased the rest of Zond as well as a German company with gear box technology. These combined capabilities enabled Enron Wind, as it was now called, to build bigger, better-operating wind turbines, improving wind economics and establishing a reputation as the leading wind company. But then fraudulent accounting sent Enron into a downward spiral that culminated in a spectacular financial collapse in autumn 2001.

In 2002 General Electric stepped in and bought Enron's wind business out of bankruptcy. The price was $328 million. But that was really just a down payment in the sense that a great deal of investment and manufacturing know-how were needed to bring the turbines up to GE's strict standards and ensure reliability. "The industry was fundamentally broken," recalled Victor Abate, the head of wind development at GE. "We needed to go through and rigorously re-engineer it to make it a mainstream technology." In so doing, it substantially increased the capacity factor for wind generation.[20]

Wind by then was beginning to boom in Europe. Already in 2000, Europe's installed capacity was five times greater than the United States', where there were repeated struggles over renewing the tax credit. The leaders were Germany and Spain, which by 2005, with their generous feed-in tariffs, accounted for 70 percent of Europe's wind capacity.

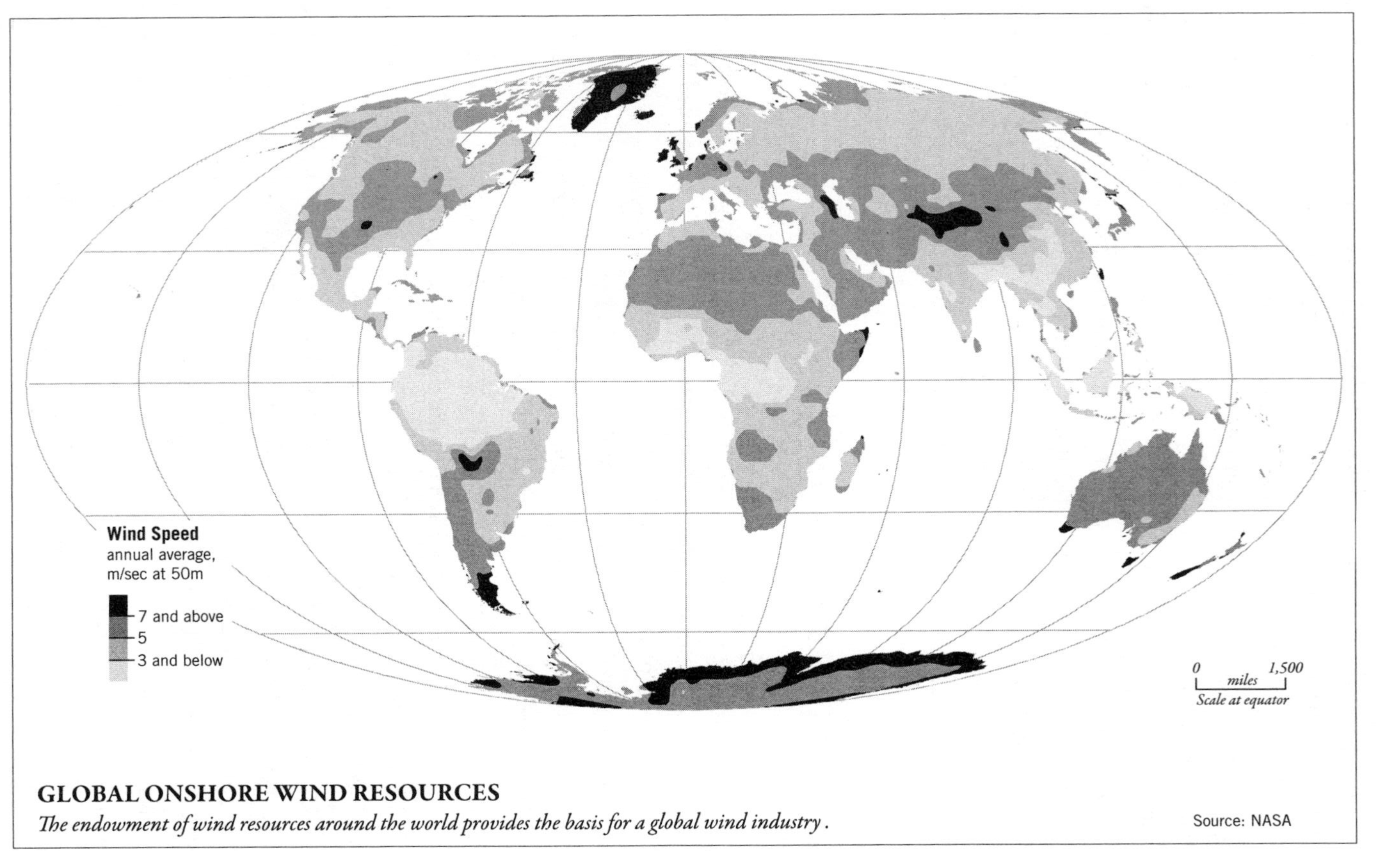

GLOBAL ONSHORE WIND RESOURCES

The endowment of wind resources around the world provides the basis for a global wind industry .

Source: NASA

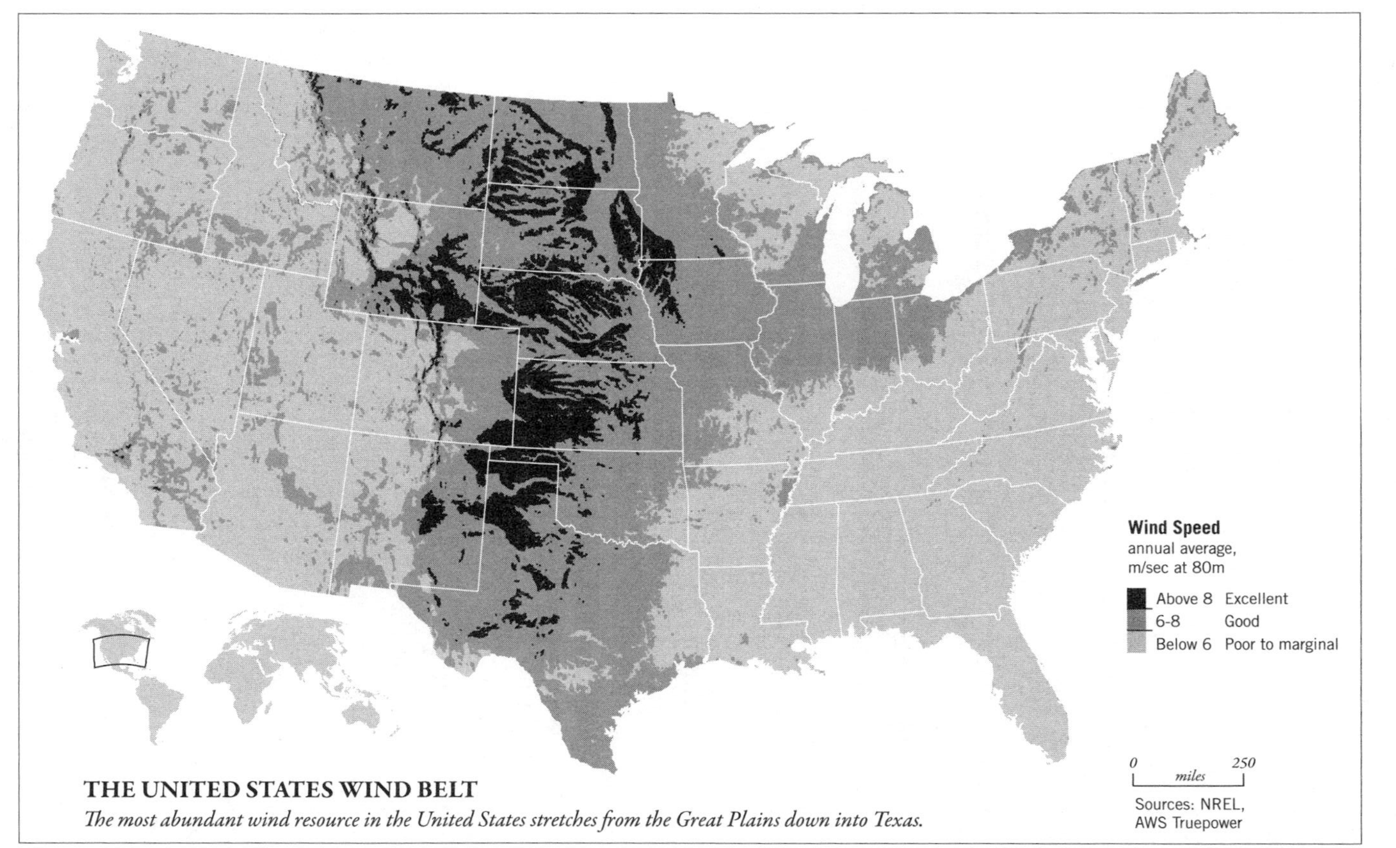

THE UNITED STATES WIND BELT

The most abundant wind resource in the United States stretches from the Great Plains down into Texas.

But 2005 was also the year that wind really picked up speed in the United States, driven by the renewable portfolio standards. Between 2005 and 2009, installed capacity grew at an average annual growth rate of about 40 percent. In terms of absolute capacity, that growth was equivalent to adding about twenty-five new nuclear reactors (but in terms of actual generation of electricity, it was equivalent to more like nine nuclear power plants).[21]

China was a latecomer to wind. But it leapfrogged to the top in terms of adding new capacity and will account for the largest growth in wind generation for years to come. As Liu Zhenya, president of China's State Grid Corporation, explained, China plans to build several "Three Gorges of wind," meaning that its commitment to expanding wind power will far outstrip even the Three Gorges Dam mega-hydroelectric project.[22]

China's push for wind is driven by the country's awesome need for new electric power of any kind, and by a strong policy commitment to clean energy as a growth sector. It is also a way to reduce dependence on coal, at least relatively, and thus reduce pollution. And China has the wind resources to make good on this commitment, especially in the northwest, including Inner Mongolia. "Many regions of China suffer from very strong winds," said Wu Guihui of China's National Energy Administration. "Originally these winds were seen by people as a natural disaster. Now these winds are a very precious resource."[23]

Globally, wind has become a substantial growth industry both financially and physically. In 2009 worldwide sales of wind-generating equipment totaled $64 billion. A standard turbine today turns out a hundred times as much electricity as one did in 1980.

Among the wind majors, Vestas and GE are the global leaders. In the United States, GE is dominant, with almost half of the total market share, while Vestas leads in the rest of the world. In the West, other major market participants include Siemens, the Spanish company Gamesa, the German company Enercon, Japan's Mitsubishi, and what was Clipper Windpower, James Dehlsen's subsequent company, purchased by United Technologies in 2010. But there are also significant companies growing up in the developing world.[24]

Tulsi Tanit ran a business making polyester yarn for saris and dresses in the northwestern Indian state of Gujarat. One day in 1990, visiting his father-in-law, he was flipping through a magazine when he came upon a photograph of a wind turbine. He had never seen one before; he was a mechanical engineer, and it piqued his interest. But then he forgot about it. What he could not forget, however, were the big problems that the lack of reliable, steady electric power—endemic to India—was creating for his business. He recalled the photograph, and in 1993, fearing for the future of the business, said to his brothers, "Let's invest in a turbine." They bought a turbine from a Vestas dealer, but then they found that they were completely on their own when it came to installing it and tying it into their own system. They learned a lot from that.

Tanit saw the opportunity to supply wind power to other Indian factories that, like his own, were shut down during part of the day owing to chronic interruptions in electricity and that needed to hedge against prices. In 1995 he founded Suzlon. He bought part of a German company and was soon supplying turbines, along with their installation, to hundreds of other textile factories. He enabled them to sell extra electricity back into the grid. He also led the lobbying effort for tax incentives from the Indian government. Finally, Tanit concluded that building turbines beat making saris and dresses and, in 2000, he exited the textile business altogether. By 2011 Suzlon was operating in thirty-two countries. "Wind hedges the power cost," he said. "That is the beauty of wind." As to the development of Suzlon itself, he explained, "Always the best ideas come when you are under pressure."[25]

Two of the largest five wind companies in the world are Chinese, Goldwind and Sinovel. As a global competitor, Chinese wind companies have benefited from both generous government supports and the country's low-cost manufacturing base. Domestic growth has been further stimulated by the government requirement that wind turbines be 70 percent "local content"; that is, made in China. Western competitors are bracing to see to what degree Chinese companies become low-cost global suppliers over the next few years, as they have done in solar. But China is not yet a major exporter. For all their heft, Chinese companies will have to establish the same global reputation for reliability and service as their Western counterparts. And wind turbines—which can weigh hundreds of tons—are not easy to ship.

"ON THE CUSP"

Building turbines is one business. Developing wind farms—acquiring sites, getting regulatory approval, buying turbines, negotiating purchase contracts with utilities for the power—is another. Three of the four biggest developers in the world are the Spanish companies Iberdrola and, next door in Portugal, Acciona and EDP Renováveis.[26]

The biggest wind developer in North America—and the second biggest on a global basis—is NextEra Energy Resources, formerly known as Florida Power & Light, FPL. Its base is Florida, where it operates the largest conventional utility business in the state in a service area that includes Miami. Its wind business stretches across 26 states and Canadian provinces. It was not obvious why NextEra would become a player in wind. After all, its home state of Florida has just about the worst wind resources of any part of the country. As it turned out, accident preceded strategy.

In the late 1980s, FPL, as it was then called, lent money to wind projects as part of a general diversification program. When the wind business went into a steep decline, some of those projects went into bankruptcy. FPL found, to its surprise, that it was now the proud owner of wind farms. It also discovered that these businesses could make money. As a result, it developed the technical skills necessary to manage wind power.

At the end of the 1990s, however, hardly anyone wanted to be in the wind business. The hot place to be was natural gas–fired merchant power plants, and—rather late—NextEra started to get on that bandwagon. The company's wind developers "felt smothered," recalled Lew Hay III, at the time the chief financial officer. "They were convinced that they were on the cusp." Hay led a strategic review that concluded that it was going to be tough to make money in natural gas–fired power. By comparison, wind looked better.

Shortly after, the giant natural gas–fired boom turned into a huge bust, creating a number of power business bankruptcies; it was to NextEra's good fortune that it had been so slow getting in. The company was largely unscathed, except for one thing: it was stuck with orders for 30 or so gas-fired turbines from General Electric. But there was another timely break. General Electric had just bought Enron's wind business and was looking for wind customers. Hay

UTILITY SCALE WIND: GROWING UP

2.5 megawatt wind turbine

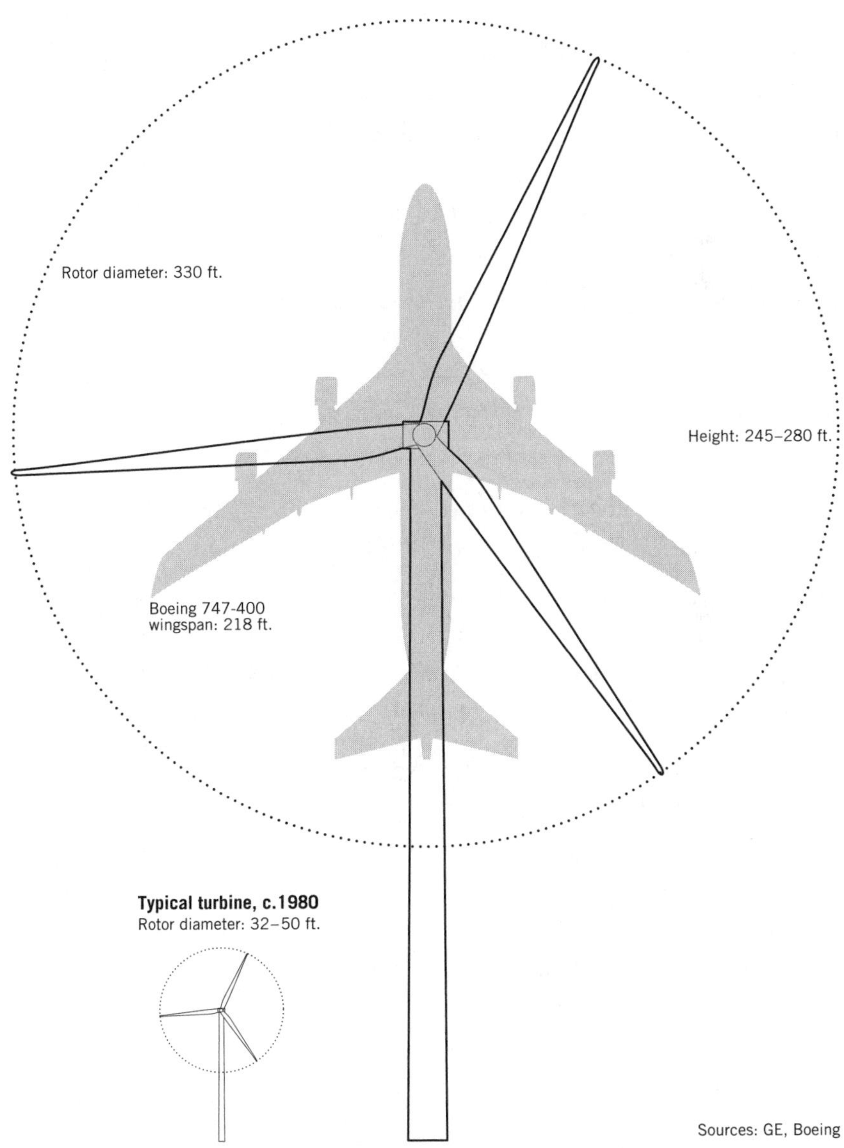

Sources: GE, Boeing

was able to persuade GE to swap the orders for gas turbines to wind turbines. This was actually helpful for GE, as it provided most of its first major orders as a supplier of wind turbines.

NextEra was now seriously committed to the wind business. "We were so out in left field compared with what other companies were doing," said Hay, by now CEO. "The Wall Street analysts were very skeptical. Investors kept asking, 'What are you doing?'" To Hay's great irritation, they also kept asking, "Is this a hobby?" NextEra became the largest operator of wind power in the United States—by 2010, over 20 percent of total installed wind capacity. For NextEra what makes wind a good business, beyond the absence of CO_2 and other airborne pollution, is the basic economics of the business. As Hay put it: "The fuel is free." In so saying, he sounded remarkably like Herbert, the twelfth-century English clergyman and the pioneering advocate of free wind.[27]

BUT HOW BIG?

But how big can wind get? Twenty percent of electricity by 2030 would be as large a contribution as nuclear today. Certainly the United States has a great deal of good wind resources. Some hold out the vision of a vast wind corridor down through the Midwest. In the 1930s, the powerful winds that came down through that corridor blew away the topsoil and created the Dust Bowl, impoverishing millions of people and uprooting many of them. Today those winds are recognized as a great natural resource, a bounty of nature to be harvested—if the transmission is there.

But scale is a challenge. There has been a continuing drive for height and breadth in wind turbines. The bigger the better because size translates into more electricity generation.

One problem is just getting the large turbine to the site. If a turbine is too big, it does not fit on a truck; it is not easy to move a 25-story tower, lying on its side, down the highway with a police escort. Lifting it into position and securing it is another challenge. If the turbines get much larger, the roads they travel down will have to be reinforced. Then there is concern about the stresses on the large blades and other components. Currently, the typical turbine is 2.5 megawatts. Many think that sheer logistics will not allow them to get much bigger than 3 megawatts, at least on land. Today's efforts are focused on improving blade designs and power electronics and overall efficiency, and on the development and use of lighter, tougher materials.

Cost is another constraint. In order to utilize lesser-quality wind resources, either the costs of the turbines have to come down or technology has to find ways to capture more of the wind's energy. While the wind is free, the wind-powered electricity system is not. Delivering it to consumers can be expensive. If the cost of additional backup generation is included in the calculations, wind can become more expensive than competitive sources, and thus can require continuing subsidies.

THE CHALLENGE OF "INTERMITTENCY"

A reason for this disparity emerges out of the interaction of electricity demand and the way wind is produced. The demand for electricity is continually fluctuating, as people turn their lights and computers on and off, as factories run their motors, and as temperatures rise and air-conditioning kicks in. To respond almost instantaneously, the grid requires power sources that, in industry parlance, are dispatchable. That is, they can be turned on and their power dispatched within seconds. Most generating capacity is dispatchable with a 95 percent assuredness.

But wind is not dispatchable. This intermittency makes it difficult to compare with other sources. As with solar cells, a megawatt of installed wind capacity does not turn out the same amount of electricity as a megawatt of coal-fired capacity. Because of intermittency, the actual electrical output of a wind turbine—its net capacity factor—is only about a third of its rated capacity. Even where the wind resource is very good, turbines usually generate electricity only 30 to 40 percent of the time, perhaps in a few areas up to 50 percent. Moreover, the profiles of winds and overall power demand do not necessarily match up well. In many locations, winds tend to be at their best at night and in the spring and autumn. But peak demand is in the daytime, and in the summer and winter. During one heat wave in California, for instance, the California Energy Commission found that only 6 percent of the rated capacity was available.[28]

This intermittency is the great challenge to substantial future growth. Public Service Company of Colorado, a subsidiary of Xcel Energy, currently has the largest share of its total electricity coming from wind of any utility in the nation, almost 15 percent. It has found that it can integrate this wind electricity into its grid without having to build additional backup by changing the way it operates its other power sources, including coal, bringing them up and down to balance the wind. But Colorado is also blessed with high-quality wind resources that are not too far from population centers.

Others argue that one cannot build enough wind farms to stamp out intermittency as a big problem. An executive of one California utility summed it up this way: "Wind tends to blow when we don't need it, at night. And when it gets hot, it's not blowing." In the view of many utilities, every new megawatt of wind needs a good deal of backup from other new generation. In the United States, that means that a wind-fired generation system generally needs to be accompanied by a parallel gas-fired generation system. Which means a substantial increase in costs. As wind power grows in China, intermittency will become a more significant challenge. As a result, Liu Zhenya, the president of China's State Grid, has observed that the multiple "Three Gorges of wind" that are to be built will have to be "bundled" with natural gas, coal, and nuclear.[29]

A second source of high costs comes from what are called the integration costs. Wind farms, by their nature, are highly spread out and are often in remote regions. "There's great wind in Wyoming, but there are only 500,000 people in the state, and it's an awfully long way to California," said an executive from one of the major turbine companies. As a result, a great deal of additional investment in transmission lines is needed to get the wind to the grid and on to consumers, and at the same time balance out the variability of the load. That will require hundreds of billions of dollars in new investment and an enormous amount of regulatory procedure, battles over right-of-ways, and contention among the many different owners of transmission lines.[30]

The number one priority, above all others, in operating the grid is to keep it stable. Without that, this complex entity called the grid goes down, regions are blacked out, and people lose their power. Wind is not a stable source, and thus connecting it to the grid creates additional challenges, the mitigation of which adds further to the costs.

However, some argue that these obstacles of intermittency and integration can be effectively dealt with through expanded and improved transmission and a more flexible grid that can take advantage of high-quality wind resources that are spread out from one another. "The dependability of wind is enhanced by its geographic dispersion," says James Dehlsen. Jon Wellinghoff, chairman of the FERC, said that "diversity of wind along the coast" means that the United States can "provide that wind on almost a constant basis."[31]

There is one further constraint: Environmental opposition. Many environmental groups strongly support wind. Others do not. They do not want wind farms on federal lands and in wilderness areas. Opposition also comes from local residents who do not like either the sight of these new towers intruding into their lives and their vistas or the whooshing noise of the blades.

Local opposition to wind development is an international phenomenon. Germany has been very open to siting wind turbines. Not Britain. Although it has the best wind resources in Europe, Britain also has very strong opposition to on-land development on visual and noise grounds. "I tried to put together a project in Britain for five years," said a European wind developer. "It was hell."[32]

Some worry that, if pushed too fast, the additional costs of wind (and other renewables) could result in a rate shock, which would create a backlash against renewables. Some countries, like Spain, have already experienced rate shock from the high cost of subsidies for investing in renewables.

Certainly, the costs can be modified by innovation, and much effort will go into that. Also putting a cost on carbon would change the relative economics in the energy marketplace in a way definitely favorable to wind. And some nations may also decide the cost differential is something they should assume in order to generate growing amounts of electricity, carbon-free. But there is an important distinction: carbon-free certainly does not mean cost-free.[33]

"MARINIZED": THE OFFSHORE FRONTIER

These cost issues become most stark when considering the new frontier of wind technology: Offshore. Planting turbines in ocean waters provides access to stronger and more frequent wind. There are no obstacles to break up the flow—no mountains, no valleys, no buildings, no trees. The European Union has embraced offshore wind as the essential element for achieving its "20 percent by 2020" renewable target. In 2010 the world's largest offshore wind farm—a $1.2 billion project that includes 100 wind turbines with a total capacity of 300 megawatts—opened in the U.K. off the coast of Kent. Currently, offshore wind makes up only a tiny fraction of Europe's wind capacity, but the targets are very big. The U.K. is aiming for 33 gigawatts of offshore wind capacity by 2020, and Germany is targeting 10 gigawatts over the same time period.[34]

Offshore turbines can be much bigger because they do not have to be transported over roads. They can be assembled, like oil platforms, in docks and then floated out to sea on barges. Thus, while three-megawatt turbines may be the limit on land, seven or even ten megawatts may be doable at sea. So big are some of the ones now planned that they will actually have heliport landing platforms atop them.

Yet the EU targets constitute a tremendous challenge. Costs are estimated at two to three times that of onshore wind. Also, the technical difficulties are much multiplied offshore because the environment is so harsh.

Planting these giants securely into the seabed is no easy thing. To operate in marine settings, turbines have to be redesigned in order, in the new lingo, to be "marinized." They need to be able to withstand the enormous, relentless stresses from the tides and waves, from the salt, from the winds themselves, and from the storms that, with no mercy, will pound and assault them. Corrosion is a big problem. So is the risk that water will get in through the vents and damage the electronics. Also they are much harder to repair. It may take as much as six weeks to get out into a turbulent sea to fix a damaged gear box, which would mean a substantial loss of production. "It's ironic," said a turbine manufacturer. "You look for the windiest places you can find. But then you have to wait for the wind to die down, and the weather to improve, to work on them." The integration costs are also higher. Extra-durable cables have to be laid that will connect each of the turbines to a substation and to the land. These cables will have to be much tougher than on land, and that will add to the integration costs.[35]

The one industry that offshore wind will have to turn to for the skills and capabilities to operate in the demanding offshore environment is the industry that has learned over many decades how to withstand the onslaught of winds and waves and storms: the offshore oil and gas industry. Indeed, while a new class of vessels is being built for the construction of offshore wind farms, when they are not available, vessels for building oil platforms can also suffice.

The operating experience from the first wave of offshore wind farms shows how big are the challenges. But Europe will push ahead. Good onshore sites are being exhausted, and thus its climate-change objectives leave it no choice. Yet even coming close to achieving Europe's overall goals on offshore wind will not be easy, especially in the projected time frame. But in order to promote offshore wind, high feed-in tariffs and other subsidies will be put in place along with regulatory policies. "Offshore wind will happen," said one longtime European wind developer. "The force of will of government will make it happen."[36]

In the United States, the prospects are less developed and more uncertain. Nothing more clearly demonstrates that than the struggle over Cape Wind, the proposed 130-turbine wind park in the Nantucket Sound between Cape Cod, Martha's Vineyard, and Nantucket. This battle—fought between landowners, sailors, Native American tribes, and local residents on one side, and developers and clean energy advocates on the other, with various environmental groups arrayed on both sides of the struggle—has been going on now for more than a decade in both Massachusetts and Washington, D.C. The project was long opposed by the late Massachusetts senator Ted Kennedy. In 2010 the state's senior senator, John Kerry, proclaimed that the project would mean "jobs and clean energy for Massachusetts"; the state's junior senator, Scott Brown, worried that the Cape Wind project would "jeopardize industries that are vital to the Cape's economy . . . [and] impact aviation safety and the rights of Native American tribes in the area."[37]

At this point the main offshore frontier remains the waters off Europe.

Despite all the development, and all that has been learned over more than three decades, it is still early days for wind as a scalable industry. But its share will certainly grow as governments and publics seek carbon-free electric generation. It is one alternative that can clearly deliver today. New research programs are seeking ways to drive technological development, optimize operations and manufacturing, increase flexibility in relation to the grid, and push down costs.

It has certainly taken a long time. But wind today is part of the landscape of the electric power industry. Indeed, so much is already happening today that—though it might pain some of the pioneers and they might even regard it as the most backhanded of compliments—wind has reached a stage where it is no longer really an "alternative." It is becoming a "conventional" energy source—still relatively small and facing its own constraints and challenges, but increasingly visible on the landscape of electric power and surely still on a fast track to growth.

31

THE FIFTH FUEL—EFFICIENCY

One energy resource has the potential to have the biggest impact of all, at least in the next several years. It may seem the simplest in terms of its rationality, and yet the hardest to wrap one's mind around. After all, it does not flow like a liquid through a pipeline, or like electrons over a wire. You can't pump it into your car, or store it in a tank. It lacks the imposing scale of a 25-story wind turbine or the heft of a power plant. It has neither the panache of an electric car nor the longer-term promise of renewables.

Some call it the "fifth fuel." Many would not even think of it as a fuel or an energy source. Yet in terms of impact, it certainly is. It goes by different names—*conservation, energy efficiency, energy productivity.* It could even be called *energy ingenuity*—applying greater intelligence to consumption, being more clever about how energy is used—using less for the same or greater effect. Whatever the name, it is a high-quality resource in a world of rising income, greater mobility, and a growing population. But capturing it is not all that easy. Nor is it free. It requires investment, measured in both time and money.

Over the years, conservation was sometimes seen as a penalty, a heavy cost, a cutting-back, a reduction in living standards, a form of self-denial. Developing countries sometimes suspected it was a ruse to deny them the opportunity for a higher standard of living. That has all changed. A global consensus is emerging around the key—and essential—role of energy efficiency, and about its scale. Call it a "C-change" in attitudes.[1]

The traditional reasons for emphasizing conservation were in response to costs and high prices, and in order to increase energy and reduce stress on the environment. Greater efficiency was embedded in good engineering practice.

But in the last few years, two new imperatives have reinforced this C-change. One is climate change. The more efficient the use of energy, the less carbon is released into the atmosphere. The other is economic growth itself. Rapid economic expansion in emerging market nations means a major surge in world energy consumption, and thus in the call on energy resources. The new consensus recognizes that improved energy efficiency is required for sustaining this economic growth without putting unsustainable burdens on the world's energy supplies and its capacity to invest in a timely way.

As a result of all these factors, the C-change is happening around the world. China has explicitly put energy efficiency at the top of its energy policy, with a goal of doubling efficiency. The European Union has set a target for a 20 percent improvement in energy efficiency by 2020. In Russia President Dmitry Medvedev has set a goal of reducing the energy intensity of the Russian economy by 40 percent by 2020. In the United States the Obama administration has focused on energy efficiency investments as an engine of economic growth. "One of the fastest, easiest, and cheapest ways to make our economy stronger and cleaner," said President Obama, "is to make our economy more efficient."[2]

REAL EFFICIENCY GAINS

One reason for confidence about the potential of energy efficiency is that a great deal has already been achieved, more than many recognize. The United States uses less than half as much energy for every unit of GDP as it did in the 1970s. A good part of the improvement is certainly pure efficiency. A new car in the 1970s might have averaged 13.5 miles to every gallon. Today, on a fleet average basis, a new car is required to get 30.2 miles per gallon. Insulation and heating controls in a new house today are much more effective than in previous decades. Some of the gain also reflects structural changes in the U.S. economy. The economy has gotten "lighter," as Alan Greenspan put it. In his words, "Today it takes a lot less physical material to produce a unit of output than it did in generations past." Less of the economy—and thus of measurable GDP—is devoted to energy-intensive manufacturing, and those processes have gotten much more efficient in themselves. More of the economy is devoted to services and to information technologies and lighter industries, much of which did not even exist in the 1970s. Part of the structural change also represents the shift of energy-intensive manufacturing to countries with lower costs. U.S. iron and steel output actually declined by almost half in the last three decades.[3]

But various studies suggest that somewhere between half and two thirds of the change in the energy ratio represents real efficiency gains (as opposed to the structural changes in the economy); that is, greater energy ingenuity, less energy needed to accomplish certain activities, whether it is to move people about, heat homes, or turn hydrocarbons into chemicals and plastics.[4]

This is a global phenomenon. Japan has doubled its energy efficiency over the same period, although it started off being a much more energy-efficient country to begin with. Europe has improved as well, though in percentage terms not as much as the United States. But, like Japan, it started from a more efficient base.

For the country with what is now the second-largest economy in the world, the challenge is different. For the first two decades of economic reform, China was becoming increasingly energy efficient. However, at the beginning of this century, as it went into high gear as the workshop of the world and its industries went into overtime to supply global markets, it became less efficient. Both because of that and because of the absolute growth in its energy consumption, the Chinese government has raised conservation to be a national priority. To ensure that both Chinese economic decision makers and the public paid attention to the significance of that goal, Premier Wen Jiabao went out of his way to emphasize the importance in the title of a speech, "Attach Great Importance, Pay Close Attention to Implementation, and Further Strengthen Energy Conservation and Emission Reduction."[5]

JIENENG JIANPAI

In 2004 an alarming calculation reached the desks of China's leadership. It showed that if China consumed oil at the same ratio as the United States, by

2030 it would be using more oil than the entire current world production. That drove home the compelling urgency of efficiency. The 11th Five Year Plan in 2006 adopted the slogan *Jieneng Jianpai*—"Save Energy! Cut Emissions!"—as a pillar for economic development, and it set ambitious targets for energy conservation. *Jieneng Jianpai* became a ubiquitous slogan in public spaces—in subways, on buses, in newspapers and magazines, on television. Yet consumption was still growing at a rapid rate. By 2007 Chinese overall energy demand had more than doubled from what it had been in 2000.[6]

So worrying was this trend that one critic that year lambasted the country's energy and environmental performance: "Industrial sectors with high energy consumption and high pollution have grown too rapidly," he said. "The contradictions between economic development on the one hand and resources and the environment on the other have become sharper." To top off this critique, he added, "The masses have much to complain about environmental pollution."[7]

That critic happened to be Premier Wen himself. The pressures for reform are coming from many directions—from rising demand for and increasing imports of oil, mounting pollution, international criticism on carbon emissions, risk of local militancy—and the increasingly vocal concerns of the growing middle class and the party cadres themselves.

The government is promoting policies to moderate energy demand and reduce pollution at the same time. This is both for energy objectives and to lay the basis, in the words of Premier Wen Jiabao, for a "new industrial system"—competitive new industries based on low-carbon technologies that would make China a leader in "green energy."[8]

China has set a broad national goal of quadrupling the economy by 2020, as compared with 2000, while restraining the growth in energy demand to a doubling. This is a very ambitious objective, and it is being pursued in many ways. The "Top 1000 Program" aims to cut energy consumption among China's largest energy-using enterprises, which by themselves represent a third of the country's entire energy consumption. Today China's fuel-efficiency standards for vehicles are stiffer than those of the United States.[9]

But Beijing has been cautious about using the price mechanism to reduce demand. One senior official was asked why China still controls retail petroleum prices, partly shielding consumers from world prices. He summed up the reasons simply: "Farmers, the army, and taxi cab drivers." In other words, Beijing wants to mitigate the price burdens for rural Chinese, many of them struggling at the lower end of the income table, and avoid stimulating outbreaks of discontent and violence in the countryside. The military certainly will not welcome higher burdens from energy costs. As for taxi cab drivers, that was a metaphor about fear of triggering urban protests against rising petroleum prices. Thus the movement toward price decontrol has been gradual and incomplete. Fear of inflation has led to a reluctance to allow electric power prices to rise to match the increase in coal prices, resulting in disruptions in power supplies.

Critical to reshaping energy demand are provincial and local government officials, who implement the central government's policies, and thus have an enormous impact on the shape of the economy. Local leaders are graded on economic growth and job creation in their region or locality. Today, however, they are also evaluated in terms of how they do in promoting greater energy efficiency and environmental protection. "Now a mayor is under great pressure," commented a mayor of a city of eight million. His role as head of a major Chinese city goes far beyond that of his opposite numbers in cities elsewhere in the world. His responsibilities include employment and job creation, as well as raising living standards and salaries and reducing income inequality. Pushing rapid economic growth is the mechanism for meeting all these targets. "I have to keep economic development going, but on the other hand I have to take care of reducing energy consumption." However, he can wield, as he put it, "government administrative measures" to help him. That means, for instance, that he has the power to consolidate the more than 300 paper manufacturing facilities in his locality, down to just 20 in order to raise energy efficiency.

In 2010 Premier Wen sternly announced that improving energy efficiency was so critical that the government would use an "iron fist" to improve it. This was followed by an order from the government for the swift closure of more than 2,000 of the most energy-inefficient steel mills, cement works, and other factories in the country. Also provinces were instructed to stop providing discounted electric power to energy-intensive industries. In some localities, firms were ordered to shut operations for part of the week to ensure that energy-saving targets were met.[10] The Twelfth Five Year Plan, adopted in March 2011, reinforced the energy-saving goals.[11]

INDUSTRY: HOW LOW THE FRUIT?

In Europe, Japan, and North America, the part of the economy that is best organized to become more energy efficient is industry. In the United States that sector consumes about a third of total energy. One of the fundamental things that companies do is strive to understand and manage their costs and quantify the paybacks on their investments. This is particularly true of the larger, more energy-intensive companies that do the hefty job of converting raw materials into the industrial products that, in turn, are made into things that people buy. They have the scale, the organization, and the urgent need to manage big costs like energy. It is less true of smaller firms that do not have the flexibility or capacity to home in on their energy usage or of companies that are more energy-light to begin with.

The last few decades have seen major gains in industrial energy efficiency. The price shocks of the 1970s started the process. Then in the 1980s the introduction of new computer systems enabled companies to manage processes much more effectively than previously, reducing energy usage. Energy itself became a focus again beginning around 2000, as costs started to rise.

Although industry has become much more efficient over the past decades, still the potential for significant savings remains. For one thing, technology is not static, and technological change is always opening up new opportunities. Advanced sensors and new computer controls, for instance, are providing "opportunities that could have barely been imagined in 1980."[12]

Changes in operations and maintenance, perhaps leavened with a little investment, can lead to low-cost gains. Other savings require larger capital investment in new equipment, facilities, or retrofitting—that is, modernizing and updating—part of an existing facility. The potential for efficiency across industry may be great. But volatility—the way that prices can rapidly move up and down—can be a real challenge. Companies are more likely to invest the money and effort—and stick with it—if they believe that prices will be high enough to have a significant impact on their costs and bottom line.

"ASPIRATIONS"

Dow Chemical—the largest U.S-based chemical company and one of the world's largest industrial consumers of energy—provides a casebook for what is possible. Its annual bill for energy and feedstocks is almost $30 billion. It uses the equivalent of one million barrels per day of oil. Between 1995 and 2005, Dow reduced its energy use on a worldwide basis, per pound of product, by 25 percent. Those savings are a big number; the same amount of energy would have been more than enough to supply electricity to all of California's residents for a year. From Dow's point of view, it was more than worth the effort—$9 billion of savings from an investment of $1 billion. But how did this get done?

In the mid-1990s, Dow's top management set a target for reducing its energy use by 20 percent over a ten-year period. It was what Dow CEO Andrew Liveris called an "aspirational goal"—meaning that it was not very carefully calculated. Rather the message initially was "go figure it out." Said Liveris, "Every aspect of the system rewards and incentivizes the engineer, the plant person, the person who's managing the car fleet, the rail fleet, to find ways to save energy. It's part of our DNA."[13]

But two major obstacles stood in the way: The first was organizational—the efficiency had to be seen as important in itself, not just a by-product of good maintenance. That required organizational redesign. It began with the appointment of a Global Efficiency Leader, who became the Keeper of Technology for the company, with the mandate to implement aggressive energy conservation plans globally. This leader sponsored teams and networks within the company that identified opportunities and then figured out how to capture them. Accountability for meeting targets was set at the factory level, along with the promotion of what the company started calling "an energy efficiency mind-set."[14]

Second, the company found that it did not have consistent ways to measure energy use, so common metrics had to be worked out. This was followed up, said Richard Wells, who had responsibility for Dow's energy program, by "leveraging ideas across the company. The biggest learning was that there was no silver bullet, but a lot of basic blocking and tackling."

The 25 percent gain came from a very wide range of projects. Some of it involved building large cogeneration plants, which provide heat and power together, thus increasing efficiency and reducing the need for energy. Some was also the cumulative effect from aggregating many small things. Dow uses a lot of steam to make chemicals. "A single steam trap leaking is not a big thing," said Wells. "But you list all of them and it's a big number, and fixing them at the company level—that is a big deal."

Dow has now set a new target—another 25 percent improvement in energy efficiency by 2015. "More technology will be required in the next ten years," said Wells. "Change has to come at the molecular level."

Andrew Liveris was the one who set the new 25 percent target. "You've got to institutionalize this as part of your behavior," he said. "When you have a signal, amazing things can happen."[15]

The International Energy Agency has analyzed the world's industrial sector, which consumes a third of the world's energy and is responsible for 36 percent of carbon emissions. It concluded that up to a quarter of the sector's consumption would be reduced using "proven technology and best practices." Reducing energy consumption would in turn eliminate as much as 12 percent of the world's entire CO_2 emissions. The energy savings would be equivalent to one and a half times Japan's entire energy use. But the study did not consider new technologies that have not yet been widely dispersed. The implication? A 25 percent reduction in industrial energy use should be considered the "lower range estimate of the technical potential for energy savings and CO_2 emissions reductions in the manufacturing industry sector." In some parts of the world, it may well be higher."[16]

THE "GAME CHANGER"

One industry that really wants to save energy is the airline industry. Over the last several years, fuel has been its number one cost—25 to 35 percent of overall costs. Indeed, fuel is the largest element in the cost of an airline ticket. This only increases the drive to control those costs in an industry that lives on the margin—indeed, often enough, on very thin margins.

"Increasing efficiency in the use of jet fuel is incredibly important to us," said Jeffery Smisek, the CEO of United Airlines. "We spend significantly more on fuel than on labor, which is our next highest cost. Volatility of prices kills us. We can't price to volatility."

Airlines have been seeking higher fuel efficiency since the 1970s and, since then, the fuel efficiency of jets has more than doubled. Using the same amount of fuel, new jets carry the same amount of passengers and cargo twice as far as their older counterparts did. The gains come in many different forms. The development of winglets—the little curved pieces at the end of the wing—reduces drag and saves on fuel. The addition of these winglets now enables 737s to fly as much as 6 percent farther on the same amount of fuel. Adding life vests on such routes as New York–Miami, Dallas–Miami, and Los Angeles–Cancún satisfies a regulatory requirement so that planes can stop hugging the coasts and fly more directly over water, saving fuel. When fuel prices soar, every bit of extra weight really hurts. So planes may now fly with less potable water, lighter-weight catering carts, and fewer magazines—or no magazines at all. Making the outside skin of the airline smoother reduces drag, and painting it with lighter colors rather than darker ones reduces air-conditioning costs. Continuous descent arrivals (CDAs) save fuel on longer, more gradual descents. At some point, $60 billion or more will have to be spent to replace the current 1950s air-traffic control system in the United States with a twenty-first century system. That will save fuel because airliners will no longer have to zigzag their way across the country, tracking land-based navigation aids but instead will be guided by satellite signals on more direct routes. They will spend less time circling and will be able to make more precise approaches. All of that will save fuel.[17]

But the biggest gains of all will come from the next generation of airliners.

WHICH "20 PERCENT"?

When Boeing was deciding what its next generation of airliner would be, it invited representatives of 59 airlines to Seattle to vote on what they as customers wanted. The company was doing the R&D on designs for two different next-generation aircraft. Both designs promised 20 percent gains, but along different vectors. One was the Sonic Cruiser, which at mach 98, close to the sound barrier, would offer speeds 20 percent higher than current jets. The other was the 7E7, which promised a 20 percent gain in fuel efficiency. The Sonic Cruiser would save *time*. The 7E7—the *E* was for efficiency—would save *fuel,* which would mean a major improvement in operating economics.

There was no secret ballot that day. It was a New England town hall meeting.

Each airline representative had to take his or her company insignia and walk to the wall on one side of the room or the other and pin it under the design of either the Sonic Cruiser or the 7E7. At the end, on the Sonic Cruiser side of the room, there were exactly zero insignia; on the 7E7 side, 59. *Fuel Efficiency* had beat *Time,* 59–0.

The result is what is now known as the 787. Though much delayed, partly by the complexity of its supply chains, the 787 will—by the time it joins airline fleets—be the most fuel-efficient large airliner in the sky.

The main source of fuel efficiency improvement is in the airframe, the fuselage. That results from moving away from aluminum, the mainstay in commercial airlines since the 1950s, to lighter, stronger materials called composites or carbon laminate. Lighter means less weight and that in turn means less fuel. Carbon laminate is the material used in tennis rackets. But a tennis racket is one thing. Scaling up from tennis rackets to a 270-seat airliner with a fully loaded weight of 540,000 pounds is quite another, and that required major technological breakthroughs.

Despite the delays, the Dreamliner is an airplane that fits what many airlines want for the growth period ahead. Air travel is on a sharp ascent, especially international travel. By 2026, according to one estimate, the number of commercial airliners in operation worldwide will double from today's 18,200 to 36,400. This growth is the result of rising incomes, globalization, and more open markets. This adds to the imperative for fuel efficiency. But, as Jeffery Smisek points out, fuel prices themselves will also determine the scale of air travel. "If we have higher fuel costs, we will have smaller airlines with smaller route networks," he said. "If we have lower costs, we will have larger airlines with larger networks."[18]

To be sure, as the growth of low-fare airlines has expanded travel opportunities across populations, a backlash has emerged. Some, mainly in Britain, oppose air travel on what they describe as "moral" grounds—global warming. Its members have taken a vow of abstinence and renounced flying. The founder of the Rough Guide travel books announced that he was cutting way back on his personal flying and would stick to Britain and the train for his summer holidays. In addition, he pledged to add a section to the Rough Guides on the "negative effects of flying." In the spirit of solidarity, the competitive Lonely Planet guides stepped up with him on this. The Anglican Archbishop of London backed them by pronouncing that taking an airplane in the course of a vacation constituted a "symptom of sin."[19]

Civil aviation produces about 2 to 3 percent of total CO_2 globally. So fuel efficiency is not only an energy strategy, it is also a carbon strategy. A 20 percent improvement in fuel efficiency means about a 20 percent reduction in CO_2 emissions. Those savings will become more significant as the number of planes in the sky increases and as airlines find themselves faced with actual or proposed national and international carbon reduction regimes. Still the biggest push for efficiency will come from the customer—not those who fly as passengers, but the direct customers, those who buy and operate the airplanes—the airlines. For them, fuel efficiency is a question of economics. And it's not just a matter of operating economics. It's also survival economics.

THE RIBBON

As the world turns over its capital stock—of buildings, vehicles, equipment, and factories—efficiency will be enhanced, because they will embody higher standards of efficiency. As conservation is increasingly seen as a competitive energy source, it will be compared with other investments. In many cases, the economic case for conservation will be very compelling.

Yet with all this said, efficiency is at two great disadvantages. It does not have a sizable and vocal constituency of proponents. And it is not something that you can reach out and touch.

Andris Piebalgs was trained as a physicist in what was then the Soviet Union. Following the breakup of the Soviet Union, he became a diplomat for the now independent Baltic nation of Latvia. He was later selected to be the EU's energy commissioner; that is, the energy minister for all of Europe. For the next five years, he was at the center of the complex and contentious intricacies of energy policymaking with the 27 separate countries that compose the EU.

One evening he was in Washington, D.C., at a dinner at the home of the EU ambassador. Piebalgs had come over for a renewable energy conference that had filled the Washington Convention Center with over three thousand people and had overflowed with enthusiasm and optimism.

Over drinks before dinner, Piebalgs was asked—in light of the EU's aggressive 2020 efficiency targets—about the relative popularity of renewables versus efficiency.

"Renewables are more popular," he said. "Renewables are supply side. They provide new energy. Efficiency is something that pays back over the years. Energy efficiency involves a lot of nitty-gritty, a lot of incentives and a lot of regulations.

"And there's no red ribbon to cut." Conservation—energy efficiency—may be so *obvious* as a solution to cost and environmental issues. But there is no photo op, no opening ceremony where government officials and company executives can cut a ribbon, smile broadly into the camera, and inaugurate a grand new facility. He shook his head as he considered one of the most powerful of the life lessons he had learned from his deep immersion in global politics.

"It's very important to be able to cut a red ribbon."[20]

32

CLOSING THE CONSERVATION GAP

As people moved from the countryside and crowded into cities in the nineteenth century, urban heat waves could be ferocious in their effect. "Apprehension of a Pestilence" and "The Rising of Today's Sun Awaited with Absolute Terror" were headlines in 1878 when one such heat wave struck parts of the United States. In 1901 one of the nation's worst heat waves left hundreds and hundreds of fatalities in the East and the Midwest. Local hospitals stopped sending horse-drawn ambulances to pick up those felled by heat prostration because the horses themselves were collapsing from the heat. So severe was the heat in 1901 that for the first time ever, the New York Stock Exchange allowed its members to remove their suit jackets on the trading floor.[1]

Traditionally, buildings had been constructed to serve as the bridge between the natural elements and the human requirements for shelter, heating, cooling, and lighting. In the Southwest, forts like the Alamo used adobe walls to help stay cool during the hot days but warm during the chilly nights. In cities, stone buildings were designed with recessed windows to shade against the sun, and with central courtyards to bring light and ventilation to the interior rooms. But as people congregated in the cities and buildings rose in height, and as industrial knowledge expanded, increasingly sophisticated and varying uses of energy were employed to deliver the heat, cooling, light, and power that were required to make these structures livable and productive—and to enable cities as a whole to function.

Today in the United States, the residential and commercial sectors (including the electricity used in buildings) consume about 40 percent of total U.S. energy and three quarters of electricity, and emit substantial amounts of CO_2. In other countries, the share is even higher: in Britain, 50 percent of total energy. In China, buildings' share of energy use is much less, but that will rapidly change as that country adds at least 10 million new residential units a year. Now the challenge is not only how to construct livable buildings but also how to use all of the energy that goes into them more efficiently. That means addressing design, behavior, and the difference between the potential of efficiency and the reality—what is called the conservation gap.[2]

PATENT NUMBER 808897: "MANUFACTURED WEATHER"

Over the nineteenth century, inventors and businessmen had struggled to find a way to control the heat and humidity that could disrupt industrial processes. By the last decade of that century, crude refrigeration systems had been deployed to help sanitize the great meat-packing industry in the "hog butcher to the world," Chicago. After the heat wave of 1901, the New York Stock Exchange finally decided that it had to do something more than just permit floor traders to take off their jackets. And so it commissioned a massive refrigeration system. But the system did not work very well; the air was clammy and uncomfortable. Cooling was not enough; humidity needed to be controlled. But how?[3]

Willis Carrier was a 25-year-old engineer from Angola, New York, who had an intuition for mechanical engineering, a gift for mathematics, and a flair for visualizing solutions. Working for the Buffalo Forge Company, he had helped a magazine printer figure out how to control humidity, which was causing colored ink to end up smudged on the wrong part of the page.

Carrier himself, however, was not satisfied with his solution. Humidity—more specifically, how to produce precise levels of water vapor in the air—continued to preoccupy him. Then one evening while waiting for a train on a fog-enshrouded platform in Pittsburgh, he had a breakthrough. As he paced up and down, Carrier noticed that despite the fog, the air was dry. Reflecting on the character of the fog, he had the "flash of genius."

This flash led to Patent 808897—"Apparatus for Treating Air"—which heated or cooled water to control temperature and humidity, and helped cleanse the air. Others ridiculed his idea of "manufactured weather." The Buffalo Forge Company itself was so worried about the reputational risks from this uncertain innovation that it set up a wholly owned subsidiary named for its chief engineer, the Carrier Air Conditioning Company.[4]

But Patent 808897 worked in practice. It marked the invention of the modern air conditioner—and, along with that, provided the solution to one of humanity's most intractable living problems. By 1911 Carrier had produced the formula that came to be venerated as the Magna Carta of the air-conditioning industry. In 1922 Carrier installed an air-conditioning system in Grauman's Metropolitan Theater in Los Angeles. The first one to go into a department store was in Detroit in 1924 in response to the tendency of customers to faint from the heat, when crowding into the store on bargain days. By 1930 air-conditioning had been installed in Madison Square Garden, in both the Senate and the House of Representatives, and in the dining car of a train running between New York and Washington, D.C. The first fully air-conditioned high-rise office building went up in San Antonio, Texas, in the late 1920s. Air-conditioning began to spread around the world; by 1937 an air-conditioned bus was running between Damascus and Baghdad. After World War II, air-conditioning made it possible for Houston to shed the indolent, oppressive swampy mugginess of its summers and become the "oil capital of the world" and, eventually, the fourth-largest U.S. city. In the late 1950s, air-conditioning started to become a standard feature of homes in the warmer parts of the United States. Without it, the Sunbelt as we know it today would not exist.[5]

The skyscrapers that were built across the world in those postwar decades would have been uninhabitable without the large air-conditioning and central-heating systems developed over the past half century. HVACs—the massive heating, ventilation, and air-conditioning systems—cycle fresh air completely through buildings.

The spread of air-conditioning changed the course of global economic development and made possible the expansion of the world economy. Lee

Kuan Yew, the founder and former prime minister of modern Singapore, once described air-conditioning as "the most important invention of the twentieth century," because, he explained, it enabled the people of the tropics to become productive. Singapore's minister of the environment was a little more explicit, saying that, without air-conditioning, "instead of working in high-tech factories" Singapore's workers "would probably be sitting under coconut trees."[6]

Energy and electricity made possible the expansion of services and comfort in the residential and commercial sector. That posed no problem so long as there was little reason to worry about cost and availability of energy or about greenhouse gases. But that has changed.

Some projections now point to the potential for 15 to 20 percent improvements in energy use in buildings. Others see much greater possibilities: 25 percent across the sector and, on a cost-effective basis, as much as 50 percent in new buildings. None of that, however, is going to happen easily.

"A lot of people are convinced that the easy things have already been done," said Professor Leon Glicksman, who founded the department of building technology at MIT two decades ago. "Some people think that all the problems are solved, and that there's no need to do more. It's one of the most conservative industries I've ever encountered. There's little R&D. And it's highly fragmented. It's hard to get people together. Everybody does his or her little piece. And a lot of people don't understand that there is no silver bullet."[7]

Yet much is changing across this sector, affecting how buildings are constructed and how they work—and perhaps how people live.

GOING MAINSTREAM

The changes actually began in the 1970s with disruptions in energy supply and sharp rises in energy prices. Higher prices had their expected effect. Thermostats were lowered in the winter and raised in the summer. Homeowners put on storm windows. Government policies at both federal and state levels started to promote greater efficiency through tax incentives, regulations, and mandates.

California was a pioneer. The state was rocked hard by the 1973 oil crisis not only because of its dependence on the car but also because its utilities burned a lot of oil. The next year, Governor Ronald Reagan, convinced by arguments about frugality and reducing energy waste, overruled his own staff and approved the establishment of the California Energy Commission. Thus did Ronald Reagan become the progenitor of the commission that set about writing increasingly strict rules for energy efficiency that became a model across the United States. Other states followed.[8]

Utilities began to promote conservation through information programs and by sending energy auditors out to poke around in attics, measuring insulation, and in basements, to check out furnaces. These efforts expanded into utilities' demand side management (DSM) programs, which were aimed at helping homeowners and building operators to manage and reduce consumption. At the same time, manufacturers, prodded by mandatory standards and labeling requirements, brought more efficient appliances to market. A chaotic welter of competing state regulations was finally consolidated into uniform national standards. The federal government also started to award energy stars to appliances that were rated above average. Architects and builders focused on more efficient design. "Energy conservation did go mainstream," observed Lee Schipper of Stanford University. "Builders thirty years ago did not understand the application of double and triple glazing in windows," he said. "They do today."[9]

THE GADGIWATTS

There is a puzzle: Despite the mainstreaming of conservation, U.S. residential energy consumption is 40 percent higher than in the 1970s, and commercial building consumption has almost doubled. The reasons are growth and innovation. The number of single-family homes increased substantially; so did the number of houses with air-conditioning. The expansion in size of houses is even more striking: square footage is up about 70 percent since the 1970s. Energy use per refrigerator has been cut in half since 1993, but energy used for refrigerators per home is roughly constant because many homes now have two refrigerators.[10]

The other major reason for the growth in home energy use are the "gadgiwatts"—more and more electricity is consumed by gadgets that largely did not exist in the 1970s. In those years, 91 percent of household electricity was consumed in just seven categories—stoves, indoor lights, refrigerators, freezers, water heaters, air conditioners, and space heating. Only 9 percent was "other."

The "other" category has since grown to be 45 percent of electricity. That includes some things that were around in the 1970s, such as dishwashers and televisions. But it also includes all those devices and gadgets that have become integral to daily life and depend on "the gadgiwatts"—computers, printers, VCRs, fax machines, microwave ovens, telephones, cable services, flat-screen televisions, DVD players, smart phones, tablets, and any number of hand-held devices that need to be recharged.

The same thirst for energy and electricity exists in increasingly high-tech, highly wired office towers. Moreover, information technology has spawned whole new complexes and new demand: the thousands of data centers that house an estimated 15 million-plus servers worldwide—a number that could grow to more than 120 million by 2020. These centers draw heavily on electricity to power processors, memory, and other computer operations, and also to deliver the cooling required to remove the heat that is generated by the servers.[11]

This potential savings in energy efficiency in buildings has been described by energy economist Lawrence Makovich as the "conservation gap." But realizing conservation potential is not so easy. The auto fleet may turn over every 12 years or so, but buildings last 50, or 75, or 100 years, or more. They can be retrofitted but only up to a point. Pricing will affect the time and amount of money that building owners and operators will put into improving the energy operations of existing structures. These investments involve rate of return and trade-offs with other investments. "The question of choice and trade-offs in efficiency investments compared with other allocations of capital is often overlooked," observes a report from the World Economic Forum. "The *investment grade* test is important for sustainable investment in energy efficiency." Like any other investment, efficiency has to compete with other choices.[12]

Nonfinancial barriers also stand in the way of efficiency. One is the disconnect between the interests of the builder and the eventual buyer. Builders, who put in insulation and appliances and decide on the thickness of the walls and the quality of the windows, are building on "spec." Their focus is on keeping costs down to promote sales. New homebuyers, on the other hand, actually have to pay the monthly energy bills, and they would benefit from greater energy efficiency. By that point, the builder is long gone, but the choices made by the builder remain. Similarly, for rental units, owners may not have an incentive to put in more efficient appliances because it is the tenants who pay the energy bills.

Homeowners expect quick paybacks on efficiency investments. Lack of knowledge is a chronic issue. How many homeowners actually have any idea how much they will save with tighter insulation or by turning down the thermostat? Some of these issues can be corrected with zoning regulations and other requirements, appliance labeling in terms of energy efficiency, and dissemination of comprehensible information. Focus and measurement can bring unexpected results in commercial buildings.

Simon Property Group is one of the largest operators of shopping malls in the country, including some of the best known, ranging from Stanford Shopping Center and Laguna Hills Mall in California to the Houston Galleria to Pentagon City near Washington, D.C., and The Westchester in New York. Between 2003 and 2009, Simon reduced its energy use by 25 percent. "As much as 60 percent were generated by the implementation of best practices and by using common sense and paying attention," said George Caraghiaur, the executive at Simon responsible for energy efficiency. "That means shutting off lights, keeping doors closed, and not cooling the entire plant. Basically, it's telling our mall managers to do the kind of things our parents told us to do."[13]

Best practices also include "not easy to see" things, he said, such as proper maintenance of heating and air-conditioning systems. The other 40 percent required investment in such things as lighting, more efficient cooling systems, and management controls. The investment can be in very big new systems. It can also go into readjusting the soft drink machines so that they don't cool cans at night when no one is buying drinks because the mall is closed.

EFFICIENCY BY DESIGN

Efficiency by design is becoming part of the approach to buildings. Green building is an initiative that started off as a fringe activity and is now firmly in the mainstream. It is already changing the way buildings are constructed and is stimulating research and development in an industry—construction—in which R&D has not been anything resembling a priority.

In the 1980s a number of organizations began to develop methodologies for rating the environmental aspects of building construction, operations, and upkeep—thereby encouraging efficiency and conservation. The best known are those of the U.S. Green Building Council and its LEED, the Leadership in Energy and Environmental Design program. LEED generates a set of guidelines and certifications for new buildings and remodeling, for both energy and environmental goals. It operates on a points system with ratings ranging from "certified" to "silver" to "gold," and, the most highly prized of all, "platinum."

But devising a system to rate the environmental impact of buildings—and everything that goes into them—is no easy thing. For instance, should the environmental assessment for a building focus mainly on energy use and carbon emissions, or should it also include sustainable forestry, toxic waste disposal, urban congestion? Geography complicates matters further. Water, for instance, needs to be treated differently in Arizona than in Maine. In short, energy and environmental accounting isn't easy. As a result, some efficiency experts question the methodology of programs like LEED.

Integrated design is now seen as a key to achieving higher levels of energy efficiency in the fragmented building world. That means architects, developers, engineers, and consultants working together from initial design to the final construction. This collaboration tries to ensure that a building's walls, heating and cooling system, ventilation, and lighting are all well integrated—bringing substantial savings. For instance, a high-performance envelope—that is, the outer walls—would eliminate the need for separate heating systems near the windows and reduce the size of the main heating and cooling equipment.

Some of the most important innovations in buildings today hearken back to principles that went into buildings prior to the twentieth century and before people gained control over their environment—before they began to "manufacture weather." But of course today that means acting on those principles in far more sophisticated ways, using advanced technology and tools, and a scientific and engineering understanding that was not available even in the recent past. The thermal mass of the building is used, like those stones walls were once used, to store energy during the daytime in order to provide heating at night.

"In a way," said Leon Glicksman of MIT, "all this is going back to the solutions that evolved over the years, but with the high-tech versions." But he did add a caution: "A building is something that will last fifty or a hundred years. Some things might work the first year. But what happens if it doesn't work down the line? It's a big risk if you try something new and it doesn't work out."[14]

. . .

A factor that can have decisive impact on how buildings use energy is mind-set, the attitudes of people who use buildings. Some sense of what mind-set can do can be found in Japan, where conservation is embedded in policy and in everyday life.

MOTTAINAI: "TOO PRECIOUS TO WASTE"

Japan is the global pace-setter for optimizing energy use, and it has been such since the 1970s.

The crises of those years deeply shook Japan, which suddenly found its path of high-speed growth disrupted. The shocks also reminded the Japanese of their vulnerability as a nation in terms of energy. The resulting crises unified the nation. "Everybody worked together," Naohiro Amaya, a vice minister of the Ministry of International Trade and Industry, had remembered some years later. "The Japanese are accustomed to crises like earthquakes and typhoons. Even though the energy shock was a great shock, we were prepared to adjust." Amaya added: "Instead of using the resources in the ground, we would use the resources in our head."[15]

Thus was launched Japan's drive for energy efficiency. The Japanese would focus a good part of their considerable engineering and technical talents on energy ingenuity, on getting more value out of every unit of energy. Not every idea worked, to be sure. In the mid-1970s, in an effort to reduce the need for air-conditioning in the summertime, a new look in men's fashion was promoted for office workers. It was business suits whose jackets were short-sleeved. Despite its being modeled by the prime minister himself, the *shoene rukku*—or "energy conservation look"—somehow just never took off.

What did work was putting resources into increasing the efficiency of the energy operations and processes across Japanese society. This was not as hard as it might be for other societies. For it was really a reconnection with a cultural tradition of thrift and care that was deeply embedded in a historical experience shaped by limited land and stringency in resources. This orientation contrasts with America's historical experience, which is based on ample land and abundant resources and a vaster and more confident geography.

Yoriko Kawaguchi was Japan's minister of the environment and then its foreign minister. Today Kawaguchi sits in the upper house of Japan's parliament but still remembers her reaction when she came to the United States the first time, as a high school exchange student. "At Christmastime, my American family unwrapped presents and then threw the wrapping paper away. I was very surprised because in Japan we would carefully fold up the wrapping paper to use it again. It's what we would call *mottainai.*"

Mottainai, she explained, is a difficult word to translate into English. Indeed, it is so difficult that at one point a meeting was convened within the Japanese Ministry of Foreign Affairs to thrash it out. The conclusion was that the best translation was "too precious to waste."

"*Mottainai* is the spirit in which we have approached things over a thousand years because we never really had anything in abundance," Kawaguchi continued. "So we've had to be wise about resources. I was taught at home, every child was taught at home, that you don't leave a grain of rice on your plate. That's *mottainai.* Too precious to waste."[16]

This sense of *mottainai* has underpinned Japan's approach to energy efficiency, which was codified in the Energy Conservation Law of 1979. The law was expanded in 1998 with the introduction of the Top Runner program. It takes the most efficient appliance or motorcar in a particular class—the "top runner"—and then sets a requirement that all appliances and cars must, within a certain number of years, exceed the efficiency of the top runner. This creates a permanent race to keep upping the ante on efficiency. The results are striking: the average efficiency of videocassette recorders increased 74 percent between 1997 and 2003. Even television sets improved by 26 percent between 1997 and 2003. Further amendments to the law mandate improvements by factories and buildings, and require them to adopt efficiency plans.[17]

The government has used a wide range of tax credits to facilitate new investments. It also imposes direct fines to penalize for efficiency targets not achieved. Such fines are something unlikely to be accepted in the American system. But values, the resource position of the country, and the political system—all these make it an acceptable policy in Japan.

This commitment to efficiency was tested mightily in the new energy crisis in the summer of 2011. Owing to the Fukushima Daiichi nuclear accident, part of Japan faced a significant electricity shortfall. In such circumstances, *mottainai* was not a matter of choice, it was a duty.

A SMARTER GRID

The conservation gap can be closed through technology—or, rather, through the intersection of technology, know-how, and behavior. Kateri Callahan, the president of the Alliance to Save Energy, described the infrastructure that efficiency requires: "While other fuels need 'hard' infrastructure like pipe and transmission lines," energy efficiency requires its own infrastructure of "public policy support, education and awareness and innovative financing tools." There are also technologies that need to be integrated into that infrastructure.

All that requires changes in how utilities are regulated so that there is as clear incentive to invest in conservation as in building new plants. In the words of James Rogers, CEO of Duke Energy, "We need to create a business model in which reducing megawatts is treated the same way from an investment point of view as producing megawatts."[18]

But it also requires the deployment of technologies that, a decade or two ago, were much less developed or did not even exist. What this involves is modernizing the system of moving electricity all the way from generation to its final use in home, office, or factory. This entire effort goes by the shorthand of "smart grid." The term has become almost ubiquitous, wildly popular, and the subject of considerable enthusiasm. After all, who wants to be against a "smart grid" or in favor of a "dumb grid"? But the concept has many definitions. As the head of one of the world's largest utilities put it, "the concept of a smart grid is rich, complex, and confusing." After all, it is not a single technology but a host of technologies. Yet in one form or another, it largely comes down to the application of digital technology, two-way communication, monitoring, sensors, information technology, and the Internet. The smart grid is also something of a movement, and as such it is the recipient of substantial and increasing investment from the federal government, utilities, industry, and investors.

The best-known subset is grouped around advanced metering infrastructure, otherwise known as the smart meter. Current meters, which in some sense have been around all the way back to the days of Samuel Insull, may be read once a month. The smart meter, by contrast, is a two-way device packed with much more capability. It eliminates the need for meter reading by sending information directly back to the utility, which thus knows in great detail what is happening to its load in real time. At the same time, it provides homeowners with situational awareness about how much electricity they are using at any given moment. With the addition of a home-area network, that knowledge can be broken down appliance by appliance, so that the smart refrigerator or the smart television can talk to the smart meter. With all this knowledge—whether displayed on a control box, on the Internet, or on their cell phone—homeowners can turn things down or even turn them off to save money.

The smart meter could, when overall demand is at the highest, enable the utility to reduce usage inside the house. For instance, during a heat wave that is straining the power system, the utility could reach out to people's thermostats (with their approval) and raise the average setting from 68 degrees to 73 degrees. (Some utilities are partway there with "paging" devices that enable them to cycle off air-conditioning every 15 minutes out of every hour.) If the electric car becomes common, the smart meter would also play a crucial role in managing recharging so that it is done late at night, off-peak, when demand is the lightest. The smart meter can do one more thing: verify energy savings. That could be essential if the utility is "paying" people to be more energy efficient.

All this is directed toward achieving two objectives: One is sharing peak demand, which reduces the need to use the most expensive generating plants, saves money, and could reduce the need to build additional expensive new generating units. The second is to promote greater energy efficiency overall, which both saves energy and cuts down on CO_2 emissions.

This all sounds very compelling. Actual implementation is challenging. The first-mover among countries is Italy, which completed installing "smart meters 1.0" for 80 percent of its load in 2006. One reason Italy moved so early was to manage demand; another, to reduce electricity theft. But Italy's experience shows that integrating these new technologies is complex. Somebody has to pay for it, and it is not cheap.

Then there is the critical matter of pricing. To get the maximum value from a smart meter system, consumers have to save money by reducing their consumption during times of peak demand. But that requires "dynamic pricing," which is another way of saying paying different rates at different times of day.

With dynamic pricing, electricity costs you less if you run your dishwasher at eleven p.m. and not at seven p.m. during peak demand. However, it is not at all clear that most consumers want prices that vary or whether they actually much prefer stable, predictable prices. That will be a crucial test for the smart meter.[19]

And there is also a question of privacy. How much do consumers want to share the details of their electricity consumption with the utility, and who will own that data, anyway? To what degree do consumers want utilities and third parties to become directly involved in controlling the operation of appliances inside their homes? Maybe they will be more amenable if the utility "pays" for that right with some financial incentive. These behavioral questions will do much to determine the extent of the impact of the smart meter.

The transmission system in the United States, the high-voltage system that carries electricity from the generating plant to the substation, is not "dumb." The United States has one of the most advanced transmissions networks in the world. At the same time, it is also something of a patchwork, having been built over many years and operating under a complex overlay of federal and state regulation and multiple ownership.

But the grid does need to be made smarter and to be expanded and reconfigured to cope with the growing load of renewable energy. Traditional coal or nuclear or gas-fired generation is predictable and can be dispatched in a measured way. Renewable generation fluctuates; it depends on how much wind is blowing and whether the sun is shining. Thus, the grid needs to become more flexible and sophisticated to absorb the increasing but variable supply of renewable energy. That will require new investment in transmission capacity and in the digital capability to integrate larger amounts of renewables into the grid and keep the overall system balanced, manage voltage, and avoid disruption. That is the urgent challenge that Germany faces with its target of doubling renewables' share of its electricity to 35 percent by 2020.

The smart grid movement has one other very important objective—increasing reliability. The smart grid can enhance reliability with a "self-healing" capability. It is impossible to ensure that weather-related events, such as an ice storm or a hurricane, do not cause outages. However, what should be a minor operational problem can, on rare occasions, have a domino effect and create a blackout over a large area. Currently utilities often find out about outages only after receiving a torrent of phone calls from angry customers who suddenly find themselves stranded in the dark, groping to find a flashlight.

That would change with the smart grid. A self-healing grid includes sensors that enable real-time monitoring, and computers that would assess trouble and present options for fixing it to human operators. This would be facilitated by two-way communications between outposts along the grid and technicians back in control rooms. Increasing situational awareness for the utility could go a long way toward reducing the duration of power outages and limiting their effects. It would also help limit the fallout from an external assault—a terrorist attack on the electricity infrastructure. Overall, this part of the smart grid could speed up response to any disruptions and reduce traditional "truck roll"—the dispatch of emergency repair teams—by solving problems in the control room.[20]

The smart grid, in its entirety, could have what has been described as a "transformational impact on how utilities operate their system, interact with their customers, and conduct their businesses." It could also be a major step forward in applying technology to promote much greater energy efficiency in buildings. However, introducing a set of new technologies, which have to be integrated into an existing system, is not only complex, it also comes with risks and setbacks. There have been a number of early examples of technology glitches and cost overruns as utilities roll out pilot programs.

One possible risk will require careful assessment and attention in terms of design: to assure that a more complex system, which is more interactive and relies more on information technology and the Internet, does not open doors that make it vulnerable to hacking, cyber attacks, or outright cyber war. The threats are real. One study found that there was "little good news about cybersecurity in the electric grid and other crucial services that depend on information technology and industrial control systems. Security improvements are modest and overmatched by the threat."[21]

Overall, new technologies and new practices can do much to improve the operations throughout the electricity system and to increase the efficiency with which buildings use energy. The full impact will only become clear over time. Surprising answers are likely to emerge out of the complex mix of technology, policy, economics, and how people live their lives—just as they did in Willis Carrier's head on that fog-enshrouded platform in Pittsburgh in 1902.

PART SIX

. . .

Road to the Future

33

CARBOHYDRATE MAN

The researcher was sitting in his office in Cambridge, Massachusetts, on a sleepy May afternoon in 1978 when the phone rang. "Admiral Rickover is on the line," said the assistant's voice. In a moment the admiral himself came on. He had just read an article by the researcher, and he had a message he wanted to deliver.

"Wood—fuel of the future. Wood!" he declared in the manner of one not used to being contradicted. "Fuel of the future!"

And with not much more than that, the Father of the Nuclear Navy—and the progenitor of nuclear power—abruptly hung up.

What Rickover was pointing at that afternoon was the potential for biological energy and biomass: energy generated from plant matter and other sources, and not by fossil fuels or uranium. The nation had just gone through an oil crisis and was on the edge of another. Now the man who had created the nuclear navy in record time was announcing that the future was about "growing" fuels.

Today legions of scientists, farmers, entrepreneurs, agribusiness managers, and venture capitalists use words like "ethanol," "cellulosic," and "biomass" rather than "wood." But they share Rickover's vision of growing fuel.

The best-known agricultural fuel is ethanol: ethyl alcohol made, in the first instance, from corn or sugar. In terms of technology, it's hardly different than brewing beer or making rum. Beyond this is the "holy grail": cellulosic ethanol,

ethanol fermented and distilled on a massive scale from agricultural or urban waste or specially designed crops. Another agricultural fuel is biodiesel, made from soybeans or palm oil or even from the leftover grease from fast-food restaurants. Some argue that the still-better choices would be other biofuels, such as butanol. And then there is algae, which functions like little natural refineries.

THE BIOFUEL VISION

Whatever approaches prevail, biofuels suggest the possibility of a new era, characterized by the application of biology and biotech and understanding of the genome—the full DNA sequence of an organism—to the production of energy. The rise of the biofuels brings a new entrant into energy: the life scientist. Only in the last decade has biology begun to be applied systematically to energy.

Over this same period biofuels have generated enormous political swell in the United States, starting of course with the traditional advocates: farmers and their political allies who have always looked to ethanol as a way to diversify agricultural markets, generate additional revenues, and contribute to farm income and rural development. But there are new supporters: environmentalists (at least some), automobile companies, Silicon Valley billionaires, Hollywood moguls, along with national security specialists, who want to reduce oil imports because of worries about the Middle East and the geopolitical power of oil. More recently, they have all been joined by formidable new players: the U.S. Navy and Air Force, which are promoting biofuels development to improve combat capabilities and increase flexibility—and to diversify away from oil. The air force is experimenting with green jet fuel. The navy has a goal that half of its liquid fuels be biofuels by 2020 and laid out a vision of the "Great Green Fleet."

This broad-based political support has generated an impressive array of programs, subsidies, incentives, and federal and state mandates meant to jump-start the biofuels industry in the United States. The most compelling is the requirement that the amount of biofuels blended with transportation fuel must almost triple from about somewhere below 1 million barrels per day in 2011 to 2.35 mbd by 2022. This could be the equivalent of about 20 percent of all motor fuel in the United States. It is like adding to world supply another Venezuela or

Nigeria. The push to biofuels has been global. The European Union mandates at least 10 percent renewable energy, including biofuels, in the transport sector of each member state by 2020. India has proposed an ambitious 20 percent target for biofuels blending by 2017. But the champion is Brazil, where 60 percent of automotive motor fuel today is already ethanol.

In the biofuels vision, the process that produces fossil fuels—compressing organic matter into oil at tremendous pressure and heat deep below the earth's surface over hundreds of millions of years—could be foreshortened into a cycle measured in seasons. A larger and larger share of the world's transportation fuels would be cultivated, rather than drilled for. Hydrocarbon Man—the quintessential embodiment of the twentieth century, the century of oil—would increasingly give way over the twenty-first century to Carbohydrate Man. If this vision eventuates and biofuels do take away significant market share from traditional oil-based fuels over the next few decades, the results would reset global economics and politics. And agri-dollars would come to compete with petro-dollars.

Significant growth of ethanol use has already been registered. Today the amount of ethanol blended into gasoline is close to 900,000 barrels per day, in terms of volume, almost 10 percent of total U.S. gasoline (including blended ethanol) consumption. However, ethanol, on a volume basis, has only about two thirds the energy value of conventional gasoline, and so on an energy basis, today's ethanol consumption is the energy equivalent of 600,000 barrels per day of gasoline.

Ethanol's share in the United States is likely to grow over the next few years, although it must first contend with a "wall" on the amount of ethanol that can be blended with gasoline for use in all gas-powered vehicles. The fear is that greater concentrations of ethanol could harm engines not designed to run on biofuels.

There is also E85 fuel, which contains between 70 percent and 85 percent ethanol, but it can only be used in flex-fuel vehicles that can switch between oil and ethanol-based fuels or all-ethanol vehicles, specifically designed to accommodate this type of fuel. Currently such vehicles total only about 3 percent of the U.S. car fleet.

All this may strike many as new. But it isn't, not by any means.

THE FIRST FLEX-FUEL VEHICLE

Henry Ford did not much care for cities. "There is something about a city of a million people which is untamed and threatening," he once said. "Thirty miles away, happy and contented villages read of the ravings of the city." Not that he had illusions about rural life. "I have followed many a weary mile behind a plough and I know all the drudgery of it." The automobile would be the "messenger," the liberator, linking farms and villages to the wider world, and the tractor would overcome the drudgery of rural work, enabling the farmer to get beyond "a bare living" and become so much more productive. "What a waste it is for a human being to spend hours and days behind a slowly moving team of horses when in the same time a tractor could do six times as much work!"

Ford was keen on using the preferred auto fuel, ethanol, produced by farmers, to tie farm and city together in a mutual interdependence, a sort of social contract. "If we industrialists want the American farmer to be our customer, we must find a way to become his customer."[1]

Yet there was a huge obstacle in the way of ethanol: price. Every gallon of alcohol carried a $2.08 a gallon tax imposed as a revenue measure during the Civil War. With the discovery of vast amounts of oil in Texas and Oklahoma around the beginning of the twentieth century, gasoline had a decided cost advantage, at least in the United States. That was not the case in Europe, where auto races pitted ethanol against gasoline as a fuel. The French and German governments used tariffs and mandates to encourage alcohol fuels. Finally, in 1906, responding to farmers who were reeling from low grain prices, Theodore Roosevelt signed a bill eliminating the alcohol tax. One congressman (and a future Speaker of the House) predicted that alcohol "made from cornstalks" would soon be one of the "most pertinent factors in modern civilization."[2]

With the tax eliminated, demand shot up, and ethanol was once again locked in a great race with gasoline as to which would be the "fuel of the future."

Making good on his social contract with America's farmers, Ford ensured that the Model T, at least when he introduced it, could run on either ethanol or gasoline. It was the first flex-fuel vehicle. Later he introduced Fordson tractors that could run on alcohol as well as gasoline. With all that, however, gasoline was the dominant fuel because it cost only a third as much.

Toward the end of World War I and in the years immediately after, however, prices shot up as gasoline once again went into short supply. Alexander Graham Bell, the inventor of the telephone, hailed alcohol as "a wonderfully clean-burning fuel . . . that can be produced from farm crops, agricultural waste and even garbage." A scientist from General Motors warned that the crude oil was "being rapidly depleted" and would soon run out. The solution was alcohol fuel, he said, which was "the most direct route which we know for converting energy from its source, the sun, into a material that is suitable for use as fuel."

However, almost insurmountable obstacles to ethanol have appeared. On January 16, 1919, the Eighteenth Amendment to the Constitution made Prohibition the law of the land. Alcoholic beverages were banned. Prohibition was aimed at ending drunkenness, alcoholism, and immorality, and at protecting the family against abuse and dissolution. But it also turned millions of Americans into lawbreakers and gave an immense boost to moonshine, bathtub gin, speakeasies, bootlegging, racketeering, and the rise of organized crime.

Prohibition stopped alcohol fuels dead in their tracks. The new Constitutional amendment prohibited "intoxicating liquors" that could be ingested by humans, not fuels that could be fed to cars. But whether made into an "intoxicating drink" or into a fuel, alcohol was alcohol. Moreover, there was no telling what a farmer would really do with the alcohol.

Yet when the Great Depression led to a collapse in commodity prices and ruin for farmers across America, ethanol seemed a key element in farm relief. It would expand the market for agricultural products and, at the same time, make the farmer self-sufficient in terms of his own fuels. Opponents denounced the idea. "To force the use of alcohol in motor fuel," said one critic, "would be to make every filling station and gasoline pump a potential speakeasy." But by the time Franklin Roosevelt became president in 1933, it was widely recognized that the "Great Experiment," as Prohibition was known, was a dismal failure, and the Twenty-first Amendment to the Constitution repealed it.

Ethanol was back in business. By the late 1930s, at least 2,000 service stations across the Middle West were selling Agroblends, gasoline with some mixture of alcohol. But this was pretty limited. Rising grain prices removed the political drive. One of Henry Ford's assistants privately admitted the harsh truth: alcohol fuels could not compete economically against gasoline.[3]

BIRTH OF GASOHOL

After World War II ethanol faded away once again. Agricultural income had risen, and the political pressure dissipated. But the oil shocks of the 1970s—and the difficult economic times they brought about—hit farmers hard. Many were struggling; others were going bankrupt. Agricultural prices swooned with the economic downturn. At the same time, prices of their critical inputs—diesel fuel for their tractors, fertilizers made from hydrocarbons—shot up.

When in 1977 President Jimmy Carter launched his National Energy Plan, there was not a word about gasohol, as ethanol was called at the time. But political support built rapidly among senators and congressmen from agricultural states. The advocates found many ways to express their support, including street theater, Washington, D.C.–style. At one such event in 1977, Senator Birch Bayh of Indiana, standing on the grounds of the Capitol, opened a bottle of vodka and triumphantly poured it directly into the fuel tank of an ancient car. The engine sprang to life without a delay to the huge delight of the assembled crowd. The political support translated into legislative support—a 40-cents-a-gallon subsidy, along with additional incentives to encourage investment in ethanol facilities. Supplies began to increase.

Ethanol was no longer just a "Ma and Pa" farmer's business. Some agribusiness firms embraced it as well. Archer Daniels Midland (ADM), one of the biggest merchants of agricultural products in the world, would turn out to be decisive. Very quickly, ADM became the biggest producer of ethanol in the United States as well as its most effective political champion.[4]

The second oil shock in the late 1970s increased the political pressure for more support from the federal government. In early February 1979, a most unusual sight appeared in Washington, D.C.: a motorcade of 3,000 tractors—or a "tractorcade," as it became known—made its way down Independence Avenue, eventually reaching the Capitol, which it circled, and then finally settled in on the National Mall for an extended stay. These farmers were angry, and they were desperate, and they wanted to dramatize their need for help. They were united in their demand: a national commitment to ethanol.

The political imperative became even stronger in December 1979. On Christmas Eve 1979, the Soviet Union launched its invasion of Afghanistan. In addition to promulgating the Carter Doctrine, guaranteeing the security of the Persion Gulf, President Carter also announced a cutoff of grain exports to the Soviet Union, a business much prized by farmers.[5] But he promised enraged farmers a highly subsidized major new program for gasohol to absorb some of the now-excess corn. As Deputy Secretary of State Warren Christopher explained, "Our farmers would rather be growing grain to solve our energy problems than they would for the Soviet Union's [livestock] herds." Then, in the midst of a tough reelection campaign against Ronald Reagan, Carter did something else that would have lasting benefit for U.S. ethanol: he slapped a tariff on Brazilian ethanol to prevent it from competing with U.S. ethanol.

Ethanol in the United States really seemed to be on its way. By 1981 10,000 gasoline stations were selling gasohol. A Department of Energy task force demonstrated how far the skepticism of just a few years earlier had turned into enthusiasm. Its high scenario predicted that renewable alcohol fuels could provide more than 100 percent of U.S. gasoline by 2000.

But, instead, when oil prices collapsed a few years later, ethanol faded away. By 1986 the Agriculture Department was dismissing gasohol subsidies as a "very inefficient" means of increasing farm income. In the first half of the 1990s, very little corn was being turned into ethanol.[6]

THE MAKING OF AN ETHANOL BOOM

Yet at almost exactly the same time, ethanol received a regulatory reprieve. Under the Clean Air Act Amendment of 1990, much of the U.S. gasoline supplies were required to include extra oxygen to improve combustion and reduce pollution. Gasoline so endowed with such oxygenates became known as reformulated gasoline. At first, the favored oxygenate was an additive called MTBE—for methyl tertiary butyl ether—which was derived from petroleum. But in the late 1990s, concern mounted that MTBE could leak out of underground tanks, contaminating groundwater. The only available alternative was ethanol. As it replaced MTBE, ethanol demand started to rise again. What once had been called gasohol had a new name: E10 (90 percent gasoline, 10 percent ethanol).

Political support was also once again building. In Iowa Governor Tom Vilsack, who had previously worked as a lawyer defending farmers going through bankruptcies, was determined to help raise farm incomes and turn the state into a national laboratory for ethanol. A number of prominent senators—including Richard Lugar of Indiana, Chuck Hagel of Nebraska, and Tom Daschle of South Dakota—promoted legislation to establish mandatory targets for ethanol in the nation's motor fuel pool. The terrorist attack of September 11, 2001, provided further impetus to ethanol. For now ethanol would provide a partial alternative to oil, particularly oil from the Middle East. "We had a national economic and strategic problem," said Senator Lugar. By helping to diversify the fuel mix, ethanol would contribute to security. It would also provide an alternative to the traditional system of agricultural subsidies and controls, connect farmers to another market, and help revitalize rural communities.[7]

The real boost came with the passage of the Energy Policy Act of 2005. First, it effectively banned MTBE, forcing ethanol's major competitor off the market. Second, the act established a Renewable Fuel Standard requiring as much as 500,000 barrels per day of ethanol in the motor fuel pool by 2012. That would mean a doubling of ethanol output. But ethanol costs more than gasoline to produce. Thus, third, the act affirmed a most attractive 51-cents-a-gallon tax credit. In addition to all this, the tariff on Brazilian ethanol remained in place, preventing significant volumes of Brazilian ethanol from entering the United States.

The U.S. ethanol boom was now on. Investment in biorefineries came from all kinds of people—from farmers and farm co-ops across the Midwest, from famous businessmen, from promoters and developers, from biotech entrepreneurs, and from investment funds.

But the most prominent booster turned out to be George W. Bush, who had started his career in "Little oil"—that is, as on independent oilman. In the autumn of 2005, after hurricanes Katrina and Rita knocked out for several months oil production in the Gulf of Mexico, gasoline prices shot up. This created a political storm and threw the administration on the defensive. At the same time, the situation in Iraq was deteriorating, and Bush increasingly saw reliance on imported oil as a weakness to America's position in the world.

On a trip to California, a venture capitalist who was the co-chairman of a presidential science advisory committee told the president that renewable fuels were now the "new, new thing" among venture capitalists. Soon after, on the farm of then Brazilian President Luis Inácio Lula da Silva, near Brasilia, over what Bush called "a good old-fashioned Brazilian barbecue," Bush heard Lula explain how ethanol now had a large share of Brazil's motor fuel market. Indeed, Lula was, as the Brazilian president himself later put it, so "truly obsessed with biofuel" that Bush "almost couldn't have lunch because I wouldn't stop talking about biofuel." Meanwhile, Capitol Hill was vigorously promoting the virtues of ethanol. Ethanol as a national strategy became one of the main themes of Bush's 2006 State of the Union Address. Americans are "addicted to oil," the president declared in the speech, and he intended to end that. Bush knew that he would catch people's attention with the reference to addiction. "I kind of startled my country when, at my State of the Union, I said we're hooked on oil, and we need to get off oil," he later said. "That seemed counterintuitive, for some people, to hear a Texan say."[8]

Ethanol was now flowing into the mainstream. Biorefineries were going up at a frantic rate across the farm belt. Farmers were pooling their savings to build their own local biorefineries. Jobs were being created in rural communities where depopulation had become a way of life. Farm incomes were going up, and land prices in the Midwest were rising faster than co-op prices in New York City. The Carbohydrate Economy has been a vision—and a dream—for over a century. But a reality now? If so, how big?

BRAZIL'S "ALCOHOL"

Outside the city of Ribeirão Preto, about two hundred miles northwest of São Paulo, the road narrows to two lanes. No one goes fast, for the cars have no choice but to creep along behind long, lumbering trucks, some hauling trailers, all filled as high as possible, almost to overflowing, with sugarcane. Finally, the trucks turn off to the mill, where they line up in a great arc in an open area. One after another they get their turn. They creep forward to a wall, and then the truckbed comes up and tilts over, and tons of sugarcane come tumbling down like a waterfall, falling onto a conveyer belt, which carries the cane into the mill where it is crushed and processed. The resulting liquid is fermented and then flows as ethanol into distillation towers and then into tanks. Then the ethanol begins a new journey, this time by tank truck and pipeline to the motorists around the country.

This scene, replayed over and over in the hinterlands of Brazil, is now part of the world energy market in a way that few would have anticipated even a decade ago. In Brazil, "alcohol," as it is known locally, has become a central factor in the national energy mix, and Brazil has come to center stage for a world looking for a biofuels role model. It is already the world's largest exporter of sugar. Its geographic endowment, its experience, its capacity to grow production—all these make it a potential new energy supplier to global markets. But what makes Brazil's position particularly compelling is the fact that it is the lowest-cost producer of ethanol in the world. The reason is that its raw material is not corn but sugar, which is that much closer along the biological spectrum to the creation of ethanol.

Ethanol has been an important crop in Brazil for centuries. In the Great Depression in the 1930s, sugar prices collapsed. In response, the government ordered that motor fuel include 5 percent ethanol to create extra demand for a crop in serious oversupply and thus help prop up farmers' incomes. But after World War II, the vast surge of cheap oil washed away the ethanol market in Brazil.

By the 1970s Brazil was importing 85 percent of its oil, and its economy was booming. But the 1973 oil crisis abruptly ended what was being called the Brazilian Economic Miracle. Petroleum prices quadrupled, delivering a devastating shock to the economy. The military government responded with what it described as a "wartime economy" to meet the nation's energy crisis. Brazil, according to the universal consensus, had absolutely no prospects for petroleum. The only energy option was sugar. As part of the "war effort"—and at the strong urging of distraught sugar growers—the government established the national Pro-Alcohol program. It was backed by the slogan "Let's unite, make alcohol." As an extra incentive, fuel stations, previously closed on weekends, were granted the right to stay open on Saturdays and Sundays in order to sell ethanol—but not gasoline. Ethanol consumption increased dramatically.

Initially ethanol was added to gasoline. But by 1980, in response to the government's insistence, the Brazilian subsidiaries of the major car companies agreed to manufacture vehicles that ran exclusively on ethanol. In turn, the government made a crucial pledge, both to the companies and consumers, that there would be sufficient ethanol. It was an absolute guarantee. The actual production costs of ethanol in 1980 were three times that of gasoline, but that was hidden from consumers by huge subsidies that were paid for by a tax on gasoline.[9]

By 1985, 95 percent of all new cars sold in Brazil ran exclusively on "alcohol." However, the oil price collapse in the mid-1980s left ethanol wildly overpriced compared with gasoline. Moreover, with sugar prices rising, growers switched from ethanol back to sugar. Ethanol output dropped sharply in the second half of the 1990s. The result was a severe shortage of ethanol. The shortfall infuriated all those now-stranded owners of the new alcohol-only vehicles, devastated ethanol's credibility, and destroyed confidence in its availability. Despite the absolute promise the government had let them down. As a final act of embarrassment, Brazil had to import ethanol from the United States to help make up for its deficit in supply.

But from 2000 onward, three things brought "alcohol" back in Brazil. The first was the rising price of oil. Second, thirty years of experience and continuing research dramatically reduced production costs for ethanol.

The third was the introduction of flex-fuel autos. These are vehicles with onboard computers that can detect by "sniffing"—that is, sensing whether the fuel is gasoline, a mixture of gasoline and ethanol, or mostly ethanol—and then adjust the engine accordingly. Flex-fuel vehicles entered the Brazilian market only in late 2003. José Goldemberg, an esteemed professor at the University of São Paulo, former government official, and one of the fathers of the Brazilian ethanol development, recognized that flex-fuel vehicles were transformative. This was the inexpensive breakthrough that would put confidence back into the minds of motorists. It cost only about $100 to make a car flex-fuel and thus enable drivers not to be reliant solely on ethanol and so eliminate the risk of driving somewhere and not being able to get home. Also, around this time, he did a highly influential analysis—"the Goldemberg Curve"—that demonstrated that Brazilian ethanol with no subsidies was now cheaper than gasoline.

To say that flex-fuel vehicles "caught on" would be an understatement. In 2003 about 40,000 flex-fuel cars were sold in Brazil. By 2008 this number had surged to just over two million, and flex-fuel constituted about 94 percent of all new cars sold in Brazil. This means that the motorist at the pump can decide what is cheaper on any given day and put that fuel into the engine. With memories fresh from the ethanol shortage of the 1990s, it also means that the car owner could always get around using "old-fashioned" gasoline, even if the price of ethanol shot up again. Though no longer subsidized, Brazilian ethanol is highly competitive both at home and on the world market. Indeed, today sugarcane ethanol in Brazil is generally seen as the world's only consistently competitive biofuel.[10]

Sugar has another cost advantage over corn-based fuel. The bagasse, the leftover waste fiber from the sugarcane, is burned to generate heat and power, eliminating the need for fossil fuels and reducing costs. The sugarcane growers have an added protection, which adds to their incentive to expand output. They are not dependent on a single market, but rather can optimize output between sugar and ethanol, depending on relative prices. Even so, the expansion of the ethanol industry has proved volatile for investors.

Ethanol is certainly well established once again in Brazil. In fact, gasoline is now the "alternative" fuel, as sales of ethanol, since 2008, have outpaced gasoline. And Brazil has achieved that nirvana of energy independence. Instead of the 85 percent import dependence of the 1970s, the country is now self-sufficient and indeed it is a net exporter of oil.

Some in the United States ask why it cannot do the same. But the challenge in the two countries is not exactly on the same scale. The entire Brazilian motor fuel market is equivalent to only about 10 percent of the U.S. gasoline market. In fact, the United States currently produces about 75 percent more ethanol than Brazil. For the United States to attain market penetration equivalent to Brazil would require almost five million barrels per day—more output than any OPEC country except Saudi Arabia.

Moreover, it would be mistaken to assume that Brazil's energy independence is exclusively because of ethanol. The 1970s expectation that Brazil was virtually devoid of oil resources has turned out to be resoundingly wrong. The growth of its petroleum output is among the fastest in the world. Today the country produces about five times as much oil as it does ethanol.

With all that said, Brazil's ethanol industry is positioned for rapid expansion.

Much land is available, and it does not require cutting down rain forests. (Sugarcane cannot grow in rain forest–type conditions.) There is potential for much further innovation in the sugarcane itself and in production facilities and logistics. And if the world is willing, Brazil has the potential to take the lead in developing a very large global export market.

FOOD VERSUS FUEL

As biofuels came to the fore around the world, a debate erupted over the prospects for conventional ethanol and other biofuels, which could be summed up as "food versus fuel" and "net carbon footprint." A good deal of energy goes into the production of ethanol. But do you get more, less, or the same amount "coming out" compared with the amount of energy "going in"? The energy balance—that is, how much energy you get for the energy you expend—is controversial and not easy to measure.

It takes energy to make energy. The energy for conventional ethanol includes the diesel fuel for the tractors that plow the fields, the petrochemicals that go into the fertilizer, the fuel for the vehicles that gather the corn, the heat on which the still operates, and the fuel for the vehicles that move the ethanol from the small towns of the heartland toward the market. Changing the assumptions on all these factors will give different answers. Currently the consensus is that the net energy balance is mildly positive for corn ethanol, although the actual balance depends very much on the fuels and the costs that are incurred to make and transport the ethanol. Moreover, with greater experience in building plants and larger scale, that balance should improve somewhat more. Also, a good part of the energy input is non-oil fuels, like coal and natural gas. Indeed, increasing ethanol production is creating an important new industrial market for natural gas.[11]

But are there limits to the growth of land that can be devoted to growing crops for biofuels? Corn is the largest agricultural crop in the United States as measured by acres planted. Such is the boom in corn that it now even outranks wheat as a crop in Kansas, "the wheat state." But the use of the corn is not what most people would assume. Only about 1 percent of the corn crop is eaten directly by humans as corn. Another portion of the corn crop goes into processed foods, including high-fructose corn syrup. A much bigger share is indirect consumption through livestock, which consume about half the corn. Ethanol's share of the nation's corn crop increased sevenfold between 1995 and 2009, from 6 percent in 1995 to 41 percent in 2009. So when it comes to American corn, the real "food versus fuel" competition is "animal food versus fuel."[12]

Higher corn prices are good news for corn farmers. But they are bad news for livestock growers and dairy farmers, who depend on corn to feed their animals. Higher costs for corn also add to the price of such consumer products as soft drinks and breakfast cereals that use high-fructose corn syrup (and, by encouraging farmers to switch from barley to corn, also to the price of beer). Corn prices, as they feed through to animal feed, flow into rising food prices around the world, contributing to inflation and generating political tensions in many countries.

Rising prices created a crisis in Mexico, which imports corn from the United States for making tortillas. And with the increase in the price of corn, prices for Mexican corn also went up. As a result, the price of tortillas abruptly jumped in 2007. This created the first political crisis for President Felipe Calderón, who had been elected by a razor-thin majority. "We're a country that eats tortillas and beans," said the Mexican energy minister in the midst of the crisis. Seventy thousand people took to the streets in Mexico City to protest the high prices—tortilla prices tripled in some parts of the country—forcing the government to slap price controls on tortillas.[13]

Remarkable advances in agronomy have quadrupled the bushel yield per acre since 1950. But even with their increases in productivity, advocates of ethanol see acreage as a limit to corn-based ethanol.

A backlash against biofuels on environmental grounds has emerged, centered on concerns about the net carbon footprint of first-generation biofuels. Although biorefineries in the United States have strong local support in farming communities, opponents complain about the effects on air quality and traffic.

More broadly, criticism has risen concerning water use and increased greenhouse emissions released from the soil and from additional fertilizer production. The biofuels criticism has been significant in Europe, particularly concerning palm oil imported from Malaysia and Indonesia, where the burning of forestlands to make way for palm oil plantations emits CO_2 and disturbs biodiversity.

As a result, the EU is trying to implement sustainability safeguards for biofuels, such as "well to wheel" limits on the CO_2 content of biofuels and prohibitions on deforestation. The land-use provisions get trickier when it comes to considering what is called indirect land-use change—the "knock-on" effects of land use, an especially hot topic for the European Union. "Indirect" is when, for instance, a biofuel crop displaces a food crop, which in turn, seeking new land for cultivation, leads to deforestation and a potentially large release of carbon. How is this going to be measured? And, by the way, who is doing the measuring?[14]

For the United States, conventional ethanol and biodiesel cannot meet the expectations for biofuels. Of the 2.35 million barrels a day of biofuels that is required to be mixed into the country's motor fuel by 2022, more than half must be advanced—second generation—biofuels. Much of that is supposed to come from something that is now available in laboratories and start-ups but does not exist on a commercial scale: cellulosic ethanol.

A PROMISING FUNGUS

During World War II, some of the fiercest fighting took place in the South Pacific. As Allied troops pushed the Japanese back, island by island, they had to contend with the daunting and unexpected travails of jungle warfare. One of the most mysterious and surprising was jungle rot—molds that ate their way through tents, garments, knapsacks, boots, and belts. Samples of these organisms—eventually some 14,000—were collected and dispatched to an army laboratory in Natick, Massachusetts, west of Boston. One of the most promising was a fungus called *Trichoderma viride,* extracted from a rotted-out cartridge belt brought back from New Guinea. A biologist at Natick, Leo Spano, developed a mutant version of the fungus that he left in a water solution with ground-up leaves. When he came back to it thirty-six hours later, he found that the mutant had worked a kind of magic, turning the leaves into glucose, a type of sugar. As he looked at the sugar, he thought he saw a new future. "I realized that a tiny enzyme could change the world as we know it," he later said. "If man could direct an enzyme and improve it, the compounds could eat up our poisonous wastes and convert them to useful substances."

After the 1973 oil crisis, Spano's work drew wider attention. At a conference in Natick in 1975, Undersecretary of the Army Norman Augustine proclaimed that "we turn to the lowly fungi" to solve problems of energy, resources, and food. "I was struck," Augustine later said, "by the possibility of making a quantum leap by adopting a totally new approach that seemed to have a supportable scientific foundation." Both large companies and start-ups began to experiment with cellulosic ethanol.[15]

But in the 1980s as oil prices declined and then collapsed, attention faded away. Funding for long-term R&D disappeared. A few stragglers still continued to play with the technology. A Canadian company, Iogen, founded with great hopes in the 1970s, just managed to stay in business by developing enzymes that, among other things, made feed more digestible for chickens and pigs.

But by the beginning of the twenty-first century, a conjunction of developments—renewed support and ambitious targets for biofuels, combined with energy security and a growing focus on climate change—created fertile soil for the rebirth of interest in cellulosic ethanol.

"SWITCH—WHAT?"

Until 2006 very few Americans had ever even heard of something called switchgrass. But one person who certainly had was David Bransby, a South African–born professor who now taught at Auburn University in Alabama. He had written his Ph.D. on grasslands science and had spent decades working on prairie grasses, one of which was switchgrass, which grows in thick tangles, eight or nine feet high. But he didn't get much attention outside his discipline. Then Alabama's Senator Jeff Sessions visited Bransby's switchgrass field and came away impressed by the grass's potential as a fuel source, and one potentially superior to corn. At a meeting at the White House, prior to the "addicted to oil" 2006 State of the Union, Sessions made the case for switchgrass. Keen to find something new on energy, the administration listened.

One can be sure that almost all of the tens of millions of Americans tuned in to the 2006 State of the Union were mystified when President Bush called for the development of "cutting-edge methods of producing ethanol . . . from wood chips and stalks, or switchgrass." Wood chips, sure. But switchgrass? What was this switchgrass? Professor Bransby from Auburn University had a somewhat different reaction. "I nearly fell off my chair when I was watching it in my living room," he later said.[16]

The "holy grail" is the term sometimes applied to cellulosic ethanol and other advanced biofuels. If achieved, these biofuels could be transformational, dramatically changing the supply balance and, at the same time, significantly reducing greenhouse gas emissions from transportation. Unlike the electric car, they would not require an entirely new infrastructure. To the end user—the motorist or the airline—the change would be essentially invisible. Life would not change. But biofuels would transform the energy system—in terms of how energy is produced, who produces it, and how the revenues flow.

Much effort now is going into their development. Life sciences have been recruited into the energy business. And also in a way that never happened before, the financial resources are there to back up this undertaking—from governments, entrepreneurs, and venture capital and private equity firms.

Moreover, the major international oil companies have in the last few years made significant commitments to various kinds of advanced biofuels research, some of them on a very large scale. BP is providing $500 million to the Energy Biosciences Institute, a collaboration between the University of California, Berkeley, the Lawrence Berkeley National Laboratory, and the University of Illinois. ExxonMobil has committed $600 million to work with Synthetic Genomics, a firm founded by Craig Venter, a mapper of the human genome. Chevron, Shell, ConocoPhillips, Total, and Statoil have all formed biofuels-related partnerships. And, of course, Brazil's Petrobras is also active in biofuels. Venture capitalists have, meanwhile, funded a number of start-ups.

While going down many different pathways, these ventures are all trying to get to the same destination: a new source of transportation fuel that is commercial, competitive, available at scale—and does not require a whole new infrastructure.

The know-how exists today to break down plant materials and agricultural waste and turn them into ethanol. The challenge is to do it in a way that is both economic and large scale. It is a big challenge. "We always knew you could use enzymes to treat fiber and turn wood into sugar," said the executive of one of the original cellulosic ethanol firms, which has been at it since the 1970s. "That's not the issue. It's at what cost and whether it can be done in an industrial-scale environment quickly."[17]

The uncertainty arises from the nature of the problem. The researchers are challenging the anatomy of the plant itself. They are trying to wrest from plants and other materials something these organic materials are not designed to give up easily.

The basic issue for ethanol is how to release the sugars that can be fermented and then distilled into alcohol fuel. With cane sugar, one is already almost there. Corn needs to be ground down and treated to release the sugars. Cellulosic ethanol is still more complicated. As the name indicates, cellulosic ethanol is derived from the sugars that are embedded in the long complex chains of carbohydrates that comprise cellulose and hemicelluloses. They are still further away from being fuels. They are meant to be tough. After all, they are the walls of the plant. The cellulose and the hemicellulose, along with the lignin, are what give the plant its structural integrity. They are what enables a tree to stand up straight.

And here is the core barrier—to break down the body armor that protects the sugar. The cellulose and the hemicellulose need to be separated from the lignin and then broken down into sugars suitable for fermentation into ethanol (ethyl alcohol). This can be accomplished through what is called enzymatic conversion; that is, the application of specialized enzymes. More has to be done on enzymes to make them more competitive.

The raw material for cellulosic ethanol is cheap. It may be crop residues or agricultural waste; for instance, the leftover corn stover or straw from wheat cultivation or the bagasse that is a waste product from fermenting sugarcane. It can also be other agricultural residue or wood waste or even some kinds of garbage. Or it can be obtained from various kinds of grasses that are grown on marginal land, such as the aforementioned switchgrass or micanthus or sorghum, a cousin of sugarcane.

But costs of processing are still high. It is estimated that building the facilities for manufacturing cellulosic ethanol can be four times as expensive or more as that for corn-based ethanol.

THE FORGOTTEN CHALLENGE

There is also what has been called the "daunting logistics"—the "forgotten challenge." For compared with oil, biomass has a very low energy density. Therefore, a lot of it has to be gathered, and the costs of doing all that gathering, transporting, and storing are high. The energy density of oil is such that transporting it halfway around the world is economic. By contrast, biomass has what has been described as an "inherently local nature," which, according to some, makes a 50-mile radius a potential outer limit. Consider a 6,000-barrel-per-day cellulosic plant. It could require as many as 50,000 semitrailer trips per year to supply it.

The refinery also needs a steady source of supply. If material is being harvested once or twice a year, then it needs to be stored, which is yet another logistical problem. Matter rots and decays. All this adds to the cost. And then, eventually, there will also be a price on the raw material itself.[18]

The industry cannot go to scale unless these logistical challenges can be met. One way to do that is by changing the raw material in the upstream—that is, the plant itself.

"TOUGHER THAN PEOPLE MAY HAVE EXPECTED"

Inspiration comes in many shapes. For Richard Hamilton, it came during the tenth grade in the form of an article in *Newsweek* about the IPO of Genentech in October 1980. This was the first public offering of a company from the new biotech industry, and it marked the opening of a whole new age of biotechnology.

The Genentech story captured Hamilton's imagination. By the time he was in college, when people asked him what he wanted to do, he would knowingly reply, "Biotech." They would look at him blankly. After all, this was still the early days for biotech.

After getting a Ph.D. in molecular biology, Hamilton spent a year as a postdoc at Harvard, where he honed ideas about using biotechnology and genetic engineering to create designer plants. He helped launch a company, Ceres, in 1997, to focus on plant genes. It was not until 2004, as the ethanol boom was building, that he focused on using biotech to create plants specifically designed as fodder for fuels to cope with the logistical challenges that will come with the growth of a cellulosic industry. Indeed, Hamilton and others in this field are bringing a new biological perspective to biofuels.

"Many people are focused on the refining technology and have worried less about feedstock," he said. "But this will change as the industry tries to scale. High-yield density is one of the key enablers because of the logistics. Overall, cellulosic ethanol has proved to be tougher than people may have expected. The biggest challenge is that the timelines are determined by the life cycles of living organisms. We are dependent on the passage of seasons to see the results of our work.

"Our crops did not just spring forth from a mythical garden of Eden," added Hamilton. "They have been bred and improved by man." He held up his hand and pointed to his fingernail. "This is how big the first ears of corn were. We have had agriculture for 10,000 years. We did not know that DNA was the genetic material until 1946. The Green Revolution in the late 1960s was an example of beginning to apply modern biology to plant improvement."[19]

Many of the people working in this field are applying the know-how that emerged from the sequencing of the human genome. Calling on the new fields of bioinformatics and computational biology, and using what is called high-throughput experimentation, they seek to identify specific genes and their functions. The aim is to speed up the process of evolution, selecting for characteristics that will make such tall grasses as miscanthus and switchgrass effective energy crops that can grow in marginal lands that would not be cultivated for food. That means selecting for such objectives as speedy growth, accessibility of the sugars, resistance to drought, and lower requirements for fertilizer. The ultimate objective: to increase substantially the number of "gallons per acre."

There are other approaches. One is to heat biomass to very high temperatures and create a syngas that can, in a process analogous to turning coal into liquids, be transformed into liquid fuel. Another is to use hydrolysis, combining water and acids, under pressure and at high temperatures, to decompose biomass and turn it into ethanol.

The focus of refining technology is increasingly on drop-ins, otherwise known as "fungible molecules" or "green molecules." The aim is, using catalysts, to turn sugars into hydrocarbons that in performance and content are virtually identical with conventional hydrocarbon fuels: gasoline, diesel fuel, and jet fuel. If this works on scale, it would mean products that could be dropped seamlessly into the existing fuel supply system with no requirement for any infrastructure changes. As it is, ethanol must be shipped and stored separately from gasoline because ethanol mixes so easily with the small amounts of water in gasoline pipelines and storage tanks.

ALGAE: THE LITTLE REFINERIES

Another potential biofuel source is algae, single-cell creatures at the bottom of the food chain in oceans, lakes, and ponds. Algae are little refineries; they absorb sunlight and CO_2 and produce oxygen (about 40 percent of the world's supply) and bio-oils. Those oils are, in molecular terms, very suitable for the production of gasoline and diesel and jet fuel. They are also, theoretically, very efficient. At work, on land or in ponds of brackish water or in more-controlled bioreactors, they could turn out, on a per-acre basis, about three times as much fuel as a palm plantation and about six times as much as a corn farm.

Some teams are trying to do this by naturally breeding strains of algae, while others are seeking to apply the genome and develop a fully functioning super-algae that could have significant impact on global energy supply.

One basic challenge in all the algae work is to find the most productive strains of algae and then maintain the stability of the algae population—which has proved very challenging—and do all this at commercial scale.

WHAT IS POSSIBLE FOR BIOFUELS

What will be the timing and impact of commercial cellulosic ethanol and other advanced biofuels? That is the subject of much argument. Some say it is almost within reach; to others, it remains a major research problem. Some who come from Silicon Valley, with its short life cycles for software and computers, might project that same kind of time frame of twenty-four to thirty-six months for biofuels. If one's point of reference is biotechnology, then a time horizon might be five to ten years. If one comes from the conventional oil and gas industry, with its very long development cycles and with its experience of the complexity and scale of the distribution system, then the thinking might be in terms of 15 to 20 years.

What is ultimately possible? A bold assessment comes from Steven Koonin, a theoretical physicist and former provost at California Institute of Technology, former chief scientist for BP, and current undersecretary of science at the Department of Energy. He suggests that biofuels could eventually supply 20 percent of global motor fuel demand in a manner that is environmentally responsible."[20]

When one thinks about this vision, it is breathtaking, for it does suggest a future in which hydrocarbons give way, increasingly, to carbohydrates and other biological sources of energy. However, in terms of getting there, many "ifs" are along the way—about technology, price, scale, and the environment—before Carbohydrate Man could really begin to overtake Hydrocarbon Man on the highways of the world.

34

INTERNAL FIRE

Thomas Edison was, by the end of the nineteenth century, not just the most famous American in the world. With so many inventions and innovations, he had shaped much of what was called the Age of Edison. He was also, of course, the patriarch of the American electric power industry. And so it was not surprising that when the executives of the Edison Illuminating Companies gathered for their annual convention in New York in August 1896, the guest of honor at the closing banquet was the great man himself.

The conversation at the head table got around to one of the big questions of the day, electric batteries and cars. Someone called attention to a person farther down the table, the chief engineer from the Detroit Edison Company, Henry Ford. He had just built what he called a "quadricycle," but it was powered by gasoline, not by a battery.

The 33-year-old Ford was shifted into the seat next to the hard-of-hearing Edison. In response to Edison's many questions, Ford sketched out a design on the back of a menu. Edison was very impressed that the vehicle carried its own fuel—what he called "hydrocarbon." The problem with electric cars, said Edison, is that they "must keep near a power station" and the battery was, in any event, too heavy. Edison told Ford to stick with gasoline and the internal combustion engine. To emphasize his point, Edison struck his fist down on the table. "You have the thing," he said to Ford. "Keep at it."

Ford later said, "That bang on the table was worth worlds to me." It was a blessing; for Ford revered Edison as "the greatest man in the world." And now "the man who knew most about electricity in the world had said that for the purpose my gas motor was better," said Ford. "And this at a time when all the electrical engineers took it as an established fact that there could be nothing new and worthwhile that did not run by electricity."

Ford had harbored his own doubts. "I wondered a little whether I might not be wasting my time," he added. But with Edison's commendation, "I went on at least twice as fast as I should have otherwise."[1]

Yet the race for personal mobility was still wide open. Indeed, two years later, in 1898, when the *New-York Sun* marveled that at a busy street corner in New York City "there may be seen cars propelled by five different methods of propulsion," the gasoline-powered car did not even make the bottom of the list.[2]

But within a decade or so, by about 1910, the race would be just about over. The automobile operating with an internal combustion engine would be the victor. And ever since, the automobile has defined personal mobility, which—along with heat, light, and cooling—is one of the fundamental characteristics of modern life.

FUEL FOR THE FUTURE?

The amount of energy embodied in oil-derived fuels is tremendous, and these fuels can be stored conveniently as a stable, easy-to-use liquid. If oil is king, its realm of unquestioned supremacy is road transportation. Yet the world's demand for mobility is only going to grow, and enormously so as the populations in emerging markets achieve income levels that put cars within their reach.

But how will that demand for mobility be fueled?

A decade ago, the answer seemed pretty clear: more of the same. Transportation would continue to be based on oil. No longer. A new race for the future of transportation has begun. Its outcome will determine what kind of automobiles people around the world will be driving two or three decades from now and whether oil keeps its preponderant position on the road (and in the air). Will vehicles primarily continue to be powered by the familiar internal combustion engine—the ICE—fueled by gasoline or diesel, but with increasing efficiency?

Will the existing and new biofuels be an increasingly important part of the mix, displacing petroleum but meaning relatively little change in cars themselves? Will the vehicles be natural gas–fueled? Or will they be hybrids—vehicles that meld the internal combustion engine with a second drive train, electric, to gain much greater efficiency? Or, more radically, will the real winner be the out-and-out electric vehicle, which fills up not at the gas pump but at the wall socket? Further out, there is the possibility of hydrogen-fed fuel cell–powered cars.

There is another possibility as well: that new kinds transportation systems will emerge that challenge current assumptions about the ways people travel. This may be the necessary response to the impending gridlock that could paralyze so many of the world's megacities.

What we do know is that nothing fast will happen to change the world's auto fleet. It is too large, and the turnover of the existing fleet is too slow—the average life of a car is 12 to 15 years. That is true in the developed world. In fast-growing emerging markets, however, where people who do not own cars are now acquiring them, the answer will be somewhat different—or perhaps very different—because they do not have a large existing stock of cars to replace.

The race has been reopened by a confluence of factors, beginning with heightened concern about energy security, conflict in the Middle East, the risks from a global supply system, and volatility of oil prices. A second reason is sustainability. When the motorized car first appeared more than a century ago, it provided an immediate solution to the growing challenge of sustainability of rapidly growing cities, an enormous environmental and pollution and health problem that threatened to choke these cities and threaten human health: This was the manure from the vast and ever-growing number of horses that pulled carts and wagons and carriages and trolleys through the expanding cities of the late nineteenth century. Motorization took the horses off the streets.

Today great progress has been made in cleaning up the exhaust coming out of auto tailpipes. But emissions are still a problem for many cities around the world. Moreover, as the engine burns gasoline or diesel fuel, it emits CO_2 out of the tailpipe. And thus concerns about climate change are driving efforts to find an engine that does not add to the carbon stock. Another reason for the new race is sheer scale—anxiety about the ability of the world to meet the additional demand for oil that economic growth in emerging markets will generate.

The ambition is great: to transform the auto fleet and the infrastructure that supports it and, at the same time, to deliver vehicles that meet the functionality that motorists want at a price that they—and society—are willing to pay. This is no small undertaking. The stakes are huge in this new race: the fuel of the future for the automobile, the shape of tomorrow's transportation, and global political and economic power. This time out, the total purse to the winners will be measured in trillions of dollars.

THE STEAM ENGINE

In 1712 Thomas Newcomen invented the first mechanical steam engine, used to pump water out of coal mines. Many decades later, the Scottish inventor James Watt dramatically improved the design and efficiency of the steam engine, bringing it, as one historian wrote, "within reach of all branches of the economy." The result was the "Age of Steam."

Around the same time, a Swiss engineer, Nicolas Joseph Cugnot, with funding from France's King Louis XV, developed a steam-powered vehicle that would transport artillery on the battlefield at speeds approaching five miles per hour, carrying four passengers. Cugnot's mechanical beast performed badly and was vexingly unbalanced for traversing the French countryside. The king finally gave up on Cugnot and cut off the funding.[3]

Over the nineteenth century, enormous advances were made in the steam engine, which powered not only the mills and factories of the Industrial Revolution but also the railways and ships. By the latter decades of the nineteenth century, the steam engine was a highly developed machine that tied together the world. By then, however, a competitor had appeared.

HERR OTTO

In 1864 a 31-year-old entrepreneur, Eugene Langen, made his way to a workshop on Gereonswall street in the city of Cologne, Germany, where he heard an "erratic thrashing." Inside the shop, Langen found Nikolaus Otto experimenting with one of his gas-engine designs. Langen had been told that Otto was doing something interesting, and he was curious to meet Otto, who was one of a number of German inventors and tinkerers trying to capture the energy of combustion more efficiently than was possible with a steam engine.

Nikolaus Otto's family was not very well off, and he struggled to make ends meet by selling tea and sugar and doing other odd jobs. Despite his lack of formal technical training, he was intuitive and afflicted with "an obsession with engines." He was also hungry for a breakthrough, for he was deeply in debt. Langen had little in common with Otto. He was an investor; by his early thirties he had already successfully started several different businesses. But Langen was taken by Otto's experiments and decided to put up some money.

Within three years, Otto had achieved a breakthrough, a dramatically more efficient engine design. It won a gold medal at the 1867 Paris Exposition, and soon this initial engine was in high demand. Langen and Otto eventually formed a new company, Gasmotoren-Fabrik Duetz AG, named for a Cologne suburb, and took on new hires, including two brilliant engineers, Gottlieb Daimler and Wilhelm Maybach. However, the new company's prospects were uncertain. Try as they did, they could not get their engines to break what seemed at the time an insurmountable barrier: three horsepower.

The engineers were very much at odds as to which way to go. Otto wanted to work on a new kind of engine, an internal combustion engine. Daimler was highly skeptical. Meanwhile, competing inventors and engineers were busily trying to find their own breakthroughs. A friend of Langen's, a professor named Franz Reulleaux, warned him that while they dithered among themselves, competitors were moving ahead. Reulleaux argued that they should pursue Otto's idea for an internal combustion engine. "Get with it," he declared. "Herr Otto must get off of his hind legs, and Herr Daimler must get off his front."

Otto's mechanism would draw air and fuel into a cylinder through a valve, compress it, combust that charge, and exhaust the spent charge in four stokes. Daimler, now the chief technologist of the tiny company, continued to object. He dismissed Otto's ideas as "a waste of time."

But Langen placed his bet on Otto. Daimler had missed the significance of the increased power and efficiency offered by Otto's design. Within six months they had prototyped an engine that not only exceeded the performance of any engine currently available, but could also shatter the three-horsepower barrier. The device was a commercial success.[4]

The development of the "Otto cycle" engine in 1876 marked the introduction of the modern internal combustion engine. It combined valves, a crankshaft, spark plugs, and a single cylinder in a way that allowed the fuel and gases to harness the energy of combustion with dramatically fewer energy losses, and thus with greater efficiency. On top of all of that, it was also more reliable.

By 1890 a German auto industry, founded on the internal combustion engine, had been born. Otto and Karl Benz, who used Otto's patent for his first three-wheeler, were among the pioneers of the German auto industry. And so was Gottlieb Daimler, who had split off from Otto and founded his own company. By the middle-1890s, Daimler was even distributing his cars in America through the piano maker William Steinway. Daimler's and Benz's firms were to be merged in the twentieth century into one company, Daimler-Benz. But Daimler and Benz apparently never met each other.

THE RACE

For at least a decade, Germany and France—the latter with such engineers as Armand Peugeot and Louis Renault—led the world in motor transportation.

The auto industry was much slower to develop in Britain, despite its preeminence in engineering. "Friends" of the railway industry pushed through Parliament the Red Flag Act, which aimed to protect the transportation franchise of the railways. Under the Red Flag Act "road locomotives"—that is, cars—could go no faster than two miles an hour in cities. (A walker, at three miles an hour, could beat that.) In rural areas, drivers could accelerate their cars up to all of four miles an hour. And to add extra safety, drivers had to be preceded by someone walking sixty yards in front who would wave a red flag during daylight hours and carry a lantern after dark. The Red Flag Act meant less incentive to use autos, as their speed and utility were severely constrained.

On the other side of the Atlantic, in the United States, cars were starting to appear on the street, but they were mainly steamers or electrics. In 1892 one newspaper reported that "a novelty in the way of a wagon propelled by electricity was seen on the streets of Chicago yesterday . . . The run was made in 22 minutes. The owners found this time respectable—given traffic and the difficulty of negotiating large crowds drawn to the vehicle."[5]

It was not until 1893 that the first successful gasoline-powered car was built in the United States, based on an article in *Scientific American* describing one of Daimler's vehicles. Thereafter, an increasing number of innovators were attracted to the internal combustion engine, many of them in the Great Lakes region, particularly around Detroit. Among the more obsessed was a farm boy from Dearborn, Michigan, who had a fascination with machinery and a natural intuition for how things worked—and could work. This was that youthful chief engineer of the Edison Illuminating Company of Detroit, Henry Ford.[6]

ELECTRIC OR GASOLINE?

In 1899, Edison's blessing still ringing in his ears, Ford left Edison Detroit to work full time on automobiles powered by internal combustion engines.

But the steamer and the electric car still held the lead. The first police car in America, which took to the road in Akron, Ohio, in 1899, was an electric vehicle. (The Akron police chief had decided it would be cheaper than paying for horse teams and their feed. Its first run was to arrest a citizen who was drunk and disorderly.) In 1900, 2,370 cars were reported to be on the streets of New York City, Boston, and Chicago. Most of them were either steam cars, such as the Stanley Steamer, or electrics. Gasoline-powered cars were far in the rear.[7]

Electric cars were favored by many, including "ladies" and, later, by doctors doing house calls. They were quiet, clean, and easy to control. There was no soot, and unlike internal combustion engines, they did not need to be cranked in order to start, sparing motorists the tiring, repetitive activity that could easily break a wrist.

Yet the internal combustion engine that Nikolaus Otto had first developed was being refined and improved, and it was beginning to overtake both electrics and steam autos in terms of power and reliability.

Electrics were vexed by three major problems: cost, range, and recharging. The 1902 Phaeton, for instance, had a range of just 18 miles and could go no faster than 14 miles per hour. Steamers, for their part, suffered from low efficiency. They also required long warm-up times and large quantities of water. Moreover, steamers had even less range before needing to be replenished with water than electric cars on a single charge. Internal combustion engines—ICEs—for their part, needed just fuel, could go longer distances, and, by comparison to electrics and steamers, they produced remarkable amounts of power. But they needed to be cranked.[8]

But it was still not clear which type of engine was going to prevail.

NATURE'S SECRET

By 1900 Thomas Edison had concluded, contrary to what he had told Henry Ford, that an electric vehicle would be preferable to the gasoline-powered cars. Edison complained that those noisy, smelly, sooty, unreliable horseless carriages, fueled by gasoline, could not be the vehicle of the future. He was convinced that he could solve the battery problem with a lightweight, reliable new design with sufficient storage to provide a superior alternative. "I don't think Nature would be so unkind as to withhold the secret of a good storage battery, if a real earnest hunt were made for it," Edison wrote to a friend. He had conquered lighting, electric generation, recording, and cinema. Why not transport?

In 1904, after much hard work, Edison released, to great fanfare, what he labeled the type E battery. It "revolutionized the world of power," reported the press. Ever the showman, Edison promised "a miniature dynamo in every home . . . an automobile for every family." But the E battery did not perform as promised and tended to leak. Discouraged but indomitable, Edison returned to the laboratory and redoubled efforts.[9]

During this time, there were certainly critics of motorized transport, as there often is with disruptive technologies, and they were not just from the "horse interests." Some thought the auto was a passing fad, a "useless nuisance" as a character in a popular novel put it. One of the sharpest critics was the president of Princeton University, Woodrow Wilson. In 1906, seven years before he moved into the White House as president of the United States, Wilson declared that cars were "a picture of the arrogance of wealth" and that "nothing spread socialistic feeling in this country more than use of the automobile."[10]

But such opposition could not hold back the tide of enthusiasm. America had caught what a buyer called "the Horseless Carriage fever." One writer declared, "The automobile is the idol of the modern age. . . . The man who owns a motorcar gets for himself, beside the joys of touring, the adulation of the walking crowd" and, better yet, "is a god to the women." But it was still not yet clear in what kind of car the new deity would travel.[11]

Through it all, one person had a clear view of what transportation should look like. "The greatest need today," Henry Ford wrote in 1906, "is a light, low-priced car with an up-to-date engine of ample horsepower, and built of the very best material." That was the car he was determined to build.

In 1908 Ford debuted his first Model Ts. They were light, sturdy, powerful, and priced at only $825. (That was the base price; headlights, windshield, and a roof were all extra.) A few years later came the revolutionary change in manufacturing. Ford introduced the assembly line to mass-produce the car. (The concept was adapted from what had been observed as the "disassembly" line for cattle in a Chicago slaughterhouse.) Every ninety-three minutes a new Model T bumped off the line. The price of a Model T went down by as much as two thirds, at one point as low as just $260.[12]

The unflagging Edison was not about to quit on the electric car. He reappeared with the type A battery by 1910. This battery promised 60 miles on a single charge and a seven-hour charging time. It was adopted in small vans—like the Detroit Electric and the Baker Runabout—that department stores used for deliveries. Edison was convinced that batteries would be a major component in the future of transportation. He triumphantly wrote to Samuel Insull in 1910, promising the electricity tycoon a major new market for electricity. Or, as Edison put it, "to add many electric Pigs to your big Electric Sow."[13]

But Edison was too late. Ford's Model Ts were capturing a rapidly growing share of the rapidly growing market and were soon a runaway success. Moreover, with the invention of the electric ignition, motorists no longer had to crank their vehicles, which canceled out one of the decided advantages of the electric car and sealed the victory for the internal combustion engine. Ford had made good on his promise to build a car not just for the wealthy but for "the great multitude" and available to any "man making a good salary." He had transformed the automobile from a luxury good into a mass-market product.

By 1920 half the cars in the world were Model Ts. By the time it was discontinued, over 15 million Model Ts had been sold, a record that held for 45 years. By then, the internal combustion engine had long since become the heart and soul of the modern automobile.

THE NEW FUEL

But how were these cars to be fueled? The answer was gasoline. The internal combustion engine also saved the oil industry. For its first 40 years, the oil industry had been a lighting business. Its main product was kerosene, poured into lamps and used around the world for illumination. John D. Rockefeller became the richest man in the world as an illumination merchant. But around the beginning of the twentieth century, the rapid advent of electricity was beginning to take away most of the lighting market.

But just in time, the automobile drove onto the scene.

Up until then, gasoline was mostly a waste product, an explosive and flammable fraction from refining, which was not of very much use to anyone. But in the dawning automobile age, it turned out that gasoline was a very effective energy packet when poured into an internal combustion engine. By 1911 gasoline had overtaken kerosene as the number one oil product. Major new oil discoveries in the American Southwest, beginning in January 1901 with the blowout at Spindletop, near Beaumont, Texas, assured that there would be adequate supplies of oil.

But there was still another big problem—distribution—getting the gasoline to motorists. Most gasoline was sold in cans by grocery or general stores, which was pretty inconvenient. In 1907 the *National Petroleum News* ran a small, inconsequential story that reported, "A new way of reaching the auto gasoline trade direct is being tried with reported success in St. Louis by the Auto Gasoline Co." The headline was "Station for Autoists." The "dump," as one person called it, was probably the first gas station in the United States. The network of gas stations that developed, hundreds of thousands by the end of the 1920s, was as crucial as the roads. Oil had become the fuel of that mobility.[14]

THE HALCYON DAYS

In the 1950s and 1960s, the decades after the Second World War, America was truly the land of the automobile. The development of the suburbs, the building out of new highway and road systems, and the proliferation of the automobile—these went hand in hand. Cars were a major obsession of American life. New cars were sold on the basis of looks, horsepower, performance, and, one way or the other, sex appeal. Fuel efficiency was declining, but that didn't matter, because gasoline was 25 cents a gallon and gas stations seemed to have sprung up on almost every commercial corner.

And then, with the oil crisis of 1973, everything changed. A furious political battle erupted in Washington over proposed legislation to regulate automobile fuel efficiency. This was something that had never been regulated before. At the forefront of the opposition were the major auto companies—General Motors, Chrysler, and Ford—often referred to simply as "The Big Three."

"We do not want any handouts, we do not want any taxes, and we do not want any regulations," declared the president of General Motors in a congressional hearing in 1975. "We do not like that sort of thing." Industry executives believed that the market, and the market alone, should be the regulator of how their cars were built; that is, consumers should decide what they wanted. Moreover, gearing up quickly to produce smaller cars would be costly, and the automakers worried what would happen if consumers changed their minds and switched back to bigger cars again, leaving them with idle production lines and vast parking lots filled with unsold small cars.

In the fevered energy politics of the 1970s, Detroit lost this battle. New regulations, the Corporate Average Fuel Efficiency—known as "CAFE"—Standards were enacted in 1975, requiring car companies to double fuel efficiency of their auto fleet from the then current 13.5 miles per gallon to 27.5 by 1985.

A few years later, Henry Ford's grandson, Henry Ford II, acknowledged that "the law requiring greater fuel efficiency in motor vehicle usage has moved us faster toward conservation goals than competitive, free-market forces would have done." Still he pleaded for Washington to "give up" on pushing for tighter post-1985 fuel-efficiency standards.[15]

GETTING MOBBED

Regulation is often, as in this case, a substitute for the market. From an economist's point of view, a more market-based approach to moderating demand—to put it in plain English, a higher tax on gasoline—is more efficient and far better than prescriptive regulations. That kind of tax would send a clear signal, keeping fuel efficiency firmly fixed in the minds of auto buyers, as it does in Europe, where taxes and duties on gasoline today can be more than $4 a gallon, compared with an average of about 40 cents in the United States (of which 18.4 cents is federal tax). The tax burden can fall more heavily on lower-income people. But a tax would make auto manufacturers confident that they could reengineer their output toward higher efficiency and not be stuck with those parking lots full of unwanted and unsold highly efficient vehicles when gasoline prices fell again. A tax is also simpler and less likely to lead to distortions. It provides incentive for continuing innovation. By contrast, a target under regulation also becomes a ceiling. Once reached, there is no strong incentive to push further.

That, at least, is how economists generally view things. However, economists do not run for office all that often; and what for the economist is the rational solution can be for a politician a recipe for electoral disaster.

Philip Sharp, who served in Congress for 20 years and chaired the House Energy Subcommittee (and is now head of Resources for the Future), will never forget what happened one Saturday morning after he voted for a five-cent increase in the federal gasoline tax. "I went into a post office when I was back in my district," he recalled, "and I was mobbed by furious constituents."[16]

That is not exactly the kind of popular reaction that a politician wants to court when running for reelection (although Sharp himself was reelected several more times). So regulation, despite its relative drawbacks, does have a great advantage: it does not look like a tax.

In other words, regulation can be a second-best solution, at least from an economist's perspective, but a more doable solution from a political prospective. And that was certainly the case with the 1975 fuel-efficiency legislation. As the automobile fleet rolled over, the savings in gasoline consumption added up, and massively so. It was as though a giant "oil field under Detroit" had been discovered. By the mid-1980s, the fuel-efficiency standards had saved about two million barrels of oil per day compared with what would have been consumed had the averages stayed at 1973 levels. That was as much as was being produced at its peak on Alaska's North Slope oil field, the other great breakthrough for United States energy policy during those years.[17] Those standards would also have a major impact on the world's automobile industry.

THE JAPANESE ARRIVE

An odd and unfamiliar car might have been seen fleetingly on the streets of Los Angeles and San Francisco in the late 1950s. It was Toyota's Toyopet S30 Crown, the first Japanese car to be brought officially to the United States. In Tokyo, Toyopets were used as taxis. But in the United States the Toyopet did not get off to a good start; the first two could not even get over the hills around Los Angeles. It is said that the first car delivered in San Francisco died on the first hill it encountered on the way to inspection. An auto dealer in that city drove it 180 times in reverse around the public library in an effort to promote it, but to no avail. The Toyopet, priced at $1,999, was anything but a hit. Over a four-year period, a total of 1,913 were sold. Other Japanese automakers also started exporting to the United States, but the numbers sold remained exceedingly modest, and the cars themselves were regarded as cheap, not very reliable, oddballs, and starter cars (lacking the vim and panache of what was then the hot import, the Volkswagen Beetle).

But the explosion in oil prices in the mid-1970s, and corresponding new focus on fuel efficiency, created a port of entry for auto imports, especially from Japan. As a result, those efficient little cars suddenly gained attention and popularity. Over time the Japanese cars began to move upmarket, establishing a growing reputation for quality and reliability.[18]

By the mid-1980s, when oil and gasoline prices collapsed, the share of household budget going for auto fuel shrunk back to a small amount. Once again, as in the old days, new-car buyers fixed instead on price, performance, and reliability—and, of course, on how the car looked. Fuel efficiency plummeted down the list of concerns, if it still made the list at all. But U.S. manufacturers still had to meet their efficiency targets. At the same time, foreign automakers, particularly the Japanese, were now broadening their appeal and demonstrating their ability to meet the demands of a wider public. They were entrenching themselves in the U.S. market and were pursuing a strategy that made them increasingly less "foreign." Japanese auto manufacturers began to put down roots—opening plants, research-and-development centers, design facilities, and joint ventures around the United States. This helped offset vehement domestic opposition that came both from the Big Three and from unionized autoworkers.

THE NEW PASSION

Because it was required to do so under U.S. automotive regulations, Detroit produced the smaller, high-efficiency cars as sort of lost-leaders to ensure compliance with the CAFE fuel-efficiency standards. But its focus was increasingly on a category of larger vehicles called "light trucks," and in particular, a type of vehicle that had never really even existed before.

This shift began in the 1980s when Chrysler introduced a new kind of light truck code-named during development as the "T-115." But soon it would be better known as the minivan. By then, the fuel-efficiency standards had effectively killed the station wagon as a major vehicle class. The station wagon had been the emblematic conveyance of pre-1973 suburban life. But the fleet averages for fuel efficiency left little room for the traditional station wagon, which was heavier than the typical car and used more gasoline. It had to be squeezed out if the automakers were to make their fleet averages for cars.

However, minivans had the great merit of counting as something altogether different—light trucks. This would have major implications for fuel consumption. When the original 1975 fuel-efficiency regulations were written, the target standards were lower for light trucks—20.7 miles per gallon—compared with the 27.5 mpg for cars. In fact, not much thought had been given to such vehicles because they were such a small share of the market: cars comprised over 80 percent of total new vehicles sold, and pickup trucks and vans were mostly driven by farmers and tradesmen. The idea of the minivan and SUV was not even a glimmer in Detroit's mind.

But now with the minivan it was possible to have a vehicle that provided the functionality desired by many drivers—indeed, that exceeded the functionality of the station wagon—without pushing automakers into the penalty box on fuel efficiency. Vans, once the province of delivery people and plumbers and electricians, had become the favorite family vehicle. These new minivans had enough room for parents, children, friends, sporting gear, luggage, and pets, and came equipped with such family-friendly and parent-useful features as a sliding door on the right-hand side and a coffee holder. Chrysler, in the words of a competitor, had hit a "home run" with the minivan.

Chrysler had also opened the door for another new vehicle entrant when it purchased the Jeep from now-defunct American Motors. What had originally been a rugged wartime workhorse now became the "sports utility vehicle"—better known as the SUV. In 1990 Ford brought out its four-door Explorer, and demand for SUVs really took off. In addition to minivans and SUVs, people who had no need at all for pickup trucks started buying pickup trucks. All these vehicles—minivans, SUVs, and pickups—were classified in the same "light truck" category. And Americans could not get enough of them. By the mid-1990s people were talking optimistically of a new "Golden Age of America Autos." And Chrysler, a few years earlier on the brink of failure, was now crowned the "world's most successful automaker."[19]

The Ford Explorer quickly became the most popular SUV. Its main competitor, General Motors, was caught off guard; it had assumed in the early 1990s that higher oil and gasoline prices were ahead, and thus it had been anticipating that consumers would want more-efficient cars and higher fuel economy. But in the face of the massive demand for Ford's Explorer and other SUVs, it had to pivot and play catch-up. It responded with the Chevy Blazer, but it was not moving fast enough.

"Sometimes a certain kind of vehicle gets hot for no logical reason," said Rick Wagoner, the former CEO of General Motors. And the SUVs and minivans got very hot. "Demand outstripped supply," recalled Wagoner. "We would wake up every morning and go into the market and find that we didn't have enough product. We just didn't have enough capacity for the larger engines required for these bigger vehicles. At every board meeting, we got the same question. 'Why don't you have more truck capacity?' "

The light trucks even came to define a new demographic: the suburban "soccer mom." By the time of the 1996 presidential election, she had become a coveted and critical bloc, courted by both parties. But it was not just moms. It was also dads and young adults. By the late 1990s, America's traditional love affair with the automobile had turned into a torrid passion for SUVs.[20]

This rapid move from cars to trucks had major implications for U.S. fuel use, for a new minivan or SUV was 25 percent less fuel efficient than a new car, and the number of light trucks on the roads was rapidly increasing.

But there was also "price" behind the "passion." A decade of extremely cheap gasoline facilitated the emergence of the SUV and trucks. The price of gasoline was so low that it was virtually irrelevant to the consumers; in fact, in 1998 gasoline made up a smaller proportion of U.S. household spending than it had in the 1950s and 1960s. In real terms, gasoline was cheaper than it had been at any time since records started being kept.[21]

The effect of price was demonstrated in a study that compared the United States and Europe. In Europe, where fuel prices were much higher owing to taxes, 50 percent of the new technology in automobiles was directed at fuel efficiency. But in America, once the efficiency targets were reached, only 20 percent of the new technology in cars went toward fuel efficiency. The other 80 percent of new technology went into such things as performance, safety, size, accessories, utility, and what has been described as "luxury." For instance, in the twenty years between 1987 and 2007, horsepower increased 85 percent.[22]

By 2000, sales of less fuel-efficient light trucks in the United States had overtaken that of traditional cars. At the same time, people drove many more miles, whatever the vehicle. The average car put on about 30 percent more miles in 2003 compared with 1985: 12,300 miles per year compared with 9,400 miles. Also, the total number of vehicles on the road increased as the U.S. economy and population both expanded. For all these reasons, gasoline consumption had increased by almost 50 percent between 1985 and 2003.

Overall, a kind of division of labor had settled over the auto market. Detroit concentrated its big guns on the bigger vehicles—SUVs and vans—while the Japanese, Koreans, and other manufacturers captured a growing share of the car market, increasingly with cars manufactured in the United States, as well as with imports. The SUVs were more profitable, which helped the American automakers cope with a competitive disadvantage compared with the foreign companies. This was the "legacy costs"—employee health and retirement costs, negotiated in the fat years with the United Auto Workers, which foreign companies did not have to bear. These costs have been estimated at $1,500 to $2,000 per vehicle—more than the cost of the steel that goes into the vehicle. In such circumstances, there was little incentive for American companies to risk a billion dollars and five years of product development to produce a new, more fuel-efficient model that relatively few would want.[23]

The thinking was different in Japan.

REMAKING OF AUTOMOBILE

In the late 1980s, Toyota's chairman, Eiji Toyoda, who had driven the company's phenomenal growth over many decades, began to worry that complacency and self-satisfaction were enveloping Japan during its great economic bubble and that these sentiments might infect Toyota. Over the next couple of years, he brooded about the future of the automobile itself: How would concerns about the environment and energy security affect the future of the industry? Toyoda challenged the company to come up with a car for the twenty-first century that would be more efficient than its best-selling Corolla and that would be environmentally conscious. The cultural values of *mottainai*—"too precious to waste"—underlay this initiative. In Japan, with virtually no oil, the fragility of energy supplies was an ever-present concern in a way that was not the case for American automakers. The 1991 Gulf War dramatized the risks from dependence on oil.

All these elements went into the mandate for a new car. The research team was called G21—for "global twenty-first century."

Still the mandate was pretty vague. From a cost and quality perspective, the G21 team came to a crucial conclusion: electric cars and fuel-cell cars were just too far away. By 1994 the team homed in on the idea of yoking together two parallel drive trains—one gasoline-fired; the other, battery-based. They called it a "hybrid." The attraction of the hybrid design was that it would employ existing infrastructure and take advantage of the power density of liquid fossil fuels. They went through more than a hundred different configurations before settling on the fundamental design. Some in the company figured that the likelihood of success was only 5 percent. And some even questioned whether what they were coming up with were "really cars" at all or whether what they were calling a hybrid would be more appropriately described as a mutant.[24]

In stop-and-go city driving, the car, which would become known as the Prius, would employ its electrical motor. But when an extra boost was needed, a small, hyperefficient internal combustion engine would kick in. At high speeds, the internal combustion engine would take over altogether. The battery would be partly recharged by the gasoline engine. But it would also be recharged by capturing the kinetic energy—dissipated as heat when cars brake—and turning that into electricity. (Indeed, about two thirds of the energy produced by the internal combustion engine is dissipated either as heat or through the exhaust pipe.) They called this regenerative braking. In this way, what traditionally was a waste product—heat—was transformed into something much more useful—electricity. The heat was "too precious to waste."

It was very challenging to implement the concept, for the engineers had to take two different engine systems and make them work seamlessly. Moreover, the G21 team was under intense pressure to get the car ready by 1997, to coincide with the Kyoto climate-change conference. Working at hyperspeed in terms of designing wholly new cars, they made the deadline, just barely.

But the Prius still needed to be accepted in the marketplace. Honda actually beat Toyota into the U.S. market with its own hybrid—the Insight—released in 1999. Honda was following a different strategy—"hybridizing" its well-known Civic model rather than creating a wholly new car. The Prius, by contrast, was an entirely new model. It went on sale in the United States in 2000.

For the first couple of years, neither Toyota nor Honda made much headway in the U.S. marketplace with their hybrids. It was only around 2003, with concerns rising about climate change and gasoline prices, that a second-generation Prius, larger and more powerful, caught the public's imagination and started to become the poster car for the hybrid-generation.

Sales of the Prius and other hybrids began to accelerate. They still cost several thousand dollars more than comparable models, and there was some debate as to how many thousands of miles motorists would have to drive to make up for the difference. *Consumer Reports* may have questioned whether a hybrid was actually superior to a high-mileage car from a dollar-savings point of view, taking into account vehicle as well as fuel costs, but that was not the point. Although there were tax incentives to encourage hybrid purchases, the hybrid was about more than just incentives and economics. Driving a Prius was also a statement—both to others and oneself—about the owner's concern about the environment, climate change, and oil dependence. As time went on, hybrids gained cachet: in a statement about environmental consciousness, movie stars arrived at the Academy Awards in chauffeur-driven Priuses.[25]

WHAT ABOUT PLAN B?

Rising prices at the gasoline pump after the turn of the century made car buyers once again aware of the fuel bill for a car, and painfully so for an SUV. For Detroit this was the beginning of the nightmare. In 2004, for the first time since they began to take hold, the market share for SUVs and other light trucks began to slide. Yet the American automakers did not really have a real Plan B. "Light trucks" is how the companies made money, and "light trucks" seemed to be what buyers truly wanted. But not for much longer. As prices at the pump climbed, SUV sales slipped, putting pressure on the American companies. They tried to buy time—and hoped for a turnaround—by cutting prices, offering rebates, and providing 0 percent financing.[26]

The politics were changing, too. Increasing gasoline prices were fueling the public's rising ire. Moreover, in some parts of the public, concerns about oil imports and global warming were also gaining traction. All these were coming together to create a coalition in favor of doing something that had not been possible for three decades: raising fuel-efficiency standards.

Detroit, with its shrinking workforce, shuttered plants, and reduced footprint, no longer had its old political clout. Now senators from states where Toyotas or Nissans or Hondas were produced did not worry much about the fate of General Motors or Ford or Chrysler. When Toyota announced that it was investing $1.3 billion in an assembly plant in his state, creating thousands of jobs, Mississippi Senator Trent Lott declared, "We are warriors on your behalf."

Just as important, there was a growing technical consensus that much more could be done to improve efficiency, as much as 40 to 50 percent by 2030, with existing internal combustion technologies. The National Research Council, representing the National Academy of Sciences and the National Academy of Engineering, made that argument, although it diplomatically added a politically somewhat-unpalatable observation: "There is a marked inconsistency between pressing automotive manufacturers for improved fuel economy from new vehicles on the one hand and insisting on low real gasoline prices on the other."[27]

NEW STANDARDS

As oil prices headed toward $100 a barrel in the second half of 2007 and as conflict continued in the Middle East, political opposition to higher fuel-efficiency standards melted away. The Energy Security and Independence Act of 2007, for the first time in thirty-two years, raised the fuel-efficiency standards: to thirty-five miles per gallon by 2020. The new target applied to both cars and SUVs and other light trucks. It could mean a savings of as much as two million barrels per day, compared with the previous standard. The legislation also initiated, for the first time, the process for regulating the fuel efficiency of large commercial trucks. This was the same legislation that also mandated the use of 2.3 million barrels a day of biofuels by 2022.

In signing the bill, President George W. Bush called it "a major step" toward "reducing our dependence on oil, fighting global climate change, expanding the production of renewable fuels," and making the country "stronger, cleaner and more secure."[28]

There was an unexpected bump at the very end of the legislative road. After the congressional vote for the new standards, the legislation still needed to be signed into law by the president. For that to happen, the bill had to be physically delivered to the White House, which meant that someone had to actually drive it up Pennsylvania Avenue. And that is what a congressional clerk did on the afternoon of December 19, 2007—in what is normally a very standard, unremarkable activity. Except that this piece of legislation—so bitterly contested by the U.S. automakers—was delivered in a fuel-efficient hybrid Prius, manufactured by the Japanese company Toyota. Not only was Toyota the great rival of General Motors, it was also at that moment in the process of overtaking GM as the number one auto manufacturer in the world. And not everybody believed that it was just an accident. An outraged congressman from Michigan denounced the delivery by Prius as a calculated "slap in the face of every American autoworker."

This embarrassing incident, though indeed accidental, seemed to symbolize how the world was changing. Sales of the Prius had taken off to such an extent that the head of Toyota in the United States called it "the hottest car we've ever had." The shift in consumer demand—and from one automotive era to another—was made starkly apparent in the marketplace. In 2007 Americans bought more Priuses than Ford Explorers, which had previously been the top-selling SUV and, indeed, the vehicle that had been emblematic of the American SUV for a decade and of the passionate embrace of the light truck. But now the small, fuel-efficient hybrid, which some had dismissed as a mutant, had unexpectedly toppled the mighty SUV.[29]

35

THE GREAT ELECTRIC CAR EXPERIMENT

Arie Haagen-Smit was an avid gardener with an abiding fascination with plants. In his professional work at the California Institute of Technology in Pasadena, next to Los Angeles, Haagen-Smit focused on the physiology of plants, particularly the chemistry of their odors and flavors. The Dutch-born professor achieved worldwide recognition for his work on plant hormones and the flavor components of wine, onions, and garlic. He also identified the active agent in marijuana.[1]

In 1948 Haagen-Smit was investigating something that deeply intrigued him: the chemical basis of the flavor of pineapples. One afternoon he stepped out of his lab for a break and a breath of fresh air. But there wasn't any fresh air. Instead he found himself immersed in what he later called "that stinking cloud that rolled across the landscape every afternoon." His own lungs were under attack. The assailant was the smog that often settled over Southern California and had become a pervasive part of life in Los Angeles.

At the time a fierce argument was raging over the source of the smog. Was it caused by industrial pollution, or by the million and a half backyard incinerators that residents used to dispose of their trash? Or could it be something else, the rapidly swelling population of automobiles? Right there, on the spot, Haagen-Smit decided that, using his skills at microchemistry, "it would not be difficult to find out what smog really was." He put aside his beloved pineapples and turned to creating smog in a test tube.

Haagen-Smit was right: it was not difficult. "We hit the jackpot with the first nickel," he later said.[2]

Haagen-Smit established that the real culprit was what came out of the automobile tailpipes—emissions from incompletely burned gasoline—along with gases released from storage tanks and auto gas tanks. For this discovery, along with his subsequent focus on air pollution, Haagen-Smit became known as "the Father of Smog." He was not thrilled with the title; if he was the father, he would ask, who was the mother?

Haagen-Smit may have identified the cause of smog, but solving it was a confused, complex, and often contentious process that went on for many years. When Haagen-Smit first reported his findings, critics dismissed him as a "scientific Don Quixote." Some were stunned by Haagen-Smit's discovery that the automobile that made possible the Southern California way of life was also the scourge of that lifestyle. One citizen wrote to the *Los Angeles Times* in shock: "We have created one of the finest networks of freeways in the country, and suddenly wake up to discover that we have also created a monster."[3]

Haagen-Smit's discovery in 1948 would eventually lead to what some believe could be the most important development in transportation since Henry Ford's Model T—the massive effort in the twenty-first century to bring back something that had disappeared from the roads at the beginning of the twentieth century: An automobile with no tailpipe at all. The electric car.

THE RACE RESUMES

Oil had held its seemingly impregnable position as king of the realm of transportation for almost a century. By the beginning of the twenty-first century, however, people were beginning to question how long oil would—or should—hold on to its crown. Yet as late as 2007 in the debate over the future of automotive transportation, the electric car was only a peripheral topic. Biofuels were the focus.

Within a few years, however, the electric car would move onto center stage. It could, said its proponents, break the grip of oil on transportation, allowing motorists to unplug from turbulence in the oil-exporting world and high prices at the pump. It could help reduce pollution and offset the carbon emissions that precipitate climate change. And it could provide a powerful answer to the great puzzle of how the world can accommodate the move from one billion cars to two billion. The electric car is powered by electricity that can be generated from any number of different sources, none of which need be oil. Perhaps more than any other technology, the electric car represents a stark alternative road to the future for the global energy system.

The electric vision rapidly became so compelling that expectations for electric cars far exceed the actual impact such cars might have on the world's auto fleet in terms of numbers, at least in the next decade or two. Yet their presence in the fleet, even if small, will change attitudes about both oil and autos far ahead of the numerical impact. In decades further out, the effect could be much larger. There are, however, two big questions: Can they deliver the performance that is promised at a cost that is acceptable? And will consumers choose to make them a mainstream purchase as opposed to a niche product?

In the meantime, very big bets are now being placed on the renewed race—between the battery and the internal combustion engine, between electricity and oil—that was supposedly decided a century ago. The outcome will have enormous significance in terms of both economics and geopolitics.

The conviction is also growing that electric vehicles could constitute a great "new industry," the epitome of cleantech, and the means to leapfrog to leadership in the global auto industry. This is a big opportunity for companies, entrepreneurs, and investors. But it is seen as much more than an opportunity in the marketplace. A French government minister has declared that "the battle of the electric car" has begun. "Electric vehicles are the future and the driver of the Industrial Revolution," said one of Europe's economic leaders. By 2010 the Obama administration had provided $5 billion in grants and loan guarantees to battery makers, entrepreneurs, major auto companies, and equipment suppliers to jump-start the electric car and build out the infrastructure systems that would support it. "Here in the United States," Obama announced, "we've created an entire new industry."[4]

This, indeed, is a game of nations. For countries like China and Korea, it is the opportunity to take a dominant position in a critical growth sector. Conversely, success in electric transportation may be required if the traditional leading countries in automobiles—the United States, Japan, and Germany—are to maintain their positions. If batteries are to be the "new oil," then the winners in battery know-how and production can capture a decisive new role in the world economy—and the rewards that will go with that.

"THE VALLEY OF SMOKES"

Long before the first Spanish settlers came to Southern California, the local Indians had called the region the Valley of Smokes, owing to the haze that hung over it, the result of natural emissions combined with smoke from fires. The geography of Southern California is shaped like a bowl, hemmed in with an ocean on one side and mountains surrounding the rest of it. This creates a particular climatic condition called a temperature inversion, in which cooler air off the ocean gets trapped below warmer air and stagnates, breeding pollution. The pollutants rise up into the warmer air, where sunlight acts upon them in a photochemical process, transforming them into the smog that then settles over the basin.

The first modern smog attacks had hit Los Angeles during World War II, as industrial production ramped up to meet the needs of mobilization. In response, in 1945 Los Angeles established a Bureau of Smoke Control. But as smog attacks continued after World War II and their severity and range increased, it was evident that the smoke was not being controlled. In fact, it got worse.

CITY UNDER SIEGE

In the first days of October 1954, the attack began, with no warning. It went on relentlessly for the next several weeks. The conditions for the assault were perfect: the days were hot, and the air just hung there, stagnant, not a breath of wind at all; a dense blue-gray haze that settled over and suffocated the Los Angeles Basin. It stung the lungs, making every breath a source of pain. It burned the throat; it irritated the eyes, causing them to itch and hurt and water and sometimes swell up; it caused lasting respiratory ailments.

Visibility was reduced to such an extent that drivers on the new freeways had to flick on their headlights in midafternoon, traffic slowed to a crawl, and accidents became endemic. Los Angeles International Airport was closed and planes diverted. At schools, outdoor physical education and recess were canceled, and students were kept inside.

The city was under siege. Panic and paralysis gripped the area. Police phone lines were swamped by callers, but there was nothing the police could do. "Angered Citizens Voice War on Smog Demand" was the front-page headline in the *Los Angeles Times*. The mayor of Los Angeles, hauled in front of a grand jury, said there was nothing he could do save issue a proclamation "to halt automobile traffic and to direct people to stay home." Housewives, marching in Pasadena to protest smog, donned gas masks. So did businessmen gathering for their regular Optimists Club meeting, although the gas masks did make it hard to eat lunch. Behind them, a big placard grimly declared "Why Wait Till 1955—We Might Not Even Be Alive." Something had to be done.

But then, at the end of October, the smog disappeared as quickly as it had arrived. "City Revels in Nearly Perfect Smog-Free Day," reported the *Times*. A few days later, it declared outright victory: "clear, bright skies" were back. The attack was over—but only until the next smog attack.[5]

THE AIR RESOURCES BOARD

The smog attack of 1954—"the worst attack ever"—was the turning point. If smog was going to be banished, government regulation would have to launch a protracted counterattack on automobile emissions. The war against smog was a long one. Over the next decades, Los Angeles was still registering more than a hundred days a year of smog alerts. One smog attack was so severe that Governor Ronald Reagan went on television to urge the public to "limit all but absolutely necessary auto travel." The smog problem was made even more difficult by the continued flow of new residents; between 1950 and 1980, California's population literally doubled, and the area was said to have "the greatest concentration of motor vehicles in the world."[6]

In 1967, Governor Reagan signed legislation setting up a new agency, the California Air Resources Board. CARB, as the agency became known, was the true successor to the Bureau of Smoke Control. Reagan appointed as its first chairman none other than the "Father of Smog," Professor Arie Haagen-Smit. No longer seen as a "scientific Don Quixote," Haagen-Smit had achieved what was described as a "worldwide reputation as the prime authority on air pollution." Now, as chairman of CARB, he could do something about the pollution. He would become, as one auto executive put it, "judge and jury" for the auto industry, a role that the agency has played ever since.[7]

That same year, California's severe pollution problems, along with its rapidly growing political heft, persuaded the U.S. Congress to grant California unusual authority. The state was given the right to regulate emissions so long as its standards were higher than the federal government's.

The powers of CARB also expanded beyond the state. For Congress granted other states the unusual option of choosing whether to adhere to either federal emission standards or those set by CARB for the state of California. This made Sacramento, along with Washington, a national regulator of air quality.

Eventually its position would also turn the California Air Resource Board into the de facto national authority. This role stems from the fact that, by itself, California represents about 12 percent of the nation's car market. Other parts of the country, particularly the Northeast and Florida, take their cues from CARB. The overall result is that CARB's ability to regulate auto emissions covers a third of the nation's auto sales. And if a third of the fleet is under orders, the other two thirds will follow, as it is very hard for automakers to make two different sets of the same model. Thus, if CARB issues an order with major impact on automobile design, it is likely to be a quasi-national regulation. And, given the scale of the U.S. market, the impact would be felt on the rest of the world. As the head of the agency said, with some modesty in 2011, "CARB punches above its weight."

CARB, along with another agency, the South Coast Air Quality District, sought to reduce emissions with what were called technology-forcing regulation, compelling industry to come up with solutions by certain deadlines. Over time the technological solutions were found. The most important was the catalytic converter, which assured a thorough burn of the gasoline and thus much reduced smog-inducing emissions. By the 1990s the number of annual smog-alert days had dwindled to fewer than ten. And by the end of the 1990s, the smog-causing emissions coming out of the tailpipe of a new car were only 1 percent of what they had been in the 1970s; 99 percent had been eliminated.[8]

Technology-forcing regulation had worked on smog. CARB also wanted to exercise its mandate in an effort to eliminate all tailpipe emissions. It did so by ordering the introduction of the ZEV, or zero-emissions vehicle. The aim was nothing less than to find a replacement for the internal combustion engine or set in motion a transition to alternative fuels. In 1990 CARB issued its most ambitious technology-forcing regulation to date. It was the regulation that would reopen the door to the electric car. It ordered that by 1998 2 percent of all new cars sold in California had to be ZEVs, zero-emission vehicles, and 10 percent by 2003. That meant no emissions at all out of the tailpipe, which was another way of saying no tailpipe and no internal combustion engine.

Major car companies set out to deliver exactly that. Considerable investment went into the effort. Yet it was all but an abject failure. "Who Killed the Electric Car?" is the question a documentary film asks about General Motors' EV1—Electric Vehicle 1—which was designed to meet CARB's stringent regulations and on which GM spent a billion dollars. While the film places primary guilt on the auto industry, the answer is something else. As a CARB member put it, "The one real culprit" was "the battery." Batteries sufficient to provide the range and driving time that people wanted simply did not exist at the time.

Another killer was lack of public acceptance. Several of the car makers leased their EV models to drivers. In addition to leasing, Toyota actually tried to sell an all-electric version of the RAV4, its small SUV. This was in the same period in which it was introducing the Prius. The uptake on the Prius by consumers was many, many times greater than that for the RAV4.

"We kept hearing about pent-up demand for electric vehicles," recalled one Toyota executive. "Well, it turned out that the initial pent-up demand was about 50 vehicles."[9]

Thereafter, despite "gobs and gobs of advertising" and considerable government subsidies, the RAV4 sold at the less than brisk rate of about five vehicles a week. That worked out to a little over 250 vehicles a year, whereas a model needs at least 100,000 sales a year to be anything more than a "niche." Sufficient numbers of people simply were not interested in buying electric cars, and CARB eventually had to back away, however reluctantly, from this particular order. But only for a time.

THE RETURN OF THE EV

With the opening of the new century, several factors started to converge to give new life to the electric vehicle.

Environmental pollution from auto exhausts has created anguish and been a major topic of public policy in the United States. In the decades since, other urban areas, from Mexico City to Beijing, have come to suffer under similar affliction and have also sought to find relief from air pollution. Moreover, now there was something new: concern about climate change. Although transportation on a global basis is responsible for about 17 percent of CO_2 emissions, the absolute volume of emissions is large and could get much larger. Rising oil prices also renewed interest. The electric car held out the prospect of insulating consumers from high prices, and blunting the impact of oil price shocks.

One other development built support. The introduction of hybrids had a major impact on the psychology of motorists. Hybrids served as a kind of mental bridge to electric cars by creating public acceptance of battery-driven vehicles and what they could mean: a much larger role for electricity in transportation.

This convergence propelled the electric car out of the automotive museum and back onto the street. Today, in contrast to a century ago, there are two primary types of electrically powered vehicles. One is a direct lineal descendant of the sort that Thomas Edison sought to get out on the road, a pure battery-operated electric vehicle: the EV. It operates only on electricity and is charged from an electric socket. But now there is a variant, the plug-in hybrid electric vehicle, the PHEV. It is an immediate descendant of the hybrid but is much more of an electric vehicle than the Prius-type hybrid. It is "plugged in" to its primary fuel source: electricity. However, after the plug-in hybrid runs for some distance on electricity and the battery runs down, a combustion engine takes over, either recharging the battery or directly providing power to propel the car, or both.

Research and experimentation with plug-in hybrids had been going on for decades, but hardly anyone paid notice. That changed in 2007 when GM unveiled its PHEV Chevy Volt as a sporty concept car at the Detroit Auto Show. Its public debut got so much attention and created such a clamor that GM decided to actually push the Volt into production. Within 12 months the model would come to symbolize the shift in focus from biofuels to EVs.

By the time of the 2008 presidential campaign, "Detroit's plug-in electric car, the Chevrolet Volt," said one political observer, had become "a must-have prop for U.S. presidential candidates." Despite GM's crushing economic problems, candidates Barack Obama and John McCain could not get close enough to the vehicle. McCain proudly announced that "the eyes of the world are now on the Volt." For his part, Barack Obama promised during the campaign to have a million such plug-in hybrids and electric cars on the road by 2015.[10]

THE ROAD MAP

Since then, policy support both for plug-ins and pure electric vehicles has grown significantly around the world, as has a great wave of energy-associated innovation, a good deal of it supported by government policies and mandates. This wave has been powered as well by scientific and technological curiosity and by the economic prospects.

In the United States, policy entrepreneurs, supported by NGOs, have had a strong impact in making the case. The Electrification Coalition, established in 2009, laid out a "road map" for the electric car that was adopted by both Democrats and Republicans alike.

The coalition's chairman, Frederick Smith, founder and CEO of FedEx, made clear that FedEx itself was very interested in moving toward electric vehicles to deliver its parcels. But Smith saw much more than that. "We cannot let electric vehicles turn into another niche product," he said. "We cannot allow their use to be limited to environmentalists and technological enthusiasts. To make our nation's investment worthwhile—and, more importantly, to truly combat our oil dependence—we must put ourselves on the pathway toward millions, then tens of millions, and then hundreds of millions of electric cars and trucks."

As Fred Smith saw it, meeting the needs exclusively with oil in a world in which the number of automobiles was going to double would be challenging and risky. That made diversifying fuel sources critical, and electricity, with improving batteries, looked like the most practical way. The need for charging was not such a great obstacle. "You have to plug in the car, but I plug in my BlackBerry every night because of the value I get from the BlackBerry."[11]

The bankruptcies of General Motors and Chrysler and the multibillion-dollar bailouts by the federal government put the Obama administration in a strong position to advance the electric car. It applied the recession-battling stimulus spending to that same end. A road map had already been laid out by David Sandalow in two books he had written prior to becoming assistant secretary of energy in the Obama administration—*Freedom from Oil* and *Plug-in Electric Vehicles: What Role for Washington.* The legislation that came out of Congress to promote the adoption of the electric car followed the map closely. It included tax credits for manufacturing electric cars, tax credits for buyers of electric cars, tax credits for recharging stations—at home and in public spaces.

In the new century, CARB, now much more focused on global warming, returned with an order requiring automakers to introduce zero-emission vehicles on a revised schedule: by 2012 automakers would be required to begin introducing ZEVs into the California market. The initial target was small and it would include fuel-cell vehicles, but the number was slated to ramp up very fast. This fueled a new urgency for automakers to find their way to deploy an all-electric car.

But there was still the problem of the battery, which had defeated the ZEV the first time.

The core of electric vehicles is the battery. The move toward electric cars would require a major technological advance in batteries. The basic lead-acid battery goes back to the second half of the nineteenth century. Other types of batteries were introduced subsequently, but the lead-acid battery remained the mainstay of the auto industry.

However, in the 1970s and 1980s, researchers, beginning in an Exxon laboratory, were figuring out how lithium, the lightest of metals, could provide the basis for a new rechargeable battery. The oil crises of the 1970s and the fear of a lasting shortage of petroleum had sparked interest in reviving the electric car. In 1976, Congress approved funding for "Electric and Hybrid" research. That same year, *Forbes* reported that "the electric car's rebirth is as sure as the need to end our dependence on imported oil." A number of automobile companies were working on electric vehicles. In 1979, in the middle of the Iranian oil crisis, *Fortune* announced, "Here Come the Electrics." But then the price of oil went down, it turned out that the world was amply supplied with petroleum, and the interest in electric cars once again faded away.

But the work on lithium batteries could be put to very good use for another big need. In 1991, Sony took the lead and introduced lithium-ion batteries in consumer electronics. These smaller, more efficient batteries enabled laptop computers to run faster and longer on a single charge. And lithium batteries were decisively important for something else. They made it possible to shrink the size of cell phones enormously, and thus powered the cell phone revolution. In theory, the greater density of lithium batteries, combined with their lower costs, could make them a more viable and competitive battery for EVs—better than both the nickel-metal-hydride batteries used in the first hybrids and the lead-acid battery that is customary today in automobiles. But that was all in theory. No one had yet road-tested the idea.[12]

ELECTRIC DRIVE

While regulators were at one end of the spectrum in terms of promoting the electric car, at the other end were inventors and tinkerers and entrepreneurs and a small clutch of electric-car enthusiasts, many in California.

Among the EV activists was Al Cocconi, who had been part of GM's ill-fated EV1 program. Cocconi took the idea of the EV1 and turned it into an electric supercar called the tzero. It could go from 0 to 60 miles per hour in a blazing 4.1 seconds.

In 2003 Cocconi came into contact with two Silicon Valley entrepreneurs straight out of the dot-com boom. One of them, Elon Musk, was a cofounders of PayPal. After selling it to eBay, Musk launched SpaceX, a commercial space shuttle business, which Musk intended to be a way station to his larger ambition—enabling people to colonize Mars. The other entrepreneur, Martin Eberhard, offered Cocconi $150,000 in investment for him to experiment with a different kind of battery: a pack composed of lithium-ion batteries, lots and lots of lithium-ion batteries. Cocconi took the money, made the modification, and the car hit 60 miles per hour in only 3.6 seconds.[13]

Not long after, Eberhard and Musk joined forces and together licensed Cocconi's technology. They saw the potential for electrification with lithium-ion batteries and wanted to move the electric car into the mainstream. The lighter weight and greater energy density of these lithium batteries meant they were a potential game-changer for the EV concept.

But the electric vehicle simply could not compete on the basis of economics. However, Musk and Eberhard theorized that it could compete in an arena that mattered very much in California and certainly to their Silicon Valley peers—style, verve, performance, and hype. It would combine the values represented by a Prius with those of a sports car. Instead of something that looked like an oversize golf cart or an egg on wheels, they would build an iconic electric sports car. And they would call it Tesla in honor of the eccentric genius and inventor who in the nineteenth century had conceived the idea of alternating current, which George Westinghouse had used to achieve victory over Thomas Edison's direct current.

Based on a Lotus Elise chassis with additional customization, the two-seater Roadster was intended to be an expensive but dashing sports car, priced at a level that made it affordable only for people who didn't care much about price. If all went well, it would be a stepping-stone to a generation of more sedate but more economically competitive electric vehicles.

Building the Tesla would not be easy. It melded almost seven thousand off-the-shelf lithium-ion batteries of a laptop into a formidable superbattery. The engineering and design challenges for this new kind of car were enormous, and milestone after milestone was missed. "We hugely underestimated the challenge," J. B. Straubel, Tesla's chief technology officer, observed. "Almost every major system on the car, including the body, HVAC, motor, power electronics, transmission, and battery pack, had to be redesigned, retooled, or switched to a new supplier." It was a hard slog for the Roadster both in terms of the technology and money.

Still the Tesla was demonstrating something of signal importance to the auto industry: that the lithium-ion battery was adaptable to the car, and that made the EV a good deal more practical. This was, said Robert Lutz, the former vice chairman of GM, "the crowbar that helped break up the logjam." The first Tesla was delivered in 2008. In 2009 Tesla won a $465 million loan guarantee from the U.S. government, and it subsequently brought in both Daimler and Toyota as investors and partners. In June 2010, it went public—in the first auto IPO in the United States since Ford went public in 1946—and in the aftermath of the IPO, its market capitalization was $2 billion. By that point Tesla had sold about a thousand of its Roadsters. Less than a year later, the company opened its showroom in Washington, D.C., a half dozen blocks from the White House.[14]

The Tesla Roadster can be an exhilarating car to drive—0 to 60 in under four seconds—but its price point was not made for a mass market. The starting price was $109,000—or "only" $101,500 with the $7,500 tax credit from the federal government. Moreover, recharging the car with a standard 110-volt outlet would take about 32 hours. With a 220-volt outlet, it's 4.5 hours, although fast charging is promised down the road. The Roadster is described as a "limited edition vehicle," to be succeeded by Tesla's luxury sedan, the Model S.

Whatever Tesla's ultimate commercial prospects, it did something notable. It demonstrated that the electric car could be something far more than an egg on wheels or a golf cart. A green car could also be a supercar.[15]

Meanwhile, other entrepreneurs joined the fray, trying to find different niches through different business models. Coda, with one leg in California and the other in China, is seeking to come up with a modestly priced electric car that would be lost next to a Tesla Roadster but would be available to a lot more pocketbooks.

Shai Agassi, a young software executive, launched his EV concept with a very different business model. His company wouldn't make the cars. Instead it would own the batteries that it would lease to motorists. It would also establish, in place of gas stations, new "battery stations" into which motorists would drive when the battery ran down. There an attendant would swap out the battery and replace it with a recharged battery.

In 2007 Agassi officially launched his company Better Place. By 2010 the company had raised $700 million, and it was planning to launch recharging networks in both Israel and Denmark, in partnership with Renault, which had designed a new car to go with the system. One of many challenges, however, is lack of standardization in battery size. EVs and PHEVs are likely to compete on the size, weight, and range of their batteries. Standardization has still yet to occur for the lead-acid batteries that have been starting internal combustion engine vehicles for many decades now.

In theory, however, the Better Place experience for motorists is intended to be the functional equivalent of pulling into a gas station and filling up. Except that, with the battery exchange, there will be no self-service.

TAKING A LEAF

Today all the major automakers are moving, with varying degrees of conviction, toward an electric-car offering. Certainly all car companies would be more than happy to find some way to blunt their vulnerability to high oil prices. But among the major international companies, none has been more fervent about the electric car than the Nissan-Renault alliance. And no one more outspoken than its joint CEO, Carlos Ghosn.

Ghosn is about as international as an executive of a global company can be. Raised in both Lebanon and Brazil and educated further in France, he ran Michelin Tires in the United States, and then became a senior executive at Renault. After Renault formed an alliance with Japan's Nissan, Ghosn set out to rescue Nissan, which was teetering on collapse with $20 billion of debt. He became famous for bringing Nissan back from the brink and ended up as the CEO of both companies.

Toyota has its hybrid, Prius. Honda is the "engine company," focused on the superior characteristics of a more-efficient internal combustion engine. By contrast, going "all-electric" gives Nissan a distinctive leadership. The opportunity emerged by accident out of the company's financial wreck.

When Ghosn arrived at Nissan in Japan in 1999, he slashed costs almost everywhere. But something about the battery program gave him pause. "Nissan had been working on the electric battery for 18 years," said Ghosn. "I was really struck by those engineers when I met with them. They thought that an electric car could be feasible and affordable. I had no clue, but I was very impressed by their passion." Despite Nissan's perilous financial condition, that was one cut he did not make. "Sometimes you only connect the dots afterward," he added.

By 2002 Nissan had what it considered a breakthrough in lithium-ion technology. "After 2003, Nissan was out of turn-around," said Ghosn. "But I was very surprised by the amount of criticism that we were getting for not having a hybrid. I asked myself why there was so much passion about this. I realized how strong were the public's concerns around the environment. At the same time, the price of oil was going up. Also, very strong environmental regulations were coming out of California. We couldn't fulfill them without some kind of new technology. We needed to think out of the box. We needed to jump-start the electric. That was the only solution. You can't go from 850 million to 2 billion cars without an environmental car." Nissan had what its engineers believed was the technology. Ghosn gave the go-ahead to go all-out for a new all-electric car.

The reaction within the company was diverse. Some were puzzled. Why, they asked, didn't Nissan try instead to build a competitive hybrid? Others were enthusiastic that the company was trying to take leadership in a new technology.

While Nissan would also develop its own hybrids, Ghosn looked at it only as a bridge technology. "If you have an efficient battery for a hybrid, why not go all the way and go for electric cars?" he said. "It has the most zero emissions of anything."

And so if Nissan was going to spend several billion dollars to develop a new car, it would be for an all-electric car. "No tailpipe," said Ghosn. Not a drop of gasoline. And it was not going to just be a car for the motor show. It was going to be an affordable car for the mass market." In the autumn of 2010, Nissan went to market with the Leaf—which stands for Leading, Environmentally friendly, Affordable, Family car. It rolled into showrooms with a 600-pound pack of lithium-ion batteries and promised an average driving range of around 90 to 100 miles and a top speed of 90 miles per hour. Nissan is targeting that 10 percent of its sales in 2020 will be EVs. "The only thing that is missing is real scale, and to achieve that, we have to cut costs of the battery," said Ghosn.

"The race to zero emissions has begun," he declared. For him, it was truly the world according to CARB. "This is not a bet," he said. "The only question about zero emissions is, When? Do we do it do now or in five years? Our competitors may see it differently." But Nissan believes "it is now."[16]

CHARGE IT

For most of the previous two decades, the center of the advanced battery world has been in Asia, in Japan, and in South Korean. While the United States was pushing ahead, the Japanese and South Korean companies have redoubled their own efforts. After all, it was a Korean company, LG Chem, that made the Chevy Volt battery cells. In response to America's new politics of electric cars, it hastened to open a plant in Michigan.

Backed by strong government incentives, the U.S. industry is expanding rapidly. The Obama administration projects America to host 40 percent of the world's advanced automotive battery manufacturing capacity by 2015, as opposed to 2 percent when Obama took office.[17]

But the battery is only half of the equation; the other is charging—getting electricity into the car reliably and with speed and convenience. Japanese companies have formed an industrial consortium whose name is a pun on "Won't you at least have some tea?" The idea is that charging time needs to be speeded up and that it should take no more time than having a cup of tea. Currently, a Chevy Volt requires four to ten hours to recharge—and that would be quite a number of cups of tea. But various researchers are trying to find the pathway that would reduce charging to something less than the time required to drink a hot cup of tea; that is, the time it takes to fill up with gasoline.

WHERE WILL THE ELECTRICITY COME FROM?

The current general theory of electric cars is that they would recharge overnight, when demand is at its lowest. This would create a new market for electric power companies and, at the same time, balance out the load. And it would be a very big market. Charging a car overnight would take about as much electricity as would be used by two houses over twenty-four hours. In other words, were EVs to become ubiquitous, electric power companies would be virtually doubling their residential load without the need to build much more capacity.

Over the last few years, a compelling new vision has taken shape: Wind and solar will generate the new supplies of electricity. That electricity will then be wheeled long-distance over a much-expanded and modernized transmission system. And then, when it gets to dense urban areas, the electricity will be managed by a smart grid that will move it through the distribution system, into the household or the charging station, and finally it will be fed into the battery of an electric car. Some even take the vision further and imagine that cars will act as storage systems, "roving" batteries, which, when idle, will feed electricity back into the grid.

But that is quite different from the electric system that exists today in which renewables provide less than 2 percent of the power. Lee Schipper, a professor at Stanford University, argues that many EVs will become what he dubs EEVs—"emissions elsewhere vehicles." That is, the emissions and greenhouse gases associated with transportation will not come out of the tailpipe of the car but potentially from the smokestack of a coal-fired power plant that generates the electricity that is fed into the EV. So one also has to take into account how the power is generated. Is it uranium or coal or wind? Or something else? Will it be natural gas, with about half the CO_2 emissions of coal and now a much more abundant fuel because of the breakthrough on shale gas worldwide? This last prospect also provides an alternative to burning natural gas in engines as a mass-market fuel. Natural gas would in effect become a motor fuel, but indirectly, by generating more of the electricity that ends up in the battery of an electric car.[18]

How fast can an electric-vehicle future happen? On a global basis, estimates for new-car sales in 2030 of EVs and PHEVs, depending upon the scenario, range between 10 percent and 32 percent of total annual sales. Under the most optimistic of the scenarios, the penetration of such vehicles (in other words, the total number of EVs and PHEVs in the global fleet) would be 14 percent.[19]

The policies of governments will be one of the critical determinants in the actual outcome. For it is such policies—regulations, incentives, and subsidies—that today are promoting the development of the electric car and on which the current economics depend. Innovation could change that calculus and drive down costs, just as Henry Ford did with the Model T. That is one of the primary arguments for the policies and incentives and subsidies: they are meant to stimulate greater scale and significant cost-cutting innovation. One critical question, therefore, is how stable will be those policies that are now aimed at making electricity the mainstay of the auto fleet? After all, energy policies have shown the recurrent characteristic of being "pendulumatic," moving in one direction and then another, and then back again.

"THERMAL RUNAWAY"?

EVs are already in production and in the marketplace. But as a product for a mass market, it remains a great experiment with big hurdles still to be surmounted.

Batteries still need to be smaller, weigh less, charge more quickly, and be able to last much longer on a single charge. They also need to prove that they can be long lived, despite the continuing charging and discharging. It will have to be demonstrated that problems like "thermal runaway"—destructive overheating—do not occur. In addition to propelling the vehicle, batteries also need sufficient capacity to power all the other accoutrements that drivers expect, from power steering and air-conditioning to the traveling entertainment center. And the cost needs to come down substantially—unless governments are willing and capable of providing continuing subsidies on a very large scale.[20]

Batteries are now a focus of intense and well-funded research around the world, aimed at addressing these questions. The entire effort is also very competitive—indeed, a global "battery race." At the same time, there is a global debate as to where the "learning curve" battery technology is and how fast it can come down.

Infrastructure is the second challenge. Today's automobile system could not operate without the dense network of gasoline stations built up over so many decades. A large fleet of electric cars will need a similar network of charging stations. One car in a neighborhood can be easily accommodated with an extension cord. But what happens to the transformers in the power system when everybody on the block, and on the next block, and on the next three blocks decides to recharge at the same time?[21]

Moreover, it is necessary to get beyond the "hand raisers"—those who put their names in the order book prior to the release of a model—and the early adopters. In the 1990s General Motors "subsidized the hell out of the EV1," said former GM CEO Rick Wagner. "But if customers don't want to buy, it's hard to do." The EV has to attract a large population of drivers. To that end, charging stations need to be built and powered around urban areas and into the countryside to ensure convenience and reliability—and to ensure that people don't get stranded.[22]

Government can implement only so many regulations, incentives, and subsidies. Buyers have to find the price, functionality, performance, and reliability that they want. That will take time to demonstrate. Specifically, what is called range anxiety—the fear of being stranded with a rundown battery—will be a major factor in what consumers actually do.

Perhaps the answer to consumer needs will be to parse those needs—different cars for different purposes. People may use a small urban electric

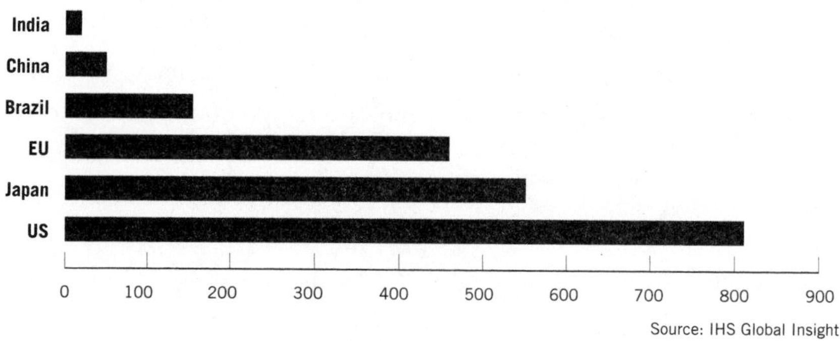

runabout for local needs and commuting—a sort of modern version of the Detroit Electrics and Baker Runabouts of the early twentieth century—and drive a bigger oil-fueled or hybrid car for longer trips or weekend getaways. At the same time, as when any kind of new product is introduced, there is always the risk of the unexpected in terms of operations or performance that could negatively affect public acceptance of EVs as a category.

Finally, there is the matter of power supply. It is generally assumed that sufficient unused electric power–generating capacity, especially at night, is available to accommodate a large fleet of electric cars. That may well be the case, but major growth in electric cars would be a very major new draw on the electric-power industry. What happens if people don't charge their EVs at night? What happens if instead large numbers of people decide to recharge during peak demand? How will the system cope?

Then there are the emerging issues. In addition to motion and emissions, the internal combustion engine also produces noise. Early on, silence was a big selling point for electric cars (and hybrids). Yet sound is part of the sensory and situational awareness for safety both for drivers and for pedestrians and bicyclists. Visually impaired groups have raised concerns about the dangers of silent vehicles. In Japan automakers have started making synthesized engine sound available in response to guidelines from the government-sponsored CCCRQHOV, or Committee for the Consideration of Countermeasures Regarding Quiet Hybrid and Other Vehicles. That safety need will have to be met in the United States and Europe as well.

And what kind of sound should it be? Carlos Ghosn has been among those at Nissan vetting sounds. "It should be something that sounds like an electric car," he said, "pleasant, not too much, but enough."[23]

ASIA FIRST?

Given all of the various hurdles, where might be the first major market for EVs?

Some Asian megacities present a combination of circumstances that appear conducive for the spread of EVs. Their physical infrastructure is still being built out, and thus is more ripe for "greenfield" development of charging stations and other equipment than older urban areas in the United States and Europe. At the same time, air pollution in these cities can be stifling, and coughing, disgruntled citizens have been pressing governments to improve air quality.

Asian countries may also be helped along by the fact that a much greater percentage of their residents are, or will be, first-time (or second-time) car buyers. This means they have fewer preconceived notions of what a car "should be" in terms of size and performance, as compared with their counterparts in more advanced countries. Moreover, many residents of developing Asian megacities, especially those in China, already have the experience of being transported in EVs, at least the two-wheel variety, in the form of electric bicycles.

"People want to have a car in the family," said one senior Chinese official. "The government cannot prevent that trend. But very important is what kind of car." And new policies make clear that Beijing wants a growing proportion of those cars to be electric.[24]

The Chinese government has categorized "New Energy Vehicles" as one of its seven strategic sectors for economic development. It is bolstering this commitment with significant subsidies that will make purchasing EVs more feasible and more attractive. Additionally, national and local governments are instituting EV procurement programs for their own fleets, ensuring a market for the vehicles.

Though the role of the state is more pronounced in China than in the United States, the most prominent Chinese electric car company, at least internationally, is a private one called BYD. It began in 1995 as a greenfield battery company, started by a then twenty-nine-year-old chemistry graduate named Chuanfu Wang. The company began by manufacturing nickel-cadmium batteries and then transitioned to manufacturing lithium-based batteries to compete with batteries made by Sanyo and Sony. By 2002, within just seven years of its founding, BYD had become one of the world's top four manufacturers of rechargeable batteries for cell phones. Wang was celebrated in China as the "Battery King." BYD had achieved this preeminence by ruthless technical intensity, beating the Japanese on costs, and, as Wang put it, by "much trial and error." In addition, as Wang said, "In China, people of my generation put work first and life second."[25]

In 2003 BYD bought a derelict state-owned auto company. By 2008 it had the best-selling sedan in China. That same year, Warren Buffett bought 10 percent of the company for $230 million; the company started selling what it said was the first mass-produced plug-in hybrid—though sales were minuscule. Two years later it introduced all-electric cars with the aim of conquering not only the Chinese market but also the global market, just as it did with its batteries. In 2011 it dispatched its F3DM plug-in hybrid to the United States to begin undergoing the regulatory process for the American market and to go on display in Omaha, Nebraska, at the annual meeting of Warren Buffett's company, Berkshire Hathaway.[26]

THE HYDROGEN HIGHWAY

But the electric car is not the only zero-emissions option. From a theoretical standpoint, a fuel cell is a very attractive device. It is similar to a battery in that it extracts energy from chemicals in the form of electricity. It also has no moving parts. However, unlike a rechargeable battery, which has to be recharged with electricity that is produced somewhere else, or a single-use chemical battery, a fuel cell typically uses onboard gaseous hydrogen to generate its own electricity. It is a bit like a battery with a gas tank. Fuel cells combine hydrogen and oxygen electrochemically. As a result, the only things that hydrogen fuel cells emit are electricity and water, and, crucially, they have the potential to provide power density that can compete with liquid fuels.

Hydrogen and the fuel cell first got serious automotive attention after California's original 1990 zero-emissions edict. Among automotive companies, Honda, Toyota, and GM have continued to be boosters of fuel-cell technology.

In its early years, the George W. Bush administration promoted research for the fuel-cell auto, what it called the "freedom car."

Fuel cells continue to face major challenges. The fuel cells themselves—the device that converts hydrogen or another chemical feedstock into electricity—are expensive and will require substantial investment and breakthroughs for commercialization. One industry estimate is that their price would have to be reduced by a factor of twenty for them to become somewhat economical.[27]

If the cells themselves are expensive, so is the hydrogen that is now mainly used in oil refineries and petrochemical plants to make high-quality products. Hydrogen does not exist independently in nature. It has to be manufactured from something else, which today, primarily, is natural gas, although it could also be manufactured using nuclear power. Storing and transporting hydrogen for automotive applications is also technically complex and certainly costly. As electric cars require considerable investment for the stations and infrastructure that will charge batteries, so hydrogen vehicles will require a good deal of investment in infrastructure—in this case, in hydrogen-fueling stations.

When he was governor of California, Arnold Schwarzenegger launched with much fanfare a network of hydrogen-fueling stations that he dubbed "California's Hydrogen Highway to the Environmental Future." But that particular highway did not get all that far. By 2010 there were fewer than two dozen stations in the entire state selling hydrogen fuel.[28]

Another possibility is a fuel cell powered by natural gas rather than hydrogen—so-called solid oxide fuel cells. Some think, however, that natural gas fuel cells are better suited for stationary uses, such as off-grid power generation, rather than as power sources for automobiles.

WHAT ABOUT NATURAL GAS?

A potential rival to the EV would be the NGV—otherwise known as the natural gas vehicle. This is a vehicle powered by an internal combustion engine but that uses natural gas, instead of gasoline or diesel, as fuel.

Despite the fact that natural gas often costs significantly less than gasoline on an energy basis, natural gas vehicles make up only 1 percent of the total light vehicles in the world. They are primarily taxicabs and other vehicles in Asia and Latin America. There was a spurt of NGV sales in Italy, owing to significant tax subsidy. In the United States, NGVs amount to less than one tenth of 1 percent of the total vehicles on the road.[29]

Any significant expansion of NGVs would face major challenges beyond the cost of converting an existing gasoline vehicle to run on natural gas or of manufacturing a natural gas vehicle. Billions of dollars would also have to be spent to create a natural gas fueling infrastructure, just as is the case with the recharging infrastructure for electric cars. Because of the lower energy density of natural gas, vehicles fueled by it would have less range or fewer miles per tank. Natural gas cars would also need to give up trunk space to accommodate a natural gas tank. Moreover, NGVs would be competing against increasingly more fuel-efficient, conventional internal combustion engine cars, reducing the economic advantage, as well as going against strong policy support for biofuels and electric cars. Finally, natural gas vehicles may not be the most efficient way to use natural gas in the transportation sector. Generating electricity with natural gas and then using it to fuel a vehicle could prove more cost-effective than burning the natural gas directly in the vehicle.

One possible market for NGVs are centralized fleets of taxis, trucks, and buses that go relatively short distances and can be easily and cheaply refueled at a central depot. Another market is heavy-duty long-distance trucks that would operate on low-temperature liquefied natural gas. But the challenges include the need for LNG refueling terminals, the higher costs of LNG trucks, and the much lower energy density of LNG compared with diesel, which would be problematic when it comes to hauling heavy loads. It would also limit the secondhand market for the trucks, which is an important element in the economics of their owners.

THE CARS OF THE FUTURE

Electric cars, hybrids, biofuels, natural gas vehicles, more efficient internal combustion engines, fuel cells at some later date—the race to reshape transportation and for "the car of the future" is once again on. Or, perhaps, it will be plural—"the cars of the future." In the last race, a century ago, the internal combustion engine won hands down—on the basis of cost, convenience, performance, and range. But this time there may not be a single winner but rather different vehicles for different purposes.

One way or the other, oil's almost total domination over transportation will either be whittled away or more drastically reduced. Cars will certainly get more efficient. It seems pretty certain that electricity will play a bigger role in transportation, either in hybrids or all-electric vehicles. Considerable effort continues to go into second-generation biofuels. Regardless of what powers cars, they are likely to get smaller in coming years, in part as baby boomers in the United States, Europe, and Japan retire. Moreover, surprises in the quest for a clean, secure form of transportation may well happen.

In shaping the future, developing countries will be critical participants in a way they have not been in the past. Emerging markets will fuel growth in the global auto market, and thus the direction of technology as well as environmental standards. China's surpassing the United States as the world's largest car market in 2009 was a landmark. As a result of this shift, the policies of governments in developing countries will have increasingly greater impact on the global auto market. Indeed, a day may well come when China, because of the dynamism of its market, becomes the defining force for the world auto industry, or when a Chinese environmental regulatory agency becomes the new CARB for the world.

The key criteria for victory, or at least a place in the winner's circle, will be the delivery of increasingly efficient cars that also meet the tests of environment, energy security, cost, and performance. The contest will require major advances in technology and multibillion-dollar investments, and it certainly will be shaped in part by the preferences of governments. In such uncertain circumstances, companies are hedging their futures by placing multiple bets to the degree that they can. "We're investing billions and billions, and basically we're going for everything—from diesel to hybrids to batteries," said Dieter Zetsche, the CEO of Daimler.

"We have taken the point of view that fuel efficiency is important to all customers," said Bill Ford, Ford's chairman. "But we still don't know what the winning technology will be. Any (long-term) sales projections today don't mean anything. So many different things are at play. I can't give a number. It's throwing a dart."[30]

TO THE FUTURE

Where does this leave oil and the internal combustion engine? Probably in an assured position of dominance at least for the next two decades. But there will be much more efficient internal combustion engines. Cars based on the ICE technology can come into today's fleet quickly. And they will not require a new infrastructure system.

Internal combustion engines do a remarkable job of generating power in an affordable and compact package. The secret to the success of the ICE lies in the energy density of liquid fuels—simply put, oil. The small size and power output of the gasoline and diesel-fuel engines will continue to make them fierce competitors—technologically speaking. Moreover, the scope certainly exists for improving the efficiency of cars—whether in gasoline and diesel engines themselves, or through "lightweighting" cars with new materials, and thus reducing emissions.

"A key question is how to halve the fuel consumption of the 2035 car fleet," observed John Heywood, professor of mechanical engineering at Massachusetts Institute of Technology and the former director of the university's Sloan Automotive Laboratory. "We can make vehicles that are twice as good as those today," says Heywood. "But the next question is, how many? If it's only 15 percent of the fleet, it's of little impact. If it's 95 percent, it's a hell of a big thing."[31]

Yet one near certainty is that the transportation system of today will evolve significantly over the coming decades. Energy efficiency and lower emissions will continue to be major preoccupations. If issues of cost and complexity and scale can be conquered, the battery will begin to push aside oil as the motive force for much of the world's automotive transportation. But the internal combustion engine is unlikely to be shunted aside easily. The new contest may, for some time, be less decisive than when Henry Ford used his Model T to engineer victory for the internal combustion engine against the electric car.

But the race has certainly begun. The outcome will do much to define our energy world in the decades ahead in terms of where we get our energy, how we use it, and who the winners will be. But it is much too soon for anyone to take a victory lap.

CONCLUSION: "A GREAT REVOLUTION"

Sadi Carnot, the son of one of Napoléon's ministers of war and himself a soldier as well as a scientist, was convinced that one reason for Britain's victory in the Napoleonic wars at the beginning of the nineteenth century was its mastery of energy, specifically the steam engine. Determined to right that balance and impelled by deep curiosity as to how the steam engine actually worked, Carnot undertook a study that he published in 1824 as *Reflections on the Motive Power of Fire.* To his disappointment, it received virtually no attention at the time of publication. Carnot would die a few years later, at age 36, during a cholera epidemic with no knowledge of the profound impact his work would have. For he had written what was almost certainly the first systematic analysis of how man had actually harnessed energy. His work would prove a crucial input into the formulation of the second law of thermodynamics, and the "Carnot cycle" would become a staple of engineering.

But Carnot never had any doubt about the wider significance of his analysis. He recognized that he was describing not only what happened inside an engine but also a transformation in human affairs. For the invention of "heat engines," using "combustibles," as he called them, "seemed to produce a great revolution in the civilized world." Humanity had broken the bonds that, except for rudimentary wind and water power, had been set by the muscles of man and beast. It was indeed a revolution. More than a century after Carnot, Hyman

Rickover actually tried to quantify what had been achieved. "Each locomotive engineer uses the energy equivalent to that of 100,000 men," said the admiral, "each jet pilot, of 700,000 men." Today that quantity would be all that much greater.

This harnessing of energy is what makes possible the world as we know it. The bounty can be measured in terms of virtually everything we do in the course of a day. But can we bet on that for the future?

The growth in world energy demand in the coming decades will be very large. The increase alone will be greater than all the energy that the world consumed in 1970. This increase is really a measure of success—of a more prosperous global economy, of rising standards of living, of billions of people moving out of poverty. In terms of oil, North America, Europe, and Japan have already reached peak demand. Because of demographics, increased efficiency, and substitution, their petroleum consumption will be flat or declining.

The story will be entirely different in emerging markets owing to the continuing globalization of demand. Over the next couple of decades, two billion people—about a quarter of the world's population—will gain a significant "pay raise." They will likely move from a per capita income of under $10,000 a year to an income of between $10,000 and $30,000 a year. Even with much improved efficiency in energy use, their rising incomes will be reflected in much greater need for energy. How will that need be met? What kind of energy mix would make this possible without crisis and confrontation? The answers to these questions will be critical to the future.

The security issue that surrounds supply will continue to be a fundamental concern. Again and again, experience has demonstrated that the threats to reliability and security of supply can come in unexpected ways. Who thought that hurricanes in the Gulf of Mexico could lead to the biggest disruption of oil in American history and necessitate the dispatch of emergency oil supplies from Europe and Japan? And as economies and technologies change, security concerns take new forms. A decade ago, U.S.–Chinese relations were not a critical factor in global energy security. The Internet has ratcheted up the risks to the energy system, notably to the electric grid on which so much depends, including the very operation of the Internet.

The scale of energy flows from the Middle East and North Africa, and particularly the Persian Gulf, make that region central to the security of oil and natural gas supplies. The upheavals across North Africa and the Middle East have transformed the politics of the region and changed the relationship between governments and their people. At the same time, they have upended at least part of the geostrategic balance that has underpinned stability. This means greater uncertainty about the future of the region in which resources are so concentrated. And that kind of uncertainty and potential political volatility—and risks of crisis—increase concerns about vulnerability and energy security. These perceptions of greater risk translate into an increased risk premium in the price of oil, one that reflects the still-evolving new geopolitics of the region.

Policies related to access to energy and its production can have major impact on the timeliness of investment and the availability of supply—and thus on energy security. Policies can constrain supply and limit access. But the effects can also be positive, encouraging investment and technological advance. For years, it has been customary to say that the United States imports "two-thirds" of its oil. But today, at least, the United States imports only 50 percent of its oil. This is the result of greater fuel efficiency in the auto fleet, growth in domestic production from both the offshore and "tight oil," and increased use of biofuels. Technological advances have turned North Dakota into the fourth largest oil-producing state in the United States. The largest source of U.S. oil imports is a resource that did not really even exist on a commercial basis in the 1970s—Canadian oil sands.

The interaction of environmental concerns with energy will continue to shape the larger energy marketplace. The biggest question is climate change and carbon. Over 80 percent of world energy continues to be supplied by what Carnot called the "combustibles"—carbon-based fuels. About 75 to 80 percent of world energy is expected to be carbon based two decades from now. The growing importance of the climate change question ensures that this ratio will be strongly challenged both politically and technologically as people strive to decarbonize energy.

While climate is the mega-issue, many other environmental questions will affect supply. Coal—the source of 40 percent of world electricity—is challenged about other emissions. Two of the most important innovations that are particularly important to energy security—oil sands, and shale gas, and tight oil—encounter determined opposition. Some seek changes in how these supplies are produced; some do not want them produced at all. How these issues are resolved will have decisive importance on the availability of energy and the security of supply. The accident at the Fukushima Daiichi nuclear site in Japan has led to a reconsideration of nuclear power around the world, as well as accelerating the drive for new designs and passive safety features.

A move away from Carnot's combustibles has already begun, but we are in the early stage of a transition—or at least a remixing of the energy mix. It represents, in one form, a shift from the carbon-based fuels, predominant since the beginning of the Industrial Revolution, to noncarbon-based fuels. But it has a second form as well. It is also a transition to a more energy-lean world that operates at a much higher level of energy efficiency. In transportation, that shift to greater efficiency is already evident, both in miles per gallon and in the spread of hybrid technology. Biofuels will likely have a growing presence, but to gain significant market share, they need to reach the second generation. As for the electric car, it is too early to assess how far and how fast it will penetrate the global auto fleet.

One sector stands out in terms of future growth—electric generation. Worldwide electricity consumption could almost double over two decades. Renewables have played a role in power generation for years in the form of hydropower. But in many countries its growth is either circumscribed or blocked altogether by environmental opposition. Another existing technology for electric generation is geothermal power, which uses steam created by deep heat in the earth to drive turbines. While an important contributor in some regions, geothermal is limited by geology and the availability of the right kind of "hot rocks" underground.

The two big new noncarbon sources for generating electricity are wind and solar. They have registered great advances and much technological maturing since the "rays of hope" of the 1970s and early 1980s. Further advances, which will lower costs, are still to come. At this point, significant businesses in themselves, they are still small when measured against the scale of the power business. They still need to demonstrate that they can provide large-scale reliable electricity competitively—or that society decides it is willing to pay additional costs through subsidies or with carbon charges. As these sources grow, how they are integrated into the overall grid becomes a more pressing question.

Are we on the edge of a new stage in the "great revolution" of energy?

History demonstrates that energy transition generally takes a long time. It took almost a century before oil overtook coal as the number one energy source.

The pace of technological advance is not the only factor affecting the speed of any transition. Another factor is the law of long lead times. The energy system is large and complex, with an enormous amount of embedded capital. It does not turn over with anything like the speed of mobile phones. A power plant may have a sixty-year life span or even more. A major new oil field may require a decade or more between exploration and first production. Even the automobile fleet, despite the impression created by the annual introduction of new models, does not change that quickly. It can take five years to develop a new model and then the fleet itself only turns over at the rate of about 8 percent in a typical year.

And yet things can change quickly. Shale gas took two decades to begin to register in the marketplace. But once it did, in a matter of just a few years, it dramatically changed the economics not just of natural gas but of competitors, from nuclear power to wind power.

By 2030, overall global energy consumption may be 35 or 40 percent greater than it is today. The mix will probably not be too different from what it is today. Hydrocarbons will likely be somewhere between 75 and 80 percent of the overall supply. One can imagine a host of factors—from political upheavals and military conflicts to major shifts in the global economy to changes in pricing and regulation or significant technological breakthroughs—that change this picture more decisively. But that law of long lead times still remains. It is really after 2030 that the energy system could start to look quite different as the cumulative effect of innovation and technological advance makes its full impact felt.

In the meantime, the elements shaping the future of energy are many, their interactions complex and sometimes confusing, and the differences in interests and perspectives considerable. All this makes forging a coherent "energy policy" a challenging matter. Indeed, "energy policy" is often shaped by policies that are not even seen as "energy" in their focus. But history suggests that certain principles will be useful in making decisions in the future.

The first is to start with the recognition of the scale, complexity, and importance of the energy foundations on which a world economy depends, whether it is today's $65 trillion or $130 trillion two decades from now. There is much to be said for an ecumenical approach that recognizes the contribution of the range of the energy options. Churchill's famous dictum about supply—"variety, and variety alone"—still resounds powerfully. Diversification of oil resources needs to be expanded to diversification among energy sources—conventional and "new." This represents a realization that there are no risk-free options and that the risks can come in many forms.

Energy efficiency remains a top priority for a growing world economy. Remarkable results have already been achieved, but technologies and tools not available in earlier decades are now at hand. The real advances, whether in developed or developing nations, will be embodied in behavior and value, but especially in investment—new processes, new factories, new buildings, new vehicles. There are many obstacles, ranging from financing to the fact that efficiency usually comes without the opportunity for good "photo ops." There is "no ribbon to cut."

Sustainability is now a fundamental value of society. Environmental priorities need to continue to be integrated into the production and consumption of energy. They should be analyzed and assessed in terms of impact and scale and cost-benefit analysis, assuring access to energy, with appropriate environmental safeguards.

The whole sweep of Carnot's great revolution—from the steam engine start-up of James Watt in the eighteenth century and the oil start-up of Colonel Edwin Drake in the nineteenth century to the latest cleantech start-ups to be spun out of Sand Hill Road and whatever is currently bubbling in the lab—demonstrates that the advances of energy are the result of innovation and conviction. Developing new knowledge and "applying science" come with a price tag. But without sustained long-term support for the entire innovation chain, the world will pay a much larger price.

As we have seen in these pages, there are many parts to the quest. But fundamental to it, and underpinning everything else, is the search for knowledge, which advances technology and promotes innovation. Sadi Carnot captured a transcendent truth when he wrote about "the great revolution." But it was more a prediction when he penned those words for it was the very early days in this energy enterprise. What has been accomplished since could not possibly have been imagined. The challenges of meeting rising energy needs in the decades ahead, of assuring that the resources are available on a sustainable basis to support a growing world, may seem daunting; and, indeed, when one considers the scale, they truly are. Meeting them requires, among other things, the responsible and efficient use of energy, sound judgment, consistent investment, statesmanship, collaboration, long-term thinking, and the thoughtful integration of environmental considerations into energy strategies.

But what provides for reasoned confidence is the increasing availability of what may be the most important resource of all—human creativity. A famous geologist once said, "Oil is found in the minds of men." We can amend that to say that the energy solutions for the twenty-first century will be found in the minds of people around the world. And that resource base is growing.

The globalization of demand may be shaping tomorrow's needs. But it is accompanied by a globalization of innovation. The generation of knowledge and the application of science have increasingly become a worldwide endeavor; and the links and interactions, amplified by ever-widening information and communications systems, multiply the speed and impact of what can be accomplished. This means that the resource base of knowledge and creativity is expanding. This will fuel the insight and ingenuity that will find the new solutions.

This is not a blind faith, by any means. There is no assurance on timing for the innovations that will make a difference. There is no guarantee that the investment at the scale needed will be made in a timely way, or that government policies will be wisely implemented. Certainly, lead times can be long, and costs will have to evolve. As this story has shown, the risks of conflict, crisis, and disruption are inherent. Things can go seriously wrong, with dire consequences. Thus, it is essential that the conditions are nurtured so that creativity can flourish. For that resource will be critical for meeting the challenges and assuring the security and sustainability of the energy for a prosperous, growing world. That is at the heart of the quest, it is as much about the human spirit as it is about technology, and that is why this is a quest that will never end.

ACKNOWLEDGMENTS

I have many people to thank and to acknowledge from the half decade I have worked on this book.

Foremost, I am very fortunate to have as my editor Ann Godoff at Penguin Press. She clearly saw what this book could be before I did, worked with me to conceptualize it and think through the issues, and provided guidance and continuing dialogue from which I greatly benefited. Her commitment was critical throughout. My deep thanks to her.

Also at Penguin Press, Virginia Smith was my shepherd, and I greatly appreciate the intelligence, care, and very thoughtful editing she brought to the process. To others at Penguin Press, I would like to express appreciation for their great efforts, especially to John Sharp, Amanda Dewey, Tracy Locke, and Elisabeth Calamari.

I am very grateful to the team members with whom I worked closely in researching, shaping, and producing this book. Over several years, Levi Tillemann-Dick, a young scholar of considerable talent, brought insight, creativity, his own deep interest in energy and engines, and a good deal of fortitude to this undertaking. His incisive analysis and thoughtful perspective were essential. His own work on the reemergence of the electric car will be an important contribution to the energy field. Jeff Meyer, who joined at a critical time, was wholly committed to this project. I greatly benefited from his judgment, curiosity, and relentless research, and from his experience and broad overview—all of which he will apply in his own continuing work on energy. Both Levi and Jeff recognized that the final mile of a quest can be a very long one, and they were there for every last foot.

Amy Kipp expertly organized me, managed everything that needed to be managed, coordinated on multiple fronts, and maintained the balance. I count on her greatly and am very grateful. Ellen Perkins was devoted to the evolving manuscript, kept it moving, and knew the story as well as anyone.

Suzanne Gluck at William Morris Endeavor was engaged with this book from day one. I have respected and relied on her judgment as agent, reader, and friend. And certainly I am very grateful to my old friend Jim Wiatt, whom I wisely followed and who was keen that I do this book.

My appreciation certainly to William Goodlad and Karen Browning at Penguin Press in London for the British and international edition.

I want to acknowledge Steve Weisman, gifted writer and shrewd critic, for his advice and careful reading and friendship, all of which has been true for so many projects over so many years. And deep thanks to James Rosenfield, with whom I founded what is now IHS Cambridge Energy Research Associates (IHS CERA) and with whom I have had so many adventures. He was a bulwark as I was writing this book, bringing his customary rigor and sense of structure to this enterprise.

The photo section was a project in itself. A great team came together to shape it into a story in its own right. Special credit goes to Ruth Mandel, expert in visual imagery and really gifted in bringing photo to the story, and for whom tireless is an understatement. Margaret Johnson, with her great knowledge of archives and her expertise in telling stories in pictures, joined us just in time. The talented and creative Kathy Nave did an extraordinary job in bringing the visual images into a coherent whole and executing it with verve.

Here I owe special thanks and acknowledgment to Sue Lena Thompson, with whom I have worked to such great benefit over the years. She visualized and conceptualized the photo section. And I am grateful to her for the spirit and wisdom she brought, as she did to *The Prize* and *Commanding Heights.*

I thank Ginny Mason for the distinctive and superb maps, and Sean McNaughton for the excellent graphics. The images they created help bring the geography and numbers in the story to life. Keith Rushworth of IHS also helped much with maps. In terms of the manuscript, I thank Anthony Martinez, who worked with me early on in the research and helped lay out the direction; and

Russ Burns and Matt Vredenburgh, who worked intensively on the documentation. Freda Amar joined just in time to be part of the final phase.

Jerre Stead, the chairman and chief executive officer of IHS, supported this project from the beginning and shared his perspectives and insight throughout. His leadership has brought IHS to its position at the crossroads of the global economy. At IHS, I would also particularly like to thank Scott Key, Mike Sullivan, Steve Green, Jane Okun Bomba, Jonathan Gear, and Dave Carlson, as well as Rich Walker and Ed Mattix.

At IHS CERA, I'm blessed with wonderful colleagues who every day, with great expertise, help paint the picture of energy in its global setting. I feel that all of them helped me in one way or another, and I'm grateful to all. I do want to thank those who read and critiqued all or substantial parts of the book or contributed in other very significant ways: Bhushan Bahree, James Burkhard, Thane Gustafson, David Hobbs, Peter Jackson, Lawrence Makovich, James Placke, Matt Sagers, Jone-Lin Wang, and K. F. Yan.

Other CERA colleagues who also contributed and helped me include: Atul Arya, Mary Barcella, Aaron Brady, Jean-Marie Chevalier, James Clad, Jackie Forrest, Tiffany Groode, Samantha Gross, Kate Hardin, John Harris, Bob Ineson, Ruchir Kadakia, Matt Kaplan, Rob LaCount, Jeff Marn, Thomas Maslin, Wolfgang Moehler, Gig Moineau, David Raney, Laurent Ruseckas, Susan Ruth, Enrique Sira, Leta Smith, Michael Stoppard, Xiaolu Wang, Irina Zamarina, and Xizhou Zhou.

I also want to thank the expert colleagues at the sister organizations, IHS Global Insight, IHS Jane's, IHS Herold, and IHS Emerging Energy Research.

I would like to express appreciation to those who read parts of the manuscript and who contributed to my thinking and understanding: William Antholis, Nariman Behravesh, Christopher Beauman, Simon Blakey, Len Blavatnik, John Browne, Cai Jin-Yong, Jamil Dandany, John Deutch, Erica Downs, Charles Ebinger, Daniel Esty, Christopher Frei, John Fritts, David Goldwyn, Peter Gorelick, Todd Harvey, John Heimlich, Chris Hunt, Jack Ihle, Sultan al-Jaber, Jan Kalicki, Yoriko Kawaguchi, Doug Kimmelman, Pierre Lapeyre, Richard Lester, David Leuschen, Robert Maguire, Michael Makovsky, Ernest Moniz, Edward Morse, Ibrahim al-Muhanna, Moises Naim, Masahisa Naitoh, Kenneth Pollack, Peter Rose, Tyler Priest, David Rubenstein, Lee Schipper,

Gordon Shearer, George Shultz, Frank Verrastro, Julian West, Mason Willrich, Barry Worthington, and Arthur Yan.

I would also like to thank Strobe Talbott and the Brookings Institution, for the opportunity to participate in the Energy Security Initiative and chair the Energy Security Roundtable; Klaus Schwab at the World Economic Forum and Roberto Bocca, and Pawel Konzal at its Energy Community; Richard Levin, John Gaddis, and Ernesto Zedillo for the opportunity to engage on a regular basis with the faculty and students at Yale University; Patti Domm and her colleagues at CNBC.

Last, but hardly least, is my deep gratitude to my family, my biggest supporters and my toughest critics. Experience has taught them to be patient and forgiving, at least up to a point. Alex and Rebecca brought their own knowledge of history and perspectives on this story to the continuing discussion. My wife, Angela Stent, has been through all my book projects. This is a better book for her eye and for the critical judgment that characterizes her own work. Her love and support have been sustaining all along this considerable journey. To her the thanks is lasting.

Daniel Yergin

CREDITS

Photo insert #1:

1. Gary Kieffer/DOD/Time & Life Pictures/ Getty Images
2. Alexsey Druginyn, STF/RIA Novosti
3. Vincent Laforet/AFP/Getty Images
4. N/A
5. Alexsey Druginyn, STF/RIA Novosti
6. Royal Dutch Shell/Newscast
7. Courtesy of Marty Miller
8. OPEC
9. BP
10. Henny Ray Abrams/AFP/Getty Images
11. Ed Kashi/VII
12. GOES 12 Satellite, NASA, NOAA
13. © Kimberly White/Reuters/Corbis
14. Rob McKee
15. Photo by Eric Draper. Courtesy of the George W. Bush Presidential Library
16. AFP/Getty Images
17. Courtesy of The New York Public Library, www.nypl.org
18. Image used with the permission of CME Group, Inc. © 2011. All rights reserved.
19. Shane Bevel
20. Daniel Acker/Bloomberg via Getty Images
21. General Motors
22. Da Qing Oil Field Iron Man Museum. Photo courtesy of Petroleum Industry Press.
23. White House Photograph. Courtesy of the Gerald R. Ford Library
24. Hu Guolin/Imaginechina
25. Zhao Bing/Imaginechina
26. World Economic Forum
27. Sergey Guneev, STF/RIA Novosti
28. © Underwood & Underwood/Corbis
29. Marion King Hubbert Collection, Box #133, American Heritage Center, University of Wyoming
30. Marion King Hubbert Collection, Box #83, American Heritage Center, University of Wyoming
31. The Richard Nixon Presidential Library & Museum
32. Courtesy of The Huntington Library, San Marino, California
33. Anadarko Petroleum Corporation
34. Eliana Fernandes/Petrobras Image Bank
35. John Mosier/ZUMA Press
36. Michael Jacobsen
37. © Yann Arthus-Bertrand/Corbis
38. Courtesy of Barco. Copyright Saudi Aramco; All Rights Reserved
39. Copyright Saudi Aramco; All Rights Reserved
40. Chris Hondros/Getty Images
41. AP Photo/Bill Foley
42. AP Photo/Iranian President's Office
43. Reuters/Fadi al-Assaad
44. www.EastepPhotography.com
45. Cliff Roe
46. Scott Goldsmith
47. Edison National Historic Site
48. Charles Hoff/New York Daily News Archive via Getty Images
49. GE Theater/Courtesy Ronald Reagan Library
50. Hank Walker/Time & Life Pictures/Getty Images
51. © Guy Christian/Hemis/Axiom/ axiomphotographic.com
52. DigitalGlobe via Getty Images

Photo insert #2:

53. The Granger Collection, New York City; All rights reserved
54. Louis Agassiz, *Études sur les glaciers*. Neuchâtel, Jent et Gassmann, 1840.
55. Reproduced by permission of Bridgette Khan
56.–58. Scripps Institution of Oceanography Archives, UC San Diego Libraries
59. © World History/Topham/The Image Works
60. Dwight D. Eisenhower Presidential Library
61. Alan Richards photographer. From The Shelby White and Leon Levy Archives Center, Institute for Advanced Study, Princeton, New Jersey, USA
62. ABC News
63. © *Manchester Daily Express*/SSPL/The Image Works
64. Scanpix/Sipa Press
65. George Bush Presidential Library and Museum
66. Photo provided by the office of Representative Edward Markey
67. Courtesy of the Ronald Coase Institute, Photographer: David Joel
68. Bjorn Sigurdson/AFP/Getty Images
69. Artwork by William J. Hennessy Jr./CourtroomArt.com
70. Courtesy: Jimmy Carter Library
71. Bill Pierce/Time & Life Pictures/Getty Images
72. AP Photo
73. N/A
74. AP Photo
75. © Ron Sachs/CNP/Corbis
76. AP Photo/Marcio Jose Sanchez
77. Georges F. Doriot in classroom, 1963. Harvard Business School Archives Photograph Collection: Faculty and Staff, Baker Library Historical Collections, Harvard Business School (olvwork377919)
78. Bloomberg/*BusinessWeek*
79. Mark Coggins
80. Andy Freeberg
81. ETH-Bibliothek Zurich, Image Archive
82. Reprinted with permission of Alcatel-Lucent USA Inc.
83. National Air and Space Museum, Smithsonian Institution
84. White House Photo
85. Sandia National Laboratories
86. Photo courtesy of John Perlin, from *From Space to Earth*
87. Suntech Power
88. The Western Reserve Historical Society, Cleveland, Ohio
89. Jim Dehlsen, Ecomerit Technologies, LLC
90. Courtesy of Vestas Wind Systems A/S
91. © 2011 Ripley Entertainment Inc. Image courtesy of ASHRAE
92. Carrier Corporation
93. *The Straits Times* © Singapore Press Holdings Limited. Reprinted with permission.
94. Rob Benson Photography
95. Lifang Wang/Xinhua News Agency
96. Ken Feil/*The Washington Post*/Getty Images
97. Reprinted with permission of the DC Public Library, Star Collection, © *Washington Post*
98. Mario R. Durán Ortiz
99. © Richardo Azoury/Olhar Imagem
100. Photo by R. L. Oliver. Copyright © 2006 *Los Angeles Times*. Reprinted with permission.
101. © Bettmann/Corbis
102. Courtesy of the Archives, California Institute of Technology
103. AP Photo/Steve Yeater
104. From the collections of The Henry Ford
105. Cincinnati Museum Center/Getty Images
106. AP Photo/Mark Humphrey
107. Courtesy of Alden Jewell
108. Mark Sullivan/WireImage/Getty Images
109. White House Photo
110. Tesla Motors

NOTES

Prologue

1. George H. W. Bush and Brent Scowcroft, *A World Transformed* (New York: Vintage, 1999), p. 312 ("Nothing will happen"); "The Gulf War," *Frontline,* PBS, aired January 9, 1996 (Egypt's president); cable, U.S. Embassy in Baghdad to Secretary of State, July 25, 1990 ("disputes"); *Al-Hayat,* March 15, 2008.
2. Bush and Scowcroft, *A World Transformed,* p. 317 ("crisis du jour"); Richard Haass, *War of Necessity, War of Choice: A Memoir of Two Iraq Wars* (New York: Simon and Schuster, 2009), pp. 61–62; interview with Boyden Gray.
3. Bush and Scowcroft, *A World Transformed,* pp. 330, 365.
4. Haass, *War of Necessity, War of Choice,* p. 148 ("classic containment"); Martin Indyk, *Innocent Abroad: An Intimate Account of American Peace Diplomacy in the Middle East* (New York: Simon and Schuster, 2009), pp. 40–43, 165 ("dual containment"); Charles Duelfer, *Hide and Seek: The Search for Truth in Iraq* (New York: Public Affairs, 2009), pp. 117–60.
5. Interview with James Placke; Jeffrey Meyer and Mark Califano, *Good Intentions Corrupted: The Oil-for-Food Scandal and the Threat to the U.N.* (New York: Public Affairs, 2006), ch. 4; Independent Inquiry Committee into the United Nations Oil-for-Food Programme, *Report on the Manipulation of the Oil-for-Food Programme,* United Nations, October 27, 2005.
6. Haass, *War of Necessity, War of Choice,* p. 162.
7. Joseph Stanislaw and Daniel Yergin, "Oil: Reopening the Door," *Foreign Affairs* 72, no. 4 (1993), pp. 81–93.

Chapter 1: Russia Returns

1. *New York Times,* December 26, 1991.
2. Interview with Valery Graifer.
3. Vagit Alekperov, introduction to *Dabycha,* the first Russian edition of *The Prize.*
4. Yegor Gaidar, *Collapse of an Empire: Lessons for Modern Russia,* trans. Antonina Bouis (Washington, DC: The Brookings Institution, 2007), p. 102.
5. Interview with Mikhail Gorbachev, *Commanding Heights;* Thane Gustafson, *Crises Amid Plenty: The Politics of Soviet Energy under Brezhnev and Gorbachev* (Princeton: Princeton University Press, 1989), pp. 103–36.
6. Gaidar, *Collapse of an Empire,* pp. 105–9, 239.
7. Interview with Yegor Gaidar; Thane Gustafson, *Wheel of Fortune: The Politics of Russian Oil Under Yeltsin and Putin* (forthcoming), p. 10 (government computers); Anders Aslund, *Russia's Capitalist Revolution: Why Market Reform Succeeded and Democracy Failed* (Washington, DC: Peterson Institute for International Economics, 2007), p. 107 ("wildly").
8. Interview with Vagit Alekperov ("revelation"); Gustafson, *Wheel of Fortune,* pp. 5–14, 54 ("destroying

the oil sector"); Vagit Alekperov, *Oil of Russia: Past, Present, and Future* (Minneapolis: East View Press, 2011), p. 324.

9. Alekperov, *Oil of Russia,* p. 326; Vadim Volkov, *Violent Entrepreneurs: The Use of Force in the Making of Russian Capitalism* (Ithaca: Cornell University Press, 2002), ch. 6.
10. Interview with Vagit Alekperov ("hardest thing"); Alekperov, introduction to *Dabycha* ("Soviet legacy"); Gustafson, *Wheel of Fortune,* p. 38 (walk to work).
11. Chrystia Freeland, *Sale of the Century: The Inside Story of the Second Russian Revolution* (London: Abacus, 2009), pp. 114–23, ch. 8; David E. Hoffman, *The Oligarchs: Wealth and Power in the New Russia* (New York: Public Affairs, 2005), chs. 5, 12.
12. Freeland, *Sale of the Century,* pp. 187, 384; Hoffman, *The Oligarchs,* ch. 18; Mikhail Fridman, "How I Became an Oligarch," Speech, Lvov, November 14, 2010.
13. Interviews with Archie Dunham and Lucio Noto.
14. Interview with Archie Dunham.
15. *Wall Street Journal,* September 27, 2010.
16. John Browne, *Beyond Business* (London: Weidenfeld and Nicolson, 2010), ch. 8.
17. John Browne, pp. 144–51; German Khan interview in *Vedomosti,* January 20, 2010.
18. Peter Baker and Susan Glasser, *Kremlin Rising: Vladimir Putin's Russia and the End of the Revolution* (Potomac Books, 2007), chs. 15, 17; Vladimir Putin, *First Person: An Astonishingly Frank Self-Portrait by Russia's President* (New York: Public Affairs, 2000); Angela Stent, "An Energy Superpower" in Kurt Campbell and Jonathon Price, *The Politics of Global Energy* (Washington, D.C.: Aspen Institute, 2008), pp. 78, 95.

Chapter 2: The Caspian Derby

1. Peter Hopkirk, *The Great Game: The Struggle for Empire in Central Asia* (New York: Kodansha International, 1994), p. 1.
2. *New York Times,* April 26, 2005.
3. Strobe Talbott, "A Farewell to Flashman: American Policy in the Caucasus and Central Asia," speech, July 21, 1997.
4. *New York Times,* October 4, 1998 ("our strategy"); Jan Kalicki, "Caspian Energy at the Crossroads," *Foreign Affairs,* September–October 2001.
5. Robert Tolf, *The Russian Rockefellers: The Saga of the Nobel Family and the Russian Oil Industry* (Stanford: Hoover Institution Press, 1976), pp. xiv ("Russian Rockefeller"), 53–55; Steve LeVine, *The Oil and the Glory: The Pursuit of Empire and Fortune on the Caspian Sea* (New York: Random House, 2007), p. 146; Ronald Suny, "A Journeyman for the Revolution: Stalin and the Labor Movement in Baku," *Soviet Studies,* no. 3, 1972; Simon Sebag Montefiore, *Young Stalin* (New York: Vintage, 2008), p. 187 ("the Oil Kingdom").
6. Daniel Yergin, *The Prize: The Epic Quest for Oil, Money, and Power* (New York: Free Press, 2009), p. 220 ("The Bolsheviks will be cleared"); Geoffrey Jones, *The State and the Emergence of the British Oil Industry* (London: Macmillan, 1981), pp. 209–11 (Bolsheviks); Alexander Stahlberg, *Bounden Duty: The Memoirs of a German Officer, 1932–1945,* trans. Patrica Crampton (London: Brassey's, 1990), pp. 226–27 ("Baku oil").
7. LeVine, *The Oil and the Glory,* pp. 50–51; Jeffrey Goldberg, "The Crude Face of Global Capitalism," *New York Times, Sunday Magazine,* October 4, 1998.
8. LeVine, *The Oil and the Glory,* p. 209 "all roads"; Terry Adams, "Baku Oil Diplomacy and 'Early Oil' 1994–1998: An External Perspective," in *Azerbaijan in Global Politics: Crafting Foreign Policy* (Baku: Azerbaijan Diplomatic Academy, 2009), p. 228 ("disruptive").
9. LeVine, *The Oil and the Glory,* p. 179 ("native son"); Heydar Aliyev, interview, *Azerbaijan International,* Winter 1994, pp. 7–9 ("core leadership").
10. Adams, "Baku Oil Diplomacy," p. 2 ("Mission Impossible").
11. "Early Oil North or West," Report, n.d.
12. Interview with Jan Kalicki.
13. LeVine, *The Oil and the Glory,* p. 350.
14. John Browne, speech, CERA "Tale of Three Seas" Conference, June 20, 2001; Frank Verrastro,

"Caspian and Central Asia: Lessons Learned from the BTC Experience," Center for Strategic and International Studies, *White Paper,* April 2009 ("arrange and negotiate").

15. David Woodward to author (fax machine).
16. Nick Butler, "Energy: The Changing World Order," speech, July 5, 2006 ("engineering project"); *Washington Post,* October 4, 1998 ("real country").

Chapter 3: Across the Caspian

1. Nursultan Nazarbayev, *The Kazakhstan Way,* trans. Jan Butler (London: Stacey International, 2008), pp. 88–89; Steve LeVine, *The Oil and the Glory: The Pursuit of Empire and Fortune on the Caspian Sea* (New York: Random House, 2007), pp. 97–100.
2. Nazarbayev, *The Kazakhstan Way,* p. 93 ("raw materials"); LeVine, *The Oil and the Glory,* p. 92 ("frozen in time").
3. LeVine, *The Oil and the Glory,* pp. 93–94.
4. Yegor Gaidar, *Days of Defeat and Victory,* trans. Jane Ann Miller (Seattle: University of Washington Press, 1999), p. 39 ("trump card"); Nazarbayev, *The Kazakhstan Way,* pp. 1, 112 ("coma," "fundamental principle"); Nursultan Nazarbayev, *Without Right and Left* (London: Class Publishing, 1992), p. 148 ("appendage"); LeVine, *The Oil and the Glory,* p. 117.
5. Nazarbayev, *The Kazakhstan Way,* pp. 95–96 ("contract," Yeltsin); interview with Richard Matzke; LeVine, *The Oil and the Glory,* p. 239 ("prolonged and bitter"); *Washington Post,* October 6, 1998 ("their oil").
6. LeVine, *The Oil and the Glory,* p. 253.
7. Interviews with Ronald Freeman, Lucio Noto, and Jan Kalicki.
8. Interview with Richard Matzke.
9. *Wall Street Journal,* August 28, 2007; *Petroleum Intelligence Weekly,* October 18, 2010.
10. Kabildyn cited a book . . . need to search out . . .
11. John J. Maresca, testimony, U.S. House of Representatives Committee on International Relations, Subcommittee on Asia and the Pacific, February 12, 1998 ("Central Asia," cost-effectiveness); Interview with John Imle and Marty Miller; Steve Coll, *Ghost Wars: The Secret History of the CIA, Afghanistan, and Bin Laden, from the Soviet Invasion to September 10, 2001* (New York: The Penguin Press, 2004), pp. 309–10.
12. Mikhail Gorbachev, "Soviet Lessons from Afghanistan," *International Herald Tribune,* February 4, 2010.
13. Ahmed Rashid, *Taliban: Militant Islam, Oil and Fundamentalism in Central Asia* (New York: Yale University Press, 2000), ch. 3 (Islamic Emirate).
14. *Christian Science Monitor,* February 9, 2007 ("alien"); interviews; *Washington Post,* October 5, 1998 ("implement").
15. Coll, *Ghost Wars,* pp. 309–13 ("no policy," "authorized"); interview with John Imle; "Political and Economic Assessment of Afghanistan, Iran, Pakistan, and Turkemnistan/Russia," Unocal Report, September 3, 1996 ("involvement").
16. Unocal Report ("scenario"); Coll, *Ghost Wars,* pp. 331, 342 ("spiritual leaders").
17. Rosita Forbes, *Conflict: Angora to Afghanistan* (London: Cassell, 1931), p. xvi ("anathema"); interviews with John Imle and Marty Miller.

Chapter 4: "Supermajors"

1. Kenichi Ohmae, *The Borderless World: Power and Strategy in the Interlinked Economy* (New York: HarperCollins, 1991).
2. *New York Times,* December 1, 1997 ("reasonable"); *Petroleum Intelligence Weekly,* December 8, 1997 ("economic stars").
3. Carmen Reinhart and Kenneth Rogoff, *This Time Is Different: Eight Centuries of Financial* Folly (Princeton: Princeton University Press, 2009), pp. 18, 157 ("darling"); Timothy J. Colton, *Yeltsin: A Life* (New York: Basic Books, 2008), p. 411–15 (93 percent); interview with Stanley Fischer, *Commanding Heights;* interview with Robert Rubin, *Commanding Heights.*
4. *New York Times,* December 26, 1998 ("understatement"), January 10, 1999 (cafeteria).

5. Interview with Robert Maguire ("roster"); *Petroleum Intelligence Weekly,* August 31, 1998 ("Were he alive today"); Douglas Terreson, "The Era of the Super-Major," Morgan Stanley, February 1998.
6. Ronald Chernow, *Titan: The Life of John D. Rockefeller Sr.* (New York: Random House, 1998), pp. 554–55; Daniel Yergin, *The Prize: The Epic Quest for Oil, Money, and Power* (New York: Free Press, 2009), chs. 2, 5.
7. Interview with Lucio Noto ("could survive").
8. Interview with Laurance Fuller; interview with John Browne; interview with Samuel Gillespie; John Browne, *Beyond Business* (London: Weidenfeld and Nicolson, 2010), pp. 67–71; Joseph Pratt, *Prelude to Merger: A History of Amoco Corporation, 1973–1998* (Houston: Hart Publications: 2000), pp. 85–86; U.S. Federal Trade Commision, "BP/Amoco Agree to Divest Gas Stations and Terminals to Satisfy FTC Antitrust Concerns," press release, December 30, 1998 ("competition"); Amoco Corp., Proxy Statement/Prospectus, October 30, 1998.
9. Browne, *Beyond Business,* p. 72 ("lap of BP").
10. Interviews with Lee Raymond, Samuel Gillespie, and Lucio Noto; Exxon Corp., *Form S-4 Registration Statement Under the Securities Act of 1933,* April 5, 1999; *New York Times,* December 1, 1998.
11. William J. Baer, testimony, U.S. House of Representatives Committee on Commerce, Subcommittee on Energy and Power, March 10, 1999.
12. *Wall Street Journal,* December 1, 1999.
13. Robert Pitofsky, testimony, U.S. Senate Committee on Commerce, Science, and Transportation, Subcommittee on Consumer Affairs, April 25, 2001 ("prices high"); Jeremy Bulow and Carl Shapiro, "The BP Amoco-ARCO Merger: Alaskan Crude Oil (2000)," in *The Antitrust Revolution,* ed. John Kwoka Jr. and Lawrence White (New York: Oxford University Press, 2008), p. 141 (half a cent), p. 149 ("protect competition"); Browne, *Beyond Business,* pp. 73–74.
14. Interviews with Thierry Desmarest and Vera de Ladoucette.
15. Interviews with David O'Reilly and William Wicker, *New York Times,* October 17, 2000 (Bijur).
16. *Washington Post,* November 19, 2001; interview with Archie Dunham.
17. Interview with Mark Moody-Stuart; Keetie Sluyterman, *Keeping Competitive in Turbulent Markets 19 History of Royal Dutch Shell* (Oxford: Oxford University Press, 2007), pp. 381–95.
18. Interview with David O'Reilly.

Chapter 5: The Petro-State

1. Moises Naim, *Paper Tigers and Minotaurs: The Politics of Venezuela's Economic Reform* (Washington, DC: Carnegie Endowment, 1993), p. 19; Herbert Adams Gibbons, *The New Map of South America* (London: Jonathan Cape, 1929), pp. 249, 252–53.
2. Daniel Yergin, *The Prize: The Epic Quest for Oil, Money, and Power* (New York: Simon and Schuster, 1990), p. 507 ("the devil").
3. Terry L. Karl, *The Paradox of Plenty: Oil Booms and Petro-States* (Berkeley: University of California Press, 1997); Michael L. Ross, "The Political Economy of the Resource Curse," *World Politics* 51 (1999): 297–322 ("rent-seeking behavior"); Christina Marcano and Alberto Barrera Tyszka, *Hugo Chávez,* trans. Kristina Cordero (New York: Random House, 2007), p. 15 (Venezuelan academics).
4. Naim, *Paper Tigers and Minotaurs,* p. 24 ("reversed Midas touch"); interview with Ngazi Okonjo-Iweala.
5. Karl, *The Paradox of Plenty,* p. 71, 123 ("change the world!" "couldn't lose"); Marcano and Tyszka, *Hugo Chávez,* p. 5 ("magical liquid"); Gustavo Coronel, *The Nationalization of the Venezuelan Oil Industry: From Technocratic Success to Political Failure* (Lexington, MA: Lexington Books, 1983).
6. Karl, *The Paradox of Plenty,* p. 72 ("trap"); Naim, *Paper Tigers and Minotaurs,* pp. 34–35.
7. Marcano and Tyszka, *Hugo Chávez,* p. 59; Naim, *Paper Tigers and Minotaurs,* pp. 100–4.
8. Marcano and Tyszka, *Hugo Chávez,* pp. 4, 29, 43.
9. Marcano and Tyszka, *Hugo Chávez,* ch. 17.
10. Interview with Luis Giusti.
11. Interview with Luis Giusti.
12. *Middle East Economic Survey,* December 8, 1997 (Jakarta).
13. *New York Times,* December 6, 1998 ("reeling").
14. Interview with Luis Giusti (fire Giusti); Nicholas Kozloff, *Hugo Chávez: Oil, Politics, and the*

Challenge to the U.S. (New York: Palgrave McMillan, 2006), p. 13; *BusinessWeek* (International Edition), October 26, 1998; Marcano and Tyszka, *Hugo Chávez,* p. 107 (Caldera).

15. Chávez quotes in *New York Times,* April 10, 1999, May 2, 1999, July 27, 2000; Richard Gott, *Hugo Chávez and the Bolivarian Revolution* (London: Verso, 2005), p. 13 ("same sea").
16. Brian A. Nelson, *The Silence and the Scorpion: The Coup Against Chávez and the Making of Modern Venezuela* (New York: Nation Books, 2009), pp. 125–26 (chief of security); *New York Times,* July 28, 2000 ("annihilate," "devils").
17. Bernard Mommer, *Changing Venezuelan Oil Policy,* Oxford Institute for Energy Studies, April 1999; *Middle East Economic Survey,* July 8, 2002.
18. Gott, *Hugo Chávez and the Bolivarian Revolution,* p. 170.
19. *Petroleum Intelligence Weekly,* September 18, 2000 ("soaring oil prices"), September 25, 2000 ("brewing energy crisis").

Chapter 6: Aggregate Disruption

1. Adam Smith, *Paper Money (New York: Summit Books, 1981),* p. 229.
2. *Petroleum Intelligence Weekly,* November 11, 2002.
3. Cristina Marcano and Alberto Barrera Tyszka, *Hugo Chávez: The Definitive Biography of Venezuela's Controversial President* (New York: Random House, 2007), p. 145 ("a great human network"); Brian A. Nelson, *The Silence and the Scorpion: The Coup Against Chávez and the Making of Modern Venezuela* (Nation Books: New York, 2009), pp. 14, 74.
4. Marcano and Tyszka, *Hugo Chávez,* pp. 173, 175, 180.
5. Nelson, *The Silence and the Scorpion,* pp. 246–47.
6. Interview with Ngozi Okonjo-Iweala.
7. Ricardo Soares de Oliveira, *Oil and Politics in the Gulf of Guinea* (New York: Columbia University Press, 2007), pp. 73–79; Nicholas Shaxson, *Poisoned Wells: The Dirty Politics of African Oil* (New York: Palgrave Macmillan, 2007), pp. 16–19; Xavier Sali-i-Martin and Arvind Subramanian, "Addressing the Natural Resource Curse: An Illustration from Nigeria," International Monetary Fund Working Paper, July 2003; Peter M. Lewis, *Growing Apart: Oil, Politics, and Economic Change in Indonesia and Nigeria* (Ann Arbor: University of Michigan Press, 2007), ch. 5.
8. Transparency International, *Global Corruption Report 2004.*
9. WAC Global Services, "Peace and Security in the Niger Delta: Conflict Expert Group Baseline Report," Working Paper for SPDC, December 2003 ("criminalization"); Stephen Davis, *The Potential for Peace and Reconciliation in the Niger Delta,* Coventry Cathedral, February 2009, pp. 67–68, 101–33 ("new dimension"); Stephen Davis, "Prospects for Peace in the Niger Delta," presentation, CSIS Africa Program, June 15, 2009; IRIN Africa, "Nigeria: Piracy Report Says Nigerian Waters the Most Deadly," July 27, 2004 ("international waters"); *Petroleum Intelligence Weekly,* October 4, 2004 ("pushed").
10. Jane's World Insurgency and Terrorism, "Nigeria Delta Groups," March 6, 2006.
11. *Financial Times,* June 7, 2006 (Greenspan).
12. National Oceanic and Atmospheric Administration, "Hurricane Katrina: A Climatological Perspective, Preliminary Report," October 2005; Ivor van Heerden and Mike Bryan, *The Storm: What Went Wrong and Why During Hurricane Katrina—the Inside Story from One Louisiana Scientist* (New York: Viking, 2006), ch. 4.
13. U.S. Department of Energy, *Impact of the 2005 Hurricanes on the Natural Gas Industry in the Gulf of Mexico Region: Final Report* 2006, p. 2; U.S. Department of Energy, "Hurricanes Katrina and Rita Chronology"; U.S. Department of Energy, "Department of Energy's Hurricane Response Chronology, as Referred to by Secretary Bodman at Today's Senate Energy and Natural Resources Committee Hearing," October 27, 2005.

Chapter 7: War in Iraq

1. Interview with Philip Carroll. Michah Sifry and Christopher Cerf, *The Iraq War Reader: History, Documents, and Opinions* (New York: Simon and Schuster, 2003), p. 618 ("addiction"); Richard Haass, *War of Necessity, War of Choice: A Memoir of Two Iraq Wars* (New York: Simon and Schuster, 2009), p. 162; Paul Pillar, "Intelligence, Policy, and the War in Iraq" *Foreign Affairs* 85, no. 2 (2006)

("broad consensus"), p. 20; Report to the President, March 31, 2005, *The Commission on the Intelligence Capabilities of the United States Regarding Weapons of Mass Destruction,* pp. 157–87.

2. *New York Times,* February 10, 2003 ("indisputable"); interview ("no evidence").
3. *New York Times,* October 7, 2004 ("deceiving"); Sifry and Cerf, *The Iraq War Reader,* p. 413 (chemical and biological); interview.
4. Catherine Collins and Douglas Frantz, *Fallout: The True Story of the CIA's Secret War on Nuclear Trafficking* (New York: Free Press, 2011), p. 23; Laura Bush, *Spoken from the Heart* (New York: Scribner, 2010), pp. 242, 277; George W. Bush, *Decision Points* (New York: Crown, 2010), p. 253; Haass, *War of Necessity, War of Choice,* p. 234 ("unable to prevent"); Pillar, "Intelligence, Policy, and the War in Iraq," p. 21 ("any analysis").
5. Thomas E. Ricks, *Fiasco: The American Military Adventure in Iraq* (New York: Penguin Press, 2007), chs. 2–3; interview with John Negroponte ("toughest message").
6. *New York Times,* August 27, 2002 ("infinitely more difficult"); Sifry and Cerf, *The Iraq War Reader,* p. 269 ("materialize"); Ricks, *Fiasco,* p. 30; George Packer, *The Assassin's Gate: America in Iraq* (New York: Farrar, Straus and Giroux, 2005), ch. 4; Michael R. Gordon and Bernard E. Trainor, *Cobra II: The Inside Story of the Invasion and Occupation of Iraq* (New York: Random House, 2006), pp. 72–73.
7. Haass, *War of Necessity, War of Choice,* p. 206 ("true threat"); Ricks, *Fiasco,* pp. 5, 65 ("not have an easy time").
8. Interview with John Negroponte.
9. Bob Woodward, *Plan of Attack* (New York: Simon and Schuster, 2004), p. 323; interview ("proposal to invest").
10. Donald Rumsfeld, "The Future of Iraq," speech, School of Advanced International Studies, Johns Hopkins University, Washington, DC, December 5, 2005 ("speed and agility"); *Washington Post,* February 27, 2003 (Gen. Shinseki); Donald Rumsfield, "Beyond Nation Building," speech, Intrepid Sea-Air-Space Museum, New York City, February 14, 2003; Gordon and Trainor, *Cobra II,* pp. 459, 506 (Franks). Also Donald Rumsfeld, *Known and Unknown: A Memoir* (New York: Sentinel, 2011), pp. 482–83; 649–51.
11. Pillar, "Intelligence, Policy, and the War in Iraq," p. 22 ("strong wind"); Brent Scowcroft, "Don't Attack Saddam," *Wall Street Journal,* August 15, 2002; interview with Brent Scowcroft; Haass, *War of Necessity, War of Choice,* p. 226 ("all else is jeopardized"); International Monetary Fund, "Iraq: Macroeconomic Assessment," October 21, 2003 (government revenues); Ricks, *Fiasco,* pp. 96–98 ("its own reconstruction").
12. Gordon and Trainor, *Cobra II,* p. 459.
13. Interview with Philip Carroll; Thomas Ghadhban, CERA, "Expansion of Iraq's Crude Oil Production Capacity," presentation, "Tale of Three Cities" conference, January 20–22, 2006 (twenty-three were put into production); Issam al-Chalabi, "Oil in Postwar Iraq," presentation, CERA "Tale of Three Cities" conference, January 11–13, 2003.
14. Interview with Philip Carroll; L. Paul Bremer III and Malcolm McConnell, *My Year in Iraq: The Struggle to Build a Future of Hope* (New York: Simon and Schuster, 2006), p. 61.
15. Gordon and Trainor, *Cobra II,* p. 481 ("civil servants"); interview with Aleksander Kwaśniewski; Bremer and McConnell, *My Year in Iraq,* pp. 36–39; Terence Adams to author.
16. "Iraq's Come Back: Consequences for the Oil Market and the Middle East," CERA, January 2004; *New York Times,* March 17, 2008 (expletive); Gordon and Trainor, *Cobra II,* pp. 483–84 ("incendiary").
17. Rumsfeld, *Known and Unknown,* pp. 473–78 ("stuff happens"); Gordon and Trainor, *Cobra II,* pp. 46, 465, 472, 575; *New York Times,* October 19, 2004; Bush, *Decision Points,* pp. 257–59.
18. Gordon and Trainor, *Cobra II,* pp. 489–95, 579.
19. Jeremy Greenstock, "What Must be Done Now," *Economist,* May 6, 2004.
20. Interview with Rob McKee; Vera de Ladoucette and Leila Benali, "Iraqi Production: More (but Slower) Growth ahead," CERA, November 12, 2003 (Baath plan).
21. *Petroleum Intelligence Weekly,* June 21, 2004; Michael Makovsky, "Oil's Not Well in Iraq," *Weekly Standard,* February 19, 2007; Michael Makovsky, "Iraq's Oil Progress," *Weekly Standard,* August 25, 2008.

Chapter 8: The Demand Shock

1. Michael Wallis, *Oil Man: The Story of Frank Phillips and Phillips Petroleum* (New York: Doubleday, 1988), p. 123 ("oil fever").
2. *Petroleum Intelligence Weekly,* February 6, 2004; interview.
3. Guy Caruso, testimony, U.S. Senate Subcommittee on Energy and Water Development, June 25, 2008; *Wall Street Journal,* April 26, 2004 ("guidelines," "curious," "skeptically").
4. IHS CERA, "Capital Costs Analysis Forum—Upstream," January 2009.
5. Ke Tang and Wei Xiong, "Index Investment and the Financialization of Commodities" January 2011, p. 13 ("co-move").
6. Daniel O'Sullivan, *Black Gold, Paper Barrels and Oil Price Barrels* (London: Harriman House, 2009).
7. Joe Roeber, *The Evolution of Oil Markets: Trading Instruments and Their Role in Oil Price Formation* (Royal Institute of International Affairs, 1993).
8. CME Group, "2010 Commodities Trading Challenge: Competition Rules and Procedures" ("anticipating").
9. Interview.
10. Jim O'Neill to author; Jim O'Neill, "Building Better Global Economic BRICs, Goldman Sachs Global Economics Paper No. 66, November 30, 2001; *Financial Times,* January 15, 2010.
11. Interview with Mark Fisher.
12. Interview with Robert Shiller. Shiller's definition of a speculative bubble: "A situation in which news of price increases spur investor enthusiasm, which spreads by psychological contagion from person to person, in the process amplifying stories that might justify the price increases and bringing in a larger and larger class of investors, who, despite doubts about the real value of an investment, are drawn to it partly through envy of others' successes and partly through a gambler's excitement." In the case of oil, hower, it would seem that many of the investors had deep convictions but few doubts about what they took to be the "real"—or future—value of petroleum. See Robert Shiller, *Irrational Exuberance,* 2nd ed. (New York: Broadway Books, 2005), p. 2.
13. Peter Jackson and Keith Eastwood, "Finding the Critical Numbers: What Are the Real Decline Rates of Global Oil Production?," IHS CERA, November 2007.
14. Mohsin S. Khan, "The 2008 Oil Price 'Bubble,'" policy brief, Peterson Institute for International Economics, August 2009; *Wall Street Journal,* August 17, 2010.
15. CalPERS, "CalPERS Sets Guidelines for New Asset Class—Commodities, Forestland, Inflation-Linked Bonds," February 19, 2008; *Bloomberg,* February 28, 2008; *Petroleum Intelligence Weekly,* May 12, 2008; interview with David Davis.
16. *Wall Street Journal,* May 17, 2008 ("more oil"); Jeffrey Curie et al., "A Lesson from Long-Dated Oil: A Steadily Rising Price Forecast," Goldman Sachs *Energy Watch,* May 16, 2008 ("structural bull market").
17. Edward Morse, "Oil Dot-com," Lehman Brothers Energy Special Report, May 2008; interview with Edward Morse; *Petroleum Intelligence Weekly,* June 2, 2008 ("biggest ramification").
18. *New York Times,* May 23, 2008 ("gouging the American public"); May 22, 2008 ("ethical compass").
19. Interview, *Bloomberg,* June 16, 2008 (travel industry); interview with David Davis.
20. *New York Times,* June 23, 2008, June 20, 2008 ("deliberately chosen"); *Wall Street Journal,* June 23, 2008, Associated Press, June 20, 2008 (memo).
21. Interview with David Davis; *Oil Bubble or New Reality: How Will Skyrocketing Oil Prices Affect the U.S. Economy: Hearings Before the Joint Economic Committee, U.S. Congress, 110th Congress, 2nd Session,* June 25, 2008, p. 10.
22. California State Board of Equalization, Fuel Taxes Division, Statistics & Reports—2008, at http://www.boe.ca.gov/sptaxprog/spftrpts08.htm.
23. The Pew Campaign for Fuel Efficiency, *A History of Fuel Economy: One Decade of Innovation, Two Decades of Inaction,* January 2, 2011.
24. Admiral Dennis Blair, testimony, U.S. Senate Committee on Commerce, Science and Transportation, May 3, 2007; Energy Security Leadership Council, *Recommendations to the Nation on Reducing U.S. Oil Dependence,* December 2006.
25. Interviews; James Hamilton, "Oil and the Economy: The Impact of Rising Global Demand on the

U.S. Economy," hearings, Joint Economic Committee, U.S. Congress, May 20, 2009, pp. 27–29; interview with Rick Wagoner, *Petroleum Intelligence Weekly,* July 14, 2008.

26. International Energy Agency, *World Energy Outlook 2010* (Paris: OECD/IEA, 2010), pp. 605–11.
27. *New York Times,* July 16, 2008; *Petroleum Intelligence Weekly,* July 21, 2008.
28. Benjamin S. Bernanke, "Economic Policy: Lessons from History," speech, Center for the Study of the Presidency and the Congress, April 8, 2010; Hilary Till, "The Oil Markets: Let the Data Speak for Itself," EDHEC Working Paper, October 2008, p. 22.
29. *Financial Times,* September 8, 2009.
30. Interview with Robert Shiller.

Chapter 9: China's Rise

1. PetroChina Company Limited, *Global Offering,* March 27, 2000.
2. Cheng Li, ed., *China's Emerging Middle Class: Beyond Economic Transformation* (Washington, D.C.: Brookings Institution Press, 2010).
3. George W. Bush, *Decision Points* (New York: Crown, 2010), p. 427.
4. Interview with Zhou Qingzu; interview with Wang Tao; Eliot Blackwelder, "Petroleum Resources of China and Siberia," *Mining and Metallurgy* 187, July 1922 ("never produce").
5. H. C. Ling, *The Petroleum Industry of the People's Republic of China* (Palo Alto: Hoover Institution Press, 1975), p. 237; Yu Qiuli, minister of petroleum from 1958 to 1964, from Yu Qiuli, *YuQiuli: Huiyilu (Memoirs)* (Beijing: Liberation Army Press, 1996), p. 1003, cited in Erica Downs, "China's Quest for Oil Self-Sufficiency in the 1960s," unpublished manuscript, 2001, p. 5 ("cut off").
6. Erica Downs, "China's Quest for Oil Self-sufficiency in the 1960s."
7. Ling, *The Petroleum Industry of the People's Republic of China,* pp. 152–59, 188–89, 209, 230–39; interview with Zhou Qingzu.
8. Interview with Zhou Qingzu.
9. Henry A. Kissinger to the President, May 7, 1971; Kissinger to Ambassador Farland, June 22, 1971; Kissinger to Farland, late June 1971, the National Security Archive; Henry A. Kissinger, *White House Years* (Boston: Little Brown, 1979), pp. 738–41.
10. Erica Downs, "China's Energy Rise," in Brantly Womack, *China's Rise in Historical Perspective* (Lanham, MD: Rowman & Littlefield, 2010), p. 181 ("petroleum export–led"); Downs III, p. 24 ("must export"); Daniel Yergin and Joseph Stanislaw, *The Commanding Heights: The Battle for the World Economy* (New York: Simon and Schuster, 2002), ch. 7.
11. Joseph Fewsmith, *Dilemmas of Reform in China: Political Conflict and Economic Debate* (New York: M. E. Sharpe, 1994), p. 17.
12. Interview.
13. Interview with Zhou Qingzu; PetroChina Company Limited, *Global Offering,* p. 73.
14. Interview with Zhou Jiping.
15. Julie Jiang and Jonathan Sinton, *Overseas Investments by Chinese National Oil Companies* (Paris: International Energy Agency, 2011), p. 22; Erica Downs, *Inside China Inc.: China Development Bank's Cross-Border Energy Deals,* John L. Thornton China Center Monograph Series, no. 3, March 2011 (Washington, DC: Brookings Institution, 2011).
16. *Moscow Times,* September 28, 2010 ("new start").
17. Interview ("throwing a match"); Frank J. Gaffney Jr., Statement of Frank J. Gaffney Jr., hearing, "National Security Implications of the Possible Merger of the China National Off-shore Oil Corporation (CNOOC) with Unocal Corporation," before the Committee on Armed Services, House of Representatives, July 13, 2005, pp. 6, 8; interview with Fu Chengyu; *Xinhua,* October 12, 2006 ("talking about the win-win"); Chevron, "Chevron Acquires Interest in Three Deepwater Exploration Blocks in China," September 7, 2010 ("welcome the opportunity"); interview.
18. Erica S. Downs, "Business Interest Groups in Chinese Politics: The Case of the Oil Companies" in *China's Changing Political Landscape: Prospects for Democracy,* ed. Cheng Li (Washington, DC, Brookings Institution, 2008); interview with Zhou Jiping; Jiang and Sinton, *Overseas Investments by Chinese National Oil Companies,* pp. 7, 25; Erica Downs, "Who's Afraid of China's Oil Companies?" *Energy Security: Economics, Politics, Strategy, and Implications* (Washington, DC: Brookings Institution Press, 2010), ch. 4; Fu Chengyu, speech, CERAWeek, February 2006; interviews.

Chapter 10: China in the Fast Lane

1. Interviews.
2. *Far Eastern Economic Review,* February 2004 ("certain powers").
3. *Time,* June 28, 2004; *Wall Street Journal,* July 9, 2004.
4. *Voice of America,* July 29, 2010 ("lifeline of our commerce").
5. *Far Eastern Economic Review,* April 2006; *Wall Street Journal,* October 4, 2010 ("hegemon"); Office of the Secretary of Defense, U.S. Department of Defense, "Military and Security Developments Involving the People's Republic of China 2010"; *Washington Post,* July 31, 2010; See Wang Jisi, "China's Search for a Grand Strategy," *Foreign Affairs,* March–April 2011, p. 71 ("reckless"). For a discussion of the emergence of the "core interest" concept, see Michael Swaine, "China's Assertive Behavior, Part 1, 'On Core Interests,'" *China Leadership Monitor,* No. 34 (2011).
6. Hu Jintao, speech, G8 Summit, St., Petersburg, July 2006 (dilemmas); interview ("exporting to America"); Zhou Jiping, "Embracing the Low Carbon Economy of Sustainable Energy Development," speech, International Petroleum Technology Conference, Doha, December 7, 2009.
7. Interview.
8. Kelly Sims Gallagher, *China Shifts Gears: Automakers, Oil, Pollution, and Development* (Cambridge: Massachusetts Institute of Technology Press, 2006), pp. 2, 34–36, 63–79, 172; Jim Mann, *Beijing Jeep: A Case Study of Western Business in China* (Boulder: Westview Press, 1997); *Wall Street Journal,* June 8, 2004.
9. *New York Times,* December 22, 2010.
10. The World Bank and State Environmental Protection Agency of the People's Republic of China, *Cost of Pollution in China: Economic Estimates of Physical Damages,* 2007; Daniel H. Rosen and Trevor Houser, *China Energy: A Guide for the Perplexed,* China Balance Sheet Project, Center for Strategic and International Studies and the Peterson Institute for International Economics, May 2007, pp. 13, 42.
11. Liu Zhenya, "Strong Smart Grid," speech, July 26, 2010.
12. Julie Jiang and Jonathan Sinton, *Overseas Investments by Chinese National Oil Companies: Assessing the Drivers and Impacts* (Paris: International Energy Agency, 2011), p. 20.

Chapter 11: Is the World Running Out of Oil?

1. Kenneth S. Deffeyes, *Hubbert's Peak: The Impending World Oil Shortage* (Princeton: Princeton University Press, 2001), pp. ix, 10, 158 ("chaos," Thanksgiving); Michael C. Ruppert, "Colin Campbell on Oil: Perhaps the World's Foremost Expert on Oil and the Oil Business Confirms the Ever More Apparent Reality of the Post 9-11 World," The Wilderness Publications, 2002 ("extinction"); Oil Depletion Analysis Centre, "New Oil Projects Cannot Meet World Needs This Decade," The Wilderness Publications, November 16, 2004 ("unbridgable"); *Independent,* June 14, 2007; UK Energy Research Centre, *Global Oil Depletion: An Assessment of the Evidence for a Near Term Peak in Global Oil Production* (London, 2009), p. x .
2. International Energy Agency, *World Energy Outlook 2010* (Paris: International Energy Agency, 2010), p. 139.
3. Ali Larijani, speech, Arab Strategy Forum, Dubai, UAE, December 5, 2006 ("expiration date").
4. Daniel Yergin, *The Prize: The Epic Quest for Oil, Money, and Power* (New York: Free Press, 2008), p. 36 (Archbold).
5. H. A. Garfield, *Final Report of the U.S. Fuel Adminstrator, 1917–1919* (Washington, DC: GPO, 1921), p. 8 ("walk to church"); Francis Delaisi, *Oil: Its Influence on Politics,* trans. C. Leonard Leese (London: Labour Publishing, 1922), pp. 86–91 (Curzon); *National Petroleum News,* October 29, 1919, p. 51 ("ever-increasing decline"); Dennis J. O'Brien, "The Oil Crisis and the Foreign Policy of the Wilson Administration, 1917–1921," Ph.D. dissertation, University of Missouri, 1974 ("necessary supply").
6. Robert Goralski and Russell W. Freeburg, *Oil & War: How the Deadly Struggle for Fuel in WWII Meant Victory or Defeat* (New York: William Morrow, 1987); Arthur J. Marder, *Old Friends, New Enemies: The Royal Navy and the Imperial Japanese Navy* (Oxford: Oxford University Press, 1981), pp. 166–7 ("scarecrows"); Basil Liddell Hart, *The Rommel Papers,* trans. Paul Findlay (New York: Da Capo Press, 1985), p. 453.
7. Donella Meadows, Dennis Meadows, Jorgen Randers and William Behrens III, *The Limits to Growth: A Report for the Club of Rome's Project on the Predicament of Mankind* (New York: Signet Books, 1974).

8. *Chemical Week,* July 19, 1978 ("twilight").
9. *Independent,* June 14, 2007 ("glass").
10. William E. Akin, *Technocracy and the American Dream: The Technocratic Movement 1900–1941* (Berkeley: University of California Press, 1977), ch. 6. *The Leading Edge* 2, no. 2 (February 1983) ("manpower and raw materials"); Tyler Priest, "Peak Oil Prophecies: Oil Supply Assessments and the Future of Nature in U.S. History," unpublished paper, p. 17 ("hieroglyphics"); Fred Meissner, "M. King Hubbert as a Teacher," presentation, Geological Society of America Annual Meeting, Seattle, Washington, 2003 ("comprehend"); David Doan, "Memorial to M. King Hubbert," *Geological Society of America* Memorials 24 (1994), p. 40.
11. Interview with Pete Rose; Priest, "Peak Prophecies," pp. 18, 21–22 ("mathematician that he is"), fn. 52–53 (Broussard).
12. *Washington Post,* April 7, 1974 ("light post").
13. M. King Hubbert, speech, American Petroleum Institute, March 8, 1956 ("blip in the span of time"); *Chemical Week,* July 19, 1978 (lifetimes); T. N. Narasimhan, "M. King Hubbert: A Centennial Tribute," *Ground Water* 41, no. 5 (2003), p. 561 ("period of non-growth").
14. Colin Campbell and Jean Laherrere, "The End of Cheap Oil," *Scientific American,* March 1998 ("only minor deviations"); Peter Jackson, "Why the 'Peak Oil' Theory Falls Down," IHS CERA, November 2006, Steven Gorelick to author; Peter R. Rose to author.
15. Interview with Pete Rose ("very static view"); William L. Fisher, "How Technology Has Confounded U.S. Gas Resource Estimates," *Oil and Gas Journal* 42, no. 3 (1994).
16. Leonardo Maugeri, "Squeezing More Oil from the Ground," *Scientific American,* October 2009, pp. 56–63; "The Benefits of DOFF: A Global Assessment of Potential Oil Recovery Increases," IHS CERA, August 19, 2005 (digital oil field).
17. Matthew R. Simmons, *Twilight in the Desert: The Coming Saudi Oil Shock and the World Economy* (Hoboken: John Wiley, 2006) (central tenet).
18. Interview with Khalid Al-Falih ("robust").
19. Interview with Mark Moody-Stuart; Peter McCabe, "Energy Resources: Cornucopia or Empty Barrel?" *AAPG Bulletin* 82, no. 11 (1998), pp. 2110–34 (revisions and additions); McCabe, "Energy Resources," p. 2131 ("symmetrical"). A good case study of "not running out" is provided by the Permian Basin, one of only two "super giant" oil fields in the Lower 48.
20. Peter Jackson, Jonathan Craig, Leta Smith, Samia Razak and Simon Wardell, "'Peak Oil' Postponed Again," IHS CERA, October 2010. For two thoughtful and highly informative analyses on depletion and "running out," see Steven Gorelick, *Oil Panic and the Global Crisis: Predictions and Myths* (Oxford: Wiley-Blackwell, 2010) and Leonardo Maugeri, *The Age of Oil: The Mythology, History, and Future of the World's Most Controversial Resource* (Westport: Praeger, 2006), chs. 16–20.

Chapter 12: Unconventional

1. Rod Lathim, *The Spirit of the Big Yellow House* (Santa Barbara: Emily Publications, 1995), pp. 33–47; William Leffler, Richard A. Pattaroizzi, and Gordon Sterling, *Deepwater Exploration and Production: A Non-Technical Guide* (Tulsa: Pennwell, 2011), ch. 1.
2. Peter Jackson, Jonathan Craig, Leta Smith, Samia Razak, and Simon Wardell, "Peak Oil Postponed Again: Liquids Production Capacity to 2030," IHS CERA, 2010.
3. John S. Ezell, *Innovations in Energy: The Story of Kerr-McGee* (Norman: University of Oklahoma Press, 1979), pp. 152–69.
4. Tyler Priest, *The Offshore Imperative: Shell's Search for Petroleum in Postwar America* (College Station: Texas A&M Press, 2007), p. 245.
5. James Burkhard, Pete Stark, and Leta Smith, "Oil Well Blowout and the Future of Deepwater E&P," IHS CERA, 2010. In the late 1970s, deepwater was considered anything over six hundred feet. Today two thousand feet is a customary definition for the point at which deepwater begins.
6. *New York Times,* December 26, 2010, May 7, 2010, September 7, 2010, May 28, 2010; *Wall Street Journal,* May 27, 2010; BP, *Deepwater Horizon Accident Investigation Report,* September 8, 2010; National Commission on the BP Deepwater Horizon Oil Spill and Offshore Drilling, *Deep Water: The Gulf Oil Disaster and the Future of Offshore Drilling,* January 2011. Det Norske Veritas, *Forensic Examination of Deepwater Horizon Blowout Preventer,* final report, Volume 1, March 20, 2011.

7. Tony Hayward, speech, Cambridge Union Society, November 10, 2010 ("could not happen").
8. U.S. Department of Interior, "Increased Safety Measures for Energy Development on the Outer Continental Shelf," May 27, 2010, p. 6.
9. National Commission on the BP Deepwater Horizon Oil Spill and Offshore Drilling, "Stopping the Spill: The Five-Month Effort to Kill the Macondo Well," Staff Working Paper, number 6; Bloomberg, September 19, 2010.
10. Federal Interagency Solutions Group, *Oil Budget Calculation: Deepwater Horizon*; November 2010.
11. Terry Hazen et al., "Deep Sea Oil Plume Enriches Oil-Degrading Bacteria," *Science* 330, no. 6001 (2010), pp. 204–8; *New York Times*, September 20, 2010.
12. *Wall Street Journal,* January 7, 2011.
13. Barack Obama, speech, Andrews Air Force Base, March 31, 2010.
14. BP America, *Deepwater Horizon Accident Investigation Report,* pp. 11, 32.
15. National Commission on the BP Deepwater Horizon Oil Spill and Offshore Drilling, *Deepwater: The Gulf Oil Disaster and the Future of Offshore Drilling,* ch. 4.
16. IHS Global Insight, *The Economic Impact of the Gulf of Mexico Offshore Oil and Natural Industry and the Role of the Independents,* July 21, 2010, pp. 9–11.
17. Interview with José Sergio Gabrielli de Azevedo ("had to go offshore"); *Upstream Online,* May 4, 2009 (Lula).
18. U.S. Senate Foreign Relations Committee, Subcommittee on International Economic Policy, "Overview on Global Energy Security Issues," April 8, 2003.
19. IHS CERA, *The Role of Canadian Oil Sands in US Oil Supply,* Canadian Oil Sands Dialogue, April 2010.
20. Paul Chatsko, *Developing Alberta's Oil Sands: From Karl Clark to Kyoto* (Calgary: University of Calgary Press, 2004), pp. 97–98 ("promising way"); Arthur M. Johnson, *The Challenge of Change: The Sun Oil Company 1945–1977* (Columbus: Ohio State University, 1983), p. 131 ("enamored"); Peter McKenzie Brown, Gordon Jaremko and David Finch, *The Great Oil Age* (Calgary: Detselig, 1993), p. 75 ("important role").
21. Chatsko, *Developing Alberta's Oil Sands,* p. 218 ("single most important"); IHS CERA, *Oil Sands Technology: Past, Present, and Future,* Canadian Oil Sands Energy Dialogue, January 2011.
22. Energy Resources Conservation Board, "ERCB Conditionally Approves Tailings Plan for Shell Muskeg River Project," press release, September 20, 2010.
23. IHS CERA, *Oil Sands, Greenhouse Gases, and US Oil Supply: Getting the Numbers Right,* Canadian Oil Sands Dialogue, September 2010.
24. U.S. Geological Service Survey, "An Estimate of Recoverable Oil Resources of the Orinoco Oil Belt," October 2009; Associated Press, May 2, 2007 ("bosses made us come"); Reuters, May 2, 2007; *Houston Chronicle,* May 5, 2007 ("our bosses"); EFE news service, May 1, 2007; *Financial Times,* May 1, 2007.
25. Guy Elliott Mitchell, "Billions of Barrels Locked Up in Rocks," *National Geographic,* February 1918, p. 201; *Washington Post,* June 16, 1979 ("doing without").
26. Leta Smith, Sang-Won Kim, Pete Stark, and Rick Chamberlain, "The Shale Gale Goes Oily," IHS CERA, 2011.
27. Interview with John Hess.
28. Peter Jackson, Jonathan Craig, Leta Smith, Samia Razak, and Simon Wardell, "'Peak Oil' Postponed Again: Liquids Production Capacity to 2030," IHS CERA, 2010.

Chapter 13: The Security of Energy

1. Rondo Cameron and Larry Neal, *A Concise Economic History of the World* (Oxford: Oxford University Press, 2002), p. 118.
2. Randolph S. Churchill, *Winston Churchill,* vol. 2, *Young Statesman, 1901–1904* (London: Heinemann, 1968), p. 529; Winston S. Churchill, *The World Crisis,* vol. 1 (New York: Scribners, 1928), pp. 130–36 ("navel supremcy"); Winston S. Churchill, *Churchill,* vol. 2, *Companion Volume,* part 3, 1926–27 ("less size").
3. John DeNovo, "Petroleum and the United States Navy Before World War I," *The Mississippi Valley Historical Review* 41, no. 4, March 1955, pp. 641–56; Aurthur A. Hardinge, *A Diplomatist in the East* (London: Jonathan Cape, 1928), p. 280 ("knocked down"); Parliamentary Debates, Commons, July 17, 1913, pp. 1474–77 ("variety").

4. Interview with Richard Fairbanks.
5. James Woolsey.
6. Robert J. Lieber, *The Oil Decade: Conflict and Cooperation in the West* (New York: Praeger, 1983), p. 19.
7. 106th Cong. Rec., 2nd Session, vol. 146, part 13, p. 19330 ("SPR was created").
8. Bruce A. Beaubouef, *The Strategic Petroleum Reserve: U.S. Energy Security and Oil Politics, 1975–2005* (College Station: Texas A&M University Press, 2007), ch. 5, epilogue.
9. *Wall Street Journal,* July 29, 2003; Bassam Fattouh and Coby van der Linde, *The International Energy Forum: Twenty Years of Consumer-Produce Country Dialogue in a Changing World* (Riyadh: IEF, 2011), pp. 51, 61, 99–100; interviews.
10. North American Electric Reliability Corporation and the U.S. Departmnt of Energy, *High-Impact, Low-Frequency Event Risk to the North American Bulk Power System,* June 2010, pp. 29–30. Dennis C. Blair, "Annual Threat Assessment of the U.S. Intelligence Community for the Senate Select Committee on Intelligence," February 2, 2010 ("severely threatened"); *Wall Street Journal,* May 18, 2011 ("bad new world").
11. Joseph McClelland, Testimony Before the Committee on Energy and Natural Resources, U.S. Senate, May 5, 2011 (smart grid).
12. *Cybersecurity Two Years Later: A Report of the CSIS Commission on Cybersecurity for the 44th Presidency* (Washington, DC: CSIS, 2011), p. 1 ("steamboats"); Charles Ebinger and Kevin Massey, "Enhancing Smart Grid Cybersecurity in the Age of Information Warfare," Brookings Energy Security Initiative, February 2011; Bruce Averill and Eric A. M. Luijf, "Canvassing the Cyber Security Landscape: Why Energy Companies Need to Pay Attention," *Journal of Energy Security,* May 2010.
13. U.S. Energy Information Administration, "World Oil Transit Chokepoints," EIA website.
14. Donna J. Nincic, "The 'Radicalization' of Maritime Piracy: Implications for Maritime Energy Security," *Journal of Energy Security,* December 2010; *Jane's Navy International,* September 28, 2010.

Chapter 14: Shifting Sands in the Persian Gulf

1. R. W. Ferrier, *The History of the British Petroleum Company, Vol. I, 1901–1932* (Cambridge: Cambridge University Press, 1982), p. 161 (Albania); Mira Wilkins, *The Maturing of Multinational Enterprise: American Business Abroad from 1914 to 1970* (Cambridge: Harvard University Press, 1974), pp. 215–17 ("total loss"); Daniel Yergin, *The Prize: The Epic Quest for Oil, Money, and Power* (New York: Free Press, 1991), ch. 20 ("prize") and chs. 24, 27, 29, Epilogue for the oil crisis.
2. Ali Al-Naimi, "Achieving Energy Stability in Uncertain Times," speech, CERAWeek, February 10, 2010; Ali Al-Naimi, speech, Center for Strategic and International Studies, May 2, 2006.
3. *Jane's Intelligence Review,* January 1, 2007 (legitimate target); Thomas Hegghammer, *Jihad in Saudi Arabia* (Cambridge: Cambridge University Press, 2010), p. 215 (safe house).
4. *Jane's Intelligence Review,* May 1, 2006; *Financial Times,* August 27, 2007; Peter Bergen and Bruce Hoffman, *Assessing the Terrorist Threat: A Report of the Center's National Security Preparedness Group,* Bipartisan Policy Center, September 10, 2009; *The National Interest,* May 13, 2009 (economic warfare); Ali Al-Naimi, speech, Center for Strategic and International Studies, May 2, 2006.
5. *Washington Post,* March 26, 2011.
6. United Nations Development Programme and Arab Fund for Economic and Social Development, *Arab Human Development Report 2002* (New York: United Nations, 2002).
7. Navtej Dhillon and Tarik Yousef, eds., *Generation in Waiting: The Unfulfilled Promise of Young People in the Middle East* (Washington, DC: Brookings Institution, 2009).
8. Clay Shirky, "The Political Power of Social Media," *Foreign Affairs* 90, no. 1 (2011), pp. 28–41.
9. Marcus Noland and Howard Pack, *The Arab Economies in a Changing World* (Washington, DC: Peterson Institute, 2007), pp. 99–111.
10. David Hobbs and Daniel Yergin, "Fiscal Fitness: How Taxes at Home Help Determine Competitiveness Abroad," IHS CERA, August 2010; interview with Lucian Pugliaresi.
11. Bhushan Bahree, "Fields of Dreams: The Great Iraqi Oil Rush: Its Potential, Challenges, and Limits" IHS CERA, March 2010.
12. *Middle East Economic Survey,* October 11, 2010, October 18, 2010.
13. Michael Axworthy, *A History of Iran: Empire of the Mind* (New York: Basic Books, 2010), p. 271 ("stupidity").

14. Kenneth Pollack, *The Persian Puzzle: The Conflict Between Iran and America* (New York: Random House, 2004), pp. 267, 286.
15. Karim Sadjadpour, *Reading Khamenei: The World View of Iran's Most Powerful Leader* (Washington, DC: Carnegie Endowment for International Peace, 2009), pp. vi, 15; interview with Archie Dunham.
16. Interview.
17. *New York Times,* March 10, 1995 (Christopher).
18. Pollack, *The Persian Puzzle*, pp. 272, 282 (executive order); interview with Archie Dunham.
19. Axworthy, *A History of Iran,* p. 277 ("constitutional government"); Robin Wright, *The Iran Primer: Power, Politics, and U.S. Policy* (Washington, DC: US Institute of Peace Press, 2010), p. 140.
20. Madeleine Albright, *Madame Secretary: A Memoir* (New York: Miramax, 2003), pp. 319–26.
21. David Frum, *The Right Man: An Inside Account of the Bush White House* (New York: Random House, 2005), ch. 12 ("axis of evil"); James Dobbins, *After the Taliban: Nation-Building in Afghanistan* (Washington, DC: Potomac Books, 2008), pp. 121–22, 142–44 ("hunt down the Taliban"); Pollack, *The Persian Puzzle,* pp. 346–47 (military cooperation).
22. *New York Times,* September 24, 2010 ("declining American economy"); Twenty Quotes (embraces Shia islam); Joshua Teitelbaum, "What Iranian Leaders Really Say About Doing Away With Israel," Jerusalem Center for Public Affairs, 2008 ("wipe Israel off the map"); Axworthy, *A History of Iran,* pp. 290, 321 ("erased from the pages of time").
23. Islamic Republic News Agency, December 5, 2006 ("good neighborliness").
24. U.S. Energy Information Administration, "Strait of Hormuz," *World Oil Transit Chokepoints,* February 2011 (Strait of Hormuz).
25. Rodney A. Mills, "Iran and the Strait of Hormuz: Saber Rattling or Global Energy Nightmare," Naval War College, 2008, p. 1 ("unlimited period"); U.S. Energy Information Administration, "China," Country Analysis Brief, November 2010; Anthony H. Cordesman, "Iran, Oil, and the Strait of Hormuz," Center for Strategic and International Affairs, March 26, 2007; Caitlin Talmadge, "Closing Time: Assessing the Iranian Threat to the Strait of Hormuz," *International Security* 33 no. 1 (2008) pp. 82–117; William D. O'Neil, "Correspondence: Cost and Difficulties of Blocking the Strait of Hormuz," *International Security* 33, no. 3 (2008/2009), pp. 190–98.
26. Pollack, *The Persian Puzzle,* pp. 258–59.
27. *Christian Science Monitor,* September 24, 2008 ("end of times," "heavens"); *New York Times,* November 28, 2010.
28. *Guardian,* November 28, 2010 ("46 seconds"); *Wall Street Journal,* January 4, 2010 ("Iranian Tactic").
29. X" (George F. Kennan), "The Sources of Soviet Conduct," *Foreign Affairs* 25 no. 4 (1947), pp. 566–82.
30. Eric Edelman, Andrew Krepinevich Jr., and Evan Braden Montgomery, "The Dangers of a Nuclear Iran: The Limits of Containment," *Foreign Affairs* 90 no. 1 (2011), pp. 66–81.

Chapter 15: Gas on Water

1. Thomas D. Cabot, *Beggar on Horseback: The Autobiography of Thomas D. Cabot* (Boston: David R. Godine, 1979), pp. 46 ("opinion"), p. 75 ("dreamt"); Cabot II, p. 118 ("expropriated").
2. Cabot II, p. 131 (extreme refrigeration); Malcolm Peebles, *Evolution of the Gas Industry* (New York: New York University Press, 1980) p. 187 ("intrigued"); Bureau of Mines study (investigation).
3. Hugh Barty-King, *New Flame: How Gas Changed the Commercial, Domestic, and Industrial Life of Britain between 1813 and 1984* (Tavistock: Graphmitre, 1984), pp 237–42 ("high speed gas"); Stephen Howarth, Joost Jonker, Keetie Sluyterman and Jan Luiten van Zanden, *The History of Royal Dutch Shell: Powering the Hydrocarbon Revolution 1939–1973,* vol. 2 (New York: Oxford University Press, 2007), p. x.
4. Fred von der Mehden and Steven W. Lewis, "Liquefied Natural Gas from Indonesia: The Arun Project," in *Natural Gas and Geopolitics: From 1970 to 2040,* eds. David G. Victor, Amy M. Jaffe, and Mark H. Hayes (Cambridge University Press, 2006), p. 101 (Cook Inlet).
5. Roosevelt to Ickes, August 12, 1942, OF4435, Franklin D. Roosevelt papers ("lying idle").
6. Robert Stobaugh and Daniel Yergin, eds., *Energy Future: Report of the Energy Project at the Harvard Business School* (New York: Vintage, 1983), p. 70.
7. Cabot II, p. 134 ($5 million).
8. Interview with Gordon Shearer.

9. Fred von der Mehden and Steven W. Lewis, "Liquefied Natural Gas from Indonesia: The Arun Project," 2006; interview ("crown jewels").
10. Interviews ("able to do much").
11. Kohei Hashimoto, Jareer Elass, and Stacy Eller, "Liquefied Natural Gas from Qatar: The Qatargas Project," prepared for the *Geopolitics of Natural Gas Study,* a joint project of the Program on Energy and Sustainable Development at Stanford University and the James A. Baker III Institue for Public Policy of Rice University, December 2004, p. 10.
12. Interview with Lucio Noto.
13. Interview with Abdullah bin Hamad *al-Attiyeh.*
14. Blake Roberts and Marcela Rosas, "Ripple Effect: Increased LNG Demand in Japan and the United Kingdom to Reduce LNG Flow to North America," CERA, July 20, 2007; Institute for Energy Economics Japan, "Impacts on International Energy Markets of Unplanned Shutdown of Kashiwazaki-Kariwa Nuclear Power Station," April 2008.

Chapter 16: The Natural Gas Revolution

1. Dan Steward, *The Barnett Shale Play: Phoenix of the Fort Worth Basin - A History* (Fort Worth: Fort Worth Geological Society, 2007), p. 32 (geological research).
2. *Houston Chronicle,* November 14, 2009 ("what we're going to do").
3. Steward, *The Barnett Shale Play,* p. 122–23, 141–42 (shut down, good deal of money); interview with Dan Steward.
4. Steward, *The Barnett Shale Play,* p. 142 ("light sand fraccing"); interview with Dan Steward; interview with Lawrence Nichols.
5. Teddy Muhlfelder, "The Shale Gale," IHS CERA, 2009.
6. Mary Lashley Barcella, "The Shale Gale Comes of Age: Resetting the Long-term Outlook for North American Natural Gas Markets," IHS CERA, February 2011.
7. IHS CERA, *Fueling North America's Energy Future: The Unconventional Natural Gas Revolution and the Carbon Agenda,* March 2010; MIT Energy Initiative, *The Future of Natural Gas: An Interdisciplinary MIT Study* (Cambridge: Massachusetts Institute of Technology, 2011).
8. Leta Smith, "Shale Gas Outside of North America: High Potential but Difficult to Reach," IHS CERA, April 2009 (recoverable shale gas).
9. John C. Harris, "Australian LNG: First Come, First Served," IHS CERA, January 28, 2011.
10. *Time,* February 16, 1970; Willy Brandt, *My Life in Politics* (New York: Viking, 1992); Angela Stent, *From Embargo to Ostpolitik: The Political Economy of West German-Soviet Relations 1955–1980* (Cambridge: Cambridge University Press, 2002), p. 173 ("Economics").
11. Angela E. Stent, *Soviet Energy and Western Europe* (New York: Praeger, 1982), p. 81.
12. *New York Times,* September 5, 1982 ("wounded by a friend"); August 3, 1982 (ignore the embargo).
13. *Bloomberg,* June 27, 2008.
14. IHS CERA, *Securing the Future: Making Russian-European Gas Interdependence Work* (2007), ch. 1.
15. Thone Gustafson and Matt Sagers, "Gas Transit Through Ukraine: The Struggle for the Crown Jewels," CERA, 2003.
16. Christine Telyan and Thane Gustafson, "Russia and Ukraine's New Gas Agreement: What Does It Mean and How Long Will It Last," IHS CERA, 2006; Robert L. Larsson, *Russia's Energy Policy: Security Dimensions and Russia's Reliability as an Energy Supplier* (Stockholm: Swedish Defense Research Agency, 2006) (shockwaves); *New York Times,* January 5, 2006 ("dependence on Russia").
17. Katherine Hardin, Sergej Mahnovski, and Leila Benali, "Filling a Southern Gas Pipeline to Europe: Export Potential and Costs for Gas Sources Compared," IHS CERA, 2010 (Kurdistan).
18. Peter Jackson, "Evolution of the Structure of the European Gas Market," IHS CERA, March 2011; Peter Jackson, et al., "The Unconventional Frontier: Prospects for Unconventional Gas in Europe," IHS CERA, February 2011.

Chapter 17: Alternating Currents

1. Jone-Lin Wang, "Why Are We Using More Electricity?," *Wall Street Journal,* March 10, 2010.
2. Jill Jonnes, *Empires of Light: Edison, Tesla, Westinghouse, and the Race to Electrify the World* (New York: Random House, 2004), p. 84.

3. Thomas Hughes, *Networks of Power: Electrification in Western Society 1880–1930* (Baltimore: Johns Hopkins University Press, 1993), p. 42 ("dynamos"); IEEE Global History Network, "Pearl Street Station," at http://www.ieeeghn.org/wiki/index.php/Pearl_Street_Station (electricity bill).
4. Matthew Josephson, *Edison: A Biography* (New York: Wiley, 1992), pp. 133–34 ("most useful citizen") p. 434; Robert Conot, *Thomas Edison: A Stroke of Luck* (New York: Bantam, 1980), p. 132 ("could not explain"); Jannes, *Empires of Light* ("minor invention").
5. Paul Israel, *Edison: A Life of Invention* (New York: John Wiley & Sons, 1998), p. 166 ("subdivided"); Jonnes, *Empires of Light,* p. 59 ("scientific men"); Hughes, *Networks of Power,* pp. 19–21 ("Edison's genius").
6. Hughes *Networks of Power,* p. 22; Israel, *Edison,* p. 167 ("enabled him to succeed").
7. Robert Friedel, Paul Israel and Bernard Finn, *Edison's Electric Light: The Art of Invention* (Baltimore: Johns Hopkins University Press, 2010), p. 30–31 ("expensive experimenting"); Jonnes, *Empires of Light,* p. 76 ("Capital is timid"), pp. 3–11 ("experimental station").
8. Randall Stross, *The Wizard of Menlo Park: How Thomas Edison Invented the Modern World* (New York: Three Rivers Press, 2007), p. 126; Jonnes, *Empires of Light,* pp. 195–97 ("Westinghoused").
9. There were 27.5 million recorded visitors to the Chicago World's Fair in 1893, at a time when the total population of the United States was 65 million; Erik Larson, *The Devil in the White City: Murder, Magic, and Madness at the Fair That Changed America* (New York: Vintage Books, 2004), pp. 4–5; J. P. Barrett, *Electricity at the Columbian Exposition* (Chicago: R.R. Donnelley & Sons Company, 1894), pp. xi, 16–18; David Nye: *Electrifying America: Social Meanings of a New Technology* (Cambridge: Massachusetts Institute of Technology Press, 1992), p. 38.
10. John F. Wasik, *The Merchant of Power: Sam Insull, Thomas Edison, and the Creation of the Modern Metropolis* (New York: Palgrave Macmillan, 2006), pp. 7, 10–11; Forrest McDonald, *Insull: The Rise and Fall of a Billionaire Utility Tycoon* (Washington, DC: BeardBooks, 2004), pp. 15–20.
11. Hughes, *Networks of Power,* p. 220 ("had to go to Europe").
12. Richard F. Hirsh, *Technology and Transformation in the American Electric Utility Industry* (Cambridge: Cambridge University Press, 1989), p. 19 ("begin to realize").
13. Alfred E. Kahn, *The Economics of Regulation: Principles and Institutions,* vol 2. (Cambridge: Massachusetts Institute of Technology Press, 1998), p. 117; Hughes, *Networks of Power,* p. 206.
14. Alfred E. Kahn, *The Economics of Regulation: Principles and Institutions,* vol. 1 (Cambridge: Massachusetts Institute of Technology Press, 1998), pp. 11–12, 43 ("fair interpretation"); Samuel Insull, *The Memoirs of Samuel Insull: An Autobiography,* ed. Larry Plachno (Polo, Illinois: Transportation Trails, 1992), pp. 89–90.
15. Hughes, *Networks of Power,* p. 182 ("most important city," "toasted bread"), p. 227 ("remaining last").
16. Hirsh, *Technology and Transformation in the American Electric Utility Industry,* p. 17; Jonnes, *Empires of Light,* p. 368; *New York Times,* July 17, 1938 ("cheapest way").
17. *Time,* May 14, 1934 ("presiding angel"); McDonald, *Insull,* p. 238 ("my name").
18. McDonald, *Insull,* p. 282.
19. U.S. Energy Information Agency, "Public Utility Holding Company Act of 1935: 1935–1992." January 1993, p. 6; *Time,* May 14, 1934 ("I have erred").
20. Frederick Lewis Allen, *Since Yesterday: The 1930's in America* (New York: Harper & Row Publishers, 1986), p. 75 ("I wish my time"); *New York Times,* June 12, 1932 ("foresight"); McDonald, *Insull,* p. 277 ("too broke").
21. Wasik, *The Merchant of Power,* p. 236; *Time,* May 14, 1934; McDonald, *Insull,* p. 314 ("to get" the Insulls); *New York Times,* July 17, 1938.
22. Arthur Schlesinger, Jr., *The Age of Roosevelt,* vol. 3, *The Politics of Upheaval* (Boston: Houghton Mifflin, 1960), p. 304 (FTC).
23. Hughes, *Networks of Power,* p. 204 ("difficult concepts"); Schlesinger, *The Age of Roosevelt,* vol. 3, *The Politics of Upheaval,* pp. 303–12 ("private socialism"); Kennth S. Davis, *FDR: The New Deal Years 1933–1937* (New York: Random House, 1986), pp. 529–37.
24. Robert Caro, *The Path to Power* (New York: Vintage Books, 1990), pp. 379, 504.
25. Kenneth T. Jackson, *Crabgrass Frontier: The Suburbanization of the United States* (New York: Oxford University Press, 1987), pp. 231–33; Michael J. Bennett, *When Dreams Came True: The G.I. Bill and the Making of Modern America* (Washington, DC: Brassay's, 2000), p. 287.

26. Ronald Reagan, *Reagan: A Life in Letters,* eds. Kiron Skinner, Annelise Anderson and Martin Anderson (New York: Free Press, 2003), p. 143 ("won't fly").
27. Ronald Reagan with Richard G. Hubler, *Where's the Rest of Me?* (New York: Duell, Sloan and Pearce, 1965), p. 273 ("most electric house"); Lou Cannon, *Governor Reagan: His Rise to Power* (New York: Public Affairs, 2003), p. 111 ("more refrigerators"), ch. 6; Nancy Reagan with William Novak, *My Turn: The Memoirs of Nancy Reagan* (New York: Random House, 1989), p. 128 (Hoover Dam).
28. General Electric, "Ronald Reagan and GE," webpage at http://www.ge.com/reagan/video.html.

Chapter 18: The Nuclear Cycle

1. David Holloway, *Stalin and the Bomb: The Soviet Union and Atomic Energy 1939–1956* (New Haven: Yale University Press, 1996), p. 220.
2. Richard G. Hewlett and Jack M. Holl, *Atoms for Peace and War, 1953–1961: Eisenhower and the Atomic Energy Commission* (Berkeley: University of California Press, 1989), ch. 1.
3. Hewlett and Holl, *Atoms for Peace and War, 1953–1961,* pp. 23–65 ("national importance"), ("Project Wheaties"); Stephen E. Ambrose, *Eisenhower: Soldier and President* (New York: Simon and Schuster, 1990), p. 339 ("scare the country"); Robert Ferrell, ed., *The Eisenhower Diaries* (New York: W. W. Norton, 1981), p. 234 ("racing towards catastrophe"); Dwight D. Eisenhower, speech, 470th Plenary Meeting of the United Nations General Assembly, December 8, 1953 ("Peaceful power").
4. Jimmy Carter, *White House Diary* (New York: Farrar, Straus and Giroux, 2010), p. 28 ("Widely considered").
5. Hyman Rickover, *No Holds Barred: The Final Congressional Testimony of Admiral Hyman Rickover* (Washington, DC: Center for Study of Responsive Law, 1982), p. 78 ("coincidence").
6. Interview with Admiral Hyman Rickover, *60 Minutes,* CBS, December 1984 ("stay alive"); Francis Duncan, *Rickover: The Struggle for Excellence* (Annapolis: Naval Institute Press, 2001), chs. 1–3.
7. Duncan, *Rickover,* p. 83 ("foremost engineers"); interview with Admiral Hyman Rickover, *60 Minutes,* CBS, December 1984 ("get things done").
8. Hyman Rickover, testimony, Joint Economic Committee, U.S. Congress, January 31, 1982.
9. Duncan, *Rickover,* p. 143 ("unknown to industry").
10. Interview with Admiral Hyman Rickover, *60 Minutes,* CBS, December 1984.
11. Jimmy Carter, *Why Not the Best?* (New York: Bantam Books, 1976).
12. Duncan, *Rickover,* pp. 2, 157–58; *Time,* January 11, 1954; William Anderson, *Nautilus 90 North* (New York: World Publishing Corp, 1959), p. 203.
13. Robert Darst, *Smokestack Diplomacy: Cooperation and Conflict in East-West Environmental Politics* (Cambridge: Massachusetts Institute of Technology, 2001), pp. 138–39.
14. Hewlett and Holl, *Atoms for Peace and War, 1953–1961,* pp. 192–95; *Time,* November 2, 1953; *New York Times Magazine,* December 20, 1953; *New York Times,* September 17, 1954 ("too cheap to meter").
15. Duncan, *Rickover,* p. 2 ("first full-scale"); Hewlett and Holl, *Atoms for Peace and War, 1953–1961,* p. 421.
16. Irving C. Bupp and Jean-Claude Derian, *Light Water: How the Nuclear Dream Dissolved* (New York: Basic Books, 1978), p. 50 ("cheapest of all").
17. Bupp and Derian, *Light Water,* ch. 4, including p. 82 ("traumatic").
18. Daniel Yergin,"The Terrifying Prospect: Atomic Bombs Everywhere," *Atlantic Monthly,* April 1977, p. 47.
19. Interview with George Kistiakowsky.
20. Bupp and Derian, *Light Water,* p. 122 ("copious amounts"); *Report of the President's Commission on the Accident at Three Mile Island,* October 1979.
21. *Report of the President's Commission on the Accident at Three Mile Island*; *New York Times,* April 2, 1979; *Time,* April 9, 1979.
22. Letter from H. G. Rickover to President Jimmy Carter, December 1, 1979, staff officer, office to the senator, Box 158, Folder 12/5/79, Canton Library.
23. Interview with Jean Blancard; Bupp and Derian, *Light Water,* pp. 105–11.
24. Philippe de Ladoucette to author.
25. *Time,* May 26, 1986.

26. Philippe de Ladoucette to author.
27. Masahisa Naitoh to author.

Chapter 19: Breaking the Bargain

1. *San Francisco Chronicle,* November 5, 1998; *Washington Post,* November 5, 1998; *Sacramento Bee,* November 4, 1998.
2. Daniel Yergin and Joseph Stanislaw, *The Commanding Heights: The Battle for the World Economy* (New York: Touchstone, 2002), ch. 12.
3. Margaret Thatcher, *The Downing Street Years* (London: HarperCollins, 1995), p. 684 ("genuine competition"); John Baker, "The Successful Privatization of Britain's Electricity Industry," in Leonard S. Hyman, *The Privatization of Public Utilities* (Vienna, VA: Public Utilities Reports, 1995).
4. Yergin and Stanislaw, *The Commanding Heights,* pp. 363–65; interview with Elizabeth Moler.
5. Lawrence Makovich, *Crisis by Design: California's Electric Power Crunch,* CERA, pp. viii, 1, 3, 36–38.
6. Interview with Mason Willrich; Paul L. Joskow, "California's Electricity Crisis," *Oxford Review of Economic Policy* 17, no. 3 (2001), pp. 365–88 ("wholesale market institutions").
7. Lawrence Makovich, "Beyond California's Power Crisis: Impact, Solutions, and Lessons," CERA, March 2001, pp. vi, 33.
8. Interview with John Bryson; CERA, "Restructuring by the Pound," April 25, 1997.
9. James L. Sweeney, *The California Electricity Crisis* (Stanford, CA: Hoover Institution Press, 2002), pp. 120–22.
10. Interview with John Bryson; *Fortune,* February 5, 2001 ("madness," "cannot run a business").
11. Sweeney, *The California Electricity Crisis,* p. 132; Gray Davis, "California: State of the State Address," January 9, 2001, on Web site of Democratic Leadership Council ("energy nightmare," "price gouging," "out-of-state profiteers," "hostage," "on sleep mode," "brink of blackouts").
12. James L. Sweeney, "California Electricity Restructuring, the Crisis, and Its Aftermath," in *Electricity Market Reform: An International Perspective,* eds. Fereidoon P. Sioshansi and Wolfgang Pfaffenberger (Oxford: Elsevier, 2006), p. 331 ("untested system"); Sweeney, *The California Electricity Crisis,* p. 203 ("20 minutes," "plunder").
13. Sweeney, *The California Electricity Crisis,* p. 136 ("more electricity they sold").
14. Sweeney, *The California Electricity Crisis,* pp. 224–26, 280; interviews.
15. Federal Energy Regulatory Commission, *Report on Plant Outages in the State of California,* February 1, 2001 ("did not discover").
16. *Houston Chronicle,* March 22, 2007; *Los Angeles Times,* June 16, 2002 (for the traders). For the fall of Enron, Kurt Eichenwald, *Conspiracy of Fools: A True Story* (New York: Broadway Books, 2005) and Bethany McLean and Peter Elkind, *The Smartest Guys in the Room: The Amazing Rise and Scandalous Fall of Enron* (New York: Portfolio, 2004).
17. James Sweeney, "The California Energy Crisis," Conference on Ethics and Changing Energy Markets, Notre Dame University, October 28, 2004.
18. Arnold Schwarzenegger, inauguration speech, Sacamento, CA, November 17, 2003; CNN.com, October 7, 2003 ("slow to act"); *New York Times,* November 12, 2003 ("bummer").
19. Interview with Joseph Kelliher.
20. Jone-Lin Wang, "The Power Generation Landscape and Recent Developments," U.S. Federal Energy Regulatory Commission, Conference on Merchant Generation Assets by Public Utilities, June 10, 2004 ("unintended hybrid").
21. California Independent System Operator, "2009 Annual Report," p. 7.

Chapter 20: Fuel Choice

1. International Energy Agency, *World Energy Outlook 2010* (Paris: International Energy Agency, 2010), p. 227.
2. Jone-Lin Wang, "Playing to Strength—Diversifying Electricity," *Wall Street Journal,* February 2006.
3. U.S. Energy Information Administration, "International Energy Statistics," 2009.
4. The Sierra Club, "Stopping the Coal Rush" Web page, at http://www.sierraclub.org/environmentallaw/coal/.

5. Ayaka Jones and Patricia DiOrio, "Staying Power: Can US Coal Plants Dodge Retirement for Another Decade?," IHS CERA, 2011.
6. Massachusetts Institute of Technology, *The Future of Coal: Options for a Carbon-Constrained World,* 2007, p. x.
7. MIT, *The Future of Coal,* pp. ix, 15, 43.
8. John Deutch, *The Crisis in Energy Policy: The Godkin Lecture* (Cambridge: Harvard University Press, 2011), ch. 3; IHS CERA, *Fueling North America's Energy Future: The Unconventional Natural Gas Revolution and the Carbon Agenda,* 2010, pp. vii–2.
9. Interview with Shirley Jackson.
10. United States Nuclear Regulatory Commission, "Reactor License Renewal," February 16, 2011, at http://www.nrc.gov/reactors/operating/licensing/renewal.html.
11. Carol Browner, CNBC interview, February 16, 2010.
12. Gregory Jaczko, "A View from the Nuclear Regulatory Commission," speech, March 1, 2010.
13. IHS CERA unpublished paper, "Small Nuclear Reactors—The Promise and the Reality."
14. Douglas Frantz and Catherine Collins, *Fallout: The True Story of the CIA's Secret War on Nuclear Trafficking* (New York: Free Press, 2011), pp. 82–86; Robert G. Joseph, *Countering WMD: The Libyan Experience* (Fairfax, VA: National Institute Press, 2009), ch. 1.
15. William Langewiesche, *The Atomic Bazaar: The Rise of the Nuclear Poor* (New York: Farrar, Straus and Giroux, 2007), p. 173.
16. World Nuclear Association, "Reactor Database."
17. Reuters, December 27, 2009.
18. Interview.
19. *World Nuclear News,* June 10, 2008 ("absolutely wrong"); Reuters, November 10, 2010.
20. European Nuclear Society, "Nuclear Power Plants, Worldwide," at http://www.euronuclear.org/info/encyclopedia/n/nuclear-power-plant-world-wide.htm.
21. World Nuclear News, January 8, 2011 ("insufficient"); *New York Times,* March 21, 2011 ("changed everything"); Reuters, April 15, 2011 ("exit").
22. *Dallas Morning News,* April 19, 2011 ("month after month").
23. John Rowe, speech, CERAWeek, March 2011.

Chapter 21: Glacial Change

1. John Tyndall, *The Glaciers of the Alps* (Boston: Ticknor and Fields, 1860), p. 11.
2. Tyndall, *The Glaciers of the Alps,* p. 21 ("sentiment"); A. S. Eve and C. H. Creasey, *Life and Work of John Tyndall* (London: Macmillan, 1945), p. 23 ("language").
3. Tyndall, *The Glaciers of the Alps,* p. 17 ("ancient glaciers").
4. Horace Bénédict de Saussure, *Voyage dans de Alps* (Geneva: Chez Les Principaux Libraires, 1834).
5. James Rodger Fleming, *Historical Perspectives on Climate Change* (New York: Oxford University Press, 1998), p. 61 ("mathematical theory").
6. Elizabeth Cary Agassiz, ed., *Louis Agassiz: His Life and Correspondence,* vol. 1 (Cambridge: Riverside Press, 1886), pp. 263–64 ("shroud"); Edward Lurie, *Louis Agassiz: A Life in Science* (Baltimore: Johns Hopkins University Press, 1988), pp. 80–102 ("beloved fossil fishes," "God's great plough").
7. Eve and Creasey, *Life and Work of John Tyndall,* p. 86 ("gases not natural"); Fleming, *Historical Perspectives on Climate Change,* pp. 68–69 ("in my hands"); Mike Hulme, "On the Origin of the 'Greenhouse Effect': John Tyndall's 1859 Interrogation of Nature," *Weather* 64, no. 5 (2009), pp. 121–23 ("experimentally based account").
8. Fleming, *Historical Perspectives on Climate Change,* pp. 58–71 ("tendency to accumulate," "every variation"); Eve and Creasey, *Life and Work of John Tyndall,* p. 279 ("my poor darling").
9. Svante Arrhenius, "On the Influence of Carbonic Acid in the Air Upon the Temperature of the Ground," *The London, Edinburgh and Dublin Philosophical Magazine and Journal of Science,* April 1896, pp. 237–76 ("absorption of the atmosphere"); Julia Uppenbrink, "Arrhenius and Global Warming," *Science* 272, no. 5265 (1996), p. 1122.
10. Spencer Weart, "The Discovery of Global Warming" and "The Carbon Dioxide Greenhouse Effect," *The Discovery of Global Warming,* at http://www.aip.org/history/climate/co2.htm (three thousand

years); Svante Arrhenius, *Worlds in the Making: The Evolution of the Universe,* tr. H. Borns (New York: Harper & Brothers, 1908), p. 63 ("more abundant crops").

11. Gustaf Arrhenius Oral History, Scripps Institution of Oceanography Library, April 11, 2006.
12. John Steinbeck, *The Grapes of Wrath* (New York: Penguin Books, 2006), p. 4.
13. G. S. Callendar, "Can Carbon Dioxide Influence Climate?," *Weather* 4 (1949), pp. 310–14 ("chequered history").
14. Fleming, *Historical Perspectives on Climate Change,* p. 115.
15. Weart, "The Discovery of Global Warming" and "The Carbon Dioxide Greenhouse Effect," ("marketplace of ideas"); Fleming, *Historical Perspectives on Climate Change,* p. 113 ("abandoned").

Chapter 22: The Age of Discovery

1. Roger R. Revelle Oral History, The Bancroft Library, University of California, Berkeley, 1986; Judith Morgan and Neil Morgan, *Roger: A Biography of Roger Revelle* (San Diego: Scripps Institution of Oceanography, 1996), p. 89 ("a lot of imagination"), pp. 44–45.
2. *San Diego Daily,* June 27, 1990.
3. Morgan and Morgan, *Roger,* p. 19; Gustaf Arrhenius Oral History Project, Scripps Institution of Oceanography Library, April 11, 2006 ("extreme stretch"); David M. Hart and David G. Victor, "Scientific Elites and the Making of US Policy for Climate Change Research, 1957–74," *Social Studies of Science* 23 (1993), p. 648 ("carbon-cycle").
4. Nancy Scott Anderson, *An Improbable Venture: A History of the University of California, San Diego* (La Jolla: University of California San Diego Press, 1993), pp. 32–33 ("unexpected discoveries"); October 10, 1949, Proposed University of California Mid-Pac Expedition, p. 20 ("featureless plain"); Morgan and Morgan, *Roger,* p. 86 ("best-known").
5. Ronald Rainger, "Patronage and Science: Roger Revelle, the U.S. Navy, and Oceanography at the Scripps Institution," *Earth Sciences History* 19:1 (2000), pp. 58–89; Arrhenius Oral History ("stratified").
6. R. Revelle and H. Suess, "Carbon Dioxide Exchange Between Atmosphere and Ocean and the Question of an Increase of Atmospheric CO_2 During the Past Decades," *Tellus,* 9, no. 1, 1957; Spencer Weart, "Roger Revelle's Discovery," *The Discovery of Global Warming,* http://www.aip.org/history/climate/Revelle.htm.
7. Arrhenius Oral History ("grand experiment"); Hart and Victor, "Scientific Elites," p. 656 ("curiosity").
8. Mark Bowen, *Thin Ice: Unlocking the Secrets of Climate Change on the World's Highest Mountains* (New York: Henry Holt, 2005), pp. 110–11.
9. Sydney Chapman, *IGY: Year of Discovery* (Ann Arbor: University of Michigan Press, 1959), p. 54 ("metal loses its strength"); *Time,* May 4, 1959.
10. Stephen E. Ambrose, *Eisenhower: Soldier and Statesman* (New York: Simon & Schuster, 1990), pp. 13–39; David Eisenhower, *Eisenhower at War: 1943–1954* (New York: Random House, 1986), pp. 241–53; Sverre Petterssen, *Weathering the Storm: Sverre Petterssen, the D-Day Forecast, and the Rise of Modern Meteorology,* ed. James Rodger Fleming (Boston: American Meteorological Society, 2001), chs. 16–19; *New York Times,* June 6, 1964.
11. Roger R. Revelle, "Sun, Sea and Air: IGY Studies of the Heat and Water Budget of the Earth," *Geophysics and the IGY,* Geophysical Monograph, no. 2. American Geophysical Union, July 1958, pp. 147–53 ("dark age"); Ronald Fraser, *Once Around the Sun: The Story of the International Geophysical Year* (New York: Macmillan Company, 1958), p. 37 ("man-made").
12. Hart and Victor, "Scientific Elites," p. 651 ("adequately documented"); Arrhenius Oral History ("historic event").
13. Charles David Keeling, "Rewards and Penalties of Monitoring the Earth," *Annual Review of Energy and the Environment* 23 (1998), pp. 25–82.
14. Keeling, "Rewards and Penalties of Monitoring the Earth," p. 30.
15. Revelle Oral History ("never been interested"); Keeling, "Rewards and Penalties of Monitoring the Earth," pp. 78–79 ("keen interest").
16. Spencer Weart, *The Discovery of Global Warming* (Cambridge: Harvard University Press, 2003), pp. 128–29.
17. Revelle Oral History ("most beautiful"); Arrhenius Oral History ("I'm sorry").

18. Keeling, "Rewards and Penalties of Monitoring the Earth," p. 48 ("present trends"); Weart, *The Discovery of Global Warming,* p. 38 ("central icon").
19. Alan D. Hecht and Dennis Tirpak, "Framework Agreement on Climate Change: A Scientific and Policy History," *Climactic Change* 29 (1995), p. 375.
20. The White House, *Restoring the Quality of Our Environment: Report of the Environmental Pollution Panel,* November 1965, pp. 126–27 ("almost certainly"); Hubert Heffner to Dr. Daniel P. Moynihan, January 26, 1970, Moynihan Papers, Nixon Library; Steven R. Weisman, *Daniel Patrick Moynihan: Portrait in Letters of an American Visionary* (New York: Public Affairs, 2010), p. 202 ("get involved").
21. Betty Friedan, "The Coming Ice Age," *Harper's,* September 1958; G. J. Kukla and R. K. Matthews, "When Will the Present Interglacial Period End?" *Science* 178, no. 4057 (1972), pp. 190–91 ("global cooling"); Hecht and Tirpak, "Framework Agreement on Climate Change," p. 376 (Defense Department climate analysis); S. I. Rasool and S. H. Schneider, "Atmospheric Carbon Dioxide and Aerosols: Effects of Large Increases on Global Climate," *Science* 173, no. 3992 (1971), pp. 138–41 ("trigger an ice age"); James Fleming, *Historical Perspectives on Climate Change* (New York: Oxford University Press, 1998), p. 132 (U.S. National Science Board report); Wallace Broecker, "Climate Change: Are We on the Brink of a Pronounced Global Warming?" *Science* 189, no. 4201 (1975), pp. 460–63 ("discount the warming effect").
22. Hecht and Tirpak, "Framework Agreement on Climate Change," p. 377 ("propelling concern"). Thomas Peterson, William Connolley, and John Fleck disagree, strongly arguing that it is a "popular myth" and a "falsehood" to say that "in the 1970s the climate science community was predicting 'global cooling.' "The Myth of the 1970s Global Cooling Scientific Consensus," Thomas C. Peterson, William M. Connolley, John Fleck, "The Myth of the 1970s Global Cooling Scientific Consensus," *Bulletin of the American Meteorological Society,* Volume 89, Issue 9, pp. 1325–37. They come to their conclusion by surveying "peer-reviewed literature," including a number of citations of various articles, between 1965 and 1979. In part, they blame "the news media" for the "myth." Yet, as the reply to Moynihan suggested, there was a clear division among scientists in those years. As the father of climate modeling, Syukuro Manabe said of his early research, "At that time, no one cared about global warming . . . Some people thought maybe an Ice Age is coming." However, by the end of the 1970s, the weight had clearly shifted away from cooling, toward warming, except for the "nuclear winter." In short, there was no obvious "consensus" either way that characterized the entire decade.
23. *Newsweek,* April 28, 1975; "What Is Happening to Our Climate," *National Geographic,* November 1976, *Time* magazine, August 19, 1976.
24. R. P. Turco, O. B. Toon, T. P. Ackerman, J. B. Pollack, and Carl Sagan, "Nuclear Winter: Global Consequences of Multiple Nuclear Explosions," *Science* 222, no. 4630 (1983), pp. 1283–92.
25. Hart and Victor, "Scientific Elites," pp. 657–61 ("advertant"); Weart, *The Discovery of Global Warming,* p. 5 (Kennedy); Martin Campbell-Kelly and William Aspray, *Computer: A History of the Information Machine* (Boulder, CO: Westview Press, 2004), p. 79 ("considerable temerity").
26. Norman Macrae, *John von Neumann: The Scientific Genius Who Pioneered the Modern Computer, Game Theory, Nuclear Deterrence, and Much More* (American Mathematical Society, 2008), pp. 5, 248 ("last words").
27. Macrae, *John von Neumann,* pp. 52, 250, 266, 325, 369; Stanislaw M. Ulam, *Adventures of a Mathematician* (Berkeley: University of California Press, 1991), pp. 4, 203, 245.
28. Campbell-Kelly and Aspray, *Computer,* pp. 3–4 ("computers"); Macrae, *John von Neumann,* p. 234 ("modern mathematical modeling").
29. Macrae, *John von Neumann,* pp. 298, 302 ("phenomena").
30. Spencer Weart, "Government: The View from Washington, DC," *The Discovery of Global Warming,* at http://www.aip.org/history/climate/Govt.htm ("warfare"); Macrae, *John von Neumann,* pp. 298, 316 ("jiggle," "weather predictions"); *New York Times,* February 9, 1957 ("electronic brain").
31. Norman Phillips, "Jule Charney, 1917–1981," *Annals of the History of Computing* 3, no. 4 (1981), pp. 318–19; Norman Phillips, "Jule Charney's Influence on Meteorology," *Bulletin of the American Meteorological Society* 63, no. 5 (1982), pp. 492–98; John M. Lewis, "Smagorinsky's GFDL: Building the Team," *Bulletin of the American Meteorological Society* 89, no. 9 (2008), pp. 1339–53; Macrae, *John von Neumann,* pp. 316–20.

32. " 'Suki' Manabe: Pioneer of Climate Modeling," *IPRC Climate* 5, no. 2 (2005), pp. 11–15; Syukuro Manabe and Richard Wetherald, "Thermal Equilibrium of the Atmosphere with a Given Distribution of Relative Humidity," *Journal of Atmospheric Sciences* 24, no. 3 (1967), pp. 241–59; Spencer Weart, "General Circulation Models of Climate," *The Discovery of Global Warming*, at http://www.aip.org/history/climate/GCM.htm.
33. Interview with Fred Krupp.
34. Macrae, *John von Neumann*, p. 3245–326 (most prominent meteorologist); James G. Speth, *Red Sky at Morning: America and the Crisis of the Global Environment* (New Haven: Yale University Press, 2005), p. 3; interview with Rafe Pomerance; *Report of an Ad Hoc Study Group on Carbon Dioxide and Climate*, Woods Hole, Massachusetts, July 23–27, 1979, to the Climate Research Board, Assembly of Mathematical and Physical Sciences, National Research Council (Washington, D.C.: National Academy of Sciences, 1979) ("incontrovertible evidence").
35. "Effects of Carbon Dioxide Buildup in the Atmosphere," Hearing, U.S. Senate Committee on Energy and Natural Resources, April 3, 1980.
36. George M. Woodwell, Gordon J. MacDonald, Roger Revelle, and Charles Keeling, "The Carbon Dioxide Report," *Bulletin of the Atomic Scientists* 35, no. 8 (1979), pp. 56–57.
37. Speth, *Red Sky at Morning*, pp. 2–9.
38. Jonathan Overpeck, "Arctic Environmental Change of the Last Four Centuries," *Science* 278, no. 5341 (1997).
39. Walter Munk, "Tribute to Roger Revelle and His Contributions to Studies of Carbon Dioxide and Climate Change," *Colloquium on Carbon Dioxide and Climate Change*, National Academy of Sciences, Irvine, CA, November 13–15, 1995 ("exile"); Revelle Oral History.
40. Roger R. Revelle, Lecture Notes, Mc6 Box 55, Folder "Natural Sciences 118," Scripps Institution of Oceanography Archives.
41. Al Gore, *An Inconvenient Truth* (New York: Rodale Books, 2006), p. 10; Al Gore, *Earth in the Balance: Ecology and the Human Spirit* (New York: Rodale Books, 2006), p. 5 ("rest of my life"); Hecht and Tirpak, "Framework Agreement on Climate Change," p. 381 ("deeply disturbed").

Chapter 23: The Road to Rio

1. Mathew Paterson, *Global Warming and Global Politics* (London: Routledge, 1996), p. 32; interview with Robert Stavins, *New York Times*, June 26, 1988 ("For the Midwest").
2. Interviews with Tim Wirth and David Harwood; Tim Wirth interview, *Frontline*, PBS.
3. *New York Times*, June 23, 1988; James Hansen interview, *Frontline*, PBS; James Hansen, testimony, U.S. Senate Energy and Natural Resources Committee, June 23, 1988.
4. " 'Suki' Manabe: Pioneer of Climate Modeling," *IPRC Climate* 5, no. 2 (2005), p. 14 ("They weren't too impressed"); interview with Tim Wirth ("huge event"); *New York Times*, August 23, 1988 ("almost overnight").
5. Roger R. Revelle to Mancur Olson, September 2, 1988, Mc A6, Box 19, Folder "Correspondence August 1988," Revelle papers.
6. Spencer Weart, *The Discovery of Global Warming* (Cambridge: Harvard University Press, 2003), p. 151 (Villach); Mohamed T. El-Ashry, "Climate Change, Clean Energy, and U.S. Leadership," AAAS Science and Technology Policy Fellows Programs, 30th Anniversary Symposium, May 13, 2004.
7. Richard Elliott Benedick, *Ozone Diplomacy: New Directions in Safeguarding the Planet* (Cambridge: Harvard University Press, 1998).
8. Richard Kerr, "Hansen vs. the World on the Greenhouse Threat," *Science* 244, no. 4908 (1989), pp. 1041–43.
9. Tim Wirth to Roger R. Revelle, July 15, 1988, Roger R. Revelle to Tim Wirth, July 18, 1988, Roger R. Revelle to Jim Bates, July 14, 1988, Mc A6, Box 19, Folder "Correspondence July 1988," Revelle papers.
10. James E. Hansen, Wei-Chyung, and Andrew A. Lacis, "Mount Agung Eruption Provides a Test of Global Climactic Perturbation," *Science* 199, no. 4333 (1978), pp. 1065–68 ("simultaneous studies"); *Audubon*, November–December 1999 ("captivated," "best proof"); James Hansen, "Climate Threat to the Planet: Implications for Energy Policy and Intergenerational Justice," Jacob Bjerknes Lecture, American Geophysical Union, December 17, 2008 ("Venus Syndrome").

11. Andrew Revkin, "Endless Summer: Living with the Greenhouse Effect," *Discover,* October 1988.
12. George H. W. Bush, press release, September 1, 1988, George Bush Presidential Library; *New York Times,* September 2, 1988 ("White House effect"); Alan D. Hecht and Dennis Tirpak, "Framework Agreement on Climate Change: A Scientific and Policy History," *Climactic Change* 29 (1995), p. 383.
13. *Time,* August 20, 1923, June 11, 1934, June 19, 1939, August 19, 1955.
14. *Sports Illustrated,* March 13, 1989; *Time,* August 6, 1934 ("U.S. Sahara"); *New York Times,* September 4, 1988 ("packing our bags"); Irving M. Mintzer and J. A. Leonard, "Visions of a Changing World," in *Negotiating Climate Change: The Inside Story of the Rio Convention,* eds. Irving M. Mintzer and J. A. Leonard (Cambridge: Cambridge University Press, 1994), p. 52 ("science fiction").
15. Daniel Yergin and Joseph Stanislaw, *The Commanding Heights: The Battle for the World's Economy* (New York: Touchstone, 2002), pp. 95–96.
16. Margaret Thatcher, *The Downing Street Years* (London: HarperCollins, 1993), pp. 640–41; Margaret Thatcher, speech to the Royal Society, September 27, 1988.
17. Weart, *The Discovery of Climate Change,* p. 12 ("indispensable man"); Bert Bolin, *A History of the Science and Politics of Climate Change: The Role of the Intergovernmental Panel on Climate Change* (Cambridge: Cambridge University Press, 2008), p. 23 ("As chairman"); interview with Danel Esty.
18. Bolin, *A History of the Science and Politics of Climate Change,* pp. 48–49, 58; James Baker, speech, in *Department of State Bulletin,* April 1989.
19. Interview with Daniel Esty.
20. Bolin, *A History of the Science and Politics of Climate Change,* p. 63.
21. W. K. Reilly, *Breakdown on the Road from Rio: Reform, Reaction, and Distraction Compete in the Cause of the International Environment, 1993–94,* Arthur and Frank Payne Lecture, Stanford University ("bet your economy"); interview with William Reilly ("dined out"); George Will, *Washington Post,* May 31, 1992 ("red roots").
22. Interview with John Sununu; *Los Angeles Times,* March 2, 1990 ("nuclear power fights").
23. Cable from American Embassy in Bonn to White House, March 13, 1992, Folder 45045-020, George H. W. Bush Presidential Library; *New York Times,* May 9, 1989; *New York Times,* March 24, 1992.
24. George H. W. Bush, press conference, April 10, 1992.
25. *New York Times,* June 13, 1992 ("lone holdout").
26. *New York Times,* June 14, 1992 ("second to none," "Darth Vader"); interview with William Reilly.
27. Irving M. Mintzer and J. Amber Leonard, eds., *Negotiating Climate Change: The Inside Story of the Rio Convention* (Cambridge: Cambridge University Press, 1994), ch. 1, appendix ("dangerous anthropogenic interference").
28. Interview with William Reilly.

Chapter 24: Making a Market

1. Michael Sandel, "It's Immoral to Buy the Right to Pollute," op-ed, *New York Times,* December 17, 1997; interview with Fred Krupp.
2. Ronald Coase autobiography, Nobel Prize Web site ("underrate your abilities").
3. Ronald Coase, "The Problem of Social Cost," *Journal of Law and Economics,* vol. 3, (1960), pp. 1–44 ("externalities").
4. John H. Dales, *Pollution, Property & Prices: An Essay in Policy-making and Economics* (Toronto: University of Toronto Press, 1968), ch. 6; David Montgomery, "Markets in Licenses and Efficient Pollution Control Programs," *Journal of Economic Theory* 5, no. 3 (1972), pp. 395–418.
5. Richard Nixon, "Message to the Congress," August 10, 1970 ("war on pollution"); Robert W. Hahn, "Economic Prescriptions for Environmental Problems: How the Patient Followed the Doctor's Orders," *Journal of Economic Perspectives* 3, no. 2 (1989), pp. 97–98.
6. Harold Williamson, Ralph Andreano, Arnold Daum, and Gilbert Klose, *The American Petroleum Industry: The Age of Energy, 1899–1959* (Evanston, IL: Northwestern University Press, 1963), p. 409.
7. Interviews with C. Boyden Gray and William Martin.
8. Hahn, "Economic Prescriptions for Environmental Problems," pp. 95–114.
9. Interview with Robert Stavins.

10. Robert Stavins, ed., *Project 88: Harnessing Market Forces to Protect the Environment* (Washington, D.C.:1988) ("incentive systems").
11. Richard Conniff, "The Political History of Cap and Trade," *Smithsonian,* August 2009 (Canadian prime minster).
12. Interview with C. Boyden Gray; Bruce A. Ackerman and Richard B. Stewart, "Reforming Environmental Law: The Democratic Case for Market Incentives," *Columbia Journal of Environmental Law* 171, no. 3 (1988).
13. Interviews with Fred Krupp and C. Boyden Gray.
14. Kathy McCauley, Bruce Barron, and Morton Coleman, *Crossing the Aisle to Cleaner Air: How the Bipartisan "Project 88" Transformed Environmental Policy* (Pittsburgh: University of Pittsburgh, 2008), p. 25 ("totally different concept"); Robert N. Stavins, "What Can We Learn from the Grand Policy Experiment? Lessons from SO_2 Allowance Trading," *Journal of Economic Perspectives* 12, no. 3 (1998), p. 74 ("decision-making").
15. Joseph Goffman and Daniel J. Dudek, "The Clean Air Act Acid Rain Program: Lessons for Success in Creating a New Paradigm," presentation, 88th Annual Meeting, Air & Waste Management Association, June 18–23, 1995, pp. 5, 7, 9. Whether Goffman and Dudek were aware of it or not, they, too, were channeling an "academic scribbler." For they were echoing the historic 1945 article by Frederich von Hayek about "the use of knowledge in society": that a dispersed market with many decision-makers, coordinated through a price system, is going to be better informed, quicker, and more innovative than a centrally directed economy. See Frederich A. Hayek, "The Use of Knowledge in Society," *American Economic Review* 35, no. 4 (1945), pp. 519–30.
16. Stavins, "What Can We Learn from the Grand Policy Experiment?," p. 69.
17. Environmental Protection Agency, "Acid Rain and Related Programs: 2008 Highlights," December 2009; Environmental Defense Fund, "The Cap and Trade Success Story," February 12, 2007; Lauraine G. Chestnut and David M. Mills, "A Fresh Look at the Benefits and Costs of the U.S. Acid Rain Program," *Journal of Environmental Management* 77 (2005), pp. 252–66.
18. A. Denny Ellerman, Paul L. Joskow, Richard Schmalensee, Juan-Pablo Montero, and Elizabeth M. Bailey, *Markets for Clean Air: The U.S. Acid Rain Program* (Cambridge: Cambridge University Press, 2000), p. 314 ("impossible to believe"); interview with Joseph Goffman; Fred Krupp, "The Making of a Market-Minded Environmentalist," *Strategy + Business* 51 (2008), pp. 1–7.
19. Bert Bolin, *A History of the Science and Politics of Climate Change: The Role of the Intergovernmental Panel on Climate Change* (Cambridge: Cambridge University Press, 2008), pp. 87–89, 112–13 ("best estimated"); Richard A. Kerr, "It's Official: Humans Are Behind Most of Global Warming," *Science* 291, no. 5504 (2001), p. 566.
20. Bolin, *A History of the Science and Politics of Climate Change,* pp. 108, 139.
21. Bolin, *A History of the Science and Politics of Climate Change,* pp. 137, 182, 196 ("lacked the scientific knowledge"); Richard S. Linzden, "Taking Greenhouse Warming Seriously," *Energy and Environment* 18, no. 7–8 (2007), pp. 937–50 ("iconic claim").
22. Interview.
23. Interviews with Stuart Eizenstat, David Sandalow, and Joseph Goffman.
24. Interview with Stuart Eizenstat.
25. Interview with Chuck Hagel.
26. Krupp, "The Making of a Market-Minded Environmentalist," pp. 1–7 (policies and measures); interview with Stuart Eizenstat ("three issues").
27. Interview with Stuart Eizenstat.
28. Bolin, *A History of the Science and Politics of Climate Change,* pp. 151, 159.
29. Interviews with Chuck Hagel and others.

Chapter 25: On the Global Agenda

1. Tony Blair, *A Journey: My Political Life* (New York: Knopf, 2010), pp. 554–60.
2. Nicholas Stern to author; Nicholas Stern, *The Global Deal: Climate Change and the Creation of a New Era of Progress and Prosperity* (New York: Public Affairs, 2009), p. 204.
3. Interviews with James Connaughton ("zippo") and Jeffrey Kupfer; Christine Todd Whitman, *It's My Party Too: The Battle for the Heart of the GOP and the Future of America* (New York: Penguin, 2005)

pp. 170-73; Ron Suskind, *The Price of Loyalty: George W. Bush, the White House, and the Education of Paul O'Neill* (New York: Simon & Schuster, 2004), pp. 88, 99, 121–22; Paul O'Neill, *Science, Politics, and Global Climate Change* (Pittsburgh: Alcoa, 1998).

4. Interview with Donald Evans.
5. Interview with James Mahoney; Granger Morgan, H. Dowlatabadi, M. Henrion, D. Keith, R. Lempert, S. McBrid, M. Small, T. Wilbanks, eds., *Best Practice Approaches for Characterizing, Communicating, and Incorporating Scientific Uncertainty in Decisionmaking* (Washington, D.C.: National Oceanic and Atmospheric Administration, 2009).
6. Blair, *A Journey*, p. 311 ("masterstroke").
7. Interview with David King; David King, "The Science of Climate Change: Adapt, Mitigate or Ignore?" *The Ninth Zuckerman Lecture,* October 31, 2002; David King, "Climate Change Science: Adapt, Mitigate, or Ignore?" *Science* 303, no. 5655 (2004), pp. 176–77.
8. CENTRA Technology Inc. and Scitor Corporation, "Russia: The Impact of Climate Change to 2030: Geopolitical Implications," September 2009.
9. Interview with Richard Sandor; Richard Sandor, "Market Based Solutions for Climate Change," paper, September 1, 2004.
10. Intergovernmental Panel on Climate Change, *Climate Change 2007: The Physical Science Basis* (New York: Cambridge University Press, 2007), pp. 2, 12, 85–88; Al Gore remarks at the *Wall Street Journal* Eco-Nomics conference, March 3, 2009.
11. Nicholas Stern, *The Economics of Climate Change: The Stern Review* (Cambridge: Cambridge University Press, 2007); *Economist,* November 2, 2006.
12. Interviews with William Nordhaus and Nicholas Stern.
13. John Browne, *Beyond Business* (London: Weidenfeld and Nicolson, 2010), p. 80; John Browne, speech, Stanford University, May 19, 1997.
14. Daniel C. Esty and Andrew S. Winston, *Green to Gold: How Smart Companies Use Environmental Strategy to Innovate, Create Value, and Build Competitive Advantage* (New Haven: Yale University Press, 2006); Global Climate "Backgrounder," February 25, 1997 ("radical reductions").
15. Al Gore, Nobel Peace Prize Lecture, Oslo, Norway, December 10, 2007.
16. Rajendra Pachauri, "Energy and Growth: Beyond the Myths and Myopia," *Energy Journal* 10, no. 1 (1989), p. 12 ("continuing insularity"); "A Conversation with Nobel Prize Winner Rajendra Pachauri," *Yale Environment 360,* June 3, 2008 ("alarm"); interview with Rajendra Pachauri, CERAWeek, February 11, 2008 ("no room").
17. Nancy Pelosi, speech, Johns Hopkins University Commencement, May 21, 2009.
18. Transcript, "Departments of Veterans Affairs and Housing and Urban Development and Independent Agencies Appropriations for 1999—Part 7—Environmental Protection Agency," U.S. House of Representatives Appropriations Committee, 1998; Carol Browner, speech, MIT Energy Initiative, April 13, 2009; George W. Bush, letter to Chuck Hagel, March 13, 2001 ("not a 'pollutant'").
19. Edward Markey, speech, MIT Energy Initiative, April 13, 2009 ("most important"); Opinion of the Supreme Court, *Massachusetts et al. v. Environmental Protection Agency,* April 2, 2007, 549 U.S. 497, pp. 2–3, 16; *New York Times,* October 30, 2006.
20. Interviews with Samuel Bodman and Paula Dobriansky; George W. Bush, State of the Union Address, Washington, D.C., January 23, 2007; George W. Bush, *Decision Points* (New York: Crown, 2010), p. 347.

Chapter 26: In Search of Consensus

1. Barack Obama, "Remarks on Jobs, Energy Independence, and Climate Change," January 26, 2009.
2. Interview with Ed Markey.
3. Erica Downs, "China's Energy Rise" in *China's Rise in Historical Perspective,* ed. Brantly Womack (Lanham, MD: Rowman and Littlefield Publishers, 2010), p. 190.
4. Joanna A. Lewis, "China's Strategic Priorities in International Climate Change Negotiations," *Washington Quarterly* 31, no. 1 (Winter 2007–8), pp. 155–74 (four-year study); National Development and Reform Commission, "China's National Climate Change Program," People's Republic of China, June 2007 ("further intensify"); Kenneth Lieberthal, "U.S.-China Clean Energy

Partnership: Progress, Prospects and Recommendations," Brookings Institution, September 2009 (possible consequences); *New York Times,* September 8, 2009 ("win-win").

5. Isabel Hinton, "In India, A Clear Victor on the Climate Front," *Yale Environment 360,* March 1, 2010 ("kiss of death"); Jairam Ramesh, speech to Parliament, December 3, 2009; *Wall Street Journal,* March 8, 2010 ("bread-and-butter").
6. United Nations Framework Convention on Climate Change, "Draft Decision: Proposal by the President, Copenhagen Accord," December 18, 2009 ("international measurement"); William Antholis and Strobe Talbott, *Fast Forward: Ethics and Politics in the Age of Global Warming* (Washington, D.C.: Brookings Institution Press, 2010), ch. 5 ("variable geometry"); interview with David Sandalow; Eric Pooley, *The Climate War: True Believers, Power Brokers, and the Fight to Save the Earth* (New York: Hyperion, 2010), pp. 423–41.
7. Pennsylvania State University, "RA-1O Final Investigation Report Involving Dr. Michael E. Mann," June 4, 2010.
8. *Hindu,* January 19, 2010 (many glaciers, "iota"); *Guardian,* November 9, 2009 ("standstill," "arrogant"); Isabel Hinton, "In India, A Clear Victor on the Climate Front," *Yale Environment 360,* March 2, 2010 ("copied"); *Times* (London), January 21, 2010 ("astrologer"); *Bloomberg,* January 20, 2010 ("pathetic state").
9. Dmitry Medvedev, speech, August 4, 2010; Reuters, August 23, 2010 (Vladimir Putin).
10. *New York Times,* December 16, 2010 ("command-and-control"); Associated Press, January 3, 2011 ("unable to legislate"); *New York Times,* December 9, 2010.

Chapter 27: Rebirth of Renewables

1. Jimmy Carter, *White House Diary* (New York: Farrar, Straus and Giroux, 2010), p. 332; *New York Times,* June 21, 1979; *Time,* July 7, 1979.
2. The White House, "Fact Sheet: President Obama Highlights Vision for Clean Energy Economy," April 22, 2009; Evan Osnos, "Green Giant: Beijing's Crash Program for Clean Energy," *New Yorker,* December 21, 2009 (Hu Jintao); *Guardian* (London), May 14, 2010 (Cameron).
3. Harvey Strum, "Eisenhower's Solar Energy Policy," *Public Historian* 6, no. 2 (1984), pp. 37–55.
4. Interview with Denis Hayes; *New York Times,* April 23, 1970 ("speech somewhere"); *Time,* January 4, 1971 ("issue of the year").
5. Interview with Scott Sklar.
6. *New York Times Magazine,* March 16, 1975 ("eco-freaks"); interview with Denis Hayes; Amory B. Lovins, "Energy Strategy: The Road Not Taken?" *Foreign Affairs,* October 1976; Denis Hayes, *Rays of Hope: The Transition to a Post-Petroleum World* (New York: W. W. Norton, 1977).
7. Jimmy Carter, speeches, February 2, 1977, and April 18, 1977; Carter, *White House Diary,* p. 41; interview (sweater).
8. Interview with Denis Hayes; *BusinessWeek,* October 9, 1978 ("public imagination").
9. *BusinessWeek,* September 8, 1980.
10. Jimmy Carter, speech, July 15, 1979 ("crisis of the American spirit"); *Wall Street Journal,* December 11, 2008 ("gnawing on a rock").
11. Robert W. Righter, *Wind Energy in America: A History* (Norman: University of Oklahoma Press, 1996), p. 222 (white elephants); interview with Denis Hayes; discussion.
12. Interview with A. L. Shrier.
13. *Washington Post,* May 14, 2008 ("joke"); *Economist,* September 25, 1993 ("graveyard"); *Wall Street Journal,* December 11, 2008; interview with Scott Sklar.
14. Interview with Taichi Sakaiya (Kotaro Ikeguchi).
15. *Business Japan,* February 1978 ("bureaucrat-novelist"); interview with Taichi Sakaiya.
16. Rolf Wustenhagen and Michael Bilharz, "Green Market Development in Germany: Effective Public Policy and Emerging Customer Demand," *Energy Policy* 34 (2006), pp. 1681–96 ("almost accidental").
17. Interviews with Gerhard Schroeder, Hermann Scheer, and Hans-Josef Fell; *Time,* August 26, 2002 ("solar crusader").
18. Interview with Gerhard Schroeder.
19. *New York Times,* May 16, 2008 ("turbocharger").
20. Interview with Hans-Josef Fell; Ministry for Environment, Conservation, and Nuclear Safety,

"Development of Renewable Energy Sources in Germany in 2009—Graphics and Tables," Federal Republic of Germany, September 2010; "Renewables Support Policies in Europe: 2011 Country Comparisons," IHS Emerging Energy Research, 2011.

21. *New York Times,* April 22 and April 23, 1990 (Earth Day); interview with Scott Sklar.
22. Barry G. Rabe, *Statehouse and Greenhouse: The Emerging Politics of American Climate Change Policy* (Washington, D.C.: Brookings Institution Press, 2004), pp. 49–62; "North American Renewable Power Outlook, 2010–2015," IHS CERA, November 2010; *Sacramento Bee,* April 13, 2011 ("can't be afraid"); *Los Angeles Times,* April 13, 2011 ("didn't get my name").
23. Interview with Michael Eckhart.
24. "Green Tech" blog at CNET News, March 5, 2008.
25. Interview with Takayuki Ueda.
26. Huang Liming, "Financing Rural Renewable Energy: A Comparison Between China and India," *Renewable and Sustainable Energy Reviews* 13, no. 5 (2009), pp. 1096–1103; Yingqi Liu and Ari Kokko, "Wind Power in China: Policy and Development Challenges," *Energy Policy* 38, no. 10 (2010), pp. 5520–29.
27. Interview.
28. "Renewable Energy Law" People's Republic of China, February 28, 2005; "Medium- and Long-Term Development Plan for Renewable Energy," People's Republic of China, September 2007.
29. Wen Jiabao, speech, World Economic Forum, January 28, 2009; *New York Times,* September 8, 2010.
30. International Energy Agency, *World Energy Outlook 2010* (Paris: International Energy Agency, 2010).
31. Barack Obama, State of the Union Address, January 27, 2010.
32. REN21, *Renewables 2010 Global Status Report,* September 2010, pp. 13–30.
33. Interview with Denis Hayes.
34. *Christian Science Monitor,* September 10, 2010; *New York Times,* October 6, 2010.

Chapter 28: Science Experiment

1. Clay Christensen, *The Innovator's Dilemma* (Cambridge: Harvard University Press, 2003).
2. Steven Chu autobiography, Nobel Prize Web site.
3. Interviews with Raymond Orbach and John Tully.
4. Chu autobiography, Nobel Prize Web site.
5. Vernon W. Ruttan, *Is War Necessary for Economic Growth?: Military Procurement and Technology Development* (Oxford: Oxford University Press, 2006), pp. 21–27.
6. Robert Solow, "Growth and After," Nobel Prize lecture, November 18, 1987; Steven Koonin, "From Energy Innovation to Energy Transformation," pp. 4, 8–10 (scrubbers); MIT Energy Initiative, *The Future of Natural Gas: Interim Report* (Cambridge: Massachusetts Institute of Technology Press, 2010) (coal bed methane).
7. DOE, "DOE Nobel Laureates" and "Laboratories," U.S. Department of Energy.
8. Secretary of Energy Advisory Board, *Task Force on Strategic Energy R&D, Energy R&D: Shaping Our Nation's Future in a Competitive World* (Washington, DC: GPO, 1995), p. 1 ("deficit"); Kelly Gallagher, Ambuj Sagar, Diane Segal, Paul de Sa, and John P. Holdren, "DOE Budget Authority for Energy, Research, Development, and Demonstration Database," Ending the Energy Stalemate: A Bipartisan Strategy to Meet America's Energy Challenges (Washington, DC: National Commission on Energy Policy, 2004) (low point).
9. Interview with William Draper III, *Commanding Heights,* PBS; *New York Times,* June 26, 1989 ("adventure capital").
10. Spencer E. Ante, *Creative Capital: Georges Doriot and the Birth of Venture Capital* (Boston: Harvard Business Press, 2008), pp. 80–88, 198.
11. Interview with Samuel Bodman; Ante, *Creative Capital,* pp. 109, 126 ("peaceful life"), 198; *Charter of the Massachusetts Institute of Technology,* at http://libraries.mit.edu/archives/mithistory/charter.html.
12. David Packard, *The HP Way* (New York: Collins Business Essentials, 1995), p. 22.
13. Tom Perkins, *Valley Boy: The Education of Tom Perkins* (New York: Gotham Books, 2007); interview with Ray Lane.
14. Interview with Nancy Floyd.
15. Interview with Ira Ehrenpreis.

16. Interview with Ray Lane; Kleiner Perkins, "MoneyTree Report," PricewaterhouseCoopers, January 21, 2011, at https://www.pwcmoneytree.com/MTPublic/ns/moneytree/filesource/exhibits/10Q4MT Release_FINAL.pdf.
17. Interview with Robert Metcalfe; Susan Hockfield, Inaugural Address, Massachusetts Institute of Technology, May 6, 2005, at http://web.mit.edu/hockfield/speeches/2005-inaugural-address.html.
18. Steven Koonin, "From Energy Innovation to Energy Transformation," p. 6 ("decades"); interviews with Ray Lane and Ernest Moniz.
19. Steven Chu, speech, CERAWeek, March 9, 2010; interview with Matt Rogers; U.S. Secretary of Energy Advisory Board Meeting, TK, p.16 ("rolling the dice"); President's Council of Advisors on Science and Technology, *Accelerating the Pace of Change in Energy Technologies Through an Integrated Federal Energy Policy* (Washington, DC: Office of the President, 2010), pp. 3–5.
20. President's Council of Advisors, *Accelerating the Pace of Change in Energy Technologies through an Integrated Federal Energy Policy*, pp. 13–14 (comparative funding). ARPA-E was proposed in the influential National Academies: report, *Rising Above the Gathering Storm: Energizing and Employing America for a Brighter Economic Future* (Washington, DC: National Academies Press, 2007).

Chapter 29: Alchemy of Shining Light

1. Walter Isaacson, *Einstein: The Life of a Genius* (New York: Simon and Schuster, 2009), ch. 4 ("lazy dog"); Albrecht Folsing, *Albert Einstein: A Biography*, tr. Ewald Osers (New York: Penguin, 1997), pp. 77, 95 ("exceedingly thorough," "depressed").
2. John Stachel, ed., *Einstein's Miraculous Year: Five Papers That Changed the Face of Physics* (Princeton: Princeton University Press, 1998), pp. 177–98; Isaacson, *Einstein*, pp. 94–101.
3. Interview with Jean Posbic ("explained it all").
4. Interview with Ernest Moniz.
5. John Perlin, *From Space to Earth: The Story of Solar Electricity* (Cambridge: Harvard University Press, 2002), p. 18 (Siemens).
6. Albert Einstein, Nobel Prize in Physics, 1921, at http://nobelprize.org/nobel_prizes/physics/laureates/1921/.
7. Perlin, *From Space to Earth*, pp. 4, 25–26, 31, 202; *New York Times*, April 26, 1954 ("almost limitless"); *Time*, October 17, 1955.
8. Stephen E. Ambrose, *Eisenhower: Soldier and President* (New York: Simon and Schuster, 1984), chs. 18, 19; Deborah Cadbury, *Space Race: The Epic Battle Between America and the Soviet Union for Dominion of Space* (New York: HarperPerennial, 2006), p. 173 ("Kaputnik").
9. Perlin, *From Space to Earth*, pp. 41–44 ("roofs"); John Perlin, "Solar Power: The Slow Revolution," *Invention and Technology* 18, no. 1 (2002).
10. Interview with Peter Varadi; Peter Varadi, lecture, 19th European Photovoltaic Solar Energy Conference, June 7–11, 2004.
11. Interview with Paul Maycock.
12. Interview with Paul Maycock.
13. Interview with Peter Varadi.
14. Interviews with Naohiro Amaya ("very apprehensive") and Taichi Sakaiya; Daniel Yergin, *The Prize: The Epic Quest for Oil, Money, and Power* (New York, Simon and Schuster, 1991), p. 688 (Ginza).
15. Paul D. Maycock and Edward N. Stirewalt, *A Guide to the Photovoltaic Revolution: Sunlight to Electricity in One Step* (Emmaus: Rodale, 1985), pp. 67–69.
16. Sanyo Corporation, "Solar Global Site," at http://www.sanyo.com/solar/history/index.html; Sharp Corporation, "Solar Global Website," at http://sharp-solar.com/index.html; International Energy Agency, "National Survey Report of PV Power Applications in Japan 2002," May 2003 ("solar roofs"); interview with Atul Arya ("shocked").
17. Interviews with Jean Posbic, Hermann Scheer, and Anton Milner.
18. *Wall Street Journal*, October 12, 2006 ("by accident"); *Time*, October 17, 2007; Bill Powell, "China's New King of Solar," *Fortune*, February 11, 2009.
19. Interview with Shi Zhengrong.
20. Associated Press, September 8, 2009; *New York Times*, September 9, 2009.
21. European Photovoltaic Industry Association and Greenpeace, *Solar Generation 6: Solar Photovoltaic Electricity Empowering the World 2011*, http://www.epia.org/.

22. Cleantech Group, "Clean Technology Venture Investment Totaled $5.6 billion in 2009 Despite Non-binding Climate Change Accord in Copenhagen, Finds the Cleantech Group and Deloitte," press release, January 6, 2010; Peachtree Capital Advisors, *2010 Greentech M & A Review,* January 12, 2011.
23. Interview with David Carlson.
24. Daniel Clery, "Sending African Sunlight to Europe, Special Delivery," *Science* 329, no. 5993 (2010) pp. 782–83 (Desertec); *Fortune,* July 21, 2008 (land rush).
25. Lawrence Makovich, Patricia DiOrio, and Douglas Giuffre, "Renewable Portfolio Standards: Getting Ahead of Themselves," IHS CERA, 2008 (another layer); interviews with Paul Maycock and Anton Milner.
26. Interview with Paul Maycock.

Chapter 30: Mystery of Wind

1. Raymond Chandler, "Red Wind," in *Trouble Is My Business* (New York: Vintage, 1988), p. 162.
2. U.S. Department of Energy, *20% Wind Energy By 2030: Increasing Wind Energy's Contribution to U.S. Electricity Supply* (Springfield, VA: U.S. Department of Commerce National Technical Information Service, 2008); Global Wind Energy Council and Greenpeace International, "Global Wind Energy Outlook 2010," October 2010.
3. Edward J. Kealey, *Harvesting the Air: Windmill Pioneers in Twelfth-Century England* (Berkeley: University of California Press, 1987), ch. 6.
4. Lynn White Jr., *Medieval Technology & Social Change* (London: Oxford University Press, 1964), pp. 88–89; Carlo M. Cipolla, *Before the Industrial Revolution: European Society and Economy 1000–1700* (New York: W. W. Norton, 1993), p. 144 ("distant announcement").
5. W.O.A., "The Storage of Wind Power," *Scientific American* XLIX, no. 2 (1883), p. 17; Robert Righter, *Wind Energy in America: A History* (Norman: University of Oklahoma, Norman Press, 1996), pp. 45–47, 52 ("more than offset").
6. Righter, *Wind Energy in America,* p. 94 ("Cheapest Power").
7. Palmer Putnam, *Putnam's Power from the Wind,* ed. Gerald Koeppl (New York: Van Nostrand Reinhold, 1982), p. 3 ("surprisingly high").
8. *New York Times,* August 31, 1941.
9. Righter, *Wind Energy in America,* p. 136 ("precursor").
10. Righter, *Wind Energy in America,* p. 174 ("We thought").
11. John Berger, *Charging Ahead: The Business of Renewable Energy and What It Means for America* (Berkeley: University of California Press, 1997), p. 157 ("suspend you"); interview with Chris Hunt; Righter, *Wind Energy in America,* p. 171 ("eyesore").
12. Interview with James Dehlsen.
13. Interview with James Dehlsen; Ole Sonnichsen, *The Winner: The Dramatic Story of Vestas* (Copenhagen: Gads Forlag, 2009).
14. Henry Nielsen, Keld Nielsen, Flemming Petersen, and Hans Siggaard Jensen, "Risø National Laboratory: Forty Years of Research in a Changing Society," Risø National Laboratory, 1998, pp. 3, 19 ("peaceful use"); Ole Sonnichsen, *The Winner,* p. 18.
15. Interview with James Dehlsen; Peter Asmus, *Reaping the Wind: How Mechanical Wizards, Visionaries, and Profiteers Helped Shape Our Energy Future* (Washington, DC: Island Press, 2001), pp. 42–43, 119; Righter, *Wind Energy in America,* p. 181 (90 percent).
16. Berger, *Charging Ahead,* p. 155; Righter, *Wind Energy in America,* pp. 230–31.
17. *Forbes,* July 18, 1983; Righter, *Wind Energy in America*, p. 209; Asmus, *Reaping the Wind,* p. 127 ("tax farms").
18. Interview with James Dehlsen; *Washington Post,* November 17, 1991.
19. Interview with Robert Kelly.
20. Interview with Victor Abate.
21. World Wind Energy Association, *World Wind Energy Report 2009* (Bonn: World Wind Energy Association Head Office, 2010).
22. Liu Zhenya, speech, Washington, D.C., April 24, 2009.
23. Interview ("precious resource").
24. IHS Emerging Energy Research, "Global Wind Turbine Markets and Strategies: 2010–2025," p. 1.13.

25. Interview with Tulsi Tanit ("beauty of wind"); *Wall Street Journal,* April 18, 2008 ("under pressure").
26. IHS Emerging Energy Research, "Global Wind Plant Ownership Rankings 2009," June 2010, p. 5.
27. Interview with Lew Hay III.
28. Lawrence Makovich, Patricia DiOrio, and Douglas Giuffre, "Renewable Portfolio Standards: Getting Ahead of Themselves," IHS CERA, February 2008 (6 percent).
29. "PG&E Corp. Q2 Earnings Call," transcript, August 6, 2008 ("gets hot"); Liu Zhenya, speech, Washington, D.C., April 24, 2009.
30. Interview ("awfully long way").
31. Interview with James Dehlsen; Jon Wellinghoff interview, GreenMonk, April 15, 2010, at http://www.ferc.gov/media/videos/wellinghoff/2010/04-15-10-wellinghoff-transcript-part-2.pdf.
32. Interview.
33. IHS CERA, "Renewable Portfolio Standards: Getting Ahead of Themselves," 2008; IHS CERA, "Comparing the Full Cost of Wind Generation to Other Options in Texas," 2008.
34. BBC News, September 23, 2010.
35. Interview ("windiest places").
36. Interview.
37. *Boston Globe,* April 28, 2010.

Chapter 31: The Fifth Fuel—Efficiency

1. National Academy of Sciences, *Real Prospects for Energy Efficiency in the United States* (Washington, DC: National Academies Press, 2010), p. 4; ExxonMobil, *Outlook for Energy: A View to 2030,* December 2010.
2. World Economic Forum and IHS CERA, *Energy Vision Update 2010: Towards a More Energy Efficient World,* 2010, p. 12; Barack Obama, "Remarks by the President on Energy," June 29, 2009.
3. Alan Greenspan, *The Age of Turbulence: Adventures in a New World* (New York: Penguin Press, 2007), p. 492.
4. Scott Murtishaw and Lee Schipper, "Disaggregated Analysis of U.S. Energy Consumption in the 1990s: Evidence of the Effects of the Internet and Rapid Economic Growth," *Energy Policy* 29, no. 15 (2001) pp. 1335–56.
5. Wen Jiabao, speech, National Teleconference on Energy Conservation and Emission Reduction, April 27, 2007.
6. Erica Downs, "China's Energy Rise," in *China's Rise in Historical Perspective,* ed. Brantly Womack (Lanham, MD: Rowman & Littlefield, 2010), p. 181 (*Jieneng Jianpai*).
7. Wen Jiabao, speech, National Teleconference on Energy Conservation and Emission Reduction, April 27, 2007.
8. BBC Worldwide Monitoring, March 5, 2010.
9. Joanna I. Lewis, "Decoding China's Climate and Energy Policy Post-Copenhagen," German Marshall Fund Policy Brief, June 2010; Hongyan H. Oliver, Kelly Sims Gallagher, Donglian Tian, and Jinhua Zhang, "China's Fuel Economy Standards for Passenger Vehicles," Energy Technology Innovation Policy research group, John F. Kennedy School of Government, Harvard University, March 2009.
10. Interview with Chinese mayor; *Financial Times,* October 27, 2010 ("iron fist"); *New York Times,* August 10, 2010.
11. Allison Hannon, Ying Liu, Jim Walker, Changhua Wu, *Delivering Low Carbon Growth: A Guide to China's 12th Five Year Plan* (The Climate Group with HSBC: March, 2011).
12. Neal Elliott and Anna Shipley, "Impacts of Energy Efficiency and Renewable Energy on Natural Gas Markets," American Council for an Energy-Efficient Economy, April 2006, pp. 11, 21.
13. Andrew Liveris, speech, CERAWeek, March 11, 2010.
14. Dow Corporation, "Dow Sustainability—Energy Efficiency and Conservation," at http://www.dow.com/commitments/goals/energy.htm.
15. Andrew Liveris, speech, CERAWeek, March 11, 2010; interview with Richard Wells; Andrew Liveris, *Wall Street Journal* 2008 Eco-Nomics Conference; interview with Andrew Liveris.
16. International Energy Agency, *Tracking Industrial Energy Efficiency and CO_2 Emissions: In Support of the G-8 Plan of Action* (Paris: International Energy Agency, 2007), pp. 19, 34.
17. Jeffery Smisek, speech, CERA Week, March 11, 2011; John Heimlich, "The Economic Climbout for US Airlines," ATA Economics, June 2, 2011, presentation, January 24, 2007 (higher fuel efficiency).

18. U.S. International Air Passenger and Freight Statistics, Federal Communications Commission, 2007 (sharp ascent); David Nielson, chief engineer for Airport Strategy at Boeing, "Boeing's Contribution to Aviation Sustainability," Pacific Basin Development Council, August 27, 2007 (By 2026); Jeffery Smisek, speech, CERA Week, March 11, 2011.
19. *Observer,* January 29, 2006 ("negative effects"); Rough Guides, press release, March 1, 2006; *Times* (London), July 23, 2006; *Lonely Planet: Discover Europe* (2010), p. 790.
20. Interview with Andris Piebalgs.

Chapter 32: Closing the Conservation Gap

1. *Chicago Tribune,* July 16, 1878 ("Apprehension").
2. Leon Glicksman, "Energy Efficiency in the Built Environment," *Physics Today* 61, no. 7 (2008), p. 2.
3. Gail Cooper, *Air-Conditioning America: Engineers and Controlled Environment, 1900–1960* (Baltimore: Johns Hopkins University Press, 1998), pp. 9–10; *Mechanical Engineering,* May 2000 (jackets).
4. Claude Wampler, "Dr. Willis H. Carrier: Father of Air Conditioning," The Newcomen Society of England, 1949; Margaret Ingels, *Willis Haviland Carrier: Father of Air Conditioning* (Louisville: Fetter Printing Company, 1991), pp. 33–34 ("manufactured weather").
5. Ingels, *Willis Haviland Carrier,* pp. 63–79 (Madison Square Garden); "The Milam Building," American Society of Mechanical Engineers, 1991 (high-rise); *Popular Mechanics,* July 1939 (Damascus and Baghdad).
6. *New York Times,* June 2, 2002.
7. Interview with Leon Glicksman.
8. Gary Simon to author.
9. Interview with Lee Schipper.
10. National Association of Home Builders, *Housing Facts, Figures, and Trends,* May 2007, p. 13; National Petroleum Council, "Residential Commercial Efficiency," July 18, 2007, p. 12.
11. Jone-Lin Wang, "Why Are We Using More Electricity?" *Wall Street Journal,* March 10, 2010 ("gadgiwatts"); The Climate Group, "Smart 2020: Enabling the Low Carbon Economy in the Information Age," 2008 (120 million); G. I. Meijer, "Cooling Energy-Hungry Data Centers," *Science* 328, no. 5976 (2010), pp. 318–19.
12. Lawrence Makovich, "Meeting the Power Conservation Investment Challenge," IHS CERA, 2007 ("conservation gap"); World Economic Forum and IHS CERA, *Energy Vision Update 2010: Towards a More Energy Efficient World,* 2010, p. 4 ("*investment grade*").
13. Interview with George Caraghiaur.
14. Glicksman, "Energy Efficiency in the Built Environment," pp. 3–6 ("high-tech versions"); interview with Leon Glicksman; U.S. Green Buildings Council Web site, http://www.usgbc.org.
15. Interview with Naohiro Amaya.
16. Interview with Yoriko Kawaguchi.
17. Ministry of Economy, Trade and Industry, *Top Runner Program,* rev. ed., March 2010, athttp://www.enecho.meti.go.jp/policy/saveenergy/toprunner2010.03en.pdf.
18. Kateri Callahan, "Building the Infrastructure for Energy Efficiency," in World Economic Forum and IHS CERA, *Energy Vision Update 2010: Towards a More Energy Efficient World,* 2010, p. 24 ("public policy support"); James Rogers, speech, CERAWeek, February 15 2008.
19. IHS CERA, *Smart Grid: Closing the Gap Between Perception and Reality* (2010); Brookings Institution Center for Technology and Innovation, "Smart Grid Future: Evaluating Policy Opportunities and Challenges after the Recovery Act," forum, July 14, 2010.
20. *Scientific American,* August 13, 2008.
21. Sewart Baker, Natalie Filipiak, and Katrina Timlin, "In the Dark: Crucial Industries Confront Cyberattacks," (CSIS and McAfee: 2011).

Chapter 33: Carbohydrate Man

1. Henry Ford and Samuel Crowther, *My Life and Work* (Garden City: Doubleday, Page & Co., 1923), pp. 188–200; Henry Ford, "Automobiles and Soybeans: An Interview with Arthur van Vlissingen, Jr.," *Rotarian,* September 1933.

2. Steven R. Weisman, *The Great Tax Wars: Lincoln—Teddy Roosevelt—Wilson: How the Income Tax Transformed America* (New York: Simon & Schuster, 2002); Hal Bernton, William Kovarik, and Scott Sklar, *The Forbidden Fuel: Power Alcohol in the Twentieth Century* (New York: Boyd Griffin, 1982), p. 10 ("made from cornstalks") .
3. Bernton, Kovarik, and Sklar, *The Forbidden Fuel,* pp. 1–13 ("wonderfully clean-burning," "rapidly depleted," "direct route," "potential speakeasy"); Reynold Wik, *Henry Ford and Grass-roots America* (Ann Arbor: University of Michigan Press, 1973), p. 249 (secretary).
4. *Washington Post,* October 13, 1977 (Birch Bayh); *Fortune,* October 1, 1990.
5. Steve Coll, *Ghost Wars: The Secret History of the CIA, Afghanistan, and Bin Laden, from the Soviet Invasion to September 10, 2001* (New York: Penguin Press, 2004), pp. 46–52; Jimmy Carter, *White House Diary* (New York: Farrar, Straus and Giroux, 2010), p. 382 ("sharpest message"); Jimmy Carter, Address to the Nation, January 4, 1980.
6. *New York Times,* January 7, 1980 (Warren Christopher); Bernton, Kovarik, and Sklar, *The Forbidden Fuel,* p. 105 (high scenario); *Washington Post,* August 3, 1986 ("very inefficient").
7. Interview with Richard Lugar; Brent D. Yacobucci, "Fuel Ethanol: Background and Public Policy Issues," Congressional Research Service, March 3, 2006 (E10); Richard G. Lugar and R. James Woolsey, "The New Petroleum," *Foreign Affairs* 78, no. 1 (1999), pp. 88–102 (mandatory targets).
8. *New York Times,* November 7, 2005 ("good old-fashioned"); "President Bush and President Lula Discuss Biofuel Technology," White House, March 9, 2007 ("truly obsessed," "couldn't have lunch"); George W. Bush, State of the Union Address, January 31, 2006 ("addicted to oil"); "Bush, da Silva Deliver Joint Remarks," CNN, November 6, 2005; *Wall Street Journal,* August 9, 2006 ("kind of startled").
9. Interview with José Goldemberg; Frederick Johnson, "Sugar in Brazil: Policy and Production," *The Journal of Developing Areas* 17, no. 2 (1983), pp. 243–56 (prices collapsed); William S. Saint, "Farming for Energy: Social Options under Brazil's National Alcohol Programme," *World Development* 10, no. 3 (1982), pp. 223–38 ("wartime economy"); Werner Baer and Claudio Paiva, "Brazil," in *The Political Economy of Latin America in the Postwar Period,* ed. Laura Randall (Austin: University of Texas Press, 1997), pp. 70–110 (no prospects); Marc Weidenmier, Joseph Davis, and Roger Aliaga-Diaz, "Is Sugar Sweeter at the Pump? The Macroeconomic Impact of Brazil's Alternative Energy Program," National Bureau of Economic Research, Working Paper No. 14362, October 2008; U.S. Congress, House of Representatives, Committee on Science and Technology, Subcommittee on Energy Development and Applications, 96th Congress, Venezuela and Brazil Visit—January 13–20, 1980 (Washington, DC: GPO), January 1980.
10. Interview with José Goldemberg; José Goldemberg, "Ethanol for a Sustainable Energy Future," *Science* 315, no. 5813 (2007), pp. 808–10; UNICA Sugarcane Industry Association Web site, at http://english.unica.com.br/dadosCotacao/estatistica/ (flexfuel).
11. The sometimes intense debate about the energy balance for ethanol has been going on since the late 1970s. John Deutch, *Energy Policy in Crisis: The Godkin Lecture* (Cambridge: Harvard University Press, 2011), ch. 5.
12. Corn Farmers Coalition, "Factbook," at http://www.cornfarmerscoalition.org/fact-book/; U.S. Department of Agriculture Economic Research Service, "U.S. Domestic Corn Use," at http://www.ers.usda.gov/Briefing/Corn/Gallery/Background/CornUseTable.html.
13. Interview with Georgina Kessel Martínez; *Washington Post,* January 27, 2007.
14. International Energy Agency, *Technology Roadmap: Biofuels for Transportation* (Paris: OECD/IEA, 2011), pp. 16–20.
15. Bernton, Kovarik, and Sklar, *The Forbidden Fuel,* pp. 74–75 (Leo Spano); *Washington Post,* Outlook, "Some Trash Can Be Really Sweet," November 11, 1975, p. 1011 ("lowly fungi"); Norm Augustine to author ("quantum leap").
16. *Nightline,* ABC, aired January 23, 2007 (Bransby); Bush, State of the Union Address, January 31, 2006.
17. Government of Canada, "Iogen—Canada's New Alchemists," Innovation in Canada Series, February 15, 2005.
18. Tiffany Groode, "Breaking through the Wall: Identifying the Main Barriers to Increasing Biofuels Production," IHS CERA, 2009 ("daunting logistics," "local nature"); Paul A. Willems, "The Biofuels Landscape: Through the Lens of Industrial Chemistry," *Science* 325, no. 5941 (2009), pp. 707–10.

19. Interview with Richard Hamilton; *Newsweek,* October 27, 1980.
20. Interview with Steven Koonin.

Chapter 34: Internal Fire

1. William Adams Simonds, *Edison: His Life, His Work, His Genius* (Indianapolis: Bobbs-Merrill, 1934), pp. 273–75; Douglas Brinkley, *Wheels for the World: Henry Ford, His Company, and a Century of Progress* (New York: Viking, 2003), pp. 25–26; Henry Ford (with Samuel Crowther), *Edison as I Knew Him* (New York, Cosmopolitan, 1930), pp. 1–12.
2. David A. Kirsch, *The Electric Vehicle and the Burden of History* (New Brunswick: Rutgers University Press: 2000), p. 1 ("five different methods").
3. C. Lyle Cummins, *Internal Fire: The Internal Combustion Engine, 1673–1900* (Wilsonville, OR: Carnot Press, 1976); David Landes, *The Unbound Prometheus: Technological Change and Industrial Development in Western Europe, from 1750 to Present,* 2nd ed. (New York: Cambridge University Press, 2003), p. 102 ("within reach"); "The Lotus Leaf: Evolution and Standardization of the Automobile Source," *Lotus Magazine* 7, no. 4 (1916), pp. 183–92 (Cugnot).
4. Cummins, *Internal Fire,* pp. 138–72.
5. *Chicago Tribune,* August 8, 1892 ("a wagon propelled"); James Flink, *The Automobile Age* (Cambridge: Massachusetts Institute of Technology Press, 1990), p. 2 (Red Flag Act).
6. Flink, *The Automobile Age,* p. 13.
7. Brinkley, *Wheels for the World,* p. 32; *Akron Beacon Journal,* June 20, 1999 (first police car); Carl Sulzberger, "An Early Road Warrior: Electric Vehicles in the Early Years of the Automobile," *IEEE Power and Energy Magazine* 2, no. 3 (2004), pp. 66–71.
8. U.S. Department of Energy, "History of Electric Vehicles: The Early Years (1890 to 1930)" (Phaeton, steamers); James Flink, *America Adopts the Automobile, 1895–1910* (Cambridge: Massachusetts Institute of Technology Press, 1970), pp. 242, 273.
9. Matthew Josephson, *Edison: A Biography* (New York: John Wiley and Sons, 1992), pp. 407–14.
10. Brinkley, *Wheels for the World,* pp. 114–15 ("useless nuisance").
11. John B. Rae, *American Automobile Manufacturers: The First Forty Years* (Philadelphia: Chilton Company, 1959), p. 33 ("fever"); Flink, *America Adopts the Automobile, 1895–1910,* pp. 50, 64 ("god to the women").
12. Brinkley, *Wheels for the World,* p. 100 ("greatest need today"); Ford Corporation, "Model T Facts," at http://media.ford.com/article_display.cfm?article_id=858.
13. Josephson, *Edison: A Biography,* p. 423 ("electric Pigs").
14. *National Petroleum News,* February 5, 1936 ("dump").
15. Robert Stobaugh and Daniel Yergin, eds., *Energy Future: A Report of the Energy Project at the Harvard Business School* (New York: Ballantine Books, 1979), p. 183 ("handouts"); Henry Ford II, speech, White House Conference on Balanced National Growth and Economic Development, January 30, 1978 ("moved us faster"); *Los Angeles Times,* January 21, 1979 ("give up").
16. Interview with Philip Sharp.
17. *Popular Science,* July 1992; Amory Lovins, "Energy Strategy: The Road Not Taken?," *Foreign Affairs* 55, no. 1 (1976), pp. 65–96.
18. David Halberstam, *The Reckoning* (New York: Avon Books, 1994), p. 304; Daniel Sperling and Deborah Golden, *Two Billion Cars: Driving Toward Sustainability* (Oxford: Oxford University Press, 2009), p. 19, Toyota Web site.
19. Interview with Rick Wagoner ("home run"); *Fortune,* May 1, 1995; *Fortune,* April 11, 1994 ("Golden Age"); *Fortune,* January 10, 1994 ("most successful").
20. Interview with Rick Wagoner ("truck capacity"); *New York Times,* October 20, 1996; *New York Times,* October 27, 1996.
21. IHS CERA, "Gasoline and the American People," November 2006.
22. David L. Greene, "Policies to Increase Passenger Car and Light Truck Fuel Efficiency," testimony, U.S. Senate Committee on Energy and Natural Resources, January 30, 2007.
23. Ibid.
24. Toyota Motor Corporation spells its name differently from the name of the family that founded the company. The motor company was established in 1937 as a spin-off of the family's weaving

concern. *Fortune,* June 26, 2009; Toyota Motor Corporation, at http://www.toyota.com/html/hybridsynergyview/2005/summer/hybridhistory.html; *Fortune,* February 24, 2006 ("global twenty-first century"); *Fortune,* February 24, 2006 ("really cars").

25. Sperling and Golden, *Two Billion Cars,* p. 170 (missed the point); *Fortune,* February 24, 2006 (Academy Awards).
26. Congressional Budget Office, *Effects of Gasoline Prices on Driving Behavior and Vehicle Markets* (Washington, DC: GPO), January 2008, p. 32.
27. *Time,* October 6, 1961 ("vice versa"); *International Herald Tribune,* March 7, 2007 ("warriors"); National Research Council, *Effectiveness and Impact of Corporate Average Fuel Economy Standards* (Washington, DC: National Academies Press, 2002), pp. 4–5 ("marked inconsistency").
28. *New York Times,* December 19, 2007.
29. Associated Press, December 20, 2007 ("slap in the face"); Sperling and Golden, p. 65 ("hottest car"); *Financial Times,* January 11, 2008.

Chapter 35: The Great Electric Car Experiment

1. "A. J. Haagen-Smit," in *World of Chemistry* (Thomson Gale Publishers, 2005). Arie Haagen-Smit, et al., "A Physiologically Active Principle from Cannabis Sativa (Marihuana)," *Science* 91, no. 2373 (1940), pp. 602–3.
2. *Los Angeles Times,* March 19, 1977 ("stinking cloud," "not be difficult").
3. *Los Angeles Times,* November 5, 1954.
4. Tiffany Groode and Levi Tillemann-Dick, "The Race to Build the Electric Car," *Wall Street Journal Special Section,* March 9, 2011; Agence France-Presse, October 1, 2009 ("battle"); Reuters, July 30, 2008 ("Industrial Revolution"); Barack Obama, speech, February 19, 2010.
5. *Los Angeles Times,* October 14, 1954; *Los Angeles Times,* October 21, 1954 ("dangerous intensity," Housewives); *Los Angeles Times,* October 26, 1954; *Los Angeles Times,* October 27, 1954 ("City Revels"); *Los Angeles Times,* November 7, 1954 ("clear, bright skies").
6. Kevin Starr, *Golden Dreams: California in an Age of Abundance, 1950–1963* (New York: Oxford, 2009), p. 260 ("worst attack ever"); South Coast Air Quality Management District, "Upland, Calif., Had Last Stage III Smog Alert in U.S.," May 1997, at http://www.aqmd.gov/news1/Archives/History/stage3.html ("auto travel"); Chip Jacobs and William Kelly, *Smogtown: The Lung-Burning History of Pollution in Los Angeles* (New York: Overlook Press, 2008), p. 162 ("greatest concentration").
7. *Los Angeles Times,* March 22 1977; *Los Angeles Times,* March 19, 1977.
8. South Coast Air Quality Management District, *The Southland's War on Smog: Fifty Years of Progress Toward Clean Air,* May 1997; Mary Nichols, remarks, *Wall Street Journal* Eco-Nomics Conference, March 4, 2011.
9. Daniel Sperling and Deborah Golden, *Two Billion Cars: Driving Toward Sustainability* (Oxford: Oxford University Press, 2009), p. 24 ("real culprit"); interview with Tom Stricker.
10. *Bloomberg,* July 18, 2008.
11. Interview with Fred Smith; Fred Smith, testimony, U.S. Senate Energy and Natural Resources Committee, June 22, 2010.
12. Seth Fletcher, *Bottle Lightning: Superbatteries, Electric Cars, and the New Lithium Economy* (New York: Hill and Wang, 2011), pp. 30–35; National Research Council, *Transition to Alternative Transportation Technologies: Plug-in Hybrid Electric Vehicles* (Washington, DC: National Academies Press, 2010), p. 9.
13. *Fortune,* July 11, 2008.
14. *Fortune,* July 1, 2010 (lithium-ion batteries); *New Yorker,* August 24, 2009 ("hugely underestimated," "logjam"); Elon Musk, "In the Beginning," Tesla Blog, June 22, 2009 ("redesigned"); *Wired,* October 2010; Robert Lutz to author.
15. Scott Doggett, "32 Hours Needed to Charge at Tesla Roadster Using Common Electrical Outlet," Edmonds.com, July 7, 2008, at http://blogs.edmunds.com/greencaradvisor/2008/07/32-hours-needed-to-charge-a-tesla-roadster-using-common-electrical-outlet.html.
16. Interview with Carlos Ghosn; *Fortune,* February 19, 2010 ("mermaid," "not a bet").
17. *Bloomberg,* July 15, 2010.

18. Interview with Lee Schipper ("emissions elsewhere").
19. IHS CERA, "Automotive Scenarios 2010"; Electrification Coalition, *Electrification Roadmap: Revolutionizing Transportation and Achieving Energy Security* (Washington, DC: Electrification Coalition, 2009).
20. Interview with Steve Koonin.
21. Calvin Timmerman, "Smart Grid's Future: Evaluating Policy Opportunities and Challenges after the Recovery Act," Brookings Institution, July 24, 2010.
22. Interview with Rick Wagoner.
23. Interview with Carlos Ghosn.
24. Zhang Guobao, speech, U.S.-China Strategic Forum on Clean Energy Cooperation, Brookings Institution, January 18, 2011.
25. *Fortune,* April 13, 2009.
26. Reuters, December 29, 2009.
27. Interview with Tom Stricker.
28. California Fuel Cell Partnership, "Station Map," at: http://www.cafcp.org/stationmap.
29. Mary Barcella, "Natural Gas for Transportation: Niche Market or More?" IHS CERA, October 13, 2010.
30. Dieter Zetsche, remarks, *Wall Street Journal* Eco-Nomics Conference, March 13, 2008; Bill Ford, remarks, *Wall Street Journal* Eco-Nomics Conference, March 3, 2011.
31. Interview with John Heywood.

BIBLIOGRAPHY

I want to express great appreciation to the following people for sharing their observations, experience, and insights. Most of the interviews were conducted for the book; a few were conducted prior to commencing this book.

Interviews

Victor Abate
Terence Adams
Vagit Alekperov
Naohiro Amaya
Abdullah bin Hamad al-Attiyeh
Jose Sergio Gabrielli de Azevedo
Jean Blancard
Samuel Bodman
John Browne
John Bryson
George Caraghiaur
Phil Carroll
Guy Caruso
Fu Chengyu
James Connaughton
David Davis
James Dehlsen
Thierry Demarest
Paula Dobriansky
Archie Dunham
Michael Eckhart
Ira Ehrenpreis
Stuart Eizenstat
Daniel Esty
Donald Evans
Richard Fairbanks
Khalid Al-Falih
Hans-Josef Fell
Mark Fisher
Nancy Floyd
Ronald Freeman
Yegor Gaidar
Carlos Ghosn
Samuel Gillespie
Luis Giusti
Leon Glicksman
Joseph Goffman
Jose Goldemberg
Valerii Graefer
C. Boyden Gray
Wu Guihui
Richard Haass
Chuck Hagel
Richard Hamilton
David Harwood
Lew Hay III
Denis Hayes
John Hess
John Heywood
Chris Hunt
John Imle
Shirley Jackson
Zhou Jiping
Jan Kalicki
Yoriko Kawaguchi
Joseph Kelliher
Robert Kelly
David King
George Kistiakowsky
Steve Koonin
Fred Krupp
Jeffrey Kupfer
Aleksander Kwasniewski
Philippe de Ladoucette
Ray Lane
Andrew Liveris
Amory Lovins
Rob McKee
Robert Maguire
James Mahoney
Ed Markey
Georgina Kessel Martinez
Richard Matzke
Paul Maycock
Robert Metcalfe
Marty Miller
Anton Milner
Elizabeth Moler

Ernest Moniz
Mark Moody-Stuart
Ed Morse
Masahisa Naitoh
John Negroponte
Larry Nichols
William Nordhaus
Lucio Noto
Ngozi Okonjo-Iweala
Jim O'Neill
Raymond Orbach
David O'Reilly
Rajendra Pachauri
Andris Piebalgs
James Placke
Rafe Pomerantz
Jean Posbic
Joseph Pratt
Lucian Pugliaresi
Zhou Qingzu
Lee Raymond
William Reilly
Robert Righter
Matt Rogers
Peter R. Rose
Taichi Sakaiya (Kotaro Ikeguchi)
David Sandalow
Richard Sandor
Hermann Scheer
Lee Schipper
James Schlesinger
Gerhard Schroeder
Brent Scowcroft
Philip Sharp
Gordon Shearer
Robert Shiller
A. L. Shrier
Scott Sklar
Jeffery Smisek
Robert Stavins
Nicholas Stern
Dan Steward
Tom Stricker
John Sununu
Tulsi Tanit
Wang Tao
George Tenet
John Tully
Takayuki Ueda
Peter Varadi
Rick Wagoner
Charles Wald
Richard Wells
William Wicker
Mason Willrich
Tim Wirth
Shi Zhengrong
Liu Zhenya

Other Interviews

Heydar Aliyev. *Azerbaijan International.* Winter 1994.
Gustaf Arrhenius. Oral History Project. Scripps Institution of Oceanography Library.
Commanding Heights. PBS. 2001. http://www.pbs.org/wgbh/commandingheights.
    William Draper III
    Stanley Fischer
    Mikhail Gorbachev
    Robert Rubin
James Hansen. *Frontline.* PBS. January 10, 2007.
Roger Revelle. Oral history. The Bancroft Library. University of California. Berkeley, 1986.
Admiral Hyman Rickover. *60 Minutes.* CBS. December 1984.
Tim Wirth. *Frontline.* PBS. January 17, 2007.

Data and Statistical Sources

A very wide range of data sources underpin the narrative. The most important and easily accessible are the extraordinary resources of the EIA—the U.S. Energy Information Administration. Two other important sources are the International Energy Agency and the BP Statistical Review, and the tables that support it. Extensive use has been made of the IHS CERA and IHS energy databases and those of IHS Emerging Energy Research and IHS Global Insight, covering a wide range from upstream field-by-field data to solar panel shipments to economic growth. Other important sources are the International Monetary Fund and the CIA *World Factbook*, along with many government agencies around the world, industry and trade associations, nongovernmental organizations, and other organizations.

Selected Bibliography

Ackerman, Bruce A., and Richard B. Stewart. "Reforming Environmental Law: The Democratic Case for Market Incentives." *Columbia Journal of Environmental Law* 171, no. 13 (1988).

Adams, Terry. "Baku Oil Diplomacy and 'Early Oil' 1994–1998: An External Perspective." In *Azerbaijan in Global Politics: Crafting Foreign Policy*. Baku: Azerbaijan Diplomatic Academy, 2009.

Agassiz, Elizabeth Cary, ed. *Louis Agassiz: His Life and Correspondence.* Vol. 1. Cambridge: The Riverside Press, 1886.

"A. J. Haagen-Smit." In *World of Chemistry*. Tampa, Fl: Thomson Gale Publishers, 2005.

Akerlog, George A., and Robert J. Shiller. *Animal Spirits: How Human Psychology Drives the Economy, and Why It Matters for Global Capitalism.* Princeton: Princeton University Press, 2009.

Albright, Madeleine. *Madame Secretary: A Memoir.* New York: Miramax, 2003.

al-Chalabi, Issam. "Oil in Postwar Iraq." Presentation. June 2003.

Alekperov, Vagit. Introduction to *Dabycha* (first Russian edition of *The Prize*).

———. *Oil of Russia: Past, Present, and Future.* Minneapolis: East View Press, 2011.

Ambrose, Stephen E. *Eisenhower: Soldier and President.* New York: Simon & Schuster, 1990.

Amoco Corp, Proxy Statement/Prospectus, October 30, 1998.

Anderson, William. *Nautilus 90 North.* New York: World Publishing Corp., 1959.

Ante, Spencer E. *Creative Capital: George Doriot and the Birth of Venture Capital.* Boston: Harvard Business Press, 2008.

Antholis, William, and Strobe Talbott. *Fast Forward: Ethics and Politics in the Age of Global Warming.* Washington: Brookings Institution Press, 2010.

Arrhenius, Svante. "On the Influence of Carbonic Acid in the Air upon the Temperature of the Ground." *The London, Edinburgh, and Dublin Philosophical Magazine and Journal of Science,* April 1896.

———. *Worlds in the Making: The Evolution of the Universe.* Translated by H. Borns. New York: Harper & Brothers, 1908.

Aslund, Anders. *Russia's Capitalist Revolution: Why Market Reform Succeeded and Democracy Failed.* Washington, D.C.: Peterson Institute for International Economics, 2007.

Asmus, Peter. *Reaping the Wind: How Mechanical Wizards, Visionaries, and Profiteers Helped Shape Our Energy Future.* Washington, D.C.: Island Press, 2000.

Averill, Bruce, and Eric A. M. Luijf. "Canvassing the Cyber Security Landscape: Why Energy Companies Need to Pay Attention." *Journal of Energy Security,* May 2010.

Axworthy, Michael. *A History of Iran: Empire of the Mind.* New York: Basic Books, 2010.

Bahree, Bhushan. "Fields of Dreams: The Great Iraqi Oil Rush: Its Potential, Challenges, and Limits." IHS CERA. March 2010.

Baker, John. "The Successful Privatization of Britain's Electricity Industry." In Leonard S. Hyman, *The Privatization of Public Utilities.* Vienna, Va.: Public Utilities Reports, 1995.

Baker, Peter, and Susan Glasser. *Kremlin Rising: Vladimir Putin's Russia and the End of Revolution.* Washington, D.C.: Potomac Books, 2007.

Baker, Stewart, Natalie Filipiak, and Katrina Timlin. *In the Dark: Crucial Industries Confront Cyberattacks.* Santa Clara, CA: CSIS and McAfee, 2011.

Barrett, J. P. *Electricity at the Columbian Exposition.* Chicago: R.R. Donnelley & Sons Company, 1894.

Barty-King, Hugh. *New Flame: How Gas Changed the Commercial, Domestic, and Industrial Life of Britain between 1813 and 1984.* Tavistock: Graphmitre, 1984.

Beaubouef, Bruce A. *The Strategic Petroleum Reserve: U.S. Energy Security and Oil Politics, 1975–2005.* College Station: Texas A&M University Press, 2007.

Benedick, Richard Elliott. *Ozone Diplomacy: New Directions in Safeguarding the Planet.* Cambridge: Harvard University Press, 1998.

Bergen, Peter. *The Longest War: The Enduring Conflict between America and Al-Qaeda.* New York: Free Press, 2011.

Bergen, Peter, and Bruce Hoffman. *Assessing the Terrorist Threat: A Report of the Center's National Security Preparedness Group.* Bipartisan Policy Center. September 10, 2009.

Berger, John. *Charging Ahead: The Business of Renewable Energy and What It Means for America.* Berkeley: University of California Press, 1997.

Bernton, Hal, William Kovarik, and Scott Sklar. *The Forbidden Fuel: Power Alcohol in the Twentieth Century.* New York: Boyd Griffin, 1982.

Blackwelder, Eliot. "Petroleum Resources of China and Siberia." *Mining and Metallurgy* 187 (1922).

Blair, Dennis. "Annual Threat Assessment of the U.S. Intelligence Community for the Senate Select Committee on Intelligence," February 2, 2010.

Blair, Tony. *A Journey: My Political Life.* New York: Knopf, 2010.

Bolin, Bert. *A History of the Science and Politics of Climate Change: The Role of the Intergovernmental Panel on Climate Change.* Cambridge: Cambridge University Press, 2008.

Bowen, Mark. *Thin Ice: Unlocking the Secrets of Climate Change on the World's Highest Mountains.* New York: Henry Holt and Company, 2005.

BP America. *Deepwater Horizon Accident Investigation Report.* September 8, 2010.

Brandt, Willy. *My Life In Politics.* New York: Viking, 1992.

Bremer III, L. Paul, and Malcolm McConnell. *My Year in Iraq: The Struggle to Build a Future of Hope*. New York: Simon & Schuster, 2006.

Brinkley, Douglas. *Wheels for the World: Henry Ford, His Company, and a Century of Progress*. New York: Viking Penguin, 2003.

Broecker, Wallace. "Climate Change: Are We on the Brink of a Pronounced Global Warming?" *Science,* 189, no. 4201 (1975).

Brown, Peter McKenzie, Gordon Jaremko, and David Finch. *The Great Oil Age*. Calgary: Detselig, 1993.

Browne, John. *Beyond Business*. London: Weidenfeld and Nicolson, 2010.

Bryce, Robert. *Gusher of Lies*. New York: Public Affairs, 2008.

———. *Power Hungry: The Myths of "Green" Energy and the Real Fuels of the Future.* New York: Public Affairs, 2010.

Bulow, Jeremy, and Carl Shapiro. "The BP Amoco-ARCO Merger: Alaskan Crude Oil (2000)." In *The Antitrust Revolution*. Edited by John Kwoka Jr. and Lawrence White. New York: Oxford University Press, 2008.

Bupp, Irving C., and Jean-Claude Derian. *Light Water: How the Nuclear Dream Dissolved.* New York: Basic Books, 1978.

Bush, George H. W., and Brent Scowcroft. *A World Transformed*. New York: Vintage, 1999.

Bush, George W. *Decision Points.* New York: Random House, 2010.

Bush, Laura. *Spoken from the Heart*. New York: Scribner, 2010.

Cabot, Thomas D. *Beggar on Horseback: The Autobiography of Thomas D. Cabot*. Boston: David R. Godine, 1979.

Cadbury, Deborah. *Space Race: The Epic Battle Between America and the Soviet Union for Dominion of* Space. New York: Harper Perennial, 2006.

Callendar, G. S. "Can Carbon Dioxide Influence Climate?" *Weather* 4 (1949).

Cameron, Rondo, and Larry Neal. *A Concise Economic History of the World*. Oxford: Oxford University Press, 2002.

Campbell, Colin, and Jean Laherrere. "The End of Cheap Oil." *Scientific American*, March 1998.

Campbell-Kelly, Martin, and William Aspray. *Computer: A History of the Information Machine*. Boulder: Westview Press, 2004.

Cannon, Lou. *Governor Reagan: His Rise to Power*. New York: Public Affairs, 2003.

Carnot, Sadi. *Reflections on the Motive Power of Fire.* Translated by R. H. Thurston. Mineola, N.Y.: Dover Publications, 1988.

Caro, Robert. *The Path to Power*. New York: Vintage Books, 1990.

Carter, Jimmy. *White House Diary*. New York: Farrar. Straus & Giroux, 2010.

———. *Why Not the Best?* New York: Bantam Books, 1976.

Chandler, Raymond. "Red Wind." In *Trouble Is My Business*. New York: Vintage, 1988.

Chapman, Sydney. *IGY: Year of Discovery*. Ann Arbor: University of Michigan Press, 1959.

Chastko, Paul. *Developing Alberta's Oil Sands: From Karl Clark to Kyoto*. Calgary: University of Calgary Press, 2005.

Chernow, Ronald. *Titan: The Life of John D. Rockefeller Sr.* New York: Random House, 1998.

Chestnut, Lauraine G., and David M. Mills. "A Fresh Look at the Benefits and Costs of the U.S. Acid Rain Program." *Journal of Environmental Management* 77 (2005).

Christensen, Clay. *The Innovator's Dilemma*. New York: Collins Business Essentials, 2006.

Chu, Steven. "Autobiography." Nobel Prize in Physics. 1997.

Churchill, Randolph S. *Winston Churchill.* Vol. 2, *Companion Volume, Part 3, 1926–27.* Boston: Houghton Mifflin, 1969.

———. *Winston Churchill.* Vol. 2, *Young Statesman, 1901–1904.* London: Heinemann, 1968.

Churchill, Winston S. *The World Crisis: 1911–1918.* New York: Scribner, 1931.

Cipolla, Carlo M. *Before the Industrial Revolution: European Society and Economy 1000–1700.* New York: Norton, 1993.

Clery, Daniel. "Sending African Sunlight to Europe. Special Delivery." *Science* 329, no. 5993 (2010).

Coase, Ronald. Autobiography. Nobel Prize in Economics. http://nobelprize.org/nobel_prizes/economics/laureates/1991/coase-autobio.html.

———. "The Problem of Social Cost." *The Journal of Law and Economics* 3 (1960): 1–44.

Cohn, Roger. "Conversation with Nobel Prize Winner Rajendra Pauchari." *Yale Environment 360*. June 3, 2008.

Coll, Steve. *Ghost Wars: The Secret History of the CIA, Afghanistan, and bin Laden from the Soviet Invasion to September 10, 2001*. New York: Penguin Press, 2004.

Collins, Catherine, and Douglas Frantz. *Fallout: The True Story of the CIA's Secret War on Nuclear Trafficking*. New York: Free Press, 2011.

Colton, Timothy J. *Yeltsin: A Life*. New York: Basic Books, 2008.

Commission on the Intelligence Capabilities of the United States Regarding Weapons of Mass Destruction. *Report to the President of the United States*. March 31, 2005.

Committee on America's Energy Future. *America's Energy Future: Technology and Transformation*. Washington, D.C.: National Academies Press, 2009.

Congressional Budget Office. *Effects of Gasoline Prices on Driving Behavior and Vehicle Markets*. January 2008.

Conniff, Richard. "The Political History of Cap and Trade." *Smithsonian Magazine*, August 2009.

Conot, Robert. *Thomas Edison: A Stroke of Luck*. New York: Bantam, 1980.

Cooper, Gail. *Air-Conditioning America: Engineers and the Controlled Environment, 1900–1960*. Baltimore: Johns Hopkins University Press, 1998.

Cordesman, Anthony H. "Iran, Oil, and the Strait of Hormuz." Center for Strategic and International Affairs, March 26, 2007.

Coronel, Gustavo. *The Nationalization of the Venezuelan Oil Industry: From Technocratic Success to Political Failure*. Lexington, Ky. : Lexington Books, 1983.

CSIS Commission on Cybersecurity for the 44th Presidency. *Cybersecurity Two Years Later: A Report of the CSIS Commission on Cybersecurity for the 44th Presidency*. Washington, D.C.: CSIS, 2011.

Cummins, C. Lyle. *Internal Fire: The Internal Combustion Engine, 1673–1900*. Lake Oswego, Or.: Carnot Press, 1976.

Dales, John H. *Pollution, Property & Prices: An Essay in Policy-making and Economics*. Toronto: University of Toronto Press, 1968.

Darst, Robert. *Smokestack Diplomacy: Cooperation and Conflict in East-West Environmental Politics*. Cambridge: Massachusetts Institute of Technology, 2001

Davis, Kenneth S. *FDR: The New Deal Years, 1933–1937*. New York: Random House, 1986.

Davis, Stephen. *The Potential for Peace and Reconciliation in the Niger Delta*. Coventry: Cathedral. February 2009.

Deffeyes, Kenneth S. *Hubbert's Peak: The Impending World Oil Shortage*. Princeton: Princeton University Press, 2001.

Delaisi, Francis. *Oil: Its Influence on Politics*. Translated by C. Leonard Leese. London: Labour Publishing, 1922.

De Novo, John. "Petroleum and the United States Navy Before World War I." *The Mississippi Valley Historical Review*, 41, no. 4 (1955).

de Saussure, Horace-Benedict. *Voyage dans les Alps*. Geneva: Chez Le Pricipaux Libraires, 1834.

Deutch, John. *Energy Policy in Crisis: The Godkin Lecture*. Cambridge: Harvard University Press, 2011.

———. "The Good News About Gas: The Natural Gas Revolution and Its Consequences." *Foreign Affairs* 90, no. 1 (2011).

Dhillon, Navtej, and Tarik Yousef. eds. *Generation in Waiting: The Unfulfilled Promise of Young People in the Middle East*. Washington, D.C.: Brookings Institution Press, 2009.

Doan, David. "Memorial to M. King Hubbert." *Geological Society of America Memorials* 24 (1994).

Dobbins, James. *After the Taliban: Nation-Building in Afghanistan*. Washington, D.C.: Potomac Books, 2008.

Downs, Erica. "Business Interest Groups in Chinese Politics: The Case of the Oil Companies." In *China's Changing Political Landscape: Prospects for Democracy*. Edited by Cheng Li. Washington, D.C.: Brookings Institution Press, 2008.

———. *China Inc.: China Development Bank's Cross-Border Energy Deals*. Washington, D.C.: Brookings Institution Press, 2011.

———. "China's Energy Rise." In *China's Rise in Historical Perspective*. Edited by Brantly Womack. New York: Rowman and Littlefield, 2010.

———. "China's Quest for Oil Self-sufficiency in the 1960s." Unpublished paper, 2001.

———. "Who's Afraid of China's Oil Companies?" In *Energy Security: Economics, Politics, Strategy, and Implications*. Washington, D.C.: Brookings Institution Press, 2010.

Duelfer, Charles. *Hide and Seek: The Search for Truth in Iraq*. New York: Public Affairs, 2009.
Duncan, Francis. *Rickover: The Struggle for Excellence*. Annapolis, Md.: Naval Institute Press, 2001.
Ebinger, Charles, and Kevin Massey. "Enhancing Smart Grid Cybersecurity in the Age of Information Warfare." Brookings Energy Security Initiative, February 2011.
Eichenwald, Kurt. *Conspiracy of Fools: A Trace Story*. New York: Broadway Books, 2005.
Edelman, Eric, Andrew Krepinevich Jr., and Evan Braden Montgomery. "The Dangers of a Nuclear Iran: The Limits of Containment." *Foreign Affairs* 90, no. 1 (2011).
Eisenhower, David. *Eisenhower at War: 1943–1954*. New York: Random House, 1986.
El-Ashry, Mohamed T. "Climate Change, Clean Energy, and U.S. Leadership." AAAS Science and Technology Policy Fellows Programs. 30th Anniversary Symposium. May 13, 2004.
Electrification Coalition. *Electrification Roadmap: Revolutionizing Transportation and Achieving Energy Security*. November 2009.
Ellerman, Denny, Paul L. Joskow, Richard Schmalensee, Juan-Pablo Montero, and Elizabeth M. Bailey. *Markets for Clean Air: The U.S. Acid Rain Program*. Cambridge: Cambridge University Press, 2000.
Energy Security Leadership Council. *Recommendations to the Nation on Reducing U.S. Oil Dependence*. December 2006.
Esty, Daniel C., and Andrew S. Winston. *Green to Gold: How Smart Companies Use Environmental Strategy to Innovate, Create Value, and Build Competitive Advantage*. New Haven: Yale University Press, 2006.
Eve, A. S., and C. H. Creasey. *Life and Work of John Tyndall*. London: Macmillan, 1945.
Exxon Corp, Form S-4 Registration Statement Under the Securities Act of 1933, April 5, 1999.
Ezell, John S. *Innovations in Energy: The Story of Kerr-McGee*. Norman: University of Oklahoma Press, 1979.
Fattouh, Bassam, and Coby van der Linde. *The International Energy Forum: Twenty Years of Consumer-Produce Country Dialogue in a Changing World*. Riyadh: International Energy Forum, 2011.
Federal Energy Regulatory Commission. *Report on Plant Outages in the State of California*, February 1, 2001.
Ferrell, Robert, ed. *The Eisenhower Diaries*. New York: W.W. Norton, 1981.
Ferrier, R. W. *The History of the British Petroleum Company, Vol I, 1901–1932*. Cambridge: Cambridge University Press, 1982.
Fewsmith, Joseph. *Dilemmas of Reform in China: Political Conflict and Economic Debate*. New York: M.E. Sharpe, 1994.
Fisher, William L. "How Technology Has Confounded U.S. Gas Resource Estimates." *Oil and Gas Journal* 42, no. 3 (1994).
Fleming, James. *The Callendar Effect: The Life and Work of Guy Stewart Callendar*. Boston: American Meteorological Society, 2007.
———. *Historical Perspectives on Climate Change*. New York: Oxford University Press, 1998.
Fletcher, Seth. *Bottled Lightning: Superbatteries, Electric Cars, and the New Lithium Economy*. New York: Hill and Wang, 2011.
Flink, James. *America Adopts the Automobile: 1895–1910*. Cambridge: MIT Press, 1970.
———. *The Automobile Age*. Cambridge: MIT Press, 1990.
Folsing, Albrecht. *Albert Einstein: A Biography*. Translated by Ewald Osers. New York: Penguin, 1997.
Forbes, Rosita. *Conflict: Angora to Afghanistan*. London: Cassell, 1931.
Ford, Henry. "Automobiles and Soybeans: An Interview with Arthur van Vlissingen. Jr." *The Rotarian*, September 1933.
Ford, Henry, and Samuel Crowther. *My Life and Work*. Garden City, N.Y.: Doubleday, Page & Co., 1923.
Fraser, Ronald. *Once Around the Sun: The Story of the International Geophysical Year*. New York: The Macmillan Company, 1958.
Freeland. Chrystia. *Sale of the Century: The Inside Story of the Second Russian Revolution*. London: Abacus, 2009.
Friedan, Betty. "The Coming Ice Age." *Harper's*, September 1958.
Friedel, Robert, Paul Israel, and Bernard Finn. *Edison's Electric Light: The Art of Invention*. Baltimore: Johns Hopkins University Press, 2010.
Friedman, Thomas. *Hot, Flat, and Crowded: Why We Need a Green Revolution*. New York: Farrar, Straus, and Giroux, 2008.
Frum, David. *The Right Man: An Inside Account of the Bush White House*. New York: Random House, 2005.
Gaidar, Yegor. *Collapse of an Empire: Lessons for Modern Russia*. Translated by Antonina Bouis. Washington, D.C.: Brookings Institution Press, 2007.

———. *Days of Defeat and Victory*. Translated by Jane Ann Miller. Seattle: University of Washington Press, 1999.

Gallagher, Kelly Sims. *China Shifts Gears: Automakers, Oil, Pollution, and Development*. Cambridge: MIT Press, 2006.

Gallagher, Kelly, Ambuj Sagar, Diane Segal, Paul de Sa, and John P. Holdren. "DOE Budget Authority for Energy, Research, Development, and Demonstration Database." In "Ending the Energy Stalemate: A Bipartisan Strategy to Meet America's Energy Challenges." Washington, D.C.: National Commission on Energy Policy, 2004.

Garfield, H. A. *Final Report of the U.S. Fuel Adminstrator, 1917–1919*. Washington, D.C.: GPO, 1921.

Gibb, George, and Evelyn Knowlton. *History of Standard Oil Company (New Jersey)*. Vol. II, *The Resurgent Years 1911–1927*. New York: Harper and Brothers, 1956.

Gibbons, Herbert Adams. *The New Map of South America*. London: Jonathan Cape, 1929.

Glicksman, Leon. "Energy Efficiency in the Built Environment." *Physics Today* 61, no. 7 (2008).

Goffman, Joseph, and Daniel J. Dudek. "The Clean Air Act Acid Rain Program: Lessons for Success in Creating a New Paradigm." Presentation. 88th Annual Meeting. Air & Waste Management Association. June 18–23, 1995.

Goldemberg, José. "Ethanol for a Sustainable Energy Future." *Science* 315, no. 5813. (2007).

Goralski, Robert, and Russell W. Freeburg. *Oil & War: How the Deadly Struggle for Fuel in WWII Meant Victory or Defeat*. New York: William Morrow, 1987.

Gorbachev, Mikhail. "Soviet Lessons from Afghanistan." *International Herald Tribune*. February 4, 2010.

Gordon, Michael, and Bernard Trainor. *Cobra II: The Inside Story of the Invasion and Occupation of Iraq*. New York: Vintage Press, 2007.

Gore, Al. *Earth in the Balance: Ecology and the Human Spirit*. New York: Rodale Books, 2006.

———. *An Inconvenient Truth*. New York: Rodale Books, 2006.

Gorelick, Steven M. *Oil Panic and the Global Crisis*. Hoboken, N.J.: Wiley-Blackwell, 2010.

Gott, Richard. *Hugo Chavez and the Bolivarian Revolution*. New York: Verso Press, 2005.

Graetz, Michael J. *The End of Energy: The Unmaking of America's Environment, Security, and Independence*. Cambridge: MIT Press, 2011.

Greenspan, Alan. *The Age of Turbulence: Adventures in a New World*. New York: Penguin, 2007.

Greenstock, Jeremy. "What Must Be Done Now." *The Economist*, May 6, 2004.

Groode, Tiffany, and Levi Tillemann-Dick. "The Race to Build the Electric Car." *Wall Street Journal*, Special Section, March 9, 2011.

Gustafson, Thane. *Capitalism Russian-Style*. Cambridge: Cambridge University Press, 1999.

———. *Crises Amid Plenty: The Politics of Soviet Energy under Brezhnev and Gorbachev*. Princeton: Princeton University Press, 1989.

———. *Wheel of Fortune: The Politics of Russian Oil Under Yeltsin and Putin*. Forthcoming.

Haagen-Smit, Arie, et al. "A Physiologically Active Principle from Cannabis Sativa (Marihuana)." *Science* 91, no. 2373 (1940).

Haass, Richard. *War of Necessity, War of Choice: A Memoir of Two Iraq Wars*. New York: Simon & Schuster, 2009.

Hahn, Robert W. "Economic Prescriptions for Environmental Problems: How the Patient Followed the Doctor's Orders." *Journal of Economic Perspectives*. 3, no. 2 (1989).

Halberstam, David. *The Reckoning*. New York: Avon Books, 1994.

Hansen, James. "Climate Threat to the Planet: Implications for Energy Policy and Intergenerational Justice." Jacob Bjerknes Lecture. American Geophysical Union. December 17, 2008.

Hansen, James, Wei-Chyung, and Andrew A. Lacis. "Mount Agung Eruption Provides a Test of Global Climactic Perturbation." *Science* 199, no. 4333 (1978).

Hardinge, Arthur A. *A Diplomatist in the East*. London: Jonathan Cape, 1928.

Hart, Basil Liddell, ed. *The Rommel Papers*. Translated by Paul Findlay. New York: Da Capo Press, 1985.

Hart, David M., and David G. Victor. "Scientific Elites and the Making of U.S. Policy for Climate Change Research, 1957–74." *Social Studies of Science* 23 (1993).

Hayek, Frederich A. "The Use of Knowledge in Society." *American Economic Review* 35, no. 4 (1945).

Hayes, Denis. *Rays of Hope: The Transition to a Post-Petroleum World*. New York: W.W. Norton, 1977.

Hazen, Terry, et al. "Deep Sea Oil Plume Enriches Oil-Degrading Bacteria." *Science* 330, no. 6001 (2010).

Hecht, Alan D., and Dennis Tirpak. "Framework Agreement on Climate Change: A Scientific and Policy History." *Climactic Change* 29 (1995).

Hegghammer, Thomas. "Deconstructing the Myth About al-Qa'ida and Khobar." *CTC Sentinel* 1, no. 3 (2008).

———*Jihad in Saudi Arabia*. Cambridge: Cambridge University Press, 2010.

Hewlett, Richard G., and Jack M. Holl. *Atoms for Peace and War, 1953–1961: Eisenhower and the Atomic Energy Commission*. Berkeley: University of California Press, 1989.

Hinton, Isabel. "In India. A Clear Victor on the Climate Front." *Yale Environment 360*. March 2, 2010.

Hirsh, Richard F. *Technology and Transformation in the American Electric Utility Industry*. Cambridge: Cambridge University Press, 1989.

Hoffman, David E. *The Oligarchs: Wealth and Power in the New Russia*. New York: Public Affairs, 2005.

Holloway, David. *Stalin and the Bomb: The Soviet Union and Atomic Energy 1939–1956*. New Haven: Yale University Press, 1996.

Hopkirk, Peter. *The Great Game: The Struggle for Empire in Central Asia*. New York: Kodansha International, 1994.

Howarth, Stephen, Joost Jonker, Keetie Sluyterman, and Jan Luiten van Zanden. *The History of Royal Dutch Shell*. New York: Oxford University Press, 2007.

Huber, Peter W., and Mark P. Mills. *The Bottomless Well*. New York: Basic Books, 2005.

Hughes, Thomas. *Networks of Power: Electrification in Western Society 1880–1930*. Baltimore: Johns Hopkins University Press, 1993.

Hulme, Mike. "On the Origin of the 'Greenhouse Effect': John Tyndall's 1859 Interrogation of Nature." *Weather* 64, no. 5 (2009).

IHS CERA. *Energy Scenarios*. 2010.

———. *Fueling North America's Energy Future: The Unconventional Natural Gas Revolution and the Carbon Agenda*. 2010.

———. *Gasoline and the American People*. 2006.

———. *Oil Sands Greenhouse Gases, and U.S. Oil Supply: Getting the Numbers Right*. Canadian Oil Sands Dialogue. 2010.

———. *Oil Sands Technology: Past, Present, and Future*. Canadian Oil Sands Energy Dialogue. 2011.

IHS Global Insight. *The Economic Impact of the Gulf of Mexico Offshore Oil and Natural Gas Industry and the Role of the Independents*. 2010.

Independent Inquiry Committee into the United Nations Oil-for-Food Programme. *Report on the Manipulation of the Oil-for-Food Programme*. United Nations. October 27, 2005.

Indyk, Martin. *Innocent Abroad: An Intimate Account of American Peace Diplomacy in the Middle East*. New York: Simon & Schuster, 2009.

Ingels, Margaret. *Willis Haviland Carrier: Father of Air Conditioning*. Louisville Ky.: Fetter Printing Company, 1991.

Insull, Samuel. *The Memoirs of Samuel Insull: An Autobiography*. Edited by Larry Plachno. Polo, Ill.: Transportation Trails, 1992.

Intergovernmental Panel on Climate Change. *Climate Change 2007: The Physical Science Basis*. New York: Cambridge University Press, 2007.

International Energy Agency. *Technology Roadmap: Biofuels for Transportation*. Paris: OECD/IEA, 2011.

———. *Tracking Industrial Energy Efficiency and CO_2 Emissions: In Support of the G-8 Plan of Action*. Paris: International Energy Agency, 2007.

———. *World Energy Outlook 2010*. Paris: International Energy Agency, 2010.

Isaacson, Walter. *Einstein: The Life of a Genius*. New York: Simon & Schuster, 2009.

Israel, Paul. *Edison: A Life of Invention*. New York: John Wiley & Sons, 1998.

Jackson, Kenneth T. *Crabgrass Frontier: The Suburbanization of the United States*. New York: Oxford University Press, 1987.

Jackson, Peter. "Why the 'Peak Oil' Theory Falls Down." IHS CERA, 2006.

Jackson, Peter, et al. *The Unconventional Frontier: Prospects for Unconventional Gas in Europe*. IHS CERA, 2011.

Jackson, Peter, Jonathan Craig, Leta Smith, Samia Razak, and Simon Wardell. "'Peak Oil' Postponed Again: Liquids Production Capacity to 2030." IHS CERA, 2010.

Jackson, Peter, and Keith Eastwood. "Finding the Critical Number: What Are the Real Declines Rates of Global Oil Production?" IHS CERA. November 2007.

Jacobs, Chip, and William Kelly. *Smogtown: The Lung-Burning History of Pollution in Los Angeles*. New York: Overlook Press, 2008.

Jiang, Julie, and Jonathan Sinton. *Overseas Investments by Chinese National Oil Companies*. Paris: International Energy Agency, 2011.

Jisi, Wang. "China's Search for a Grand Strategy." *Foreign Affairs*, 90, no. 2 (March–April 2011).

Johnson, Arthur M. *The Challenge of Change: The Sun Oil Company 1945–1977*. Columbus: Ohio State University Press, 1983.

Johnson, Frederick. "Sugar in Brazil: Policy and Production." *The Journal of Developing Areas* 17, no. 2 (1983).

Jones, Geoffrey. *The State and the Emergence of the British Oil Industry*. London: Macmillan, 1981.

Jonnes, Jill. *Empires of Light: Edison, Tesla, Westinghouse, and the Race to Electrify the World*. New York: Random House, 2004.

Joseph, Robert G. *Countering WMD: The Libyan Experience*. Fairfax: National Institute Press, 2009.

Josephson, Matthew. *Edison: A Biography*. New York: John Wiley and Sons, 1992.

Joskow, Paul L. "California's Electricity Crisis." *Oxford Review of Economic Policy*, 17, no. 3 (2001).

Kahn, Alfred E. *The Economics of Regulation: Principles and Institutions*. Cambridge: MIT Press, 1998.

Kalicki, Jan H. "Caspian Energy at the Crossroads." *Foreign Affairs*, 80, no. 5 (2001).

Kalicki, Jan H., and David L. Goldwyn. *Energy and Security: Toward a New Foreign Policy Strategy*. Baltimore: Johns Hopkins University Press, 2005.

Karl, Terry L. *The Paradox of Plenty: Oil Booms and Petro States*. Berkeley: University of California Press, 1997.

Kealey, Edward J. *Harvesting the Air: Windmill Pioneers in Twelfth Century England*. Berkeley: University of California Press, 1987.

Keeling, Charles David. "Rewards and Penalties of Monitoring the Earth." *Annual Review of Energy and the Environment* 23, 1998.

Kerr, Richard A. "It's Official: Humans Are Behind Most of Global Warming" *Science* 291, no. 5504 (2001).

———. "Hansen vs. the World on the Greenhouse Threat." *Science*, 244, no. 4908 (1989).

Khan, Mohsin S. "The 2008 Oil Price 'Bubble.'" Policy Brief. Peterson Institute for International Economics. August 2009.

King, David. "Climate Change Science: Adapt, Mitigate, or Ignore?" *Science* 303, no. 5655 (2004).

Kirsch, David A. *The Electric Vehicle and the Burden of History*. Rutgers University Press: 2000.

Kissinger, Henry. *On China*. New York: Penguin Press, 2011.

———. *White House Years*. Boston: Little Brown, 1979.

Koonin, Steven. "From Energy Innovation to Energy Transformation." (Unpublished paper.)

Kozloff, Nikolas. *Hugo Chávez: Oil, Politics, and the Challenge to the U.S.* New York: Palgrave Macmillan, 2006.

Krupp, Fred. "The Making of a Market-Minded Environmentalist." *Strategy + Business* 51 (2008).

Krupp, Fred, and Miriam Horn. *Earth: The Sequel: The Race to Reinvent Energy and Stop Global Warming.* New York: W. W. Norton & Company, 2009.

Kukla, G. J., and R. K. Matthews. "When Will the Present Interglacial Period End?" *Science*, 178, no. 4057 (1972).

Kvendseth, Stig S. *Giant Discovery: A History of Ekofisk Through the First 20 Years*. Tananger, Norway: Phillips Petroleum, 1988.

Landes, David. *The Unbound Prometheus: Technological Change and Industrial Development in Western Europe From 1750 to Present*. Second edition. New York: Cambridge University Press, 2003.

Langewiesche, William. *The Atomic Bazaar: The Rise of the Nuclear Poor*. Farrar, Straus & Giroux, 2007.

Larson, Erik. *The Devil in the White City: Murder, Magic, and Madness at the Fair That Changed America*. New York: Vintage Books, 2004.

Larsson, Robert L. *Russia's Energy Policy: Security Dimensions and Russia's Reliability as an Energy Supplier.* Stockholm: Swedish Defense Research Agency, 2006.

Lathim, Rod. *The Spirit of the Big Yellow House*. Santa Barbara: Emily Publications, 1995.

Leffler, William, Richard A. Pattaroizzi, and Gordon Sterling. *Deepwater Exploration and Production: A Non-Technical Guide*. Tulsa, Okla.: Pennwell, 2011.

LeVine, Steve. *The Oil and the Glory: The Pursuit of Empire and Fortune on the Caspian Sea*. New York: Random House, 2007.
Lewis, Joanna. "China's Strategic Priorities in International Climate Change Negotiations." *Washington Quarterly* 31, no. 1 (Winter 2007–8).
———. "Decoding China's Climate and Energy Policy Post-Copenhagen." German Marshall Fund Policy Brief. June 2010.
Lewis, John M. "Smagorinsky's GFDL: Building the Team." *Bulletin of the American Meteorological Society* 89, no. 9 (2008).
Lewis, Peter M. *Growing Apart: Oil, Politics, and Economic Change in Indonesia and Nigeria*. Ann Arbor: University of Michigan Press, 2007.
Lieber, Robert J. *The Oil Decade: Conflict and Cooperation in the West*. New York: Praeger, 1983.
Liming, Huang. "Financing Rural Renewable Energy: A Comparison Between China and India." *Renewable and Sustainable Energy Reviews* 13, no. 5 (2009).
Ling, H. C. *The Petroleum Industry of the People's Republic of China*. Palo Alto: Hoover Institution Press, 1975.
Linzden, Richard S. "Taking Greenhouse Warming Seriously." *Energy and Environment*. 18, no. 7-8 (2007).
Liu, Yingqi, and Ari Kokko. "Wind Power in China: Policy and Development Challenges." *Energy Policy* 38, no. 10 (2010).
"Lotus Leaf: Evolution and Standardization of the Automobile Source, The ," *Lotus Magazine*, 7, no. 4 (1916).
Lovins, Amory. "Energy Strategy: The Road Less Traveled?" *Foreign Affairs* 55, no. 1 (1976).
Lugar, Richard G., and R. James Woolsey. "The New Petroleum." *Foreign Affairs* 78, no. 1 (1999).
Lurie, Edward. *Louis Agassiz: A Life in Science*. Baltimore: Johns Hopkins University Press, 1988.
McCabe, Peter. "Energy Resources: Cornucopia or Empty Barrel?" *AAPG Bulletin* 82:11 (1998).
McCauley, Kathy, Bruce Barron, and Morton Coleman. *Crossing the Aisle to Cleaner Air: How the Bipartisan "Project 88" Transformed Environmental Policy*. Pittsburgh: University of Pittsburgh Press, 2008.
McDonald, Forrest. *Insull: The Rise and Fall of a Billionaire Utility Tycoon*. Washington, D.C.: BeardBooks, 2004.
MacKay, David J. C. *Sustainable Energy—Without the Hot Air*. Cambridge, U.K.: UIT Cambridge, 2009.
McKinsey Global Institute. *Preparing for China's Urban Billion*. McKinsey & Company. March 2009.
McLean, Bethany, and Peter Elkind. *The Smartest Guys in the Room: The Amazing Rise and Scandalous Fall of Enron*. New York: Portfolio, 2004.
Macrae, Norman. *John von Neumann: The Scientific Genius Who Pioneered the Modern Computer, Game Theory, Nuclear Deterrence and Much More*. American Mathematical Society, 2008.
Makovich, Lawrence. "Beyond California's Power Crisis: Impact, Solutions, and Lessons." CERA. March 2001.
———. "Meeting the Power Conservation Investment Challenge." IHS CERA (2007).
———. "The 'Smart Grid Narrative' and the 'Smarter Grid.'" IHS CERA (2011).
Manabe, Syukuro, and Richard Wetherald. "Thermal Equilibrium of the Atmosphere with a Given Ditribution of Relative Humidity." *Journal of Atmospheric Sciences* 24, no. 3 (1967).
Mann, Jim. *Beijing Jeep: A Case Study of Western Business in China*. Boulder: Westview Press, 1997.
Marcano, Cristina, and Alberto Barrera Tyszka. *Hugo Chavez: The Definitive Biography of Venezuela's Controversial President*. New York: Random House, 2007.
Marcel, Valerie. *Oil Titans: National Oil Companies in the Middle East*. Washington, D.C.: Brookings Institution Press, 2006.
Marder, Arthur J. *Old Friends, New Enemies: The Royal Navy and the Imperial Japanese Navy*. Oxford: Oxford University Press, 1981.
Massachusetts Institute of Technology. *The Future of Nuclear Power*. Cambridge: MIT Press, 2003.
Massachusetts Institute of Technology Energy Initiative. *The Future of Coal: Options for a Carbon-Constrained World*. Cambridge: MIT Press, 2007.
———. *The Future of Natural Gas: Interim Report*. Cambridge: MIT Press, 2010.
Matarrese, Lynne. *The History of Levittown, New York*. Levittown, N.Y.: Levittown Historical Society, 1977.
Maugeri, Leonardo. *The Age of Oil: The Mythology, History, and Future of the World's Most Controversial Resource*. Westport, Conn.: Praeger, 2006.
———. "Squeezing More Oil from the Ground." *Scientific American*, October 2009.
———. *Beyond the Age of Oil: The Myths, Realities, and Future of Fossil Fuels and Their Alternatives*. Translated by Jonathan T. Hine Jr. Santa Barbara: Praeger, 2010.

Maycock, Paul D., and Edward N. Stirewalt. *A Guide to the Photovoltaic Revolution: Sunlight to Electricity in One Step*. Emmaus, Pa.: Rodale, 1985.

Meadows, Donella, Dennis Meadows, Jorgen Randers, and William Behrens III. *The Limits to Growth: A Report for the Club of Rome's Project on the Predicament of Mankind*. New York: Signet Books, 1974.

Meijer, G. I. "Cooling Energy-Hungry Data Centers." *Science* 328, no. 5976 (2010).

Meissner, Fred. "M. King Hubbert as a Teacher." Presentation. Geological Society of America Annual Meeting. Seattle. (2003).

Meyer, Jeffrey, and Mark Califano. *Good Intentions Corrupted: The Oil-for-Food Scandal and the Threat to the U.N.* New York: Public Affairs, 2006.

Meyer, Karl E., and Shareen Blair Brysac. *Tournament of Shadows: The Great Game and the Race for Empire in Central Asia*. New York: Basic Books, 1999.

Mills, Rodney A. "Iran and the Strait of Hormuz: Saber Rattling or Global Energy Nightmare." Naval War College. Newport, R.I. Unpublished paper. (2008).

Mintzer, Irving M., and J. Amber Leonard, eds. *Negotiating Climate Change: The Inside Story of the Rio Convention*. Cambridge: Cambridge University Press, 1994.

Mommer, Bernard. *Changing Venezuelan Oil Policy*. Oxford U.K.: Oxford Institute for Energy Studies, April 1999.

Montefiore, Simon Sebag. *Young Stalin*. New York: Vintage, 2008.

Montgomery, David. "Markets in Licenses and Efficient Pollution Control Programs." *Journal of Economic Theory,* 5, no. 3 (1972).

Morgan, Granger, H. Dowlatabadi, M. Henrion, D. Keith, R. Lempert, S. McBrid, M. Small, and T. Wilbanks, eds. *Best Practice Approaches for Characterizing, Communicating. and Incorporating Scientific Uncertainty in Decisionmaking*. Washington, D.C.: National Oceanic and Atmospheric Administration, 2009.

Morgan, Judith, and Neil Morgan. *Roger: A Biography of Roger Revelle*. San Diego: Scripps Institution of Oceanography, 1996.

Morse, Edward. "Oil.Com." Lehman Brothers Energy Special Report. May 2008.

Munk, Walter. "Tribute to Roger Revelle and His Contributions to Studies of Carbon Dioxide and Climate Change." Colloquium on Carbon Dioxide and Climate Change. National Academy of Sciences. Irvine, Calif., November 13–15, 1995.

Murtishaw, Scott, and Lee Schipper. "Disaggregated Analysis of US Energy Consumption in the 1990s: Evidence of the Effects of the Internet and Rapid Economic Growth." *Energy Policy* 29, no. 15 (2001).

Naim, Moises. *Paper Tigers & Minotaurs: The Politics of Venezuela's Economic Reform*. Washington, D.C.: Carnegie Endowment, 1993.

Narasimhan, T. N. "M. King Hubbert: A Centennial Tribute." *Ground Water* 41, no. 5 (2003).

National Academy of Sciences. *Real Prospects for Energy Efficiency in the United States*. Washington, D.C.: National Academies Press, 2010.

National Commission on the BP Deepwater Horizon Oil Spill and Offshore Drilling. *Deep Water: The Gulf Oil Disaster and the Future of Offshore Drilling: Report to the President*. January 2011.

National Development and Reform Commission. "China's National Climate Change Program." People's Republic of China. June 2007.

National Oceanic and Atmospheric Administration. "Hurricane Katrina: A Climatological Perspective. Preliminary Report." October 2005.

National Research Council. *Effectiveness and Impact of Corporate Average Fuel Economy Standards*. Washington, D.C.: National Academies Press, 2002.

———. *Transition to Alternative Transportation Technologies: Plug-in Hybrid Electric Vehicles*. Washington, D.C.: National Academies Press, 2010.

Nazarbayev, Nursultan. *The Kazakhstan Way*. Translated by Jan Butler. London: Stacey International, 2008.

———. *Without Right and Left*. London: Class Publishing, 1992.

Nelson, Brian A. *The Silence and the Scorpion: The Coup Against Chavez and the Making of Modern Venezuela*. New York: Nation Books, 2009.

Nielsen, Henry, Keld Nielsen, Flemming Petersen, and Hans Siggaard Jensen. "Riso National Laboratory—Forty Years of Research in a Changing Society." Frederiksborgvej, Denmark: Riso National Laboratory, 1998.

Nincic, Donna J. "The 'Radicalization' of Maritime Piracy: Implications for Maritime Energy Security." *Journal of Energy Security*. December 2010.

Noland, Marcus, and Howard Pack. *The Arab Economies in a Changing World.* Washington, D.C.: Peterson Institute, 2007.

Nordhaus, William. *A Question of Balance: Weighing the Options on Global Warming Policies.* New Haven: Yale University Press, 2008.

North American Electric Reliability Corporation. *High-Impact, Low-Frequency Event Risk to the North American Bulk Power System.* June 2010.

Nye, David. *Electrifying America: Social Meanings of a New Technology.* Cambridge: MIT Press, 1992.

O'Brien, Dennis J. "The Oil Crisis and the Foreign Policy of the Wilson Administration, 1917–1921." PhD dissertation. University of Missouri, 1974.

Ohmae, Kenichi. *The Borderless World: Power and Strategy in the Interlinked Economy.* New York: Harper-Collins, 1991.

Oil Depletion Analysis Centre. "New Oil Projects Cannot Meet World Needs This Decade." Ashland, Ore.: From the Wilderness Publications, November 16, 2004.

Oliver, Hongyan, Kelly Sims Gallagher, Donglian Tian, and Jinhua Zhang. "China's Fuel Economy Standards for Passenger Vehicles." Energy Technology Innovation Policy Research Group. John F. Kennedy School of Government. Harvard University. March 2009.

O'Neil, William D. "Correspondence: Cost and Difficulties of Blocking the Strait of Hormuz." *International Security.* 33, no. 3 (2008/2009).

O'Neill, Jim. "Building Better Global Economic BRICs." Goldman Sachs Global Economics Paper No. 66. November 30, 2001.

O'Sullivan, Daniel. *Black Gold. Paper Barrels and Oil Price Barrels.* London: Harriman House, 2009.

Overpeck, Jonathan. "Arctic Environmental Change of the Last Four Centuries." *Science* 278, no. 5341 (1997).

Pachauri, Rajendra. "Energy and Growth: Beyond the Myths and Myopia." *Energy Journal* 10, no. 1 (1989).

Packard, David. *The HP Way.* New York: Collins Business Essentials, 1995.

Packer, George. *The Assassin's Gate: America in Iraq.* New York: Farrar, Straus & Giroux, 2005.

Paterson, Matthew. *Global Warming and Global Politics.* London: Routledge, 1996.

Peachtree Capital Advisors. *2010 Greentech Annual M&A Review.*

Peebles, Malcolm. *Evolution of the Gas Industry.* New York: New York University Press, 1980.

Perkins, Tom. *Valley Boy: The Education of Tom Perkins.* New York: Gotham Books, 2007.

Perlin, John. *From Space to Earth: The Story of Solar Electricity.* Cambridge: Harvard University Press, 2002.

———. "Solar Power: The Slow Revolution." *Invention and Technology* 18, no. 1 (2002).

PetroChina Company Limited. *Global Offering.* March 27, 2000.

Petterssen, Sverre. *Weathering the Storm: Sverre Petterssen, The D-Day Forecast, and the Rise of Modern Meteorology.* Edited by James Rodger Fleming. Boston: American Meteorological Society, 2001.

Pew Campaign for Fuel Efficiency. *A History of Fuel Economy: One Decade of Innovation, Two Decades of Inaction.* Washington, D.C.: January 2, 2011.

Phillips, Norman. "Jule Charney, 1917–1981." *Annals of the History of Computing* 3, no. 4 (1981).

———. "Jule Charney's Influence on Meteorology." *Bulletin of the American Meteorological Society* 63, no. 5 (1982).

Pillar, Paul. "Intelligence, Policy, and the War in Iraq." *Foreign Affairs* 85, no. 2 (2006).

Pollack, Kenneth. *The Persian Puzzle: The Conflict Between Iran and America.* New York: Random House, 2004.

Pooley, Eric. *The Climate War: True Believers, Power Brokers, and the Fight to Save the Earth.* New York: Hyperion, 2010.

Pratt, Joseph A. *Prelude to Merger: A History of Amoco Corporation, 1973–1998.* Houston: Hart Publications: 2000.

President's Council of Advisors on Science and Technology. *Accelerating the Pace of Change in Energy Technologies through an Integrated Federal Energy Policy.* Washington, D.C.: Office of the President, 2010.

Priest, Tyler. "Peak Oil Prophecies: Oil Supply Assessments and the Future of Nature in U.S. History." Unpublished paper.

———. *The Offshore Imperative: Shell's Search for Petroleum in Postwar America.* College Station: Texas A&M University Press, 2007.

Putnam, Palmer. *Putnam's Power from the Wind.* Edited by Gerald Koeppl. New York: Van Nostrand Reinhold, 1982.

Rabe, Barry G. *Statehouse and Greenhouse: The Emerging Politics of American Climate Change Policy*. Washington, D.C.: Brookings Institution Press, 2004.

Rae, John B. *American Automobile Manufacturers: The First Forty Years*. Philadelphia: Chilton Company, 1959.

Rainger, Ronald. "Patronage and Science: Roger Revelle, The U.S. Navy, and Oceanography at the Scripps Institution." *Earth Sciences History* 19, no. 1 (2000).

Rashid, Ahmed. *Taliban: Militant Islam, Oil and Fundamentalism in Central Asia*. New Haven: Yale University Press, 2000.

Rasool, S. I., and S. H. Schneider. "Atmospheric Carbon Dioxide and Aerosols: Effects of Large Increases on Global Climate." *Science* 173, no. 3992 (1971).

Reagan, Nancy, with William Novak. *My Turn: The Memoirs of Nancy Reagan*. New York: Random House, 1989.

Reagan, Ronald, with Richard G. Hubler. *Where's the Rest of Me?* New York: Duell, Sloan and Pearce, 1965.

Reagan, Ronald. *Reagan: A Life in Letters*. Edited by Kiron Skinner, Annelise Anderson, and Martin Anderson. New York: Free Press, 2003.

Reilly, W. K. "Breakdown on the Road from Rio: Reform, Reaction, and Distraction Compete in the Cause of the International Environment, 1993–94." Arthur and Frank Payne Lecture. Stanford University.

Reinhart, Carmen, and Kenneth Rogoff. *This Time Is Different: Eight Centuries of Financial Folly*. Princeton: Princeton University Press, 2009.

REN21. *Renewables 2010 Global Status Report*. September 2010.

Report of the President's Commission on the Accident at Three Mile Island. October 1979.

Revelle, Roger. "Sun. Sea and Air: IGY Studies of the Heat and Water Budget of the Earth." *Geophysics and the IGY.* Geophysical Monograph No. 2. American Geophysical Union. July 1958.

Revelle, Roger, and Hans Suess. "Carbon Dioxide Exchange Between Atmosphere and Ocean and the Question of an Increase of Atmospheric CO_2 during the Past Decades." *Tellus* 9, no. 1 (1957).

Revkin, Andrew. "Endless Summer: Living with the Greenhouse Effect." *Discover*, October 1988.

Rickover, Hyman. *No Holds Barred: The Final Congressional Testimony of Admiral Hyman Rickover*. Washington, D.C.: Center for Study of Responsive Law, 1982.

Ricks, Thomas E. *Fiasco: The American Military Adventure in Iraq*. New York: Penguin, 2007.

Righter, Robert. *Wind Energy in America: A History*. Norman: University of Oklahoma Press, 1996.

Roberts, Paul. *The End of Oil: On the Edge of a Perilous New World*. Boston: Houghton Mifflin, 2004.

Rockwell, Theodore. *The Rickover Effect: How One Man Made a Difference.* Bloomington: iUniverse, 2002.

Roeber, Joe. *The Evolution of Oil Markets: Trading Instruments and Their Role in Oil Price Formation.* Energy and Environment Program of the Royal Institute of International Affairs, Chattham House, 1993.

Rosen, Daniel H., and Trevor Houser. *China Energy: A Guide for the Perplexed.* China Balance Sheet Project. Center for Strategic and International Studies and the Peterson Institute for International Economics. May 2007.

Ross, Michael L. "The Political Economy of the Resource Curse." *World Politics* 51 (1999).

Rumsfeld, Donald. *Known and Unknown: A Memoir.* New York: Sentinel, 2011.

Ruppert, Michael C. "Colin Campbell on Oil: Perhaps the World's Foremost Expert on Oil and the Oil Business Confirms the Ever More Apparent Reality of the Post 9-11 World." Sherman Oats, Calif.: In The Wilderness Publications, 2002.

Ruttan, Vernon W. *Is War Necessary for Economic Growth? Military Procurement and Technology Development*. Oxford: Oxford University Press, 2006.

Sadjadpour, Karim. *Reading Khamenei: The World View of Iran's Most Powerful Leader*. Washington, D.C.: Carnegie Endowment for International Peace, 2009.

Saint, William S. "Farming for Energy: Social Options under Brazil's National Alcohol Programme." *World Development* 10, no. 3 (1982).

Sali-i-Martin, Xavier, and Arvind Subramanian. "Addressing the Natural Resource Curse: An Illustration from Nigeria." International Monetary Fund Working Paper. July 2003.

Schlesinger, Arthur, Jr.. *The Age of Roosevelt.* Vol. 3, *The Politics of Upheaval.* Boston: Houghton Mifflin: 1960.

Shaxson, Nicholas. *Poisoned Wells: The Dirty Politics of African Oil.* New York: Palgrave Macmillan, 2007.
Shiller, Robert. *Irrational Exuberance.* Second edition. New York: Broadway Books, 2005.
Shirky, Clay. "The Political Power of Social Media." *Foreign Affairs,* 90, no. 1 (2011).
Sifry, Micah, and Christopher Cerf. *The Iraq War Reader: History, Documents, and Opinions.* New York: Simon & Schuster, 2003.
Simmons, Matthew R. *Twilight in the Desert: The Coming Saudi Oil Shock and the World Economy.* Hoboken, N.J.: John Wiley, 2006.
Simonds, William Adams. *Edison: His Life, His Work, His Genius.* Indianapolis: Bobbs-Merrill, 1934.
Smith, Adam. *Paper Money.* New York: Summit Books, 1981.
Soares de Oliveira, Ricardo. *Oil and Politics in the Gulf of Guinea.* New York: Columbia University Press, 2007.
Solow, Robert. "Growth and After." Nobel Prize Lecture. November 18, 1987.
Sonnichsen, Ole. *The Winner: The Dramatic Story of Vestas.* Copenhagen: Gads Forlag, 2009.
South Coast Air Quality Management District. *The Southland's War on Smog: Fifty Years of Progress Toward Clean Air.* May 1997.
Sperling, Daniel, and Deborah Golden. *Two Billion Cars: Driving Toward Sustainability.* Oxford: Oxford University Press, 2009.
Speth, James Gustave. *Red Sky at Morning: America and the Crisis of the Global Environment.* New Haven: Yale University Press, 2005.
Stachel, John, ed. *Einstein's Miraculous Year: Five Papers That Changed the Face of Physics.* Princeton: Princeton University Press, 1998.
Stahlberg, Alexander. *Bounden Duty: The Memoirs of a German Officer, 1932–1945.* Translated by Patricia Crampton. London: Brassey's, 1990.
Starr, Kevin. *Golden Dreams: California in an Age of Abundance, 1950–1963.* New York: Oxford, 2009.
State Council of the People's Republic of China. "Renewable Energy Law." February 28, 2005.
Stavins, Robert N. "What Can We Learn from the Grand Policy Experiment? Lessons from SO_2 Allowance Trading." *Journal of Economic Perspectives,* 12, no 3 (1998).
———, ed. *Project 88: Harnessing Market Forces to Protect the Environment.* Washington, D.C.: 1988.
Steinbeck, John. *The Grapes of Wrath.* New York: Penguin Books, 2006.
Stent, Angela. *From Embargo to Ostpolitik: The Political Economy of West German-Soviet Relations 1955–1980.* New York: Cambridge University Press, 1981.
———. *Soviet Energy and Western Europe.* New York: Praeger, 2003.
Stern, Nicholas. *The Economics of Climate Change: The Stern Review.* Cambridge: Cambridge University Press, 2007.
———. *The Global Deal: Climate Change and the Creation of a New Era of Progress and Prosperity.* New York: Public Affairs, 2009.
Steward, Dan. *The Barnett Shale Play: Phoenix of the Fort Worth Basin—A History.* Fort Worth: Fort Worth Geological Society, 2007.
Stobaugh, Robert, and Daniel Yergin, eds. *Energy Future: A Report of the Energy Project at the Harvard Business School.* New York: Ballantine Books, 1979.
Stross, Randall. *The Wizard of Menlo Park: How Thomas Edison Invented the Modern World.* New York: Three Rivers Press, 2007.
Study Group on Carbon Dioxide and Climate (JASON). *Carbon Dioxide and Climate: A Scientific Assessment.* Climate Research Board, Assembly of Mathematical and Physical Sciences, National Research Council. Woods Hole, Mass. July 23–27, 1979.
Strum, Harvey. "Eisenhower's Solar Energy Policy." *The Public Historian* 6, no. 2 (1984).
"'Suki' Manabe: Pioneer of Climate Modeling." *IPRC Climate* 5, no. 2 (2005).
Sulzberger, Carl. "An Early Road Warrior: Electric Vehicles in the Early Years of the Automobile." *IEEE Power and Energy Magazine* 2, no. 3 (2004).
Suny, Ronald. "A Journeyman for the Revolution: Stalin and the Labor Movement in Baku. June 1907–May 1908." *Soviet Studies* 3 (1972).
Suskind, Ron. *The Price of Loyalty: George W. Bush, the White House, and the Education of Paul O'Neill.* New York: Simon & Schuster, 2004.
Sweeney, James L. *The California Electricity Crisis.* Stanford: Hoover Institution Press, 2002.

———. "California Electricity Restructuring: The Crisis and Its Aftermath." In *Electricity Market Reform: An International Perspective.* Edited by Fereidoon P. Sioshansi and Wolfgang Pfaffenberger. Oxford: Elsevier, 2006.

———. "The California Energy Crisis." Conference on Ethics and Changing Energy Markets. Notre Dame University. October 28, 2004.

Talbott, Strobe. "A Farewell to Flashman: American Policy in the Caucasus and Central Asia." Speech. July 21, 1997.

———. *The Russia Hand.* New York: Random House, 2002.

Talmadge, Caitlin. "Closing Time: Assessing the Iranian Threat to the Strait of Hormuz." *International Security* 33, no. 1 (2008).

Tang, Ke, and Wei Xiong. "Index Investment and the Financialization of Commodities," March 2011.

Teitelbaum, Joshua. "What Iranian Leaders Really Say About Doing Away with Israel." Jerusalem Center for Public Affairs, 2008.

Terreson, Douglas. "The Era of the Super-Major." Morgan Stanley. February 1998.

Thatcher, Margaret. *The Downing Street Years.* London: HarperCollins Publishers, 1995.

Till, Hilary. "The Oil Markets: Let the Data Speak for Itself." EDHEC Working Paper. October 2008.

Tolf, Robert. *The Russian Rockefellers: The Saga of the Nobel Family and the Russian Oil Industry.* Stanford: Hoover Institution Press, 1976.

Transparency International. *Global Corruption Report 2004.*

Tucker, William. *Terrestrial Energy: How Nuclear Power Will Lead the Green Revolution and End America's Energy Odyssey.* Savage, Md.: Bartleby Press, 2008.

Turco, R. P., O. B. Toon, T. P. Ackerman, J. B. Pollack, and Carl Sagan. "Nuclear Winter: Global Consequences of Multiple Nuclear Explosions." *Science* 222, no. 4630 (1983).

Tyndall, John. *The Glaciers of the Alps.* Boston: Ticknor and Fields, 1860.

Ulam, Stanislaw M. *Adventures of a Mathematician.* Berkeley: University of California Press, 1991.

UK Energy Research Centre. *Global Oil Depletion: An Assessment of the Evidence for a Near Term Peak in Global Oil Production.* London (2009).

United Nations Development Programme and Arab Fund for Economic and Social Development. *Arab Human Development Report 2002.* New York: United Nations, 2002.

United Nations Framework Convention on Climate Change. "Draft Decision: Proposal by the President. Copenhagen Accord." New York: United Nations, December 18, 2009.

U.S. Congress, House of Representatives, Committee on Science and Technology, Subcommittee on Energy Development and Applications, 96th Congress. *Venezuela and Brazil Visit—January 13–20, 1980.* Washington, D.C.: GPO, January 1980.

U. S. Department of Energy. *Impact of the 2005 Hurricanes on the Natural Gas Industry in the Gulf of Mexico Region: Final Report.* 2006.

———. *20% Wind Energy by 2030: Increasing Wind Energy's Contribution to U.S. Electricity Supply.* Springfield, Va.: U.S. Department of Commerce National Technical Information Service, 2008.

U.S. Department of Interior. "Increased Safety Measures for Energy Development on the Outer Continental Shelf." May 27, 2010.

U.S. Secretary of Energy Advisory Board, Task Force on Strategic Energy R&D. *Energy R&D: Shaping Our Nation's Future in a Competitive World.* Washington, D.C.: U.S. Government Printing Office, June 1995.

U.S. Senate Energy and Natural Resources Committee. "The Greenhouse Effect: Impacts on Current Global Temperature and Regional Heat Waves." June 23, 1988.

U.S. Supreme Court. *Massachusetts et al. v. Environmental Protection Agency.* 549 U.S. 497. April 2, 2007.

Uppenbrink, Julia. "Arrhenius and Global Warming." *Science* 272, no. 5265 (1996).

van Heerden, Ivor, and Mike Bryan. *The Storm: What Went Wrong and Why During Hurricane Katrina—The Inside Story From One Louisiana Scientist.* New York: Viking, 2006.

Varadi, Peter. Lecture, 19th European Photovoltaic Solar Energy Conference. June 7–11, 2004.

Verrastro, Frank. "Caspian and Central Asia: Lessons Learned from the BTC Experience." White Paper. Center for Strategic and International Studies. April 2009.

Victor, David G., Amy M. Jaffe, and Mark H. Hayes, eds. *Natural Gas and Geopolitics: From 1970–2040.* New York: Cambridge University Press, 2006.

Volkov, Vadim. *Violent Entrepreneurs: The Use of Force in the Making of Russian Capitalism.* Ithaca: Cornell University Press, 2002.

WAC Global Services. "Peace and Security in the Niger Delta: Conflict Expert Group Baseline Report." Working Paper for Shell Petroleum Development Company. December 2003.

Wampler, Cloud. "Dr. Willis H. Carrier: Father of Air Conditioning." The Newcomen Society of England, 1949.

Wang, Jone-Lin. "Playing to Strength—Diversifying Electricity." *Wall Street Journal,* February 2006.

———. "Why Are We Using More Electricity?" *Wall Street Journal*, March 10, 2010.

Wasik, John F. *The Merchant of Power: Sam Insull, Thomas Edison, and the Creation of the Modern Metropolis*. New York: Palgrave Macmillan, 2006.

Weart, Spencer. *The Discovery of Global Warming.* Cambridge: Harvard University Press, 2003.

———. *The Discovery of Global Warming*. Web site: http://www.aip.org/history/climate/index.htm#contents.

Weidenmier, Marc, Joseph Davis, and Roger Aliaga-Diaz. "Is Sugar Sweeter at the Pump? The Macroeconomic Impact of Brazil's Alternative Energy Program." National Bureau of Economic Research. Working Paper No. 14362. October 2008.

Weisman, Steven R. *Daniel Patrick Moynihan: Portrait in Letters of an American Visionary*. New York: Public Affairs, 2010.

———. *The Great Tax Wars: Lincoln—Teddy Roosevelt—Wilson: How the Income Tax Transformed America.* New York: Simon & Schuster: 2002.

White, Lynn, Jr. *Medieval Technology & Social Change.* London: Oxford University Press, 1964.

The White House. *Restoring the Quality of Our Environment: Report of the Environmental Pollution Panel.* November 1965.

Whitman, Christine Todd. *It's My Party Too: The Battle for the Heart of the GOP and the Future of America.* New York: Penguin, 2005.

Wik, Reynold M. *Henry Ford and Grass-roots America.* Ann Arbor: University of Michigan Press, 1973.

Wilkins, Mira. *The Maturing of Multinational Enterprise: American Business Abroad from 1914 to 1970.* Cambridge: Harvard University Press, 1974.

Willems, Paul A. "The Biofuels Landscape: Through the Lens of Industrial Chemistry." *Science* 32, no. 5941 (2009).

Williamson, Harold, Ralph Andreano, Arnold Daum, and Gilbert Klose. *The American Petroleum Industry: The Age of Energy. 1899–1959.* Evanston: Northwestern University Press, 1963.

Woodward, Bob. *Plan of Attack.* New York: Simon & Schuster, 2004.

Woodwell, George, Gordon J. MacDonald, Roger Revelle, and Charles Keeling. "The Carbon Dioxide Report." *Bulletin of the Atomic Scientists* 35, no. 8 (1979).

The World Bank and State Environmental Protection Agency of the People's Republic of China. *Cost of Pollution in China: Economic Estimates of Physical Damages*. 2007.

World Economic Forum and IHS CERA. *Energy Vision Update 2010: Towards a More Energy Efficient World.* 2010.

Wright, Robin. *The Iran Primer: Power, Politics, and U.S. Policy*. Washington, D.C.: U.S. Institute of Peace Press, 2010.

Wustenhagen, Rolf, and Michael Bilharz. "Green Energy Market Development in Germany: Effective Public Policy and Emerging Customer Demand." *Energy Policy* 34, no. 13 (2006).

Yacobucci, Brent D. "Fuel Ethanol: Background and Public Policy Issues." Congressional Research Service. March 3, 2006.

Yergin, Daniel. *The Prize: The Epic Quest for Oil, Money, and Power*. New York: Free Press, 2009.

Yergin, Daniel, and Thane Gustafson. *Russia 2010 and What It Means for the World.* New York: Vintage, 1995.

Yergin, Daniel, and Joseph Stanislaw. *Commanding Heights: The Battle for the World Economy.* New York: Touchstone, 2002.

———. "Oil: Reopening the Door." *Foreign Affairs* 72, no. 4 (1993).

INDEX